Information Diffusion Management and Knowledge Sharing:

Breakthroughs in Research and Practice

Information Resources Management Association
USA

Volume I

IGI Global
DISSEMINATOR OF KNOWLEDGE

Published in the United States of America by
IGI Global
Information Science Reference (an imprint of IGI Global)
701 E. Chocolate Avenue
Hershey PA, USA 17033
Tel: 717-533-8845
Fax: 717-533-8661
E-mail: cust@igi-global.com
Web site: http://www.igi-global.com

Library of Congress Cataloging-in-Publication Data

Names: Information Resources Management Association, editor.
Title: Information diffusion management and knowledge sharing : breakthroughs in research and practice / Information Resources Management Association, editor.
Description: Hershey, PA : Information Science Reference, [2020] | Includes bibliographical references and index.
Identifiers: LCCN 2019023057 (print) | LCCN 2019023056 (ebook) | ISBN 9781799804178 (hardcover) | ISBN 9781799804185 (ebook) | ISBN 9781799804185¬(ebook) | ISBN 9781799804178¬(hardcover)
Subjects: LCSH: Information technology. | Information behavior. | Information society
Classification: LCC HD30.2 .I525 2020 (ebook) | LCC HD30.2 (print) | DDC 658.4/038--dc23
LC record available at https://lccn.loc.gov/2019023057

British Cataloguing in Publication Data
A Cataloguing in Publication record for this book is available from the British Library.

For electronic access to this publication, please contact: eresources@igi-global.com.

List of Contributors

Agresta, Thomas P. / *University of Connecticut Healthcare Center, USA* 253
Ahsan, Mohammad / *National Institute of Technology, India* 807
Alali, Haitham / *Amman Arab University, Jordan* 676
Al-Busaidi, Kamla Ali / *Sultan Qaboos University, Oman* 658
Alim, Sophia / *Independent Researcher, UK* 690
Almunawar, Mohammad Nabil / *Universiti Brunei Darussalam, Brunei* 623
Alsewi, Salem Meftah Jebriel / *Misurata University, Libya* 676
Amin, Nurul Afiqah Hj Nor / *Universiti Brunei Darussalam, Brunei* 623
Arfini, Selene / *University of Chieti and Pescara, Italy* 843
Arslan, Aykut / *Piri Reis University, Turkey* 557
Asim, Yousra / *COMSATS Institute of Information Technology, Pakistan* 319
Bertok, Peter / *RMIT University, Australia* 185
Bertolotti, Tommaso / *University of Pavia, Italy* 843
Besar, Nurul Nazira / *Universiti Brunei Darussalam, Brunei* 623
Bhatia, M.P.S. / *Netaji Subhash Institute of Technology, India* 897
Cao, Yang / *Virginia Tech, USA* 879
Carugati, Andrea / *Aarhus University, Denmark & IESEG School of Management (LEM - CNRS UMR 9221), France* 382
Carvalho, Nuno / *Universidade de Coimbra, Portugal* 403
Chang, Hsia-Ching / *University of North Texas, USA* 823
Chang, Yu-Wei / *China Jiliang University, China* 513
Charoensukmongkol, Peerayuth / *National Institute of Development Administration, Thailand* 858
Chen, Hsin / *University of Bedfordshire, UK* 1
Chen, Xin / *Virginia Tech, USA* 879
Cheng, Yun-Shan / *National Central University, Taiwan* 513
Chou, Seng-cho T. / *National Taiwan University, Taiwan* 823
Chugh, Ritesh / *Central Queensland University, Australia* 745
Conover, Joanne / *University of Connecticut, USA* 253
Cristina de la Escosura, María / *Universidad Complutense de Madrid, Spain* 135
Csepregi, Anikó / *University of Pannonia, Hungary* 761, 785
Cubbage, Jayne / *Bowie State University, USA* 27
Dalkir, Kimiz / *McGill University, Canada* 490, 711
del Mar Rodríguez, María / *Universidad Complutense de Madrid, Spain* 135
Demurjian, Steven A. / *University of Connecticut, USA* 253

Diamond, Michael / *Pomona College, USA* 253
Edwards, John S. / *Aston University, UK* 344
Escámez de Vera, Diego M. / *Universidad Complutense de Madrid, Spain* 135
Fang, Youjia / *Virginia Tech, USA* 879
Franchi, Enrico / *University of Parma, Italy* 473
Gaál, Zoltán / *University of Pannonia, Hungary* 761
Garcia-Murillo, Martha / *Syracuse University, USA* 113
Georgiadou, Elli / *University of Middlesex, UK* 533
Giangreco, Antonio / *IESEG School of Management (LEM-CNRS UMR 9221), Catholic University of Lille, France* 382
Gomes, Isabel / *ISCTE, Portugal* 403
Grant, Susan B. / *Brunel University, UK* 588
Gustafson-Pearce, Olinkha / *Brunel University, UK* 588
Harker, Lee-Anne Lesley / *Cape Peninsula University of Technology, South Africa* 358
Hasnan, Amy Suliza / *Universiti Brunei Darussalam, Brunei* 623
Hsu, Ping-Yu / *National Central University, Taiwan* 513
Jha, Chandan Kumar / *Madden School of Business, Le Moyne College, USA* 300
Joshi, Mahesh / *RMIT University, Australia* 745
Kedjar, Saadia / *University of Bejaia, Algeria* 185
Ko, Lok Wan Lorraine / *Nottingham University, UK* 1
Kővári, Edit / *University of Pannonia, Hungary* 785
Kumari, Madhu / *National Institute of Technology, India* 807
Lakaraju, Sandeep / *Dakota State University, USA* 277
Lawrence, Japhet Eke / *Nigerian Defence Academy, Nigeria* 45
Lin, Yi-Chun / *National Taiwan University, Taiwan* 823
Lozano, David Serrano / *Universidad Complutense de Madrid, Spain* 135
Magnani, Lorenzo / *University of Pavia, Italy* 843
Malik, Ahmad Kamran / *COMSATS Institute of Information Technology, Pakistan* 319
Manzoor, Amir / *Bahria University, Pakistan* 66
Marques, Marco E. / *FUMEC University, Brazil* 174
Mola, Lapo / *SKEMA Business School, LSMRC, France* 382
Natarajan, M. / *Jimma University, Ethiopia* 726
Obermayer, Nora / *University of Pannonia, Hungary* 761, 785
Okolie-Osemene, James / *Wellspring University, Nigeria* 642
Oladokun, Olugbade / *University of Botswana, Botswana* 155
Olfman, Lorne / *Claremont Graduate University, USA* 424
Pal, Shantanu / *The University of St. Andrews, UK* 94
Pal, Triveni Lal / *National Institute of Technology, India* 807
Pastor, Elena Duce / *Universidad Autónoma de Madrid, Spain* 135
Pessoa, Cláudio Roberto Magalhães / *FUMEC University, Brazil* 174
Poggi, Agostino / *University of Parma, Italy* 473
Popa, Simona / *University of Murcia, Spain* 452
Ramanathan, Ramakrishnan / *University of Bedfordshire, UK* 1
Ramanathan, Usha / *Nottingham Trent University, UK* 1
Rossignoli, Cecilia / *Università degli Studi di Verona, Italy* 382
Salim, Juhana / *Universiti Kebangsaan Malaysia, Malaysia* 676

Sánchez, Yaira K. Rivera / *University of Connecticut, USA* 253
Shao, Xian / *University of Connecticut, USA* 253
Shiau, Wen-Lung / *Ming Chuan University, Taiwan* 513
Siakas, Dimitrios / *Citec, Finland* 533
Siakas, Kerstin / *Alexander Technological Educational Institution of Thessaloniki, Greece* 533
Singh, Tajinder / *National Institute of Technology, India* 807
Song, Zheng / *Virginia Tech, USA* 879
Soto-Acosta, Pedro / *University of Murcia, Spain* 452
Szabó, Lajos / *Corvinus University of Budapest, Hungary* 761
Tari, Abdelkamel / *University of Bejaia, Algeria* 185
Tomaiuolo, Michele / *University of Parma, Italy* 473
Twum-Darko, Michael / *Cape Peninsula University of Technology, South Africa* 358
Virkar, Shefali / *University of Oxford, UK* 220
Walia, Rhythm / *Netaji Subhash Institute of Technology, India* 897
Wang, Chen-Ya / *National Open University, Taiwan* 823
Wang, Tianzi / *Virginia Tech, USA* 879
Wang, Yong / *Dakota State University, USA* 277
Weiss-Randall, Debra / *Florida Atlantic University, USA* 13
Wohlers de Almeida, Marcio / *State University of Campinas – UNICAMP, Brazil* 113
Wu, Bing / *Tongji University, China* 603
Xu, Dianxiang / *Boise State University, USA* 277
Yener, Serdar / *Sinop University, Turkey* 557
Yi, Jingbing / *Xi'an Jiaotong University, China* 424
Yuan, Xinwei / *Xi'an University of Technology, China* 424
Zaber, Moinul / *University of Dhaka, Bangladesh* 113
Zulu, Saul F. C. / *University of Botswana, Botswana* 155
Zwayda, Yousef / *Misrata University, Libya* 676

Table of Contents

Preface xiv

Volume I

Section 1
Diffusion Theory

Chapter 1
A Study on Green Characteristics of RFID using Innovation Diffusion Theory 1
Ramakrishnan Ramanathan, University of Bedfordshire, UK
Lok Wan Lorraine Ko, Nottingham University, UK
Hsin Chen, University of Bedfordshire, UK
Usha Ramanathan, Nottingham Trent University, UK

Chapter 2
Using Diffusion of Innovations Theory to Encourage Workers to Make Healthy Food Choices and Engage in Physical Activity 13
Debra Weiss-Randall, Florida Atlantic University, USA

Chapter 3
Establishing a Media Literacy Cognate at Historically Black Colleges and Universities: A Comparative Analysis of Existing Courses and Potential of Implementation 27
Jayne Cubbage, Bowie State University, USA

Chapter 4
Examining the Factors that Influence ICT Adoption in SMEs: A Research Preliminary Findings 45
Japhet Eke Lawrence, Nigerian Defence Academy, Nigeria

Section 2
Diffusion Tools and Technologies

Chapter 5
Online Communities of Practice and Web 2.0 66
Amir Manzoor, Bahria University, Pakistan

Chapter 6
Information Sharing and Communications with Mobile Cloud Technology: Applications and Challenges 94
Shantanu Pal, The University of St. Andrews, UK

Chapter 7
Information and Communication Technologies as Drivers of Social Unrest 113
Martha Garcia-Murillo, Syracuse University, USA
Moinul Zaber, University of Dhaka, Bangladesh
Marcio Wohlers de Almeida, State University of Campinas – UNICAMP, Brazil

Chapter 8
Fasti Congressuum: A Useful Online Tool for Congresses and Call for Papers 135
Elena Duce Pastor, Universidad Autónoma de Madrid, Spain
María Cristina de la Escosura, Universidad Complutense de Madrid, Spain
Diego M. Escámez de Vera, Universidad Complutense de Madrid, Spain
María del Mar Rodríguez, Universidad Complutense de Madrid, Spain
David Serrano Lozano, Universidad Complutense de Madrid, Spain

Section 3
Information Control and Management

Chapter 9
Document Description and Coding as Key Elements in Knowledge, Records, and Information Management 155
Olugbade Oladokun, University of Botswana, Botswana
Saul F. C. Zulu, University of Botswana, Botswana

Chapter 10
Information Technology and Communication Management in Supply Chain Management 174
Cláudio Roberto Magalhães Pessoa, FUMEC University, Brazil
Marco E. Marques, FUMEC University, Brazil

Chapter 11
Access Control and Information Flow Control for Web Services Security 185
Saadia Kedjar, University of Bejaia, Algeria
Abdelkamel Tari, University of Bejaia, Algeria
Peter Bertok, RMIT University, Australia

Chapter 12
The Politics of Access to Information: Exploring the Development of Software Platforms and Communications Hardware in the Digital Age 220
Shefali Virkar, University of Oxford, UK

Chapter 13
Role-Based Access Control for Mobile Computing and Applications 253
Yaira K. Rivera Sánchez, University of Connecticut, USA
Steven A. Demurjian, University of Connecticut, USA
Joanne Conover, University of Connecticut, USA
Thomas P. Agresta, University of Connecticut Healthcare Center, USA
Xian Shao, University of Connecticut, USA
Michael Diamond, Pomona College, USA

Chapter 14
Analysis of Healthcare Workflows in Accordance with Access Control Policies 277
Sandeep Lakaraju, Dakota State University, USA
Dianxiang Xu, Boise State University, USA
Yong Wang, Dakota State University, USA

Chapter 15
Information Control, Transparency, and Social Media: Implications for Corruption 300
Chandan Kumar Jha, Madden School of Business, Le Moyne College, USA

Chapter 16
A Survey on Access Control Techniques for Social Networks 319
Yousra Asim, COMSATS Institute of Information Technology, Pakistan
Ahmad Kamran Malik, COMSATS Institute of Information Technology, Pakistan

Section 4
Knowledge Sharing in Business

Chapter 17
Knowledge Sharing: At the Heart of Knowledge Management.. 344
John S. Edwards, Aston University, UK

Chapter 18
Understanding Knowledge Sharing in an Organization: A Perspective of Actor-Network Theory 358
Michael Twum-Darko, Cape Peninsula University of Technology, South Africa
Lee-Anne Lesley Harker, Cape Peninsula University of Technology, South Africa

Chapter 19
Business Intelligence System Design and its Consequences for Knowledge Sharing, Collaboration, and Decision-Making: An Exploratory Study 382
Lapo Mola, SKEMA Business School, LSMRC, France
Cecilia Rossignoli, Università degli Studi di Verona, Italy
Andrea Carugati, Aarhus University, Denmark & IESEG School of Management (LEM - CNRS UMR 9221), France
Antonio Giangreco, IESEG School of Management (LEM-CNRS UMR 9221), Catholic University of Lille, France

Chapter 20
Knowledge Sharing between Enterprises of the Same Group 403
Nuno Carvalho, Universidade de Coimbra, Portugal
Isabel Gomes, ISCTE, Portugal

Chapter 21
How Do Institution-Based Trust and Interpersonal Trust Affect Interdepartmental Knowledge Sharing? 424
Xinwei Yuan, Xi'an University of Technology, China
Lorne Olfman, Claremont Graduate University, USA
Jingbing Yi, Xi'an Jiaotong University, China

Volume II

Chapter 22
Antecedents and Consequences of Adopting Social Networking Technologies for Knowledge Sharing in Small Firms: 452
Pedro Soto-Acosta, University of Murcia, Spain
Simona Popa, University of Murcia, Spain

Chapter 23
Social Media for Online Collaboration in Firms and Organizations 473
Enrico Franchi, University of Parma, Italy
Agostino Poggi, University of Parma, Italy
Michele Tomaiuolo, University of Parma, Italy

Chapter 24
The Role of Human Resources (HR) in Tacit Knowledge Sharing 490
Kimiz Dalkir, McGill University, Canada

Chapter 25
The Effects of Individual and National Cultures in Knowledge Sharing: A Comparative Study of the U.S. and China 513
Yu-Wei Chang, China Jiliang University, China
Ping-Yu Hsu, National Central University, Taiwan
Wen-Lung Shiau, Ming Chuan University, Taiwan
Yun-Shan Cheng, National Central University, Taiwan

Chapter 26
The Influence of National and Organisational Culture on Knowledge Sharing in Distributed Teams 533
Kerstin Siakas, Alexander Technological Educational Institution of Thessaloniki, Greece
Elli Georgiadou, University of Middlesex, UK
Dimitrios Siakas, Citec, Finland

Section 5
Knowledge Sharing in Education

Chapter 27
Relationship Between the Motivational Language of School Administrators and Tacit Knowledge Sharing of Teachers 557
Serdar Yener, Sinop University, Turkey
Aykut Arslan, Piri Reis University, Turkey

Chapter 28
The Use of Virtual Environments for Knowledge Sharing in Distance Learning Education, with a View to Informing Industry 588
Olinkha Gustafson-Pearce, Brunel University, UK
Susan B. Grant, Brunel University, UK

Chapter 29
Identifying the Influential Factors of Knowledge Sharing in E-Learning 2.0 Systems 603
Bing Wu, Tongji University, China

Chapter 30
Knowledge Sharing Using Web 2.0: Preferences, Benefits and Barriers in Brunei Darussalam's Tertiary Education 623
Nurul Afiqah Hj Nor Amin, Universiti Brunei Darussalam, Brunei
Amy Suliza Hasnan, Universiti Brunei Darussalam, Brunei
Nurul Nazira Besar, Universiti Brunei Darussalam, Brunei
Mohammad Nabil Almunawar, Universiti Brunei Darussalam, Brunei

Chapter 31
Facilitating Knowledge Sharing on Social Media for Students of International Relations and Conflict Studies in Nigeria 642
James Okolie-Osemene, Wellspring University, Nigeria

Section 6
Knowledge Sharing in Healthcare

Chapter 32
Inter-Organizational Knowledge Sharing System in the Health Sector: Physicians' Perspective 658
Kamla Ali Al-Busaidi, Sultan Qaboos University, Oman

Chapter 33
Knowledge Sharing Success Model of Virtual Communities of Practice in Healthcare Sector 676
Haitham Alali, Amman Arab University, Jordan
Juhana Salim, Universiti Kebangsaan Malaysia, Malaysia
Yousef Zwayda, Misrata University, Libya
Salem Meftah Jebriel Alsewi, Misurata University, Libya

Chapter 34
Insights Into Tweets Associated With Congenital Heart Disease 690
Sophia Alim, Independent Researcher, UK

Section 7
Social Media

Chapter 35
The Role of Technology and Social Media in Tacit Knowledge Sharing 711
Kimiz Dalkir, McGill University, Canada

Chapter 36
Exploring Knowledge Sharing over Social Media 726
M. Natarajan, Jimma University, Ethiopia

Chapter 37
Challenges of Knowledge Management amidst Rapidly Evolving Tools of Social Media 745
Ritesh Chugh, Central Queensland University, Australia
Mahesh Joshi, RMIT University, Australia

Chapter 38
Leveraging Knowledge Sharing over Social Media Tools 761
Nora Obermayer, University of Pannonia, Hungary
Zoltán Gaál, University of Pannonia, Hungary
Lajos Szabó, Corvinus University of Budapest, Hungary
Anikó Csepregi, University of Pannonia, Hungary

Chapter 39
Knowledge Sharing Relation to Competence, Emotional Intelligence, and Social Media Regarding Generations 785
Nora Obermayer, University of Pannonia, Hungary
Anikó Csepregi, University of Pannonia, Hungary
Edit Kővári, University of Pannonia, Hungary

Chapter 40
Sentiment Based Information Diffusion in Online Social Networks 807
Mohammad Ahsan, National Institute of Technology, India
Madhu Kumari, National Institute of Technology, India
Tajinder Singh, National Institute of Technology, India
Triveni Lal Pal, National Institute of Technology, India

Chapter 41
Consumer Sentiment in Tweets and Coupon Information-Sharing Behavior: An Initial Exploration 823
Chen-Ya Wang, National Open University, Taiwan
Yi-Chun Lin, National Taiwan University, Taiwan
Hsia-Ching Chang, University of North Texas, USA
Seng-cho T. Chou, National Taiwan University, Taiwan

Chapter 42
The Diffusion of Ignorance in On-Line Communities 843
Selene Arfini, University of Chieti and Pescara, Italy
Tommaso Bertolotti, University of Pavia, Italy
Lorenzo Magnani, University of Pavia, Italy

Chapter 43
Contribution of Mindfulness to Individuals' Tendency to Believe and Share Social Media Content 858
Peerayuth Charoensukmongkol, National Institute of Development Administration, Thailand

Chapter 44
Modelling Propagation of Public Opinions on Microblogging Big Data Using Sentiment Analysis and Compartmental Models 879
Youjia Fang, Virginia Tech, USA
Xin Chen, Virginia Tech, USA
Zheng Song, Virginia Tech, USA
Tianzi Wang, Virginia Tech, USA
Yang Cao, Virginia Tech, USA

Chapter 45
Modeling Rumors in Twitter: An Overview 897
Rhythm Walia, Netaji Subhash Institute of Technology, India
M.P.S. Bhatia, Netaji Subhash Institute of Technology, India

Index xix

Preface

One of the greatest commodities in the modern era of technology is information. Information gathering, sharing, and privacy remain topics of great interest among professionals and researchers in conjunction with ensuring information quality. Ideas and information, benign or otherwise, can be shared with thousands through as little effort as the click of a mouse. It is the ease with which knowledge can be shared that raises questions among experts worldwide about the management systems that host information, how this information is disseminated, and to whom this information is released.

While the internet and social media have made positive aspects of information management and knowledge sharing more accessible, they have also allowed greater exploitation of the flaws within these systems. The phenomena of misinformation and its dissemination has become a prevalent criticism of social media, despite its ability to circulate researched facts with comparable ease. New knowledge management technologies also create dilemmas for businesses and other organizations that must balance convenience with security and quality.

Knowledge sharing and information management systems are increasingly essential to the success of businesses, organizations, and social life in the age of the internet. Ensuring the usability of these systems while mitigating the pitfalls is critical in fostering success for those utilizing these technologies and recognizing their effects on traditional methods. Ensuring that appropriate systems are utilized and effective management techniques are employed to foster successful technological integration for information diffusion and mindful knowledge sharing is crucial for organizational success.

The everchanging landscape surrounding the diverse applications of different scientific areas can make it very challenging to stay on the forefront of innovative research trends. That is why IGI Global is pleased to offer this two-volume comprehensive reference that will empower librarians, managers, information systems specialists, and professionals with a stronger understanding of information diffusion management and knowledge sharing.

This compilation is designed to act as a single reference source on conceptual, methodological, and technical aspects and will provide insight into emerging topics including but not limited to information leakage, peer influence, social networking, information management systems, information governance, and social influence. The chapters within this publication are sure to provide readers with the tools necessary for further research and discovery in their respective industries and/or fields.

Information Diffusion Management and Knowledge Sharing: Breakthroughs in Research and Practice is organized into seven sections that provide comprehensive coverage of important topics. The sections are:

1. Diffusion Theory
2. Diffusion Tools and Technologies
3. Information Control and Management

4. Knowledge Sharing in Business
5. Knowledge Sharing in Education
6. Knowledge Sharing in Healthcare
7. Social Media

The following paragraphs provide a summary of what to expect from this invaluable reference source:

Section 1, "Diffusion Theory," opens this extensive reference source by highlighting the latest trends in knowledge dissemination and methods for the transfer of ideas. In the first chapter in this section, "A Study on Green Characteristics of RFID Using Innovation Diffusion Theory," the authors, Prof. Ramakrishnan Ramanathan from the University of Bedforshire, UK; Prof. Lok Wan of Nottingham University, UK; Hsin Chen from the University of Bedforshire, UK; and Usha Ramanathan of Nottingham Trent University, UK, examine the theory of innovation diffusion and its applications in the prediction of administrative technology adoption. In the second chapter, "Using Diffusion of Innovations Theory to Encourage Workers to Make Healthy Food Choices and Engage in Physical Activity," Prof. Debra N. Weiss-Randall, Florida Atlantic University, USA offers insights into the applications of diffusion of innovations in corporate environments for encouraging healthy lifestyles in employees and reducing absenteeism and boosting productivity. This chapter is followed by "Establishing a Media Literacy Cognate at Historically Black Colleges and Universities: A Comparative Analysis of Existing Courses and Potential of Implementation," in which the author, Prof. Jayne Cubbage, from Bowie State University, USA, explores the demand for, and practicality of employing media literacy courses at Historically Black Colleges and Universities across the United States. In the final chapter in this section, "Examining the Factors that Influence ICT Adoption in SMEs: A Research Preliminary Findings," the author, Prof. Japhet Eke Lawrence, Department of Mathematics and Computer Science, Nigerian Defence Academy, Kaduna, Nigeria, offers insight into the factors and influences of SMEs' decisions in adopting ICT in business.

Section 2, "Diffusion Tools and Technologies," includes chapters on emerging technological advancements which impact the dissemination of ideas and innovations. In the first chapter in this section, "Online Communities of Practice and Web 2.0," Prof. Amir Manzoor, Bahria University, Pakistan, discusses the use of online tools to release knowledge through an appropriate channel so that it becomes usable. In the second chapter in this section, "Information Sharing and Communications with Mobile Cloud Technology: Applications and Challenges," the author, Prof. Shantanu Pal, The University of St. Andrews, UK, examines the use of mobile and cloud technologies and their impact on the computing capabilities of their users. This chapter is followed by "Information and Communication Technologies as Drivers of Social Unrest," in which the authors, Prof. Martha Garcia-Murillo, Syracuse University, USA; Prof. Moinul Zaber, University of Dhaka, Bangladesh; and Prof. Marcio Wohlers de Almeida, State University of Campinas (UNICAMP), Brazil, explore how information and communication technologies (ICTs) are alleviating frictions associated with gathering and distributing information. In the final chapter in this section, "Fasti Congressuum: A Useful Online Tool for Congresses and Call for Papers," the authors, Prof. Elena Duce Pastor, Universidad Autónoma de Madrid, Spain and Profs. María Cristina de la Escosura, Diego M. Escámez de Vera, María del Mar Rodríguez, and David Serrano Lozano, from the Universidad Complutense de Madrid, Spain, provides a critical case study on methods for organization of distributed knowledge.

Section 3, "Information Control and Management," presents coverage on novel strategies for overseeing the appropriate and systematic administration of knowledge and information. The first chapter in this section, "Document Description and Coding as Key Elements in Knowledge, Records, and Information

Management," authored by Profs. Olugbade Oladokun and Saul C. Zulu from the University of Botswana, Botswana, examines aspects critical to information storage and retrieval systems, such as description and coding. Another chapter contained within this section, "The Politics of Access to Information: Exploring the Development of Software Platforms and Communications Hardware in the Digital Age," by Prof. Shefali Virkar, University of Oxford, UK, provides essential research on the global policy debate over potential development contributions of information and communications technologies. Another noteworthy chapter within this section, "Analysis of Healthcare Workflows in Accordance With Access Control Policies," authored by Prof. Sandeep Lakaraju, Dakota State University, USA; Prof. Dianxiang Xu, Boise State University, USA; and Prof. Yong Wang, Dakota State University, USA, provides detailed research on the handling of sensitive data within healthcare information systems. One of the closing chapters within this section, "Information Control, Transparency, and Social Media: Implications for Corruption," by Prof. Chandan Kumar Jha, Le Moyne College, USA, focuses on the developing links between social media and corruption. The final chapter in this section, "A Survey on Access Control Techniques for Social Networks," authored by Prof. Yousra Asim, COMSATS Institute of Information Technology, Pakistan and Prof. Ahmad Kamran Malik, COMSATS Institute of Information Technology, Pakistan, explores the importance of access control in order to prevent unauthorized access to information hosted on online social networks (OSN).

Section 4, "Knowledge Sharing in Business," discusses coverage and research perspectives on the applications of information dispersing techniques and management in corporate settings. The first chapter in this section, "Knowledge Sharing: At the Heart of Knowledge Management," authored by Prof. John S. Edwards from Aston University, UK, provides compelling research on successful knowledge sharing and the need to consider all aspects of knowledge sharing including content, people, and context. Following this chapter is "Utilizing Communities of Practice to Facilitate Knowledge Sharing in the Digital Age," written by Prof. Kijpokin Kasemsap of Suan Sunandha Rajabhat University, Thailand. It explains essential aspects of knowledge sharing and perspectives on knowledge sharing behavior. Another chapter contained within this section, "Knowledge Sharing Between Enterprises of the Same Group," authored by Prof. Nuno Carvalho from the Universidade de Coimbra, Portugal and Prof. Isabel Gomes of ISCTE, Portuagal, is an exploratory study that seeks to promote investigation into knowledge sharing between enterprises of the same enterprise group. Another noteworthy chapter within this section, "Social Media for Online Collaboration in Firms and Organizations," authored by Profs. Enrico Franchi, Agostino Poggi, and Michele Tomaiuolo from the University of Parma, Italy, explores the role of social capital in the participation in online social networking activities. The final chapter in this section, "The Influence of National and Organisational Culture on Knowledge Sharing in Distributed Teams," authored by Prof. Kerstin Siakas, Alexander Technological Educational Institution of Thessaloniki, Greece; Prof. Elli Georgiadou, University of Middlesex, UK; and Prof. Dimitrios Siakas, Citec, Finland, examines distributed teams and knowledge use and sharing methods of members on these teams.

Section 5, "Knowledge Sharing in Education," discusses coverage and research perspectives on the applications of information dispersing techniques and management in educational and learning environments. The first chapter in this section, "Relationship Between the Motivational Language of School Administrators and Tacit Knowledge Sharing of Teachers," authored by Prof. Serdar Yener, Sinop University, Turkey and Prof. Aykut Arslan, Piri Reis University, Turkey, investigates motivational language of school administrators and its effect on tacit knowledge sharing by teachers and schools. The chapter, "The Use of Virtual Environments for Knowledge Sharing in Distance Learning Education, With a View to Informing Industry," by Profs. Olinkha Gustafson-Pearce and Susan B. Grant, Brunel University,

UK, is also housed within this section. It considers how educators and industry can leverage the tools and systems of social media and virtual world technology mediums. Another noteworthy chapter within this section, “Identifying the Influential Factors of Knowledge Sharing in E-Learning 2.0 Systems,” by Prof. Bing Wu, Tongji University, China, examines the constructs of knowledge creation self-efficacy, subjective norms, perceived usefulness, and attitudes toward knowledge sharing and the intention to engage in knowledge sharing. One of the closing chapters, “Knowledge Sharing Using Web 2.0: Preferences, Benefits, and Barriers in Brunei Darussalam’s Tertiary Education,” authored by Profs. Nurul Afiqah Hj Nor Amin, Amy Suliza Hasnan, Nurul Nazira Besar, and Mohammad Nabil Almunawar from the Universiti Brunei Darussalam, Brunei, assesses the current knowledge sharing processes in tertiary education in Brunei Darussalam and identifies preferred knowledge sharing methods. The final chapter in this section, “Facilitating Knowledge Sharing on Social Media for Students of International Relations and Conflict Studies in Nigeria,” written by Prof. James Okolie-Osemene of Wellspring University, Nigeria, examines techniques for facilitating knowledge sharing for the benefit of students of international relations and conflict studies in Nigerian universities.

Section 6, “Knowledge Sharing in Healthcare,” discusses coverage and research perspectives on the applications of information dispersing techniques and management in healthcare institutions. In the first chapter in this section, “Inter-Organizational Knowledge Sharing System in the Health Sector: Physicians’ Perspective,” authored by Prof. Kamla Ali Al-Busaidi, Sultan Qaboos University, Oman, the attitudes of physicians toward the deployment of inter-organizational knowledge sharing system (IOKSS) is examined. Another chapter included within this section, “Knowledge Sharing Success Model of Virtual Communities of Practice in Healthcare Sector,” by Prof. Jaitham Alali of Amman Arab University, Jordan; Prof. Juhana Salim from the Universiti Kebangsaan Malaysia, Malaysia; Prof. Yousef Zwayda from Misrata University, Libya; and Prof. Salem Meftah Jebriel Alsewi of Misurata University, Libya, examines virtual communities of practice as an enabler of knowledge creation, sharing, and use. The final chapter in this section, “Insights Into Tweets Associated With Congenital Heart Disease,” by Prof. Sophia Alim, Independent Researcher, USA, examines the use of Twitter by healthcare professionals as an opportunity to break down boundaries with patients.

Section 7, “Social Media,” discusses coverage and research perspectives on various applications of social media as a method for managing and distributing knowledge and information. The first chapter in this section, “The Role of Technology and Social Media in Tacit Knowledge Sharing,” authored by Prof. Kimiz Dalkir from McGill University, Canada, provides compelling research on the role of technology-mediated knowledge sharing and best practices and methods for sharing tacit knowledge. Another chapter presented early within this section, “Challenges of Knowledge Management Amidst Rapidly Evolving Tools of Social Media,” by Prof. Ritesh Chugh, Central Queensland University, Australia and Mahesh Joshi, RMIT University, Australia, examines the reactions of individuals and organizations to social media technologies and how the embracing of these technologies has changed social discourse and knowledge management strategies. Another chapter contained within this section, “Leveraging Knowledge Sharing Over Social Media Tools,” by Profs. Nora Obermayer and Zoltán Gaál from the University of Panninoa, Hungary; Prof. Lajos Szabó, Corvinus University of Budapest, Hungary; and Prof. Anikó Csepregi, University of Panninoa, Hungary, provides essential perspectives on how social media tools are being used for knowledge sharing. One of the closing chapters within this section, “Contribution of Mindfulness to Individuals’ Tendency to Believe and Share Social Media Content,” authored by Prof. Peerayuth

Charoensikmongkol of the International College, National Institute of Development Administration, Thailand, explores the effect of individual tendencies to believe social media content and share it without knowing the potential consequences. The final chapter in this section, "Modeling Rumors in Twitter: An Overview," authored by Profs. Rhythm Walia and M. P. S. Bhatia from Netaji Subhash Institute of Technology, India, analyzes the influence of social media on traditional advertising and viral marketing.

Although the primary organization of the contents in this work is based on its seven sections, offering a progression of coverage of the important concepts, methodologies, technologies, applications, social issues, and emerging trends, the reader can also identify specific contents by utilizing the extensive indexing system listed at the end.

Section 1
Diffusion Theory

Chapter 1
A Study on Green Characteristics of RFID using Innovation Diffusion Theory

Ramakrishnan Ramanathan
University of Bedfordshire, UK

Lok Wan Lorraine Ko
Nottingham University, UK

Hsin Chen
University of Bedfordshire, UK

Usha Ramanathan
Nottingham Trent University, UK

ABSTRACT

Radio frequency identification (RFID) is one type of auto-identification technology that uses radio frequency (RF) waves to identify, track, and locate individual physical items. This technology has been used in many applications including manufacturing and distribution of product. While RFID is useful in improving several functions within a firm, the authors focus on the logistics function in this chapter. Applying RFID can help improve logistics in several ways. RFID can closely monitor and track positions of vehicles and assist companies to successfully manage their warehouses and supply chains. Additionally, cost savings, supply chain visibility, and new process creation have been identified as three key benefits of RFID adoption. In spite of significant number of research studies on RFID, there is a limited amount of published knowledge on the discussion of the drivers or influencing factors that lead logistics industry to consider RFID. Given the increasing importance of green issues, there is a need to understand how the perceived positive green characteristics are affecting the level of adoption of the RFID technology. The aim of this chapter is therefore to explore the factors affecting logistics service providers' intention to use RFID, with special emphasis on its environmental friendly green characteristics. The theory of diffusion of innovations is used to develop a conceptual model of factors influencing RFID adoption.

DOI: 10.4018/978-1-7998-0417-8.ch001

INTRODUCTION

Radio frequency identification (RFID) is one type of auto-identification technology that uses radio frequency (RF) waves to identify, track and locate individual physical items. This technology has been used in many applications including manufacturing and distribution of products (Lin & Ho, 2009a,b). While RFID is useful in improving several functions within a firm, we focus on the logistics function in this study. Applying RFID can help improve logistics in several ways. Lin (2009) points out that the capabilities of RFID to closely monitor and track positions of vehicles can assist companies to successfully manage their warehouses and supply chains. Additionally, cost savings, supply chain visibility, and new process creation have been identified as three key benefits of RFID adoption (Roh et al., 2009). Wamba (2012) claims that RFID can be useful in integrating supply chains by improving shipping and receiving processes, automatically trigger specific processes, foster higher level of information sharing among supply chain partners and finally promote the use of new business processes.

In spite of significant number of research studies on RFID, there is a limited amount of published knowledge on the discussion of the drivers or influencing factors that lead logistics industry to consider RFID. Given the increasing importance of green issues, there is a need to understand how the perceived positive green characteristics are affecting the level of adoption of the RFID technology. The aim of this paper is therefore to explore the factors affecting logistics service providers' intention to use RFID, with special emphasis on its environmental friendly green characteristics. The theory of diffusion of innovations (Rogers, 2010) is used to develop a conceptual model of factors influencing RFID adoption.

LITERATURE REVIEW

Background of RFID Technology and the Literature

An RFID system consists of three primary components: the tag or transponder; the readers; and the middleware. It is always connected to an enterprise application system for data processing in support of business activities (Wang, et al., 2010). RFID uses tags with embedded chips within a product, pallet, or case. These chips help to store and transmit information about the specific unit to RFID readers (which are radio frequency transmitters) (Attaran, 2007). According to Wang, et al. (2010), the middleware is an intermediate layer between the RFID readers and the enterprise application systems. It is used for reader and device management to provide a common interface to configure, monitor, deploy, and issue commands directly to readers; data management to filter raw data and pass on only useful information to the appropriate applications; application integration to provide integrated RFID data and connect disparate applications within the enterprise; and partner integration to provide collaborative solutions like business-to-business integration between trading partners.

In recent years, there has been a growing interest and attention among consultants, academics and researchers worldwide on RFID. This is indicated by the increasing volume of articles on the subject in trade publications and scholarly journals. A steadily increasing number of logistics companies adopt RFID for efficient identification of physical items, and hence several recent studies suggested that the interest of researchers in RFID should continue (Riedel, et al., 2008; Li, et al., 2010; Pedroso, et al., 2009). Li et al. (2010) classified the literature of RFID into three areas: RFID general overview, analytical studies, and empirical studies. In this chapter, a theoretical perspective to the adoption of RFID using the theory of diffusion of innovations is provided. This theory is briefly described and hypotheses based on tenets of this theory have been developed in the next section.

INNOVATION DIFFUSION THEORY AND THE RESEARCH HYPOTHESES

The theory of innovation diffusion (Rogers, 2010) is one of the most widely applied theories in the prediction of organizational level technology adoption (Wang et al., 2010). It provides the basic model of how perceived innovation characteristics affect the rate of adoption of innovation (Zhang et al., 2010).

Five Characteristics of Innovation

Rogers (2010) proposed five attributes that are key influencers on the acceptance of an innovation. These characteristics are relative advantage, compatibility, complexity, trialability and observability.

- **Relative Advantage:** The extent to which people believe that the innovation is better than the traditional one. Robinson (2009) highlighted that the greater the perceived relative advantage of an innovation, the more rapid its rate of adoption is likely to be. In this study, intention to use RFID is used as the dependent variable and the following hypothesis is proposed to link relative advantage of using RFID with the intention to use:
  H1: Relative advantage will have a positive effect on intention to use RFID.
- **Complexity:** The extent to which an innovation is perceived as relatively difficult to understand and use (Wang, et al., 2010). Potential users may not have confidence in the RFID technology if it is complex to understand (Wang, et al., 2010). The following hypothesis is proposed:
  H2: Complexity will have a negative effect on intention to use RFID.
- **Compatibility:** The degree to which an innovation is perceived as consistent with the existing values, past values, and needs of potential adopters (Luo, et al., 2007). High compatibility has been identified as a facilitator for innovation adoption (Wang, et al., 2010). The following hypothesis is proposed:
  H3: Compatibility will have a positive effect on intention to use RFID
- **Trialability:** The extent to which people believe that there are chances for the innovation to be experienced before deciding whether to adopt it or not (Zhang, et al., 2010). However, Wang et al. (2010) excluded the trialability in their research model. This is because they observed that trialability was not consistently related to innovation adoption. Hence, this attribute is not included for further analysis in this study.
- **Observability:** The degree to which the results of an innovation are visible to others (Luo, et al., 2007). The easier it is for individuals to observe the benefits of RFID, the more likely they are to adopt it (Robinson, 2009). This leads to our next hypothesis.
  H4: Observability of benefits (excluding green benefits) will have a positive effect on intention to use RFID.
- **Observability of Green Benefits:** Of a new technology is gaining more and more attention in the literature given the growing interests in environmentally friendly technologies (Dukovska-Popovska, et al., 2010; Krigslund et al., 2010). Hence it will be worthwhile to specifically examine

the influence of green characteristics on the company's intention to use RFID. Hence, the final hypothesis links observability of green benefits of RFID with intention to use the technology.
H5: Observability of green benefits will have a positive effect on intention to use RFID.

RESEARCH METHODOLOGY

This study has used a questionnaire survey to verify the hypotheses. Details of the research methodology are provided in this section.

Construct Measures

An intensive literature study was undertaken to identify the principal construct measures. The questionnaire consisted of two parts: one for RFID adoption, and the other one for assessing the measurement items relating to Innovation Diffusion theory. A 7-point Likert Scale has been used for all items in this study.

Sample Selection and Data Collection

During June – August 2011, data for this study were collected using a questionnaire survey administered in the UK. Contact details of UK Logistics companies were obtained from the Chartered Institute of Logistics and Transport in the UK (CILT(UK)). These companies were selected as the sample population of this study. The CILT (UK) is a pre-eminent independent professional body for individuals associated with logistics, supply chains and all transport throughout their careers. The CILT (UK) was chosen to be the major source of companies' contact information because its Knowledge Centre has the most comprehensive, accurate and up-to-date database of Logistics companies in the UK. A total of 174 questionnaires were received, of which 107 were usable for further analysis.

Measure Purification and Data Analysis

The Statistical Package for the Social Sciences (SPSS), a computer program for statistical analysis, has been used to run factor analysis, reliability analysis, correlation analysis and regression analysis in this study.

Data Analysis

In the context of RFID, most of the questionnaire items loaded into factors as expected based on theory except for 8 items: T1S; T1CR; T5OBT_A; T5OBI; T5OBA; T5OBS; T5OBIS; and T5OBIV (please see Table 3 for full description of the items). These items loaded on to more than once factor and hence they were eliminated. Table 1 shows that the factor analysis resulted in five factors that measure the independent variables.

The Cronbach's alphas for independent variables ranged from 0.217 to 0.933. These values support the contention that all the factors, except for Complexity (T3U and T3D), had adequate reliability. As the Cronbach's alpha value of Complexity is below the threshold level of 0.65, items of Complexity were

Table 1. Confirmatory factor analysis and Cronbach's alpha for Independent variables

Items		Component				
		1	2	3	4	5
Relative Advantage						
T1D	My company expects RFID to help quick data capture and analysis.	.866				
T1R	My company expects RFID to help immediate reward.	.890				
T1RoI	My company expects RFID to help increase return on investment.	.907				
T1CA	My company expects RFID to help gain competitive advantage.	.910				
T1G	My company expects RFID to help improve company's green image.	.768				
T1S	My company expects RFID to help improve safety.	Eliminated, due to cross-loadings				
T1CR	My company expects RFID to help meet customer requirements.					
Compatibility						
T2I	RFID is compatible with existing information infrastructure.		.975			
T2R	RFID is compatible with the existing regulation in the Logistics industry.		.977			
T2E	RFID development is compatible with my firm's existing experiences/practices with similar systems.		.973			
T2B	The changes introduced by RFID are consistent with my firm's existing beliefs/values.		.737			
Complexity						
T3U	My company believes that RFID is complex to use.			.759		
T3D	My company believes that RFID development (i.e. procedures for facilitating wider adoptions) is a complex process.			.759		
Observability of Benefits						
T5OBRoI	My company observed return on investment is increased from RFID adoption.				.865	
T5OBCS	My company observed customer service level is improved from RFID adoption.				.845	
T5OBC	My company observed cost is saved from RFID adoption.				.910	
T5OBT	My company observed item tracking and tracking is improved from RFID adoption.				.830	

continues on following page

Table 1. Continued

Items		Component				
		1	2	3	4	5
T5OBT_A	My company observed time is saved from RFID adoption.	Eliminated, due to cross-loadings Eliminated, due to cross-loadings				
T5OBI	My company observed inventory is reduced from RFID adoption.					
T5OBA	My company observed data accuracy is improved from RFID adoption.					
T5OBS	My company observed item security is improved from RFID adoption.					
T5OBIS	My company observed information sharing is improved from RFID adoption.					
T5OBIV	My company observed inventory visibility is improved from RFID adoption.					
Observability of Green Characteristics						
T5OGTC	My company observed reduced emission of toxic components from RFID adoption.					.854
T5OGR	My company observed reduced resource consumption from RFID adoption.					.917
T5OGW	My company observed reduced wastes from RFID adoption.					.866
T5OGEC	My company observed reduced energy consumption from RFID adoption.					.825
T5OGP	My company observed reduced paperwork from RFID adoption.					.745
Cronbach's Aplha		0.914	0.933	0.217	0.882	0.890
Kaiser-Meyer-Olkin (KOM) Measure of Sampling Adequacy		0.840	0.787	0.500	0.766	0.621
Average Variance Extracted (AVE)		75.659	84.869	57.618	74.487	71.097
Sig.		0.000	0.000	0.413[a]	0.000	0.000

[a]The factor complexity has been removed from further analysis because of unacceptable Cronbach's alpha, KMO statistics and significance value.

considered unacceptable and thus were removed. In addition, the AVE values of all variables exceed the minimum acceptable threshold level of 50%, suggesting a good fit of the internal structure of the model.

As shown in Table 1, the KMO values of all variables are 0.50 or above, and the Bartlett's test is significant as all Significance (Sig.) values are smaller than 0.05 except for Complexity that had been removed. Therefore factor analysis for the independent variables is appropriate.

The results of the factor analysis and reliability analysis for the dependent variable (Intention to Use) are shown in Table 2. It shows that the factor analysis resulted in one factor for the dependent variable, i.e. Intention to Use. The Cronbach's alpha of the dependent variable (intention to use) is 0.669, which is exceeding the acceptable coefficient alpha of 0.65, and thus this value support the view that the independent variable had adequate reliability. In addition, the AVE value is well above 50%, suggesting a good fit of the internal structure of the model. As shown in Table 2, the KMO value of dependent

Table 2. Confirmatory factor analysis and Cronbach's alpha results for Dependent variable

Items		Component
		1
Intention to Use		
FutureUiC	Company's future plan in RFID adoption	.895
FutureTiLI	Future trend of RFID adoption in the UK Logistics industry	.799
Stage	Stages regarding RFID adoption	.860
Cronbach's Aplha		0.669
Kaiser-Meyer-Olkin (KOM) Measure of Sampling Adequacy		0.682
Average Variance Extracted (AVE)		72.626
Sig. value		.000

variable is 0.50 or above, and the Bartlett's test is significant as the Sig. value is 0.000. Therefore factor analysis for the dependent variables is also appropriate.

Regression Analysis

Regression analysis was run for the variables of Innovation Diffusion theory. Results are shown in Table 3. The regression does not suffer from multi-collinearity issues since all variable inflation factors are well below the recommended threshold of 10 (Hair et al., 2010). However the results show insufficient evidence for support of three hypotheses (H1, H3, H4), suggesting that the relative advantage, compatibility and observability of benefits of RFID are insignificant in predicting intention to use the technology. The results also show that the observability of green characteristics is significant predictor of intention to use RFID. These findings only support one hypothesis (H5). Thus our results show that, except for the observability of green benefits, all other independent variables of Innovation Diffusion theory do not seem to have significant effect on the prediction of the intention to use RFID.

Table 3. Regression analysis predicting intention to use RFID

Predictors	Std. Beta Coeff.	Hypotheses	Hypothesized Effect	Hypotheses Supported?
Relative advantages	-.011	H1	No effect	No
Compatibility	-.081	H3	No effect	No
Observability of benefits	.071	H4	No effect	No
Observability of green characteristics	.449*	H5	Significant	Yes

* Regression is significant at the level of $p < 0.1$.

DISCUSSION

Relative Advantage

This study has found that relative advantage did not have a significant influence on RFID adoption in the UK Logistics industry. The finding is consistent with those of Wang et al. (2010) in the context of RFID adoption in Taiwanese manufacturing industry and is somewhat similar to the findings of Lee and Kim (2007) on Internet-based Information Systems implementation in Korea. Wang et al. (2010) found that, while relative advantage is not a significant discriminator, this does not mean that the firms perceive RFID technology has a low level of relative advantage. The average perceived relative advantage levels of this study is 5.61, which is above the neutral assessment of 3.5. Thus this implied that companies believe adopting RFID is beneficial for their competitive edge. Therefore the reason for making relative advantage an insignificant discriminator of RFID adoption could be because firms still have no confidence in the RFID system, as it is still in its infancy and relatively new to them. As long as firms think that they do not have sufficient technical capabilities to adopt new technology, they would rather maintain their current systems (Wang et al., 2010).

Compatibility

Compatability was found to have no significant effect on company decisions to adopt RFID technology. The finding of this study is contrary to that of Wang et al. (2010) and Lee and Kim (2007). Wang et al. (2010) observed that compatibility is positively related to RFID adoption in the Taiwanese manufacturing industry. Lee and Kim (2007) explained that the implementation of new technology is encouraged when the system is compatibile with the existing work procedures and value systems because firms want to be less hampered by unstructured task characteristics and to have a greater opportunity to make the tasks compatible with processes. However, in this case, compatibility is not relevant to predicting the intention to use RFID. The average percieved relative advantage levels of this study is 5.64, which is above the neutral assessment of 3.5. Thus this indicated that most respondents felt that RFID technology is compatible with their organizational infrastructure, practices and needs. However, as most adoption decision (71%) is still at the dicussion stage with no firm commitment to pilot studies, there is a lack of perceived compatibility of RFID with the existing infrastructure and the uncertainties as to its compatiblity with organizational practices and thus this makes compatability an insignificant discriminator of RFID adoption.

Observability of Benefits

Results of this study show that observability of benefits did not have significant effect on company decisions to adopt RFID technology. In the prior literature, Zhang et al. (2010) studied the people's perceptions and attitudes toward adoping E-learning and explored key factors affecting E-learning adoption behavior in China. They observed that the perception on observability had the minimum weight in comparison with other factors. This implied that fewer companies believed that the benefits of RFID technology are visible compared to other factors. Moreover, Tornatzky & Klein (1982) found that of those five factors in Innovation Diffusion theory, only compatiblity, relative advantage and complexity are consistently related to innovation adoption. Hence many prior studies (e.g., Lee and Kim, 2007; Tornatzky & Klein,

1982; Wang et al., 2010) directly excluded the trialability and observability constructs in their research models. Tornatzky & Klein (1982) also reasoned that there may be a signficant relationship between observability and adoption of new technology because their findings were often hampered by the small number of studies reporting first-order correlational data.

Observability of Green Characteristics

As highlighted earlier, the inclusion of observability of green characteristics as an innovation attribute of RFID is a primary contribution of this research. Though this attribute was not included in prior studies on innovation diffusion, a very limited number of studies (e.g. Dukovska-Popovska et al., 2010) observed that the applications of RFID in supply chain operations could support a firm's green initiatives. Our finding reveal that observability of green characteristics is a significant predictor of RFID adoption and have positive effect on company's intention to use RFID technology. It indicates that companies are progressively aware about the green-related practices or benefits in RFID adoption, which might be due to the raising attention of the escalating deterioration of the environment, such as increasing level of all types of pollutions, diminishing natural resources and overflowing waste sites, and also due to increasing enviromental pressures on companies by different stakeholders (Kassinis & Vafeas, 2006; Ramanathan et al., 2014b). Moreover, in comparison with other factors in the Innovation Diffusion theory, it is found that green-related benefits of RFID technology were more visible to companies. This may be due to the fact that the governments/authority bodies have been playing an important role by imposing climate policies to protect the environment in the EU bv For instance, under the EU Emission Trading Scheme (ETS), large companies within the EU are requested to monitor their carbon dioxide emissions and provide a report annually, which is to ensure the company has not exceeded their annual emission allowance (Dukovska-Popovska et al., 2010). Therefore, green issues in the logistics industry has gained progressive attention by companies and thus the observability of green characteristics has slightly positive effect on the company's intention to use RFID.

In summary, the finding that only green characteristics seem to have significant relationship with intention to adopt RFID is somewhat counter-intuitive but there have been several previous studies (Lee & Kim, 2007; Tornatzky & Klein, 1982; Wang et al., 2010) in which one or more characteristics of innovation have been found to be insignificant. Since the measurement scales for measuing innovation characteristics are drawn from existing literature, this startling result is not due to issues related to measurement. The main contribution from this study is the fact that green characteristics of RFID seem to be a rather predominantly important driver of its adoption in the UK logistics industry. Our study points to the need for expanding innovation characteristics to include environmental friendliness of technologies. It may be possible to expand measurement scales of innovation characteristics to include environmental benefits of new technologies. For example, relative advantage, complexity or trialability can also include some elements of environmental friendliness gained by using a technology. In this sense, this study suggests extention of the theory of diffusion of innovations from an environmental perspective.

CONCLUSION

Since RFID technology has been regarded an important technology that can provide strategic and operational advantages, it is necessary to understand what determines RFID adoption in the logistics industry. This study is to explore the level of current adoption and future trends of RFID technology, and to examine the influencing factors on RFID adoption in the UK logistics industry. Based on Innovation Diffusion theory (Rogers, 2010), this study developed and validated a research model to examine the influence of contextual factors on RFID adoption.

This study has provided valuable insight into the determinants of RFID adoption in the UK logistics industry. It has found that observability of green characteristics to be facilitators of RFID adoption. Contrary to prior literature and hypotheses of this study, the relative advantage, compatibility and observability of benefits are observed to have no effect on the companies' intention to use RFID. This might be due to the fact that, as RFID technology is still in its infancy and a significant number of implementation questions remain unanswered, firms may have doubts about whether RFID meets their benefits effectively. Furthermore, RFID technology may be in its early stages of development, where firms are influenced by mainstream fashions and tend to be cost sensitive and risk averse. Hence, companies may still prefer to wait and see how well and in what direction RFID technology develops. They will not apply RFID technology without solid proof of guaranteed performance and benefits. This study found one significant facilitator of RFID adoption (i.e. observability of green characteristics), which was not explored in the prior RFID adoption research. This may be due to the fact that the governments/authority bodies have been playing an important role by imposing climate policies to protect the environment in the EU (Dukovska-Popovska et al., 2010).

This study can be extended further. This study only explores the influences of factors on the adoption of RFID technology in UK logistics industry. While there are differences between the UK and other countries in political structures, cultural background, historical perspective, social value, and so on, logistics service providers in different countries may have different views on the influences of these influential factors on the adoption of RFID technology (Lin & Ho, 2009a). Hence it will be worthwhile to advance a cross-national comparative study on the adoption of RFID technology among logistics industries in the UK and in other countries (Lin & Ho, 2009a). This study explores the influences of factors on the adoption of RFID technology in UK logistics industry based on the Innovation Diffusion theory. It will be worthwhile to apply other technology adoption theories to take other possible influential factors on the adoption of RFID technology into considerations in further studies. Finally, more items to measure environmental friendliness of new technologies in terms the five innovation characteristics – relative advantage, compatibility, complexity, trialability and observability – can be included in future RFID studies.

REFERENCES

Attaran, M. (2007). RFID: An enabler of supply chain operations. *Supply Chain Management: An International Journal, 12*(4), 249–257. doi:10.1108/13598540710759763

Dukovska-Popovska, I., Lim, M. K., Steger-Jensen, K., & Hvolby, H. H. (2010). RFID Technology to Support Environmentally Sustainable Supply Chain Management. In *Program for the IEEE International Conference on RFID-Technology and Applications*, (pp. 291-295). IEEE.

Hair, F. J., Black, W. C., Babin, B. J., & Anderson, R. E. (2010). *Multivariate Data Analysis* (7th ed.). Upper Saddle River, NJ: Pearson Prentice Hall.

Kassinis, G., & Vafeas, N. (2006). Stakeholder pressures and Environmental performance. *Academy of Management Journal, 49*(15), 145–159. doi:10.5465/AMJ.2006.20785799

Krigslund, R., Popovski, P., Dukovska-Popovska, I., Pedersen, G. F., & Manev, B. (2010). Using ICT in Greening: The Role of RFID. In *Towards Green ICT* (pp. 97–116). Denmark: River Publishers.

Lee, S., & Kim, K. (2007). Factors affecting the implementation success of Internet-based information systems. *Computers in Human Behavior, 23*(4), 1853–1880. doi:10.1016/j.chb.2005.12.001

Li, S., Godon, D., & Visich, J. K. (2010). An exploratory study of RFID implementation in the supply chain. *Management Research Review, 33*(10), 1005–1015. doi:10.1108/01409171011084003

Lin, C. Y. & Ho, Y. H. (2009a). RFID technology adoption and supply chain performance: an empirical study in China's logistics industry. *Supply Chain Management: An International Journal*, 369-378.

Lin, C. Y., & Ho, Y. H. (2009b). An Empirical Study on the Adoption of RFID Technology for Logistics Service Providers in China. *International Business Research, 2*(1), 23–36. doi:10.5539/ibr.v2n1p23

Lin, L. C. (2009). An integrated framework for the development of radio frequency identification technology in the logistics and supply chain management. *Computers & Industrial Engineering, 57*(3), 832–842. doi:10.1016/j.cie.2009.02.010

Luo, Z., Tan, Z., Ni, Z., & Yen, B. (2007). *Analysis of RFID Adoption in China.* IEEE International Conference on e-Business Engineering. 10.1109/ICEBE.2007.35

Pedroso, M. C., Zwicker, R., & de Souza, C. A. (2009). RFID adoption: Framework and survey in large Brazilian companies. *Industrial Management & Data Systems, 109*(7), 877–897. doi:10.1108/02635570910982256

Ramanathan, R., Ko, L. W. K., Chen, H., & Ramanathan, U. (2014a). Green characteristics of RFID technologies: An exploration in the UK logistics sector from innovation diffusion perspective. In I. Lee (Ed.), RFID Technology Integration for Business Performance Improvement (pp. 158–180). IGI Global.

Ramanathan, R., Poomkaew, B., & Nath, P. (2014b). The impact of organizational pressures on environmental performance of firms. *Business Ethics (Oxford, England), 23*(2), 169–182. doi:10.1111/beer.12042

Riedel, J., Pawar, K. S., Torroni, S., & Ferrari, E. (2008). A survey of RFID awareness and use in the UK logistics industry. In *Dynamics in Logistics* (pp. 105–115). Springer Berlin Heidelberg. doi:10.1007/978-3-540-76862-3_9

Robinson, L. (2009). *A summary of Diffusion of Innovations.* Available at: http://www.enablingchange.com.au/Summary_Diffusion_Theory.pdf

Rogers, E. M. (2010). *Diffusion of innovations.* Simon and Schuster.

Roh, J. J., Kunnathur, A., & Tarafdar, M. (2009). Classification of RFID adoption: An expected benefits approach. *Information & Management, 46*(6), 357–363. doi:10.1016/j.im.2009.07.001

Tornatzky, L. G., & Klein, K. J. (1982). Innovation Characteristics and Innovation Adoption Implementation: A Meta-Analysis of Findings. *IEEE Transactions on Engineering Management, EM-29*(1), 28–45. doi:10.1109/TEM.1982.6447463

Wamba, S. F. (2012). Achieving supply chain integration using RFID technology: The case of emerging intelligent B-to-B e-commerce processes in a living laboratory. *Business Process Management Journal*, *18*(1), 58–81. doi:10.1108/14637151211215019

Wang, Y. M., Wang, Y. S., & Yang, Y. F. (2010). Understanding the determinants of RFID adoption in the manufacturing industry. *Technological Forecasting and Social Change*, *77*(5), 803–815. doi:10.1016/j.techfore.2010.03.006

Zhang, L., Wen, H., Li, D., Fu, Z., & Cui, S. (2010). E-learning adoption intention and its key influence factors based on innovation adoption theory. *Mathematical and Computer Modelling*, *51*(11-12), 1428–1432. doi:10.1016/j.mcm.2009.11.013

KEY TERMS AND DEFINITIONS

Compatibility: The degree to which an innovation is perceived as consistent with the existing values, past values, and needs of potential adopters.

Complexity: The extent to which an innovation is perceived as relatively difficult to understand and use.

Diffusion of Innovations: A theory to help understand how new innovations get accepted at an organizational level.

Green Characteristics: The characteristics of a technology that helps in improving environmental sustainability of an organization that embraces the technology.

Observability: The degree to which the results of an innovation are visible to others.

Relative Advantage: The extent to which people believe that an innovation is better than the traditional one.

RFID: Radio frequency identification (RFID) is one type of auto-identification technology that uses radio frequency (RF) waves to identify, track and locate individual physical items.

Trialability: The extent to which people believe that there are chances for the innovation to be experienced before deciding whether to adopt it or not.

ENDNOTE

1 This chapter draws heavily from Ramanathan et al. (2014a).

This research was previously published in the Encyclopedia of E-Commerce Development, Implementation, and Management edited by In Lee; pages 1913-1922, copyright year 2016 by Business Science Reference (an imprint of IGI Global).

Chapter 2
Using Diffusion of Innovations Theory to Encourage Workers to Make Healthy Food Choices and Engage in Physical Activity

Debra Weiss-Randall
Florida Atlantic University, USA

ABSTRACT

Employers want workers to be as healthy as possible, to reduce absenteeism and to boost productivity. The challenge is getting employees to adopt healthy behaviors, a daunting task in our obesogenic society, which promotes a sedentary lifestyle and a diet high in saturated fat, sodium, and sugar. We are seeing an epidemic of obesity and type 2 diabetes, two preventable diseases that impair quality of life and increase healthcare costs. Rogers' Diffusions of Innovations (DOI) theory explains how and why people adopt new behaviors. Rogers observed how some workers were resistant to change. He categorized people according to how long it took them to adopt an innovation. He found that certain attributes were characteristic of early adopters, the opinion leaders that organizations need to win over to facilitate acceptance of an innovation. This chapter explores how DOI theory can be applied to the workplace to promote healthy behaviors.

INTRODUCTION

On January 11, 1964, Luther L. Terry, M.D., Surgeon General of the U.S. Public Health Service, issued a warning to the American people that smoking was hazardous to one's health and was a cause of lung cancer and laryngeal cancer as well as the main cause of chronic bronchitis. The Surgeon General's Advisory Committee on Smoking and Health had reviewed more than 7,000 articles relating to smoking and disease before issuing its report. The response of the American public was tepid (Centers for Disease Control and Prevention, 2009). Why was that the case? For one thing, smoking is highly addictive, and

DOI: 10.4018/978-1-7998-0417-8.ch002

smoking cessation is difficult and uncomfortable. In addition, changing behavior is a complex process that takes time. There are some—the early adopters—who are in the vanguard of behavior change and lead the pack. The rest of the crowd takes much longer to believe that they should change their behavior and to actually adopt a new behavior. The new behavior, or innovation, does not take hold automatically. Its acceptance and adoption requires an effective health education campaign (Oldenburg & Parcel, 2002). The Diffusion of Innovations Theory provides a roadmap for promoting and gaining widespread acceptance of an innovation.

After the 1964 Surgeon General report, warning labels were put on cigarette packages. Tobacco companies continued to promote cigarette smoking on the radio television, movies, and print media with icons such as Joe Camel and Marlboro Man. Cigarettes were associated with being cool, sexy, and hip. The jingles for the commercials were catchy—even a young child could pick up the tune and repeat it. In 1969, the U.S. Surgeon General issued another smoking report that warned that low birthweight was associated with tobacco use (Report of the Surgeon General, 1969). Under pressure, Congress passed the Public Health Cigarette Smoking Act, which banned cigarette commercials from radio and TV, effective January 2, 1971. Print sources such as magazine continued to advertise cigarettes, and movies still glamorized smoking cigarettes. Additional federal restrictions were passed, banning cigarette advertising on billboards, and smoking on airplanes.

The next step in tobacco control was to take the diffusion of innovations to the state level. Slowly, a tipping point was reached, and the onus was on the smoker to leave and smoke outside. Individual states created tobacco-free areas, then tobacco-free buildings, and then tobacco-free campuses and workplaces. Of course, there are some who complain that smokers get "too many breaks" at work, because they have to go outside. But it is well worth it so that the non-smoking employees are not exposed to secondhand smoke. The ultimate goal is to get all smokers to stop and to prevent young people from starting. One step in the right direction is the refusal of CVS to sell cigarettes. Otis Brawley, Chief Medical Officer for the American Cancer Society, called CVS's an "an act of corporate courage," and added "the Cancer Society has pressured pharmacies to ban cigarettes for several years. Studies show that being forced to travel just two extra blocks can deter someone from buying cigarettes" (Szabo, 2014).

Refraining from tobacco use is one of the leading national health indicators for adults in the United States today (Healthy People, 2020). Other key health indicators include eating a healthy diet, getting adequate exercise, maintaining a healthy weight, refraining from substance abuse, and getting regular clinical preventive services such as cancer screenings. A full list of the 26 leading health indicators is found on the *Healthy People 2020* website (Healthy People, 2020).

It is important for workplace management to understand how to use the *DOI* theory to improve compliance from employees with their lifestyle health factors. The focus of this chapter is on applying *DOI* to the workplace and developing strategies for its successful implementation in improving employees' nutrition and physical activity level.

BACKGROUND: DIFFUSIONS OF INNOVATION THEORY

Everett M. Rogers first published his seminal work *Diffusion of Innovations Theory* in 1962. The fifth edition of his work was published in 2003, a year before he died. By the time he wrote his final edition of *Diffusion of Innovations* (2003), the theory had become so widely recognized as a valuable framework for social change that Rogers estimated that there were approximately 5,200 publications about

DOI theory. Rogers grew up on a farm in Iowa and became interested in the diffusion of agricultural innovations after watching how farmers responded to the availability of new technology to improve agricultural output and efficiency. He noticed that some farmers delayed adopting innovations that would have been profitable for them. He wondered why some farmers adopted innovations while other resisted. Rogers enrolled in graduate school at Iowa State to study rural sociology and the diffusion of agricultural innovations (Rogers, 2003). He developed a generalized diffusion theory, and posited that his theory explained social change, a fundamental human process.

Rogers (2003, pp. 11-12) defined innovation as "an idea, practice, or object that is perceived as new by an individual or other unit of adoption" and diffusion as "the process in which an innovation is communicated through certain channels over time among the members of a social system." The four main elements of DOI are innovation, communication channels, time, and the social system.

The perceived characteristics of an innovation influences its rate of adoption. Rogers (2003) lists the following five characteristics as the most predictive of the adoption rate:

- Relative advantage (the degree to which the innovation is perceived to be an improvement over the status quo)
- Compatibility (the degree to which the innovation is perceived to be consistent with target audience's existing values, experiences, and needs)
- Complexity (the degree to which the innovation is perceived to be difficult to understand and use)
- Trialability (the degree to which the innovation can be experimented with on a limited basis)
- Observability (the degree to which the results of the innovation are visible to others)

The first two characteristics—relative advantage and compatibility—are particularly important. The less complex an innovation appears to be to the target audience, the more likely they are to adopt it more readily. Another characteristic Rogers (2003) cites is the ability to re-invent the innovation, that is, to make it one's own by customizing it. Re-inventability makes an innovation more attractive to the target audience (Rogers, 2003).

A communication channel is the means by which the innovation is communicated from one individual to others. Mass media channels such as radio, television, and newspapers are an effective way to reach large numbers of people. Interpersonal channels are face-to-face exchanges between people. The third main type of communication channel is interactive communication using the Internet (Rogers, 2003).

The amount of time that it takes from the introduction of an innovation to its eventual adoption is known as the "innovation decision process." This process generally unfolds in a time-ordered sequence that follows five stages, as shown in Table 1.

Table 1. Stages in the adoption process

Knowledge	First exposure to innovation
Persuasion	Individual actively seeks information about innovation
Decision	Individual weighs pros/cons of adopting innovation and makes a decision
Implementation	Individual employs the innovation and forms an opinion of its usefulness
Confirmation	Individual finalizes his/her decision to adopt the innovation

(Rogers, 2003)

As Rogers noted in his own early years living on an Iowa farm, some individuals adopt innovations fairly easily and quickly, while other take years to adopt the innovation, even though there is visible evidence of its benefits to others. Adoption also may be by an organization rather than an individual.

The *Transtheoretical Model Stages of Change* (Prochaska et al., 1992), one of the most widely used models for behavior change, works in tandem with Rogers' *DOI* theoretical framework. In the *Stages of Change*, an individual goes through five stages in making a behavior change. The first stage is pre-contemplation, when it becomes clear that the individual has a problem but he or she is not yet ready to address it; the second stage is contemplation, when the individual is seriously thinking about overcoming the problem; the third stage is preparation, when the individual intends to take action in the immediate future and is actively planning for it; the fourth stage is action, when the individual changes his or her behavior to overcome the problem; and the fifth stage is maintenance, when the individual consolidates and maintains the behavior change. In Rogers' *DOI* theory, the knowledge stage corresponds with pre-contemplation; the persuasion stage corresponds with contemplation; the decision stage corresponds with preparation; the implementation stage corresponds with action; and the confirmation stage corresponds with maintenance (Rogers, 2003; Prochaska et al., 1992).

Innovativeness is "the degree to which an individual or other unit of adoption is relatively earlier in adopting new ideas than the other members of the system" (Rogers, 2003, p. 22). Rogers (2003) classifies members of a social system on the basis of their innovativeness, that is, the amount of time it takes them to adopt an innovation; Rogers's five categories of adoptors are shown in Table 2.

Innovators, the first to adopt an innovation, are active information seekers who are able to cope with higher levels of uncertainty than are the other categories of adopters. They tend to have more mass media exposure and more extensive interpersonal networks than do the other categories of adopters. Diffusion of innovations takes place within the context of a social system. The norms, or established behavior patterns, of the social system influence the rate of adoption of an innovation. Opinion leaders—those who influence the perceptions of others in the social system—are important players in the adoption or rejection of an innovation. Understanding the differences between early adoptors and later adoptors is an important part of the process of creating a tipping point in an organization, to persuade the majority of the members of the organization to adopt the innovation. Table 3 sums up the differences between early adoptors and later adoptors in terms of three variables—socioeconomic status, personality values, and communication behaviors:

Convincing individuals (or organizations) to change their behavior requires more than education about the consequences of adopting the innovation. It also requires a social marketing campaign, to persuade people about the relative advantages of the innovation vis-a-vis the status quo (Rogers, 2003), as well as policy changes to make the environment more supportive of the innovation. The anti-smoking campaign

Table 2. Categories of adoptors

Innovators	Individual finalizes his/her decision to adopt the innovation
Early adopters	Respected opinion leaders, willing to try new ideas
Early majority	Thoughtful individuals, careful but accepting change more quickly than the average
Late majority	Skeptical individuals, will try something new only after majority is using it
Laggards	Traditional people critical of new ideas, will accept change only if it has become mainstream

(Rogers, 2003)

Table 3. Early adoptors vs. late adoptors

	Early Adoptors	Late Adoptors
1. Socioeconomic Status	More years of formal education More likely to be literate Higher social status (income, lifestyle, occupational prestige, self-perceived identification with a social class) A greater degree of upward social mobility Have larger-sized units (farms, schools, companies)	Few years of formal education Less likely to be literate Lower social status (income, lifestyle, occupational prestige, self-perceived identification with a social class) A lesser degree of upward social mobility Have smaller-sized units (farms, schools, companies)
2. Personality Variables	Have greater empathy Are less dogmatic Have a greater ability to deal with abstractions Have greater rationality Have more intelligence Have a more favorable attitude toward change Are better able to cope with uncertainty and risk Have a more favorable attitude toward science Are less fatalistic Have higher aspirations	Have less empathy Are more dogmatic Have a lesser ability to deal with abstractions Have lesser rationality Have less intelligence Have a less favorable attitude toward change Are less able to cope with uncertainty and risk Have a less favorable attitude toward science Are more fatalistic Have lower aspirations
3. Communication Behavior	Have more social participation Greater interpersonal connectedness Are more widely travelled and cosmopolite	Have less social participation Less interpersonal connectedness Are less widely travelled and cosmopolite

(Rogers, 2003)

in the United States demonstrates that a very intense and long-term effort may be necessary to diffuse an innovation. Most individuals do not readily change their lifestyle habits, even in the face of observable evidence that it is in their best interests.

Rogers posited that the adoption of an innovation using the five categories of adopters follows a normal bell curve, shown in Figure 1. Rogers (2003) notes that "The adopter classification system is not symmetrical, in that there are three adopter categories to the left of the mean and only two to the right" (p. 281). He notes that "one solution would be to break laggards into two categories, such as early and late laggards," but he opts not to do so because "laggards seem to form a fairly homogeneous category" (Rogers, 2003, p. 281).

Figure 1.

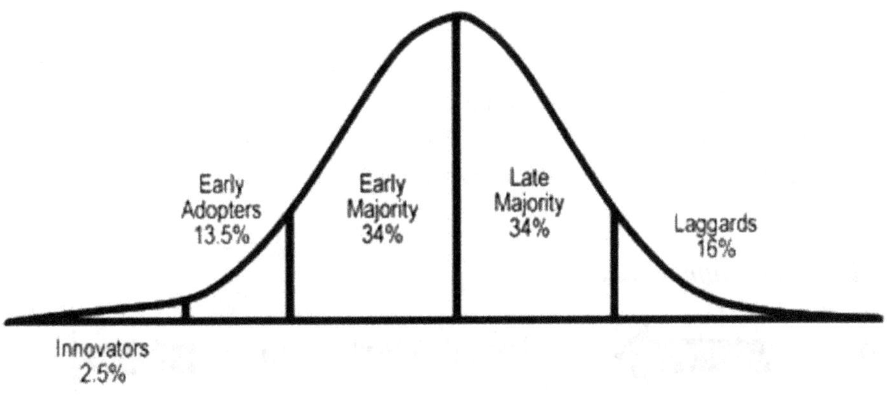

In a normal bell curve, 68% of the individuals fall within 1 standard deviation of the mean, and 95% fall within two standard deviations from the mean. In Rogers' bell curve, the early and late majority form the 68%, the early adopters add another 13.5%, but the laggards do not make a symmetrical 13.5%; instead they take up the whole right tail of the curve at 16%. This phenomenon drives home the point of how hard it is to get some people to change!

DISCUSSION: APPLICATIONS IN THE WORKPLACE

Leaders who plan to diffuse innovations in the workplace should use the distinctive characteristics of the different adopter groups for audience segmentation; i.e., market the innovation using messages and communication channels tailored for each adopter category. In addition, employees will be more likely to have a positive attitude toward change if they are part of the process. Leaders should include the early adoptors in the process of persuading the late adoptors to change (Stichler, 2011).

Leaders who wish to implement an innovation using *DOI* theory need to focus time and resources on the first, on education--making the employees aware and knowledgeable about all aspects of the change—and next, on using persuasive social marketing techniques to address their attitudes toward the change. Social marketing uses media to promote a new product, idea, or behavior, and thereby to change the target population's attitude and increase the acceptability of the innovation (Simons-Morton et al., 1995). After individuals' attitudes have changed, there is one more step—passing laws to support the change, such as banning smoking in the workplace. Healthy behavior change moves along a continuum from education (knowledge), to marketing, to laws supporting the innovation, as shown in Figure 2. To return to our earlier example, the U.S. Surgeon General's 1964 report on smoking informed the public about the dangers of tobacco (education); subsequently the anti-smoking message was diffused around the country using various communication channels (e.g., PSAs, warnings on packages) and messages (social marketing); next, laws were passed banning cigarette commercials on TV, banning smoking on airplanes, and eventually creating tobacco-free campuses and workplaces. The anti-smoking movement has made progress, but it took a long time because of the profound change required to adopt a new social norm enforced through practice and policy.

Managers seeking to improve the health of their employees must encourage the adoption of healthy behaviors. Healthy eating and adequate physical exercise together form the prime defense against obesity, a disease that is of great concern to employers due to its role in premature morbidity and mortality, as well as its astronomically high medical costs.

More than one-third of American adults and 17% of youth are obese, defined as having a Body Mass Index (BMI) of 30 or greater (Ogden et al., 2014). In certain groups, the prevalence is even higher; non-Hispanic blacks and Hispanics have age-adjusted prevalence rates of obesity of 47.8% and 42.5%, respectively, compared to rates of 32.6% for non-Hispanic whites and 10.8% for non-Hispanic Asians (Ogden et al., 2014). Obesity rates vary with age; prevalence is 39.5% among adults aged 40-59 years

Figure 2. Continuum of healthy behavior change

Education → Social Marketing → Law

old, 30.3% among adults aged 20-39, and 35.4% among adults over age 60 (Ogden et al., 2014). Obesity is very costly; Finkelstein et al's study (2009) found that "across all payers, obese people had medical spending that was $1,429 greater than spending for normal-weight people in 2006" (p. w825). Being obese or overweight (BMI of 25 to 29.9) is associated with an increased risk of morbidity from hypertension, dyslipidemia, type 2 diabetes, coronary heart disease, stroke, gallbladder disease, osteoarthritis, sleep apnea and respiratory problems, and endometrial, breast, prostate, and colon cancers. In addition, obese adults and youth may experience social stigmatization and discrimination (NHLBI Obesity Education Initiative Expert Panel, 1998).

The fight against obesity comprises two main components:

1. Changing eating habits to include high-fiber, low-fat items; and
2. Increasing the level of physical activity.

In the case studies that follow, employers used the following strategies to encourage employees to make healthy food choices, exercise, and maintain a healthy weight:

- Providing nutritional and physical activity information
- Placing posters about healthy eating at high-traffic areas in the workplace
- Adding healthy choice foods to vending machines and company cafeterias
- Giving employees frequent reminders about healthy food choice in point-of-purchase messages and lunch tips on pay stubs
- Offering free or discounted gym memberships
- Offering incentives, such as cash rewards and products (e.g., T-shirts and mugs)
- Offering health coaching
- Offering weight management
- Making sure that workplace policies included specific statements about providing access to healthy food choices.

The following case studies help us to understand how and under what conditions people adopt these recommended healthy behaviors. A common theme throughout is the importance of management and supervisor buy-in.

A CANADIAN STUDY: ADOPTING AND IMPLEMENTING NUTRITIONAL GUIDELINES

Recreational facilities in Canada are ubiquitous and provide an affordable source of physical activities that families can go to after school and on the weekends; 80% of them sell food (Olstad et al., 2012). In a multiple case study in Alberta, Canada, the *DOI* theoretical framework was used to determine why and how healthy food choices were adopted by the recreational facility managers; the researchers selected *DOI* because it is "a socio-environmental paradigm [that] provides a framework for understanding obesity as a consequence of the complex and dynamic interplay between individuals…and their environments" (Olstad et al, 2012, p. 2). The mixed methods study looked at adoption and implementation of Alberta's nutritional guidelines and the nature of the food environment within three case studies: an adopter, a semi-adopter and a non-adopter. The study found that the key to adoption and implementation of Alberta's nutritional guidelines was the nutrition-related knowledge, perceptions, and beliefs of the managers. Compared to non-adopters, facilities that had adopted the nutritional guidelines in stocking their vending machines had greater availability of "choose most often" food and beverage items, and their vending machine items contained fewer calories on average. In the full adopter facility, revenues from food declined 17% in the first year of implementation. Clearly, more social marketing needs to be done to influence the attitudes of those buying food at the recreational facilities! The researchers noted that stronger government measures, combined with partnerships between recreation centers, on the one hand, and industry and schools, on the other, might help facilitate adoption of Alberta's nutritional guidelines (Olstad et al., 2012).

A NETHERLANDS STUDY: A NUTRITION LABELLING INTERVENTION IN WORKSITE CAFETERIAS

In the Netherlands, 35%-40% of workers eat their lunch out in worksite cafeterias (The Netherlands Nutrition Center, 2005). With so many workers eating out on a daily basis, it is vital to provide healthy food choices and, further, to pinpoint which factors are most influential in encouraging workers to make healthy food selections. In 2006, the *Choices* nutrition logo was introduced in the Netherlands; the logo appeared on products that qualified as healthy choices based on international recommendations by the World Health Organization (Vyth et al., 2011). The aim of the Netherlands cafeteria study was to use *DOI* theory to study which attributes influence the implementation of the *Choices* logo. Catering managers of 316 cafeterias in the Netherlands completed questionnaires, with a response rate 49.8% (Vyth et al., 2011).

The best predictors for the frequency of offering fresh *Choices* products (all significant) were compatibility (consistency with the beliefs of the catering manager; OR ¼ 1.52), voluntariness (perception of the implementation as voluntary; OR ¼ 0.50), result demonstrability (ability to communicate the implementation; OR ¼ 1.52) and complexity in the sense of time (time needed for implementation; OR ¼ 0.70). The best predictors for frequency of using *Choices* promotion material were voluntariness (OR ¼ 0.54), result demonstrability (OR ¼ 1.51), and relative advantage (perceived advantage of the implementation) (Vyth et al, 2011), (OR ¼ 1.44) were the best predictors (all significant).

UNITED STATES WORKSITE INTERVENTION PROGRAM TO INCREASE PHYSICAL ACTIVITY

In 2012 in the United States, 29.6% of adults engaged in no leisure-time physical activity; 50.0% (age adjusted) of adults met the national guidelines for aerobic physical activity (at least 150 minutes per week of moderate physical activity, or 75 minutes per week of vigorous physical activity, or an equivalent combination) (Healthy People, 2020). Despite progress (in 2008, 36.2% of US adults were sedentary and only 43.5% met physical activity guidelines), 50% of the US adult population still is not meeting national physical activity guidelines (Healthy People, 2020). The aim of The Physical Activity and Lifestyle Study was to address multiple barriers to physical activity in 60 departments at a large southeastern university (Gazmararian et al., 2013). Departments were randomly assigned to one of five conditions:

1. Control
2. Gym membership
3. Gym + PA education
4. Gym + time during the workday
5. Gym + PA education + time during the workday

Providing paid time during the workday for physical activity, giving workers free gym membership, and providing free PA education were innovations intended to motivate workers and to reduce barriers (time, money, knowledge) to engaging in physical activity (Gazmararian et al., 2013). Data was collected at baseline, and again after six weeks, three months, six months, and nine months. Data on physical activity intensity and quantity were measured using the 7-Day Physical Activity Recall (PAR) instrument for the 410 participants. The results showed no significant improvement when a group received gym alone compared to the control group. However, gym + PA education, gym + time, and gym + PA education + time were all significantly better than the control group control (RR 1.51 [1.15, 1.98], RR 1.46 [1.13, 1.88], RR 1.28 [1.01, 1.62]), with results sustained over the 9-month trial. The researchers had hypothesized that adding a third component would further increase PA over that associated with two components, but it did not, suggesting that adding another component is not necessarily more effective (Gazmararian et al., 2013).

THE AUSTRALIAN NATIONAL WORKPLACE HEALTH PROJECT

The largest trial of worksite wellness done in Australia was implemented at 20 worksites to assess four key behaviors affecting employee health--cigarette smoking, unhealthy food choices, physical inactivity, and unsafe levels of alcohol use. A two-by-two factorial design was used to test two different interventions: sociobehavioral and environmental. First, participants were asked to complete a survey and undergo a Health Risk Appraisal (HRA). The control groups in the trial received only the HRA and general advice (minimal condition). Worksites were randomly allocated to conditions (Simpson et al., 2000).

Participants receiving the sociobehavioral intervention were given tailored counseling that followed *Stages of Change* principles; they also received self-instructional material supplemented by group instruction. The environmental intervention encouraged employees to modify aspects of their physical, information, and policy environments at work to improve their health. For example, in the arena of healthy eating, the physical environment was altered by placing posters about healthy eating at strategic locations in the worksite and by adding low-fat, high-fiber food items to vending machines; strategies that targeted the information environment included point-of-purchase message about healthy food choices and take-home messages for healthy lunch tips on pay stubs; policy changes included the addition of specific statements about providing access to healthy food choices (Simpson et al., 2012). During the 12 months of the trial, the response rate was 73%. Results for participants in the intervention groups compared with those in the control group showed more physical activity (500-600 MET minute/week) and fiber intake (0.66–0.80 servings/day of fruit and vegetables), and decreased fat consumption (1.4–1.7) (Simpson et al., 2000).

UNITED STATES NATIONAL HEALTHY WORKSITE PROGRAM

In October 2011, the Centers for Disease Control and Prevention (Centers for Disease Control and Prevention, 2014) began the National Healthy Worksite Program (NHWP), to assist employers in implementing health promotion programs that provide prevention activities, reduce chronic illness and disability, and improve worker productivity (Centers for Disease Control and Prevention, 2014). Eight communities were selected for inclusion in the program, based on need, including significant health disparities; 115 businesses are now part of NHWP. The NHWP assesses employees' needs, and then develops employee plans that offer health coaching, weight management and physical activity through changes in the work environment. The PA plan may include time during the workday; the healthy eating plan may include nutritional and caloric information on food items in worksite cafeterias and vending machines, as well as access to nearby farmers' or garden markets (Centers for Disease Control and Prevention, 2014).

NHWP provides a model for businesses that wish to develop a worksite wellness program. The CDC's tool kit *Workplace Health Promotion* provides guidance for business managers about doing a needs assessment, and then planning, implementing, and evaluating a Workplace Health Promotion Program (Centers for Disease Control and Prevention, 2014). The CDC's tool kit *Steps to Wellness* gives an overview of national PA guidelines and offers suggestions about how to incorporate physical activity programs into the workplace, with examples of successful worksite PA programs (Centers for Disease Control and Prevention, 2014).

FUTURE RESEARCH IMPLICATIONS

According to a recent study sponsored by the U.S. Department of Labor and the U.S. Department of Health and Human Services (Mattke et al., 2013), the numbers of firms offering worksite wellness programs has been increasing. In 2013, 51% of U.S. businesses had worksite wellness programs; most offered both screenings and interventions covering primary prevention (risk reduction), secondary prevention (disease management), and health promotion (e.g., healthy food items in vending machines and cafeteria). Seventy-nine percent of the programs offered nutrition interventions, and 72% offered fitness activities (Mattke et al., 2013). A concern was increasing participation rates, as only 46% of employees underwent screenings, and a fifth or less followed through after being identified as needing an intervention. Incentives were popular, usually in the form of gym discounts, cash incentives, and novelty items such as T-shirts, coffee mugs, and gift cards. Cash incentives for HRA completion increased participation, especially over the threshold of $50 (Mattke et al., 2013). A recent meta-analysis (Hutchinson & Wilson, 2011) found employees were more likely to support workplace interventions that used motivation enhancement such as motivational interviewing or the use of rewards. This finding is in line with the *Transtheoretical Model Stages of Change* and *DOI* theory.

Five key facilitators of successful worksite wellness programs were identified:

- Effective communication strategies (broad outreach and clear messaging)
- Opportunity for employees to engage (convenience and accessibility of programs)
- Leadership engaged at all levels (buy-in from direct supervisors is crucial)
- Use of existing resources and relationships
- Continuous evaluation

Encouraging healthy eating habits and regular physical activity should be implemented at the policy level as part of an integrated approach to weight management that includes healthy work scheduling, policies governing meal and break times, well-equipped, clean break room for meals, and management support for rest, movement breaks, and flex time. Stress management is another factor that impacts weight management (Nobrega et al., 2014).

CONCLUSION

Changing ingrained lifestyle behaviors such as eating habits and physical activity (or lack of it) is a slow process. Recall how long it took for anti-smoking laws to protect the public from cigarette smoke! Rogers would be the first to tell you that those late majority and laggards delay full diffusion of an innovation. The adoption process requires changing the social norms, so that, for example, eating a low-fat, high-fiber diet becomes the accepted norm, replacing the previous norm of fatty fried foods and soda.

The first step in changing social norms is to educate the public, such as the U.S. Surgeon General did about the dangers of cigarette smoking in 1964. The second step, social marketing, plays a key role in facilitating adoption of healthy lifestyle behaviors. Purveyors of a healthy message use mass media to persuade consumers. A good example of this is filmmaker Morgan Spurlock's 2004 film *Supersize Me,* which helped to raise public consciousness about the dangers of sugary soda and fatty junk food. One diabetic man was shown downing several gallons of soda even after becoming blind. Fortunately, he changed his behavior in time to regain his eyesight! (Clearly, this man was a laggard and serious soda addict.) In *Supersize Me,* Spurlock points out the ridiculous financial disparities between those marketing healthy food and those marketing candy and McDonalds: the 5 A Day Fruit and Vegetable Campaign spent $2 million a year on promotion, while McDonald's spent $1.4 billion on direct advertising and Hershey's spent $200 million—David and Goliath (*Supersize Me*, 2004)! As a result of the impact of Spurlock's film, McDonald's stopped making Supersize fries; subsequently, the fast food chain stopped frying potatoes in saturated fat after consumers sued McDonald's. So, progress is occurring, albeit slowly; its pace can be accelerated with the use of mass media, which reach millions of people quickly. Social marketing in the workplace may include, for example, appealing posters of people exercising, combined with a gym incentive. The third step in changing social norms is policy changes. An example of this is implementing a no-smoking policy in the workplace, which has become more acceptable to employees in recent years as the social norm has changed from smoking to non-smoking.

In conclusion, the *Diffusion of Innovations* theory is a useful framework for worksite wellness programs that seek to improve employees' food choices and physical activity level. Worksite wellness programs are a good organizational vehicle for dispensing health promotion using *DOI* in conjunction with the *Stages of Change* model. For worksite wellness programs to be effective, there must be effective communication, employee engagement, and buy-in from the firm leadership, especially the direct supervisors. Partnerships with industry are helpful in dispensing healthier food choices in vending machines and workplace cafeterias. In addition, incentives such as gift cards, gym memberships, and novelty items are useful to motivate employees to participate. The workplace is where most adults spend almost two-thirds of their waking time during the week. Employers have a captive audience! The workplace is a wonderful avenue for promoting healthy behaviors using *DOI*, provided that management buys in and serves as role models and facilitators.

REFERENCES

Centers for Disease Control & Prevention. (2009). Smoking and Tobacco Use. History of the Surgeon General's Reports on Smoking and Health. Retrieved from http://www.cdc.gov/tobacco/data_statistics/sgr/history/index.htm

Centers for Disease Control & Prevention. (2014). National Healthy Worksite Program. Fighting obesity in the workplace. Retrieved from http://www.cdc.gov/nationalhealthyworksite/program-news/news-archives.html

Centers for Disease Control and Prevention. (2015). Adult Obesity Facts, United States. Retrieved from http://www.cdc.gov/obesity/data/adult.html

Finkelstein, E. A., Trogden, J. G., Cohen, J. W., & Dietz, W. D. (2009). Annual medical spending attributable to obesity: Payer-and service-specific estimates. *Health Affairs*, *28*(5), w822–w831. doi:10.1377/hlthaff.28.5.w822 PMID:19635784

Gazmararian, J. A., Elon, L., Newsome, K., Schild, L., & Jacobson, K. L. (2013). A randomized prospective trial of a worksite intervention program to increase physical activity. *American Journal of Health Promotion*, *28*(1), 32–40. doi:10.4278/ajhp.110525-QUAN-220 PMID:23470188

Healthy People. 2020. (2015). *Physical Activity: Objectives*. Washington, D.C. U.S. Department of Health and Human Services. Retrieved from http://www.healthypeople.gov/2020/topics-objectives/topic/physical-activity/objectives

Hutchinson, A. D., & Wilson, C. (2011). Improving nutrition and physical activity in the workplace: A meta-analysis of intervention studies. *Health Promotion International*, *27*(2), 238–249. doi:10.1093/heapro/dar035 PMID:21733915

Mattke, S., Liu, H., Caloyeras, J. P., Huang, C. Y., Van Busum, K. R., Khodyakov, D., & Shier, V. (2013). *Workplace wellness programs study: a research report*. Santa Monica, CA: Rand Corporation. Sponsored by the U.S. Department of Labor and the U.S. Department of Health and Human Services.

NHLBI Obesity Education Initiative Expert Panel. (1998). The Evidence Report NIH Publication No. 98-4083. National Institutes of Health. National Heart, Lung, and Blood Institute in cooperation with The National Institute of Diabetes and Digestive and Kidney Diseases.

Nobrega, S., Champagne, C., Punnett, L., Abreu, M., & Kernan, L. (2014). *Understanding and counteracting the obesogenic work environment*. Lowell, MA: Center for the Promotion of Health in the New England Workplace.

Ogden, C. L., Carroll, M. D., Kit, B. K., & Flegal, K. M. (2014). Prevalence of Childhood and Adult Obesity in the United States, 20112012. *Journal of the American Medical Association*, *311*(8), 806–814. doi:10.1001/jama.2014.732 PMID:24570244

Oldenburg, B., & Parcel, G. S. (2002). Diffusion of innovations. In K. Glanz, B. K. Rimer, & F. M. Lewis (Eds.), *Health behavior & health education* (3rd ed., pp. 312–334). San Francisco, CA: Wiley & Sons.

Olstad, D. L., Raine, K. D., & McCargar, L. J. (2012). Adopting and implementing nutrition guidelines in recreational facilities: Public and private sector roles. A multiple case study. *BMC Public Health*, *12*(376), 1–20. doi:10.1186/1471-2458-12-376 PMID:22632384

Prochaska, J. O., DiClemente, C. C., & Norcross, J. C. (1992). In search of how people change: Applications to addictive behaviors. *The American Psychologist*, *47*(9), 1102–1114. doi:10.1037/0003-066X.47.9.1102 PMID:1329589

Public Health Service Review. (1967). (Supplement). Washington, D.C.: U.S. Department of Health, Education and Welfare. Retrieved from http://profiles.nlm.nih.gov/ps/access/NNBBLH.pdf

Reports of the Surgeon General. (1969). The Health Consequences of Smoking: 1969

Rogers, E. M. (1962). *Diffusion of innovations* (1st ed.). New York, NY: Free Press.

Rogers, E. M. (1983). *Diffusion of innovations* (3rd ed.). New York, NY: Free Press.

Rogers, E. M. (1995). *Diffusion of innovations* (4th ed.). New York, NY: Free Press.

Rogers, E. M. (2002). *Diffusion of innovations* (5th ed.). New York, NY: Free Press.

Simons-Morton, B. G., Greene, W. H., & Gottlieb, N. H. (1995). *Introduction to health education and health promotion* (2nd ed.). Long Grove, IL: Waveland Press.

Simpson, J. M., Oldenburg, B., Owen, N., Harris, D., Dobbins, T., Salmon, A., ... Saunders, J. B. (2000). The Australian National Workplace Health Project: Design and baseline findings. *Preventive Medicine*, *31*(3), 249–260. doi:10.1006/pmed.2000.0707 PMID:10964639

Spurlock. M. (2004). *Supersize Me* [Motion picture]. USA.

Stichler, J. F. (2011). Leading Change. *Nursing for Womens Health*, *15*(2), 166–170. doi:10.1111/j.1751-486X.2011.01625.x PMID:21504551

Szabo, E. (2014, February 5). CVS decision comes amid renewed anti-smoking efforts. *USA Today.* Retrieved from http://www.usatoday.com/story/news/nation/2014/02/05/smoking-cvs-health/5230621/

The Netherlands Nutrition Center. (2005). *Masterplan Prevention of Overweight 2005-2010.* The Hague: The Netherlands Nutrition Center.

Vyth, E. L., van der Meer, E. W., Seidell, J. C., & Steenhus, I. H. (2011). A nutrition labelling intervention in worksite cafeterias: An implementation evaluation across two large catering companies in the Netherlands. Retrieved from http://www.ncbi.nlm.nih.gov/pubmed/21693473

KEY TERMS AND DEFINITIONS

Adoption: Uptake of a health education program by a target audience.

Cosmopolite: Describes a person who tends to have interpersonal networks outside of, rather than within, his or her social system.

Diffusion: The process by which an innovation is communicated over time among the members of a social system.

Dissemination: Active approach for knowledge transfer from the resource system to the users.

Everett M. Rogers: (1931-2004): An American sociologist who developed the Diffusion of Innovation Theory, which has been widely used in communications, technology, and health education, including hygiene, family planning, and cancer prevention.

Innovation: An idea, practice, or object that is perceived as new by an individual or other unit of adoption.

Obesegenic: Promoting obesity.

This research was previously published in the Encyclopedia of Strategic Leadership and Management edited by Victor X. Wang; pages 1781-1793, copyright year 2017 by Business Science Reference (an imprint of IGI Global).

Chapter 3
Establishing a Media Literacy Cognate at Historically Black Colleges and Universities:
A Comparative Analysis of Existing Courses and Potential of Implementation

Jayne Cubbage
Bowie State University, USA

ABSTRACT

This study explores the need as well as the feasibility of implementing a media literacy cognate at Historically Black Colleges and Universities nationwide. Of the approximately 40 colleges and universities with media studies or communications departments or schools, only three offer a named media literacy course. Similarly, of the communications and media programs with ACEJMC accreditation, only one, Howard University offers a media literacy course. Using diffusion of information theory to explore the knowledge of and eventual adoption of media literacy courses at HBCUs, the study seeks to provide an introduction to schools about their need to teach media literacy to students across the college and university curriculum.

MAIN FOCUS OF THIS CHAPTER

Media literacy training and education is paramount to the mission of HBCUs with their imperative to educate African Americans, promote a village like learning environment and provide a culturally relevant education for countless scholars who may not otherwise receive an education (Albritton, 2012; ASHE, 2010; Hale, 2006; Jones, 2013; Lovett, 2011). The implementation of media literacy at HBCUs can foster the beginning of the end to pejorative and stereotypical images in various forms of media, which have been prevalent since the dawn of the media age (Wilson, Guitierrez, & Chao, 2013). The full adaption of media literacy can usher in awareness among students and graduates about the various machinations

DOI: 10.4018/978-1-7998-0417-8.ch003

of media, the intentions of media producers and creators, which in many cases, are designed to continue the subjugation and oppression of African Americans and other marginalized groups in U.S. society (Wilson, et al., 2013). With increased consciousness, the realization of individual agency becomes imperative as the alternative to the continued blind consumption of harmful media messages. Media illiteracy can dampen the full benefit of new media technologies including social media and its ability to equalize and address political and social ills. The benefits of new media will not be realized if end users lack complete awareness of the empowering potential of media literacy, (Mercea 2014; Nakagawa & Arzubiaga, 2014; Thevenin, 2012).

Several scholars have noted that media literacy, often defined as the ability to access, analyze, produce and act upon media messages (Hobbs, 2010; Milhailidis, 2009; Potter, 2011) is a vital 21st century skill necessary for full participation and awareness in a democratic society (UNESCO, 2015, http://www.unesco.org/new/en/communication-and-information/media-development/media-literacy/). Additionally, media literacy is considered paramount in building critical thinking and fostering increased participation in the creation and production of media. Media literacy can also serve as an equalizing factor in media and educational institutions. Media literacy when realized is ripe with emancipatory potential and liberation for media audiences across racial, geographic and all other socioeconomic strata (Mercea, 2014; Thevenin, 2012).

Several educational organizations have touted the multiple benefits of media literacy in post secondary education. The Association of American Colleges and Universities (AACU 2015, https://www.aacu.org) suggests a need for an updated approach to education in the 21st century with a focus on inclusiveness and diversity of ideas and educational approaches that change the dynamic of teaching and learning that allow for an interactive approach among other suggestions. The National Communication Association (NCA, 2015, https://www.natcom.org/Tertiary.aspx?id=236&terms=media%20literacy) formulated a list of Media Literacy Standards and Competencies for K-12 educators, and lists media literacy (along with mass communication) as one of its areas of concentration. The Accrediting Council for Education in Journalism and Mass Communication (ACEJMC, 2015, https://www2.ku.edu/~acejmc/) has also touted the importance of media education assessment and a well-rounded and diversified curriculum in communication studies (ACEJMC, 2015, https://www2.ku.edu/~acejmc/).

Given the need for increased media literacy among all populations in the United States today, this chapter seeks to explore the feasibility of implementing a media literacy cognate consisting of three media literacy courses at HBCUs. The research of van der Linde (2010) provides a rough outline of courses which may be implemented to include an introductory and theoretical course, a hands-on practicum/media production course and thirdly an advocacy and action-oriented course, which will teach students how to engage with the media and create campaigns to petition or to foster greater audience involvement in the production and discussion with media executives. This cognate would be implemented at HBCUs nationwide. The idea of instituting a media literacy cognate at HBCUs is synergistically aligned with fostering deeper engagement and retention for students and universities. The need for media literacy is a commonality every member of society shares via his or her participation and consumption of media (Byrne, 2009; Kellner & Share, 2005).

Previously, in industrialized societies, such as the United States, when knowledge was sought, one consulted a written text to gain information or to become enlightened about a particular topic. In the 21st century when knowledge or information is sought, individuals, more often than not, consult a media text first (Potter, 2011).

In a media saturated society such as the United States, it is widely known that many citizens are spending a great deal of time with media on a daily basis compared to other industrialized nations. It has been found that the average American media audience member is reported to have consumed 279 minutes of television, 163 minutes using a tablet, 134 minutes using a smart phone, 87 minutes listening to radio, 28 minutes reading newspapers and 27 minutes reading a magazine—daily. That's a total of 718 minutes or nearly 12 HOURS spent EACH DAY for the AVERAGE citizen in the United States on media usage. These figures do not account for cell phone usage, as smart phones were only measured for their data retrieval capabilities (Johnson & Kellstedt, 2013; Graber, 2010; Lindsay, 2006; Stastita.com, 2014, http://www.statista.com/statistics/270781/average-daily-media-use-in-the-us/)

Conversely, in measured data sets, groups of color, specifically, African Americans, consume more media than all other racial groups in the United States on a daily basis. More specifically, African Americans consume more media across all media platforms, particularly television, social media and smart phone usage; specifically text messaging (Nielsen, 2015; http://www.nielsen.com/us/en/insights/news/2015/multifaceted-connections-african-american-media-usage-outpaces-across-platforms.html; Consoli, 2014; http://www.broadcastingcable.com/news/currency/mbpt-spotlight-nielsen-cross-platform-consumption-data-offers-message-marketers-african-americans-spend-more-time-most-media-platforms-hispanics/134561; NNPA, 2013, http://nnpa.org/wp-content/uploads/2013/06/African-American-Consumer-Report-2013.pdf)

Most media platforms are funded using advertising dollars making the overwhelming majority of media production in the United States a for-profit enterprise—*a business*. Also, while the United States comprises 8% of the global population, its citizens consume over 50 percent of all advertising messages on a daily basis (Kubey, 2003; Potter, 2011). Comparatively speaking, African Americans, who consume more media on a daily basis than all other groups, are subject to media messages and advertising more often than other racial ethnicities on a daily basis.

Media Literacy Defined

As mentioned previously, media literacy is generally defined as the ability to access, analyze, produce and act upon media messages (Hobbs, 2010; Hobbs & Moore, 2013; Potter, 2011; Milhailidis, 2009). What is media literacy and what importance does it hold for media consumers? Despite some fragmentation in approach in the research area, generally media literacy scholars agree on a core set of principles that define the concept and provide operational language for its application for media audiences and producers.

Potter (2011) defines media literacy as the ability to access, analyze and produce media. Hobbs (2010) adds to the definition of media literacy calling it a "constellation of life skills that are necessary for full participation in a media saturated society" and include the ability to responsibly choose media materials, determining the author, purpose and point of view of media messages, create media messages of their own and take appropriate actions within a community to social action and solve media problems. Hobbs and Moore (2013), further define media literacy as the ability to access, analyze, create, reflect and act upon media messages. The National Association for Media Literacy Education, NAMLE (2015, http://namle.net/publications/media-literacy-definitions/) provides a working definition in the same vein. Milhailidis (2009) defines the tenets of media literacy as the "5 A's of Media Literacy" accordingly as: *access* to media, *awareness* of its power, *assessment* of its coverage of global events and issues, *appreciation* for media's role in a "civilized" society and *action* to encourage better communication across social divides (pp. 3-6), (emphasis added).

More pointedly and directed to the need for increased media literacy training and awareness, Kellner and Share (2005) also offer five core concepts of media literacy as follows: 1. *All media messages are "constructed". 2. Media messages are constructed using a creative language with its own rules. 3. Different people experience the same media message differently. 4. Media have embedded values and points of view. 5. Most media messages are organized to gain profit and/or power.*

Although the media literacy movement in the United States is more than 50 years old, there is still not widespread knowledge of or adaptation of the concept in society despite the near ubiquitous presence of the media in the lives of the citizenry today (Kubey, 1998; 2003). Additionally, the existing media literacy movement, while largely benevolent and well-intentioned, has done little to address the needs of communities of color, which are known to consume larger quantities of media on a daily basis and are thus subject to greater amounts of predatory advertisements as well as pejorative and stereotypical images which abound (Wilson, et al., 2013). As such, this study seeks to ask and answer the following research questions:

RQ1: Which HBCUs have the capacity to implement a media literacy cognate within an existing communications studies department and introduce a cognate to a general education curriculum?

RQ2: What factors allow for favorable implementation of a media literacy cognate; department size, existing courses on media literacy, knowledgeable faculty, departmental budget, student demand?

RQ3: What barriers exist to implementing a media literacy cognate? Using the diffusion of information/innovation theory, this study will focus on surveying communications departments at HBCUs to access their capability of implementing a media literacy cognate into the existing curriculum.

From a theoretical perspective information diffusion theory, which was introduced by Everett Rogers in 1962 (Baron & Davis, 2009, p. 277) can aptly be applied to the media literacy movement in the United States. The stages of adoption of a new idea are awareness via mass media or other methods, adoption by a small group of innovators called early adaptors. The third step in the process is when a group of so-called opinion leaders consider the idea useful or one that holds value and they try it for themselves. If the opinion leaders like the idea well enough, they in turn introduce the idea to their friends, who are known as opinion followers. After adoption of an idea by opinion followers, the final group, late adopters accept the idea or concept and make the appropriate changes, (p. 277). Abelman and Dalessandro (2015) echo this process in detailing the steps taken by HBCUs to institute core visions (p. 109).

Issues, Controversies, Problems

The purpose of this study is determine which HBCUs are poised to implement a 3-course media literacy cognate to be offered within the general education curriculum in addition to existing communications studies. Once determined, the study will offer important foundational evidence to schools about the importance of adding a widely adopted and required media literacy cognate to students across the curriculum. The first course, course number one would be introductory in nature and titled, Introduction to Media Literacy. The course would provide a theoretical overview of the themes, practices and concepts of media literacy across all media disciplines and practices and would directly address the first two components of media literacy; access and analyze media messages.

The second course would be titled Production Practicum: Media Literacy Production Skills and Application, where students would gain hands-on knowledge of video and audio production, web development, writing skills for media (blogs, news sites, production scripts), producing, editing, social media site development and app creation along with other practical skills necessary in both digital and legacy media formats. This course would cover the third component of media literacy and impart the ability to produce media messages.

Course number three would be titled, Media Literacy Action and Advocacy, which would provide a template and course of action for media consumers seeking to engage media executives and producers about offensive content. Additionally, students would receive direction on how to launch productive media campaigns. The course would address the final component of media literacy to impart the ability to act upon media messages and would also include discussions of previous successful campaigns and their mechanics. The course would also include an entrepreneurial component to encourage would-be entrepreneurs to begin their own media ventures.

Review of Literature

Several scholars (ASHE, 2010; Hale, 2006; Harris, 2012) have noted the key importance of HBCUs both historically and for the foreseeable future as a key component in the continued journey of African Americans to gain economic and social equality. They (Abelman & Dalessandro, 2015; Jones, 2013; Lovett, 2011), speak of the unique institutional vision of HBCUs as well as the components of implementation for a successful and widely accepted vision among university stakeholders; students, faculty and staff. While other scholars (Albritton, 2012; Conrad & Kim, 2006; Lovett, 2011; Wynne (2005) speak of the primary history of the institutions, which were established during Reconstruction with the mission of educating newly freed men and women (Lovett, 2011; Shexnider, 2013) as well as providing the impetus for social change and the uplifting of a people. Still other scholars, (Albritton 2012; Lovett, 2011; Willie, Reddick, & Brown, 2006) provide an historical overview of HBCUs, discuss the relevance of HBCUs in today's educational and economic climate, calling the institutions vital for imparting culturally relevant experiences for young Black men and women and providing important nurturing, historical grounding amid a family-like setting.

Other scholars (Jeter, 2002; Mattox Berry, 2003) address communications and journalism programs at HBCUs. Jeter (2002) discusses mass communication and journalism curricula at HBCUs and he provides an historical analysis of the evolution of such studies in Black institutions of higher education. Noting that Florida Agricultural and Mechanical University (also known as FAMU) became the first HBCU to receive accreditation from the ACEJMC in 1981. Mattox Berry (2003) provides an overview of the accreditation process among HBCUs with journalism and communications programs noting that only seven schools are accredited. The number of ACEJMC accredited HBCUs remains the same in 2016. Still other scholars address the unique ability and significance of HBCUs to provide culturally relevant training in journalism and mass communications to students of color where they may face increased levels of adversity by enrolling in similar programs at PWIs (Biswas, Perkins, & Izard, 2012; Mihalidis, 2006).

Another researcher, (Schmidt, 2012; 2013) found a significant disconnect between faculty and students at PWIs as faculty perceived their course offerings to include substantial coverage on media literacy while students felt the offerings fell woefully short of what was necessary to consider themselves to be truly media literate.

METHOD

The method of the study is a comparative analysis (Cresswell, 2014) of the course offerings of media programs and departments at HBCUs and those of PWIs or TWIs, which offer media literacy courses and programs. A textual analysis and interpretive data analysis, which outlines patterns and themes, are hallmark to qualitative research design (p.17). The comparative analysis is a method often used to establish commonalities between two similar entities, which then offer the basis of direction for establishing a balance between the differences found in the items compared.

As mentioned previously, the top 10 largest schools by enrollment were examined. Secondly, the researcher also examined schools with journalism or mass communication programs that hold accreditation by the ACEJMC. Also *U.S. News & World Report* publishes annual rankings of the top HBCUs in the nation. The top 10 schools on the publication's list were also analyzed for this study. Finally, by way of comparison, the researcher examined TWIs and PWIs that currently offer one or more named media literacy courses and colleges and universities that offer a full degree-granting program of study or certificate in the subject.

METHOD OF ANALYSIS

In order to compare or survey media literacy offerings at HBCUs, and as noted previously, the author compiled the list of schools to be included in the survey, the top 10 largest 4-year colleges and universities, based upon enrollment numbers from the White House Initiative on HBCUs enrollment estimates (http://www.ed.gov/edblogs/whhbcu/one-hundred-and-five-historically-black-colleges-and-universities/, 2015), schools or departments with ACEJMC accreditation, the top 10 HBCUs as ranked by *U.S. News & World Report*, (http://colleges.usnews.rankingsandreviews.com/best-colleges/rankings/hbcu).

Once each list was compiled, the researcher searched the schools' department of media and communications or journalism programs (if they exist) to search for courses on media literacy. No personal contact was made to each department by the author. There may be courses in media literacy currently in development which, have not been implemented or that are not visible on department websites.

Courses not specifically titled media literacy were not considered for this study. While many courses in journalism and communications curriculum address some forms of media literacy, if they are not specifically covering each facet of media literacy (the ability to access, analyze, produce and act upon media messages), and are not specifically designed with fostering the complete skill set of media literacy they are not apt to be considered media literacy without revision to its description and syllabus. Schmidt (2013) notes that often faculty members believe they are addressing media literacy within their courses, when in fact upon polling students about core competencies and subjects addressed, it is revealed that there is a tendency among faculty to overestimate the amount of actual media literacy competencies addressed in their classes (p. 148). For this study, course syllabi were not examined.

Similarly among TWIs or PWIs, which offered at least one course in media literacy, the same examination process occurred. The researcher viewed the department course requirements and descriptions as well as the university course catalogue and bulletins for full course descriptions.

FINDINGS

As noted previously, the offerings of named media literacy courses at HBCUs are near non-existent. Although, many departments offer courses that partially address media literacy concepts, they simply use another name for the course.

As indicated in Table 1 Top 10 HBCUs based on student enrollment, of the schools surveyed, only 3 of the largest top 10 schools, Howard University and Prairie View A&M University and Morgan State University have named media literacy courses. A description of the Howard University course, SCOM 203 Digital Media Literacy was not found on the university web site, or in the course bulletin as of this writing. Prairie View A&M's course, COMM 2643 Media Literacy is described as follows:

COMM 2643. Media Literacy (3-0) Credit 3 semester credit hours. Students will develop an appreciation for and analyze creative artifacts in a variety of media, such as film, television, new media, and social media. Clips, screenings, and other examples familiarize students with a variety of cultures; prompt students' consideration of different points of view; and provide a basis for critical, creative, and innovative written, oral, and visual communication about works of art. Prerequisite: ENGL 1123. (2015, http://www.pvamu.edu/lcom/home/course-offerings/communication/).

Morgan State University's course COM 203, Media Literacy in a Diverse World is described on the School of Global Journalism and Communication website as follows:

COMM 203 – Media Literacy in a Diverse World – Three hours; 3 credits - This course examines mass media and the social, economic and psychological roles and impacts that they have in different societies. Emphasis will be placed on how media shape perceptions about race, religion, gender, ability, sexual orientation, etc. Students will learn how media shape our perceptions about other nations and shape other nations' perceptions about us. Students will also learn the roles media play in helping to shape

Table 1. Top 10 HBCUs (4-Year Colleges & Universities) based on student enrollment

School/State	Enrollment	Media Literacy Course
1. North Carolina Agricultural & Technical State University (North Carolina)	10,725	No
2. Howard University (District of Columbia)	10,265	Yes
3. Florida Agricultural & Mining University (Florida)	10,241	No
4. Jackson State University (Mississippi)	9,508	No
5. Texas Southern University (Texas)	9,233	No
6. Tennessee State University (Tennessee)	9,027	No
7. Prairie View A&M (Agricultural & Mining) University (Texas)	8,429	Yes
8. Morgan State University (Maryland)	7,698	Yes
9. North Carolina Central University (North Carolina)	7,687	No
10. Norfolk State University (Virginia)	6,027	No

Note: Based on listings from the National Center for Education Statistics Undergraduate Enrollment 5,000 to 20,000 (results are for combined enrollment, undergraduate and graduate): http://nces.ed.gov/COLLEGENAVIGATOR/?s=all&en=5000&ex=20000&sp=4

and reflect culture and the important roles that media consumers play in the mass communication process. [Formerly BROA 200/TELC 202] (FALL/SPRING). (2015, http://www.morgan.edu//Documents/ACADEMICS/academic_catalog/undergrad/2014-2015/ucat_SGJC.pdf).

While the course offered by Morgan State University is named media literacy, it provides no indication in the description of how the course will teach students to engage or act upon media messages that they find offensive or averse to their sensibilities. The ability to analyze media messages and to create those messages while apt falls short of a complete media literacy definition. This matter reaches far beyond a case of semantics surrounding whether or not a course is simply named media literacy or whether a course offers the full spectrum of media literacy concepts. A media literacy cognate or other appropriately designed course will specifically add the emancipatory and empowerment component that will provide a call for action for all media consumers to act upon media messages which are not to their liking.

As indicated in Table 2 Top 10 HBCUs in *U.S. News & World Report*, of the top 10 HBCUs in the *U.S. News & World Report* rankings, only Howard University offers a named media literacy course, SCOM 120 Digital Media Literacy.

The final category for HBCUs is illustrated in Table 3 HBCUs with ACEJMC accreditation. While the other categories contain at least 10 listings, there are only 7 HBCUs with schools or departments of communications or media studies that hold such accreditation as of this writing in 2016. The table is a reflection of the most recent publication of accredited colleges and universities by state listed at, http://www2.ku.edu/~acejmc/STUDENT/PROGLIST.SHTML. Of the seven ranked schools with ACEJMC accreditation, only Howard University offers a course on media literacy, as noted previously.

For TWIs or PWIs, universities with media literacy programs are listed in Table 4 PWIs with degree granting or certificate programs in media literacy. As shown, Appalachian State University offers both a Masters in Education with a focus in media literacy for future educators as well as a graduate certificate in media literacy.

Table 2. Top 10 HBCUs in U.S. News & World Report Ranking, 2015

School/State	Enrollment	Media Literacy Course
1. Spelman College (Georgia)	2,135	No
2. Howard University (District of Columbia)	10,265	Yes
3. Morehouse College (Georgia)	2,109	No
4. Hampton University (Virginia)	4,393	No
5. Tuskegee University (Alabama)	3,103	No
6. Xavier University of Louisiana (Louisiana)	2,976	No
7. Fisk University (Tennessee)	772	No
8. Florida Agricultural & Mining University (Florida)	10,241	No
9. Claflin University (South Carolina)	1,866	No
10. North Carolina Agricultural & Technical State University (North Carolina)	10,725	No

Note: Based on top 10 HBCUs from U.S. News & World Report Annual College Ratings, Historically Black Colleges and Universities Ranking, 2015.

Source: http://colleges.usnews.rankingsandreviews.com/best-colleges/rankings/hbcu and National Center for Education Statistics http://nces.ed.gov/COLLEGENAVIGATOR (results are for combined enrollment, undergraduate and graduate)

Table 3. HBCUs with ACEJMC accreditation listed by student enrollment

School/State	Enrollment	Media Literacy Course
1. North Carolina Agricultural & Technical State University (North Carolina)	10,725	No
2. Howard University (District of Columbia)	10,265	Yes
3. Florida Agricultural & Mining University (Florida)	10,241	No
4. Norfolk State University (Virginia)	6,027	No
5. Southern University & Agricultural & Mining College (Baton Rouge) (Louisiana)	6,330	No
6. Grambling State University (Louisiana)	4,504	No
7. Hampton University (Virginia)	4,393	No

Source: ACEJMC Accrediting Council on Education in Journalism and Mass Communications, 2015 http://www2.ku.edu/~acejmc/STUDENT/PROGLIST.SHTML and National Center for Education Statistics http://nces.ed.gov/COLLEGENAVIGATOR (results are for combined enrollment, undergraduate and graduate)

Table 4. TWIs/PWIs with media literacy programs; degree granting or certificates

School/State	Named Media Literacy Program	Degree
Appalachian State University* (North Carolina)	Media Literacy	Master of Arts
Sacred Heart University (Connecticut)	Media Literacy and Digital Culture	Master of Arts
Southern Illinois University (Illinois)	Media Literacy	Post Baccalaureate Certificate
University of Florida (Florida)	Media Literacy Education**	Master of Arts
Webster University (Missouri)	Media Literacy	Master of Arts

Source: http://namle.net/community/caucuses/grad-student/schools-orgs/, 2007. *Program undergoing revisions, 2015
**Education with an area of Concentration

As of this writing the program is in the process of being revamped and students are directed to take courses in digital media. Sacred Heart University in Fairfield, CT also offers graduate programs in media literacy in the Department of Communication and Media Studies including two concentration choices; Children, Health and Media and Media and Social Justice.

Of the schools offering degrees in media literacy, Webster University's offerings are the most extensive. The MA in Media Literacy offers multiple courses named media literacy along with other courses, which address the concept at various levels. Additionally, the offerings for the program include courses titled Comparative Approaches to Media Literacy (MEDC 5480), Integrated Studies in Media Literacy (MEDC 5981), International Media Literacy (MEDC 5370), Topics in Media Communications: Video and Media Literacy (MEDC 5550). Note the majority of electives are named to reflect the emphasis on media literacy with the subject of the course title. The other courses are also an integral part of the program and serve to lay the foundation in communication studies and research as well as introduce and address current practices and existing media structures today.

The data included in Table 5 PWIs with one or more named media literacy course offered reveal the universities with at least one named media literacy course. Many universities have been listed as offering media literacy courses, which do not carry the name of media literacy in the course title. They were not examined for this study.

Table 5. TWIs/PWIs with one or more named media literacy course offered

School/State	Media Literacy Course Graduate or Undergraduate	Program
Columbia University (New York)	Practice of Media Literacy (Graduate)	Education
Ithaca College (New York)	Media Literacy and Popular Culture (Undergraduate) Special Topics in Media Literacy (Undergraduate)	Communication and Culture
Oklahoma State University (Oklahoma)	Media Literacy Across the Curriculum (Graduate)	Education
University of Texas Austin (Texas)	Media Literacy for Prospective Teachers (Graduate)	Education
University of Connecticut (Connecticut)	Media Literacy in an Information Age (Graduate)	Education
University of Massachusetts Amherst (Massachusetts)	Media Literacy (Graduate)	Continuing Education and Professional Studies
Webster University (Missouri)	Media Literacy (Undergraduate) Studies in Media Literacy (Undergraduate) Topics in Media Literacy (Undergraduate) Senior Seminar in Media Literacy (Undergraduate)	Media Communications as a Minor Concentration

Source: http://namle.net/community/caucuses/grad-student/schools-orgs/, 2007.

As with the listings for HBCUs and their offered media literacy courses, the course descriptions for PWI/TWIs that also offer at least one or more named media literacy course at the undergraduate level are listed below. Ithaca College in New York offers two courses in media literacy through their Department of Communication and Culture in the School of Communications, *CLTC 11000 Media Literacy and Popular Culture* and *CLTC 23000—23099 Special Topics in Media Literacy*. While the first course, CLTC 1000 a 3-credit undergraduate course is general in its offerings of media literacy, it offers a tepid introduction to the action component by offering to "examine the effects of media messages on beliefs, attitudes, and behaviors…" (http://ithaca.smartcatalogiq.com/2012-2013/Undergraduate-Catalog/Course-Descriptions/CLTC-Culture-and-Communication/10000/CLTC-11000) The second course listed, CLTC 23000—23099 Special Topics in Media Literacy and offered as a multiple credit course to be taken in intervals may afford the best opportunity to explore the full spectrum of media literacy concepts. A partial listing reads, "…Each year the seminar will focus on a different topic reflecting current issues in and media literacy curricula developed at the college…" (http://ithaca.smartcatalogiq.com/en/2012-2013/Undergraduate-Catalog/Course-Descriptions/CLTC-Culture-and-Communication/20000/CLTC-23000).

Similarly, Webster University in Missouri offers at least two media literacy courses at the undergraduate level in the School of Communications in the Department of Media Communications. There are two courses: *MEDC 1630 Media Literacy*, a 3-credit introductory course and *MEDC 2630 Studies in Media Literacy*, which "…deepens the theoretical foundations and practical applications of the field of media literacy…" (http://www.webster.edu/catalog/current/undergraduate-catalog/courses/medc.html).

DISCUSSION

To revisit the research questions in this study, the researcher found the following:

RQ1: Which HBCUs have the capacity to implement a media literacy cognate within an existing communications studies department and introduce a cognate to a general education curriculum?

Based on information provided by universities and course descriptions, the most logical assertion for suitability is implementing media literacy programs at HBCUs with ACEJMC accreditation. Such programs are easily the most poised to establish full media literacy curriculum in their schools. Because of the rigorous nature of accreditation by the ACEJMC, accredited schools have shown themselves willing and able to stand at the forefront of academic excellence and scholarly rigor within the field of journalism and mass communication. Secondly are the schools, which have media literacy courses, yet do not have or are currently seeking ACEJMC accreditation. Prairie View and Morgan State have each implemented a single media literacy course, revealing some discussion among faculty and school leadership about the importance of media literacy and those schools are uniquely poised to expand programs to a multiple course offering and to begin the process of opening courses to the entire student population. Following those schools that have already established courses would be the well-known institutions with *U.S. News & World Report* Top HBCU Rankings. The reasoning here, is that these schools are often considered top-tier among HBCUs which enjoy the best reputations. Once the general population becomes more aware of media literacy and its importance, these schools, considered innovative in their own right, are behooved to begin offering courses in media literacy by matter of course as they are top ranked.

RQ2: What factors allow for favorable implementation of a media literacy cognate; department size, existing courses on media literacy, knowledgeable faculty, departmental budget, student demand? As noted in RQ1, implementation of a media literacy cognate is dependent on several factors, including school ranking and accreditation, existing offerings of media literacy and general acceptance of the idea for the need for media literacy courses first within journalism and communications programs. Although many schools have budgetary constraints to consider, the option of swapping media literacy courses with other dormant courses in the curriculum may provide alternative options for departments and programs. Faculty in various departments and programs may consider revising courses that partially address media literacy within a program to provide the full spectrum of media literacy tenets (foster the ability to access, analyze, produce and act upon media message) in each class and to increase the ultimate benefit of offering such courses.

RQ3: What barriers exist to implementing a media literacy cognate? Beyond the traditional barriers that prevent the adaptation of new ideas in society and in the academy, the primary barriers to wide scale implementation of a media literacy cognate at HBCUs are lack of education about media literacy and awareness of its necessity, college and university culture and politics, lack of student awareness and limited demand, budgetary constraints, existing curriculum mandates and unwillingness to add more courses to the current course load for students seeking to graduate within five years. The last factor is a major consideration as many HBCUs struggle with retention rates and often see students leave school when there are even slight barriers and challenges, (Schexnider, 2013). However, offering culturally relevant courses, and culturally relevant media literacy courses, may actually improve retention at HBCUs.

Regarding the comparisons of courses, from a review of course descriptions of media literacy courses, none of the listed courses among HBCUs offer within a span of one semester a full offering of a media literacy curriculum. Researchers (Schmidt, 2013: Silverblatt, Ferry & Finan, 2004) have asserted that media literacy courses should be designed to "enable students to fully comprehend and act on the content, form purpose and effects of media messages," (p. 136). The course offered by Howard University, Digital Media Literacy SCOM 203, is not described in the university bulletin, nor does a description of the course appear on the School of Communications website for any of the undergraduate departments for a comparative review as of this writing. Although there has been no review of the course syllabus for this course or any of the others, its title: "Digital Media Literacy" also suggests a focus on electronic and new media technologies omitting print media from the offerings within the course. The other two courses, COMM 2643 Media Literacy offered by Prairie View University includes a description which reads more like an aesthetic appreciation of media offerings rather than a full analysis and critique of media messages and techniques. A partial description reads, "...Students will develop an appreciation for and analyze creative artifacts in a variety of media, such as film, television, new media, and social media. Clips, screenings, and other examples familiarize students with a variety of cultures; prompt students' consideration of different points of view; and provide a basis for critical, creative, and innovative written, oral, and visual communication about works of art..." (https://www.pvamu.edu/lcom/home/course-offerings/communication/). In the framework of access, analyze, produce and act upon, the final tenet is notably missing from this course description. Also, the course offered at Morgan State University, COMM 203 Media Literacy in a Diverse World omits similar information from its course description. A partial description reads, "...This course examines mass media and the social, economic and psychological roles and impacts that they have in different societies. Emphasis will be placed on how media shape perceptions about race, religion, gender, ability, sexual orientation, etc. Students will learn how media shape our perceptions about other nations and shape other nations' perceptions about us. Students will also learn the roles media play in helping to shape and reflect culture and the important roles that media consumers play in the mass communication process..." (http://www.morgan.edu//Documents/ACADEMICS/academic_catalog/undergrad/2014-2015/ucat_SGJC.pdf). Of particular note in this course description is the addressing of media consumers. However, the description only notes, "students will learn the roles media play in helping to shape and reflect culture and the important roles consumers play in the mass communication process..." What is most likely lacking among media consumers is the ability to leverage their relationship with advertisers and media producers in a meaningful way. That skill set and pathway must be specifically addressed and taught in media literacy courses (Schmidt, 2012; 2013).

The course offerings and descriptions at PWIs fared no better. Missing from the description of all listed offerings in schools with one or more media literacy course is the final tenet of "act upon" media messages. While more than a few schools were found to have offered at least one media literacy course, those schools, like HBCUs appear to offer courses that merely introduce the topic of media literacy and provide no emancipatory potential or method of agency to contact media producers or corporations in the event that end users are not satisfied with media messages or themes or as an avenue to discuss more equitable distribution of air time and production spaces. The programs that incorporate media literacy into their education departments are imparting the skill set for K-12 educators to be used within their classroom. The best and most suitable treatment of media literacy at the college and university level are the degree and or certificate granting programs offered by Appalachia State University, Sacred Heart University, Southern Illinois University, University of Florida and Webster University. A review of course descriptions at these universities reveal some, if slight treatment of the act upon media messages tenet of media literacy, these programs are best poised to expand course offerings or to revise courses to reflect each of the components of media literacy.

FUTURE RESEARCH DIRECTIONS

The study can be expanded by holding direct conversations via a survey or focus groups with department leaders and faculty who teach media courses at HBCUs to determine their knowledge and awareness of media literacy concepts and how they may apply them more directly to their existing curricula by either adding new courses or revising and updating existing courses such as public speaking, for instance, which is generally required for all majors. Also, a more concise examination of existing degree granting and certificate programs at PWIs is necessary to determine best practices on the road to incorporating media literacy curricula at HBCUs.

SOLUTIONS AND RECOMMENDATIONS

The media literacy tapestry is vast. There are multiple definitions, approaches and applications of media literacy in practice by a range of organizations, media practitioners, educators, policymakers and scholars today.

Adoption of a media literacy curriculum that features at least one course or most beneficially three courses which cover each of the tenets of media literacy, the ability to access, analyze, produce and act upon media messages will assist in the process of helping students to productively engage the media industry on multiple levels to enhance dialogue to create more appropriate and suitably representative media images for marginalized and often stereotyped ethnic groups in the United States. Today, communications departments can take the mantle of media literacy upon themselves, by making a firm commitment to educate themselves about the concept and its importance in their own lives and in the lives of students at HBCUs. Faculty can attend media literacy workshops and conferences, sit on curriculum committees at their own university and advocate for such classes to be added, visit schools that have incorporated media literacy into their curriculum and seek syllabi from other institutions to gather ideas.

As noted previously, media literacy training and education is paramount to the mission of HBCUs. Its implementation will foster the beginning of the end to pejorative and stereotypical images, which have been prevalent since the dawn of the media age. The full adaption of media literacy can usher in awareness among students and graduates about the various machinations of media and create a more informed and empowered citizenry in the process.

REFERENCES

AACU. (2015). The LEAP challenge, education for a world of unscripted problems. Retrieved from: https://aacu.org/leap

Abelman, R., & Dalessandro, A. (2009). The institutional vision of historically Black colleges and universities. *Journal of Black Studies*, *40*(2), 105–134. doi:10.1177/0021934707307828

Albritton, T. J. (2012). Educating our own: The historical legacy of HBCUs and their relevance for educating a new generation of leaders. *The Urban Review*, *44*(3), 311–331. doi:10.100711256-012-0202-9

ASHE Higher Education Report. (2010). Unearthing promise and potential: Our nation's historically Black colleges and universities. *ASHE Higher Education Report* (Special issue), *35*(5), 1-134.

Baron, S. J., & Davis, D. K. (2009). *Mass communication theory foundations, ferment, and future*. Stamford, CT: Cengage.

Becker, L. B., Vlad, T., & Simpson, H. (2013). Annual survey of journalism & mass communication enrollments. Retrieved from http://www.grady.uga.edu/annualsurveys/Enrollment_Survey/Enrollment_2013/2013EnrollCombined.pdf

Biswas, M., Perkins, L., & Izard, R. (2012). Selection of universities by students in journalism and mass communication courses: Do criteria differ between Caucasian and Minority students? *Journalism & Mass Communication Education*, *62*(2), 164–183. doi:10.1177/1077695812440946

Byrne, S. (2009). Media literacy interventions: What makes them boom or boomerang? *Communication Education*, *58*(1), 1–14. doi:10.1080/03634520802226444

Chen, G. M. (2007). Media (literacy) in the United States. *China Media Research*, *3*(3), 87–103.

Consoli, J. (2014, October 3) MBPT Spotlight: Nielson cross-platform consumption data offers message for marketers: African-Americans spend more time on most media platforms than Hispanics. *Broadcasting & Cable*. Retrieved from http://www.broadcastingcable.com/news/currency/mbpt-spotlight-nielsen-cross-platform-consumption-data-offers-message-marketers-african-americans-spend-more-time-most-media-platforms-hispanics/134561

Creswell, J. W. (2014). *Research design qualitative, quantitative and mixed methods approaches*. Thousand Oaks, CA: Sage.

Gallien, L. B., & Peterson, M. S. (Eds.). (2005). *Instructing and mentoring the African American college student*. Boston: Pearson.

Hale, F. W. (Ed.). (2006). *How Black colleges empower Black Students: Lessons for higher education*. Sterling, VA: Stylus.

Harris, O. D. III. (2012). From margin to center: Participating in village pedagogy at historically Black colleges and universities. *The Urban Review*, *44*(3), 332–357. doi:10.100711256-012-0199-0

Hobbs, R. (2010). Digital and media literacy: A plan of action. (The Aspen Institute). Retrieved from http://www.knightcomm.org/wp-content/uploads/2010/12/Digital_and_Media_Literacy_A_Plan_of_Action.pdf

Hobbs, R., & Moore, D. C. (2013). *Discovering media literacy: Teaching digital media and popular culture in elementary school.* Thousand Oaks, CA: Corwin. doi:10.4135/9781506335445

Jeter, P. (2002). Journalism and mass communication education at HBCUs: History and current issues. *Education, 123*(1), 200–204.

Jones, W. A. (2013). Prestige among Black colleges: Examining the predictors of HBCU peer academic reputation. *Journal of African-American Studies, 17*(2), 129–141. doi:10.100712111-012-9231-4

Kellner, D., & Share, J. (2005). Toward critical media literacy: Core concepts, debates, organizations and policies. *Discourse Studies in Politics of Education, 26*(3), 369–386. doi:10.1080/01596300500200169

Kim, M. M., & Conrad, C. F. (2006). The impact of historically Black colleges and universities on the academic success of African-American students. *Research in Higher Education, 47*(4), 399–427. doi:10.100711162-005-9001-4

Kubey, R. W. (1998). Obstacles to the development of media education in the United States. *Journal of Communication, 48*(2), 58–69. doi:10.1111/j.1460-2466.1998.tb02737.x

Kubey, R. W. (2003). Why U.S. media education lags behind the rest of the English-speaking world. *Television & New Media, 4*(4), 351–370. doi:10.1177/1527476403255808

Lovett, B. L. (2011). *America's historically Black colleges and universities.* Macon, GA: Mercer University Press.

Mattox Berry, C. (2003). HBCUs seek accreditation. *Quill, 91*(3), 30–31.

Mercea, D. (2015). Making Sense of Democratic Institutions Intertextually Communication on Social Media as a Civic Literacy Event Preceding Collective Action. *Communication Review, 18*(3), 2014. do i:10.1080/10714421.2015.1058102

Mihailidis, P. (2006). Media literacy in journalism/mass communication education: Can the United States learn from Sweden? *Journalism & Mass Communication Education, 60*(4), 416–428.

Mihailidis, P. (2009). Connecting cultures: New dynamics in global media literacy. *Afterimage, 37*(2), 37–41.

Nakagawa, K., & Arzubiaga, A. E. (2014). The Use of Social Media in Teaching Race. *Adult Learning, 25*(3), 103–110. doi:10.1177/1045159514534190

National Association for Media Literacy Education. (2007, November). Core principles of media literacy education in the United States. Retrieved from http://namle.net/publications/core-principles

Nielsen. (2015). Multifaceted connections, African-American media usage outpaces across platforms. Retrieved from http://www.nielsen.com/us/en/insights/news/2015/multifaceted-connections-african-american-media-usage-outpaces-across-platforms.html

Nielsen Media Rankings. (2010) Retrieved from http://blog.nielsen.com/nielsenwire/wp-content/uploads/2009/08/2009-2010-dma-ranks.pdf

NNPA. (2013). Resilient, receptive and relevant the African-American consumer 2013 report. Retrieved from http://nnpa.org/wp-content/uploads/2013/06/African-American-Consumer-Report-2013.pdf

O'Neil, B. (2010). Current policy developments in European media literacy. *International Journal of Media and Cultural Politics*, *6*(2), 235–241. doi:10.1386/mcp.6.2.235_3

Potter, J. W. (2011). *Media literacy* (5th ed.). Thousand Oaks, CA: Sage. doi:10.1093/OBO_dataset_home

Schexnider, A. J. (2013). *Saving Black colleges*. New York: Palgrave Macmillan. doi:10.1057/9781137323460

Schmidt, H. C. (2012). Essential but problematic: Faculty perceptions of media literacy at the university level. *Qualitative Research Reports in Communications*, *13*(1), 10–20. doi:10.1080/17459435.2012.719204

Schmidt, H. C. (2013). Addressing media literacy within higher education: A comparison of faculty and student perceptions. *The Northwest Journal of Communications*, *41*(1), 133–159.

Share, J. (2015). *Media literacy is elementary* (2nd ed.). New York: Peter Lang.

Statista.com. (2014). Average daily media use in the U.S. Retrieved from: http://www.statista.com/statistics/270781/average-daily-media-use-in-the-us/

Taylor, H. (2007). Black spaces: Examining writing major at an urban HBCU. *Composition Studies*, *35*(1), 99–112.

Thevenin, B. (2012, May). Discovering media literacy's emancipatory potential. *Paper presented at the annual meeting of the International Communication Association, Phoenix, AZ*. Retrieved from http://citation.allacademic.com/meta/p556213_index.html

Tyner, K. (2009). Media literacy and the tyranny of the narrative. *Afterimage*, *37*(2), 3–10.

UNESCO. (2015). Media literacy. Retrieved from http://www.unesco.org/new/en/communication-and-information/media-development/media-literacy/

van der Linde, F. (2010). The necessity of a media literacy module within journalism or media studies curricula. Global Media Journal African Edition, 4(2), 1-15.

White House Initiative on HBCUs (WHHBCU). (2015). Retrieved from http://www.ed.gov/edblogs/whhbcu/one-hundred-and-five-historically-black-colleges-and-universities/

Willie, C. V., Reddick, R. J., & Brown, R. (Eds.). (2006). *The Black college mystique*. Lanham, MD: Rowman & Littlefield.

Wilson, C. C., Gutierrez, F., & Chao, L. M. (2013). *Racism, sexism and the media*. Thousand Oaks, CA: Sage.

ADDITIONAL READING

Buckingham, D. (2007a). Digital media literacies: Rethinking media education in the age of the Internet. *Research in Comparative and International Education*, *2*(1), 43–45. doi:10.2304/rcie.2007.2.1.43

Buckingham, D. (2007b). Media education goes digital: An introduction. *Learning, Media and Technology*, *32*(2), 111–119. doi:10.1080/17439880701343006

Christ, W. G. (2004). Assessment, media literacy standards, and higher education. *The American Behavioral Scientist*, *48*(1), 92–96. doi:10.1177/0002764204267254

Considine, D. M. (2002). Media Literacy: National developments and international origins. *Journal of Popular Film & Television*, *30*(1), 7–16. doi:10.1080/01956050209605554

Goetz, S. K., Brown, D. S., & Schwarz, G. (2005). Teachers need media literacy, too! *Yearbook of the National Society for the Study of Education*, *104*, 104–179.

Goodman, S. (2003). *Teaching youth media: A critical guide to literacy, video production, and social change*. New York: Teachers College Press.

Hobbs, R. (1998). The seven great debates in the media literacy movement. *Journal of Communication*, *48*(1), 6–32. doi:10.1111/j.1460-2466.1998.tb02734.x

Potter, W. J. (2004). *Theory of media literacy: A cognitive approach*. Thousand Oaks, CA: Sage. doi:10.4135/9781483328881

Silverblatt, A., Ferry, J., & Finan, B. (2004). *Approaches to media literacy: A handbook*. Armonk, NY: M.E. Sharpe.

KEY TERMS AND DEFINITIONS

ACEJMC: The Accrediting Council for Education in Journalism and Mass Communication education of the AEJMC, the Association for Education in Journalism and Mass Communication. Currently, there are 7 HBCU accredited journalism or mass communications programs.

Accreditation: The process of approval by a professional organization with a set of standards and measures that consider an educational program or school a member based on a list of standards.

Communication Studies: Curriculum studies that focus on communication technologies, specifically interpersonal or mass communication processes, theory and components.

Diffusion of Innovation/Information Theory: A theory that explains how innovations are introduced and adopted by various communities, (Baron & Davis, 2009, p. 277).

Digital Literacy: a set of core media processing competencies focusing specifically in the digital, converged and new media realm that allow media consumers to access, analyze, create, reflect and act upon messages and methods parceled by the media industries.

HBCU: An historically Black college or university with specific designation by the U.S. Department of Education, which either currently serves or was instituted to serve African Americans.

Higher Education: Education beyond grade 12. Also considered post-secondary education.

Journalism and Mass Communication Education: Education on the collegiate level that trains, educates and prepares students for careers in the mass communication industries including journalism, public relations, marketing and advertising.

Media Education: Curriculum studies post secondary or K-12 that focuses on media and media production can include journalism, video and audio production, communication theory, law, ethics and other related components of media.

Media Literacy: A set of core media processing competencies that allow media consumers to access, analyze, create, reflect and act upon messages and methods parceled by the media industries.

P/HIS: A predominately or Hispanic serving institution, colleges and universities with a higher than average or predominate number of Hispanic or Latino enrollees, and whose mission is to serve members of the Spanish speaking population.

TWIS/PWIS: Traditionally or predominately White institutions, that were founded to serve and whose enrollment today remains comprised of mostly White students.

This research was previously published in Administrative Challenges and Organizational Leadership in Historically Black Colleges and Universities edited by Charles B. W. Prince and Rochelle L. Ford; pages 213-236, copyright year 2016 by Information Science Reference (an imprint of IGI Global).

Chapter 4
Examining the Factors that Influence ICT Adoption in SMEs:
A Research Preliminary Findings

Japhet Eke Lawrence
Nigerian Defence Academy, Nigeria

ABSTRACT

Many opportunities have been made available through the use of Information communication technologies (ICT) in organizations in general, and particularly in Small to medium-sized enterprises (SMEs) with the early adopters' successes well publicized. Thus, many organizations not taking advantages of the ICT are currently examining their options. The purpose of this study is to examine the factors that influence SMEs' decision in adopting ICT in business. The diffusion theory, the technology acceptance model and information richness will provide the theoretical foundation for this study. Currently in the data collection phase, the owner/manager or someone responsible for IT employed by the SMEs will be surveyed in this cross-industry study. Preliminary results from the study are reported as well as sample questions resulting from the study to be used in the final survey questionnaire.

INTRODUCTION

Information communication technologies (ICT) are radically changing the face of business and organizations. ICTs (especially the computer, Internet, mobile telephony) provide a great deal of opportunities, as well as challenges for SMEs. ICTs seem to be giving a significant leverage to organisations in general, particularly SMEs. The impacts manifest themselves in many ways, ranging from virtual communication through mobile phone and web technology which increase awareness due to better quality information and images. Technologies are being adopted and incorporated into nearly all organizations, particularly the Internet which has the potential to radically change the way business is conducted. The Internet offers a competitive edge and a gateway to the global marketplace. Electronic commerce is enabled by the wide spread presence of information technology and the increasing use of networks, especially the Internet which have the ability to deliver cost effective on-line services for SMEs.

DOI: 10.4018/978-1-7998-0417-8.ch004

The use of ICT is widely seen as critical for the competitiveness of SMEs in the emerging global market. In an increasingly global world, both information and information technology are of great significance to organisations of all sizes. Businesses both large and small need information to succeed in today's rapidly changing environment. SMEs need to be able to process data and use information effectively when conducting their day-to-day operations.

The use of IT has the potential to play an increasingly important role in organisations by enabling them to substantially gain competitive advantage and compete successfully. The effective use of ICT can add significant value to an organisation in terms of productivity increase and performance improvements (Lawrence, 2009).

The role of information technology has been seen as increasingly important amongst companies as a mechanism to increase productivity, reduce costs and facilitate flexibility.

There is a growing interest in the use of ecommerce as a means to perform business transactions. Through the use of ecommerce, organisations are able to connect with their trading partners for ''just in time production'' and ''just in time delivery'', which improve their competitiveness globally. Lawrence (2002) clearly demonstrates that the use of ICT provides SMEs with substantial benefits in several areas crucial for their business success. Subsequent study by Lawrence (2013) shows that the appropriate use of electronic commerce technologies by SMEs can be an important factor in facilitating business growth, contribute to productivity, efficiency, and enable access to global markets.

As Kalakota and Whinston (1997) suggest, the role of SMEs is a key factor in the growth of economies in general and the emerging electronic marketplace in particular. The growth of the Internet has opened up a vast arena. The Internet provides more opportunities for businesses, particularly SMEs to sell their products and services to a global audience than they would have been able to afford to reach using the traditional methods. It offers a new paradigm for business that allows global trading and there are potentially few limits to growth (Levy and Powell 1999). The use of Internet technology presents a unique opportunity for SMEs to participate in electronic commerce and extend their capabilities and grow in a global market.

The establishment of an environment in which SMEs are able to grow and prosper in the emerging global business is considered critical to the development and expansion of businesses in the economy. The identification and encouragement of new business opportunities for SMEs based on ICT has been the priority of most governments, particularly the British government. ICTs are seen as playing an increasingly important role in the growth performance of SMEs and these are taking on new significance in most countries of the world (OECD, 2000). The advent of Internet-based electronic commerce allows smaller firms to expand their customer base, enter new product markets and rationalize their businesses (Lawrence, 2009). The paper is structured as follows. The section following this introduction discusses the main research area of concern, followed by literature review, then the methodology and finally, the paper presents some conclusions.

Conceptual Background

Literature search shows that SMEs posses' specific attributes (Auger and Gallaugher, 1997) that distinguish them from the large organisations most often studied in regards to information systems usage (Cragg and King 1993). Other studies (Lawrence, 2013, 2009; MacGregor et al, 1998; Auger and Gallaugher, 1997) have shown that SMEs' characteristics are different from larger organizations. It is argued that SMEs differ from large companies in the way they develop their corporate strategies and their technology policies

(Lawrence, 2008; MacGregor et al, 1998). Large companies typically have well-defined processes for developing and implementing strategies through a corporate planning process (Pool et al, 2006). While SMEs often use less structured approaches, strategies and policies that may not be formulated but may 'emerge' from a set of actions and experiments (Lawrence, 2008).

MacGregor et al (1998), Cragg and King (1993) and DeLone (1988) show the differences in management style between large businesses and SMEs. These studies have shown that among other characteristics, SMEs tend to have a small management team (often one or two individuals). SMEs are strongly influenced by the owner and the owner's personal habits. SMEs have little control over their environment (this is supported by the studies of Poon et al, 1996; Barnes et al, 2008 and Lawrence, 2008). SMEs have strong desire to remain independent. Other research studies show (Lawrence, 2002, 2013; DeLone, 1988) that small businesses tend to be more risky than their larger organisation. Most SMEs lack technical expertise (Cragg and King, 1993; Blili and Raymond 1993). Most SMEs lack adequate capital to undertake technical improvements (Wymer and Regan, 2005; Auger and Gallaugher, 1997) and most SMEs suffer from inadequate organizational planning (Lawrence, 2013).

Majority of SMEs may be too small to be able to employ a dedicated IT expert (Wymer and Regan, 2005; Auger and Gallaugher, 1997; Lawrence, 2002) and most SMEs lack resources and expertise both financial and intellectual and especially in terms of management of new technologies (Van Toorn et al, 2006; Caldeira and Ward, 2002; MacGregor et al, 1998; Igbaria et al, 1997) to buy consultancy advice. These authors agree that SMEs are more vulnerable because of their lack of financial and human resources (Wymer and Regan, 2005), as well as information resources that are needed to sufficiently understand and master the organisation and its environment. Many SMEs do not possess the technological background, which would enable them to use and evaluate IT, or lack the time to explore it (Barnes et al, 2008). SMEs find themselves caught in a trap and lack of resources means that while there may be an aggregate demand for IT service and advice, individually. The varying nature of that demand makes it uneconomical for other firms to provide a service meeting that demand. It is often the skill and enthusiasm of the owner-manager that typically drives the business forward and shapes the character of investment decisions (Barnes et al, 2008; Dixon et al, 2002). Yet the need to remain flexible and innovative is the criteria for survival and success for SMEs.

On the other hand, Cameron and Clarke (1996) add that some of the features of SMEs' made information technology use ideal for their businesses. These include flexibility and their ability to change and adapt quickly to innovations compared to large organisations (Blili and Raymond, 1993), which are very slow to respond to change. SMEs are generally less formal in their organisational and managerial practices and have less sophisticated IT capabilities and expertise than larger organisations. They are less likely to suffer 'lock-in' with respect to existing plants; technologies or organisational structure. SMEs tend to exhibit more informal communication and a less bureaucratic mode of operation and less rigid functional divisions.

SME is chosen as the main context of this research because of the strategic importance of this sector to growth and job creation. Businesses in this sector include those which are flexible to new working patterns and who are innovators in the adoption of new business practice. Although the definition of what constitutes small to medium enterprise varies from country to country, the benefits of growth in the SME sector are significant. There is no clear understanding of what SME is. The term small to medium-sized enterprises incorporates two primary classifications - small business and medium business. The Department of Trade and Industry in the UK (DTI, 2007) defines SME as a company employing between 1-249 employees. The current study based on DTI SME defines small business thus: as being independently owned and managed; being closely controlled by owners/managers who also contribute most, if not all, of the operating capital, having the principal decision making functions resting with the owner/manager; with total number of employees less than 50. While medium-sized enterprise is defined as business that is larger than small business and smaller than large business with total employees greater 50 and less than 250.

SMEs are extremely important to many countries, in some countries these group of organisations provide the foundation for the entire economy (Lawrence, 2013), their contribution to the economy cannot be over emphasised. SME comprises firms that make up the significant proportion of UK industry (99.8%), and are therefore very important to the UK economy. They account for more than 59% of private sector employment in the UK and currently are contributing most of the private sector employment growth (BERR, 2008).

According to the Observatory of European SMEs (2007), the average SME across all

European enterprises employ 6.8 people. At both the European Union (EU) and national level, SMEs lie at the heart of policy making with the emphasis on encouraging enterprise and promoting business growth. SMEs are an important link to boosting the levels of innovation in the national economy and fostering greater competition both domestically and increasingly, internationally.

In Canada, where SMEs account for 45% of GDP, much of the economy's growth, 60% of all jobs in the economy, and 75% of net employment growth. SMEs are an integral part of the country's economic fabric and are important to the economy. "The success of SMEs affects the well-being of the Canadian society as engines of job creation, economic growth and innovation" (CFIB, 2000). This is because more dynamic ICT-based service sectors are dominated by smaller enterprises. In most OECD countries, this trend is linked to rationalization in large firms, which are downsizing and outsourcing more functions to SMEs. The result is that more and more SMEs are providing business services, including marketing, staff training, and technical testing to other services and manufacturing enterprises (OECD, 2000). Apart from the economic significance of SMEs, the sector's social significance is widely recognized. In many cases, SMEs reflect the more personal and unique characteristics of a community than larger firms do. SMEs often serve specific market niches, the very presence of which can be a manifestation of special social and cultural characteristics. The greater independence and entrepreneurial nature of SMEs are thought to embody desirable social values and their presence is regarded as an important source of social stability (Lawrence, 2013).

Barnes et al (2008) argue that the advent of the digital economy has made the adoption and use of ICT a significant issue for most SMEs. Yet, many SMEs find themselves in a difficult situation. Research shows (Barnes et al, 2008; Turban et al, 2008) that SMEs may be too small to be able to employ a dedicated IT expert and lack the resources to buy consultancy advice. SMEs often have limited experience in selecting, implementing and evaluating suggested IT solutions. Barnes et al (2008) note that SMEs find themselves caught in a trap, lack of resources means that while there may be an aggregate demand for IT service and advice, individually, the varying nature of that demand makes it uneconomical for other firms to provide a service meeting that demand.

Given the strategic importance of the SME sector to growth and job creation and the large base of current Internet users as well as potential users, the success of SMEs gaining business leverage from the Internet is critical to the future of global economies (Lawrence, 2002; Poon and Swatman, 1999). It is therefore of importance that insight be gained into the issues affecting the adoption and use of ICT in SMEs. Furthermore, knowing the factors that influence adoption of ICT would explain why SMEs adopt or do not adopt this phenomenon. The author believes that an understanding of the factors that influence SMEs decision to adopt the technology in business may provide an avenue for policy-makers and practitioners to influence the rate of adoption of the Internet and consequently, the speed of electronic commerce.

Literature Review

Information systems and information technology innovations are increasingly being used to derive organizational changes intended to deliver significant performance improvement (Lawrence, 2013). Organisations both large and small need information to succeed in today's rapidly changing environment, they need to be able to process data and use information effectively when conducting their day-to-day operations (Walsham, 1993). There is an emerging consensus that to a greater extent ICTs have significantly impacted on the way business is conducted globally (OECD, 2004; World Economic Forum, 2004).

Understanding why organisations accept or reject technological innovation has proved to be one of the most challenging issues in information systems research (Swanson, 1988). Researchers have studied IT outcomes and diffusion processes since the inception of the IS field (Gefen and Straub, 1997). A summation of the implementation literature (Swanson, 1988) highlighted independent variables such as management commitment and user involvement as influential factors in the adoption of innovations. Other studies cited factors such as job tenure, uncertainty, competition and feedback (Kwon and Zmud, 1987).

There is a bourgeoning body of work on IS innovation diffusion (Rogers, 1983; Tornatzky and Klein, 1982; Davis, 1989) which focussed on factors such as relative advantage, complexity and ease of use that examined the overall impact of these variables on adoption of technological innovation. Many studies have investigated the effects of a wide range of variables, drawn primarily from diffusion of innovation theory (Ginzberg 1980); much relevant empirical work has been conducted in the past few years, most notably by Bayer and Melone (1989), Markus (1987), Orlikowski (1993), Kwon and Zmud (1987), Cooper and Zmud (1990). Other researchers have studied the impact of users' internal beliefs and attitude on usage behaviour (DeSanctis 1983), and how these internal beliefs and attitudes are, in turn, influenced by various external factors, including the system's technical design characteristics (Benbasat and Dexter 1986; Benbasat et al, 1986) and user involvement in system development. While a large number of other studies have considered factors that lead to successful adoption and use of innovation in organisation. These studies are particularly helpful in the effort to understand the factors that influence the adoption of ICT in SMEs. However, in each of these studies, one must use caution in applying concepts derived from the large organisational context to the SME context (Mason, 1997).

The focus of this study is to quantitatively and qualitatively examine the adoption and usage of ICT in SMEs. The researcher hopes to propose a more enriched model for conceptualising the technological, organisational, environmental and contextual issues around the adoption and usage of ICT —issues that have been largely missing from contemporary discussions of ICT adoption and usage (Orlikowski, 1993). The study aims to build on the work done so far by using grounded theory technique to develop a theory designed to contribute toward a fuller understanding of the factors that influence SMEs' decision in adopting and using ICT in business.

This study will interrogate three key theoretical issues on the role of ICT in SMEs: (a) the diffusion of innovation theory (b) technology acceptance model and (c) information richness theory. These theoretical perspectives offer differing, but overlapping insight into the factors that influence organisations, particularly SMEs to adopt and use information technologies in general and in particular ICT. These perspectives sweep in crucial insights that could not have been obtained by reliance on a single perspective. The use of these models will widen the scope of the enquiry and pools the lessons learned from research that spans disciplines and methodologies and provides insights that may help to extend the depth and breadth of understanding of the adoption of ICT in business. Thus, the study sought to build on and extend these extant models and previous research on diffusion, adoption and implementation, by providing adoption model, propositions, and data designed to increase the understanding of the factors that influence the adoption and use of ICT in SMEs. Each theory will be briefly introduced for the purpose of this proposal.

The *diffusion theory* (Rogers, 1983) addresses the communication and adoption of innovations (ideas, practices, or objects "perceived as new by an individual or other unit of adoption") through certain channels, over time, and across members of an organization.

Diffusion is aimed at developing a better understanding of dissemination of new ideas through communities of potential adopters who may then make the decision to adopt the idea.

The theory identifies factors that facilitate or hinder technology adoption. These factors include characteristics of the technology, characteristics of adopters, and the means by which adopters learn about and are persuaded to adopt the technology (Rogers 1983). It provides well-developed concepts and a large body of empirical results applicable to the study of ICT adoption. The main elements of diffusion theory are innovation, communication channels, time and social systems. To understand the theory and its limitation, one needs to understand the ways in which these components relate to the diffusion of an innovation.

Most past studies on adoption have used Roger's (1983) diffusion of innovations theory to identify the attributes of innovation that influence technological adoption at individual or organisational level. As Rogers points out, innovation diffusion has emerged as one of the most multidisciplinary research topics in social sciences today, as well as studies concerned with the adoption of information technologies (Fichman, 1992). The diffusion theory offers potentially useful insights into the reasons surrounding the widespread uptake of new ideas such as the ICT in organisation (Galliers and Swan, 1999). Much of the theory was developed in the context of adopters making voluntary decisions to accept or reject an innovation based on the benefits they expect to accrue from their own independent use of the technology.

The currency of Rogers' theory of diffusion is supported by the fact that researchers continue to use this model as a basis for their own study (e.g. Mason, 1997; Fichman, 1992; Brancheau and Wetherbe, 1990). It provides a useful perspective on challenging topics in the IT field, such as how to improve technology assessment, adoption and implementation. The theory provides well-developed concepts and a large body of empirical results applicable to the study of technology adoption and use in organisation. In his review and analysis of eighteen published empirical studies of IT adoption and diffusion, Fichman (1992) reported that no critical review existed that focused specifically on the application of diffusion theory to the adoption of information technologies. Fichman identified the assumptions implicit in the diffusion of innovation theory and concluded that the theory found strong support only when the context met the assumptions of diffusion theory.

Frambach (1993) found that organisational adoption of innovations has received less attention in literature than innovation adoption in individual users. Wolfe (1994) argued that most often, the adoption of innovation could not be understood without careful attention to the personal, organisational, technological and environmental contexts with which it takes place. Within the context of ICT use in SMEs, both organisational and individual level factors are undoubtedly important in understanding the factors that influence ICT adoption in SMEs. The focus of this study is on SMEs adoption of ICT and the objective is to build and extend the diffusion theory to develop an enriched model of factors that influence ICT adoption in SMEs that considers technological, organisational as well as environmental factors. While the diffusion theory was developed from contexts outside organisations, Rogers views it as potentially applicable within organisations.

On the other hand, *the technology acceptance model* (TAM) (Davis, 1989; Davis et al, 1989) offers promising theoretical bases for examining the factors that influence the adoption of ICT in SMEs. Davis (1989) technology acceptance model is an adaptation of Ajzen and Fishbein (1980) theory of reasoned action (TRA), which is specifically meant to explain computer usage behaviour. TAM is considerably less general than TRA, designed to apply only to computer usage behaviour in organisation. The model incorporates findings accumulated from over a decade of IS research and it has been especially well suited for modelling IS usage in organisations (Davis, 1989). The goal of TAM is to provide an explanation of the determinants of computer acceptance that is general and capable of explaining user behaviour across a broad range of end-user computing technologies and user populations, while at the same time being both parsimoniously and theoretically justified.

TAM posits that two particular beliefs, perceived usefulness and perceived ease of use, are of primary relevance for computer acceptance behaviours. Davis (1989) defines perceived usefulness as "the prospective users' subjective probability that using a specific application system will increase his or her job performance within an organisational context". Within organisations, people are generally reinforced for good performance by raises, promotions, bonuses, and other rewards (Davis, 1989). A system high in perceived usefulness, in turn, is one for which a user believes in the existence of a positive use-performance relationship. Perceived ease of use, in contrast, refers to "the degree to which a prospective user believes that using a particular system would be free of effort". Effort is a finite resource that a person may allocate to the various activities for which he or she is responsible. All else being equal, Davis claims, an application perceived to be easier to use than another is more likely to be accepted by users (Davis, 1989).

Overall, perceived usefulness and perceived ease of use have shown significant associations with outcomes (Gefen and Straub, 1997). Golden et al (1992) found in their study that user perceptions of the medium's usefulness affects IT use in organisation. Adams et al (1992) reported that there were a wide variety of ways in which perceived usefulness and perceived ease of use could be applied. It may be used in organisations to make selections between contending software packages or it may also be used by researchers interested in understanding factors that influence the success of information systems. Or it may be used in studies within and across organisations by researchers who are interested in understanding the diffusion of information technology and the determinants of technology adoption. TAM has proven to be successful in predicting and explaining usage across a variety of systems. The theoretical insights of TAM thus provide a strong basis from which to examine the factors that influence adoption of ICT in SMEs

Finally, *the information richness theory* concerns the information processing requirements of tasks and capacities of media. The core premise of the theory is that information richness is an inherent, physical property of media and that a person's use of one medium, rather than another, for a particular communication transaction is the result of a choice that the person makes in an objectively rational process. Richness is defined as "the potential information—carrying capacity of data". If the communication of an item of data, such as a wink, provides substantial new understanding, it would be considered rich. If the datum provides little understanding, it would be low in richness. Information richness is defined as the ability of information and media to change understanding within a time interval. Communication transactions that can overcome different frames of reference or clarify ambiguous issues to change human understanding in a timely manner are considered rich (Daft and Lengel, 1984, 1986), while communications that require a long time to enable understanding or cannot overcome different perspectives are lower in richness.

Daft and Lengel (1984, 1986) have described communication media along a single continuum of "information richness" to explain information processing behaviour in organisations. At the core of information richness theory is the notion that what makes media more or less appropriate for particular communication tasks are inherent media characteristics (Fulk et al. 1987, Fulk and Ryu 1990). Communication media are arrayed along a continuum of "information richness" based on four criteria: "(a) facilitating feedback, (b) the ability to convey multiple cues, (c) the tailoring of messages to personal circumstances, and (d) using natural language to convey subtleties" (Daft and Lengel, 1984). The rank order of media in terms of richness is face-to-face, telephone, personal written text (letters, memos), formal written text (documents, bulletins), and formal numeric text (computer output).

Steinfield and Fulk (1990) further added electronic mail to the richness continuum at a point between the telephone and written personal text (Trevino et al, 1987). When gauged on these criteria, the richest way to communicate is face-to-face interaction because it provides immediate feedback. Daft and Lengel argue that with feedback, understanding can be checked and interpretations corrected. It allows simultaneous observation of multiple cues via ody language, facial expression and tone of voice. It conveys information beyond the spoken message, and is of a personal nature and utilises natural language, which is high in variety (Daft and Lengel 1986).

The telephone medium is somewhat less rich than face-to-face, although its feedback capability is fast, but visual cues are not available. Therefore, individuals using the telephone have to rely on language content and audio cues to reach understanding. Written communications are less rich still, because their feedback is slow and only the information that is written down is conveyed, so visual cues are limited to that which is on paper. Formal numeric documents are lowest in the information richness continuum. Daft and Lengel argue that numeric documents tend to be useful in communicating simple, quantifiable aspects of organisations. Numbers do not have the information—carrying capacity of natural language. They provide no opportunity for visual observation, feedback, or personalization. In general, face-to-face medium is believed to convey the richest information while formal numeric documents convey the least rich information.

Based on the foregoing models, the study is interested in examining how SMEs currently use ICT and the factors that influence SMEs' decision in adopting ICT in business. The study will generate specific questions that will seek to interrogate the theoretical elements of the foregoing models.

Research Questions

This study sets out to examine the adoption and usage of ICT in small to medium-sized enterprises. The study is cross-sectional in nature and the data for this study will be collected over a six-month period. The objective of the study is to ascertain how SMEs currently use ICT and to establish the factors that influence their decision in adopting this technology in business. The study aims to build on the work done so far by using grounded theory technique to develop a theory designed to contribute toward a fuller understanding of the factors that influence SMEs' decision in adopting and using ICT in business. The researcher hopes to propose a more enriched model for conceptualising the technological, organisational, environmental and contextual issues around the adoption and usage of ICT — issues that have been largely missing from contemporary discussions of ICT adoption and usage (Orlikowski, 1993).

In order to realise the research objective the study, especially the data-gathering process, will be guided by the following research questions:

- How do SMEs currently use ICT in their business?
- What are the benefits that may be gained from the use of ICT in business?
- What are the possible barriers that may prevent ICT use in business?
- What are the factors that influence SMEs' decision in adopting this technology in business?

Significance of the Study

It is true that ICTs has the potential to radically change the way business is conducted generally, empowering and offering SMEs in particular a competitive edge and a gateway to the global marketplace. The use of ICT is widely seen as critical for the competitiveness of SMEs in the emerging global market. This research will be unique in that it will be the first study to use the combination of case study and survey methods to examine ICT phenomenon in SMEs. The author maintains that in order to find out the current picture of ICT usage in SMEs and the factors that influence adoption decision. It is not only desirable but also essential that a different perspective that involves combining different research methods be employed to investigate the complex and dynamic technology like ICT adoption in SMEs. The author argues that the use of survey method alone presents a restricted view of current ICT usage and the factors that influence SMEs to adopt the technology. The survey method will pay little attention to the deeper understanding of the factors that influence adoption. No matter how rigorous the analysis might be; it will not provide a full insight into the current picture of ICT usage in SMEs and the factors that influence them in adopting the technology.

The study will hopefully generate crucial data and informed analysis about how SMEs are coping in a world driven by ICTs. In particular, it will shed more light on the factors that influence their decision in adopting ICT in business. This study is uniquely placed because it will generate theory grounded in data collected from SMEs. The study will develop an ICT adoption model based on theory-driven case study that will explain the factors that influence or inhibit SMEs decision in adopting and using ICT in business. The model will show technological, organisational and environmental factors as important constructs that explains ICT adoption and usage in organisation. It is, therefore, hoped that the work that will be presented in this study will contribute to a realistic understanding of ICT adoption and usage in organisations in general and SMEs in particular. The theory that will be generated from this study will be an original contribution to the knowledge base of the emerging field of IS.

Research Methodology

The study takes the form of exploratory and descriptive research, focusing on the usage and adoption of ICT in SMEs. Given the newness and changeable nature of the area of study, a quantitative and qualitative strategy will be adopted, which will utilise the survey and case study format, involving the collection of organisational facts from specific SME. In doing so, the research will combine the following tools: quantitative survey questionnaire administration and qualitative case study interviewing respectively. The study will focus attention on interpreting the context in which the SMEs currently use ICT and the factors that influence their decision in adopting the technology.

The search of literature shows no empirical studies have been carried out in this area that has used the combination of survey and case study to examine ICT adoption and usage in SMEs. Many of the methods that have been used to examine ICT adoption and usage in business have traditionally been either survey or case study. Neither of them has managed to provide a full insight into ICT usage and the factors that influence decisions in adopting the technology. This triangulation across various techniques of data collection is particularly beneficial in theory generation, as it will provide multiple perspectives on an issue and supply more information on emerging concepts and allows for cross-checking, and yields stronger substantiation of constructs (Eisenhardt, 1989; Glaser and Strauss, 1967; Pettigrew, 1990; Orlikowski, 1993). Danziger and Kraemer (1991) suggest that it is always best to utilise several methods of data collection to address adequately the impact of information technology. Using multiple techniques can lead to new insights and modes of analysis that is unlikely to occur if one technique alone is used (Kaplan and Duchon, 1988). The use of each technique offers a different avenue for SMEs to express their perceptions of the adoption of ICT and is more effective in addressing information systems issues.

Mitroff and Linstone (1993) report that in today's messy world, to achieve success demands that one be able to examine problems from "multiple perspectives". Each of these perspectives is of value in that it views a problem through a distinct lens and offers perceptions not encompassed by the others. None by itself suffices to deal with a complex and dynamic problem, but together they give a richer and fuller picture of the phenomenon. The survey will be combined with the case study to provide deeper insight on the factors that influence adoption and it will also complement and strengthen the findings of the research study. Robson (1993) suggests that when the purpose of the research is descriptive, then survey will be the most appropriate method however, if the purpose is exploratory then case study method will be the most appropriate. The purpose of the study is both descriptive and exploratory.

The study is cross-sectional in nature and the data collection will be in two-phases and will be collected over a six-month period. In phase one, a survey questionnaire of 400 randomly selected SMEs will be conducted across the UK, to elicit information regarding the current status of ICT usage in SMEs. The aims of using survey are threefold: (1) to describe how ICT is currently used in SMEs (2) to examine the benefits that SMEs may be gained from the use of ICT and (3) to examine some of the possible barriers that may prevent SMEs from using ICT. The use of survey in this study is important, because the analysis from the survey questionnaire might highlight issues that need to be resolved through case study interview with SMEs. The survey will be designed in this study to collect descriptive data and it will make no provision for interaction with the participants. Although it is hoped to provide a comprehensive picture of current ICT usage and to discover patterns that may be common across SMEs. However, it will not provide explanation of how and why SMEs use ICT or the factors that influence their decision in adopting the technology in business. While the survey method is very useful, Kraemer and Dutton (1991) suggest that it is greatly improved when used in conjunction with the case study method. The survey phase of this study will set much of the agenda for the qualitative phase by providing descriptive information.

Phase two of the study will be carried out using multiple case studies on some of the SMEs that have previously completed the questionnaire in phase one to elicit qualitative information to complement the shortcomings of the survey. The case study phase will be based on the results of the survey questionnaire and further review of the literature. The aim of using this method is to gain a deeper insight into the issues raised in the survey questionnaire and to understand the factors that influence SMEs decision in adopting ICT in business. It will also be used to explain and conceptualise the phenomenon of ICT usage in SMEs and to add a richer dimension to the survey data.

Case studies differ fundamentally from surveys in that the researcher generally has less presumptive knowledge of what the variables of interest will be and how they will be measured (Gable, 1994). Yin (1984) suggests that case studies are appropriate where the objective is to study contemporary events, and where it is not necessary to control behavioural events or variables. Yin (1994) defines case studies as "an empirical inquiry that investigates a contemporary phenomenon within its real life context, especially when the boundaries between a phenomenon and context are not clearly evident; and in which multiple sources of evidence are used". The contemporary phenomenon being investigated by this research is the understanding of how ICT is used within the context of small to medium-sized enterprises. The phenomenon has to be investigated in its real-life context because all the variables in that context contribute to its understanding.

Benbasat et al (1987) and Myers (1997) argue that case study method is particularly appropriate for the Study of information systems development, implementation and use within organisations. Furthermore, it is well suited to where an understanding of interactions between information technology-related innovations in organisational contexts is needed (Darke et al, 1998). Case study can be used in various ways from within different research perspectives using a variety of data collection and analysis methods, producing diverse types of research outcomes (Cavaye, 1996). Orlikowski and Baroudi (1991) note that case study methods are appropriate to generating valid interpretive knowledge, as these examine humans within their social setting. It is particularly appropriate when theoretical knowledge on the phenomenon under investigation is limited and an understanding is not well developed (Benbasat et al, 1987). These include areas where a phenomenon is dynamic and not yet mature or settled, such as ICT adoption and usage where there are few existing theories to explain the phenomenon (Lawrence, 2002).

Case study method has the ability to capture realities in greater details by studying a phenomenon in its natural context and the ability to analyse more variables than is possible using any other methods (Benbasat et al, 1987). It also provides the opportunity to ask penetrating questions and to capture the richness of organisational behaviour. However the conclusions drawn may be specific to the particular organisations studied. It provides rich, explanatory evidence that can be used to explain why and how phenomena occur. Case studies are appropriate for studying topics where attitudes and behaviours can best be understood within their natural setting. Benbasat et al (1987) further identify three strengths of case study method in information systems: (1) the researcher can study information in a natural setting, learn about the state of the art, and generate theories from practice; (2) the method allows the researcher to understand the nature and complexity of the process taking place; and (3) valuable insights can be gained into new topics emerging from the rapidly changing information systems field. The case study enables detailed study of the concepts in their own natural context. Not only will the participants discuss their interpretation of ICT usage concept, but the organisational context will also be analysed for relationships to the concept. Its use will help in more intelligent interpretation of the patterns that might be discovered in the analysis of questionnaire data. Case study provides a much richer picture of the world than can be obtained from survey (Yin, 1994), which is restricted to gathering information related to the questions on the survey instruments.

Data Analysis

Data presentation and analysis will be based on quantitative survey and qualitative case study, using the statistical package for social science (SPSS for windows) to analyse the survey while grounded theory will be used to analyse the case study data.

Data analysis in grounded theory involves specific procedures which, when applied appropriately and with vigilance will result in theory that is rigorous and well grounded in the data. The defining characteristic of grounded theory is that of a general methodology for discovering theory that is grounded in data systematically gathered and analysed. The theory evolves during actual research, and it does this through a continuous interplay between analysis and data collection; data analysis guides future data collection. Strauss and Corbin (1990) have identified three levels of analysis: (a) to present the data without interpretation and abstraction, the participants tell their own story; (b) to create a "rich and believable descriptive narrative" using field notes, interview transcripts and researcher interpretations; (c) building a theory using high levels of interpretation and abstraction. This research will combine the second and third approaches, to present rich and detailed descriptions, which allows the reader to make sufficient contextual judgements to transfer the case study findings to alternative settings. The concern here is with the multiple constructions of reality as experienced by SMEs.

The selection of grounded theory (Glaser and Strauss, 1967; Glaser, 1978; Strauss, 1987;

Strauss and Corbin, 1990, 1998) amongst a myriad of other qualitative analysis methods is to generate a descriptive and explanatory theory of the adoption of ICT rooted in the experiences of the SMEs. The objective of the study is the development of a conceptual model that explains the adoption of ICT in SMEs and it fits well with the philosophical nature of grounded theory. It is useful for understanding the contextual elements (Orlikowski 1993) that constitutes the main focus of this case study. Strauss (1987) emphasises the usefulness of the case study approach when used with grounded theory. It "is an inductive, theory discovery methodology that allows the researcher to develop a theoretical account of the general features of a topic while simultaneously grounding the account in empirical data" (Martin and Turner, 1986; Glaser and Strauss, 1967). This generative approach seems particularly useful here given that the objective of the study is the discovery of theory that explains the adoption and usage of ICT in SMEs.

Accordingly, proponents of the grounded theory advocate that an approach which concerns itself with the meanings, definitions, and interpretations which are made by the subjects of the study has greater potential for depicting their world and priorities more accurately than methods which begin by preconceiving the world and its meaning (De Burca and McLoughlin, 1996). A grounded theory is one that is discovered, developed, and provisionally verified through systematic data collection and analysis of data pertaining to a particular phenomenon (Strauss and Corbin, 1990). It offers a way of attending in details to qualitative material in order to develop systematically theories about the phenomena being studied. Turner (1981) suggests that grounded theory is particularly well suited to dealing with qualitative data of the kind gathered from participant observation, from the observation of face-to-face interaction, from semi- structured or unstructured interviews, from case-study material or documentary sources. Typically, these particular kinds of inquiry generate large amounts of data, which accumulate in non-standard and unpredictable formats. The grounded theory approach offers the researcher a strategy for sifting and analysing material of this kind. A particular strength of utilising grounded theory is that a documented record of the progress of the analysis will be generated. Hence, it is always possible to trace the derivation of any concept or model by checking back through the data and memos.

The goal of grounded theory is seeking a theory that is intimately tied with the evidence, so that the resultant theory is likely to be consistent with empirical data (Orlikowski 1993; Eisenhardt 1989). It is a general style of doing analysis that does not depend on any particular disciplinary perspectives (Strauss 1987) and, therefore, would seem to lend itself to information systems research, which can be described as a hybrid discipline. Theory is grounded when it emerges from and generates explanations of relationships and events that reflect the life experiences of those people and processes that the researcher is attempting to understand. Grounded theory is an appropriate technique for this study as it generates theory that can be used as a precursor for further investigation of this phenomenon and related issues. Other qualitative research techniques, quantitative methods, or a combination of both can then be used in subsequent studies to test, verify or extend the qualitative propositions that will emerge from this research.

A number of theoretical approaches emphasise the criticality of organisational context in shaping technology use in organisations, such a conviction also informs this research, and the use of a grounded theory methodology allows the inclusion and investigation of this key organisational element. This inductive approach relies on the researcher systematically collecting, coding, categorising and analysing data to derive the theory that explains the phenomena. The methodology facilitates "the generation of theories of process, sequence, and change pertaining to organisations, positions, and social interaction" (Glaser and Strauss, 1967).

Most IT usage models have tended to neglect the contextual aspect of technology use in literature. An approach that specifically includes elements of process and context is thus particularly appropriate here. The three characteristics of grounded theory inductive, contextual, and processual fit with the interpretive rather than positivist orientation of this research. The focus here is on developing a context-based description and explanation of the phenomenon, rather than an objective, static description expressed strictly in terms of causality (Boland, 1979, 1985; Chua, 1986; Orlikowski and Baroudi, 1991).

Preliminary Findings

The research preliminary findings will suggest that innovation adoption theories should not only account for technological factors (innovation characteristics), but also organisational and environmental factors should be included in IT adoption and use in organisation. Although the adoption of ICT in SMEs has been led by technological attributes, however, the research findings will show the importance of organisational and environmental factors in SMEs decision in adopting and using ICT in business.

The existing theories such as technology acceptance model and diffusion of innovation theory were developed with the concept of static individual computing environment in mind. As such, in today's rapidly changing IT environment, they do not provide adequate explanations of an organisation's IT usage behaviour (Kang, 1998). Further, there has been little or no previous study done to examine the applicability of these models to the SME context.

The technology acceptance model posits that both perceived ease of use and perceived usefulness correlate with system use. The model's two constructs are limited to technological attributes of usefulness of computer technology and the ease of use of the technology. The model, with its assumption of users being motivated primarily by job performance expectations from IS use, may be considered as a model of compliance. In this model, the users are motivated to use the IS to gain specific rewards. However, the model is influential in the contribution to the enduring line of IT adoption and diffusion research. It has proved useful for understanding the factors involved in organizational adoption decision making.

An alternative model that will extend the technology acceptance model and diffusion of innovation will be proposed based on the findings from a theory-driven case study. The proposed theoretical model will redress the inadequacies of these models by developing a more enrich adoption model that will consider not only the technological characteristics, but also the organisational as well as the environmental factors. Within the proposed model, each of these factors will be shown as having an influence on the decision in adopting and using ICT in SMEs.

CONCLUSION

In this paper various theoretical frameworks have been described. The paper began by discussing the ICT and small to medium-sized enterprises which formed the background to this research. The existing conceptual models of diffusion of innovation, the technology acceptance model, information richness theory and empirical studies relevant to this study have been reviewed. These models are characterised by largely positivist epistemology, however, they are found to be relevant to the adoption and use of ICT in SMEs. Some of the empirical support for the theories has consisted of laboratory type experiments, often the subjects were students, whose behaviour in this type of formal setting would probably differ quite radically from that of people carrying out everyday tasks in a real world organisation (Howcroft, 1998). A large body of research discussed focused on the technical advantages and task requirements to explain the adoption and use of technology in organisation (Schmitz and Fulk, 1991). There has been an overriding theme with most of the research in that it attempts to match media characteristics and task characteristics. These models are based on the assumption that each medium has an "objective" set of features, which can be replicated in any organisational setting, regardless of the particular context.

REFERENCES

Adams, D. A., Nelson, R. R., & Todd, P. A. (1992). Perceived usefulness, ease of use and usage of information technology: Replication. *Management Information Systems Quarterly*, *16*(June), 227–247. doi:10.2307/249577

Ajzen, I., & Fishbein, M. (1980). *Understanding attitudes and predicting social behaviour*. Englewood Cliffs, New Jersey: Prentice-Hall.

Auger, P., & Gallaugher, J.PAT AUGER JOHN M. GALLAUGHER. (1997). Factors affecting the adoption of an Internet-based sales presence for small businesses. *The Information Society*, *13*(1), 55–74. doi:10.1080/019722497129287

Barnes, D., Dyerson, R., & Harindranath, G. (2008). *If it isn't broken, don't fix it*. Retrieved from http://www.rhul.ac.uk/Management/Research/PRISM/index.html

Bayer, J., & Melone, N. (1989). A critique of diffusion theory as a management framework for understanding adoption of software engineering innovations. *Journal of Systems and Software*, *9*(2), 161–166. doi:10.1016/0164-1212(89)90018-6

Beauclair, R., & Sussman, L. (1992). Factors affecting email use. *Computers in Human Behavior*, *8*(4), 297–311. doi:10.1016/0747-5632(92)90026-B

Benbasat, I., & Dexter, A. S. (1986). An investigation of the effectiveness of colour and graphical presentation under varying time constraints. *Management Information Systems Quarterly*, *10*(1), 59–84. doi:10.2307/248881

Benbasat, I., Dexter, A. S., & Todd, P. (1986). An experimental program investigating colour-enhanced and graphical information presentation: An integration of the findings. *Communications of the ACM*, *29*(11), 1094–1105. doi:10.1145/7538.7545

Benbasat, I., Goldstein, D. K., & Mead, M. (1987). The Case Research Strategy in Studies of Information Systems. *Management Information Systems Quarterly*, *11*(3), 369–385. doi:10.2307/248684

BERR. (Business Enterprise and Regulatory Reform), (2008). Retrieved from http://stats.berr.gov.uk/ed/sme

Blili, S., & Raymond, L. (1993). Information technology: Threats and Opportunities for Small and Medium Enterprises. *International Journal of Information Management*, *13*(6), 439–448. doi:10.1016/0268-4012(93)90060-H

Boland, L. A. (1979). A Critique of Friedman's Critics. *Journal of Economic Literature American Economic Association*, *17*(2), 503–522.

Boland, L. A. (1985). Reflections on Blaug's Methodology of Economics: Suggestions for a Revised Edition. Eastern Economic Journal, 11(4), 450-454.

Bracheau, J. C., & Wetherbe, J. C. (1990). The adoption of spreadsheet software: Testing innovation diffusion theory in the context of end-user computing. *Information Systems Research*, *1*(2), 115–143. doi:10.1287/isre.1.2.115

Caldeira, M. M., & Ward, J. M. (2002). Understanding the successful adoption and us of IS/IT in SMEs: An explanation from Portuguese manufacturing industries. *Information Systems Journal*, *12*(2), 121–152. doi:10.1046/j.1365-2575.2002.00119.x

Cameron, J., & Clarke, R. (1996). Towards a Theoretical Framework for Collaborative Electronic Commerce Projects Involving Small and Medium-Size Enterprises. *Proc. of the 9th International Conference EDI-IOS*, Bled, Slovenia.

Cavaye, A. L. M. (1996). Case Study Research: A Multi-faceted Research Approach for IS. *Information Systems Journal*, *6*(3), 227–242. doi:10.1111/j.1365-2575.1996.tb00015.x

CFIB. (2000). Internet Use among Small and Medium-sized Firms. Retrieved from www.bcstats.gov.bc.ca/pubs/sbq/sbq01q1.pdf

Chua, W. F. (1986). Radical Developments in Accounting Thought. *Accounting Review*, *61*, 601–632.

Cooper, R. B., & Zmud, R. W. (1990). Information Technology Implementation Research: A Technological Diffusion Approach. *Management Science*, *36*(2), 123–139. doi:10.1287/mnsc.36.2.123

Cragg, P., & King, M. (1993). Small-Firm Computing: Motivators and Inhibitors. *Management Information Systems Quarterly*, *17*(1), 47–59. doi:10.2307/249509

Daft, R. L., & Lengel, R. H. (1984). Information richness: A new approach to managerial behaviour and organisational design. In B. Staw & L. Cummings (Eds.), *Research in Organisational Behaviour* (Vol. 6, pp. 191–233).

Daft, R. L., & Lengel, R. H. (1986). Organisational Information Requirements, Media Richness and Structural Design. *Management Science*, *32*(5), 554–571. doi:10.1287/mnsc.32.5.554

Danziger, J. N., & Kraemer, K. L. (1991). Survey Research and Multiple Operationism: The URBIS Project Methodology. In K. L. Kraemer (Ed.), *The Information Systems Research Challenge: Survey Research Methods* (Vol. 3, pp. 351–371). Boston, MA: Harvard Business School Press.

Darke, P., Shanks, G., & Broadbent, M. (1998). Successfully completing case study Research: Combining rigour, relevance and pragmatism. *Information Systems Journal*, *8*(4), 273–289. doi:10.1046/j.1365-2575.1998.00040.x

Davis, F. D. (1989). Perceived usefulness, perceived Ease of use, and user acceptance of Information Technology. *Management Information Systems Quarterly*, *13*(3), 319–340. doi:10.2307/249008

Davis, F. D., Bagozzi, R. P., & Warshaw, P. R. (1989). User acceptance of computer technology: A comparison of two theoretical models. *Management Science*, *35*(8), 982–1003. doi:10.1287/mnsc.35.8.982

De Burca, S., & McLoughlin, D. (1996). The Grounded Theory Alternative in Business Network Research. Retrieved from http://www.dcu.ie/business/research_interests.html

DeLone, W. (1988). Determinants of success for computer usage in small business. *Management Information Systems Quarterly*, (March): 50–61.

DeSanctis, G. (1983). Expectancy theory as an explanation of voluntary use of a decision support system. *Psychological Reports*, *52*(1), 247–260. doi:10.2466/pr0.1983.52.1.247

Dixon, T., McAllister, P., & Thompson, B. (2002). *The value of ICT for SMEs in the UK: A critical Literature Review*. Retrieved from http://www.cem.ac.uk/itribe.htm

DTI (Department of Trade and Industry). (2007), http://www.dti.gov.uk

Eisenhardt, K. M. (1989). Building theories from Case Study Research. *Academy of Management Review*, *14*(4), 532–550.

Fichman, R. G. (1992). Information technology diffusion: A review of empirical research. In J.I. DeGross, J. D. Becker, & J. J. Elam (Eds.), *Proceedings of the Thirteenth International Conference on Information Systems*, Dallas, TX (pp. 195-206).

Frambach, R. T. (1993). An integrated model of organisational adoption and diffusion of innovation. *European Journal of Marketing*, *27*(5), 22–41. doi:10.1108/03090569310039705

Fulk, J., & Ryu, D. (1990). *Perceiving electronic mail systems: A partial test of the social information processing model of communication media use in organisation. Paper presented to international communication association*, Dublin, Ireland

Fulk, J., Steinfield, C. W., Schmitz, J., & Power, J. G. (1987). A social information processing model of media use in organisations. *Communication Research*, *14*(5), 529–552. doi:10.1177/009365087014005005

Gable, G. G. (1994). Integrating case study and survey research methods: An example in information systems. *European Journal of Information Systems*, *3*(2), 112–126. doi:10.1057/ejis.1994.12

Galliers, B., & Swan, J. (1999). Information systems and strategic change: A critical review of business process reengineering. In W. Currie & B. Galliers (Eds.), *Rethinking Management Information Systems Oxford. University Press.*

Gefen, D., & Straub, D. W. (1997). Gender differences in the perception and use of email: an extension to the technology acceptance model. *MIS Quarterly*, December.

Ginzberg, M. J. (1980). An organisational contingencies view of accounting and information systems implementation. *Accounting, Organizations and Society*, *5*(5), 369–382. doi:10.1016/0361-3682(80)90036-7

Glaser, E. G. (1978). *Advances in the Methodology of Grounded Theory: Theoretical Sensitivity*. Mill Valley, California: Sociology press.

Glaser, E. G., & Strauss, A. L. (1999). *The Discovery of Grounded Theory: Strategies for Qualitative Research*. London, UK: Aldine Transaction.

Howcroft, D. (1998). *Spanning the Spectrum from Utopia to Dystopia: An Interpretive Field Study of the Nature and Characteristics of Internet Usage* [Unpublished PhD thesis]. UMIST, UK.

Igbaria, M., Zinatelli, N., Craig, P., & Cavaye, A. (1997). *Personal Computing Acceptance Factors in Small Firms: A Structured Equation Model*. MIS Quarterly, September.

Kalakota, R., & Whinston, A. B. (1997). *Electronic Commerce: A Manager's Guide*. Reading, MA: Addison-Wesley.

Kang, S. (1998). Information Technology Acceptance: Evolving with the Changes in the Network Environment. *Proceedings of the IEEE 31st Hawaii international conference on system science*, Hawaii.

Kaplan, B., & Duchon, D. (1988). Combining Qualitative and Quantitative Methods in Information Systems Research: A Case Study. *Management Information Systems Quarterly*, (December): 57–86.

Kraemer, K. L., & Dutton, W. H. (1991). In K. L. Kraemer (Ed.), *Survey Research in the Study of Management Information Systems, In the Information Systems Research Challenge: Survey Research Methods* (Vol. 3, pp. 3–34). Boston, Massachusetts: Harvard Business School Press.

Kwon, T. H., & Zmud, R. W. (1987). Unifying the fragmented models of information systems implementation. In R. J. Boland & R. A. Hirschheim (Eds.), *critical issues in information systems research.* New York: Wiley.

Lawrence, J. E. (2002), *The Use of Internet in Small to Medium-Sized Enterprises* [Unpublished PhD thesis]. University of Salford, UK.

Lawrence, J. E. (2008). *The Challenges and Utilization of e-Commerce: The Use of Internet by Small to Medium-sized Enterprises in the United Kingdom,* Information. *Social Justice (San Francisco, Calif.), 1*(2).

Lawrence, J. E. (2009). The Utilization of E-Commerce by Small to Medium-sized Enterprises: A U K Perspective. *Proceedings of the IADIS International Conference Information Systems*, Barcelona, Spain.

Lawrence, J. E. (2013). *Adoption and Usage of Internet in Small to Medium-sized Enterprises*. Germany: Lambert Academic Publishing.

Levy, M., & Powell, P. (1999), Emerging Technology: can the Internet add value for SMEs? *Proceedings of UKAIS Conference* (pp. 438-450).

MacGregor, R. C., Bunker, D. J., & Waugh, P. (1998), Electronic Commerce and Small / Medium Enterprises (SMEs) in Australia: An Electronic Data Interchange (EDI) Pilot Study, *Eleventh International Bled Electronic Commerce Conference*, Bled, Slovenia.

Markus, M. L. (1987). Towards a critical mass theory of interactive media: Universal access, interdependence, and diffusion. *Communication Research, 14*(5), 491–511. doi:10.1177/009365087014005003

Martin, P. Y., & Turner, B. A. (1986). Grounded theory and organisational research. *The Journal of Applied Behavioral Science, 22*(2), 141–157. doi:10.1177/002188638602200207

Mason, R. M. (1997). SME adoption of electronic commerce technologies: Implication for emerging national information infrastructure, Systems sciences *Proceedings of the thirtieth Hawaii international conference on information systems* (pp. 495-504).

Mitroff, I., & Listone, H. A. (1993). *The Unbounded Mind.* New York: Oxford University Press.

Myers, M. D. (1997). Qualitative Research in Information Systems. *Management Information Systems Quarterly, 21*(2), 241–242. doi:10.2307/249422

Observatory of European SMEs. (2007). *Competence Development in SMEs*. European Commission.

OECD. (2000). *OECD Small and Medium Enterprise Outlook.* OECD publication services.

OECD. (2004, July 3-5). ICTs, e-business and SMEs. *Paper prepared for the 2nd OECD Conference of Ministers responsible for SMEs*, Istanbul, Turkey.

Orlikowski, W. J. (1993). CASE tools as organisational change: Investigating incremental and radical changes in systems development. *Management Information Systems Quarterly, 17*(3), 309–340. doi:10.2307/249774

Orlikowski, W. J., & Baroudi, J. J. (1991). Studying Information Technology in Organisations: Research Approaches and Assumptions. *Information Systems Research, 2*(1), 1–28. doi:10.1287/isre.2.1.1

Pettigrew, A. (1990). Longitudinal field research on change: Theory and practice. *Organization Science, 1*(3), 267–292. doi:10.1287/orsc.1.3.267

Pool, P. W., Parnell, J. A., Spillan, J. E., Carraher, S., & Lester, D. L. (2006). Are SMEs meeting the challenge of integrating e-commerce into their businesses? A review of the development, challenges and opportunities. *International Journal of Information Technology and Management*, *5*(2/3), 97–113. doi:10.1504/IJITM.2006.010112

Poon, S., & Swatman, P. (1996). Small business alliances: A frame-work for Internet-enabled strategic advantage. *Proceedings of the 29th Hawaii conference in systems science*, Hawaii

Poon, S., & Swatman, P. M. C. (1999). An exploratory study of small business Internet commerce issues. *Information & Management*, *35*(1), 9–18. doi:10.1016/S0378-7206(98)00079-2

Robson, C. (1993). *Real World Research*. Oxford, UK: Blackwell Publishers.

Rogers, E. M. (1983). *Diffusion of innovation* (3rd ed.). London: Collier Macmillan Publishers.

Schmitz, J., & Fulk, J. (1991). Organisational colleagues, media richness, and electronic mail: A test of the social influence model of technology use. *Communication Research*, *18*(4), 487–523. doi:10.1177/009365091018004003

Steinfield, C. W., & Fulk, J. (1990). *Organisation and Communication Technology*. London: Sage.

Strauss, A. L. (1987). *Qualitative Analysis for Social Scientists*. Cambridge: Cambridge University Press; doi:10.1017/CBO9780511557842

Strauss, A. L., & Corbin, J. (1998). *Basics of Qualitative Research: Techniques and Procedures for developing Grounded Theory*. London: Sage Publications Ltd.

Swanson, E. B. (1988). *Information system implementation: Bridging the gap between design and utilisation*. Homewood, IL: Irwin.

Tornatzky, L., & Klein, K. (1982). Innovation Characteristics and innovation adoption-implementation: A Meta-Analysis of findings. *IEEE Transactions on Engineering Management*, *EM-29*(1), 28–45. doi:10.1109/TEM.1982.6447463

Trevino, L. K., Lengel, R. H., & Daft, R. L. (1987). Media symbolism, media richness, and media choice in organisation: A symbolic interactionist perspective. *Communication Research*, *14*(5), 553–574. doi:10.1177/009365087014005006

Turban, T., King, D., McKay, J., Lee, J., & Viehland, D. (2008). *Electronic commerce a managerial perspective*. New Jersey: Pearson Prentice Hall.

Turner, B. A. (1981). Some Practical Aspects of Qualitative Data Analysis: One Way of Organising the Cognitive Processes Associated with the Generation of Grounded Theory. *Quality & Quantity*, *15*(3), 225–247. doi:10.1007/BF00164639

Van Toorn, C., Bunker, D., Yee, K., & Smith, S. (2006). The barriers to the adoption of E-commerce by Micro Businesses, small and medium enterprises. *Proceedings of the sixth International conference on knowledge, culture, and change in organizations*, Prato, Tuscany, Italy.

Walsham, G. (1993). *Interpreting Information Systems in Organisation*. Chichester, England: John Wiley & Sons Ltd.

Wolfe, R. A. (1994). Organisational innovation: Review, critique and suggested research directions. *Journal of Management Studies*, *31*(3), 405–431. doi:10.1111/j.1467-6486.1994.tb00624.x

World Economic Forum. (2004). *Global Information Technology Report 2003-2004*. Oxford University Press, Oxford.

Wymer, S. A., & Regan, E. A. (2005). Factors influencing e-commerce adoption and use by small and medium businesses. *Electronic Markets*, *15*(4), 438–453. doi:10.1080/10196780500303151

Yin, R. K. (1984). *Case Study Research: Design and Methods*. Beverly Hills: Sage publications.

Yin, R. K. (1994). *Case Study Research, Design and Methods*. Newbury Park: Sage Publications.

This research was previously published in the International Journal of Technology Diffusion (IJTD), 6(4); edited by Ali Hussein Saleh Zolait; pages 40-57, copyright year 2015 by IGI Publishing (an imprint of IGI Global).

Section 2

Diffusion Tools and Technologies

Chapter 5
Online Communities of Practice and Web 2.0

Amir Manzoor
Bahria University, Pakistan

ABSTRACT

In contemporary Knowledge Management, communication and collaboration play very significant role. Knowledge exists within the stakeholders of an organization. Such knowledge, when extracted and harnessed effectively, can become an extremely valuable asset to achieve organizational goals and objectives. This knowledge, embedded in the people, must be properly released through an appropriate channel to make it usable. Through dialogue and discussions, using online tools, this release and reuses of knowledge can be made possible. The Community of Practice (CoP) is a useful organizing concept for enhancing collaboration, sharing knowledge, and disseminating best practices among researchers and practitioners. This chapter explores the concept of Communities of Practice and how Web 2.0 technologies can facilitate the transformation from a conventional community of practice to online community of practice for better and effective online communities of practices.

INTRODUCTION

According to Wenger (2006), a community of practice (CoP) is a group of interested parties that come together to collaborate, and hopefully learn from one another. CoP share a concern or a passion for something they do and learn how to do it better as they interact regularly.

The impact of the Internet on our lives has been pervasive. People are increasingly turning to the social interaction available on the Internet to satisfy their needs, whether these are professional or personal. The Internet offers users fast access to social contacts such as online chat groups and discussion lists to make connections with others. Richness and vitality are important components to ensure that people continue to actively participate in such a phenomenon. Online communities have their roots firmly in the 1960's Counterculture movement (Goldberger, 2003; Matei, 2005; Sun, Rau, & Ma, 2014) which

DOI: 10.4018/978-1-7998-0417-8.ch005

advocated authenticity, deeper social involvement, egalitarian ideals, individualism, less prejudice and more emotional satisfaction (Matei, 2005). From the general meeting place of people who shared ideas grew subject-specific communities and professional communities.

Online communities are being increasingly used by for professional support, guidance and inspiration (Bond, 2004; Chen & Chen, 2002; Cornu, 2004; Matei, 2005; Sun, Rau, & Ma, 2014; R. Jamali, Russell, Nicholas, & Watkinson, 2014). These have been organized around subject areas and offer participants the opportunities to develop both personally and professionally. The current popularity of online communities means that it is necessary to examine these communities and determine what characteristics are necessary for them to function effectively. The objective of this chapter is to explore how Web 2.0 technologies can facilitate developing better and effective online communities of practices. The chapter will explore the concept of Communities of Practice and the transformation from a conventional community of practice to online community of practice. . The barriers and motivations for contributing to such communities will be analyzed. The chapter will then move on to assessing how the Web 2.0 technologies facilitate Communities of Practice.

COMMUNITIES OF PRACTICE

Knowledge Management System (KMS) is also a collaborative tool. KMS can be used to create virtual Communities of Practice (CoP) (Wenger, 2006; Tsai & Bagozzi, 2014). Community is a principle feature of collaboration and sharing (Wang, Noe, & Wang, 2014). According to Rao (2002), successful knowledge management heavily relies on "groups of people who work on business-relevant topics across organizational boundaries" (p. 2). The creation of conversations among groups of interested people leads to enhancement of knowledge and business practices (Bolger, 2009). A CoP develops a "shared understanding of what it does, of how to do it, and how it is related to other communities and their practices – in all, a 'world-view' … (CoP's) are a sensible focus for Knowledge Management initiatives (sharing) some common language, purpose and ways of acting" (Walsham, 2001, p. 601). In the collaboration among like-minded people, the one idea that permeates is that multiple brains are better than one. CoPs also provide learning opportunities. As Sinclair (2006) puts it "we learn from our communities" and from our experiences "spending much of our lives learning from others and sharing our experiences and lessons learned with them in exchange" (p. 601). Such community learning promotes dialogue and development of concepts. This dialogue and concept building supports the transformation of tacit knowledge to explicit knowledge (Adams, Brock, Gordon, Grohs, & Kirk, 2014).

Most commonly, a "community of practice" (CoP) refers to a group of people united by a common goal, usually the sharing of professional knowledge or practices (Wenger, 1999; Cox, 2005). This ideal permits a community to persist over time, despite changes in the composition of the community's membership (Cox, 2005). A primary aspect of a CoP involves the cultivation of relationships between experts possessing practical knowledge of interest to the group as a whole, while a secondary concern involves the socialization of newcomers to the group. The social relationship between these two groups—established practitioners and novices—facilitates the transfer of knowledge and ensures continuity within the community (Jin, Wen, & Gough, 2010; McWilliam, 2012).

Originally for an online strategy for business, a CoP also refers to a group of individuals who share experience, comprehension, information, and resources about an area of common interest. It could be defined further as a group of individuals who share common causes, capabilities, or problems within a certain field, discipline, or context. They establish a formal community with the explicit purpose of allowing members to deepen their knowledge and expertise through ongoing interaction. This form of knowledge management and manipulation has many effects on learning in various sectors and on various scales (Saint-Onge & Wallace, 2012). There are three elements of a CoP: 1) a domain, or a defined set of issues, 2) a community, or network of relationships, and 3) practices, or standardized ways of "doing things" (Lin & Lee, 2006). These three elements—domain, community, and practices—draw upon various iterations of social and professional networking.

A CoP can be used to address any set of issues that a networked community decides to address such as collaboration on research projects, business endeavors, and technological innovations. Unlike social networking websites soliciting feedback and consumer opinion, CoPs are more than one-way channels for information dissemination or a social connection. COPs are a vehicle for knowledge management in many places at once. With differing types of knowledge, practitioners can obtain, contribute, reshape, or critique knowledge, in any manner that is consistent with a given CoP's norms and standards. This horizontal movement of communication fragments power and authority and allows more people to become producers of knowledge themselves (Wenger, 2011).

Community is not a new concept. A community is a natural part of human behavior that recognizes people need of socialization and work with others (van Winkelen, 2003). Yet CoPs are more formalized and what van Winkelen (2003) identifies as an "emergent phenomena". CoPs also contain an aspect of design and commitment and formalize their existence through the establishment of common goals and values and seek to meet predetermined needs of their participants. CoPs are also learning environments. According to Hubert, Newhouse and Vestal (2001), CoPs are groups of people who come together to share and to learn from one another. This sharing and learning occurs both face-to-face and virtually. These people are held together by a common interest in a body of knowledge. Their motivation of participation comes from their desire and need to share knowledge (Wenger, 2011).

Community members, through an ongoing daily interactions, extend their knowledge and understanding. CoPs are fundamentally social structures that foster their own learning, manage their own knowledge building and develop competencies within the group (van Winkelen, 2003). Participants become a community through interacting and experiencing common events created by the community (Tosey, 1999). CoPs differ in their effectiveness as learning communities. In some CoPs, there exist few opportunities for peripheral practice and novices find it difficult to gain entry and make a valuable contribution to the community's work. Other communities provide different ways for people to become involved at different levels of competence. Some communities religiously follow long-established traditions while others adopt their own status and practices (Wenger, 2011).

Participation in Communities of Practice

There exist many studies (Ardichvili, et al, 2003; McLure Wasko & Faraj, 2002; ;Hall & Graham, 2004; Ridings & Gefen, 2004; Zhang & Watts, 2008; Wang & Fesenmaier, 2003; Schneider, Von Krogh, & JäGer, 2013; Zhou, Wu, Zhang, & Xu, 2013; Fugelstad et al., 2012) that seek to determine what motivates/demotivates people to practice in CoPs. CoPs are not viewed as forums in which to socialize or form new relationships. According to McLure Wasko and Faraj (2000), "work units behaving as focused communities are more innovative" (p. 162). It is essential to understand what factors motivate such innovation and participation (Bolger, 2009).

Motivations for Participation

Some clear benefits for less well-informed participants to participate in any knowledge sharing activity include hope to gain more knowledge and insight of experienced people. However, there must also be some benefits for knowledge providers who are prepared to share their knowledge to these less knowledgeable members of the community. Benefits or returns for participation can be classified into two categories: tangible and intangible (McLure Wasko & Faraj, 2000; Bolger, 2009).

Tangible Returns for Participation

According to McLure Wasko and Faraj (2000), CoPs provide access to "useful information and expertise, answers to specific questions, and personal gain" (p. 163). CoPs provide quick and most up-to-date help unavailable elsewhere. CoPs are excellent source of expertise (Barab, Scott, Del Valle Martin, & Fang, 2012). Take example of online CoP that makes up DRUPAL (an interactive web-building application). While the DRUPAL technology is not revolutionary, the community that supports it is extremely proactive in knowledge collaboration (Bolger, 2009). DRUPAL is open source and members can extend DRUPAL's capabilities. Members are encouraged to develop new functionalities and make them available to the community. Members can use online forums to resolve issues they are experiencing with DRUPAL. Members can use threaded discussion forums to get help on specific problems. According to McLure Wasko and Faraj (2000), the prospect that contribution many enhance "standing in the profession, establish a reputation that will hopefully translate into a job ... generate personal clients is foremost" (p. 166).

Intangible Returns for Participation

First, motivation such as satisfaction and self-actualization, exposing expertise and gaining peer recognition for such can drive participation in the community. Second, people can view community collaboration as a challenge and encouraged to refine thinking and develop new insights. Third, some people may participate in a community for fun. They gain enjoyment through learning and sharing with others. Fourth, participants can keep themselves abreast of innovations and issues in their field. With the CoP, it may be difficult and untimely to discover (Yen, Hsu, & Huang, 2011; Bolger, 2009).

Barriers to Participation

Conversely to analyzing why people participate, barriers need to be identified. First, there is no financial reward for participating in the CoP (Bolger, 2009; Hughes, Jewson, & Unwin, 2013). Such rewards could not be possibly implemented and maintained and may not align with a community spirit. However, as Walsham (2001) states, "in a context where individuals see little in the way of financial reward for knowledge-sharing activities, it is not surprising that knowledge hoarding may take place" (p. 603). Rewards exist in some form. Rewards must be viewed as individual and personal and the benefits of the intangible returns must be emphasized over tangible returns (Jeon, Kim, & Koh, 2011). Walshman studied the benefits and limitations of computer systems in the context of CoPs. According to Walsham (2001), a "strongly individual-based reward system did not encourage collaborative behavior" (p. 603). This is an area for top management need to address to promote new CoP initiatives (Bolger, 2009).

Second, McLure Wasko and Faraj (2000) states that "People must become comfortable with their own level of expertise in order to feel their participation is valuable" (p. 169). This aspect of motivation needs to be nurtured in individuals over time. However, feeling comfortable and confident certainly becomes stronger when participation increases and positive feedback is expected (Bouchamma & Michaud, 2011).

Third, Walsham (2001) noted that there is a "danger of being seen to be politically incorrect in terms of current organisational thinking" (p. 603). Users may feel hesitant to share views in a CoP that are not strictly in keeping with top management point of view. This is particularly notable for public sector organizations (Sayed and Rowland, 2004). In their discussion of Wiki technologies in public sector, Guy (2006) noted that some aspects may "go against the organisation's acceptable usage policy (and) by their very nature provide a collective view and this may not always represent an unbiased view." (p. 4). A possible solution could be restricting access to a CoP to members only. According to Walsham (2001), that means "individuals in a community of practice may share views, knowing that their organizational superiors have no access to their exchanges" (p. 603).

WEB 2.0 TECHNOLOGIES FOR COMMUNITIES OF PRACTICE

For contemporary CoPs to be most effective, Allee (1997) argues that the World Wide Web (WWW) is an ideal location for knowledge sharing. According to Alleee, knowledge requires community and Internet is the best place that illustrates this principle. Similarly, knowledge creation and transfer was described by McLure Wasko and Faraj (2000) as "social phenomena and an integral part of a community" (p. 160). When communities use a KMS as a host platform for their collaboration, knowledge is captured, organized, formalized, distributed, and accessible to other members. The system has the power to extend and transform existing knowledge and merge it with knowledgebase of other members (Hislop, 2013).

With these social and functional considerations in mind, we should keep in mind that existing CoPs are bounded by geography and, without efficient forms of communication, community members at different geographical locations cannot get optimal benefits from the dispersion of knowledge (Jin, Wen, & Gough, 2010; Wenger, 2011). The most efficient form of communicating knowledge within a CoP has been through in-person interaction (Tierney & Palmer, 2013). However, this form of communication can severely limit the scope of the conventional CoP to immediately surrounding geography (Jin, Wen, & Gough, 2010). Web 2.0 technologies offer novel ways of undertaking efficient communication despite vast geographical distances. Web 2.0 technologies confer the capability to drastically reshape the scale and scope of CoPs.

Web 2.0 facilitates communication, information sharing, interoperability, user-centric design, and collaboration on the web. Popular Web 2.0 tools include Blogs, WIKIS, RSS Feeds, Tagging, Social Networks, and Search Engines (Brown, 2012). Web 2.0 tools are fast becoming leading tools that provides more progressive use of users time spent online "contributing (to the) contents of their Knowledge Space" (Lee & Lan, 2007, p. 49). In general, people are making extended uses of the web as intranets spread within organizations. Utilizing technologies which are already existing (such as SQL databases, message boards, JavaScript etc.) and the extension of such technologies using familiar and easy-to-use tools (such as AJAX, XML, and Flash) mean the real knowledge management side of a KMS can become its true focus (Venkatesh, Croteau, & Rabah, 2014). Nissen et al. (2000) noted that some KMS's are supportive in nature. These KMS organize, formalize, and distribute knowledge in the enterprise and support people to apply, evolve, and create knowledge in the organization. Such a KMS provides sharing of knowledge with its users and has the facility and ability to create new knowledge without having an extensive technology focus (Bolger, 2009).

Note that World Wide Web has not changed to facilitate knowledge management and the development of powerful KMS. What has changed, is the increased use of interactive trends and the discovery of powerful organizational communication across the World Wide Web. Industries are replacing standalone applications with distributed enterprise applications. The focus of the World Wide Web has changed to become a space for collaboration, enhancing creativity among people/groups who share interests (Eisenstadt & Vincent, 2012).

Web 2.0 offers increased collaboration speeds in the virtual, or online, realm, thus enhancing the functionality of CoPs. Web 2.0 allows users to transmit knowledge, research, data, and practical experience more easily (Kai-Wai Chu & Kennedy, 2011). The ubiquity of the Internet allows for interaction between experts from different areas of the globe. Expert-to-expert interaction enables communities to disseminate information more quickly and effectively. Another potential benefit of virtual CoPs is their ability to foster multiculturalism, thus expanding a community's diversity and versatility. Multicultural interaction creates a higher level of understanding and fosters an increase in social skills, and these communities exist in virtual realms because of the broad access that exists through online social networking (Hossain & Aydin, 2011). Observations and practices that are common in specific parts of the globe may become accessible worldwide when the communities become part of the virtual realm.

PLANNING FOR ONLINE COMMUNITIES OF PRACTICE

Community Planning

There exist some common pitfalls of online community projects. In the process of technology evaluation, we must remember overall goals of the online community. The process of technology evaluation should be an iterative process. In this process, user scenarios and functional requirements should be determined and supporting technologies should be examined against these scenarios and functional requirements (Bolger, 2009; Kraut et al., 2012).

Community Goals

Goals of the online community should first be clearly identified before the process of technology evaluation starts. A consensus needs to be developed about the value created by the community for its members. In addition to this, how the beneficial outcomes will be achieved in near future. Potential members must be able to clearly understand the community purpose. The goals thus guide participation and growth of memberships (Meyerhoff & Strycharz, 2013).

Audience Needs

Along with goals, understanding the needs of potential members is also important. The community's purpose determines the kind of potential members to attract. A deep understanding of the requirements and online behavior of these potential members of community is needed. Functionality a technology platform should provide depends on few things needed for active engagement of all segments of community (Meyerhoff & Strycharz, 2013).

Audience Scenarios and Functional Requirements

Community initiators need to translate community's needs and objectives into a set of clear functional priorities. These functional priorities guide technology selection and configuration (Spagnoletti & Resca, 2012). User scenarios are concise statements which describe probable tasks that potential community members would perform. These scenarios may include many steps a user takes to achieve a certain goal (such as find and download a resource). These needs not be exhaustive, but they should be enough to capture all the key illustrations pertinent to the potential members of the community (Cruickshank, 2011).

Wenger, White, and Smith (2009) developed a list of common orientations that communities can have. These orientations are as follows:

- **Meeting Support:** Some communities are formed around face-to-face meetings that can result in either follow-up online meetings or a combination of online and offline meetings. Communities formed around online meetings may provide sharing of information and decision making.
- **Open-ended Conversations:** Some communities are formed around discussions and community members take part in a series of ongoing online discussions.
- **Project-Orientations:** Communities formed around projects are based on sharing key project information.
- **Content Collection and Organization:** Content-oriented communities provide collection and categorization of content useful for community members. These communities may also develop and synthesize information and dependent on file repositories to collect and categorize content.
- **Access to Expertise:** Some communities are formed around the idea that knowledge can be useful as collected content but we still we need the right person with the right expertise. These communities make experts available to community members for questions and answers.
- **Interpersonal Relationships:** Some communities form around building and maintaining interpersonal relationships. The purpose of these communities could be explicit learning or to build/maintain a network to achieve personal/professional objectives of its members. Often closed, these communities and their members generally are very concerned about who becomes a member of the community.
- **Individual Participation:** Some communities form around user participation. In such communities, individual participate may vary from one to another. These communities offer a higher level of personalization.
- **Community Growth:** Some communities are formed around content mining. Members perform active mining of community content for valuable information. For these communities to work, active governance and accepted leadership is a must.
- **Context-Orientation:** Some communities are mission-focused and thus have a unique identity. Such communities may bring people together from different organizations or from a single organization. While some of these communities may be open or closed, the context in which they work is their key feature.

Scenarios can also be developed based on desired level of interaction, the desired kind of knowledge development, the kind of resources required for community, and community members' characteristics (Bolger, 2009; Dascalu, Bodea, Lytras, De Pablos, & Burlacu, 2014). Following is the discussion of some possible levels of interaction.

- **One-Way Dissemination of Knowledge:** In this type of interaction, producer(s) of knowledge disseminate knowledge/resources to participants who are primarily knowledge consumers. Comments might be posted and questions may be asked from participants. Participants may also post suggestions about the disseminated content /resources. However, the flow of knowledge is primarily unidirectional.
- **Shared Knowledge Development:** In this type of interaction, multiple users work in a group to achieve a common goal (e.g. managing a project) and build knowledge in multiple people at once.
- **Many-to-Many Interactions:** In this type of interaction, a small group of users is the source of knowledge for a wider group of users. However, all users are peers irrespective of whether they are knowledge provider or knowledge consumers. In these interactions, all participants act voluntarily. As such, it is the most difficult to foster. Motivating users to actually contribute knowledge can be very difficult.

However, these interactions can help in identification of relationships among users and to develop user scenarios that can guide technical requirements. Once user scenarios are identified, community initiators can prioritize them in the context of the overall community goals and members' needs. In this process, first, audience needs should be mapped to audience scenarios. Second, an importance value (on a scale of 1-5 for example) should be assigned to each audience/audience need. Third, these importance ratings should be used to prioritize the list of user scenarios. Fourth, in a parallel activity, similar importance ratings should be assigned to the community goals. Scenarios providing clear support to the most important community goals should be assigned additional priority. Some subjective analysis can also be done on top of these importance ratings to come up with the optimal set of functional priorities (Bolger, 2009).

Community designers are often tempted to create a large set of priority scenarios and technology features. However, community designers should perform a critical review of the final set of priority scenarios. The final scenarios should satisfy community goals and members' needs. The scenarios should include a few discrete, well-connected activities and provide small amount of functionality. These activities should be such that potential community members having different preferences are engaged with community without overwhelming them with technology options. Communities can be more effective when they do right a small number of activities. At their beginning, communities run into problems when they try to provide some sort of ultimate solution to many potential problems (Venkatesh et al., 2012).

Functionality and Pilot Testing

The leaders of the community need to have a set of prioritized scenarios in order determine appropriate technical functionality for the developed scenarios. Community leaders often are tempted to provide more and more functionality. However, excessive functionality can shift community focus from its core value-creating activities. Communities of professionals tend to focus on providing more functionality. This is because this audience is busy, willing to have quick technology solutions, and already overloaded with information. This audience needs quick access to information needed to do their jobs. As such, the desire of such audience is access to functionality that will help them get such information (e.g. the information needed to prepare presentation for the next meeting).

The choice of functionality plays a significant role for the community's purpose. A blog might be a better choice for a community whose key objective is knowledge sharing by a small group of knowledge providers with a large group of knowledge consumers. Using blogs, the knowledge providers can provide useful and easily consumable knowledge and get feedback from knowledge consumers. A discussion forum may be inappropriate here if knowledge consumers only want to consumer knowledge and not provide feedback to the knowledge providers. If a community's key value proposition is to connect members working on the same topics, an appropriate choice may be a discussion forum. This forum would allow its users to post and answer questions and share resources. Social networking functionality (such as user profiles and wall posts) may also help users. A blog for this community can split user's questions and conversations and might actually detract from mass of the discussion area. In both communities described above, a Wiki wouldn't work well because Wikis are often less useful for less structured communities facilitating ad-hoc, on-going knowledge sharing (Connectededucators.org, 2011).

Communities should start with a small feature set and a limited roll out w.r.t. technology and scale of community. In other words, community leaders should begin with a pilot of the community. Historically, online communities, once activated, are guided by community members who decide the community direction and purpose regardless of initial intention about the community.

This natural process pose no problems if the original community goals remain in line. Community leaders should adopt a flexible approach and be ready to accept different ways to achieve the same goals because these emerging new ways may imply modifications in technical functionality and other fine tunings to enhance the community's development. Additionally, emerging patterns of member activity may be an indication of new required functionality to improve the usability of the community. For example, an emerging pattern of members' regular access to images from discussions may suggest that providing a photo gallery functionality may be valuable feature for community. When a pilot is launched first, community designers can identify emerging activity patterns and put them into practice without risking a change in community's original direction (Valaitis, Akhtar-Danesh, Brooks, Binks, & Semogas, 2011).

Community Management

Community leaders should know that launching a community requires heavy investment of their time. Many successful communities have emerged organically due to significant effort of their members and developers. This effort included development of content for the community and norms of community interaction. Users generally do not expect very large amount of existing content from a community before becoming a member but they do expect that the available content must be seeded (Valaitis, Akhtar-Danesh, Brooks, Binks, & Semogas, 2011). Within the technological infrastructure of the community, there must exist explicit and clear directions and norms of the community. This requires skilful user experience configuration and choice of wording. User training on new technology is important but a large liability (Connected Educators, 2011).

Community users not only need static help (e.g. frequently asked questions) but also need some sort of dynamic help (such as webinars) so that they clearly understand the use of various tools and how to provide effective contribution to the community. Growing a new non-existent community requires an additional effort of recruiting participants, bringing them together, and community moderation/marketing. Community leaders must keep online discussions active and make active regular contact with the community. Community leaders must understand use of community tools by the members and the content these members consider most valuable. With this analysis, future technology use can be decided.

Web 2.0 Community Tools and their Functionality

There exist different types of valuable community tools that provide different functionalities (Bolger, 2009; Barnett, Jones, Bennett, Iverson, & Bonney, 2013; Venkatesh, Croteau, & Rabah, 2014).

Content Tools

Content Management and File Repositories: Many CoPs provide sharing and dissemination of knowledge. Community platforms should integrate traditional web content management with other forms of collaboration such as social networking. Content can be provided as either file lists with folders or as hierarchal listing of files. The amount of content a community might provide determines the choice of needed features with larger amounts of data requiring extensive browsing and organizing ability. Community size and members' familiarity with each other is also important. Smaller online communities belonging to existing offline communities often results in more useful communities.

- **Blogs:** Blogs are important tools for facilitating discussions when users want to go beyond simple questions and answers. With blogs, user can post a brief idea or opinion and invite other users for their comments. For active participation, group blogs should provide an intuitive user interface that users can use to include different forms of multimedia (such as images and videos) in blog posts. This interface should also allow highlighting the authors with their profile and pictures. With this, users can gain a clear understanding of relationships to be made and the expertise to be utilized. Examples of some blog software are WordPress, TypePad, and BlogSpot. There are other all-in-one software packages (e.g. Drupal Commons and Central Desktop) that provides blog functionality as part of their large portfolio of features.
- **Microblogs/Status Updates:** Microblogs can be called status updates. Microblogs provide anyone the ability to post short thoughts/quick observations. Twitter is one good example that users can use to send tweets (a 140-character short message). Today, microblogs provide serious community interaction. Some examples of microblog applications include Twitter and Tumblr. There are other all-in-one software packages (e.g. Jive and Drupal Commons) that provides microblog functionality as part of their large portfolio of features.
- **Wikis:** Wikis are special collaborative content development websites that users can use to add and edit pages. To develop software documentation or frequently asked questions, wikis are a good choice. Since wikis do not provide preexisting structure, they are not a good choice for novice users and often work better for more sophisticated users and for those with extensive experience of content development. Some popular examples of wiki software are MediaWiki, SocialText, PBWorks, and Confluence.

Collaborative Document Authoring Tools

One good example is Google Documents. These tools work like a familiar software (such as a word processor, spreadsheet, or a presentation tool). Simultaneous editing of a document by multiple users is possible. All edits made are tracked for reference and provide immediate feedback to principal author(s).

Some more examples of collaborative document authoring tools are NoodleTools, TitanPad, Wiggio, and Writeboard. There are other all-in-one community software packages (e.g. Basecamp and ProjectSpaces) that provides collaborative document authoring functionality as part of their large portfolio of features.

- **Social Bookmarking:** Online CoPs should be able to collect links from across the web. That allows a great deal of content, already posted somewhere else, to be brought on a single page for the community so that users can easily access it. Using social bookmarking services, community leaders and members can collect and categorize external web content. Users can also provide annotation and comments that others users of social bookmarking service can see when they visit the page. Some popular examples of social bookmarking service provides include backlinksflow.com (world renowned link builder and SEO specialist), onlywire.com (a fast, secure automation tool to submit content to the top Social Media Networks like Facebook, Twitter and Google+.), Diigo.com (a social bookmarking website which allows signed-up users to bookmark and tag webpages). Additionally, it allows users to highlight any part of a webpage and attach sticky notes to specific highlights or to a whole page), Delicious.com (a social bookmarking web service owned by Yahoo and used for storing, sharing, and discovering web bookmarks), and StumbleUpon.com (a form of web search engine that finds and recommends web content to its users and allow users to discover and rate Web pages, photos and videos that are personalized to their tastes and interests using peer-sourcing and social-networking principles).
- **Media Libraries:** In many cases, communities want to share multimedia (such as videos and images) in order both capture knowledge and build comradeship. Some community tools provide a way to do this with the tool and users can also use outside services as the primary source of their content. The outside services provide an excellent user experience. Community managers are free from the worries of hosting large amounts of user content. Some examples of these outside service providers include Flickr (an image hosting and video hosting website, and web services suite that is owned by Yahoo) and YouTube (a video-sharing website that allows users to upload, view, and share videos, and it makes use of Adobe Flash Video and HTML5 technology to display a wide variety of user-generated and corporate media video). There are other all-in-one software packages (e.g. Ning and BuddyPress) that provides this functionality as part of their large portfolio of features.

Data Visualization Tools

Data visualization tools are used by communities to share information and knowledge within the data. These tools can make this data easier for members to access, use, and share across acknowledge levels in a community. Some examples of these data visualization tools are Google Spreadsheets (part of a software office suite offered by Google within its Google Drive service. The suite allows users to create and edit documents online while collaborating with other users in real-time), Many Eyes (a web community that connects visualization experts, practitioners, academics and enthusiasts, offers this technology and expertise, along with ways to share and learn from others), Swivel, Dygraphs (allows users to explore and interpret dense data sets), ZingChart (a JavaScript charting library designed to quickly render fast, beautiful charts with big data sets), InstantAtlas,Timeline, Exhibit, Modest Maps, Leaflet, WolframAlpha (an online service that answers factual queries directly by computing the answer from externally sourced curated data, rather than providing a list of documents or web pages that might contain the answer), Visual.ly (a community platform for data visualization and infographics), and Visualize Free (Connected Educators, 2011).

Member Interaction Tools

- **User Profiles:** Social networking is valuable for large communities. This is because it can help build, strengthen, and maintain participants' relationships (Cambridge, 2010). Members connect with people to involve in new types of interactions. For social networking platforms (such as Facebook) this is especially true. The Facebook profile includes both biographic information and a history of user contributions. A rich profile feature can encourage participation, help members have a more comfortable interaction, and sharing with unknown people. For tropical communities, this aspect is because in these communities users are seeking knowledge. There exist many all-in-one software packages (such as BuddyPres and Ning) that provide user profile feature.
- **Member Comments:** Many online communities provide user comments feature. Users can post comments on content posted by others. When comments are embedded in web pages, documents, and blog posts, rich discussions on content can take place and lead to an enhancement of both quality and quantity of user interaction. Communities can use advanced comments tools to provide rich discussion threads, easy access, and tracking of an individual's comments posted across different communities. Examples of some all-in-one platforms that provide this comments functionality include Disqus (a blog comment hosting service for web sites and online communities that uses a networked platform and includes various features, such as social integration, social networking, user profiles, spam and moderation tools, analytics, email notifications, and mobile commenting) and Omeka (a free, open source content management system for online digital collections that allows users to publish and exhibit cultural heritage objects, and extend its functionality with themes and plugins).
- **Discussions:** Meaningful discussions are important for knowledge sharing. In discussions, all participants have equal status. Some example of all-in-one community platforms that provide this functionality include LinkedIn, Facebook, phpBB (a free, open-source Internet forum package written in the PHP scripting language that provide support for multiple database engines (PostgreSQL, MySQL, Oracle, SQL Server), flat message structure (as opposed to threaded), hierarchical subforums, topic split/merge/lock, user groups, multiple attachments per post, full-text search, plugins and various notification options such as e-mail, Jabber instant messaging, and ATOM feeds), and ezboard (a provider of free and paid hosted Internet forums for use by webmasters and message board administrators who have little to no experience running a web site).
- **Webinars:** These tools are generally stand-alone that run alongside other community tools. Webinars provide synchronous, virtual interaction which require simultaneous presence of all members online. Users can share their screens in real time. This could provide a more powerful and efficient way to get work done. Some examples of tools used to provide webinar services include WebEx (provides on-demand collaboration, online meeting, web conferencing and video-conferencing applications), Adobe Connect (software used to create information and general presentations, online training materials, web conferencing, learning modules, and user desktop shar-

ing), Elluminate Live (a web conferencing program that rented out virtual Spaces where virtual schools and businesses can hold classes and meetings), and Dimdim (a web-based platform for realtime, rich-media collaboration and meetings including free web conferencing service where users could share desktops, show slides, collaborate, chat, talk and broadcast via webcam).

Member Feedback and Research

- **User-Generated Ratings:** In many communities, members can rate the utility of content. Users can comment on content, rate the content, and find the ratings and usage of content by other members. For community sites that provide less content, content ratings can be a powerful tool that users can use to quickly find the most useful content and understand its use by other members of community. Some examples of such user ratings are ratings and reviews on Amazon.com and eBay and Facebook's 'Like' feature. A Like button on Facebook is a feature where the user can express that they like, enjoy or support certain content. Facebook also display the number of users who liked each content, and show a full list of them.
- **Polls and Surveys:** These tools facilitate participation and involvement from of large group of participants. This is because not all users post to a discussion forum or a blog. These tools can reduce fear among users for posting ideas in large communities. This fear factor can result in an ecosystem of non-participation where we see only few dominant participants lead a large group of hesitant participants. Examples of tools that provide these polls and surveys include SurveyMonkey; SurveyGizmo; Wufoo. Some all-in-one community platforms (such as Jive and Drupal Commons) also provide this feature as part of a portfolio of a large feature set (Connectededucators.org, 2011).

Project Coordination

- **Event Calendars:** This tool can be used to provide a central listing of events. Using this list, members can get information about upcoming events/activities and past meetings. Some all-in-one community platforms (such as Centrla Desktop and Ning) provide this functiolaity. Meetup provides online access to commercial offline events. Eventbrite (www.eventbrite.com) is a global marketplace for live experiences that allows people to find and create events in more than 150 countries.
- **Task-management Tools:** This tool is important for a more project-oriented community that require task management and milestone tracking. Some examples of such tools include BaseCamp (a web-based project-management tool) and ProjectSpace (a total project managment solution accessed by any browser platform). Some all-in-one community platforms (such as CentralDesktop) also provide this tool as part of a portfolio of a large feature set.
- **Decision-support Tools:** Groups collaborating on projects need to have discussions and develop strategies. Decision support tools can support decision-making processes by facilitating ranking of ideas, establishing consensus, and systematically analyzing a situation. Some all-in-one project management software (such as SAS Streamworks) provide decision support tools. IdeaScale and HERMES are online idea ranking and deliberation systems. IdeaScale is a cloud-based software company that licenses an innovation management platform employing the principles and practices of crowdsourcing. HERMES is a web-based system that augments classical decision making approaches by supporting argumentative discourse among decision makers.

Incentive and Recognition Services

- **Badges:** This tool can be used to indicate levels of achievement within a community in order motivate participation and help members identify experts. Users earn, give, and receive badges that indicate their achievements. These badges become part of user profile. Edmodo is an educational website that takes the ideas of a social network and refines them and makes it appropriate for a classroom. Using Edmodo, students and teachers can reach out to one another and connect by sharing ideas, problems, and helpful tips (Connected Educators, 2011). The customized versions of all-in-one community platforms (such as BuddyPress and DrupalCommons) also provide the badge functionality.
- **Rewards Systems:** This tool is a step ahead of badges that users can use to earn physical rewards for their actions performed within community. Use of this tool could increase costs but also increases incentives. Some examples of these reward system include uBoost (an online student performance recognition and rewards platform,); Webcentiv (online incentives management system that is easy to set up, highly efficient and can be accessed at any time by any number of people in any number of locations); and Love2Reward.co.uk (one of the largest providers of reward management products and services in the UK).
- **Reputation Management Systems:** This tool can help establish whether the person making a comment is reliable or not. This tool can assess a user's behavior so that other users could establish the user's history of reputation. This tool can provide added contextual information about author's general reputation. Amazon and eBay provides "rate the seller" tool. Seller ratings function like a personal referral: before making a purchase, customer can view comments as well as star ratings submitted by previous buyers. Customer can use the link sent in reminder e-mail, or rate the seller via the "Buyer Account" link after receiving item from the seller. Slashdot (a news website that features news stories on science and technology that are submitted and evaluated by its users, and each story has a comments section attached to it) and other community news sites can also provide this functionality.

Social Media and Community Sites

- **General Social Networking Sites:** Online communities have blurred boundaries mainly due to the proliferation of social networking sites. Communities provide certain activities within site and push certain activities to third-party sites. Some communities may only focus on third-party sites though it limits community functionality. On the other hand, many communities coexist with the social networking sites. These communities provide core activities occurring onsite while some activities are extended into social networks. A number of platforms support automated linking to the Facebook or LinkedIn. Many APIs are also offered by the major social networking sites for custom integration. In some cases, community mangers use both onsite and offsite communities in parallel. The Facebook API is a platform for building applications that are available to the members of the social network of Facebook. The API allows applications to use the social connections and profile information to make applications more involving, and to publish activities to the news feed and profile pages of Facebook, subject to individual users privacy settings. With the API, users can add social context to their applications by utilizing profile, friend, Page, group, photo, and event data. The API uses RESTful protocol and responses are localized and in XML format (Facebook, 2014).

- **Topic-specific Community Sites:** These sites are platforms that serve specific contemporary sectors (e.g. education sector). Many features of these sites are shared by more general-purpose communities. These sites may also include features specific to the sector which the community is serving (in this case education). These features may include privacy and control for social networking. In some cases, these sites can provide means to recruit members because may already be participants of these types of sites but in different contexts. These sites provide high level of security and privacy and are generally tailored to meet specific audience. Some examples of such sites in education sector include edmodo.com and Edublogs.org (a web-based service that archives and supports student and teacher learning by facilitating reflection, questioning by self and others, collaboration and by providing contexts for engaging in higher-order thinking).
- **Content-type-specific Social Media Sites:** These social media sites are formed around sharing of specific content. One good example is famous Youtube.com that share videos. These sites are good choice for distributing media content around which community interaction can be encouraged. Vimeo is another famous site for sharing videos. Flickr and Picasa are popular sites for sharing photos. Slideshare is a famous site for sharing presentations and Scribd for sharing documents. Swivel and Many Eyes are two famous sites for sharing data.

Supporting Utilities

- **Notifications:** For an active community, notifications are important. Email remains the primary way communities use to notify members of community activities. Busy people can use notifications sent via email to stay informed about what's happening (such as new resources and discussions) without logging in to the community site. Content syndication standards (such as RSS and Atom) and SMS notifications are generally preferred by users. Many all-in-one community platforms (such as Basecamp and Central Desktop) provide notifications feature.
- **Public and Private Content:** Many communities place much of the community content on publically accessible pages. Password protecting the resources raises the barriers to participation and some users may be discouraged to join the community. However, password protection also provide added trust and privacy and different tools can provide different level of protection. In some cases, the whole community site can be private. Other sites may make private some sections, or some content. Many all-in-one community platforms (such as Jive and Drupal Commons) allow content protection. Facebook allows a more granular protection of the content.
- **Application Programming Interface (API):** An API provides a set of rules and specifications to be followed by web-based applications in their interactions with other applications. Use of APIs is a more recent trend. APIs can be used to develop mashup applications that combine data and functionality from multiple sources to create new information (Connected Educators, 2011).
- **Centralized User Authentication and Login:** Web-based authentications services are one of the most common techniques of user authentication and login used by today's websites. Use of this feature reduces barriers to join the community because the prospective member can use a single account to access all networked resources. There are open authentication standards available such as OpenID (an open standard and decentralized protocol by the non-profit OpenID Foundation that allows users to be authenticated by certain co-operating sites, known as Relying Parties or

RP, using a third party service) and OAuth (an open standard to authorization that provides client applications a 'secure delegated access' to server resources, on behalf of a resource owner, without sharing their credentials). Famous sites such as Facebook, Twitter, Google, and Yahoo also provide authentication/login services.

- **Web Metrics:** Increasing number of web applications offering their own set of tailored web metrics. These metrics are useful to understand tools usage i.e. who uses them and for what purposes. Google Analytics (a service offered by Google that generates detailed statistics about a website's traffic and traffic sources and measures conversions and sale) and Omniture (an online marketing and web analytics service) are examples of services that provide these metrics.

Community Architecture

To provide coherent community service, desired and available functionality must be merged together. Here 'coherent' is not necessarily a single solution. Community designers need to consider the different community orientations and map them to possible functionalities. Wenger, White and Smith (2009) provided different community orientations. Knowing the functionality requirements and functionality in hand, community designers can set up a set of tools. Available community platforms can be either a single all-in-one platform or a best-of-breed package. A best-of-breed package promises to provide in one package an extensive set of tools that cater needs of each specialty. It is a good idea to first plan for a core platform for the community that serves as a base and then add additional functionality as needed.

The Core Platform

We discussed previously that online communities should concentrate on providing a focused, simple experience doing well a small number of activities. In order to do so, a core platform for community is a logical choice. This core platform provides the major functionality used by community plus some additional supporting features. There are few significant benefits of having such a core platform.

1. **Seamless User Experience**: Users learn one system that provides them a significant portion of what they need.
2. **Simplified Management:** Community designers can develop few key channels for users to interact with the community. These channels are customized to meet the community goals and user needs. Users can then be trained and supported on using these features.
3. **Cost-Effective and Easy Pilot:** Most core platform are available either as online services or as a download. This way, community leaders can start a community with low initial investment. Core platforms provide multiple configuration options to the community managers.

Most core platforms provide many common features. These common features include document repositories, announcements, blogs, member profiles, user comments, and event calendar. Most core platforms provide some sort of control over appearance of features. Community leaders can activate a limited set of features when the community is launched and add other features as the need arise.

Example Core Collaboration Platforms

There exist various core online collaboration platforms (such as HUdle, BaseCamp, Wrike, OneHub, and Google Docs) and each platform has unique characteristics. Community designers need to carefully evaluate these characteristics before selecting a core platform. Three most important defining features of these platforms are:

1. **Feature Set**: Collaboration software vary in their approach of aggregating different features such as discussion boards, event calendars, and blogs. Community initiators need to make tradeoff between having a platform with so many complex features to understand or a platform with limited number of features but easier to understand.
2. **Open Source/Proprietary**: There exist both proprietary and open-source collaborative tools. Open source tools has the advantage of low costs and no licensing requirements. Users can have full access to the source code and there also available options for commercial implementation with an active community of developers support the product. In contrast, best proprietary software can provide very smooth functioning and supported but their licensing costs are high and users have limited choices of customizations.
3. **Hosting:** Collaborative software can also be provided under Software-as-a-service (SaS) model. In this configuration, the user hosts the collaborative software. SaaS software can be easily setup and configured. They can be updated quite easily and can be scaled when needed. SaaS-based collaborative software vary considerably and may cost fortune.

   Following are the representative selection f popular core platforms.

   - **Jive SBS:** It is a full-featured commercial software. It is a commercial Java EE-based Enterprise 2.0 collaboration and knowledge management tool. Jive integrates the functionality of online communities, microblogging, social networking, discussion forums, blogs, wikis, and IM under one unified user interface. Content placed into any of the systems (blog, wiki, documentation, etc.) can be found through a common search interface. Other features include RSS capability, email integration, a reputation and reward system for participation, personal user profiles, JAX-WS web service interoperability, and integration with the Spring Framework.
   - **Drupal Commons:** It is an open source platform that provides a significant suite of tools and allow customization to unique needs. Drupal Commons is backed by a large, global, well-organized and active developer community. Drupal Commons is a ready-to-use solution for building either internal or external communities. It provides a complete social business software solution for organizations. Drupal Commons helps organize content into topic (organic) groups with blog, discussion, document, wiki, and event content types. It also allows users to create (user) relationships with each other in order to follow each other's activities on a site. Authenticated users can view a personalized dashboard containing content from all their subscribed groups (Drupal.org, 2014).
   - **Central Desktop:** It is a proprietary, hosted collaboration application that provides collaborative workspaces. Users use these collaborative workspaces for task and document management. It provides excellent integration with e-mail and allow users to send copies of emails to workspaces.

- Central Desktop also include an online file viewer that supports more than 200 different file types, improved wiki navigation and the ability to convert any file type into a downloadable PDF document. Central Desktop is an alternative to email, Microsoft SharePoint and lightweight file-sharing sites. It connects people, content and customers in the cloud, so everyone can get things done together from one private, secure, centralized website.
- **SharePoint:** SharePoint is a web application framework and platform developed by Microsoft. .SharePoint integrates intranet, content management, and document management. SharePoint is mostly used by midsize businesses and large departments. SharePoint comprises a multipurpose set of Web technologies backed by a common technical infrastructure. By default, SharePoint has a Microsoft Office-like interface, and it is closely integrated with the Office suite. The web tools are intended for non-technical users. SharePoint can provide intranet portals, document and file management, collaboration, social networks, extranets, websites, enterprise search, and business intelligence. It also has system integration, process integration, and workflow automation capabilities. Enterprise application software (such as enterprise resource planning (ERP) and customer relationship management (CRM) packages) often provide some SharePoint integration.
- **BuddyPress:** Built-upon WordPress, BuddyPress is an open-source social networking software. It provides many features of a typical social networking platforms plus a set of technologies for web developers. BuddyPress is supported by a large active body of developers. BuddyPress helps you run any kind of social network on your WordPress, with member profiles, activity streams, user groups, messaging, and more.
- **Edmodo:** Edmodo is a custom-built education social networking software. It is not a general collaboration platform. Main focus of Edmodo is to provide a safe, efficient way for teachers to have online collaboration in their classes. Edmodo provides a substantial teacher-to-teacher community area, social networking functionality, discussions, and document sharing. The easy-to-use Interface makes Edmodo easy to adopt.
- **PBWorks:** PBworks is a commercial real-time collaborative editing (RTCE). PBworks is a hosted application that uses its own proprietary software. Users can create free basic wiki workspaces or upgrade to a premium plan to access additional features, such as enhanced security features, customization through CSS, and more storage space. Workspaces can be public or private (only viewable by those who have been invited to join the workspace). The software is only available in English. A number of businesses and corporations use PBworks to create private wikis for employees.
- **Groupsite:** Groupsite is a platform that empowers the creation of social websites called Groupsites. Groupsites are collaboration communities that enable groups to communicate, share and network to make things happen. It is done by combining the most useful features of online groups and listservs (like Yahoo! Groups), collaboration software (like Sharepoint) and Social Networks (like Facebook and Linkedin). It is a hosted workspace software that provides an institutive, easy-to-use interface. It is easy to implement and offer various design themes and configuration options organizations can use based on their needs. Groupsite nicely integrates with e-mail. Users can link notifications to discussions and announcements.

- **Ning:** Users and organizations can use Ning, an online software, to create custom social network based community sites having a customized look and feel. Ning-based community sites can provide multiple features such as photos, videos, forums and blogs. Similar to Facebook 'Like' feature, a 'Like' button can also be added. Users can also integrate these sites with other sites such as Facebook, Twitter, Google and Yahoo!. It is a hosted workspace software that draws large number of users and networks. It is reliable and scalable. Ning incorporates many external applications that support APIs.
- **SocialGO:** It is an integrated social networking and collaboration software. SocialGo provides online video chat feature, is simple to setup and users can send bulletins to other users. SocialGO offers premium services whereby it builds a site on behalf of a customer. The company offers two products. SocialGO Classic is a social network builder that allows users to create a custom social network using preset configuration. SocialGO Pro is a social website builder that allows users to use advanced customization to form an online community for a group, business or interest.
- **Tomoye Community Software and Social Sites:** It is a proprietary, integrated social networking and collaboration software designed for CoPs. Multiple features (such as document sharing, blogging, wikis, videos, and Q&A) are aggregated in this software. Users can interact with the site via e-mail. This software showcases community experts displaying whether they are helpful and active. Users can rate content highlight the content they think is the most valuable. Like Jive, this software can be quite expensive if the membership of community is large.
- **Alfresco Share:** It is an open-source community software. It is designed to provide collaboration on content and projects. This collaboration is done among a geographically dispersed team of people. Alfresco Share provides social networking features, such as tagging and feeds, and collaboration tools (such as document repositories, blogs, wikis, event calendar etc.). Users can use a built-in reader to view various types of documents within the software without downloading the documents. The software can be easily setup, customized, and scaled.

Supporting Services

Selected core platforms, in most cases, don't provide some features that the community needs. Some of these features may be required for particular needs (such as webinar) to support a community's offline discussions. Many other features may be required over time. As an example, successful community may be based on a document repository. Later on, the community may decide to use a social bookmarking service to gather links.

During its growth, a community explore many technologies and can integrate various incentives tools into community architecture to support community growth and activity. Using collaborative authoring tools, communities can develop and share pieces of knowledge. A community can launch a blog to highlight community activities. These are just few examples how a community can expand beyond its core platform. Available integration tools (such as APIs, feeds, and widgets) can make certain types of integration easy but others can be difficult. There is a trade-off between the benefits of more connected system and the costs of integration required. These higher costs can be justified provided that integration results in more efficient work, further community growth, and new kinds of interaction.

Third-Party Sites and Social Media

Social media sites are special support services that can play multiple roles (e.g. to provide support to community marketing strategy). A community focused on a topic (e.g. Topic "A") may post notifications on Facebook and Twitter to reach a wider audience base. Acting as an ongoing channel for information dissemination, social media sites can use their feeds to broadcast content to members of the community. The services provided by social media sites can be significant aspects of a community. Social media sites (such as LinkedIn) can provide a community formed around discussions among professionals of many types. If audience are already using a core platform in another context, making these services part of community architecture can be valuable. Community goals can be better served by using custom applications to extend such communities.

Community designers face considerable challenge to decide about activities that should take place on social media sites. Social media site communities, with broader reach, tend to be more casual. This way these sites can identify and attract active users to their community. An example can be taken from the presidential campaign of US president Barack Obama. Obama succeeded to build large Facebook communities. However, the members of these communities didn't donate for Obama's campaign. The donors were the ones who migrated from other social media sites to sites dedicated to Obama (e.g. barackobama.com). This is a clear example of ability of social media sites to act as an excellent communication channel to strengthen community efforts (Connected Educators, 2011).

PRACTICAL/MANAGERIAL IMPLICATIONS AND RECOMMENDATIONS

Efforts to encourage use of CoPs still suffer from various shortcomings. In order encourage users to use KMS tools for collaboration a stimulus is strongly needed. We need withdraw from using traditional methods of communication (such as email) in favor of new web-based applications (such as wikis). Employees need positive enforcement and encouragement to use these new applications. Employees must also be encouraged to utilize positive aspects of these applications such as feedback and enhanced user experience.

Experts also need to realize that they are not only the contributors to these new applications but also the users of the same. McLure Wasko and Faraj (2000) points out this fact by noting that "instead of experts focusing their time and attention on creating new innovations, their role shifts from that of knowledge creators to knowledge disseminators" (p. 160). The CoPs should be a valuable tool of knowledge search for both experts and newbies alike. This task is difficult and would require adequate access to, and participation in, from all levels of the community.

For CoPs, some important considerations include keeping abreast of new technologies, learning new technologies, training users, and maintaining services. Even if these considerations are taken into account, it is remain uncertain whether or not non-participants of CoP will recognize the potential provided by new technologies for CoP. There has been some exploration about web 2.0 technologies however it is insufficient. It is important that CoP participants understand and capitalize on the opportunities available through use of these emerging technologies to maintain and sustain contact by and among communities, to alleviate the challenges of distance and isolation and the lack of inconsistent information dissemination.

Educators need to focus on organizations transition from being pure teaching organization to learning organization. Teaching organizations have traditionally been run by highly skilled professionals. Today's communities have transformed to become networks of artisans who collaborate with each other but still act individually. Ultimately, a transition is needed so that these educators work together on independent learning teams. The members of a true collaborative community have different roles but perform collectively. An analogy can be taken from hockey team where each team member plays a different role but performs collectively. Developing effective independent teams is a genuine challenge. Initially the organizations should focus on building offline teams. Once these offline teams get off the ground, online collaboration should be fostered among teams.

Technology providers have traditionally considered online communities as customer or user groups. An important shift to watch for is that how these "closed boxes" (i.e. communities) evolve into an open space where open conversations will take place. Content providers can create content and share it across different groups. Content sharing and conversations among teams of educators can build huge knowledgebase. The real challenge is to find ways to leverage these knowledgebase across communities.

A fundamental goal of education is to create cross-cultural, cross-boundary collaboration. To produce true learners of 21st century, connected educators need to develop connected learners. There exist two groups of educators today. One consists of educators that are motivated, self-directed and connected. The second group consists of educators that are overwhelmed, timid, and disconnected. The growing divide between the two groups is worrisome. Current teacher evaluation programs seldom give credit for participation in online CoPs. Teachers need to be rewarded for their participation in CoPs. A 360 degree evaluation of teachers should be done where evaluation of teacher is not limited to just administration but it also includes teacher's peers and members of CoP in which the teacher participates.

Schools are constantly introducing new programs. These programs are seldom implemented fully as teacher expect another program before the last one is fully implemented. This way, provision of even something valuable can just go through the motions of implementing it. Technology is clearly here to stay. However, the same phenomenon stand in the way of technology adoption as the teachers continue to look for what benefits they can get from this technology. With each new program, teacher expects to gain something out of its use (such as salary increase or some form of appreciation). The remedy to this is to just keep putting out more content with the hope that, as the time passes, teachers will start posting their own materials.

We are still waiting for a killer app that could give online CoPs a real boost (Bolger, 2009). Current technology allows motivated persons to stay connected at their own. Surprisingly not many young teachers in their professional lives don't seem to realize the potential of technology for their benefit. The technology vendors currently sell to a market of educators that can be called a market of artisans. To this market, vendors sell technology as it is. A market of collaborative teaching practices current doesn't seem to exist probably because vendors currently lack collaborative teaching skills. The killer app mentioned earlier is expected to change this culture and increase real demand of social-networking based learning tools by educators.

Presently many communities are operational. Another important question is how new effective CoPs can built in the presence of these existing communities. The current generation of schools can be described as closed systems with conservative curriculum. The important thing is educators need to learn from their students. Free students can teach educators in a very short period of time (let's say a week or a month). Educators are not the ones to take us where educators need to go. The important question is how education can be made a profession such as medicine or law. The learning could be considered a product and teachers need to move beyond not knowing how to use technology. While a radical forward change is not possible for everyone in education community, online CoPs are great help for majority of teachers who progress gradually.

FUTURE RESEARCH DIRECTIONS

It would be interesting to analyze whether Web 2.0 technologies impact Communities of Practice and knowledge sharing the same way in both non-profit and for-profit organizations. It would be interesting because both types of the organization cover different aspects of the KM spectrum. Research is also needed to analyze in-depth situational factors that influence the impact of Web 2.0 application on KM. The outcomes would help organizations understand which levers they have to move in order to benefit from Web 2.0. Another future research area is to conduct some quantitative research in order to derive some general conclusion about the impact of Web 2.0 on KM. Innovations in mobile technology shape how mobile workers share knowledge and collaborate on the go. There exists a concept called mobile communities of practice (MCOPs) introduced as a lens for understanding how these workers self-organize. Variations in the degree of organizational alignment and individual discretion can shape these MCOPs. Further research is needed to gain a deeper understanding of MCOPs that can provide important strategic implications practical considerations for identifying, creating, and supporting MCOPs and Online COPs.

CONCLUSION

Currently we are in the early stages of using technology that supports online CoPs. We are also beginning to understand the dynamics and values of these communities. There exist great challenges regarding access, training of users, community building and engagement and integrating these online CoPs into the existing educational communities. Besides, the online communities and technology use to build these communities provide many rewards to the users.

Knowledge Management Systems (KMS) are primarily people-driven tools. Development of light, web-based tools for CoPs can encourage participation and probably barriers of adoption and implementation of CoPs. Existing communities need efficient and effective support. Web 2.0 tools can be the most effective tools for supporting online CoPs. Implementing online CoP technology is challenging but some clear roadmaps exist for successful implementation.

Developing CoPs, based on Web 2.0 tools, need careful planning. Careful mapping of goals and scenarios is required to understand the true requirements of audience in the community. We also need to think about the purpose of the community. These considerations should guide and inform the technology selection for building CoPs. Availability of resources for community management tasks (such as user training) should be ensured. Implementation should first start with a pilot program with minimum features offered. The community can grow in unexpected ways. It is need to be assured that the expansion is consistent with goals and purpose of community. Community will evolve over time and features should be added when needed. While home-based technology should be preferred, other valuable tools should also be used. In early stages, the focus should be to have few systems flow perfectly. With the passage of time, other useful systems should be fine-tuned. This chapter contributes to the existing knowledge base of knowledge management by providing insights how Web 2.0 applications can be used for developing effective Communities of Practice.

REFERENCES

Adams, A. N., Brock, R. J., Gordon, K. A., Grohs, J. R., & Kirk, G. R. (2014). Service, Dialogue, and Reflection as Foundational Elements in a Living Learning Community. *Journal of College and Character, 15*(3), 179–188. doi:10.1515/jcc-2014-0021

Allee, V. 1997. 12 Principles of Knowledge Management. Retrieved from http://www.providersedge.com/docs/km_articles/12_principles_of_Knowledge_Management.pdf

Ardichvili, A., Page, V., & Wentling, T. (2003). Motivation and barriers to participation in virtual knowledge-sharing communities of practice. *Journal of Knowledge Management, 7*(1), 64–77. doi:10.1108/13673270310463626

Barab, S., Scott, J., Del Valle Martin, R., & Fang, F. (2012). Coming to Terms with Communities of Practice: A definition and operational criteria.

Barnett, S., Jones, S. C., Bennett, S., Iverson, D., & Bonney, A. (2013). Usefulness of a virtual community of practice and web 2.0 tools for general practice training: Experiences and expectations of general practitioner registrars and supervisors. *Australian Journal of Primary Health, 19*(4), 292–296. doi:10.1071/PY13024 PMID:23823006

Bolger, S. (2009). Investigating the viability of virtual communities of practice in the public sector.

Bond, P. (2004). Communities of Practice and Complexity: Conversation and Culture. *Organization and People, 11*(4), 1–7.

Bouchamma, Y., & Michaud, C. (2011). Communities of practice with teaching supervisors: A discussion of community members' experiences. *Journal of Educational Change, 12*(4), 403–420. doi:10.100710833-010-9141-y

Brown, S. A. (2012). Seeing Web 2.0 in context: A study of academic perceptions. *The Internet and Higher Education, 15*(1), 50–57. doi:10.1016/j.iheduc.2011.04.003

Chen, T.-L., & Chen, T.-J. (2002). A strategic analysis of the online learning community for continuing professional development of university faculty in Taiwan: A SWOT analysis. *Proceedings of the International Conference on Computers in Education 2002* (pp. 1408–1409). IEEE.

Connectededucators (2011). Technology for Online Communities of Practice. from http://connectededucators.org/wp-content/uploads/2011/03/0143_Platforms-and-Tools-march-2011.pdf

Cornu, B. (2004). Networking and collecting intelligence for teachers and learners. In A. Brown & N. Davis (Eds.), *Digital technology, communities and education* (pp. 40–45). London: Routledge Falmer.

Cox, A. (2005). What are communities of practice? A comparative review of four seminal works. *Journal of Information Science, 31*(6), 527–540. doi:10.1177/0165551505057016

Cruickshank, P. (2011). *Customer journey mapping*. Smart Cities Guide.

Dascalu, M.-I., Bodea, C.-N., Lytras, M., De Pablos, P. O., & Burlacu, A. (2014). Improving e-learning communities through optimal composition of multidisciplinary learning groups. *Computers in Human Behavior*, *30*, 362–371. doi:10.1016/j.chb.2013.01.022

Drupal.org. (2014). Drupal Commons. Retrieved from https://www.drupal.org/project/commons

Eisenstadt, M., & Vincent, T. (2012). *The knowledge web: Learning and collaborating on the net*. Routledge.

Euerby, A., & Burns, C. M. (2012). Designing for Social Engagement in Online Social Networks Using Communities-of-Practice Theory and Cognitive Work Analysis A Case Study. *Journal of Cognitive Engineering and Decision Making*, *6*(2), 194–213. doi:10.1177/1555343412440697

Facebook. (2014). Facebook. Retrieved from http://www.programmableweb.com/api/facebook

Fugelstad, P., Dwyer, P., Filson Moses, J., Kim, J., Mannino, C. A., Terveen, L., & Snyder, M. (2012). What makes users rate (share, tag, edit...)?: predicting patterns of participation in online communities. *Proceedings of the ACM 2012 conference on Computer Supported Cooperative Work* (pp. 969–978). ACM. 10.1145/2145204.2145349

Goldberg, P. (2003). Disconnected Urbanism - Metropolis Magazine. Retrieved from http://www.metropolismag.com/December-1969/Disconnected-Urbanism/

Guy, M. 2006. Wiki or Won't He? A Tale of Public Sector Wikis. Comparison of UK & US State Organisations, Changing Audiences, Participation, and Collective Intelligence. Available from: http://www.ariadne.ac.uk/issue49/guy/

Hall, H., & Graham, D. (2004). Creation and recreation: Motivating collaboration to generate knowledge capital in online communities. *International Journal of Information Management*, *24*(3), 235–246. doi:10.1016/j.ijinfomgt.2004.02.004

Hislop, D. (2013). *Knowledge management in organizations: A critical introduction*. Oxford University Press.

Hossain, M., & Aydin, H. (2011). A Web 2.0-based collaborative model for multicultural education. *Multicultural Education & Technology Journal*, *5*(2), 116–128. doi:10.1108/17504971111142655

Hughes, J., Jewson, N., & Unwin, L. (2013). *Communities of practice: Critical perspectives*. Routledge.

Jamali, R., H., Russell, B., Nicholas, D., & Watkinson, A. (. (2014). Do online communities support research collaboration? *Aslib Journal of Information Management*, *66*(6), 603–622. doi:10.1108/AJIM-08-2013-0072

Jeon, S., Kim, Y.-G., & Koh, J. (2011). An integrative model for knowledge sharing in communities-of-practice. *Journal of Knowledge Management*, *15*(2), 251–269. doi:10.1108/13673271111119682

Jin, L., Wen, Z., & Gough, N. (2010). Social virtual worlds for technology-enhanced learning on an augmented learning platform. *Learning, Media and Technology*, *35*(2), 139–153. doi:10.1080/17439884.2010.494424

Kai-Wai Chu, S., & Kennedy, D. M. (2011). Using online collaborative tools for groups to co-construct knowledge. *Online Information Review*, *35*(4), 581–597. doi:10.1108/14684521111161945

Kraut, R. E., Resnick, P., Kiesler, S., Burke, M., Chen, Y., & Kittur, N. … Riedl, J. (2012). Building successful online communities: Evidence-based social design. MIT Press.

Lee, M. R., & Lan, Y. (2007). From Web 2.0 to conversational knowledge management: Towards collaborative intelligence. *Journal of Entrepreneurship Research*, *2*(2), 47–62.

Lin, M. F., & Lee, M. (2006). E-learning Localized: The case of the OOPS project. In A. Edmundson (Ed.), *Globalization in Education: Improving education quality through cross-cultural dialogue* (pp. 168–186). Hershey, PA: Idea Group.

Matei, S. A. (2005). From counterculture to cyberculture: Virtual community discourse and the dilemma of modernity. *Journal of Computer-Mediated Communication, 10*(3), 00–00.

McLure Wasko, M., & Faraj, S. (2000). It is what one does: Why people participate and help others in electronic communities of practice. *The Journal of Strategic Information Systems*, *9*(2-3), 155–173. doi:10.1016/S0963-8687(00)00045-7

McWilliam, G. (2012). Building stronger brands through online communities. *Sloan Management Review*, *41*(3).

Meyerhoff, M., & Strycharz, A. (2013). *Communities of practice*. Wiley Online Library. doi:10.1002/9781118335598.ch20

Newhouse, H. C. B., & Vestal, W. (2001). Building and Sustaining Communities of Practice. Houston: American Productivity Centre.

Nissen, M. E., Kamel, M. N., & Sengupta, K. C. (2000). Toward integrating knowledge management, processes and systems: a position paper. *Proceedings of the AAAI Symposium on Bringing Knowledge to Business Processes, Stanford, CA*.

Ridings, C. M., & Gefen, D. (2004). Virtual community attraction: Why people hang out online. *Journal of Computer-Mediated Communication, 10*(1).

Saint-Onge, H., & Wallace, D. (2012). *Leveraging communities of practice for strategic advantage*. Routledge.

Schneider, A., Von Krogh, G., & Jäger, P. (2013). "What's coming next?" Epistemic curiosity and lurking behavior in online communities. *Computers in Human Behavior*, *29*(1), 293–303. doi:10.1016/j.chb.2012.09.008

Sinclair, N. (2006). *Stealth KM, Winning Knowledge Management Strategies for the Public Sector*. Butterworth-Heinemann.

Spagnoletti, P., & Resca, A. (2012). A design theory for IT supporting online communities. *Proceedings of the 2012 45th Hawaii International Conference on System Science HICSS* (pp. 4082–4091). IEEE. 10.1109/HICSS.2012.54

Sun, N., Rau, P. P.-L., & Ma, L. (2014). Understanding lurkers in online communities: A literature review. *Computers in Human Behavior, 38*, 110–117. doi:10.1016/j.chb.2014.05.022

Tierney, R., & Palmer, M. (2013). Participation, interaction and learner satisfaction in a professional practice wiki for teachers. *Cyberpsychology and New Media: A Thematic Reader*, 195.

Tosey, P. (1999). The peer learning community: A contextual design for learning? *Management Decision, 37*(5), 403–010. doi:10.1108/00251749910274171

Tsai, H.-T., & Bagozzi, R. P. (2014). Contribution behavior in virtual communities: Cognitive, emotional and social influences. *Management Information Systems Quarterly, 38*(1), 143–163.

Valaitis, R. K., Akhtar-Danesh, N., Brooks, F., Binks, S., & Semogas, D. (2011). Online communities of practice as a communication resource for community health nurses working with homeless persons. *Journal of Advanced Nursing, 67*(6), 1273–1284. doi:10.1111/j.1365-2648.2010.05582.x PMID:21306424

Van Winkelen, C. 2003. Inter-organisational communities of practice. Retrieved from http://www. elearningeuropa.info/directory/index.php?page=doc&doc_id=1483&doclng=6

Venkatesh, V., Croteau, A.-M., & Rabah, J. (2014). Perceptions of effectiveness of instructional uses of technology in higher education in an era of Web 2.0. *Proceedings of the 2014 47th Hawaii International Conference on System Sciences (HICSS)* (pp. 110–119). IEEE.

Venkatesh, V., Rabah, J., Fusaro, M., Couture, A., Varela, W., & Alexander, K. (2012). Perceptions of Technology Use and Course Effectiveness in the Age of Web 2.0: A Large-Scale Survey of Québec University Students and Instructors. *Proceedings of the World Conference on E-Learning in Corporate, Government, Healthcare, and Higher Education* (Vol. 2012, pp. 1691–1699).

Walsham, G. (2001). Knowledge Management: The benefits and limitations of Computer Systems. *European Journal of Knowledge Management, 9*(6), 599–608. doi:10.1016/S0263-2373(01)00085-8

Wang, S., Noe, R. A., & Wang, Z.-M. (2014). Motivating Knowledge Sharing in Knowledge Management Systems A Quasi–Field Experiment. *Journal of Management, 40*(4), 978–1009. doi:10.1177/0149206311412192

Wang, Y., & Fesenmaier, D. R. (2003). Assessing motivation of contribution in online communities: An empirical investigation of an online travel community. *Electronic Markets, 13*(1), 33–45. doi:10.1080/1019678032000052934

Wenger, E. (1999). Communities of practice: Learning as a social system. *Systems Thinker, 9*(5), 2–3.

Wenger, E. (2006). Communities of Practice: A brief introduction. North San Juan, C.A. Available from: http://www.ewenger.com/theory/index.html

Wenger, E. (2011). *Communities of practice: A brief introduction.* Retrieved from https://scholarsbank.uoregon.edu/xmlui/bitstream/handle/1794/11736/A%20brief%20introduction%20to%20CoP.pdf?sequence=1&isAllowed=y

Wenger, E., White, N., & Smith, J. D. (2009). *Digital habitats.* Stewarding Technology for Communities.

Yen, H. R., Hsu, S. H.-Y., & Huang, C.-Y. (2011). Good soldiers on the Web: Understanding the drivers of participation in online communities of consumption. *International Journal of Electronic Commerce*, *15*(4), 89–120. doi:10.2753/JEC1086-4415150403

Zhang, W., & Watts, S. (2008). Online communities as communities of practice: A case study. *Journal of Knowledge Management*, *12*(4), 55–71. doi:10.1108/13673270810884255

Zhou, Z., Wu, J. P., Zhang, Q., & Xu, S. (2013). Transforming visitors into members in online brand communities: Evidence from China. *Journal of Business Research*, *66*(12), 2438–2443.

ADDITIONAL READING

Bannister, F., 2007. The curse of benchmarking: an assessment of the validity and value of e-government comparisons. *International Review of Administrative Sciences,* 73, 171.

Bhatt, G. (2001). Knowledge Management in Organisations: Examining the Interactions between Technologies, Techniques and People. *Journal of Knowledge Management*, *5*(1), 68–75. doi:10.1108/13673270110384419

Bixler, C. H. (2002). Applying the four pillars of Knowledge Management, *KMWorldMagazine*, 11(1)

Davenport, T. H., & Prusak, L. (2006). Working Knowledge: How organizations manage what they know (pp. 3, 11). Harvard Business School Press, Boston, MA, USA.

Gladwell, M. (2002). *The Tipping Point: How little things can make a big difference*. New York, NY: Black Ray Books.

Holland, G. A. (2006). Extended Cognition and Social Constructionism as Underpinnings for Knowledge Management Practice. *Journal of Knowledge Management Practice*, 7(1).

Nonaka, I. (1991). The knowledge-creating company. *Harvard Business Review*, *69*(6), 96–104.

Orlikowski, W. J. 1992. Learning from Notes: organizational issues in groupware implementation. Proceedings of the 1992 ACM conference on Computer- supported cooperative work (pp. 362-369). ACM Press New York, NY, USA. 10.1145/143457.143549

Rowley, J. (1992). *Organising Knowledge* (2nd ed.). Hants, UK: Gower Publishing.

Senge, P. M. (1990). *The Fifth Discipline: The Art and Practice of the Learning Organization*. New York, NY: Doubleday.

Wiig, K. M. (1993). *Knowledge Management Foundations: Thinking About Thinking – How People and Organizations Create, Represent, and Use Knowledge*. Arlington, TX: Schema Press.

KEY TERMS AND DEFINITIONS

Collaboration: Collaboration is a joint effort of multiple individuals or work groups to accomplish a task or project.

Community: A community is a group of people living in the same place or having a particular characteristic in common.

Community of Practice: Community of practice is formed by people who engage in a process of collective learning in a shared domain of human endeavor.

Explicit Knowledge: Explicit knowledge is knowledge that has been articulated, codified, and stored in certain media.

Knowledge Management: Knowledge management is the process of capturing, developing, sharing, and effectively using organizational knowledge.

Tacit Knowledge: Tacit knowledge is the kind of knowledge that is difficult to transfer to another person by means of writing it down or verbalizing it.

Virtual Community: A virtual community is a community of people sharing common interests, ideas, and feelings over the Internet or other collaborative networks.

This research was previously published in Cultural, Behavioral, and Social Considerations in Electronic Collaboration edited by Ayse Kok and Hyunkyung Lee; pages 265-292, copyright year 2016 by Business Science Reference (an imprint of IGI Global).

Chapter 6
Information Sharing and Communications with Mobile Cloud Technology:
Applications and Challenges

Shantanu Pal
The University of St. Andrews, UK

ABSTRACT

The use of mobile devices (e.g., smartphones, tablet computers, and PDAs) has steadily increased in recent years. At the same time the cloud-based applications have greatly enhanced the computing capabilities to these mobile devices. Therefore, the emergence of mobile-cloud technology is promising for offloading computations to the cloud. In this chapter we explore the state-of-the-art research in mobile-cloud technology and discuss the integration of the mobile devices and cloud-based applications. We begin by describing the mobile-cloud architecture and its functional components. Next, we explore the applications (e.g., education, healthcare, disaster management, etc.) and related challenges (e.g., bandwidth utilization, latency, connectivity, etc.) with the mobile-cloud technology. Finally, we outline the issues associated to these applications that need to be improved upon for delivering a more scalable and resource-enhanced mobile-cloud technology to the users.

INTRODUCTION

Nowadays smart mobile devices (e.g., smartphones, tablet computers and PDAs) have become more popular. These devices are not limited anymore to just sending a text or making a phone call. They have become more powerful in order to execute computing resources (e.g., processing and storage) (Han, et al., 2015). With this explosive growth in the use of mobile devices and the use of accessible cloud-based applications at a user's will, helps to provide a more convenient way of offloading computations through

DOI: 10.4018/978-1-7998-0417-8.ch006

the resource-constrained mobile devices. Thus, the emergence of mobile-cloud technology (Giurgiu, et al., 2009) delivers a new platform by combining the mobile devices and cloud-based applications together, whereby improving the devices processing power and storage capacity.

Mobile-cloud technology is the abstraction of the cloud-based application that enables ubiquitous, convenient and on-demand network access to the services by the user's mobile devices through wireless networks. Moreover, the use of cloud-based applications enables the execution of rich mobile computations to these devices with a better user experience that improves the constraints related to bandwidth utilization, latency related issues or the battery power for the devices (Fernando, et al., 2013).

The term 'cloud' refers to a distributed resource pool which enables networks, servers or storage to access configurable hosted services over the Internet in a 'pay-as-you-go' manner (Armbrust, et al., 2009). This kind of service is rapidly provisioned and needs minimal management efforts to gain access by the users. Moreover, the use of cloud-based applications improves the reliability and accessibility of data through the mobile devices. Therefore, mobile-cloud technology enables users an efficient use of networks with unified elastic resources of various applications aimed at storage, processing power and extensive functionality (e.g., the low cost of applications) of the devices.

In this chapter, we explore the various applications of mobile-cloud technology in different sectors. The scope of this chapter is to outline a set of mobile-cloud based applications which includes online learning applications, mobile healthcare, automated traffic management systems etc., and then we further outline the challenges e.g., bandwidth, latency, connectivity etc. related to these applications. In addition, we discuss the possible countermeasures to address these challenges. The major contributions of this chapter are as follows:

- A comprehensive analysis of the applications scenarios with this state-of-the-art research in mobile-cloud technology.
- A detailed discussion of the existing challenges that are related to these applications with the intent to bring attention to motivate further research for a more scalable and resource-enhanced mobile-cloud technology.
- An overview of the recent research advances with the possible countermeasures to identify these challenges that need to be improved upon for a better mobile-cloud application for the users in the future.

The rest of this chapter is organized as follows. Section 'BACKGROUND' describes the background of both, this research and mobile-cloud architecture and its functional components. In Section 'APPLICATIONS AND CHALLENGES', we explore the state-of-the-art applications and related challenges and issues related to mobile-cloud technology followed by the comprehensive summary of the applications, techniques, challenges and possible countermeasures (in Section 'SUMMARY'). Finally, we present our concluding remarks in Section 'CONCLUSION'.

BACKGROUND

Mobile-cloud technology primarily focuses on the user's mobile devices to access cloud-based services through wireless network communications (Qi & Gani, 2012). This is achieved when mobile applications are deployed (i.e., mobile offloading) to the cloud servers or cloud-based applications run inside the user's mobile devices e.g., in terms of 'cloudlets' (Satyanarayanan, et al., 2009). The cloudlets are a mobility-enhanced small-scale cloud data centre that provides powerful and resource-intensive services with a lower latency.

The mobile data offloading can be done in two ways. One is through Femtocell (Chandrasekhar, et al., 2008) and another is through Wi-Fi networks (e.g., Wi-Fi access points) (Qiu, et al., 2015). Femtocell, which is an access point base station, is used for data offloading in an indoor environment. The major requirement for this is a small base station that helps gain access to an available Internet connection for data offloading. But unlike the Femtocell, offloading through a Wi-Fi access point, works in an outdoor environment using the unlicensed frequency bands.

The major components of the mobile-cloud architectures are composed of the mobile devices, mobile networks, Internet access points, cloud servers and the cloud controllers (cf. Figure 1). As illustrated in Figure 1, mobile devices connect with the mobile networks via base stations e.g., Base Transceiver Stations (BTS), access points or satellites. BTS facilitate the wireless communications between the users and the network. The mobile network then connects with the cloud servers via an Internet access point to avail cloud-based services for the users. In the cloud (in this case the infrastructure cloud), the cloud controllers process these requests to navigate to the corresponding cloud servers for providing the requested services to the users (Dinh, et al., 2013). In this chapter we use the term 'cloud' and 'infrastructure clouds' interchangeably.

However, offloading computations depends upon several issues associated with the cloud and mobile device (Giurgiu, et al., 2009; Fernando, et al., 2013). From the cloud's side, major issues are the availability of networks for communication (i.e., an accessible Internet connection), required bandwidth for data transmission and latency related issues for transmission costs (i.e., the number of required data packets for a successful communication). From the device's point of view, issues are related to limited battery power or memory size, which greatly influences such communication (Ahmed, et al., 2015).

There are several studies carried out addressing the networking issues for communication and device related concerns in mobile-cloud technology (Han, et al., 2015; Li, et al., 2009). In the former case (i.e., the networking issues), heterogeneity is a major concern for accessing a seamless cloud-based application by the users. In the context of mobile-cloud technology, heterogeneity is referred to the use of different connectivity means to access cloud-based applications. When mobile devices change their locations such connectivity also changes according to the available network infrastructure. For instance, this connectivity is limited e.g., for user's 3G/4G plan and even they vary from one place to another e.g., home, office, university or when travelling on the train.

Additionally, communications in mobile-cloud technology depends upon the device's mobility and user's movements (Li, et al., 2014). During a roaming situation, it is difficult for searching an available network connection for communication. This may cause potential vulnerabilities to the system. In such cases, the attackers may enter into the user's system when accessing a non-trusted network connection. To address such issues, the 'Intelligent Radio Network Access' architecture can be employed to secure the network from a non-trusted user's access (Klein, et al., 2010). In this architecture, the service broker provides a 'Uniform Resource Identifier' (URI) to the service user. The URI is a set of unique characters that determines a unique user's identification. It provides a context-aware service management mechanism to that user in a specific network. This in turn, improves the possibility for a secure interaction by avoiding unauthorized users access in different network connectivity. Further, a trusted connectivity

Figure 1. Mobile-cloud architecture is where the user's mobile devices are connected with the mobile network via different access points. The mobile network then communicates with the cloud servers using the Internet access points. Finally, the cloud controllers provide the requested cloud-based service to the users.

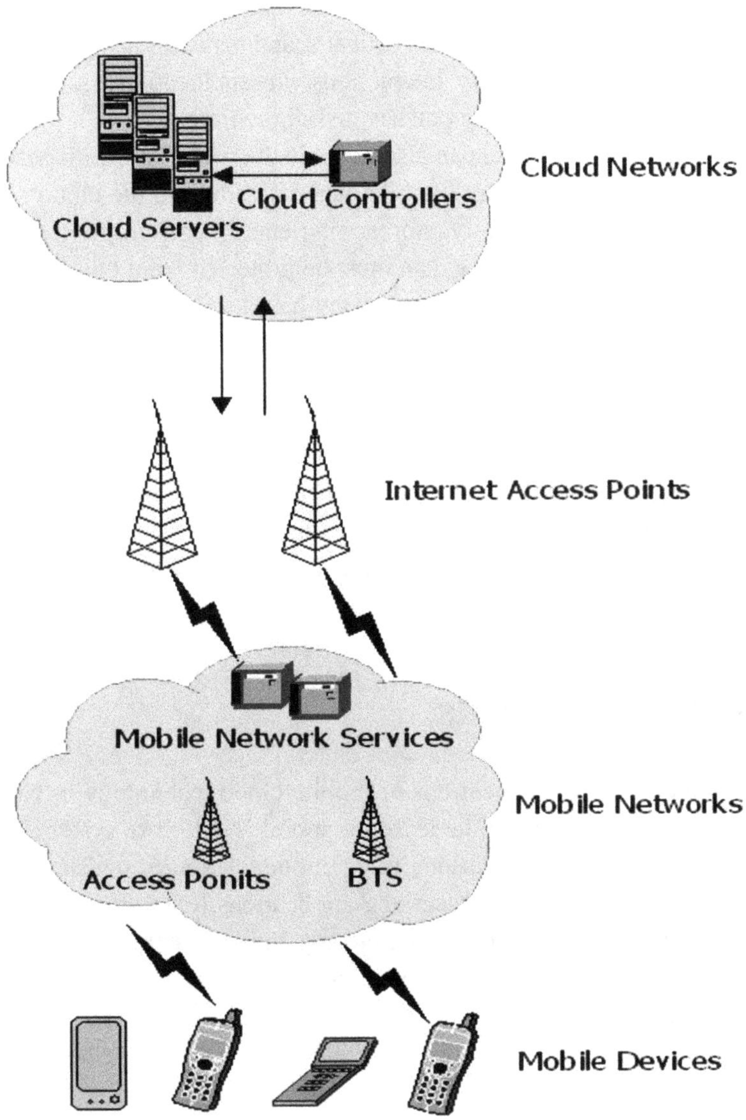

between the mobile nodes (a user in a real-life) accessing data via different network connections should be guaranteed. This connectivity must supports dynamic routing protocols that follow the node's trusted encounters between each other for controlling data exchange at runtime (Huang, et al., 2011).

In the latter case (i.e., the device's issue), battery power and memory size are the major concerns (Wang, et al., 2015). Due to the limited battery power capacity of the mobile devices, it is impractical to run these devices all the time in areas that lack a fixed infrastructure for communication. This includes rural or sparse areas or areas with high network density but full of interference access networks.

In the first case (i.e., rural or sparse areas), it is important to save the battery power for an emergency/important application. On the other hand, in the second case (i.e., high network density areas), the issues are the communication costs and data accessibility (Conti & Giordano, 2015). To address such above mentioned issues, a context-aware battery management system for mobile devices may be used (Ravi, et al., 2008). This system is able to distinguish between the user's important phone calls and other non-important activates by keeping a log of previous activates and applications. However, in the context of the mobile-cloud technology, user's mobility, interactions, present locations and various calling patterns make it difficult to predict the user's calling patterns for all the time.

Similarly, devices limited memory size can also degrade the overall network performance due to the lack of device's storage capacity. Therefore, mobile data offloading to the cloud servers is significant to improve the device's processing capacity, storage and energy consumption (Kumar & Lu, 2010). However, during a data offloading, sensitive data must be protected from other users who may cause a potential damage to the system. Upon this, cryptography-based security architecture in a mobile-cloud based infrastructure can be enforced (Sedayao, et al., 2009). In this architecture, users have the exclusive control over the private key of the encrypted data. This in turn reduces unauthorized data access by ensuring user's privacy with a trust-based access control mechanism. Furthermore, there are risks for devices being stolen or damaged. Over this, a secure data management framework can be used (Huang, et al., 2011). In this framework, users have full access control over the cloud-data which can be retrieved or transferred securely into another system. In this chapter, we further study these networking and device related issues in various mobile-cloud applications along with their challenges and potential countermeasures.

APPLICATIONS AND CHALLENGES

In this section we explore different applications of mobile-cloud technology in various scenarios and the challenges they face. This includes online learning, mobile healthcare systems, electronic business applications, online entertainment applications (e.g., mobile gaming, multimedia applications and online television streaming), information processing applications (e.g., crowdsourcing and navigation systems), social networking as well as different monitoring and management applications (e.g., wildlife monitoring and management, disaster management, smart-tourism and travel, and automated urban traffic controlling systems).

Mobile Learning

The rapid growth of mobile technology and wireless communication networks has improved the emergence of mobile learning (m-learning) technology (Ting, 2005), as it creates a convenient online learning-platform for the users which is easily accessible from virtually anywhere. The fundamental basis of the m-learning technology is the use of mobile devices for learning purposes while users are travelling. This technology is based on the electronic learning (e-learning) technology and the mobility of the devices.

For instance, the 'MobiLearn'[1] and the 'Learning Citizen Cluster'[2] are two projects that are focusing on the m-learning technology by exploring the context-sensitive approaches for mobility of the users. This helps visitors (e.g., tourists) to improve their knowledge (e.g., information of place) and helps in cultural information interchange in places e.g., museums, in social communities or to improve the information accessed through updating recent activities and interests via online. These projects aim at building a common user centric platform for collaborating information among users, service providers and service developers more easily and the use of cloud-based applications improves the overall m-learning process through these collaborations and social interactions (Dascalu, et al., 2015). Various mobile communication mechanisms can be used for the m-learning process, e.g., voice communications, real-time message exchange (e.g., text messages and emails) and the direct information interchange via document uploading between the users. Additionally, by employing a learning portal in the Internet, users can manage different activities which also support m-learning management systems. The mobile-cloud technology improves the accessibility of information among the users via a seamless learning collaboration. Documents can be shard through the cloud assisted platforms using these mobile devices. This includes GoogleDocs, Live Skydrive or Office Live.

Although mobile devices are portable and easily accessible by the users, there are several limitations related to the traditional m-learning technology which includes a weak network bandwidth for communications, low network transmission rates, limited battery power or even the device's small screen size. The use of cloud-based applications with mobile devices has introduced new ways to solve these limitations (Dinh, et al., 2013). It is now possible to use mobile devices to control cloud-based applications without maintaining a higher amount of infrastructure or resources. Utilizing a cloud-based application has several advantages e.g., higher storage capacity, faster processing and the convenient use of resources that provides learners with more scalable services in terms of data accessibility. Thereby improving the m-learning process for both out-of-classroom and in-classroom education.

However, the challenges are to originate the concept of adaptive learning to build instructional strategies and learning content for the user's personal preferences according to their needs as well as providing them with the correct information (Leung & Chan, 2003). The future research goal would be to integrate heterogeneous mobile-cloud platforms and various mobile applications seamlessly in order to provide these types of m-learning technologies to the users for a better utilization of resources and to further enhance computational capabilities. To this end, context-aware m-learning technology can be employed for improving the m-learning process (Huang & Chiu, 2015). This context-aware system helps to determine the user's personal preferences according to their needs through users' collaborations with one another in heterogeneous mobile-cloud platforms.

Mobile Healthcare

Mobile healthcare (m-healthcare) is a form of electronic healthcare (e-healthcare) technology that manages patient's clinical records as well as enabling a ubiquitous and uninterrupted access platform to provide these records to the doctors and caregivers using a mobile-based application (Silva, et al., 2015). This technology helps with treatments through constant observations without the patient's physical presence being required at the clinic or hospital. Therefore, m-healthcare technology helps reduce the cost of medical treatments. The use of cloud-based applications on mobile devices also enables a greater potential in remote healthcare services with higher bandwidth utilization, storage and a more scalable service platform overcoming the device's limitations of storage and processing capabilities.

Hoang and Chen propose a middleware based m-healthcare architecture, named 'MoCAsH' (Hoang & Chen, 2010). This architecture uses mobile sensing technology with the help of locally available mobile communication infrastructure, and then processes the data to a central cloud server. However, the proposed model relies on intelligent mobile agents and context-aware sensor records for information processing and storage which requires a continuous network connection that may be affected by the device's limited battery capacity or in a challenged network scenario (e.g., in rural areas that lack an Internet connection) .

Tang et al. propose a mobile-based home care management system through the transmission of Multimedia Messaging Services (MMS) (Tang, et al., 2010). This system is especially configured for hypertension and diabetes patients who can generate their own requirements (e.g., requesting doctor's advice or seeking advice for a particular medical treatment) through text messages using their mobile phones. Similar to the 'MoCAsH' architecture (Hoang & Chen, 2010), in this system a centralized cloud-based service management architecture has been introduced to monitor these requirements and process them to the appropriate departments or doctors according to the patient's necessity or emergency situations.

However, the secure exchange of electronic health records among clinics, doctors and caregivers, while storing and transmitting that data using resource-constraint mobile devices is still a major challenge (Williams & Maeder, 2015). To address this, strong security architecture for protecting medical records from unauthorized user access can be employed (Nkosi & Mekuria, 2010). This architecture uses cloud-based applications to distribute medical health records and implement a security protocol for an efficient cloud-based resource management in the mobile devices. In addition, to overcome the devices limited battery power capacity, the proposed architecture offloads the complex computational services to the cloud and only executes the final process on the mobile devices, which reduces the cost of communication. This architecture improves the overall bandwidth utilization and reduces the computational complexities to the mobile devices by providing a faster data processing between the devices.

Electronic Business

The use of mobile-cloud applications in electronic business (e-business) technology is rapidly increasing. These applications allow users to perform their business transactions over the Internet via their mobile devices. This is an important aspect towards the development of a faster cloud-assisted e-business technology that enables the adaptability of the device's mobility (Varshney, 2010).

Furthermore, mobile-cloud technology facilitates these applications e.g., as online photo sharing, booking online movie tickets or even online shopping from a favorite book store. These cloud-based mobile applications are more popular at present and users can instantly avail these services even when they are travelling (Hao, et al., 2013). However, it may happen that the e-commerce web-sites in the cloud may be situated far away from their customers. Therefore, a low latency for communications may cause the company to lose their business revenues. Research is promising in these areas on how to find the online retail businesses more quickly according to the user's choice and demands. To this end, context-aware, collaboration-based technology can be employed (Hoang & Jung, 2015). This would help to find a collaborative as well as mobile-adaptive local user's communication platform that may help others for finding the specific needs more quickly rather than relying on a fixed infrastructure for communication.

Online Entertainment Applications

- **Mobile Gaming:** Mobile entertainment applications are the potential for generating revenue for the enterprises (Hwang, et al., 2012). The global market of mobile games in 2010 was 66 billion US dollars and it is expected to rise to nearly 81 billion US dollars by 2016.[3] The concept of mobile gaming is to offload the large scale computing resources into the cloud servers and to use this application via mobile devices as an interface. Research is promising in the areas where multiple mobile users can communicate with each other at runtime in a collaborative platform without a direct physical involvement.

Gaming systems using mobile-cloud technology attract both the users and game developers in many ways. Users can play the same game (at a time) over a heterogeneous platform, e.g., a laptop, mobile device, personal computers or in tablet computers. This gaming system reduces the cost for both the users as well as the developers. But the challenging task is to develop a cloud-based gaming system over the heterogeneous mobile platforms which will provide high-quality audio and video streaming as well as reduce response delays at runtime (Zammit, et al., 2012). To this end, an open cloud-based gaming system, named 'GamingAnywhere' can be employed (Huang, et al., 2012). This system is able to support continuous video streaming and maintains its performance accordingly. The development of this system is based on a cloud assisted client-server model. However, research is challenging on how the users can play such games using a decentralized mobile-cloud platform.

- **Multimedia Applications:** Video, audio and photographs (e.g., multimedia streaming or photo sharing) have different delivery requirements in a distributed mobile-cloud environment. These applications need to be synchronized to provide coherent information to the mobile users for their requirements. The use of these types of multimedia applications are popular to use or play on the mobile devices, because such portable devices are easy to carry and easy to access (Cerqueira, et al., 2014). But the major challenge is an efficient scheduling of multimedia data streaming over different mobile-cloud platforms.

Upon this, an efficient scheduling algorithm for massive multimedia data flows with a heterogeneous mobile-cloud platform can be employed (Zhou, et al., 2013). The proposed scheduling architecture tries to mitigate the delays and energy related issues among the cloud servers. The use of such architecture is promising where users can share their interests with similar types of users (i.e., with the same interests) and applications.

- **Online Television Streaming:** Internet Protocol television (IPTV) services like 'Video On Demand' (VoD) and 'Live broadcast TV' are quite popular at present (Aggarwal, et al., 2012). With the advancement of mobile-cloud technology, these services have become more demanded by the users but the concerns are for a continuous need of an Internet connection, network bandwidth or usability of the mobile devices to access these services. Other challenges are how to provide a continuous streaming over these mobile-cloud platforms while the devices are changing the networks frequently, and the use of these devices in places with limited connectivity e.g., sparse areas without an infrastructure for communication or in the urban areas with full interference access networks.

To this end, the traditional Peer-to-Peer (P2P) mobile communications technique (Chang, et al., 2012), which is able to deliver the context over the Internet can be employed. This is the most common existing decentralized mobile communication technique that follows mobile ad-hoc network (MANET) communication techniques. However, the challenge is how to build a mobile-cloud assisted P2P communications system that is able to provide a high-speed data transfer (i.e., higher bandwidth utilization) to the users in areas that are limited to access an IPTV.

Another issue is the 'Instant Channel Change' (ICC) requests in IPTV. Technologies like IPTV and LiveTV typically follow the multicasting mechanism from the servers using IP multicast, with one group per TV channel. For each channel change each user needs to join the multicast group associated with that particular channel and they need to wait for enough data to be buffered before the video is displayed, which is time consuming. To address such issues, the use of a mobile-cloud based architecture that provides a faster deployment of IPTV and LiveTV services over wireless networks can be beneficial (Park, et al., 2008). The future research is encouraging where users can adopt additional functionalities that are related to improve the latency related issues and connection protocols for a seamless service to the mobile devices.

Information Processing

- **Crowdsourcing:** Using mobile-cloud technology, crowdsourcing is possible for information interchange via online activity among individuals or groups (Fernando, et al., 2012). Many mobile devices can form a domain that could allow users the ability to find useful information in a shorter range (i.e., a reasonable close distance). But the challenge is that the mobile devices need a continuous Internet connection to avail remote cloud services via Wi-Fi or a 3G network connection which is not feasible because of the bandwidth and communication related issues in sparse areas or urban areas. On the other hand, privacy and security issues are major challenges for building a secure/privacy-aware mobile crowdsourcing system (Yang, et al., 2013). To this end, a strong cryptography security framework that is used for protecting sensitive data via encryption (e.g., identity-based encryption) can be employed (Bowers, et al., 2009).
- **Navigation Systems:** Mobile devices are able to connect Global Positioning System (GPS) services for finding locations with the help of a cloud-assisted sensing system (Whipple, et al., 2009). These services can also calculate a device's location and speed with sufficient accuracy. This may be applicable when searching for specific locations (e.g., travel destinations, roads or tourist attractions). But the challenge is the need for a stable network connection for communication that will not be easily affected by natural calamities or disasters (e.g., earthquake, tornadoes or tsunami). To address this issue, architecture that is able to provide a continuous network connection for communication through opportunistic collaborations can be employed (Pelusi, et al., 2006). In such collaborations local user's mobile devices are the major components which store, carry and forward information with the other individuals in a physical proximity.

Social Networking

People can build a network with social collaborations with their peers, who share similar information, for information interchange by using mobile-cloud technology. Networking based on mobile-cloud technology called 'saba'[4] combines social, mobile and real-time users' collaborations. This helps individuals to communicate easier with others e.g., colleagues, students and customers in a more productive way. With the help of this network, users can build relationships with each other to share information. 'Zimbra'[5] is another type of enterprise community based on the mobile-cloud technology that connects people and information for sharing emails, files and helps in social interactions.

However, the major challenge is to build context-awareness systems that are able to use contextual information to change and automatically reconfigure their configurations to adapt to the context (Buchegger & Datta, 2009). In a mobile-cloud perspective, this context refers to noise, network connectivity, cost of communication, bandwidth utilization, latency, etc. that are all related to the communication. To address these issues, a context-aware data management architecture can be employed (Hoang & Jung, 2015), that adopts the situational changes according to the user's needs.

Wildlife Monitoring and Management

The use of mobile-cloud technology is promising in wildlife monitoring and several other related applications, e.g., finding the location of specific animals or to monitor their behaviors. However, the lack of infrastructure (e.g., a fixed network connection) faces major challenges in order to increase the communication opportunities and the throughput in the system. Applications are promising in the areas where the locally available P2P network communications can be integrated in such monitoring systems for an efficient collection of data and providing access of cloud-based services that may require a real-time data management (Buchegger & Datta, 2009).

To address this, a mobile-cloud based system on outdoor mobility-learning activities with the integration of wireless communication technology can be employed (Chen, et al., 2002). The proposed system is built on an ad hoc network communication that is formed with the different mobile users. For example, using mobile devices and a Wi-Fi network card the users can share an animal's information between each other. This system is based on a centralized service oriented architecture and active collaboration between the users who are participating in this monitoring system.

Disaster Management

Satyanarayanan presents a view to use mobile-cloud technology in cases of disaster and emergency situations (Satyanarayanan, 2010). The potential use of mobile-cloud technology are discussed in situations e.g., finding a lost child or in a natural disaster like an earthquake scenario. In such cases, local users can help by sharing the real-time information with one another creating a pool of resources to make further decisions accordingly with the help of the locally available network connections. However, the challenge is the efficient management of the high data traffic within the network during the time of a disaster.

To address such issues, an intelligent transportation system for disaster management with vehicular ad-hoc networks (VANETs) and mobile-cloud technology can be employed (Alazawi, et al., 2011). The proposed system is able to collect information from multiple sources and locations, including from the point of an incident. It then creates effective strategies to send updated information to the vehicles and other co-located users for finding an alternative route to the destination.

Smart-Tourism and Travel

Smart-tourism is the technology for scheduling, planning and recommendations in the tourism industry. Huag et al. present a smart travel system that consists of real-time travel searches, personal demands and task service management systems (Hung, et al., 2012). But this requires a continuous Internet connection which is difficult to gain/access in rural areas or in the high costs of Internet roaming access zones. Therefore, research is promising when travelling in areas with no Internet connection or in the high costs of Internet access zones, which may allow the use of smart-tourism applications with the help of the local users' mobile networks. To this end, mobile-cloud technology, using users' social interactions and collaborations can be used (Pelusi, et al., 2006). This would also allow users to share information locally during the time of a traditional network connection failure. Attractive incentives may further encourage users for an active participation in such communications (Scekic et al., 2013).

Urban Traffic Controlling Systems

Mobile-cloud technology is promising in the use of urban traffic communications and controlling systems. The cloud-based applications provide the resources required to use traffic strategies and efficient control of massive data transportation.

Wang et al. present an agent-based traffic controlling management system for intelligent vehicular transportation (Wang, et al., 2013). The system is based on agent-controlled network-enabled technology. The advantage of this system is that it requires less memory and processing power to control the agents than the process that is operated by traditional controlling algorithms. This system deals with a centralized server-based architecture. However, the challenge is how we can build such systems in real-time over a decentralized network that connects to a heterogeneous mobile-cloud platform. Moreover, this system requires a continuous network connection between the driver's mobile device and the cloud server that may be unavailable in areas that lack a network infrastructure for communication.

Xue et al. present a cloud storage-based traffic video detection system that is capable of processing higher amounts of video streams to generate the present traffic condition in a given area (Xue, et al., 2011). But a large amount of storage-resources are required for deploying such a system which increase the network delays. Research in these areas is promising where we could process data over the cloud and use mobile devices for streaming the data at runtime which would reduce the communication delays in the network.

To address such issue, a mobile-cloud based smart trafficking system can be used (Manolopoulos, et al., 2010). The proposed system is based on a mobile application which runs on each driver's mobile device and a traffic prediction algorithm which runs inside the cloud server. This system provides a real-time guidance to the users and reconstructs the traffic model from the collected data for the future traffic predictions.

SUMMARY

We have summarized the relevancy of mobile-cloud applications and their related challenges discussed in the previous section. We explore the major categories of these applications e.g., education, healthcare, business and entertainment, information processing and monitoring, and management. We find that the use of mobile-cloud technology is promising in all of these cases allowing users a ubiquitous networking environment for information processing and storage. The use of cloud-based applications is a major benefit for resource constraint mobile devices for offloading computations to the clouds. But from the communication point of view, available network connections, required bandwidth for data transmissions, data security and users privacy are major challenges to the mobile-cloud technology. On the other hand, from the devices point of view, limited battery power and memory size, smaller display or even different operating systems make it difficult for a seamless data communication between the devices.

In Table 1, we summarize the different application scenarios of mobile-cloud technology. We discuss the application category, the techniques used for each application, related challenges and potential countermeasures for the underlying challenges.

FUTURE RESEARCH DIRECTIONS

The uses of smart mobile devices are becoming a major part for the key transforming of information in the future of education, healthcare as well as different management and monitoring applications. In this chapter, we outline the future research directions in many areas including user's privacy and security, data confidentiality, secure data transmission between the mobile devices as well as an efficient data management infrastructure. For mobile learning purpose, context-aware m-learning technology that provides instructional strategies and learning content for the users can be used (Huang & Chiu, 2015). From the security and privacy perspective, strong security mechanisms for protecting medical-health records from unauthorized user access can be employed (Nkosi & Mekuria, 2010). A context-aware, collaboration-based information sharing technique can be enforced for information processing, electronic business and online entertainment applications (Hoang & Jung, 2015). Moreover, intelligent transportation systems for smart-tourism and travel, disaster management as well as wild life monitoring and management can be used (Alazawi, et al., 2011).

CONCLUSION

In this chapter we explore the various applications and related challenges in mobile-cloud technology. Major contributions of this chapter are as follows: first, a detailed discussion on the different applications and potential scenarios when using mobile-cloud technology and second, we explore the challenges and issues related to these applications that need to be improved upon for a more scalable and resource-enhanced data transmission in the network. Our current studies give a detailed view of the state-of-the-art research in mobile-cloud applications with the input of the emerging research issues in this area.

However, the heterogeneity of networks, limited bandwidth, context-awareness of the device, limited battery power and memory size as well as security and privacy issues to protect user's data are the major constraints to overcome for the continuation of delivering better mobile-cloud applications. We find that the use of local users' mobile network communications is promising for extending mobile-cloud applications in areas that lack an infrastructure e.g., in remote/sparse areas, but also in areas with infrastructure e.g., high density areas with full of interference access networks. In future, we plan to perform more comprehensive experiments focusing the challenges raised in this chapter.

ACKNOWLEDGMENT

The author would like to acknowledge the Scottish Informatics and Computer Science Alliance (SICSA) and the University of St Andrews, Scotland, United Kingdom. The author would like to thank the reviewers for their insightful comments on the chapter. The author would also like to acknowledge to all the researchers for their ideas and works which have been presented in this chapter.

Table 1. The table highlights the various applications of mobile-cloud technology, their techniques and related challenges with possible countermeasures.

Applications	Techniques	Challenges	Solutions/Measures
Mobile Learning	The use of smart mobile devices for m-learning purposes while users are in motion. In this, mobile devices connect to the cloud servers via an Internet access point (e.g., Wi-Fi networks) and gain advantages to the cloud-based resources (e.g., processing and storage) to improve the data accessibility for learning purposes that supports device's mobility.	The challenge is how to originate the concept of adaptive learning to build instructional strategies and learning content for the user's personal preferences according to their needs.	To employ context-aware m-learning technology for improving instructional strategies and learning content for the users (Huang & Chiu, 2015). This context-aware system uses a self-adapting algorithm that helps to automatically determine changes in user's preferences according to their needs through users' collaborations with one another in a heterogeneous mobile-cloud platform.
Mobile Healthcare	Manage patient's clinical records enabling a ubiquitous and uninterrupted access platform to make available them to doctors and caregivers using a mobile-cloud platform. This may be done by employing a mobile sensing technology for collecting data locally and then process them to a central cloud server.	The challenge is the secure exchange of electronic health records among patients, doctors and caregivers, while storing and transmitting them by using resource-constraint mobile devices.	To employ strong security mechanisms for protecting medical records from unauthorized user access (Nkosi & Mekuria, 2010). The proposed mechanism uses encryption-based security technique (e.g., identity-based encryption) for distributing medical records over the mobile and cloud platforms.
Electronic Business	E-business is the conduct of business processes that uses Internet to operate such processes over a cloud-based platform. In this, business transactions are performed by sharing information and running automated business activities between the users and companies using Information and Communication Technologies (ICT).	One of the major challenges is that, it may happen that the e-commerce web-sites (in the cloud) may be situated far away from their customers. Therefore, a low latency for communications degrades the overall e-business performance due to the inadequate network connectivity.	A context-aware, collaboration-based information sharing technique can be employed (Hoang & Jung, 2015). This would help to find a collaborative as well as mobile-adaptive communication platform available locally that may assist users to find specific answers more quickly rather than relying on a fixed infrastructure for communication.
Online Entertainment Applications	Offloading large scale computing resources/ applications into the cloud servers and to use these resources/applications via resource constraint mobile devices as an interface e.g., accessing online data streaming or live broadcasting via mobile devices.	The challenge is, an efficient scheduling of computing resources/applications (e.g., a multimedia data streaming) over different mobile-cloud platforms.	A scheduling algorithm for massive multimedia data flows in a heterogeneous mobile-cloud platform can be used (Zhou, et al., 2013). The proposed scheduling algorithm tries to mitigate the delays and energy related issues among the various cloud servers using efficient resource management techniques.
Information Processing	Many mobile devices form a platform that could allow users the ability to find useful information in a shorter range. For instance, the use of crowdsourcing technology which supports a collaborative information sharing platform with the help of the nearby mobile devices.	The challenge is the need for a stable network connection for communication between the devices that will not be easily affected by natural calamities or disasters (e.g., earthquake, tornadoes or tsunami).	An architecture that is able to provide a stable network connection for communication through users' collaborations, can be employed (Pelusi, et al., 2006). In such collaborations, local user's mobile devices become major components for storing, carrying and forwarding information with other individuals in a physical proximity.

continues on following page

Table 1. Continued

Applications	Techniques	Challenges	Solutions/Measures
Social Networking	Build a platform among various people with similar interests, activities in a network for sharing information with one another. This can be achieved by extending mobile-cloud technology in social contacts and establishing connections through individuals (via mobile devices).	The major challenge is to build context-awareness systems that are able to use contextual information (e.g., connectivity, cost, latency) to change and automatically reconfigure their configurations to adapt to the context.	Upon this, a context-aware data management architecture can be employed (Hoang & Jung, 2015). This architecture adopts the situational changes (e.g., local contexts) according to the user's needs through dynamic collaborations of services between mobile devices and cloud-assisted platforms.
Wildlife Monitoring and Management	Mobility-assisted automated management and monitoring system through the integration of wireless communication technologies and mobile devices. In this, mobile devices connect with one another via wireless local area network (WirelessLAN) for surveillance/tracking wildlife movements.	The major challenge is, how to increase the communication opportunities between various mobile devices and improve the throughput in the system though efficient users' collaborations during connection failures.	Upon this, locally available P2P network communications technology (e.g., BitTorrent) can be employed in such management and monitoring systems. This helps for an efficient collection of data and providing access to stable network services for real-time data management (Buchegger & Datta, 2009}.
Disaster Management	The use of mobile-cloud technology for disaster and emergency situations in which users share real-time information with one another located in a physical proximity. Users may broadcast useful information to their peers via Bluetooth or Wi-Fi communication technologies.	The challenge is the need for a stable network connection for an efficient management of high data traffic in the network during the time of a disaster and emergency situations.	An intelligent transportation system for disaster management with vehicular ad-hoc networks (VANETs) and mobile-cloud technology can be employed (Alazawi, et al., 2011). This is able to collect information from multiple sources and locations, including from the point of an incident. It then uses strategic algorithms to send updated information to the co-located users for an alternative route to the destination.
Smart-Tourism and Travel	Smart tourism uses mobile-cloud technology for scheduling, planning and to access/provide recommendations in the tourism industry. In this, with the help of a mobile app, a user can schedule, book and accesses (cloud-assisted) updated travel information in their mobile devices.	The major concern is the requirement for a continuous Internet connection for communication which is difficult to gain in rural/sparse areas or in areas with a high cost of Internet roaming.	To this end, mobile-cloud technology, using user's social interactions and collaborations can be enforced (Pelusi, et al., 2006). This would allow users for accessing locally available mobile networks through 'opportunistic communications', instead of relying upon a fixed infrastructure for communication.
Urban Traffic Controlling Systems	The use of cloud-assisted network enabled devices for massive data transportation to communicate and share information with one another. In this, real-time urban traffic controlling algorithm is used to manage/control system traffic and to response to the traffic conditions according to the real-time requirements.	The challenge is how to build a real-time traffic management system over a decentralized network that connects to a heterogeneous mobile-cloud platform. Moreover, this system requires a continuous network connection for connecting between the users' mobile device and the cloud server that may be unavailable in places that lack a communication infrastructure.	A mobile-cloud based smart trafficking system can be employed (Manolopoulos, et al., 2010). The proposed system is based on a mobile application which is running on each user's mobile device and a traffic prediction algorithm which is running inside the cloud server. This system provides a real-time guidance to the users and reconstructs the traffic model from the collected data for the future traffic predictions.

REFERENCES

Aggarwal, V., Gopalakrishnan, V., Jana, R., Ramakrishnan, K. K., & Vaishampayan, V. A. (2012). Optimizing cloud resources for delivering IPTV services through virtualization. In *The International Conference on Communication Systems and Networks (COMSNETS)*, (pp. 1-10). 10.1109/COMSNETS.2012.6151343

Ahmed, E., Gani, A., Khan, M. K., Buyya, R., & Khan, S. U. (2015). Seamless application execution in mobile cloud computing: Motivation, taxonomy, and open challenges. Elsevier Journal of Network and Computer Applications, 52, 154-172. doi:10.1016/j.jnca.2015.03.001

Alazawi, Z., Altowaijri, S., Mehmood, R., & Abdljabar, M. B. (2011). Intelligent disaster management system based on cloud-enabled vehicular networks. In *The IEEE ITS Telecommunications (ITST) International Conference*, (pp. 361-368). 10.1109/ITST.2011.6060083

Armbrust, M., Fox, A. R., Griffith, A. D., Joseph, R., Katz, A., Konwinski, G., … Zaharia. (2010). A View of Cloud Computing. ACM Communications, 53(4), 50-58.

Bowers, K. D., Juels, A., & Oprea, A. (2009). Hail: A high-availability and integrity layer for cloud storage. In *The ACM Conference on Computer and Communications Security (CCS)*, (pp. 187-198). 10.1145/1653662.1653686

Buchegger, S., & Datta, A. (2009). A case for P2P infrastructure for social networks opportunities & challenges. In *Annual Conference on Wireless On Demand Network Systems and Services (WONS)*, (pp. 161-168). 10.1109/WONS.2009.4801862

Cerqueira, E., Lee, E., Weng, J. T., Lim, J. H., Joy, J., & Gerla, M. (2014). Recent advances and challenges in human-centric multimedia mobile cloud computing. In *The International Conference on Computing, Networking and Communication (ICNC)*, (pp. 242-246). 10.1109/ICCNC.2014.6785339

Chandrasekhar, V., Andrews, J., & Gatherer, A. (2008). Femtocell networks: A survey. *IEEE Communications Magazine*, *46*(9), 59–67. doi:10.1109/MCOM.2008.4623708

Chang, C., Srirama, S., & Ling, S. (2012). An adaptive mediation framework for mobile P2P social content sharing. In C. Liu, H. Ludwig, F. Toumani, & Q. Yu (Eds.), Service-Oriented Computing(LNCS), (vol. vol. 7636, pp. 374-388). Springer. doi:10.1007/978-3-642-34321-6_25

Chen, Y. S., Kao, T. C., Sheu, J. P., & Chiang, C. Y. (2002). A mobile scaffolding-aid-based bird-watching learning system. In *The IEEE International Workshop on Wireless and Mobile Technologies in Education*, (pp. 15-22). 10.1109/WMTE.2002.1039216

Conti, M., & Giordano, S. (2014). Mobile ad hoc networking: Milestones, challenges, and new research directions. *IEEE Communications Magazine*, *52*(1), 85–96. doi:10.1109/MCOM.2014.6710069

Dascalu, M. I., Bodea, C. N., Moldoveanu, A., Mohora, M., Lytras, & de Pablos. (2015). A recommender agent based on learning styles for better virtual collaborative learning experiences. Computers in Human Behavior, 45, 243-253.

Dinh, H. T., Lee, C., Niyato, D., & Wang, P. (2013). A survey of mobile cloud computing: architecture, applications, and approaches. Wireless Communications and Mobile Computing, 13(18), 1587-1611. doi:10.1002/wcm.1203

Fernando, N., Loke, S. W., & Rahayu, W. (2012). Mobile Crowd Computing with Work Stealing. In *The IEEE 15th International Conference on Network-Based Information Systems (NBiS)*, (pp. 660-665).

Fernando, N., Loke, S. W., & Rahayu, W. (2013). Mobile cloud computing: A survey. *Future Generation Computer Systems*, *29*(1), 84–106. doi:10.1016/j.future.2012.05.023

Giurgiu, I., Riva, O., Juric, D., Krivulev, I., & Alonso, G. (2009). Calling the cloud: Enabling mobile phones as interfaces to cloud applications. In J. Bacon & B. Cooper (Eds.), *Middleware 2009* (Vol. 5896, pp. 83–102). doi:10.1007/978-3-642-10445-9_5

Han, Q., Liang, S., & Zhang, H. (2015). Mobile cloud sensing, big data, and 5g networks make an intelligent and smart world. *IEEE Network*, *29*(2), 40–45. doi:10.1109/MNET.2015.7064901

Hao, W., Walden, J., & Trenkamp, C. (2013). Accelerating e-commerce sites in the cloud. In *The IEEE Consumer Communications and Networking Conference* (pp. 605–608). CCNC.

Hoang, D. B., & Chen, L. (2010). Mobile Cloud for Assistive Healthcare (MoCAsH). In *The IEEE Asia-Pacific Conference on Services Computing (APSCC)*, (pp. 325-332).

Hoang, H., & Jung, J. (2015). An onto-logical framework for context-aware collaborative business process formulation. Computing and Informatics, 33(3), 553-569.

Huang, C. Y., Hsu, C. H., Chang, Y. C., & Chen, K. T. (2013). GamingAnywhere: An Open Cloud Gaming System. In *The 4th ACM Multimedia Systems Conference*, (pp. 36-47). 10.1145/2483977.2483981

Huang, D., Zhou, Z., Xu, L., Xing, T., & Zhong, N. (2011). Secure data processing framework for mobile cloud computing. In *The IEEE Conference on Computer Communications Workshops*, (pp. 614-618). 10.1109/INFCOMW.2011.5928886

Huang, Y. M., & Chiu, P. S. (2015). The effectiveness of a meaningful learning-based evaluation model for context-aware mobile learning. *British Journal of Educational Technology*, *46*(2), 437–447. doi:10.1111/bjet.12147

Hung, J. C., Hsu, V., & Wang, Y. B. (2011). A Smart-Travel System Based on Social Network Service for Cloud Environment. In *The IEEE International Conference on Intelligent Networking and Collaborative Systems (INCoS)*, (pp. 514-519). 10.1109/INCoS.2011.38

Hwang, I., Lee, Y., Park, T., & Song, J. (2012). Toward a mobile platform for pervasive games. In *The First ACM International Workshop on Mobile Gaming, ser. MobileGames'12, NY, USA*, (pp. 19-24). 10.1145/2342480.2342486

Klein, A., Mannweiler, C., Schneider, J., & Schotten, H. D. (2010). Access Schemes for Mobile Cloud Computing. In *The Eleventh International Conference on Mobile Data Management (MDM)*. IEEE.

Kumar, K., & Lu, Y. H. (2010). Cloud computing for mobile users: Can offloading computation save energy? IEEE Computer, 4(4), 51–56. doi:10.1109/MC.2010.98

Leung, C. H., & Chan, Y. Y. (2003). Mobile learning: a new paradigm in electronic learning. In *The 3rd IEEE International Conference on Advanced Learning Technologies*, (pp. 76-80). 10.1109/ICALT.2003.1215030

Li, B., Liu, Z., Pei, Y., & Wu, H. (2014). Mobility prediction based opportunistic computational offloading for mobile device cloud. In *The 17th International Conference on Computational Science and Engineering (CSE)*. IEEE. 10.1109/CSE.2014.161

Li, X., Zhang, H., & Zhang, Y. (2009). Deploying Mobile Computation in Cloud Service. In M.G. Jaatun, G. Zhao, & C. Rong (Eds.), Cloud Computing, (LNCS), (vol. 5931, p. 301-311). Springer.

Manolopoulos, V., Tao, S., Rodriguez, S., Is-mail, M., & Rusu, A. (2010). MobiTraS: A mobile application for a Smart Traffic System. In The IEEE International NEW Circuits And Systems (NEWCAS) conference, (pp. 365-368). doi:10.1109/NEWCAS.2010.5604010

Nkosi, M. T., & Mekuria, F. (2010). Cloud Computing for Enhanced Mobile Health Applications. In *The IEEE International Conference on Cloud Computing Technology and Science (CloudCom)*, (pp. 629-633). 10.1109/CloudCom.2010.31

Park, S., Jeong, S. H., & Hwang, C. (2008). Mobile IPTV Expanding the Value of IPTV. In *IEEE International Conference on Networking (ICN)*, (pp. 296-301). 10.1109/ICN.2008.8

Pelusi, L., Passarella, A., & Conti, M. (2006). Opportunistic networking: Data forwarding in disconnected mobile ad hoc networks. *IEEE Communications Magazine*, *44*(11), 134–141. doi:10.1109/MCOM.2006.248176

Qi, H., & Gani, A. (2012). Research on mobile cloud computing: Review, trend and perspectives. In *The International Conference on Digital Information and Communication Technology and its Applications (DICTAP)*. IEEE. 10.1109/DICTAP.2012.6215350

Qiu, L., Rui, H., & Whinston, A. (2015). When cellular capacity meets wifi hotspots: A smart auction system for mobile data of-oading. In *The 48th Hawaii International Conference on System Sciences (HICSS)*, (pp. 4898-4907). 10.1109/HICSS.2015.581

Ravi, N., Scott, J., Han, L., & Iftode, L. (2008). Context-aware battery management for mobile phones. In *The Sixth Annual IEEE International Conference on Pervasive Computing and Communications*, (pp. 224-233).

Satyanarayanan, M. (2010). Mobile computing: The next decade. In *The 1st ACM Workshop on Mobile Cloud Computing; Services: Social Networks and Beyond*, (pp. 51-56).

Satyanarayanan, M., Bahl, P., Caceres, R., & Davies, N. (2009). The case for vm-based cloudlets in mobile computing. IEEE Pervasive Computing, 8(4), 14-23. doi:10.1109/MPRV.2009.82

Scekic, O., Truong, H. L., & Dustdar, S. (2013). Incentives and rewarding in social computing. *Communications of the ACM*, *56*(6), 72–82. doi:10.1145/2461256.2461275

Sedayao, J., Su, S., Ma, X., Jiang, M., & Miao, K. (2009). A Simple Technique for Securing Data at Rest Stored in a Computing Cloud. In Z. Jaatun & C. Rong (Eds.), Cloud Computing, (LNCS), (vol. 5931, pp. 553–558). Springer Berlin Heidelberg. doi:10.1007/978-3-642-10665-1_51

Silva, B. M., Rodrigues, J. J., de la Torre Diez, I., Lopez-Coronado, M., & Saleem, K. (2015). Mobile-health: A review of current state in 2015. *Journal of Biomedical Informatics*, *56*, 265–272. doi:10.1016/j.jbi.2015.06.003 PMID:26071682

Tang, W. T., Hu, C. M., & Hsu, C. Y. (2010). A mobile phone based homecare management system on the cloud. In *International Conference on Biomedical Engineering and Informatics (BMEI)*. IEEE. 10.1109/BMEI.2010.5639917

Ting, R. Y. L. (2005). Mobile learning: current trend and future challenges. In *The IEEE International Conference on Advanced Learning Technologies (ICALT)*, (pp. 603-607). 10.1109/ICALT.2005.202

Varshney, U. (2001). Location Management Support for Mobile Commerce Applications. In *The 1st ACM International Workshop on Mobile Commerce*, (pp. 1-6). 10.1145/381461.381462

Wang, S., Liu, M., Cheng, X., Li, Z., Huang, J., & Chen, B. (2013). Opportunistic routing in intermittently connected mobile P2P networks. IEEE Selected Areas in Communications, 31(9), 369-378. doi:10.1109/JSAC.2013.SUP.0513033

Wang, X., Han, G., Du, X., & Rodrigues, J. (2015). Mobile cloud computing in 5g: Emerging trends, issues, and challenges. *IEEE Network*, *29*(2), 4–5. doi:10.1109/MNET.2015.7064896

Wang, Y., Huang, Y., & Louis, C. (2013). Towards a framework for privacy-aware mobile crowdsourcing. In *The International Conference on Social Computing (SocialCom)*, (pp. 454-459). 10.1109/SocialCom.2013.71

Whipple, J., Arensman, W., & Boler, M. S. (2009). A public safety application of GPS-enabled smartphones and the android operating system. In *IEEE International Conference on Systems, Man and Cybernetics*, (pp. 2059-2061). 10.1109/ICSMC.2009.5346390

Williams, P., & Maeder, A. (2015). Security and privacy issues for mobile health. In S. Adibi (Ed.), *Mobile Health, ser. Springer Series in Bio-Neuroinformatics* (Vol. 5, pp. 1067–1088). doi:10.1007/978-3-319-12817-7_44

Xue, R., Wu, Z. S., & Bai, A. N. (2011). Application of Cloud Storage in Traffic Video Detection. In *The IEEE International Conference on Computational Intelligence and Security (CIS)*, (pp. 1294-1297). 10.1109/CIS.2011.287

Zammit, S., Muscat, A., & Gauci, G. (2012). Mobile gaming on a virtualized infrastructure. In *The IEEE Mediterranean Electrotechnical Conference* (pp. 745–748). MELECON.

Zhou, L., Yang, Z., Rodrigues, J. J. P. C., & Guizani, M. (2013). Exploring blind online scheduling for mobile cloud multimedia services. IEEE Wireless Communications, 20(3), 54-61. doi:10.1109/MWC.2013.6549283

KEY TERMS AND DEFINITIONS

Cloud-Based Applications: Cloud-based applications refer to the traditional cloud-computing services. Users connect their mobile devices with the remote cloud servers via wireless networks (e.g., Wi-Fi access points) to avail these services.

Cloudlets: The cloudlets are a mobility-enhanced small-scale cloud data centre that provides powerful and resource-intensive services with lower latency.

Femtocell: Femtocell is an access point base station used for data offloading in an indoor environment. The major requirement for this is a small base station that helps gain access to an available Internet connection for data offloading.

Mobile Devices: Mobile devices are the smart mobile devices carried by the users. Smartphones and tablet computers are the most popular choices here.

Mobile Healthcare (M-Healthcare): A form of electronic healthcare (e-healthcare) technology that manages patient's clinical records as well as enabling a ubiquitous and uninterrupted access platform to provide these records to the doctors and caregivers using a mobile-based application.

Mobile Learning (M-Learning): The technology that creates a convenient learning platform for the users which is easily accessible from virtually anywhere. The fundamental basis of the m-learning technology is the use of mobile devices for learning purposes while users are travelling.

Mobile-Cloud Technology: Mobile-cloud technology is the abstraction of the cloud-based application that enables ubiquitous, convenient and on-demand network access to the services by the users' mobile devices via wireless networks.

ENDNOTES

1 http://www.mobilearn.org/

2 http://www.learningcitizen.net/

3 http://www.dfcint.com/wp/?p=311

4 http://www.saba.com/uk/social-collaboration/

5 http://www.zimbra.com/

This research was previously published in the Handbook of Research on Mobile Devices and Applications in Higher Education Settings edited by Francisco José García-Peñalvo, Laura Briz-Ponce, and Juan Antonio Juanes-Méndez; pages 53-71, copyright year 2016 by Information Science Reference (an imprint of IGI Global).

Chapter 7
Information and Communication Technologies as Drivers of Social Unrest

Martha Garcia-Murillo
Syracuse University, USA

Moinul Zaber
University of Dhaka, Bangladesh

Marcio Wohlers de Almeida
State University of Campinas – UNICAMP, Brazil

ABSTRACT

Information and communication technologies (ICTs) are alleviating frictions associated with the gathering and distribution of information, as well as reducing transaction costs related to the identifying, monitoring, and coordination of citizens dissatisfied with certain government policies. We conducted a random-effect logit tests based on a uniquely developed panel dataset of 138 countries from 2005 to 2014 to determine, ceteris paribus, whether or not ICTs play a role in facilitating changes to the status quo that gravitate against government policies. We found that ICTs although it can reduce hysteresis, the tendency to remain passive, inertia, is stronger. In addition, because ICTs are multi-purpose technologies they also support other beneficial economic and political activities which can explain why we don't see greater evidence of social unrest with these technologies. The literature on social unrest provide some clues about this phenomenon. People are willing to engage in these movements but it appears that only during a crisis.

INTRODUCTION

The goal of this chapter is to understand why information and communication technologies (ICTs) can be a powerful tool for citizens to protest against what they perceive to be unjust. We focus on the attributes of ICTs that are able to reduce friction in information gathering and distribution, as well as

DOI: 10.4018/978-1-7998-0417-8.ch007

reduce the transaction costs of searching for information and or people, monitoring their behavior, and coordinating participation among similarly concerned citizens. These attributes, we believe, can facilitate and enhance the emotional connections that people have with the problems they face. This century has seen, much more tangibly, the manner in which these technologies have facilitated, to a certain extent, social movements such as the Arab Spring in the Middle East, the Occupy and the Black Lives Matter movements in the U.S. and *Los Indignados* in Spain, among others. We believe that ICTs are opening virtual public spheres where the members of civil society are able to engage with peers and, at times of distress, to organize to protest against their governments.

Many scholars have studied social unrest and have tested different hypotheses to try to elucidate the causes of these movements. The main contribution of this paper is to make connections between neuroscience (in particular the emotional connections that are needed for people to get engaged in a social protest) and economics (in particular the manner in which fundamental concepts such as information friction and transaction costs are significantly reduced by ICTs), while also taking into consideration the contributions of the social sciences (in particular the factors that contribute to unrest). From this analysis, we find that, indeed, ICTs contribute to social manifestations of discontent.

Using data from the World Bank and other international organizations, we constructed a model to empirically determine if information technologies, specifically mobile devices and Internet access, lead to greater social unrest.

In addition to ICTs, we included three control factors that previous scholars have identified as contributors to a society's need to protest. These are: economic factors (income per capita), governance, and the size of the population.

LITERATURE REVIEW

Explaining Social Unrest

Social unrest can have different manifestations. It can be displayed in violent and uncontrolled ways, in more planned and organized public protests, and even in the form of nonviolent resistance, which, we believe, in the future may even take place exclusively online. There is a large body of scholarly work about social unrest.

Regarding social unrest specifically, Castells (2013) notes that social neuroscientists have shown that social change involves individual or collective actions that have emotional motivations. The main emotions involved in social change are fear, which results in precautionary behaviors such as withdrawal, and anger, which acts as a trigger to action. In other words, emotions push individuals towards action, which, with others, can evolve into collective action.

Castells' (2013) ideas about the role of emotional motivation in social change is supported by the social psychological theory of protest. Van Stekelenburg and Klandermans (2013), for example, have provided a sound literature review on social psychological issues explaining peoples' reasons for protesting. The authors stress that group-based emotions, including anger, are important motivators of protest participation.

The literature about protests has found that individuals are relatively slow to respond to the problems they face. There is, therefore, a delay between a problem and a reaction from citizens. Scholars have modeled the process in terms of movement from a passive state, when civil society is not engaged, to an active state, which can involve street protests, for example. This swift passage from passive to active is shown in Figure 1, which represents the delay or reluctance that people show before they decide to get involved. F1 is the point at which people are no longer satisfied with the problematic situation they are facing and decide to act. They remain active until things get better at point F2, when it is no longer justifiable or necessary to remain active.

This phenomenon is getting greater attention in other fields like economics, where, for example, Liu, Hassanpour, Tatikonda, and Morse (2012) describe how a network of individuals may or may not be willing to participate in collective action, depending on their level of risk and the number of other people engaged. For people to get engaged, they need to know that their discontent is shared by other people, and they must be willing to join in. Under an oppressive regime, nobody wants to be involved in an unsuccessful attempt to protest against their government, as this can result in severe retaliations, such as those experienced in Turkey after a failed coup attempt in July of 2015.

In this study, we were concerned only with the first part of the sigmoidal curve, as we were mainly interested in the factors that lead a society to move from passive to active, from idleness to protest, in the presence of perceived economic or political problems. In this respect, we believe that ICTs may

Figure 1. Public attitude versus perceived seriousness of the problem. (Adapted from Scheffer, Westley, & Brock, 2003)

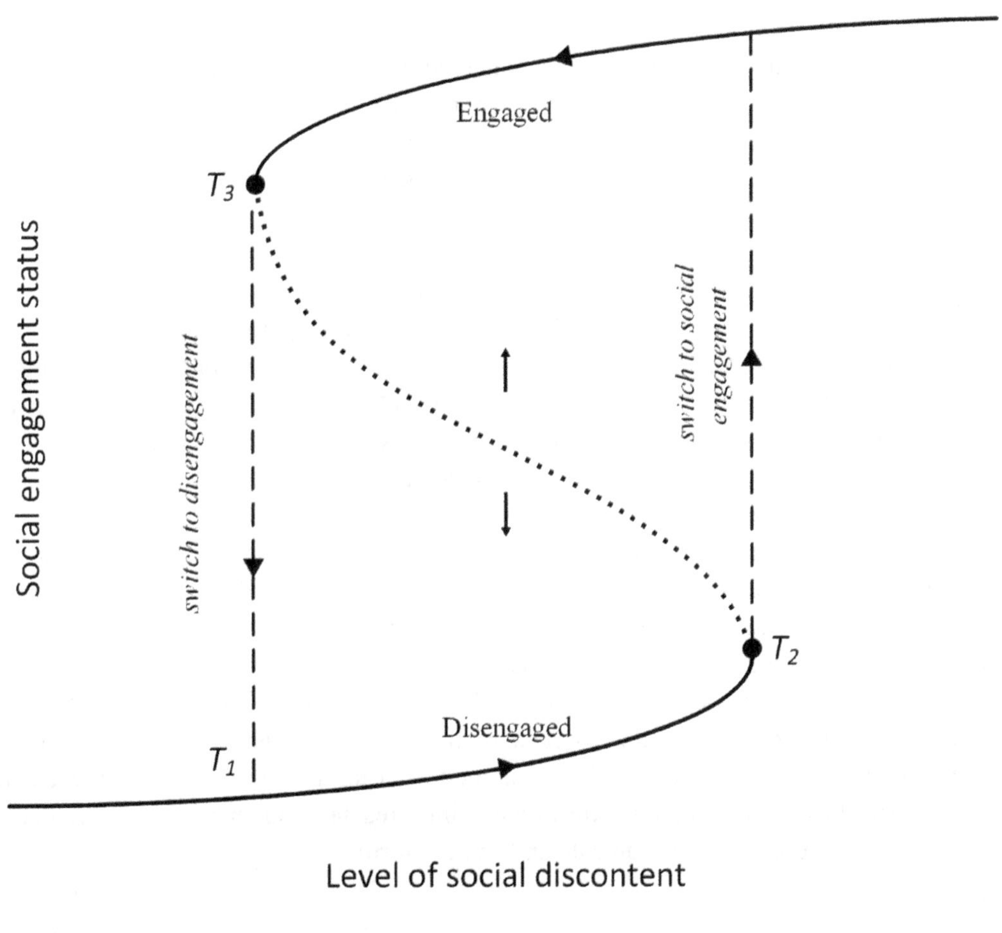

shorten the time it takes, and the frequency with which people wait, to get organized. Hysteresis, which is the tendency to remain constant in spite of changes in the environment, is analogous to the delay that we see in societies before they are willing to get engaged more visibly when faced with a problem. As Kuran (1991) explains, in the absence of information about other's people's concerns, each risk-averse citizen, falsifies his/her preference until a threshold is reach when people are willing to display their private preferences and get engaged in a public protest. We may thus find that ICTs reduce hysteresis, meaning the tendency to maintain the status quo, due to the ease with which they can make people aware of problems.

It is clear that research about social movements points to two key elements that prompt people to get involved: the dissatisfaction that they feel about a situation and an emotional connection to dissatisfied others that may prompt them to act. According to Jovanović, Renn, and Schröter (2012), social unrest is an expression of collective dissatisfaction, where the intensity of the protest depends on the level and nature of the social discontent.

Pappas and O'Malley (2014) identified four groups of causes that can lead people to take to the streets to express their dissatisfaction: economic, cultural, socio-ideological, and state-related.

There are examples in the literature that support Jovanović, Renn, and Schröter's definition. In Argentina in 1993, for example, government employees rioted and burned three government buildings, as well as the houses of local politicians and government officers. Scholars who studied the event found that the government employees had not been paid in more than three months; moreover, instances of corruption, nepotism, and police repression had led to "psychological states of indignation, frustration and/or resentment" (Auyero, 2003, p. 121).

Today, we see, potentially, more instances of this type of abuses, not necessarily because there are more of them but because ICTs have made them more public globally.

Dewey, Kaden, Marks, Matsushima, and Zhu (2012), for example, documented seven of the Arab Spring uprisings, all of which show that economic and government-related problems contributed to these social protests.

Regarding state motivators for unrest, Tunisia, Egypt, Yemen, Jordan, Bahrain, Syria, and Morocco were all governed by authoritarian regimes, and many lacked free elections and/or had restrictions imposed on the creation of new parties. In addition, they lacked transparency and showed little respect for the rule of law and the protection of civil liberties. Corruption was also prevalent in many of these countries. In Egypt, for example, President Mubarak was believed to have accumulated between $40 USD and $70 USD billion and business associates close to his son to have accumulated $1 billion USD (Jack, 2011). Similarly, people in Tunisia, Syria, and Yemen were outraged at the level of corruption and nepotism displayed by their governments.

Given this more recent evidence, we believe that information and communication technologies, as explained below, can also contribute by reducing the frictions associated with information gathering and distribution, and by reducing the costs of searching and monitoring other people's reactions and coordinating social action, making these manifestations of discontent more salient.

In isolation it is difficult for people to find out whether their discontent with government is shared and if other people are willing to protest, and could lead, we believe, to many fewer instances of social unrest.

As we will describe in the next section, ICTs can incite a faster transition from passive to active participation, due to the fact that the tipping or threshold point is reached sooner because these technologies are available to enable people to communicate and share information.

The Role of ICTs in Helping Citizens Get Organized

Previous generations faced challenges when trying to make policy changes or changes in government. These citizens did not have the tools needed to find and share information about government incompetencies, for example, nor did they have the means to coordinate their efforts against perceived injustices. ICTs have, however, improved information and access.

ICTs are "a diverse set of technological tools and resources used to communicate, and to create, disseminate, store and manage information" (Blurton, 1999). However, technology alone is not, per se, a solution to society's problems; it is the people who own them and the manner in which they use and apply them. ICTs allow people to access information and to communicate with one another, facilitating more informed decisions.

There are several reasons why ICTs can be particularly effective in coordinating people for the purpose of expressing their collective dissatisfaction with their government (Kaur & Tao, 2014): (1) ICTs are interactive, so that they can facilitate conversation, not only between two people, but among many simultaneously; (2) they are permanently available, barring any government blocks – once a population has acquired mobile phones or has access to the Internet, these tools are available to them anytime they need them; (3) they aren't bound by geography and have, in fact, a global reach, which means that social movements can coordinate and bring together people from all corners of a nation, or even the world; (4) the actual costs, as well as the transaction costs, of communication have decreased significantly, making it affordable for most people.

In his book *Networks of Outrage and Hope*, Castells (2013) highlights ten characteristics of social movements that are particular to this Internet age. The movements: (1) are networked using the Internet and wireless devices that allow for mass communication with powerful images; (2) are horizontal networks that create a sense of fellowship that helps to overcome fear and find hope, while facilitating and encouraging cooperation; (3) are triggered by a spark of outrage in a spontaneous manner; (4) become viral due to the easy dissemination of information on the Internet, which is reinforced by the demonstration effect of other social events; (5) convert indignation into an autonomous entity, which usually happens through decisions made in a space of autonomy; (6) are self-reflexive and constantly question what they want, with a governance structure that can help them avoid the pitfalls of failed movements; and (7) are generally nonviolent. However, (8) they tend to occupy public spaces to pressure political authorities and business representatives, and (9) they rarely have a focus, except in cases of rebellions against dictatorial regimes. They have many and varied demands, in order not to produce an organization or leadership, because agreements proceed from their collective decisions and detailed protest plans, and (10) they intend to transform the state but not radically change it.

These technologies are thus able to create links among people who lacked them prior to their prevalence and use in society. They expanded the "neighborhood" to reach all corners of the globe and multiply the number of channels that people have to distribute or obtain information.

We know from experimental research in psychology that people are highly influenced in their actions by the actions of others (Latane & Darley, 1968). It is clear, thus, that knowing what others are doing will influence a person's behavior. Before ICTs were more widely available, it would have taken much longer for a person to know what fellow citizens were feeling about their government. Today, the public has many tools for communicating with people they don't know. With a few keystrokes, a person can easily share information on practically any topic or event. Mobile phones, for example, allow people to connect to others through blogs, Facebook postings e-mail, tweets and SMSs. On the Internet, they can find limitless information, and with a broadband connection, they can make, share, and access videos.

We may thus find that the inertia (hysteresis) or reluctance that people may feel about getting involved can be eased by their getting to know, through these technologies, that there are many peers as dissatisfied as themselves.

ICTs as a communication resource affect people's perceptions due to a reduction of both information friction and transaction costs. Information friction stems from the limited information that the population has about the preferences and concerns of their fellow citizens. Reductions in transaction costs include a reduction of the cost of searching, which in the case of protests means both for information about a problem and for people who may have similar negative perception about it, a reduction of monitoring costs, which, for social unrest to happen, means knowing about the amount of people who may also feel discontent about a specific problem, and a reduction of coordination costs of participating in public demonstrations about the issues of concern. In the past, people had to dedicate time and resources looking for information that was spread through means such as radio, TV, newspapers, and word-of-mouth. Today it is much easier, due to the fact that people can simply subscribe to news, follow tweets or Facebook posts, and read at their leisure. This cursory awareness is, in fact, a form of monitoring that takes little effort. Coordination is another factor that has significantly changed with the spread of ICTs. In this respect, we made an important distinction that does not appear in the literature. We divided ICTs into coordination and information technologies, with cell phones being primarily a coordination tool, and the Internet primarily an information tool. Because cell phones convey short messages with basic information, people can quickly get information about the location and time of an organized event. However, if they need more in-depth information about an issue, they will find it more convenient to do it through a broadband connection, with a larger screen that allows them to navigate to multiple sources.

Information technologies, with their ability to reduce information friction and transaction costs, also enable leaders to emerge much faster. An opinion leader who finds an audience can quickly acquire a large number of followers through likes and the spreading of links to the leader's site. These leaders, as Scheffer et al. (2003) indicate, can precipitate a rapid shift in opinion.

If one looks back at work on group processes in the literature, such as the book edited by Berkowitz (1978), we find that decentralized groups, in which information is distributed and accessible to everyone, are more productive (Shaw, 1964). At the time Shaw was writing about this, we find that without these technologies the amount of information and coordination that a person could handle significantly limited the size and activities of a group. From an information-handling perspective, previously, the problems of noise and distribution were significant because there were no tools like these, and the size of the groups was consequently limited, but with these technologies, groups can correct mistakes (also they can be larger), and provide unlimited access to information flows. In sum, ICTs are able to reduce information friction when larger groups of people need to coordinate their work.

Today, even traditional media outlets have moved to the digital realm, creating what Wilson calls a media "ecosystem," a closely knit network of information producers where entities public, private and, we would argue, citizens, participate (Palmer & Perkins, 2012) These new digital information outlets have opened spaces for participation, openness, and knowledge/content creation (Palmer & Perkins, 2012).

Given the unique characteristics of these technologies, there has been greater interest in studying their role in the policy field. Lopes (2014), for example, explores the impact of social media on social movements. Using a data set that includes economic, social, and political conditions, she uncovers a relationship between those conditions and social media. Using Internet penetration as a proxy variable for social media, she found, is a strong predictor of protest activity. From this, she concludes that social media is the "latest and most revolutionary tool in the formation of social movements" (p. 5).

In fact, although there is some evidence that these technologies are not sufficient to produce social unrest (Dewey et al., 2012), some recent studies suggest that social media, which is made possible by ICTs, may have contributed to the Arab Spring (Ghannam, 2011). Thus, we expect that, given the political instability related to poverty, education, and governance factors, ICTs may lead to greater instability because people can more easily organize. From an economic perspective, this would mean an upward shift in the relationship between ICTs and protests as ICTs become more widely accessible to a population.

Figure 2 shows the increase in average subscriptions of both mobile phones and broadband, and Figure 3 provides an early indication of the growth in social unrest that has been experienced around the world over the last ten years.

Twitter was founded in 2006, and the great recession happened in 2008. We see a slight increase in social unrest just before the crisis and then a significant increase two and a half years later. These two graphs require additional scrutiny, which is the focus of the empirical analysis.

Beyond statistics, we find cases of the impact of ICTS even in a country like China, where citizens face severe limitations on their civil liberties. An example of the manner in which ICTs are becoming an important information mechanism for people to mobilize is described by MacKinnon (2009), who discusses the case of Guo Baofeng, a blogger who was arrested in 2009 by police on suspicious rape charges. At the time of his arrest, he sent a tweet that led to bloggers' organizing to get him released. One set up a campaign to get hundreds of people to mail postcards to the detention center where Mr. Guo was being held. Others organized fundraising to pay for his defense. These efforts eventually led to his release two weeks later. As MacKinnon explains, if this event had taken place ten years earlier, few people would have known of it at all through the traditional media, much less the public at large in real time.

Similarly, in 2001 in China, ICTs contributed to a social movement following an explosion at a school that killed 41 people in Jiangxi Province. The initial official report had blamed the blast to a single person. Using the Internet, parents at the school contradicted the government's explanation, explaining instead that the explosion was caused by school children who were forced to work constructing firecrackers on the school grounds. Although the government deleted many of these postings, enough remained to

Figure 2. Average subscription to mobile phones per 100 and fixed broadband subscription per 100 (in logarithmic scale) over the years 2005 to 2014. Data Source: ITU

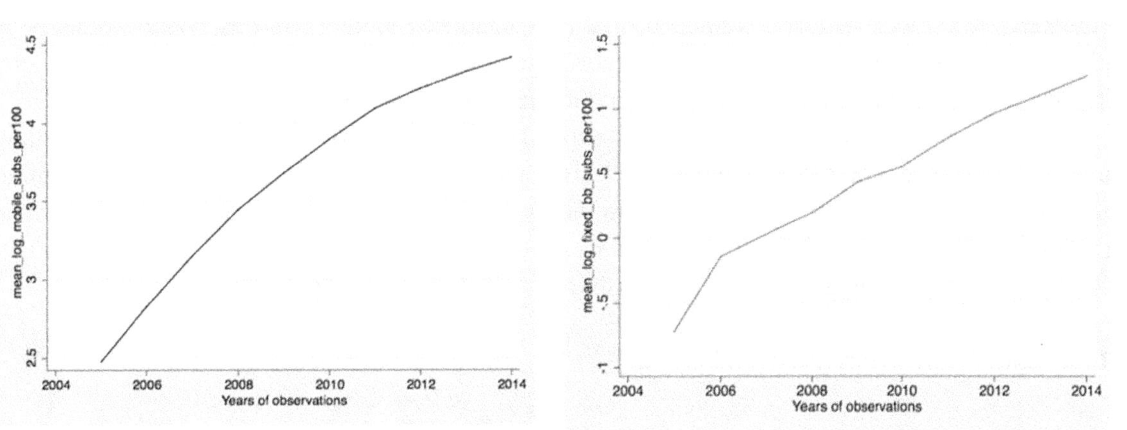

Figure 3. Increase in reports of social unrest over the years 2005 to 2014. Data Source: (Democracy, 2016)

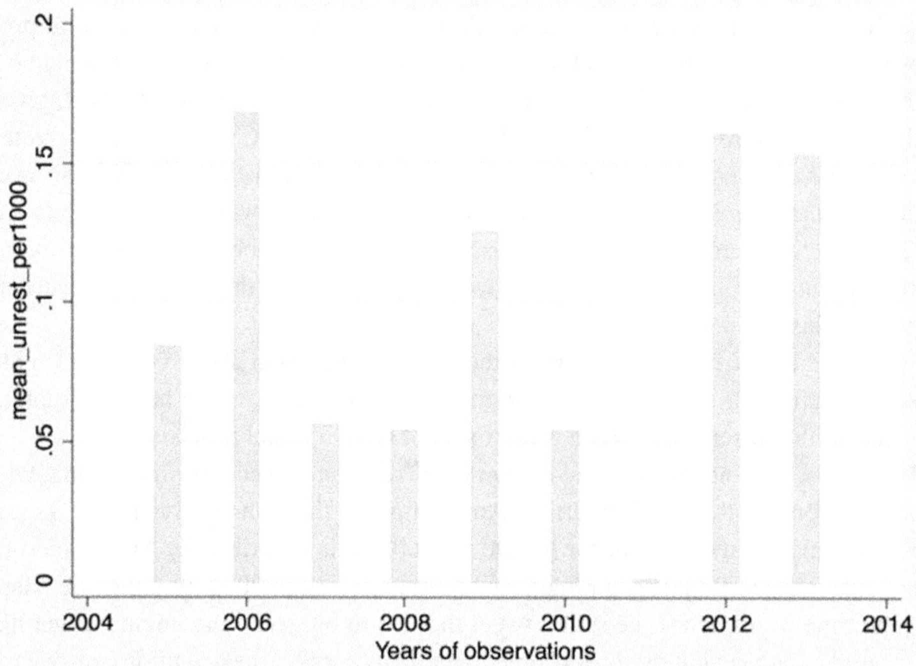

eventually lead to an unprecedented official apology by Zhu Rongji, then Prime Minister (Kalathil & Boas, 2010; C. Smith, 2001).

In Indonesia, as Lim (2003) explains, warnets (public rooms with computers) were the main source for "forbidden" information. The mailing list *Apakabar*, founded by an American, John McDougall, forwarded Indonesian-related news all over the world, including messages about corruption by Suharto and his cronies, and contributed to the online emergence of the Indonesia Communist Party (PKI). Furthermore, Indonesian students abroad coordinated through an e-mail-based newsletter, *Suara Demokrasi* (voice of Democracy). All of these channels of communication eventually contributed to the fall of President Suharto (Kalathil & Boas, 2003)

As these cases show, ICTs create spaces where citizens can express their contentions with government and feel free to criticize it. The relationships that ICTs can foster among families, friends, other people with similar interests, and civil society organizations generate spontaneous or coordinated efforts aimed at protesting a government's inability to respond to the needs of the population.

In addition to facilitating protests, ICTs also expand human emotions. ICTs, Castells (2013) believes, create horizontal networks that feed movements in both local and global dimensions, producing enthusiasm that strengthens social mobilization intentionality. It is the Internet, he argues, that turns untreated responses into movements of political importance.

In light of the preceding discussion, we wish to test the following hypothesis:

H1: ICTs are likely to increase social unrest.

While we are interested in the role of ICTs, it would be unrealistic to ignore other factors that can contribute to the emergence of these movements. Because of this, our econometric analysis includes economic factors, political factors (specifically, governance), and the size of the population as control elements that can contribute to a society's need to protest.

Other Factors That Contribute to Social Unrest

Social unrest is not an isolated phenomenon; because of this, our empirical analysis includes other factors found in the literature, described below. Figure 4 presents these additional variables.

Economic Factors

In 1970, Gurr published the book *Why Men Rebel*, in which he argues that when people are negatively affected by economic factors, such as a general economic recession or more specific feelings of deprivation, it can lead to frustration, and thus, aggression.

Figure 4. Theoretical model of factors influencing social unrest

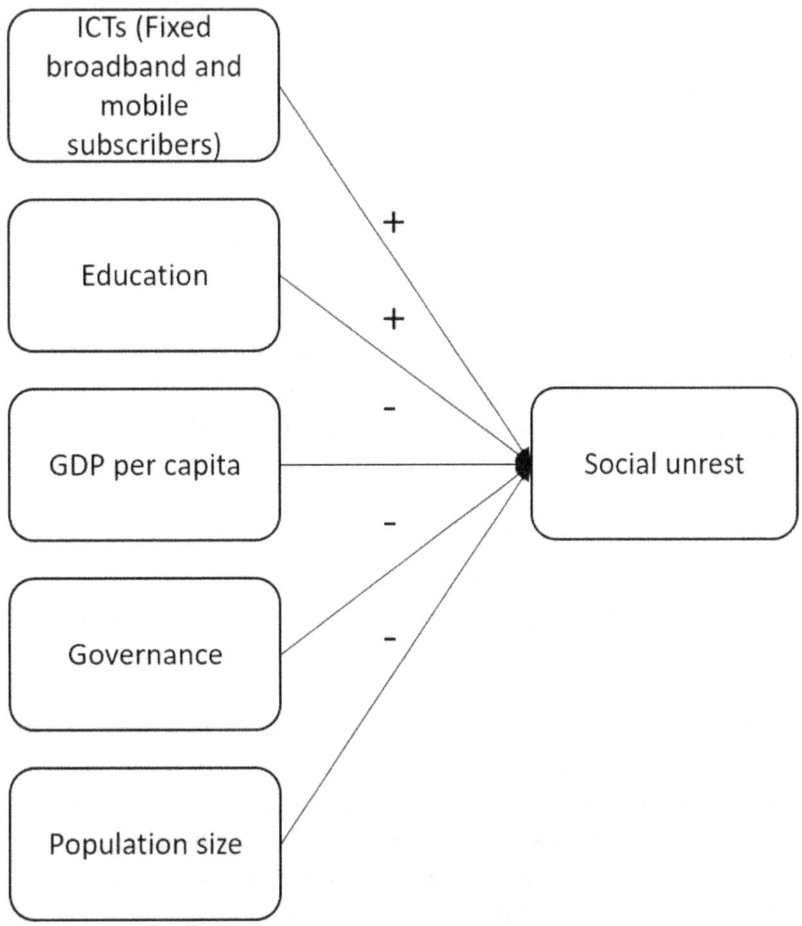

Economic conditions such as depressions and crises that lead to austerity measures can negatively affect employment opportunities and wages. Other scholars (Bohlken & Sergenti, 2010; Brandt & Ulfelder, 2011) have also found that a country is likely to experience social unrest when its economic growth is slow, while the contrary is true when its economy is growing. A similar result was found among European countries, where instances of social unrest increased when public spending as a percentage of GDP decreased, and the probability of protests almost doubled when these cuts reached 5% of GDP.

The 2008 "Great Recession" led to citizen protests. In some countries, these continued for months, while in others they dissipated relatively quickly. In the U.S. and the U.K., for example, Roberts (2013) explains, people ceased their manifestations of discontent due to quantitative easing that limited the extent to which the recession affected them.

Roubini (2011) warned about social unrest coming from inadequate economic responses to market forces. For instance, firms' cutting jobs because of inadequate consumer demand. This rational decision on the part of individual firms is destructive to society at large, and, if it is not dealt with well by governments, can generate widespread discontent.

We need to be concerned about these manifestations of discontent because of the impact they have on a country's economy. Justino (2005), for example, found a correlation between social unrest and reductions in economic growth. She argues that frequent episodes of civil unrest significantly reduce the potential for economic growth and poverty reduction. In short, civil unrest can lead to poverty. However, it is also true that poverty induces civil unrest. The magnitude of recent social and political instability in many developing countries has brought social conflict to the forefront of modern development economics.

In his book *The End of Protest - How Free-Market Capitalism Learned to Control Dissent*, Roberts (2013) presents an analysis of the factors that lead to social protest. He states that unrest is an intrinsic part of the free market model, a problem identified earlier by thinkers like Polany and Schumpeter. These authors, Roberts (2013) states, noted the natural tendency of loosely regulated markets to create discontent. However, in the United States and England, unrest emerged during the Great Recession, the worst economic crisis in a generation, but not to the extent expected, because these countries developed new methods for reconciling the neoliberal disdain for democratic politics with the immediate need to avert a total economic meltdown.

In the 19th century, politics were routinely shaped by mass action on the part of citizens in the form of strikes, demonstrations, marches, and riots. Currently, preventing crowds into mass action depends on the effectiveness of democratic institutions to give expression to public frustration about the economy (Roberts, 2013).

One of the aims of protesters since the financial crisis has been to point out the ways in which the democratic process has been undermined during the neoliberal age and to denounce democratic institutions that have been captured by well-heeled interests. In others words, the institutions that are supposed to function as the vehicle for responding to public discontent have been hobbled so that they cannot do this properly.

More recently, Della Porta (2015) presents a broad perspective analyzing social unrest under the conditions of income concentration, unemployment, and under-unemployment. She makes a distinction between the salariat, such as the 29th century's industrial workers, and the precariat. These, she argues, constitute the main participants of social unrest and encompass people without formal employment and social protection, as well as disadvantaged youth. She also explores the influence of neoliberalism and its crises on protest movements. In this respect, she argues that the precariat is reinforced by neoliberal policies that reduce social protections in favor of pro-market solutions.

Social movements do not begin only because of social inequality or political despair. They also require an emotional mobilization triggered by outrage and hopes for a possible change. They are fueled by movements in other parts of the world whose successes have been spread by the Internet.

The 1993 riot in Argentina occurred in Santiago del Estero, where almost a third of the population at the time was unable to satisfy basic needs. The city had the lowest income level and the lowest life expectancy (Auyero, 2003). When a population is living with incomes at or below the poverty line, it is reasonable to expect that, feeling pressure, they will protest to influence the government to change their circumstances (Alesina & Perotti, 1996). They have nothing to lose so that they decide to demonstrate, or even engage in acts of terrorism (Abadie, 2006). As their income increases, they grow busy with their lives, and, being a bit more satisfied, they may be more reluctant to protest, leading to greater political stability. We should thus expect that as income increases, so should stability.

We thus tested the following hypothesis:

H2: The lower the GDP per capita, the more likely social unrest.

Governance

An efficient and effective state is open, transparent, and accountable to the population (Theobald, 2002). Poor governance affects the poor, which can in turn push citizens to the streets to call for the prosecution of corrupt behavior.

Poor governance can potentially have two effects on the likelihood of protests. On one hand, it can be a powerful motivating factor that can lead people to protest when they realize how poor policy decisions and corruption are affecting their country, and them personally. For example, poorly paid, or even unpaid, government employees can take advantage of their positions to "sell favors" in the form of government services and to commit even more serious offences, such as selling weapons to drug cartels or approving lucrative public work contracts. The main concern is when money is diverted from the economy at the hands of public officials to illegally supply public services.

Governments that profit from the status quo will try to limit protest, resist any changes and simply put in place cosmetic solutions that lead the population to think that something is being done, while, in reality, the problem persists. In addition, given the personal benefits that these individuals receive and the power they hold, they can delay or block changes in government (Magee, 1989).

Examples from many countries provide evidence of a link between social unrest and ineffective or corrupt governments. In China, for example, Sun (1991) attributes to government corruption the 1989 protests in Beijing. Also in China, Chen (2000) attributes labor protests to corruption and the ineffectiveness of state enterprises that systematically eroded salaries and subjected workers to coercive labor controls.

Similarly, Lippman (2014) explains how protests in Bosnia-Herzegovina, which resulted in several torched government buildings, could be traced to pervasive government corruption in the country, and in India, the actions of Anna Hazare, who began a protest fast against public corruption, and ultimately died, was the starting point for the Hazare Movement, which resulted in protests in many sectors of the economy.

Even in a world where citizens have greater access to ICTs, governments play an important role in the success that citizens may have in using these tools to get organized. In this respect, Lessig has indicated that governments can regulate the Internet through the technical code that runs the network or through their laws and regulations (Lessig, 1999).

This is not more evident than in China, where the government decided in 1996 that connections to the Internet were going to be arranged through a two-tier system, where users connect to a first level of servers, which in turn connects to a second tier of servers controlled by the state (Kalathil & Boas, 2010). Similarly, as described by Kalathil and Boas (2003) in Saudi Arabia and the United Arab Emirates, the government uses technology that blocks both pornographic and political sites. Studies of other countries, like Egypt and Turkey (Kalathil & Boas, 2003), indicate that censorship of participation happens when governments make very public crackdowns against the use of ICTS that have political or socially inappropriate content.

In this study, we thus tested the following hypothesis:

H3: Poor governance in a country will lead to higher instances of social unrest.

METHOD AND DATA DESCRIPTION

Using data from the World Bank and other international organizations, we assembled panel data that tested the impact of ICTs on political stability through the variables of income, governance, and size of the population.

To analyze the data, we used a panel dataset from 2005-2014 encompassing 128 countries from 2005 to 2014. The dataset is unique in that it was constructed by merging data from various sources. The appendix provides a more detailed description for each of the variables, summary statistics and correlations among the variables. The data come from:

- The World Bank database, which provided us with data on GDP per capita, education enrollment and population. We used log transformations of both the GDP and population variables;
- The International Social Science Resource, produced by Witold J. Henisz, who constructed the Political Constraint Index Dataset (POLCON III), where POLCON = 0 means minimum constraint, or the most unstable political environment, and POLCON = 1 means maximum constraint, or the most stable political environment. POLCON III is an attempt to measure political constraint, that is, to recognize underlying political structures and measure their ability to support credible policy commitments (National Bureau of Economic Research, 2015). This is also our proxy variable for governance;
- The International Telecommunication Union, where data on broadband subscriptions and mobile subscriptions are available. We used the log of both broadband subscribers per 100 in the overall population and mobile subscribers per 100 in our estimations;
- The Freedom house, that reports the press freedom index of the countries of the world. The index is a numerical score calculated from evaluating the "legal environment for the media, political pressures that influence reporting, and economic factors that affect access to news and information (Freedom House, 2016)".
- The University of Illinois Urbana-Champaign which provided the dependent variable unrest, which represents a weighted conflict index taken from its Civil Unrest Data (Cline Center for Democray, 2016). The variable that indicates unrest is termed domestic9 in the estimation – it is a weighted index of the number of reports of protest in the country in question. The weighted index is based on reports of assassinations, general strikes, guerrilla warfare, government crises, purges, riots, revolutions, and anti-government demonstrations.

Tables 1 and 2 present the regression results of the cross-national panel regression conducted on the variable *social unrest*. We have used a level-log linear model to ascertain the impact of the explanatory variables on unrest variable. The model helps to reduce the effect of possible outliers and also handles the non-linear relationship between the dependent variable and some of the independent variables. Using log makes the relationship non-linear while still preserving the linear nature of the model.

The general model for the estimation is given below:

$$Unrest_{it} = \beta_0 + \boldsymbol{logICT}_{it}\beta_1 + \boldsymbol{Politic}_{it}\beta_2 + \boldsymbol{logDemographic}_{it}\beta_3 + +\varepsilon_{it},$$

Where *i* indicates countries, *t* indicates years, *unrest* is a variable that indicates number of protests (in thousands) in a country in a given year, the vector *ICT* stands for the explanatory variables: log of mobile (log_mobile_subs_per100) and broadband subscriptions (log_fixed_bb_subs_per100). *Politic* indicates the political structure variable (polcon3). *logDemographic* indicates the demographic variables, GDP per Capita PPP (log_gdp), *Population* (log_pop). *logEducation* indicates educational enrollment. Finally, ε_{it} indicates the error for that observation.

Table 1. Regression results by region

			East Asia and Ocenia	South Asia	Middle East	Africa	Europe	North America	South America
	1	2	3	4	5	6	7	8	9
VARIABLES	unrest per1000	unrest per1000	unrest per1000	unrest per1000	unrest per1000	unrest per1000	unrest per1000	unrest per1000	unrest per1000
polcon3	0.07	-0.01	0.36**	0.10	0.21	-0.24	0.08*	0.14***	-0.03
	(0.056)	(0.083)	(0.149)	(0.067)	(0.142)	(0.267)	(0.045)	(0.054)	(0.052)
log_gdp	0.04**	0.07*	-0.09**	0.02	0.02	0.19**	-0.02	-0.02*	0.02
	(0.018)	(0.037)	(0.045)	(0.039)	(0.035)	(0.079)	(0.017)	(0.010)	(0.024)
log_pop	-0.02**	-0.14***	-0.04***	-0.01	-0.03	-0.11**	-0.01	-0.00	0.01
	(0.010)	(0.028)	(0.014)	(0.005)	(0.028)	(0.054)	(0.009)	(0.001)	(0.006)
log_education enrollment	0.09	-0.30	0.70	-0.17**	-0.53	0.59	-0.77**	0.36**	0.06
	(0.177)	(0.290)	(0.758)	(0.084)	(0.437)	(0.567)	(0.379)	(0.164)	(0.442)
log_fixed_bb subs_per100	-0.02***	-0.04***	0.02	-0.01	-0.00	-0.10***	-0.01	-0.00	-0.02***
	(0.006)	(0.010)	(0.019)	(0.016)	(0.014)	(0.031)	(0.005)	(0.004)	(0.007)
log_mobile subs_per100	-0.01	0.00	-0.01	0.01	0.02	-0.09**	-0.01	-0.01	-0.01
	(0.008)	(0.013)	(0.030)	(0.008)	(0.021)	(0.038)	(0.008)	(0.006)	(0.008)
t	0.01***	0.01**	-0.01	-0.00	0.01	0.06***	0.01***	0.00***	0.00
	(0.003)	(0.004)	(0.010)	(0.008)	(0.007)	(0.018)	(0.002)	(0.001)	(0.003)
Constant	-0.03	1.79***	1.53***	-0.04	0.17	-0.19	0.25	0.21**	-0.23
	(0.249)	(0.584)	(0.500)	(0.420)	(0.597)	(1.307)	(0.215)	(0.105)	(0.221)
Observations	1,233	499	129	57	161	213	462	41	170
R-squared									
Number of cn	132	116	13	7	19	29	41	4	19

Standard errors in parentheses
*** p<0.01, ** p<0.05, * p<0.1

Table 2. Regression results by freedom index

	freedom 1	freedom 2	freedom 3	freedom 4	freedom 5	freedom 6	freedom 7
	10	11	12	13	14	15	16
VARIABLES	unrest per1000	unrest per1000	unrest per1000	unrest per1000	unrest per1000	unrest per1000	unrest per1000
polcon3	-0.02	0.11	-0.08	0.33	-0.11	-0.01	3.39*
	(0.029)	(0.066)	(0.148)	(0.229)	(0.282)	(0.055)	(1.948)
log_gdp	-0.01	0.01	0.01	-0.03	0.21	-0.01	0.48***
	(0.011)	(0.033)	(0.043)	(0.102)	(0.167)	(0.011)	(0.151)
log_pop	-0.00	0.00	-0.03	-0.08	-0.16*	0.00	-0.09
	(0.003)	(0.013)	(0.018)	(0.055)	(0.085)	(0.007)	(0.088)
log_enrollment	0.28	0.29	0.44	0.21	-0.56	-0.14*	1.40
	(0.273)	(0.213)	(0.368)	(0.823)	(0.905)	(0.077)	(1.711)
log_fixed_bb_subs_per100	0.00	-0.01	-0.01	-0.04	-0.05	0.00	-0.18***
	(0.004)	(0.008)	(0.016)	(0.025)	(0.038)	(0.005)	(0.060)
log_mobile_subs_per100	0.00	-0.01	0.00	0.05	-0.15*	0.00	-0.12*
	(0.006)	(0.014)	(0.017)	(0.038)	(0.083)	(0.007)	(0.065)
t	-0.00	0.01	0.01	-0.02	0.07***	-0.00	0.11***
	(0.001)	(0.005)	(0.008)	(0.014)	(0.025)	(0.003)	(0.043)
Constant	0.11	-0.10	0.39	1.47	0.86	0.14	-3.42
	(0.109)	(0.384)	(0.517)	(1.282)	(2.052)	(0.150)	(2.573)
Observations	482	175	160	106	82	160	68
R-squared							
Number of cn	48	31	36	33	21	30	13

Standard errors in parentheses
*** p<0.01, ** p<0.05, * p<0.1

ANALYSIS OF RESULTS

The model (1) described in the previous section was scrutinized with the help of a cross national time series data. Econometric estimations of such datasets may have systematic differences among coefficients. In order to reduce country specific biases, fixed effect (FE) estimation methods are often used. Along with country specific biases, a time series estimation may also have time specific biases. More specifically, many of the occurrences of unrest around the world may be due to global events at a specific time of a specific year. We therefore introduce a variable 't' to capture any time specific effect. In order to ensure the appropriateness of the use of FE method we conducted a Hausman test. A statistically significant p-value of the test indicates there may be a systematic difference in the coefficients, and we should prefer the fixed-effects ("within") model rather than include the random-effects ("between") model. However, in the case of the datasets we have employed, the p-value was not found to be significant. Hence we had to assume RE method over FE method. This is particularly important for variables such as Population and GDP per Capita, because they do not change much and hence would be dropped if fixed effect is assumed. Hence all the estimations in tables 1 and 2 use random effect model. In this context we would like to emphasize that, there is not much difference in both the direction and magnitude of the independent variables in RE and FE methods.

Tables 1 and 2 summarize the findings of the estimate. Estimation 1 is the cross country analysis consisting of the countries in the world that are in the dataset while estimation 2 only covers the country-year pair that do not have any 0 value for the unrest variable. Estimation 2 therefore has fewer observations and it is useful to understand the impact of the independent variables on the estimations 3-8 that are over various regions of the world. Estimation 3 is of countries in East-Asia and Oceania, estimation 4 is of south Asian countries, estimation 5 is of Middle Eastern countries, estimation 6 is of African countries, estimation 7 is of European countries, estimation 8 is of North American countries, and estimation 9 is of South American countries. Estimations 10-16 are respectively of countries grouped according to their Freedom House press freedom index. Here 1 indicates countries where press has greatest freedom while 7 indicates countries that have the least press freedom. The breakdown into these seven categories is done by Freedom House so we kept the same groupings to maintain the structure of the data.

The estimations indicate that the ICT variables of both mobile and broadband are significant and they show a negative impact on the weighted unrest index. This is contrary to what we had hypothesized. The results indicate that an increase of fixed broadband subscriptions may be associated with a decrease in the unrest index. A 1% increase in broadband subscribers results in a 2 to 4% decrease in the value of the unrest index for all countries. In Africa, the decrease is around 10% and in South America it is around 2%.

We find the same result for the mobile variable where the coefficient is significant, specifically Africa, where countries with higher penetration of mobile telephony seem to have fewer reports of unrest. This indicates that all things being equal, the more people who subscribe to the Internet via fixed broadband the less likely the country will experience unrest.

While these models capture governance in general we wanted to determine if one variable in particular, freedom of expression, could help us understand the impact of ICTs on social unrest. This is because the ability of the population to express their discontent depends on whether or not their governments allow it or repress it. This is why our second set of models clusters countries not by region but by the freedoms (1 = most free, 7 = least free) these populations are granted. Table 2 shows those results. It should be noted that for many countries their respective value changes almost every year as press freedoms changes.

The results are almost identical to the previous models where the we find that a higher penetration of broadband leads to a reduction of instances of social unrest particularly in those with the most restrictive regimes where improvements in broadband can result in a 18% decrease in social unrest.

The mobile results are similar. In the most restrictive countries we find reduced social unrest. There is a 7% reduction in social unrest due to mobile improvements in countries with a freedom index of 5 and there is an 11% reduction for countries with a freedom index of 7. We believe that these lower instances of social unrest may be due to a lesser reporting of unrests in the least free countries.

All of these findings contradict our central hypothesis, which prompted us to search for additional research on the subject. Previous work on social unrest does not include information and communication technologies but some of those works can give us some clues about the role of ICTs with respect of social unrest.

We believe that two things can be happening. First ICTs are multi-purpose technologies, which means that they indeed reduce information frictions and transaction costs but this is true for many other activities including for example the ability to start a business or access to government services, for example. Broadband affords countless activities, from education to entertainment. Because of this, access to broadband can also provide access to many other resources, many of which are not related to social unrest. In fact, it is possible that having broadband access at home provides relief from other afflictions. It is also a door to educational and business opportunities that can help alleviate some of a country's economic and political problems.

Broadband penetration entails significant fixed costs which means that in order for a country to improve broadband access to the population it needs to be able to have reached a level of economic prosperity that can afford such infrastructure.

This may indicate that as wealthy societies mostly enjoy better fixed broadband connectivity, the effect of broadband is in a sense the effect of economic prosperity. However, as table 1 shows, higher GDP per capita PPP is associated with a higher value of unrest index. This indicate that in countries that have similar GDP per capita PPP, the country that has better fixed broadband connectivity will see less unrest. The estimations show that contrary to popular belief, digital connectivity is not one of the enablers of social unrest.

The literature on social unrest also provides other clues regarding the negative effect of ICTs on social unrest. (Mancini & O'Reilly, 2013) for example argue the opposite to what we hypothesized, that ICTs could be used to effectively prevent violence and conflict but they also acknowledge the importance of other measures to that aim. More importantly the work that the OECD (Renn, Jovanovic, & Schröter, 2011) did on social unrest focuses on specific events to explain these civic manifestations. The study highlights specific events such as the Greek economic crisis, environmental disasters such as Hurricane Katrina or the H1N1 flu as triggers to public protest. This approach is similar to the one that (T. Smith, 2013) took which focused exclusively on food prices. These works point to a reality that exhibits much more difficult conditions. What does this mean within the context of the theory we proposed in the paper? It appears that the level of inertia that we see is much greater than what we had anticipated, meaning that willingness to engage in social unrest requires much harsher conditions before people feel that public demonstrations are warranted. Similarly, these technologies also afford other benefits which can help counteract the potentially negative circumstances that the society may encounter. These two factors combined may thus help explain why we don't see greater instances of unrest with the greater penetration of these technologies.

Among the control variables, we found the log of population to have a negative effect on the number of protests. Again we may be seeing the effects of inertia but these countries may also experience more free riders where many of them are simply not engaged expecting others to do so.

Of the economic variables, the log of GDP per Capita was found to be significant and negative for North America and Oceania, which includes China, Japan and Korea as well as many island countries. This, as expected, means that as the per capita income of the population increases, they are more satisfied with their government and thus less likely to engage in social protests. In Africa, GDP per capita is significant but positive. This could mean that circumstances are improving but not to their satisfaction.

As regards the governance variable, the results tables also shows that the variable *Polcon* (0 indicates most politically unstable, 1 indicates most politically stable) is significant for some regions only. For North America, Europe and Oceania countries that have experiences of social unrest, when the political circumstances improve social unrest increases. It should be noted that over the period of study these regions have experienced significant economic changes with the reduction of manufacturing jobs due to both trade and automation, stagnant income and increased income inequality, which may explain why, in spite having good governments, they show increasing social discontent.

The variable education was, significant and negative, which means that improvement in education can result in reduced instances of social unrest. The exception is North America where an increase in educational enrollment increases social unrest. This may reflect the conflicted relationship that the public education system has in both the US and Mexico where funding in many areas is considered inadequate.

The time variable is seen to have a positive impact on the unrest variable indicating that reporting of unrest is increasing over time.

POLICY IMPLICATIONS AND CONCLUSION

This paper examines the relationship between ICTs and social unrest. Our main hypothesis was that ICTs can lead to more social unrest because they reduce information friction, which can help citizens gather and distribute relevant information, reduce the transaction costs of finding fellow citizens who may feel equally dissatisfied, and also reduce the coordination costs of getting organized. These technologies, we believed, reduce the natural inertia people have for getting engaged under conditions where information is lacking. However, we have found that contrary to our belief, ICTs do not seem to increase social unrest, or at least not exclusively. This finding does not invalidate the central premise that ICTs reduce both information frictions and transaction costs. Rather, what we might be seeing is that more engaged social interaction may reduce uncertainty which may dissuade people from taking to the streets for minor reasons.

Of the two technologies, broadband, which we expected to contribute to social unrest is found to be associated with reduced reports of social unrest. This, we believe is because this general purpose technology can help alleviate some of the problems a country may be facing by opening opportunities to people. In addition, as mentioned in the theory section, before people are willing to engage in social protest there is a certain level of inertia; only when they see others concerned with similar problems protesting are they willing to participate. These results indicate that inertia was stronger than expected and other literature points to much more serious events pushing people to the streets.

From a policy perspective, the fact that ICTs are not associated with a higher level of social unrest implies that governments should not limit their use, as some governments have tried to do. Instead, investing in infrastructure such as broadband can help improve the economic and political conditions of a country. The adoption of ICTs can in fact positively affect the economic development of a nation. They could also contribute to the strengthening of democratic processes. Opportunities for policy engagement through government sites, improvements in governance through e-government initiatives, and improvements in the economic circumstances of the population through online education and business are tools that governments can use to advance the wellbeing of their populations and reduce social unrest.

Educational policy raises far-reaching issues. Increasing the education level of a country leads to productivity gains and by doing so expands the possibilities for economic growth. However, as people become more educated, they are more likely to become aware of injustices and will thus be more likely to protest, leading to more unrest and instability. This is because education provides the tools to look at information with a more critical eye whereas ICTs might lead some to emphasize viewpoints with which they are already familiar.

It is important to stress that capitalism will continue to raise income concentration, unemployment, and under-unemployment. Taking into account increments in the use of ICTs, these conditions may have the potential to lead to social unrest but only under catastrophic circumstances. If governments do not wish to spawn protest movements, it is necessary for them to prevent them through adequate economic policies or to properly respond to crisis.

This study is a first attempt to empirically ascertain the impact of ICTs on social unrest. Further analysis – of more granular datasets at the national level, for example – can help us understand the roles that these technologies play when there is widespread discontent among people.

REFERENCES

Abadie, A. (2006). Poverty, political freedom, and the roots of terrorism. *The American Economic Review, 96*(2), 50–56. doi:10.1257/000282806777211847

Alesina, A., & Perotti, R. (1996). Income distribution, political instability, and investment. *European Economic Review, 40*(6), 1203–1228. doi:10.1016/0014-2921(95)00030-5

Auyero, J. (2003). Relational riot: Austerity and corruption protest in the neoliberal era. *Social Movement Studies, 2*(2), 117–145. doi:10.1080/1474283032000139742

Berkowitz, L. (1978). *Group processes*. New York: Academic Press.

Blurton, C. (1999). New directions of ICT-use in education. Retrieved from https://goo.gl/6SgGxV

Bohlken, A. T., & Sergenti, E. J. (2010). Economic growth and ethnic violence: An empirical investigation of Hindu-Muslim riots in India. *Journal of Peace Research, 47*(5), 589–600. doi:10.1177/0022343310373032

Brandt, P. T., & Ulfelder, J. (2011). Economic growth and political instability.

Castells, M. (2013). *Networks of outrage and hope: Social movements in the internet age*. John Wiley & Sons.

Chen, F. (2000). Subsistence crises, managerial corruption and labour protests in china. *China Journal (Canberra, A.C.T.), 44*(44), 41–63. doi:10.2307/2667476

Cline Center for Democracy. (2016). Civil unrest monitoring - dataset. Retrieved from http://www.clinecenter.illinois.edu/data/speed/

Della Porta, D. (2015). *Social movements in times of austerity: Bringing capitalism back into protest analysis*. Cambridge, UK: John Wiley & Sons.

Democracy, C. C. f. (2016). Civil unrest monitoring - datasets. Retrieved from http://www.clinecenter.illinois.edu/data/speed/

Dewey, T., Kaden, J., Marks, M., Matsushima, S., & Zhu, B. (2012). The impact of social media on social unrest in the arab spring. *Final report prepared for Defense Intelligence Agency* Retrieved from https://goo.gl/pT0Pgi

Freedom House. (2016). Freedom in the world. Retrieved from https://freedomhouse.org/report-types/freedom-press

Ghannam, J. (2011). Social media in the Arab world: Leading up to the uprisings of 2011. Retrieved from https://goo.gl/a6KuSC

Gurr, T. R. (1970). *Why men rebel*. Princeton, NJ: Princeton University Press.

Jack, G. (2011). Understanding the revolutions of 2011. *Foreign Affairs, 90*(3), 8.

Jovanović, A. S., Renn, O., & Schröter, R. (2012). *Social unrest*. OECD. doi:10.1787/9789264173460-en

Justino, P. (2005). Redistribution and civil unrest. Retrieved from https://goo.gl/KYkc6c

Kalathil, S., & Boas, T. C. (2003). *Open networks, closed regimes: The impact of the internet on authoritarian rule*. Washington, DC: Carnegie Endowment for International Peace.

Kalathil, S., & Boas, T. C. (2010). *Open networks, closed regimes: The impact of the internet on authoritarian rule*. Washington, D.C.: Carnegie Endowment for International Peace.

Kaur, H., & Tao, X. (2014). *Icts and the millennium development goals*. New York: Springer. doi:10.1007/978-1-4899-7439-6

Kuran, T. (1991). Now out of never: The element of surprise in the east european revolution of 1989. *World Politics, 44*(1), 7–48. doi:10.2307/2010422

Latane, B., & Darley, J. M. (1968). Group inhibition of bystander intervention in emergencies. *Journal of Personality and Social Psychology, 10*(3), 215–221. doi:10.1037/h0026570 PMID:5704479

Lessig, L. (1999). *Code: And other laws of cyberspace*. New York: Basic Books.

Lim, M. (2003). From real to virtual (and back again). In K. C. Ho & R. Kluver (Eds.), *Asia. Com: Asia encounters the internet* (pp. 113–128).

Lippman, P. (2014). Bosnia-herzegovina protests a response to post-war corruption, impoverishment. *The Washington Report on Middle East Affairs, 33*(3), 29–30.

Liu, J., Hassanpour, N., Tatikonda, S., & Morse, A. S. (2012). Dynamic threshold models of collective action in social networks. *Paper presented at the 2012 IEEE 51st IEEE Conference on Decision and Control (CDC)*. 10.1109/CDC.2012.6426657

Lopes, A. R. (2014). The impact of social media on social movements: The new opportunity and mobilizing structure. Retrieved from https://goo.gl/Jb1OS3

MacKinnon, R. (2009). Book review: The power of the internet in china: Citizen activism online. *Far Eastern Economic Review,* September.

Magee, S. P. (1989). *Black hole tariffs and endogenous policy theory: Political economy in general equilibrium*. Cambridge University Press.

Mancini, F., & O'Reilly, M. (2013). New technology and the prevention of violence and conflict. *Stability: International Journal of Security and Development*, 2(3), 1–9.

National Bureau of Economic Research. (2015). Data. Retrieved from http://www.nber.org/data/

Palmer, N. A., & Perkins, D. D. (2012). Technological democratization: The potential role of ict in social and political transformation in china and beyond. *Perspectives on Global Development and Technology, 11*(4), 456–479. doi:10.1163/15691497-12341236

Pappas, T. S., & OMalley, E. (2014). Civil compliance and political luddism: Explaining variance in social unrest during crisis in Ireland and Greece. *The American Behavioral Scientist*, *58*(12), 1592–1613. doi:10.1177/0002764214534663

Renn, O., Jovanovic, A., & Schröter, R. (2011). Social unrest. *OECD*. Retrieved from http://www.oecd.org/governance/risk/46890018.pdf

Roberts, A. (2013). *The end of protest: How free-market capitalism learned to control dissent*. Cornell University Press.

Roubini, N. (2011). The instability of inequality. *Project Syndicate*. Retrieved from https://www.project-syndicate.org/commentary/the-instability-of-inequality

Scheffer, M., Westley, F., & Brock, W. (2003). Slow response of societies to new problems: Causes and costs. *Ecosystems (New York, N.Y.)*, *6*(5), 493–502. doi:10.100710021-002-0146-0

Shaw, M. E. (1964). Communication networks. *Advances in Experimental Social Psychology*, *1*, 111–147. doi:10.1016/S0065-2601(08)60050-7

Smith, C. (2001). China backs away from initial denial in school explosion. Retrieved from https://goo.gl/AHjpTv

Smith, T. (2013). Food price spikes and social unrest in Africa. *CCAPS Research Brief*(11).

Sun, Y. (1991). The Chinese protests of 1989: The issue of corruption. *Asian Survey*, *31*(8), 762–782. doi:10.2307/2645228

Theobald, R. (2002). Containing corruption. *New Political Economy*, *7*(3), 435–449. doi:10.1080/1356346022000018775

Van Stekelenburg, J., & Klandermans, B. (2013). The social psychology of protest. *Current Sociology*, *61*(5-6), 886–905. doi:10.1177/0011392113479314

This research was previously published in Online Communities as Agents of Change and Social Movements edited by Steven Gordon; pages 89-115, copyright year 2017 by Information Science Reference (an imprint of IGI Global).

APPENDIX

Table 3. Description of the variables used

Variable	Description
domestic9	Weighted conflict index
unrest_per1000	Weighted conflict per 1000
polcon3	Political Condition Index (POLCON = 0 most hazardous and POLCON = 1 most stable political environment.)
log_gdp	log of gdp per capita
log_pop	log of total number of inhabitants
log_fixed_bb subs_per100	log of fixed broadband subscribers per 100
log_mobile subs_per100	log of mobile subscribers per 100
enrollment	School enrollment, primary (gross), gender parity index (GPI)
log_enrollment	log of School enrollment, primary (gross), gender parity index (GPI)
pressfreedom	PR, and Freedom Rating Score Explanation: (1 = most free and 7 = least free)
region	Regions of the world
year	Years of observations

Table 4. Summary statistics

Variable	Obs.	Mean	Std. Dev.	Min	Max
domestic9	2349	721.75	2953.76	0	85625
unrest_per1000	2340	0.11	0.62	0	14.35
polcon3	2357	0.28	0.20	0	0.72
log_gdp	2680	8.76	1.30	5.47	11.63
log_pop	3165	15.18	2.34	9.15	21.04
log_fixed_bb_subs_per100	2316	0.03	2.92	-9.94	4.55
log_mobile_subs_per100	2829	3.36	1.93	-5.55	13.24
enrollment	2253	0.96	0.08	0	1.33
log_enrollment	2251	-0.04	0.09	-0.83	0.29
pressfreedom	2773	3.33	2.15	1	7
region	2880	4.03	1.88	1	7
year	3235	2007	4	2000	2014

Table 5. Correlation Matrix

	domestic9	polcon3	log_gdp	log_pop	log_fixed bb subs_per100	log_mobile subs_per100	log enrollment	Press freedom	region	year
domestic9	1									
polcon3	-0.04	1								
log_gdp	-0.09	0.29	1							
log_pop	0.25	0.06	-0.12	1						
log_fixed_ bb_subs_per100	-0.07	0.34	0.83	-0.07	1					
log_mobile subs_per100	-0.05	0.28	0.66	-0.14	0.72	1				
log_enrollment	-0.10	0.16	0.41	-0.01	0.46	0.35	1			
pressfreedom	0.08	-0.62	-0.50	0.09	-0.50	-0.3958	-0.2897	1		
region	-0.09	0.18	0.21	-0.26	0.22	0.18	0.14	-0.33	1	
year	0.06	-0.10	-0.02	0.01	0.30	0.36	0.03	0.13	-0.05	1

Chapter 8
Fasti Congressuum:
A Useful Online Tool for Congresses and Call for Papers

Elena Duce Pastor
Universidad Autónoma de Madrid, Spain

María Cristina de la Escosura
Universidad Complutense de Madrid, Spain

Diego M. Escámez de Vera
Universidad Complutense de Madrid, Spain

María del Mar Rodríguez
Universidad Complutense de Madrid, Spain

David Serrano Lozano
Universidad Complutense de Madrid, Spain

ABSTRACT

Every year, all over the world, hundreds of calls for papers are submitted and hundreds of congresses take place, all of them devoted to some aspect of antiquity. With such an enormous amount of international activity, it is rather difficult, if not impossible, for an individual researcher, or a researching group, to keep in track of every single academic activity related to their specialty, not to say of general academic activities at international scale. It is a very common phenomenon listening to complains from students, young researchers or even consolidated ones about the lack of information on some activities they would have been interested in participating in. The members of this project have checked this experience, even personally, happening in different countries, always talking about classics and antiquity studies. Fasti Congressuum was born by and for students and researchers on Antiquity as an independent project and a tool against this situation.

DOI: 10.4018/978-1-7998-0417-8.ch008

INTRODUCTION

Romans used to call *fasti* to chronologically organized records. Originally, *fasti* were the days in which public events were allowed: coming from *fas*, that which is legitimate in Gods' eyes. So, Romans exposed calendars in their cities with necessary instructions for daily life. Eventually, documents recording magistrates and most important events each year were also called *fasti*. These traditions are combined in order to name this project, *Fasti Congressuum*.

Every week, somewhere in the world, a congress, seminar, encounter, conference or workshop is hold, with a subject directly related with Antiquity. The interest generated by this period within the academic world leads to an exchange of ideas which is hard to track. *Fasti Congressuum* is born with the aim of becoming a useful tool for professionals, researchers, students and amateurs by compiling the greatest number of events as possible in a single calendar with two kinds of information: Call for Papers and Congress programs.

ORIGINS OF THE PROJECT

Every year, all over the world, hundreds of calls for papers are submitted and, consequently, hundreds of congresses take place, all of them devoted to some aspect of antiquity. With such an enormous amount of international activity, it is rather difficult, if not impossible, for an individual researcher, or even for a researching group, to keep in track of every single academic activity related to their specialty, not to say of the general calendar of academic activities at international scale.

Even at a more national or even local level, it is a very common phenomenon listening to complains from students, young researchers or even consolidated ones about the lack of information on some interesting activities they would have been interested in participating. It is known that a congress is not only a proper place to show academic work but also it is the venue where social academic networks take place. So, it is a pity when scholars do not share their job not because they have other meetings to attend or they have academic duties, but also because they do not receive any information about the event.

The members of the present project have checked this recurrent experience, even personally, happening in different countries, always talking about classics and antiquity studies. By one hand researchers have to confront those difficulties, by the other they should be as much international as they can and they must try to share their work not only for researching reasons but also for receiving a better place and foundation in their home universities.

Up to now, the way of learning about Call for papers and Congresses was limited. Researchers have easy access to their own universities' events via email and panels. In some well know universities such as Oxford or Sorbonne-Pantheon everyone can see posters of Congresses. In those universities, secretaries play an essential role in diffusion receiving information about different events and promoting them through a common space online. Most of the universities do not forget to keep in touch with the most prestigious centers, but most of researchers work in middle and small universities, which are out of this chain of information.

In small and medium universities, only local and semi local information about Congresses reach to researchers. For example, it is quite easy to promote a national Congress between colleagues but external or foreign Congresses seem too far away.

Email is other important way of events' spreading. Most of researchers try to keep in touch with colleagues via email and some of them try to share information about their own Congresses. This way may be very useful but it requires counting on contacts in order to be in the chain of communication. Young PhD applicants and young professor are not always able to be inside big mail lists easily.

The last way of information is e-mailing group. There are some e-mailing list like Classicists (1997) or Archport (2015), in which anyone can be registered and receive a wide range of different information. A big amount of congresses are diffused this way but there are some problems. The first of them is the saturation of information: a researcher can receive five or six e-mails every day. It can be a real waste of time to read everything and select useful information since those e-mailing list do not filter information. It is common to receive information about exhibitions, new articles or a Call for Papers. Tags are not employed and so information is not selected. In the end, a researcher must waste an amount of time filtering this kind of information.

After this background, it is assumed that researchers are missing important events because the information has not a clear way of diffusion and every researcher is conscious about this lack of information.

After missing an important congress which was directly related to her doctoral researching, the project founder decided to start up an idea which had been going round her head for months. Up till then, the only possibility offered by internet to access to this kind of information were subscribing to some associations' newsletters, to follow some websites with this kind of information or specific projects. The main websites we use are:

- Terra ItaliaOnlus (2008)
- Society for Classical Studies (n.d.)
- The Classical Association (2016)
- Classical Association of the Atlantic States. Classical World (2012)
- Notiziario di Antichistica (2007)
- CLASSICISTS List (1997)
- Archport list (2015)
- Conference Alerts (Conal) (2000)
- Calenda.org (2000)
- International Society of Cicero's Friends (2008)
- École Française de Rome (n.d.)
- Society for Ancient Mediterranean Religions (2008)

The problem is that these sites supply a great amount of information which can contain information on congresses but uses to include diverse facts about books, doubts, job offers or even obituaries. Besides, when coming from specific institutions or groups, the information tends to be very geographically local or really specific on its subject. Quite the opposite happens with Conference Alerts (Conal, 2000), a platform which offers information from all over the world to its users. However, Conal policy forces the users to log in and insert information on their own congresses and paying for diffusing it. This may be the reason for it being so difficult to find any congress related to Antiquity in its database. Sometimes it happens that a researcher receives two or three emails with different kind of information and has to proceed suddenly to it. If he has not time at the moment, a long list of waiting emails is unavoidable. This procedure has been demonstrated contra productive because one of the main problems of a scholarship is the lack of time every day.

Although these kinds of projects had been a strong inspiration for the FC team, they always lacked of one, or some, of the components wanted to join in *Fasti Congressuum*, like the global scale, totally open and free access or interactivity with the organizing team through direct mail contact.

Facing this situation, the FC director decided to start her own project with the intention to offer to researchers a specific and intuitive tool where finding information about congresses on Antiquity. Once the project main lines where outlined, the founder joined the first team member. In order to name the project, the team decided that it should be easily understandable for most of the reachable researchers, as well as easy to remember. Being both team members specialists on Roman History, and having them devised the project in the Capitolium (Rome, Italy), they decided to be based on roman traditions of publicly exposed urban calendars, which were full of instructions, and the traditional lists of each year most relevant individuals and events. Both of them were called *fasti* by the Romans. With this in mind, the team decided to use Latin for reflecting the idea of what they were trying to offer in the website: a list, a congress calendar. Thus *Fasti Congressuum* was born.

It must be clarified that Roman studies were not the only purpose of the project. *Fasti Congressuum* is a website about Antiquity in every aspect and every geographical area. Latin must be though as the easier and commoner alphabet in Antiquity. Designing a website in hieroglyphics or in Greek characters might be possible, but less accessible for everyone.

WEB BUILDING

Both team members divided up then the two first challenges: designing a website and organizing a model of diffusion. Counting on a zero budget, the new website must be hosted in a free platform which offered creative freedom without programming. So the team decided to employ Wix.com (2006). Web director and designer opted for a chromatic range of deep reds, whites and blacks, which gather the aesthetic elements of roman calendars. Easiness when interacting with the website was one of the main team objectives, so the site was organized around four sections: home, about us, congresses and call for papers.

The two first sections, "Home" and "About us", might look very simple. "Home" is the place in which everyone can return and see a general view of the website."About us" is the logical presentation of the project. It was important to present the *Fasti Congressuum* team as part of the research world. Young researchers, PhD applicants sometimes have confronted very soon those problems related to the lack of information about Congresses and Call for papers. It must be admitted also that young researchers have been working with educative tools in humanities all their live and are more used to improve them and use them in their benefit. A short text in *Fasti Congressuum* explains in three languages the composition of the *Fasti Congressuum* team and the main objectives of the project. This information is accessible and it was though with the idea of being transparent and clear.

The first and most visual interface for the user offers a gallery of images, a calendar, a list of post and a tags cloud for every visitor to be able to dive through the different activities displayed in the website, as well as getting in contact with the site's structure and mechanic (designed to be as simple and usable as possible).

Figure 1. Fasti Congressuum 'Home' section
Source: FC main site screenshot

- **Calendar**: provided by Google calendar (2006), including every single data uploaded to our site, along with the basic information of each CFP or congress (deadline, dates, location), including a link to its specific post. The calendar permits to check, with only one click, how many events are in the same day. The main objective of this part is to avoid scholars to miss deadlines or to waste time creating their own calendar.
- **Pictures**: Every congress has a different picture, one for the Call for Papers and other for the congress' program. Sometimes the team do not receive the official poster, in those cases it is chosen an image related to the topic of the event or to the home university.
- **Tags Cloud**: Free Wix.com (2006) version restrictions, which forbid an unlimited searching tool, makes the tag cloud the only way for the user to make thematic searches. Tags always include the kind of event (congress, call for papers), the country in which it will take place (in English), the fields to which papers belong (history, archaeology, philology, etc.), their chronological context basing on big cultures (Middle East, Egypt, Greece, Rome, Late-Antiquity) and more specific thematic instructions (religion, gender, inheritance, digital humanities, etc.)

Wishing a global scale, gathering events from all over the world, the original team built the website in three languages: Spanish, their mother tongue, English, most spread language in the academia, and Italian, due to the team professional links with this country. So the four main web sections are built. However, the kind of information to offer forced to use a blog system in order to be useful for the users

Figure 2. 'Calendar' service
Source: FC main site screenshot

Figure 3. 'Congresses' section
Source: FC main site screenshot

and manageable for editors. This system didn't allow to create new posts in each of the three languages which be automatically inserted in the two main sections ("congress", "call for papers"). So the team decided to design every post in a trilingual way.

The posts, personally created by our team and customized to every activity, they are designed to offer the essential information and links necessary for every person to be able to identify, find and join the academic activity in question. Although if an official Call for Paper of Congress program is available it is uploaded to the website, all of the posts have the same format. It permits scholars to find information easily because it will appear always in the same order and contain always the same kind of information: title, photo, deadline (for CFP), date, location (link to GoogleMaps, 2005), organizer, info (web and email), call (for CFP), registration and program (if available). The use of the form implies the smallest number of idiomatic differences and allows the post to keep being clear despite being in three languages.

We count on different ways to find information before uploading it. We offer an email address, fasti-congressuum@gmail.com, to which anyone can address us with information. We are also subscribers of different newsletters. The Fasti team also keeps in touch with Ancient History, Archaeology, Epigraphy, Ancient Law, and Ancient Philology departments, so we can receive any possible useful information

Figure 4. 'Call for Papers' section
Source: FC main site screenshot

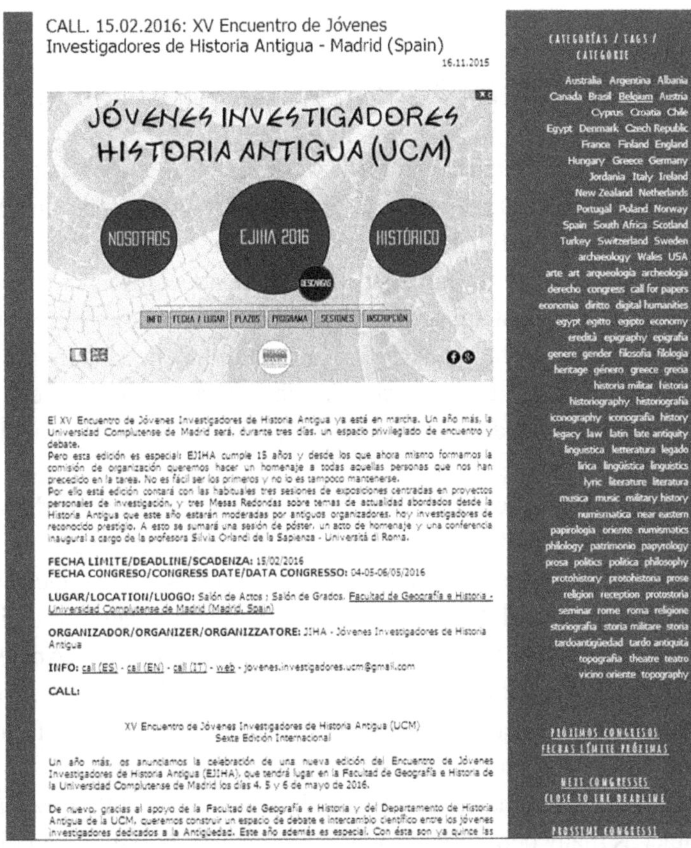

for them, as well as we always send back to each department or institution the notice of every new post concerning their activities, so the consciousness of the importance of such an interface tool can constantly be taken into account.

Not every event is automatically admitted to be published in *Fasti Congressuum*. Only those events organized by papers which can have poster and, or workshops, though not exclusively. Anyway, there must be more than two speakers and it must be aimed to a wide audience, not exclusively to the members of a college or a doctoral program. In those congresses with a generic subject, there must be at least two papers related with Ancient History. Last, series of conferences fitting the mentioned requisites are included, even when they are not celebrated in consecutive days. Thus, it is tried to build an Antiquity congress map which doesn't clash with colleges' daily formative activities, whose aim and audience don't fit this project objectives. On the other hand, a scientific and researching profile, whose aim is not merely informative to a wide audience, is pursued.

Being the website already built and the diffusing plan organized, the Project was delayed for months due to other professional duties of the team members, which made its releasing impossible. When becoming aware of the amount of information to process, the team realized the extent of the project ambition. It was necessary to gather a bigger team, which would be willing to take part for free. So, four new partners joined the project. Only then did the tentative steps towards the starting of the project were accompanied by a constant and continuous workload, which allowed publishing the website online and starting the diffusing plan.

LAUNCHING THE DIFFUSION PROCESS

When the *Fasti Congressuum* team started to create the website, they realized that the lack of information about University departments and researching centres all over the world. The first obstacle consisted of the fact that there is not a checkable official list of universities for every, or some, country. But the main objective of the project was to contact with University and Independent researchers, preferably at the same time, in order to start up with the website. *Fasti Congressuum* team has the role of uploading congresses and Call for Papers, but also need the help of scholarships, and they needed by the very first moment.

As a result of this, the team decided to start creating their own list of contacts. The main objective was to contact as many university departments as possible, as well as asking them for help in order to spread information about the website.

The phase of looking for information about universities throughout the world lasted more than one month. A sharing out of countries and geographical areas was carried out among the team members, so each of them chose one country or region (e.g. north or south America, Oceania, etc.) and looked for every single department and researching centre which could be located in their respective regions or countries. The *Fasti Congressuum* team decided to contact members of Ancient History, Ancient Archaeology, Ancient Philology, Epigraphy, Palaeography, Ancient Diplomatic, Ancient Law, Ancient Philosophy and Architecture departments, considering that these would be the fields of study in which researchers and events related with ancient history could be found. Being conscious of the amount of departments and contact information that this task would imply to deal with, it was thought that priority should be given to contact as many departments and individuals as possible, and did not miss any field related to Antiquity, over the huge amount of work it supposed.

During this process, Internet worked as the main database for the team's work. In this sense, internet was very useful since virtually every university throughout the world count on email addresses for each of their departments, as well as provide official emails of every staff member online. The original idea was to contact the main academic secretary or administrative member, as well as the head of the department staff. These two members were considered to be the best diffusion contacts, so they could resend information on *Fasti Congressuum* to every member of the department, or even professional colleagues which they could considered to be interested in the *Fasti* project, and so it was specified in our mail for initial contact.

At first sight, it was obvious that some small universities do not count on a very specific organization and gather researchers for many areas of knowledge in the same department. For example, it was found that some universities only count on one department of History, which include all the specialities of this field, and so classics or ancient history was not always represent within the university staff or the lines of study. Thus, it was a challenge to contact the right people, and it implied more hours of surfing on the Internet than it was initially expected.

When the list was eventually created, a date of starting was chosen. The website was ready, with some congresses and Call for Papers on them just to work as an example of the website way of working. The main purpose of this phase was to show the website appearance which would be soon full of congresses and Call for Papers. Checks and re-checks had been made in order to taste the reliability of an external dominium like Wix (2006).

The contact phase was then carried out. An email in four languages, (Spanish, English, French and Italian) was sent to every department and centre recorded in the mail list. Although it is known that most of scholars can read and write in English, the website has trilingual design. So, it seemed obvious that we should present the website in the three languages that it counts with. During this phase of initial contacts, some technical problems were raised, as a consequence both of the lack of experience of the *Fasti* team at this starting point, and the quite uncommon nature of the work that it was carrying out. The most notable technical difficulty faced consisted on the fact that no email service, including the one employed by the *Fasti Congressuum* team, can hold a big and continuous amount of outgoing mail in a short lapse of time without considering it as a spam activity. This was exactly what happened during the initial stage of the first round of email contacts, so the team decided to design a new protocol for this kind of massive email outgoing. Thus, the whole mail list was split in similar groups, each of them corresponding to a team member, who would be responsible of sending all the mails included in their mail list section, expanding their activity along a lengthy lapse of time, in order to prevent the spam consideration to our mails, which would totally spoil our diffusion activity.

After overcoming such difficulties, the team started to receive lots of emails with messages of congratulations and the first call for papers in few days. In some weeks, a database was created and *Fasti Congressuum* started with a big success, which was increased in the following months.

SOCIAL NETWORKS

Last but not least, we offer different ways to open access information. Our website is the main platform of information but, since we are concerned of the extremely important role of social networks in relation with the academic relationships nowadays, we also have a facebook (2004) (www.facebook.com/fasticongressuum) and a twitter (2006) account (@fasticongress). These keep in constant and updated track of every single post uploaded to *Fasti Congressuum* site, including links to each of them.

Social networks have several key roles for the *Fasti Congressuum* project. On the one hand, social networks are the most affordable way to get in touch with people involved in research that are not attached to a project or department, or who have not had previous access to the website. Furthermore, the access to the sites, the ability to share information and the free advertising that social networks provide, allows information to get much faster to people who have not already searched for general congresses or call for papers on Google, Bing or other searching platforms.

For Twitter (2006) (@fasticongress), the team has made a first approach to possible users through the twitter search box, focusing on potential followers who post tweets on Archaeology, Ancient History, Philosophy, Philology and Ancient Heritage. From this initial search, the authors have followed those users who are presumably interested on the web platform. To enhance dissemination, the team decided not to discriminate users whose interest is more focused on other periods or other related disciplines, such as Medieval Archaeology, or Teaching. *Fasti Congressuum* account on Twitter (2006) has also followed university departments and libraries. When our account has around 100 new followers and follows 200 new users, the community manager of the team checks the twitter accounts which the platform recommends and follows accounts with a possible common interest. Now the community manager does a weekly review of Twitter users, given by the social network itself, in order to expand our distribution network.

On the other hand, the way of publication in Twitter (2006) also involves a secondary diffusion of the website. Each member of the team shares on both social networks any new post of the website. By sharing the post on Twitter (2006), the team adds the hashtags relating to the place and the category "conference" or "call for papers". This has encouraged more retweets from tourism accounts, which is really interesting for the project because it makes a secondary diffusion on Heritage. Likewise, other Twitter (2006) accounts usually share publications from @fasticongress. The community manager tracked the type of user who is looking for *Fasti Congressuum*, and the members of the project can say that most followers in Twitter (2006) or Facebook (2004) are people who are dedicated to researching on the Ancient World. This is a success for the platform.

In the case of Facebook (2004), the dissemination of the website (https://www.facebook.com/fasticongressuum) has been even greater than in Twitter (2006). *Fasti Congressuum*'s diffusion policy has focused on sharing in the personal page profiles of the members of the team and in pages or groups dedicated to the spread of the Antiquity. Many users of these groups have also shared new publications. The community manager has also followed other research institutions possibly interested in the project, so they couldspread and also use the platform. The community manager also renews the web publishing in the groups in which we published initially and also in others we find.

Each post that the team uploads to the web is shared on Twitter (2006) and Facebook (2004) to facilitate daily monitoring of the web. The community manager also tries to keep the social networks updated with congresses which are starting in the same or few days and with the close deadlines to call for papers, so that users have the daily update of events. Also the Team publishes full information on some conference whose program comes later than the post itself. One of the key points of our website is daily updated information.

Social networks are also a form of direct contact with *Fasti Congressuum* team. There are users who send their conferences or some other kind of information directly through Facebook (2004) or Twitter (2006). This allows a more direct contact with the users.

It is really important to keep personal contact with social network users and also in every kind of research, so the *Fasti Congressuum* team tries to advertise the website in scientific events related to Ancient History and Digital Humanities.

The web also offers a personal newsletter for subscribers, with updates with all new activity every week or in two weeks, depending on the density of initiatives which have been promoted in that period. The newsletter is also another way to keep users informed. It is really useful for people who do not want to look for new conferences in the website every day, so they can find in their personal e-mail weekly news. For subscribing to the newsletter, the website has a little box called "*Fasti Congressuum*'s newsletter" where people just write their e-mail address and, automatically, get into a data base for subscribers. As a rule, one of the members of the group sends every Sunday the newsletter with the post uploaded that week. To take an example of real data, the week from 9th to 15th November 2015, 48 emails have been sent to the subscribers, the web has 50 visits from which 13 came from the Shot Out. A 53% of the subscribers opened the newsletter email, and the 24% of them clicked at least in one of the congresses or call for papers. Those are data just for a week because the website only lets us know for that period.

There's a correlation between the social networks and the newsletter, not just for diffusion, but also because the community manager has already verify that when all the members of the group do their own broadcasting, the number of subscribers to the newsletter grows faster. In the period since *Fasti Congressuum* is online, the website have 49 subscribers.

At the moment when the team wants to increase the number of followers in Facebook (2004), the page increase from 497 followers to 550 in a single day when the normal growth was of 3 to 6 followers per week. When it is necessary, every member put an advertising in different pages or groups where is possible to found more followers. The dissemination of the information is quite good because the members have different interests, so they can use the pages or groups related to these interests to advertise *Fasti Congressuum.*

The diverse interests and Facebook (2004) friends of the members of the project is a really important tool for diffusion because the members show to their friends the website and ask for dissemination. In spite of the so called "information society", we have notice that conversation or direct communication is even as important as global diffusion. That is the reason for using personal channels of communication related to each ones' interests, not just scientific channels but also scientific dissemination channels. As researchers, the members of the team show the website in different seminars or congresses where they take part. As the reader can see, the team has one person who works in the dissemination of the project, the community manager, but every member is ready to assume this work if it is necessary, so the team is constantly renewing the web and everyone can work in every different function. The team have decided that in order to be flexible and to assume possible new members. Another motive for this it is that *Fasti Congressuum* is a non profit tool and the project has not funding to increase the advertising.

RESULTS AND FUTURE PERSPECTIVES

Fasti Congressuum project has come a long way and experimented a notable evolution in a comparatively short time. After only six months of operation, Fasti's posts were as findable through the main online searchers as most of those from similar websites and platforms. Currently, after a little more than a year of existence, this initiative has not only grown up, but it has also reached a series of essential aims which not only guarantee that the existence of such a tool was a real need and that it has a real and increasingly important role within the academic community.

Through this politic of diffusion, hundreds of people and institutions have been contacted all throughout the world, with a high percentage of positive and collaborative responses. Particular and institutional collaboration with our platform was a touchstone for the continuity of the project, since it is the perfect indicator of recognition from the professional environment.

Second, the dissemination ability beyond our own and direct work, or self-diffusion, is another crucial objective which has been certainly fulfilled. All the members of the *Fasti Congressuum* team have had news, through a formal or a casual way, that knowledge, consciousness and, or use of the platform was being spread through different external channels, such as university directories, web or mail sharing and even mouth-to-mouth mentioning in congresses or academic environments. Of course, the team's labour of diffusion, publicity and looking for new ways of contacts will be constant, but self-diffusion is such an essential factor that had not been for it our national and international perspectives would have simply been impossible.

Third, figures were a challenge from the very beginning of this initiative, but the perspective after a whole year of work shows that it has not only been overcome, but it has also become one of the main basis for our work. In a first moment, there were reasonable doubts on the capability for such a low (or zero) budget project to get to a respectable quantity of people or to really influence at large geographical scale.

Nowadays, the information gathered from the statistic services included in our website and social networks serves as an indicator of two important factors. The first one consists in the amount of countries to which *Fasti* has reached, which is not only considerable, but also continuously increasing, even to those countries in which we haven't already started a direct round of contacts. As can be seen in Figure 5, the accumulation of the last 500 visitors to our site (roughly corresponding to the last 15 days of use) indicates a clearly greater density of visits coming from the European continent, which will be discussed later. However, a significant amount of visits can be distinguished from the American continent, and especially from the United States of America. This country represents the third national origin of use for *Fasti Congressuum* website, after Spain and Italy, since the beginning of the project, and this tendency has been maintained all through the project's life. A good sample of the mentioned tendency can be seen on Figure 6, which shows the origin of *Fasti Congressuum* website visits by country in the last 8 months, with a clear third position of the United States, well over United Kingdom as fourth country of origin, and this very same proportion is maintained month after month.

This is a really interesting statistic, since the United States were not part of our initial list of contacts, due to the great volume of searching and classifying work implied, which is currently being done. Nonetheless, the North American interest in the *Fasti Congressuum* site has been a big, and pleasant, surprise for its management team. It is also especially interesting in statistic terms due to the mentioned relation with United Kingdom as fourth country of origin, since it does not fit at all with the proportion of countries which the posts published in the *Fasti Congressuum* site are directly related to. In general, since we still don't count on final figures for our posts, the amount of events taking place in the United Kingdom which are regularly published in our official website is roughly almost three times bigger than that of congresses and call for papers concerning the United States.

Thus, this inverse relationship between posts implications and visitors country of origin represents a really useful indicator for the level of importance of certain activities in terms of diffusion. This figure reflects in a quite clear way that the impact of *Fasti Congressuum* in each country is not strictly linked with the appearance of events taking place in a country, for the indirect diffusion, that one which is performed out of the *Fasti* team hands, can be notably more important, as the American figures display.

Figure 5. Visitors map corresponding to the last 500 visits to Fasti Congressuum website Source: web-stat.com (1996)

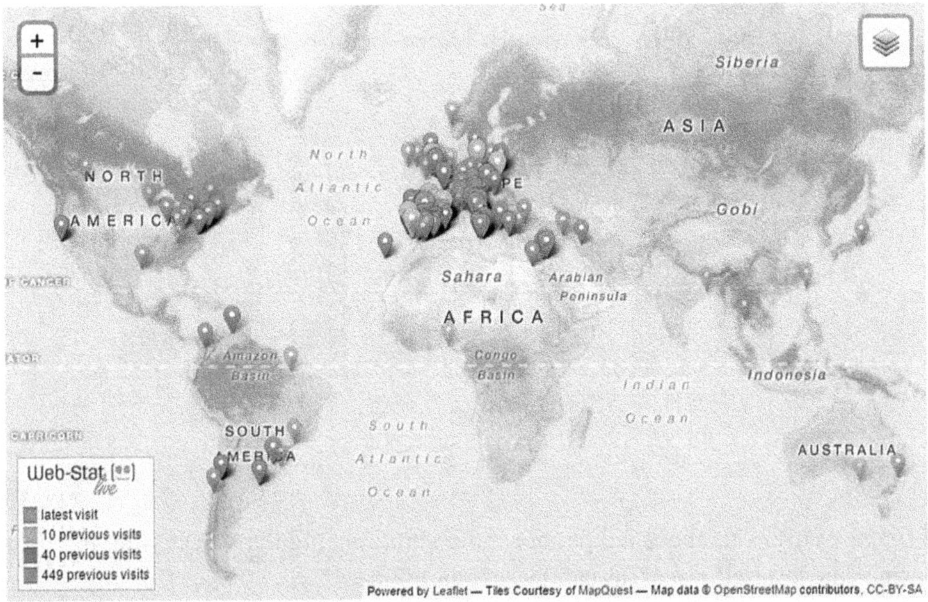

Figure 6. Top 10 countries of origin of Fasti Congressuum' visitors
Source: data from web-stat.com (1996), graphic created by the FC team.

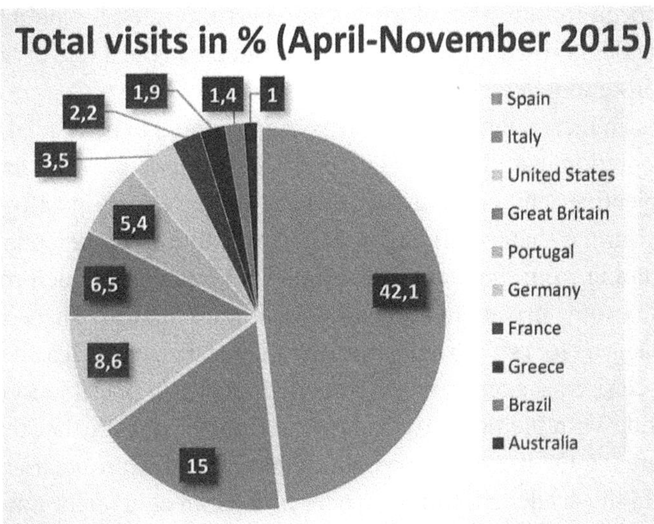

A second interesting statistic information developed after this last year, or year and a half, of work is related with the figures concerning people who have recurrently made use of *Fasti Congressuum*, which has systematically increased in scale during the first twelve months: if during the first two to six months a range of no more than one hundred people used our service (indicating a strictly personal and local scale), at roughly two months intervals the range of users have been raised by hundreds, reaching

Figure 7. Total visits to Fasti Congressuum per month, from April to November 2015 Source: data from web-stat.com (1996), graphic created by the FC team.

a sustained figure of over one thousand people and institutions regularly accessing to our information each month since the last half a year, as can be seen in Figure 7.

Even more significant is the fact that, out of the total figure of monthly visitors, the relation of new visitors and repeat visits is almost constantly under a proportion of two thirds the former and one third the latter. This statistic shows a new reflection of the diffusing success during this first year of existence. It is not a question of underestimation of the importance of loyalty in our users and visitors. On the contrary, had not it been for this base of loyal and recurring users, it would be impossible for us to count on a stable independent diffusion out of our hands. But the highest rate of new visitors implies that the amount of institutions and independent users which her about *Fasti Congressuum* and get in touch with it for the first keeps an increasing tendency. This is considered to be crucial, because as long as the number of new users is predominant it is sure that there is a positive growing tendency.

As a fourth main objective achieved, not only there is an objectively positive success after the first twelve months of work (in the shape of figures), but also a quite more personal satisfaction for every member in the team coming from the increasing number of messages which reach our mail or social networks inbox, in which some private researcher or institution not only share some relevant information, but also congratulates us for our job and stress the importance of such a site and the great need for it that there was in the classics academic world. It is not obviously possible to compare the reliability of this kind of recognition with the one provided by the figures. But, further than the personal fulfilling that provide, they are a quite interesting symptom that *Fasti Congressuum* is responding to a need which was “in the air” in the academia, so that sooner or later an equivalent initiative would have been raised somewhere else.

Having reached what is considered as a plentifully satisfactory state to the present moment, the *Fasti Congressuum* project is currently ready to face new initiatives and work for reaching prospective aims. Naturally, first of them consists on extending the base of contacts on which the site counts, personally, institutionally and internationally. This is why in this very moment the *Fasti* core mail list is being enlarged with researchers and institution from the United States of America and, hopefully in a short time, it will start incorporating information corresponding to Eastern Europe and North Africa countries.

As mentioned above, statistics concerning the habits of use of *Fasti Congressuum* website show a marked trend towards the concentration of national origin of visitors in the European continent. A tendency which was foreseeable since most of the posts published in the official website inform about events taking place in Europe, and also due to the European nature of most of the consolidated contacts of the *Fasti* team members. Within the European territory, a notable highest density of visits from Spain, Italy and United Kingdom can be identified, as it is clearly displayed on Figure 8. The vast majority of visits from Spain is quite comprehensible because the most immediate networks of contacts initially established when starting the project diffusion spread essentially through this country, due to the Spanish origin of the founding members.

Besides, the high figures of visits from Italy and the United Kingdom respond to what the organizers have identified as a linguistic phenomenon. As it has already been mentioned, the final design of *Fasti Congressuum* interface was set in a trilingual way, including information in Spanish, English and Italian. Thus, the direct access to these languages would have influenced on the marked tendencies of researchers and institutions from these countries accessing to our website.

There is actually a contrasting low figure which could also be related with this linguistic accessibility issue. It consists on the remarkable lower number of visits from France, since French is not one of the languages offered in the *Fasti Congressuum* main design. Although English is the essential working language in the current academic world, it is quite comprehensible that the absence of a mother tongue can be a reason for considering such a service as a second or third choice in contrast with the informative sites from French institutions.

Such a phenomenon is the perfect example of the kind of lesser-scale challenges which the *Fasti Congressuum* team is willing to get over in the close future, most of which are part of the diffusion politic. So, it is basic to go deep into the networks of contacts at a national scale in relation with certain countries, with initiatives such as intensifying the contacts with French institutions and particulars. Accordingly, the already mentioned mail list with the United States of America, or the planned expansion of contacts with institutions and individuals in Oceania are part of the immediate tasks of the *Fasti* team.

Figure 8. Visitors map corresponding to the last 500 visits to Fasti Congressuum website from Europe. Source: web-stat.com (1996).

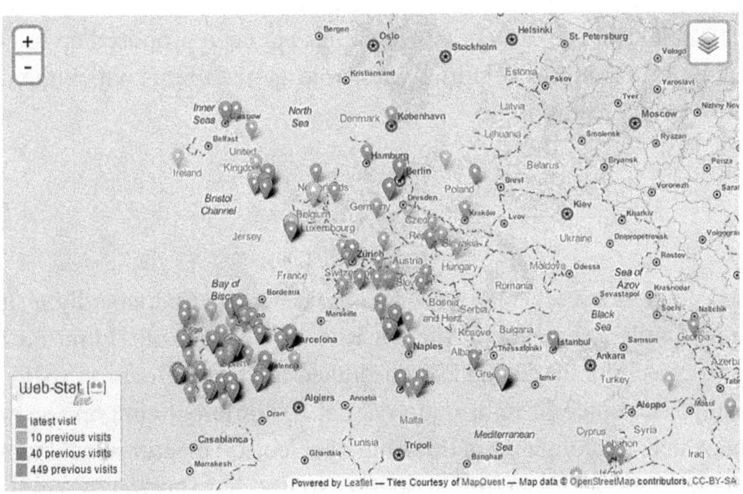

The awareness of the fact that this increasing of the number of contacts and objectives will naturally imply an increase in the amount work, has led to the decision of also enlarging the number of members implicated in the *Fasti Congressuum* management team, for which possible candidates are currently being searched and contacted.

Going a step further, the possibility of including *Fasti Congressuum* references in new platforms is currently being studied. Academia.edu (2008, September) or researchgate.net (2008, may), two of the most successful academic social networks in recent time, represent the perfect examples of the kind of environments through which the Fasti project looks to extend its roots: free and common sharing spaces with strong impact in the academic world whose cyclic publishing format, combined with the use of tools which have become essential for our job (such as tags, documents uploading and editing, etc.), fits quite well with the nature of our website.

As a further complement to this initiative, the team is looking for additional channels of transmission and consolidation of the project. These consist on the use of our past and future experience as an important element of consideration in the field of humanities and its relationship with digital tools. The importance of this area has had an obvious raise in the last decades and, though *Fasti Congressuum* is not a customary researching project (focused on a specific subject of study or material record), it could represent a referential initiative in terms of digital tools and humanities diffusion. So, taking part in eventual initiatives of discussion, presentation or even publishing with *Fasti Congressuum* not only as a tool but as the result of a job is a new line which is currently being explored by our team. Actually, this very article is a perfect example of an initial success in this sense.

Last but not least, first ideas are coming up in the team's meeting about the further information that *Fasti Congressuum* can provide. Not meaning with it the amount of dates, places and events which every day pass through our public posts, but an implicit kind of knowledge coming out of it. Being in the situation they are, the members of the *Fasti Congressuum* management team have access to a daily live image of the academic world behaviour. All the institutional initiatives, events, proposals, workshops, projects and so on which pass in front the managers' eyes give them a really interesting perspective, in real time, of the interests, concerns or novelties concerning the study of ancient history. Thus, *Fasti Congressuum* could eventually become a tool for taking the pulse to the researching world in an alternative way to the traditional following of researching tendencies or diffusion fashions.

This initiative could represent a unique way to provide information to individuals or institution on how the academia's behaviour is working and, or evolving in a certain moment, at a global, regional, national or even local scale, from a perspective which has not been proposed up to now. That is, having a broad objective view of the patterns of initiatives, subjects or formats which are raising or declining in the academic world at the greatest scale.

CONCLUSION

As it has been exposed along the present paper, *Fasti Congressuum* is, undoubtedly, an innovative, versatile and useful tool to every single researcher in Ancient History. The website (http://fasticongressuum.wix.com/fasticongressuum) was initially planned and designed by the FC Team as a way of overcoming the traditional lack of a unified source of information about the different congresses, a recurrent problem for the researcher interested in taking part in this kind of scientific meetings, as it was mentioned above. The dependence on newsletters and academic websites usually characterized by fragmentation and commonly focused in very specific areas of knowledge or geographical regions produce a considerable gap between the institutions interested in the celebration of a congress and its potential participants. The creation of a site that works as a centralized repository and a diffusing spot at the same time is, in this context, a real need for the scientific community.

But FC is also an excellent way of diffusion for the organizers of congresses. Up to now the spreading of the call for papers and congresses' programs from different researching centres depended on previously created networks of collaboration with other institutions. This implied an incredible effort for the promoters, but FC give the organizers the opportunity of a centralized, reliable and standardized free platform for an effective diffusion, at a worldwide level, of the their congresses, symposia and seminars. FC doesn't exclusively depend on the academic e-mail list compiled by its team. Through the FC e-mail account (fasticongressuum@gmail.com), organizers can interact directly and personally with the members of the team and send the basic information of their event to be included in our diffusion channels.

The use of a visual and user friendly website, translated into Spanish, Italian and English to guarantee a better international diffusion of its contents, permits an easy way of access to all the information compiled by the FC team. On one hand, the FC calendar, in which the basic information of each seminar or congress is accompanied of a direct link to its own website entry, permits the search in terms of date of celebration. On the other hand, the use of specific labels and keywords referring the contents of every single congress and its country of celebration makes the searching of encounters dedicated to specific search fields or celebrated in a precise place easier.

The stress of the project on the use of the enormous possibilities of free transmission of information given by the social media also comes from the conception of FC as an accessible and useful tool for the international diffusion of scientific encounters. The great amount of potential recipients that can be reached through our Facebook (2004) and Twitter (2006) profiles, whose number of followers rise continuously, as it was explained above, guarantee the effective spreading of the uploaded events. In addition, it has to be mentioned the fact that, since different users and official platforms directly related with the research into ancient world commonly diffuse the contents of FC accounts, so the social nature of that platforms also contribute to a exponential grow on the reach of every single new post. But the key of the relevancy of the social media is, undoubtedly, the international reach of those means of communication. Since both FC accounts receive regular visits from the five continents, they allow the effective spreading at a global level of every single call for papers and congresses included in the FC website.

At the same time, the weekly sending of the FC newsletters, which, as was exposed before, consists in a compilation of all the new posts directly linked with the website, permitting the automatic reception of all the new information in the inbox of the personal e-mail account of an increasing number of subscribers. By means of it, all the new information of the website is only one click away from interested researchers.

As a tool designed and implemented by ancient world researchers for the use of the ancient world academic community, FC fulfils, by means of the use of the potential of social media, a traditional need for effective spreading of scientific meetings in this research field. The use of an user friendly interface of the website and the continuous diffusion of its information via Facebook (2004) and Twitter (2006) gives the opportunity, to every single researcher interested in sharing the results of his/her investigation and exchanging information and ideas with other colleagues, or in the organization of a congress or seminar in his home institution, of an easy access to a huge net of diffusion of academic encounters. FC is, in conclusion, the result of a complex process of conception and design motivated by the desire of overcoming one of the most obvious and, at the same time, most ignored needs of the academic community.

REFERENCES

Academia.edu. (2008, September). Retrieved from https://www.academia.edu/

Archport Mail List. (2015). Retrieved from http://ml.ci.uc.pt/mhonarchive/archport/index.html

Calenda.org. (2000). Retrieved from http://calenda.org/

Classical Association of the Atlantic States. (n.d.). *Classical World*. Retrieved December 4, 2015, from http://caas-cw.org/wp/

CLASSICISTS Mail List. (n.d.). Retrieved from http://listserv.liv.ac.uk/cgi-bin/wa?A0=CLASSICISTS

Conal Conference Alerts. (2000). Retrieved from http://www.conferencealerts.com/

Facebook. (2004). Retrieved from www.facebook.com/fasticongressuum

Fasti Congressuum. (2015). Retrieved from http://fasticongressuum.wix.com/fasticongressuum

Google Calendar. (2006). Retrieved from https://calendar.google.com

Google Maps. (2005). Retrieved from https://www.google.es/maps

International Society of Cicero's Friends. (2012). Retrieved from https://tulliananews.wordpress.com/2015/12/04/siac-newsletter-96/

Notiziario Italiano di Antichistica. (2007). Retrieved from http://www.accademiafiorentina.it/?pg=notiziario_italiano_di_antichistica

Researchgate.net. (2008, May). Retrieved from http://www.researchgate.net/

Society for Ancient Mediterranean Religions. (2008). Retrieved from http://samreligions.org/

Society for Classical Studies. (n.d.). Retrieved from https://classicalstudies.org/

TIO Newsletter. (2008). Retrieved from http://terraitalia.altervista.org/

Twitter. (2006). Retrieved from https://twitter.com/fasticongress

Wix.com. (2006). Retrieved 2015, from http://es.wix.com/

KEY TERMS AND DEFINITIONS

Call for Papers: It is document in which new ideas for a speech in a congress is showed. When a congress is going to be celebrated, the researches in charge ask for ideas related to a topic. A researcher must write an abstract of more o lees 200-300 words and send to the committee in order to be taken into account. The call for papers is the legal document in which those conditions are explained. It usually provided information about the congress such as, city, research institution which organize it, days of the Congress.

Congress: Social encounter in the research world. A congress is the way to present news in academic world. Normally it is related to one topic and before a Call for papers it is celebrated during some days. The main propose of a Congress is to share information between colleagues. That is the reason of choosing a topic in common and to have a process of Call for papers and revision. Usually researches pronounce a speech but also listen to colleagues. Speeches are organized in sessions. The debate part, located at the end of each session is the place of discussing and interchanging ideas. Those ideas can be reflected in a posterior article or help to future investigation. In a congress extern people, such as students or other researchers are admitted just to listen to speeches but also to share their opinion in a more informal way.

Fasti Congressuum: Latin term created related to Roman calendar. Fasti were those days when working was prohibited in honor of the gods. It is also an international website in which information about Congress and Call for papers is provided.

Newsletter: It is a periodical email (every week, every month) in which regular information is provided. The main propose of a newsletter is to update information for visitors. It is not needed to go into a website because an email with the last news is received. Usually it is needed to sing up and ask for becoming a subscriber.

Seminar: Periodical reunion in at least one University or research institution. It must be organized around a topic and periodically an expert came and pronounced a speech. Every day (it usually be one day per week) only one person speak for the public and a general discussion follow the speech. It last longer than a congress, from one moth to the whole academic year.

Social Networks: It is called to every single tool which was located on the Internet network and has the finality to interact people. The main propose of this world is to connect people immediately and make easier to share information. Every person must have a personal profile with personal information that must be real. From your account it is provided a way to share information such as pictures, videos and documents. Facebook (2004) is the most popular social networks but it is not the only one.

Suscriptor: Person with an email address who ask for receiving newsletter. It is a kind of follower. Sometimes personal information is required but sometimes it is needed only to provide an email address.

Tag: Social network term. It is a title or definition that it is given to a post. It is used to define or to express any kind of information. Then it can be used to look up information about some topic. In *Fasti Congressuum* website tags are used to selection and compile different post.

This research was previously published in the Handbook of Research on Emerging Technologies for Digital Preservation and Information Modeling edited by Alfonso Ippolito and Michela Cigola; pages 26-44, copyright year 2017 by Information Science Reference (an imprint of IGI Global).

Section 3
Information Control and Management

Chapter 9
Document Description and Coding as Key Elements in Knowledge, Records, and Information Management

Olugbade Oladokun
University of Botswana, Botswana

Saul F. C. Zulu
University of Botswana, Botswana

ABSTRACT

Document description and coding are key operations to information storage and retrieval systems. Description makes it possible for users to obtain information about the documents while coding provides unique numbers to described documents, and enables users to locate, retrieve and store documents manually or electronically. Consequent upon the mass production of information and attendant information explosion, modern libraries and other information dissemination institutions, attached to various institutions, were established. A need therefore arose to put in place systems of achieving bibliographic control over the information produced and collected to facilitate its identification and location wherever it may be found. Among the major systems or tools that information professionals developed to achieve bibliographic control and organization of information include: cataloguing, classification, indexing and abstracting. Using largely documentary sources, the chapter makes a case on the critical role of document description and coding systems in information and knowledge management.

INTRODUCTION

Categorizing and description of objects and other physical entities are as old as the existence of humanity. It is through description and coding of things that humanity is able to identify and characterize them. All the things that are perceived and used, either in homes or outside the home; things made by humans or

DOI: 10.4018/978-1-7998-0417-8.ch009

natural objects such as living and non-living things, are easily identified because they have been categorised, described and coded. Assigning names to people and objects is in fact, an act of description. This chapter discusses the role of document description and coding in information and knowledge management.

GENESIS OF DOCUMENT DESCRIPTION AND CODING

Document description and coding can be traced to two major factors namely: the invention of writing, and the establishment of information and knowledge management institutions. These two indices are briefly described below to provide the context for document description and coding.

Invention of Writing

The first major factor responsible for the development of document description and coding tools can be traced to the invention of writing, as explained by Burke and Ornstein (1995) and Schmandt-Besserat (1982) and chronicled below:

- Writing initially involved coding human sound into pictures. This led to picture 'writing' demonstrated in rock paintings all over the world;
- Picture writings coded into symbols that evolved into letters and numbers used for communication in writing. Alphabet and number systems evolved from these symbols;
- The invention of alphabet and number systems standardized the symbols used to represent letters and numbers; and
- Standardization of letters and numbers, through the invention of alphabets and number systems, enable people using a particular alphabet or number system to communicate in a standardized manner.

Early writing was achieved by using various writing implements and storage media. Writing tools included various types of styluses or brushes and other predecessors of the modern writing pens and different types of inks and paints that were used to achieve writing on a surface of objects such as papyrus scrolls, animal skins, parchment, wood, stone, etc. (American Printing History Association, 2016).

The next development in the evolution of the technology of recording and production of information was the invention of printing. Printing essentially involved transferring the writing symbols (letters of the alphabet or numbers) onto a mechanical device. Printing was achieved by dipping the key containing the writing symbol (number, letter or punctuation mark) into a pad of ink and pressing it against a printing surface such as parchment, animal skin, etc. The invention of printing was significant because it mechanized writing (Prepressure, 2012; American Printing History Association, 2016).

Another milestone in the production of information materials came with the invention of the movable type in the far East, as well as Europe. For instance, Johannes Gutenberg, a German inventor and industrialist, is generally credited for having invented the first movable type in the 1450's in Europe (Prepressure, 2012). The invention of the movable type represented the mechanization of printing. Printing revolutionized the production and communication of information materials in the sense that it fostered mass production of information whose circulation cut across national boundaries.

As information production technologies based on the movable type improved, so did the rate of information production, increase. This phenomenon of mass production of information in the 1800s and 1900s came to be known as the information explosion. The information explosion was not only characterized by the production of too much information, but also by the diversity of publishing houses, languages in which information was produced, geographic dispersion of publishers and a variety of formats in which information was produced. In addition, the systematic creation of knowledge, through research, by universities and research institutes since the 1900s, also contributed and has continued to contribute to the mass production of information materials (Blackford, 2001; New World Encyclopedia, 2016).

Establishment of Information Management Institutions

As a consequence of the mass production of information and its attendant information explosion, modern libraries and other information dissemination institutions, attached to various institutions, were established. A need therefore arose to put in place systems of achieving bibliographic control over the information that was being produced and collected by these institutions to facilitate its identification and location wherever it may be found (in collections of libraries, publishing houses or in individual documents) (History Magazine, 2001). Among the major systems or tools that information professionals have developed to achieve bibliographic control and organization of information, over the past 500 years or so, include: cataloguing, classification, indexing and abstracting. These are discussed shortly in this chapter.

DOCUMENT DESCRIPTION AND CODING

Document description is the process of extracting data from a document to describe the document using international standards. Document description is an essential process that provides access to the information resources acquired in the library, archives, records and other information centres. Document coding on the other hand is the process of assigning described documents unique numbers that facilitate physical storage, location, identification and retrieval.

Document description and coding (or classifications) are central functions of any information service. Tools for document description and coding are among the key elements in information and knowledge management process. Rowley and Hartley (2014, p. xix) observe that "as availability of, and access to, information increases, the need to be able to locate and retrieve information becomes all the more pressing...so are the tools that support or assist in the process of information retrieval are becoming increasingly important and sophisticated''. In order to be able to locate, retrieve and store materials with ease, be it in the library, records, knowledge or any other information centre, the information resources must be organized. Document description is generally known to be part of 'bibliographic control or information organization' (IFLA, 2014). In her general assessment of information organization, Taylor (2004) affirms that 'retrieval of information is dependent upon its having been organised'. Taylor further declares that 'organization of information also allows us to keep a usable record of human endeavours for posterity'. Narrowing it to the ambience of the library, Adedibu, Akinboro, & Abdussalam (2012) declare that the purposes of organizing library materials are:

- To make location of library materials easy;
- To save time and space; to facilitate easy accessibility to the materials;

- To enhance effective utilization of the materials; and
- To make the library attractive to its users.

Generally, the purpose of organizing information is to ensure that information, (data, information, knowledge) is processed for storage and retrieval.

In order that the twin goal of easy retrieval and storage of information might be achieved, the development of various systems and tools used for the organization of information was facilitated. Among the major information storage and retrieval systems and tools developed to describe documents and achieve bibliographic control and organization of information are cataloguing, indexing abstracting and classification. Whilst the first three are specifically for document description, the last (classification) is for subject coding. These tools are discussed below.

CATALOGUING

Irrespective of the size or number, information materials or resources kept either in libraries, records or any information centres should be organised and made accessible with ease, as and when the need arises. In order to ensure easy accessibility, materials need to be appropriately described such that even when there are many that look similar, the standard used in describing them will distinguish one from the other. As an activity that is essentially concerned with describing documents, cataloguing is the process of creating entries for a set of bibliographic records that represent the collection accessible in a particular location. Sales (2005) sees cataloguing as the process of creating bibliographic records of works according to accepted rules or standards. Cabonero and Dolendo (2013, p. 1) also affirm that cataloguing is "an essential process that provides access to all acquired information resources for it allows people to find information needed for their personal and professional growth and development". Cabonero and Dolendo further observe that cataloguing provides access points to information resources in a way that users will be able to find the needed information or resources. The basic goal of cataloguing is to expose the physical traits and characteristics of documents so that each document may be easily identified as a distinctive entity in a collection of documents.

Cataloguing is carried out in two phases, namely: descriptive cataloguing and subject cataloguing. Descriptive cataloguing, also known as physical description, is concerned with revealing the physical characteristics or attributes of the document being described. In order to ensure uniformity and consistency in document description, an international standard, Anglo American Cataloguing Rules Second Edition Revised (AACR2R), provides the rules for cataloguing various types of information carriers. It should be noted that even though the AACR2R is still predominantly used in developing countries, it has been replaced with the introduction of Resource Description and Access (RDA) (discussed shortly) in some advanced countries of the world. In sequential order as defined in Anglo-American Cataloguing Rules (2004), a bibliographic record/entry comprises the following elements used to describe documents:

- Title, statement of responsibility area – the person(s) responsible for the intellectual content of document. Title depicts the name the document is called;
- Edition statement – usually gives an indication of the number of times the document has been revised or when additional information has been added to the document;

- Material or type of publication – usually provides information on the type of document being described, especially if the material is non-conventional i.e. microforms, sound or audio recording materials in a predominantly book environment;
- Publication details - often referred to as imprint, usually comprises place of publication, publishers and date of publication;
- Physical description – reveals the extent and size i.e. the number of pages, frames, kilobytes, etc. It also reveals whether the document has any illustrative materials or not.
- Series area is indicated only for documents written as part of a series;
- Note area - contains special features of the document not indicated in the preceding areas i.e. Index, bibliography, etc; and
- Standard availability number – peculiar to each document, this is where the ISBN (for books) or ISSN (for serials), which are the unique identifier given to each document.

Subject cataloguing is the second phase of cataloguing in bibliographic description. Also known as content description, subject cataloguing involves content analysis and providing a response to the question, to put it in the parlance of document descriptors: *what is the 'aboutness' of the document?* In a more understandable way, the question often raised when doing subject cataloguing of an item is: *what is the document about?* (Taylor, 2006; Rowley & Hartley, 2014). Hutchins (1978) asserts that the traditional view finds universal acceptance, namely that for the purposes of document indexing and information retrieval the 'aboutness' of a document is to be equated with some kind of 'summary' of its contents. The correct response to or determination of the question brings about the subject heading for a document. The cataloguer or indexer analyzes the subject contents of the document under consideration, and subsequently assigns appropriate subject heading(s) which summarizes the contents of the document. Whilst determining the 'aboutness' of the document being described, several parts of the document or the information package are usually considered. The parts of a document to examine in order to determine the subject heading include the title, introduction, preface and table of contents, among others. The Title is perceived as a distinctive phrase or words which attempts to succinctly capture or summarize the whole content of the document; the Introduction provides some hints on the contents of various sections of the document; the Preface provides the author's reasons for writing the document and the Table of Contents presents an outline, which serves as a 'map' of what the document contains, chapter by chapter and where the various elements are located in the document. Since 'there is no one correct way to determine 'aboutness' (Taylor, 2006), various aspects or parts of the document are considered before determination of the subject.

In order to select and assign subject headings to documents, a standardized list of subject headings is usually consulted to provide guidance. Probably the two most popular standard lists of subject headings are: *Sears List of Subject Headings* (SLSH) and *Library of Congress Subject Headings* (LCSH). These codes provide a controlled list of subject terms to be used as subject headings. Whilst the Sears List of Subject Headings is more useful for small public and school libraries, the LCSH is mostly used in research and academic libraries. In the traditional system, subject headings derived from subject description, are used as entries in the subject catalogue.

Once the subject or the 'aboutness' of the document is determined, the list of subject headings in use (be it SLSH, LCSH or any other) is consulted to see if the term or phrase is acceptable and usable as a subject heading or not. The preferential term 'USE' is written against the acceptable term, whilst a referral term 'SEE' is written against the terms that are rejected and not usable or acceptable. The word

'See' therefore directs the user/cataloguer to the preferred or usable term. The usable and unusable terms are often applied to describe the subjects in a document. They are often referred to as descriptors and non-descriptors respectively (Aina, 2004; Taylor, 2006).

Choice of Access Points

The catalogue of a library, information or record centre is the key and a major index to the collection of that organization or establishment. The users approach the catalogue to gain access to the holdings or collection of the organization. In order to gain access to the information or document desired, the user would require a heading for guidance. The heading, created from the document, is regarded as the main access point of a document. Generally, the users prefer and use the author as their access point. However, some prefer the title and others, the subject. Taylor (2006) declares that for any one item, one of the access points is chosen as a main entry, or primary access point, and the others become added entries. Whilst emphasising the role an author plays in the provision of access points, Aina (2004) affirms that an author is generally defined as the person chiefly responsible for the creation of the intellectual or artistic content of a document, hence, the author is expected to be the main entry point of a document.

In the traditional information, knowledge and record keeping ambience, it is important to note that each document is expected to have three access points, namely:

1. Author,
2. Title, and
3. Subject.

From the options and facts available, a cataloguer applies his/her judgement to take a decision on the option to use as the main heading or access point. The rule is that the person responsible for the intellectual content of a document is the author and is supposed to be the main entry point to the document Where a document is authored by more than one person, only one of them can be used as the heading or main entry. In the event that no author is seen in a document or when there are more than 3 authors to a document, none of them is regarded as owning the intellectual content to the document. In this respect, the title is used as the main entry. The access points of a book are usually derived from the title page often referred to as the chief source of information for a document. It should also be noted that apart from personal authors, corporate bodies like institutions (e.g. University of Botswana) or organisations (e.g. Southern African Development Community) are authors when they are responsible for the intellectual content of a document.

MARC (Machine-Readable Cataloguing Record)

As the world of information, knowledge and record management is changing from paper-centric environments to paperless electronic ones, a new system that moves with the demands of the time emerged. *Machine-Readable Cataloguing Record* (MARC) is a departure from the traditional form of making catalogue entries on paper cards. It represents modernization in cataloguing. British Library (2016) indicates that MARC is a format standard for the storage and exchange of bibliographic record and related information in machine readable form. In its attempt to simplify the definition of MARC, the Library of Congress (LoC) (2009a) breaks the phrase into two, namely: "machine readable" and "cataloguing record". Kelsey (2014) also affirms that MARC is a coding system facilitating computer manipulation of bibliographic records 'Machine readable', according to LoC means that one particular type of machine, a computer, can read and interpret the data in the cataloging record. "Cataloguing record", LoC states, means a bibliographic record, or the information traditionally shown on a catalogue card. The record includes (not necessarily in this order):

1. A description of the item,
2. Main entry and added entries,
3. Subject headings, and
4. The classification or call number (MARC records often contain much more additional information).

According to Sales (2005), MARC format was developed to standardize machine-readable bibliographic data so that all kinds of library materials can be read by a variety of automated library systems. Document description as prescribed in Anglo American Cataloguing Rules, second edition, Revised (AACR2R) is represented by a number of elements. Each element is a field and a field is an access point. These elements include the heading or main entry, which can be a personal author or corporate body; title or statement of responsibility, edition etc. LoC (2009a) states that each field is associated with a 3-digit number called a "tag."

Below is a list of the most frequently used tags or principal fields relating to AACR2R in a MARC format:

020 tag: International Standard Book Number (ISBN);
100 tag: Main entry heading: personal author;
110 tag: Main entry heading: corporate body;
245 tag: Title and statement of responsibility;
250 tag: Edition;
260 tag: Publication, etc.;
300 tag: Physical description;
490 tag: Series not in added entry form;
520 tag: Notes; and
650 tag: Topical subject heading.

It is noteworthy to indicate that MARC21 is the latest and most popular metadata standard used internationally. Developed in 2000, MARC21, according to Rowley and Hartley (2014), came into being as a result of the development and integration of the US and Canadian MARC formats. The Library of Congress (2009b) affirms that MARC21 format uses "260" "$a" "$b" and "$c" to mark the field that holds imprint data instead of storing the words "publication area," "place of publication," "name of publisher," and "date of publication" in each record. The Library of Congress (2016) declares that a MARC bibliographic record consists of three main components, defined as follows;

- The *Leader*, which is the first field of a MARC record and fixed in length at 24 character positions;
- The *Directory*, which describes series of entries containing the tag, length, and starting location of each variable field within a record. Each entry is 12 character positions in length; and
- The *Variable fields*. The data in a MARC bibliographic record is organized into *variable fields*, each identified by a three-character numeric tag stored in the Directory entry for the field.

The type of information in the field is identified by the remainder of the tag.

- 0XX Control information, identification and classification numbers, etc.;
- 1XX Main entries;
- 2XX Titles and title paragraph (title, edition, imprint);
- 3XX Physical description, etc.;
- 4XX Series statements;
- 5XX Notes;
- 6XX Subject access fields;
- 7XX Added entries other than subject or series - linking fields;
- 8XX Series added entries, holdings, etc.; and
- 9XX Reserved for local implementation.

Explaining its usefulness, Rowley and Hartley (2014) states that MARC records can be used in information retrieval, displaying citations, cataloguing, identifying new publications and resource sharing.

RESOURCE DISCOVERY AND ACCESS (RDA)

Resource Description and Access is the new cataloguing code that is replacing the age-long Anglo-American Cataloguing Rules, Second Edition (AACR2). In a release by the American Library Association (2009), it is asserted that RDA goes beyond earlier cataloguing codes in that it provides guidelines on cataloguing digital resources and places a stronger emphasis on helping users find, identify, select, and obtain the information they want. The development of RDA is known to have benefited from two conceptual models developed by the International Federation of Library Associations and Institutions (IFLA) – Functional Requirements for Bibliographic Data (FRBR) and Functional Requirements for Authority Data (FRAD).

Anhalt and Stewart (2012) observe that some of the traditional cataloguing terms will change under RDA: for instance "heading," "main entry," and "added entry" all become "access points". They note that the term "main entry," originally developed in the context of card and book catalogues, is not applicable in the online environment, using "preferred access point" instead and clarifying more precisely its relationships with works and expressions. Other key features include:

- RDA is flexible and has extensible framework for the description of resources;
- It is designed to take advantages of the new technologies;
- It is better able to work in the computer environment which gives a richer discovery experience for users;
- It has the capability to take library data from the library catalogue to the web; and
- It was designed with the users in mind to improve the users navigation of library resources.

INDEXING

Whilst cataloguing provides a guide to the documents arranged on the shelf in a library, information or record centre, indexing conducts a user to the contents of the documents. Thus indexing helps in digging deep into and retrieving relevant information contained from the documents. Indexing is the process of providing a guide to the intellectual content of a document or a collection of documents. Together with its counterpart, abstracting, Musa, Musa, and Musa (2014) affirm that these tools help users to retrieve information needed with or without little difficulty and more importantly lead users to pertinent and relevant information within the shortest time possible. As if advocating for what constitutes a good index and abstract, Cleveland and Cleveland (2013) declare for whatever purpose, what forms a good index or abstract as both are tools that lead a user to extract information that is needed with no hurdles, no false paths and no irrelevant materials. The perfect index or abstract according to these authors lead a user to totally pertinent information, hardly leads to trivial information and never lead to non-pertinent information. The result of this process is an index, which will serve as a pointer to the intellectual content in a document or a collection of documents. Whilst quoting from the British Indexing Standard (BS 3700:1988), Akinwumi (2013) states that an index is a systematic arrangement of entries designed to enable users locate information in a document. The Standard asserts that the document in this instance can be a book, a journal, an audiotape, a computer film and so on. Musa et al. (2014) declare that the process of creating an index is called indexing. Index elements can be names of people, places, topics, or subjects being discussed in a document or a collection of documents.

The index performs its function through the descriptors (subjects, topics, terms, keywords etc.) assigned to the document by the indexer. As noted above, the ultimate goal of the index is to reduce the time and efforts a user expends in accessing a topic of interest in a particular document or a set of documents which have been stored in a collection.

Types of Indexes

Categorized either by purpose, arrangement, subject, structure of search, indexes are many and varied. Some of the indexes include:

Alphabetical Index

This type of index is popular and well known to many people. Cleveland and Cleveland (2013) confirm that the term alphabetical index covers a number of different kinds of indexes, even as it is based on the orderly principles of letters of the alphabet. The National Open University of Nigeria (NOUN) (2015) also lends credence and describes it as a kind of general purpose and simple index forms that many people are familiar with. NOUN avows that one of the best known methods of index arrangement is the single alphabetical index in which names and subject entries are filed together. NOUN further reiterate that alphabetical indexes are the most common index method noting that many index types also follow this alphabetical format of arrangement not only because it is simple to create but also because it follows a known pattern which people are used to.

Author Index

The entry points in an author index are people, organizations, corporate authors, government agencies, universities etc. and users are guided to titles of documents by way of authors (Cleveland & Cleveland, 2013). Borko and Bernier (1978) suggest that a subject, concept, or topic index may be combined with the author index to give a one-alphabet product that is simply called an index.

Classified Index

This is an index where the contents are arranged systematically by classes or subject headings. The Society of American Archivists (2016) defines a classified index as a list of headings, organized into groups based on similar characteristics rather than in alphabetical order, that point to information relevant to the heading in materials organized in some other manner. Borko and Bernier (1978) made further clarification by noting that entries in an index do not need to be in alphabetical order. They assert that in a classified index, entries are arranged according to some classification scheme. It should however be noted that though classifiers have a penchant for classified items, the mind-set of users is alphabetic order, hence most users find classified indexes difficult to use.

Coordinate Index

This index makes it possible for terms to be combined or coordinated for searching purposes. The Society of American Archivists (2016) perceive this type of index as a set of rules to provide access to materials by assigning separate headings for each concept, which are then related (coordinated) during a search to retrieve materials based on the relationship among those headings.

Periodical Indexes

The role of a periodical index is critical to scholarship. This probably made Colorado State University (CSU) (2016) to observe that the most up-to-date information on a given topic is quite often published in periodicals-journals, magazines, newspapers or any other publication issued at regular intervals-rather than in books. The institution in its examination believes that a periodical index is a list of articles from a specific time period contained in a group of selected publications or that cover a group of related subjects. Organized alphabetically, they may be searched by author, title and subject in the same manner as you would in a library catalogue. There are two types of periodical indexes:

1. Individual indexes to individual journals. The publisher of the journal prepares an index, usually for a volume at the end of a year's run of the journal. The approach for this type of indexing can range from a simple, uncontrolled vocabulary to a complex indexing system with a thesaurus (Cleveland & Cleveland, 2013); and
2. Broad indexes to a group of journals. The indexing of the world periodical literature is a major enterprise cutting across many titles and specific subjects. Unlike books authored by one or two people, there are thousands of authors in an index to periodicals. Several indexers are involved in periodical indexing (Cleveland & Cleveland, 2013).

Book Indexes

These are the popular lists of words, keywords, descriptors and phrases indicating or pointing to pages of location of the terms, usually documented at the back of books. Providing further details on book indexes, Cleveland and Cleveland (2013) corroborate that these indexes are generally alphabetical, at the back of a book, giving a page location of the subject or name associated with each word. A book index pinpoints information so that the reader will not have to read, or re-read the entire book. The authors however warned that a book index is not a substitute for the information in the book, but is a pointer to the information included.

ABSTRACTING

Abstracting is the process of creating brief descriptions or summaries of the contents of documents such as books, periodical articles, or other documents. Colorado State University (CSU) (2016) describes abstracts as formal summaries writers prepare of their completed work. Abstracts, according to CSU, are important tools for readers, especially as they try to keep up with an explosion of information in print and on the Internet. An abstract is usually accompanied by a bibliographic citation to enable the user identify and/or locate the item. Cleveland and Cleveland (2013) maintain that the purpose of an abstract is to give scholars filtered access to the literature in their disciplines. According to Aina (2004), abstracts can also give the user current awareness service or a retrospective search tool so that non-current literature can be examined for pertinent information. Like an index, an abstract provides access to documents and goes further to provide the concise and accurate summary of the essential contents of a document. Quoting the International Standard Organisation (ISO) (1976), Aina observes that users of an abstract are able to:

1. Identify the basic content of a document quickly and accurately; and
2. Determine its relevance to their interests and decide whether they need to read the document in its entirety or not.

It is noteworthy to state that many documents in foreign languages usually have abstracts in English language, hence, abstracts can be used to overcome a language barrier. Such abstracts help the user to determine whether there is need to translate the original document or not. In constructing a minuscule surrogate or skeletal representation of the original document, Cleveland and Cleveland (2001) observe that the abstractor examines the following five indicators from the contents of the document:

1. **Objectives and Scope:** Why was the document written; author's purpose and motivation;
2. **Methodology:** The research method or design used to do the study is expected to be detailed;
3. **Results:** What were the findings? Does the abstractor see any factors that might affect the validity, reliability or accuracy of the results;
4. **Conclusions:** How were the objectives of the study or research questions achieved, not achieved and, or addressed should be explained. The recommendations of the researcher(s) from the study should also be mentioned; and
5. **Other Information:** Supportive information should be noted.

Types of Abstracts

There are two main types of abstracts. These are briefly described below.

1. **Informative Abstract:** Attempts to capture all the essential points in the document. It presents the actual data and information contained in the original document. An informative abstract usually covers four essential areas of the document being abstracted, and these, according to the National Open University of Nigeria (NOUN) (2015), include the Objective and scope of the work; Methods used; Results; and Conclusions. Similarly, Colorado State University (2016) presents a four-way outline when the institution declares that Informative abstracts typically follow this format:
   a. Identifying information (bibliographic citation or other identification of the document);
   b. Concise restatement of the main point, including the initial problem or other background;
   c. Methodology (for experimental work) and key findings; and
   d. Major conclusions. It represents the true surrogate of the original document
2. **Indicative Abstract:** This type of abstract gives the outlines of the topics or headings covered in a piece of writing. The outlines usually enable the reader to decide whether to read the entire document or not. Otherwise known as descriptive, indicative abstract provides an indication of the original document (Aina, 2004). It provides information on the type of documents being abstracted, the principal areas covered and how the facts are treated. The descriptive abstract is like a table of contents in paragraph form; therefore reading a descriptive abstract cannot substitute for reading the document because it does not capture the content of the piece. The descriptive abstracts are useful as alerting and selection aids (Colorado State University, 2016). Cleveland and Cleveland (2013) also stress that in most cases, the indicative abstract is somewhat shorter, written in general terms and does not give the user a progressive account of the paper's development.

Since an indicative or descriptive abstract hardly provides the actual contents, it cannot be used in place or as a true surrogate of the original.

Apart from the two main types, other variants of abstracts include:

1. **Authors' Abstracts:** Are usually prepared by author(s) of the original document. The abstracts are written along with the documents. Whilst they may not be skilled in abstracting, authors as experts in their fields can bring out essential contents from their documents (Aina, 2004);
2. **Critical Abstract:** Makes an evaluative judgement on the content of the document. It gives the depth or extent of the content and comment on various aspects of the document. The abstractor should be knowledgeable and be a subject expert of the document (National Open University of Nigeria, 2015);
3. **Discipline-Oriented Abstract:** This is abstracting of document that is of a specific area of knowledge or discipline e.g. Library and Information Science Abstract (Mortel, 2012);
4. **Professional Abstracts:** These are written by skilled professional abstractors who, for reasons of their skills and professionalism in abstracting, are capable of producing high quality abstracts in their specific subject areas (Aina, 2004); and
5. **Slanted Abstract:** Provides an abstract for the users of a particular section of a multi-purpose document (Aina, 2004).

CLASSIFICATION

Classification is a plan used in the organization of information, records and knowledge for storage and retrieval purposes. Classification involves the grouping of related records together so that they are found quickly when they are required. Classification is also basic to the effective management of various types of documents including records. All other aspects of document control are dependent on the way they have been classified. Classification, according to the Online Computer Library Center (OCLC, 2016), provides a system for organising knowledge. OCLC further notes that classification may be used to organize knowledge represented in any form, e.g., books, documents, electronic resource. Books or any materials of value are generally arranged in the library, information or record centre in a systematic way that commands easy accessibility. This arrangement is often referred to as classification.

Rowley and Hartley (2014) believe that classification and the creation of structure through categorization of knowledge is one of the most fundamental of human learning activities. Cleveland and Cleveland (2013) also affirm that classification is to put similar things into groups with some designation tag that generally captures the essence of the group. Classification is concerned with the grouping together of related or similar entities from general to specific. The determination of the subject heading(s) carried out in the second phase of cataloguing as discussed above is normally used as a basis for assigning a classification number for the item. Thus, after assigning the subject headings, the next step is to assign classification notation, which can be letters (alphabets) or numbers or combination of both, to a work. It is these notations that are used to arrange or file the documents on the shelf. When the subject heading is appropriately selected for a document the cataloguer is well guided to the classification notation/number that can be assigned to the item. Taylor (2006) asserts that whereas subject headings give a random alphabetic approach to the concepts inherent in documents, classification provides a logical, or at least a methodical approach to the arrangement of those documents.

In information storage and retrieval systems, classification is used to assign notation to documents based on the dominant subject or activity (or transaction) determined from subject/activity description. The document code is then used as a tool for the physical arrangement of documents into their storage areas. The document codes or class marks are used for the location, identification and retrieval of documents that have been committed to storage. A document is stored or shelved using the notation given to it. In bibliographic classification the classifier arranges documents into groups/classes based on subject content. In this arrangement the relationships between documents in the same class are also demonstrated (Taylor, 2006; Kelsey, 2014).

As noted, in order to arrange documents and ensure they are accessible to users, classification schemes are used. Taylor (2006) confirms that the ultimate aim of any classification system is to lead an information seeker to the information package required. In order to maintain consistency and uniformity in assigning document codes or class marks, classification codes have been developed.

Classification Principles

A good classification system should be based on international principles. The principles ensure that documents are classified in a uniform and consistent manner following international best practices. These principles include that the classification scheme should have (Schellenberg, 1956):

1. The ability to bring related files together;
2. The ability to provide room for growth when new functions are created;
3. Ability to bring records of similar retention periods together for easy disposition;
4. Ability to operate the classification scheme with limited skill and knowledge in records management; and
5. Ability of users to search for files using standardised terminologies and controlled vocabulary used in the organization.

Two of the major document classification schemes (or codes) that are used in most libraries and other information management institutions are Dewey Decimal Classification (DDC) and the American Library of Congress Classification Schemes

DEWEY DECIMAL CLASSIFICATION (DDC)

Developed by Melvil Dewey in 1876, Dewey Decimal Classification simply known as DDC arranges knowledge into 10 main disciplines/subjects and assigns them numbers. Each of the main classes is subdivided into 10 sub-classes. DDC arranges subjects from the general to the specific in a logical order and uses a decimal point to specify subject terms which results in digits of long numbers. The application of Arabic numerals and decimal makes an indefinite expansion possible.

The 10 main classes are (OCLC, 2016):

- 000 Computer Science, Information and General works;
- 100 Philosophy and Psychology;
- 200 Religion;
- 300 Social Sciences;
- 400 Language;
- 500 Natural Sciences and Mathematics;
- 600 Technology (Applied Sciences);
- 700 The Arts;
- 800 Literature and Rhetoric; and
- 900 Geography and History.

LIBRARY OF CONGRESS CLASSIFICATION

While it uses mixed notation i.e. combines letters and numbers, the Library of Congress (LoC) classification divides the entire field of knowledge into 21 groups. The main classes of LC (Library of Congress, 2016) are:

- A General Works;
- B Philosophy, Psychology. Religion;
- C Auxiliary Sciences of History;
- D World History and History of Europe etc;

- E History: America (western hemisphere);
- F History of the Americas;
- G Geography, Anthropology, Recreation;
- H Social Sciences;
- J Political Science;
- K Law of the United Kingdom, Ireland United States;
- L Education;
- M Music and books on Music;
- N Fine Arts;
- P Language and Literature;
- Q Science;
- R Medicine;
- S Agriculture;
- T Technology;
- U Military Science;
- V Naval Science; and
- Z Bibliography, Library Science, Information Resources.

The classification number is normally placed on the spine of the book, where it is easily visible.

SPECIALIZED FILE CLASSIFICATION SYSTEMS

Both the DDC and LC Classification systems are designed for the arrangement of published materials such as books, periodicals and other media in the public domain. However, these general schemes may not be very effective in organizing for the storage and retrieval of non-published materials such as reports, organizational records, museum and archival materials. It is for these reasons that special in-house classification systems have been developed. These special classification schemes are based on assigning unique numbers to documents to facilitate storage and retrieval processes. An example of how a document numbering in a specialized classification system works is given below.

Assigning Primary Class

Just like in the DDC the primary class is the main discipline (e.g. Generalities such as 025 for library science) where 0 represents Generalities and 25 library science. In an in-house scheme, the primary class is the abbreviated code for the parent organization. For example all document numbers in the United Nations will be preceded by the acronym 'UN'.

Assigning Secondary Classes

The secondary class will be derived from an acronym of an institutional unit where the document originates from (e.g. UNHCR (United Nations High Commission for Refugees)). This acronym is then added to the primary class (UN) to read as: UN/UNHCR/ (forward slanting slashes (/) are used to separate the primary from secondary classes.

Assigning the Third Class

Third level classification represents what the document is about. In the same unit of an organization, different documents may come from different areas of operations or activities. Each activity or area of operation will then be assigned a unique number. For example, under UNHCR, there could be different operations under refugees such as administration, settlements, repatriation, etc. Each of these operations will be assigned a unique number to form the third level of classification. (e.g. UN/UNHCR/01 to represent administration within UNHCR).

Assigning the Fourth Class

Fourth level class may be used to indicate the year that the document was issued (e.g. UN/UNHCR/01/2016). This arrangement will ensure that all documents on administration emanating from or going to UNHCR Administration for a particular year, are kept together. If more than one document on Administration from UNHCR was issued in 2016, the first document issued in 2016 will be represented by UN/UNHCR/01/2016/1. The second document will be assigned number UN/UNHCR/01/2016/2. The only thing that will change in the following and subsequent years will be the year when the document is issued.

CONCLUSION

It is evident from the discussion, that without putting in place systems for describing and coding of information materials, it would be virtually impossible for users to access information and enable information management institutions to achieve bibliographic control of their collections. Document description and coding saves the users time and effort in locating and retrieving information that they seek. It should be concluded that the old practices of cataloguing, indexing, abstracting and classification are still relevant even in the digital era.

REFERENCES

Adedibu, L. O., Akinboro, E. O., & Abdussalam, T. A. B. (2012). *Cataloguing and Classification of Library Resources in the 21st the Century*. In A. Tella & A. Issa (Eds.), *Library and Information Science in Developing Countries: Contemporary Issues*. Retrieved March 13, 2016, from http://www.igi-global.com/chapter/cataloguing-classification-library-resources-21st/60814

Aina, L. O. (2004). *Library and Information Science Text for Africa*. Ibadan: Third World Information Services Limited.

Akinwumi, O. S. (2013). Indexing and abstracting services in libraries: A legal perspective. *International Journal of Academic Library and Information Science*, *1*(1), 1–9. Retrieved from http://www.academicresearchjournals.org/IJALIS/PDF/2013/August/AKINWUMI.pdf

American Library Association. (2009). *Resource Description and Access (RDA): The Cataloguing Standard for the 21st Century.* Retrieved May 21, 2016, from http://connect.ala.org/files/4161/rda_brochure_pdf_49ff4c8c3b.pdf

American Printing History Association. (2016). *History of printing timeline.* Retrieved May 23, 2016, from https://printinghistory.org/timeline/

Anglo-American Cataloguing Rules (AACR2). (2004). *Cooperative Cataloguing Rules.* London: Library Association.

Anhalt, J., & Stewart, R. A. (2012). Article. *RDA Simplified. Cataloguing & Classification Quarterly, 50*(1), 33-42. Retrieved May 25, 2016, from http://www.tandfonline.com/doi/full/10.1080/01639374.2011.615378

Borko, H., & Bernier, C. L. (1978). *Abstracting Concepts and Methods.* New York: Academic Press.

Blackford, K. (2012). *Factors that influence information explosion.* Retrieved June 13, 2016, from http://thepotentialsmti.blogspot.com/2012/04/factors-that-influence-information.html#!/2012/04/factors-that-influence-information.html

British Indexing Standard. (1988). *Recommendations for preparing indexes to books, periodicals and other documents.* London: BSI British Library.

Standard, C. M. (2016). Retrieved May 27, 2016, from http://www.bl.uk/bibliographic/exchange.html

Burk, J., & Ornstein, R. (1995). *Turning points in the development of contemporary society: a report on the axe makers gift technology's capture and control of our minds and culture.* Retrieved May 26, 2016, from http://www.humanjourney.us/axemaker.html

Cabonero, D. A., & Dolendo, R. B. (2013). Cataloging and Classification Skills of Library and Information Science Practitioners in their Workplaces: A Case Analysis. *Library Philosophy and Practice (e-journal).* Retrieved May 21, 2016, from http://digitalcommons.unl.edu/libphilprac/960

Cleveland, D. B., & Cleveland, A. D. (2013). *Introduction to Indexing and Abstracting.* Libraries Unlimited.

Cleveland, D. B., & Cleveland, A. D. (2001). *Introduction to indexing and Abstracting.* Libraries Unlimited.

Colorado State University. (2016). *Types of Abstracts: Informative Abstract and Indexes.* Retrieved May 29, 2016, from http://writing.colostate.edu/guides/page.cfm?pageid=1252&guideid=59

History Magazine. (2001). *Survivor: The history of the library.* Retrieved June 26, 2016, from http://www.history-magazine.com/libraries.html

Hutchins, W. J. (1978). The concept of aboutness in subject indexing. *ASLIB Proceedings, 30*(5), 172–181. doi:10.1108/eb050629

IFLA. (2014). *Best practice for national bibliographic agencies in a digital age: Bibliographic control.* Retrieved July 21, 2016, from http://www.ifla.org/best-practice-for-national-bibliographic-agencies-in-a-digital-age/node/8911

Infoplease.com. (2016). *Information Storage and Retrieval*. Retrieved September 14, 2016 from http://www.infoplease.com/encyclopedia/science/information-storage-retrieval.html

International Standard Organization. (1976). *Documentation: Abstracts for Publication and Documentation. ISO214: 1976 E*. Geneva: ISO.

Kelsey, M. E. (2014). *Cataloguing for school librarians*. Lanham, MD: Rowman & Littlefield.

Library of Congress. (2008). *MARC 21 Bibliographic*. Retrieved July 29, 2016, from https://www.loc.gov/marc/bibliographic/bdintro.html

Library of Congress. (2009a). *Understanding MARC Bibliographic: Machine Readable Cataloguing*. Retrieved July 29, 2016, from http://www.loc.gov/marc/umb/um01to06.html

Library of Congress. (2009b). *What is a MARC Record, and why is it important*? Retrieved July 29, 2016, from http://www.loc.gov/marc/umb/um01to06.html

Library of Congress. (2016). *Library of Congress Classification Outline*. Retrieved July 29, 2016, from https://www.loc.gov/catdir/cpso/lcco/

Mortel, I. A. (2012). *Abstract and Abstracting*. Retrieved July 29, 2016, from http://www.slideshare.net/ImeAmorMortel/abstracts-abstracting

Musa, A. U., Musa, A. M., & Musa, S. (2014). An Assessment of Indexing and Abstracting Services in Nuhu Bamalli Polytechnic Library, Zaria, Nigeria. *Research on Humanities and Social Sciences, 4*(8), 21-29. Retrieved June 20, 2016, from http://iiste.org/Journals/index.php/RHSS/article/view/12474/13082

New World Encyclopedia. (2016). *Information Explosion*. Retrieved July 24, 2016, from http://www.newworldencyclopedia.org/entry/Information_explosion

National Open University of Nigeria (NOUN). (2015). *Indexing and Abstracting: LIB 811*. Retrieved July 26, 2016, from http://nou.edu.ng/uploads/fileuploads/3jVMpsYFGy1438351898.pdf

Nunberg, G. (2016). *The information explosion: a very brief history*. Retrieved July 29, 2016, from http://courses.ischool.berkeley.edu/i218/f07/QOI9-5GN.pdf

OCLC. (2016). *Introduction to the Dewey Decimal Classification 23*. Retrieved June 26, 2016, from http://www.oclc.org/content/dam/oclc/dewey/versions/print/intro.pdf

Prepressure.com. (2012). *The History of Printing*. Retrieved August 16, 2016, from https://www.prepressure.com/printing/history

Rowley, J., & Hartley, R. (2014). *Organizing Knowledge: an introduction to managing access to information*. Ashgate Publishers.

Sales, M. H. (2005). *Cataloguing and classification. Journal of Adventist Education*. Retrieved July 12, 2016, from http://circle.adventist.org/files/jae/en/jae200467021804.pdf

Schelleberg, T. R. (1956). *Modern archives: principles and techniques*. Chicago: University of Chicago Press. Retrieved June 28, 2016, from http://www.archivists.org/publications/epubs/ModernArchives-Schellenberg.pdf

Schmandt-Besserat, D. (1982). *How writing came about.* Retrieved May 26, 2016, from http://www.jstor.org/stable/pdf/20183589.pdf?_=1470831741653

Society of American Archivists. (2016). *Classified Index.* Retrieved August 29, 2016, from http://www2.archivists.org/glossary/terms/c/classified-index#.V0WF8Lh96Uk

Taylor, A. G. (2004). *The Organization of Information* (2nd ed.). Westport, CT: Libraries Unlimited.

Taylor, A. G. (2006). *Introduction to Cataloging and Classification* (10th ed.). Westport, CT: Libraries Unlimited.

ADDITIONAL READING

Joudrey, D. N. (2015). *Introduction to cataloging and classification.* Santa Barbara, CA: Libraries Unlimited.

Chan, L. M. (2007). *Cataloging and classification: an introduction.* Lanham, MD: Scarecrow Press.

Langridge, D. W. (1989). *Subject Analysis: Principles and Procedures.* London: Bowker-Saur.

Moens, M. F. (2000). *Automatic Indexing and Abstracting of Document Texts.* Boston: Kluwer Academic.

KEY TERMS AND DEFINITIONS

Abstracting: The process of creating brief descriptions or summaries of the contents of documents such as books, periodical articles, or other information carriers.

Document Coding/Classification: Document coding or document classification is the process of assigning a unique number to a document in a collection so that documents of the same subject are brought together.

Document Description: A process of describing the physical as well as content attributes of a document.

Indexing: A process of assigning document descriptors used to locate information in a document or a collection.

Information Storage and Retrieval: the systematic process of collecting and cataloging data so that they can be located and displayed on request (infoplease.com, 2016).

Subject Cataloguing: A process of determining the subject content of a document.

This research was previously published in Managing Knowledge Resources and Records in Modern Organizations edited by Priti Jain and Nathan Mnjama; pages 179-197, copyright year 2017 by Business Science Reference (an imprint of IGI Global).

Chapter 10
Information Technology and Communication Management in Supply Chain Management

Cláudio Roberto Magalhães Pessoa
FUMEC University, Brazil

Marco E. Marques
FUMEC University, Brazil

ABSTRACT

Information Management policies must be provided, according to various SCM studies. Companies that need to operate in an integrated form, have in common the necessity that these policies must be communicated, in an efficient way, to everyone involved in strategic decisions to allow effective decision-making. In addition to that, it is of utmost importance to try to understand the customer's values, thought data prospected on the market. Then, Information Management must be done in order to efficiently apply them in the day-by-day of the organizations. This chapter explores information management in SCMs.

INTRODUCTION

Modern organizations have been trying to plan their business in an efficient way with the perspective of competition that is dynamic by nature. One of the approaches that have been used is to bring the suppliers to collaborate in this planning, many authors have suggested that Supply Chain Management (SCM) as a right tool for that (New, 1997; Beske & Seuring, 2014).

According Lavastre, Gunasekaran and Spalanzani (2014), the very competitive and dynamic market induces the companies to adopt Supply Chain Management (SCM) to achieve better finance results. According to the authors the interrelation between the company and suppliers, treated as partners, is directly tied to customer satisfaction. In addition, they claim that the SCM encompasses planning and

DOI: 10.4018/978-1-7998-0417-8.ch010

management of all activities involved on the supply, purchase, manufacturing and logistics management that must include the coordination and collaboration with partners, suppliers, third part professionals and costumers channels.

Cox (2012) explains SCM both from the strategic and operational perspective. He explains that the correct implementation of SCM is directed linked with the organization relative power structures that work with then.

Eckler and Schneller (2015, p.22) state that SCM is a key factor to maximize quality and performance, and collaborate to ensure that decision-making process will be made according organization´s interests. According to them, one failure in the decision-making process can bring some risks, as for example, the organization can be excessively dependent on the suppliers. Thus, managers must focus the purchase process on the value of the product to the business. This approach could bring better results to the organization.

Seth, Goyal, and Kiran (2015) states that much effort and attention in the implementation of a SCM system are focused on the evaluating the results obtained after implementation. However, according to the authors, during implementation, greater importance should be given to planning, because is in this phase that the organizations should think in their Business Plan, which would include "the strategy and tangible benefits, resources, risks, costs and schedule". The authors suggest that the implementation of a SCM system can be split into two parts: the technological and one that contemplates organizational factors. The second one is more important than the first when implementing the SCM.

According to Seth, Goyal and Kiran (2015), SCM became important for organizations due to globalization and the increasing growth of market competition. According to the authors, the SCM aims circulation of goods and services from one end of the chain to the other, in several stages, to improve the "efficiency, effectiveness, productivity and profitability of the process as a whole" and then, SCM management becomes critical in searching for competitive advantage.

According to Seth, Goyal and Kiran (2015), besides goods and services, other factor that requires attention is information flow. It will serve as a "lubricant" that will allow those involved in the supply chain to create an integrated and coordinated chain. The flow of information gained importance with the advent of Information Technology (IT) tools, which have facilitated the exchange of information with customers (internal and external), distributors and other partners in the SC (Supply Chain). The authors call attention to the need to manage IT tools related to SCM, as these tools have a major role in the management and flow of information, from its origin (raw material) to their arrival to the customer.

According to Madhani (2015), in the past decade the organizations noticed that SCM could be more efficient to contribute to the reduction of deadlines and sales forecasts errors. However, actually, the SCM focus is on meeting customer's needs, this new focus reduces costs related to "forced markdowns or empty stocks". However, for the author, achieving a level of services that fulfil customer needs will require a greater integration between organizations areas and functions. Efficient cost management is the biggest challenge for the SCM, and only an efficient implementation of SCM can help to overcome this challenge.

According to Madhani (2015), an efficient SCM often becomes inefficient when it is not aligned with market changes. A system focused only on replacement products, for example, may fail by not knowing what is the real costumer demand, or the value that the client seeks to find on these products. Therefore, product replacement will be done in such a way that will not fulfill customer needs. To avoid this, according to the author, it is important for SCM manager's work to integrated with the organization's marketing professionals in order to draw product strategies, thus reaching the customer satisfaction.

This integration is also necessary to analyze business interests. That's where the Strategic Managers enters. According to Madhani (2015), there is a very common conflict within Marketing personnel, who prefers to work with a high level of products on stock, ready to deliver to the customer as they want them, and SCM Managers, who prefers to work with a stock with the lowest level possible, preferable with no products on stock. In the last case, SCM system should be able to meet the demand on the exact quantity. In this conflict, it is important, therefore, to keep in mind the Business Vision, translating the Organization's Needs.

Another aspect highlighted by Madhani (2015) is the integration with partner companies. An efficient SCM will depend, in addition to existing integration between the areas of the company, on a close relationship with its partners. It is important to everyone to be aligned to the company's strategies, in other to avoid a weak spot of the entire system. Only then, it would be possible to satisfy customer needs.

Green aspects have been incorporated in SCM, especially linked with the three sustainable aspects dimensions: economic, environmental and social. In this endeavor, both the Customer and Stackholder points of views were requirements discussed by Beske and Seuring (2014). Kirchoff et al. identify that the resource based theory (RBT) provides the foundation for identifying strategic green aspects on SCM.

Information Management policies must be provided, according to various SCM studies. Companies that need to operate in an integrated form, have in common the necessity that these policies must be communicated, in an efficient way, to everyone involved in strategic decisions to allow effective decision-making. In addition to that, it is of utmost importance to try to understand the customer's values, thought data prospected on the market. Then, Information Management must be done in order to efficiently apply them in the day-by-day of the organizations

INFORMATION MANAGEMENT

In order to talk about Information Management is essential to think about Business Strategy. It makes no sense to manage any information in an organization if it is not strategically aligned with organization´s business.

Drucker (1992) states that every organization has a strategy, even intuitive. It is not possible for an organization to act on the market without having a target, and in order to try to achieve this target, it must trace strategies that will allow the professionals involved in the organization to seek the same direction.

According to Chiavenato (2003), based on the authors of the Structuration Theory, the existence of an "organization, as a complex social unit which interacts with social groups", demands its adaptation with the environment that surrounds it. Jensen and Beckling (1976) and Teixeira (1998) state the organizations are composed of "people who work to meet other people needs". Therefore, the organization's professionals must accompany the adaptations demanded from the organizations. The authors of the Structuration Theory called these professionals as "Organizational Men".

Thinking strategically, as seen previously, Information Management is vital to survive in the market, which requires rapid changes in organizations, to meet the needs imposed by customers. According Estrela (2014, p.1), information is only useful when it is sorted and organized in a way that can be used at the appropriate time.

According to Estrela (2014):

... the adaptability of organizations, to business environmental changes is crucial to ensure their survival, given that organizations do not exist in a vacuum, they are inserted in a context and they need information about their customers, competitors, suppliers, partners and their market, as well as they need information about technology, new products and services, relevant legislation, among others. (ESTRELA, 2014, p. 34)

Following this concept, Peter Drucker, using Neoclassical Theory, brought the idea of a strategy focused on the customer, where the main objective is to 'give to the customer the desired value'. Andrade and Amboni (2010, p.8) stated: "an organization must remain agile, strong and lean, capable to move quickly to take advantage of the opportunities", in other words, they must be ready to meet customer-desired values.

By analyzing various SCM studies, it can be noted that, currently, it became necessary to know customers needs and the values given by them to the products they purchase. Therefore, it begins the phase of Information Management aligned with the organization processes.

According to Tarapanoff (2006, p.22), the main reason for Information Management is to "identify and optimize information resources of an organization and its information capacity, allowing the organization to learn to adapt to business environmental changes."

Imbued with this thought, it is important for Managers to understand the Information Cycle. The purpose of the Information Cycle Management (Figure 1) is to improve how the information is used in decision-making of Managers, and this cycle should be taken into consideration for the adoption of a SCM system.

The Information Cycle (IC), according to Choo (2003), Pinto and Silva (2005), Tarapanoff (2006), Silva and Ribeiro (2009), Jamil (2014), among others, starts at the moment any organization member detects a necessity of some information, as an example, at a moment can happen when there is a process of decision-making in place. This corroborates with Marchand, Ketinger and Rollins (2001). The authors consider the beginning of the Information Cycle at the moment Managers perceive: changes in the external

Figure 1. Information cycle management
Source: Marchand, Ketinger and Rollins (2001, p. 76).

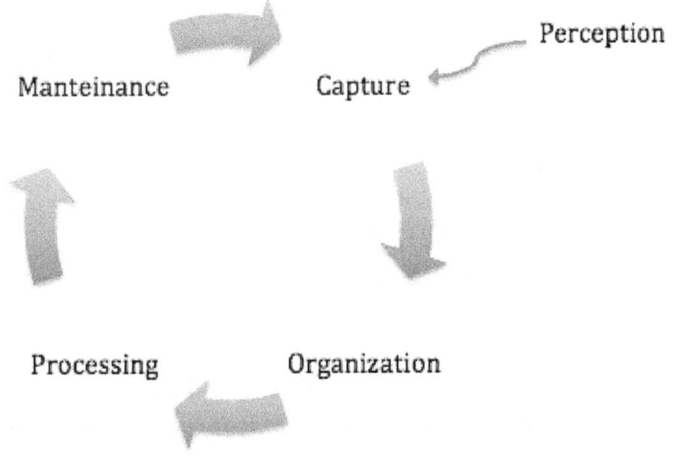

environment, in others worlds, changes of customers needs; the influence of new technologies that are necessary to collect information. This corresponds to the state “anomalous knowledge” (BELKIN, 1980).

Linking IC with SCM concepts, the organization must meet the customer’s needs and values. Two other authors, Kim and Mauborgne (2005), working with the concept of Value, have developed a strategy that was presented in a book called “The Blue Ocean Strategy”. In this strategy, the organization should build a Value Curve in order to better know customers’ expectations for the product (or service). These information can be acquired through Market research, focused on the target Customer. With this information, you can trace actions that will focus on the Perceived Value to meet Costumer needs.

Kotler (2000) developed a study that analyzes the purchase decision-making process. This analysis aims to know how it would be possible to meet Customer Satisfaction. The author has shown that the process involves five phases:

- **Problem Recognition:** The beginning of the process. It begins when the Customer recognizes a problem or need;
- **Information Searching:** The Customer will seek information about the product;
- **Alternatives Evaluation:** The attributes of interest vary depending on the product, and the Customer evaluates different options;
- **Purchase Decision**: The moment when the Customer makes the decision to buy;
- **Post-Purchase Behavior:** Everything will depend, after shopping, if the product has met the initial expectations of the Customer.

It is important to understand that when evaluating the alternatives. It is in the third phase that Customer expectations acts in order to direct Customer choice. Therefore, with a SCM project is extremely important to know these expectations, so that the organization will acquire and/or develop products and/or solutions that meet them.

To build an effective Information Management is important:

- To know how Managers will seek information to support their decision-making. This step, according to Marchand, Ketinger and Rollins (2001), prevents an information overload and defines how the organization should be organized;
- To Classify and organize the collected information (whether electronic or not) in order to ease recovery of this data. According to Alvarenga (2003), if this step is neglected it be very difficult to recover the necessary information at the appropriate time it is necessary for the Managers.

According to Tarapanoff (2006), the union of the Strategic Planning, Information Management and Knowledge Management, in an interdependent way, will create a Competitive Intelligence that will support strategic decisions to be adopted by the SCM system.

According to Silva and Ribeiro (2005), the organization should divide their activities of Information Management in two levels:

1. **Addressing Problems:** In this level professionals should handle and manage activities such as: production, processing, registration and storage, communication and use of information;

2. **Addressing Cases:** For the authors, the solution of the problems goes beyond getting documents, but rather requires a scientific study of Information Management applied to the organization and to the business environment in which it operates.

These two levels will also assist in the adoption of a SCM system, allowing Managers to have an holistic view of the organizations, and existed relationships whether inside or outside them.

It is not possible to neglect, in the adoption of an Information Management system focused on SCM, two cornerstones that together with the information will be of paramount importance to obtain success: technology and people.

Information Technology and Communication Management (ITCM)

ITCM should demand special attention because they encompass the tools that will help the company to make more accurate decisions. Then, it is important to notice "how" professionals will make choices of the tools will be used (programs, equipment, procedures, etc).

Some authors, such as Moraes and Laurindo (2003), Rodrigues, Maccari and Simões (2009), among others, all attention to growing importance that these tools have gained in the organizations, simultaneously with their technical evolution over time. ITCM has evolved from simple tools to support day routine tasks to tools that will help the Cycle of Information Management. In this way, they will provide accurate information to Managers at the right time.

The concept of ITCM, according to several authors such as Porter and Millar (1985), Seyal, Rahim and Raham (2000), Brady et al. (2002), Akan (2003), Pinto and Silva (2005), Sharma and Bhagwat (2006), Barba-Sánchez, Martínez-Ruiz and Jiménez-Zarco (2007) and Pinho, Nogueira and Franco (2014), has evolved, and now includes "information processing which means: create, produce, analyze, process, retrieve, store and transform the information in general". This processing encompass internet, e-mail, data storage, network communication and security, fax, video conferencing, software, hardware, telecommunications and applications.

Pinho, Nogueira and Franco (2014) state that organizations need to be agile in managing practices to be able to fast adapt to market changes. Its essential to achieve this goal technology is essential, because it will allow greater interactivity and flexibility. The adoption of Information and Communication Technology Management can even transform the existing business model.

But several studies show that, when choosing the tools that will be adopted, the ITC Managers do not take into account the business strategy. Pessoa (2009) show in a survey points out that strategic Managers recognize the importance of the ITCM tools, but they see them as a cost that brings no the expected benefits. The survey also points out that in none of the analyzed cases, the ITC Manager participates in the organization's strategic planning, which leads to the lack of alignment problems

Authors such as Henderson and Venkatraman (1993), Davenport (2000), Laurindo et al. (2001), Barba-Sánchez, Martínez-Ruiz and Jiménez-Zarco (2007), Silva and Ribeiro (2009), Jamil and Silva (2014) corroborate this finding and point to the lack of alignment as the main factor for the wrong investment in ITCM tools, and, consequently the results were below expectations.

Rodrigues, Maccari and Simões (2009), show in a survey made in 100 big companies, headquartered in Brazil, that ITC Managers, mostly have manage practices that sees ICT as "a solution provider" rather than as an "innovation generator". For these managers, the ITCM services are monitored and measured rather than organized, standardized, documented and disseminated. The planning of routine activities is done (printing reports, communication, tool support), but innovation actions that would bring greater benefits for the organizations are not encouraged.

PEOPLE MANAGEMENT

The lack of alignment between ITCM tools and Organization Strategy brings the necessity for organizations to incentive Managers and professionals to work in an integrated manner, following ICTM practices. If this practices fail, there is a risk of having all SCM and ITCM planning ruined. We have to get in mind that it is the people who works in an organization that really put the strategy plans in operation, through action plans that are based on their knowledge. That action plans really matters in the success or complete failure of the entire planning effort.

The change must start by the organization´s Leading Executives, when they realize that this integration requires a cultural change . Silva (2005, p. 39 and 40) draws attention to a new role, of the ITCM professionals who must know how to act in order to identify all the information produced/received by the organization and know why and how they were generated. All this knowledge will be essential to analyze, interpret and manage the information.

According to Silva, it is of paramount its importante to

... know and define what is generated on paper and in digital format, or both, so you can plan a business strategy and a model that avoids duplication of information. (SILVA 2005, p.40)

Professionals in the information age must be aligned to market changes, especially the needs and values of potential customers, and the implications of these changes in their work. They should also be proactive to ensure fast adaptation to changes, and not lose new business opportunities.

Silva (2005) states that the capabilities of ICTM professionals of the XXI century "must be founded in the theoretical and methodological supports, must be solid and comprehensive, allowing them to work in any context organic producer / information flow handler" (p. 71).

Professionals should analyze and guide the information towards the organization's business. According to Marchand, Ketinger and Rollins (2000), Managers should direct the values and behaviors of the professionals in order to meet business requirements and not individual requirements.

To analyze the alignment between personnel and business, Pessoa (2015) presented a model (Table 2), based on Luftman (2000) and Marchand, Ketinger and Rollins (2000) models, which enables Managers to assess how is the alignment of ITCM and organization's business. The model also allows the analysis whether ITC tools are in accordance with customer needs and if they are able to provide better operating results. The model becomes important when the organizations are doing the Strategic Planning, because besides the model allows Managers to know the organization current situation, it allows them to create metrics and goals to guide the organization to level 5, which in turn, would bring better results.

The model, as well as the Luftman (2000), assumes that the entire company has an alignment, even if it is minimal. In the model MAEGI model (Portuguese acronym for Strategy Alignment and Information Management Model), the strategic alignment level will be measured increasingly from level one to level five as follows:

Level 1: At this level, organizations work with isolated areas. They recognize the importance of ITCM tools but use them in an isolated way, and only to meet the routine activities (e-mail, spreadsheets, text editors, etc.). Decision making process is reactive and there is no Information Cycle Management.

Level 2: Organizations are aware of the importance Information Management Practices and how they must be alignment with organization strategy. Some Information Management tools use to support the business, but still they are still not able to make effective analysis of information. All Information Management activities are the result of the technology team effort, rather than high management directive.

Table 1. Strategy alignment and information management model (MAEGI)

Level 1	• **Information Management Practices:** Lack of Business Vision by Information Technology Managers of; lack of Information Management. • **Values and Behavior:** Employees are unaware of Information Management and there is only minimal management information necessary for the performance of daily tasks. • **Governance:** Information Management with relative priority. • **Information Management Tools:** Limited to the use of isolated computers and software • **Communication and Architecture:** Unstructured.
Level 2	• **Information Management Practices:** Only provide operational assistance and there is a project of adoption of these practices for management support. • **Values and Behavior:** Employees are unaware of Information Management and there is only the Information Management implemented for some corporate controls and formalities. • **Governance:** Information Management already seen as necessary • **Information Management Tools:** Initial existence of the Information Management tools. • **Communication and Architecture:** There is a project of business structuring tools, but communication is still done via traditional means (written and spoken communications, e-mail, electronic mail, etc.).
Level 3	• **Information Management Practices:** Adoption of practices that assist operational support, management support and processes support has been initiated. • **Values and Behavior:** Employees with minimal awareness of Information Management and there is Information Management implemented in business controls, procedures and information sharing. • **Governance:** Information Management already seen as necessary. • **Information Management Tools:** Information Management Processes already mapped and implementation has been started. • **Communication and Architecture:** There are tools to assist Information Management. Shared Communication is in place.
Level 4	• **Information Management Practices:** Adoption of practices that assist operational support, management support and processes support. • **Values and Behavior:** Employees are aware of the Information Management and there is transparency, integrity, information sharing and the existence of Information Management awareness training. • **Governance:** Information Management already seen as necessary. • **Information Management Tools:** Information Management Processes already mapped and in implementation. • **Communication and Architecture:** Existence of integrated communication and there are tools to assist organization's key sectors.
Level 5	• **Information Management Practices:** Adoption of practices that assist operational support, management support, processes support and innovation support. • **Values and Behavior:** Employees are aware of the Information Management and there is proactivity, transparency, integrity, information sharing and the existence of constant Information Management awareness training. • **Governance:** Information Management already seen as part of the Strategic Management • **Information Management Tools:** Information Management Processes implanted • **Communication and Architecture:** Integrated communication throughout the whole organization, and there are tools to assist all sector of the organization.

Source: Pessoa (2015).

Level 3: This level is the minimum level expected to organizations that have an ISO 9001 Quality System. The operational procedures and values are facing alignment and there is a minimum management in the areas of the organization. Some tools (systems and hardware) with the ability to support the Information Management are in use but Information Cycle is still not correctly managed, due to the lack of knowledge by the majority of managers regarding its importance. In addition, a lack of focus on the organization's business management can be seen.

Level 4: Communication between departments is done and Information Management tools are integrated key organizational areas. There is an awareness of the importance of participation of all personnel in the Information Cycle Management trained by professionals about this subject is already a real practice. Management practices exist and are applied in all areas with good alignment with organization´s strategy.

Level 5: At level five, all stages of the Information Management cycle are in place. There is a collective awareness of the need to work in an integrated manner. Thus, communication is completely integrated throughout all the organization. ITM tools support all processes and, together with the acquired organizations values, improve participation of the professionals, stimulating proactivity and innovation. An effective decision-making process exists due to the use of ITM tools that acquire process and interpret information.

REFERENCES

Akan, P. I. (2003). Basic-needs to globalization: Are ICTs the missing link? *Information Technology for Development, 10*(4), 261–274.

Alvarenga, L. (2003). *Representação do conhecimento na perspectiva da ciência da informação em rempo e espaço digital.* Brasil: Universidade Federal de Minas Gerais.

Andrade, R., & Amboni, N. (n.d.). *Estratégias de gestão* [Management strategies]. Elsevier.

Barba-Sánches, V., Martínez-Ruiz, M. de P., & Jiménes-Zarco, A. I. (2007). Drivers, benefits and challenges of ICT adoption by small and medium sized enterprises (SMEs): A literature review. *Problems and Perspectives in Management, 5*(1). Retrieved from http://www.businessperspectives.org/journals_free/ppm/2007/PPM_EN_2007_01_Barba-Sanchez.pdf

Beske, P., & Seuring, S. (2014). Putting sustainability into supply chain management. *Supply Chain Management*, *9*(3), 322–331.

Brady, M., Saren, M., & Tzokas, N. (2002). Integrating information technology into marketing practice – The IT realize of contemporary marketing practice. *Journal of Marketing Management, 18*(5-6), 555–577. doi:10.1362/0267257022683703

Chiavenato, I. (1999). *Introdução à teoria geral da administração, edição compacta.* Rio de Janeiro: Campus.

Choo, C. W. (1998). *The knowing organization: How organizations use information to construct meaning, create knowledge and make decisions.* New York: Oxford University Press.

Cox, A. (1999). Power, value and supply chain management. *Supply Chain Management, 4*(4), 167–175.

Da Silva, A. M. (2005). A gestão da Informação abordada no campo da CI. *Páginas a&b,* (16), 89-113.

Davenport, T. H., & Prusak, L. (2000). *Working knowledge: How organizations manage what they know*. Cambridge, MA: Harvard Business School.

Drucker, P. F. (1992). *The age of discontinuity: Guidelines to our changing society*. Harper and Row Publishers.

Eckler, J., & Schneller, E. S. (2015). Physician leaders' roles in supply chain management. *Physician Leadership Journal*. Retrieved from keliey.iupui.edu/physician-leader

Estrela, S. C. L. (2014). Modelo inde-infodecidor para a gestão de informação e a tomada de decisão. In *Gestão da informação, cooperação em redes e competitividade*. Universidade do Porto.

Henderson, J. C., & Venkatraman, N. (1993). Strategic alignment: Leveraging information technology for transforming organizations. *IBM Systems Journal, 32*(1).

Jamil, G. L. (2014). Estruturação de oficina de inteligência de mercado. In *Gestão da informação, cooperação em redes e competitividade*. Universidade do Porto.

Jensen, M. C., & Beckling, W. (1976). Theory of firm: Managerial behavior, agency cost and ownership structure. *Journal of Financial Economics, 3*(4), 305–360. doi:10.1016/0304-405X(76)90026-X

Kirchoff, J. F., Tate, L. T., & Mollenkopf, D. A. (2016). The impact of organizations on green supply chain management and firm performance. *International Journal of Physical Distribution & Logistics Management, 46*(3), 1–39. doi:10.1108/IJPDLM-03-2015-0055

Kirchoff, J. F., Tate, L. T., & Mollenkopf, D. A. (2016). The impact of organizations on green supply chain management and firm performance. *International Journal of Physical Distribution & Logistics Management, 46*(3), 1–39. doi:10.1108/IJPDLM-03-2015-0055

Laurindo, J. B. L., Shimizu, T., Carvalho, M. M., & Rabechini, R. Jr. (2001). O papel da tecnologia da informação (TI) na estratégia das empresas. *Gestão & Produção, 8*(2).

Lavastre, O., Gunasekaran, A., & Spalanzani, A. (2014). Effect of firm characteristics, supplier relationships and techniques used on supply chain risk management (SCRM): An empirical investigation on French industrial firms. *International Journal of Production Research, 52*(11), 3381–3403. doi:10.1080/00207543.2013.878057

Luftman, J. (2000). Assessing business-IT alignment maturity. *Communications of the Association for Information Systems, 4*. Retrieved from http://www.itu.dk/courses/SBIT/E2008/IT-Business%20Alignment_luftman.pdf

Lutchen, M. (2003). Managing IT as a business: A survival guide. Hoboken, NJ: John Wiley and Sons.

Madhani, P. M. (2015). Demand chain management: Enhancing customer lifetime value through integration of marketing and supply chain management. *The IUP Journal of Business Strategy, 12*(3).

Marchand, D. A., Ketinger, W. J., & Rollins, J. D. (2001). Information orientation: The link to business performance. Oxford University Press.

Moraes, R. de O., & Laurindo, F. J. B. (2003). Um Estudo De Caso De Gestão De Portfolio De Projetos De Tecnologia Da Informação. *Gestão & Produção, 10*(3), 311–328.

New, S. J. (1977). The scope of supply chain management. *Supply Chain Management, 2*(1), 15–22.

Pessoa, C. R. M. (2009). *Alinhamento estratégico entre a gestão das empresas e o setor de tecnologia da informação (TI): O momento da aquisição de soluções de tecnologia.* Dissertação de Mestrado apresentada na Universidade Fumec. Retrieved from http://www.fch.fumec.br/anexos/cursos/mestrado/dissertacoes/completa/claudio_roberto_magalhaes_pessoa.pdf

Pessoa, C. R. M. (2015). *Gestão da informação e conhecimento no alinhamento estratégico em empresas de engenharia.* Projeto de tese aprovado na Universidade Federal de Minas Gerais.

Pinho, C. S., Nogueira, M. G., & Franco, M. J. B. (2014). As TIC como uma vantage competitive para as PME: Benefícios e barreiras à sua utilização. In *Gestão da informação, cooperação em redes e competitividade*. Universidade do Porto.

Pinto, M. A., & Silva, A. M. (2005). Um modelo sistémico e integral de gestão da informação nas organizações. In *Proceedings of International Conference on Information Systems and Technology Management.* Retrieved from https://repositorio-aberto.up.pt/bitstream/10216/13461/2/63557.pdf

Porter, M. E., & Millar, V. E. (1985). How Information Gives You Competitive Advantage. *Harvard Business Review.*

Rodrigues, L. C., Maccari, E. A., & Simões, S. A. (2009). O desenho da gestão da tecnologia da informação nas 100 maiores empresas na visão dos executivos de TI. *Journal of Information Systems and Technology Management, 6*(3), 483–506. Retrieved from http://www.scielo.br/pdf/jistm/v6n3/06.pdf

Seth, M., Goyal, D. P., & Kiran, R. (2015). *Development of a model for successful implementation of supply chain management information system in Indian automotive industry.* SAGE Publications. Retrieved from http://vision.sagepub.com

Seyal, A. H., Rahim, M. M., & Raham, M. M. A. (2000). An empirical investigation of the use of information technology among small and medium business organizations: A Bruneian scenario. *The Electronic Journal of information System in Developing Countries, 2*(7), 1-17.

Sharman, M. K., & Bhagwat, R. (2006). Pratice of information system evidence from select Indian SMEs. *Journal of Manufacturing Technology Management, 17*(2), 199–223.

Silva, A. M., & Ribeiro, F. (2009). A gestão da informação na administração pública: Interface administração pública. *Grupo Algébrica, 161*(50).

Tarapanoff, K. (2006). Informação, conhecimento e inteligência em corporações: Relações e complementaridade. In *Inteligência, informação e conhecimento.* Ibict.

Teixeira, S. (1998). *Gestão das organizações.* Amadora: McGraw-Hill.

This research was previously published in the Handbook of Research on Information Management for Effective Logistics and Supply Chains edited by António Lucas Soares, George Leal Jamil, and Cláudio Roberto Magalhães Pessoa; pages 23-33, copyright year 2017 by Business Science Reference (an imprint of IGI Global).

Chapter 11
Access Control and Information Flow Control for Web Services Security

Saadia Kedjar
University of Bejaia, Algeria

Abdelkamel Tari
University of Bejaia, Algeria

Peter Bertok
RMIT University, Australia

ABSTRACT

With the advancement of web services technology, security has become an increasingly important issue. Various security standards have been developed to secure web services at the transport and message level, but application level has received less attention. The security solutions at the application level focus on access control which cannot alone ensure the confidentiality and integrity of information. The solution proposed in this paper consists on a hybrid model that combines access control (AC) and information flow control (IFC). The AC mechanism uses the concept of roles and attributes to control user access to web services' methods. The IFC mechanism uses labels to control how the roles access to the system's objects and verify the information flows between them to ensure the information confidentiality and integrity. This manuscript describes the model, gives the demonstration of the IFC model safety, presents the modeling and implementation of the model and a case study.

INTRODUCTION

Several companies have adopted the Web services technology to implement their distributed systems, because they offer cooperation and interoperability (Cantara et al., 2003; Chen, 2003). However, the opening and accessibility of the web services on Internet make them vulnerable to various attacks. Con-

DOI: 10.4018/978-1-7998-0417-8.ch011

sequently, web services security remains a significant issue which motivates many researchers to develop various security solutions (Bertino et al., 2010). Access control is the most used security mechanism at the application level.

Traditional access control models (LBAC: Lattice-based access control, RBAC: Role-based access control, etc.) are designed for the LAN-based applications such as banking applications, which are closed systems. These models are not suitable for open systems like the web services considering their distributed and decentralized aspect. Indeed, the application of these controls is based mainly on known users' identities and attributes. However, the opened, distributed and dynamic environments are confronted with a great number of unknown users. Furthermore, AC models for the web services must be decentralized and must be able to manage the trust relationships between service providers and requesters. Moreover, these models must be able to control the accesses to heterogeneous resources i.e. the methods of the web services and data which they handle.

Access control (AC) models proposed for web services are distinguished by the concepts, which are used for authentication and authorization policies definition. We can find the role-based models which adapt the RBAC model such as the models suggested by (Tari and Wonohoesodo, 2004) and (Bhatti et al., 2003). Attribute-based models for the trust management such as the models of (Hai-bo and Fan, 2006) and (Bertino et al., 2004). Hybrid models use various concepts (e.g. the role and the attribute) to fulfil the requirements of the web services such as the models suggested by (Chakraborty and Ray, 2006) and (Liu et al., 2005). (Alipour et al., 2012) proposed another type of models, which use dynamic separation of duty rules.

Absence of information flow control (IFC) between the objects of a web services system constitutes the limit of the majority of the AC models found in the literature. Indeed, these models control the direct accesses to the resources of a system but they do not perform control over the information after their dissemination or distribution (Gondara, 2011) (Esfandi and Sabbari, 2012).

The IFC was introduced for the programming languages by (Myers and Liskov, 1997) and is used in other field as the data bases (Ferrari et al., 1997). The IFC models for web services must take into account the highly dynamic and distributed aspect of web services and they must take into account the composite web services (Bryce et al., 1995).

Tari (Tari et al., 2006) proposed IFC model for the web services based on the dynamic label checking of objects handled by the web services. This model consists of an adaptation of the model of Myers and Liskov (Myers and Liskov, 1997). The model aims to ensure data confidentiality handled by a web services system by preventing the information disclosure.

This model is improved in (Bertok et al., 2009) by modifying the operation joins to ensure information confidentiality. Moreover, the label is extended to allow not only information confidentiality but also their integrity by considering writing operation in the control policies.

In (Kedjar and Tari, 2013), a new approach of web services security has been proposed which combine access control and information flow control.

In this paper, the authors propose a hybrid model for web services security, theoretical proofs of safety, its modeling and some details of its implementation. The model adopts two concepts: "role" to control user access to web services methods and, "labels" to control the role's access to system's objects and IFC between them. The model is extended to exploit the relation of hierarchy of XML data.

This paper is structured as follows. First, the model is presented and its basic components are detailed. Then, the modeling with UML diagrams is described. It is followed by a brief overview of implementation methodology. After, a case study and software validation are presented.

THE HYBRID MODEL FOR WEB SERVICES SECURITY

Presentation of the Model

The Hybrid Model for Web Services Security (HM-WSS) proposed offers at the same time the access control to web services methods, access control to the system's objects and information flow control between these objects.

HM-WSS integrates the Attribute and Role Based Access Control (ARBAC) model proposed by (Liu et al., 2005) and the IFC model (Tari et al., 2006) (Bertok et al., 2009) (Kedjar and Tari, 2013) by using the role concept introduced in the RBAC model.

The choice of the ARBAC is justified by:

1. Trust management and authentication by using the users' attributes;
2. Use of the role concept to facilitate extensibility and administration of the model;
3. Fine-grained web services by considering methods of the later and data handled;
4. Taking into account the context parameters in the AC policies.

The ARBAC model is adapted by introducing the following modifications:

1. In ARBAC model, the system resources, which the access permissions consider are the web services methods and all data they handle. In HM-WSS, the access permissions consider only the system objects. Web services methods are taken into account in the user-to-role assignment policies;
2. The user-to-role assignment policies take into account not only the users' attributes as in ARBAC but also invoked method and context parameters;
3. The permission-to-role assignment function uses the IFC rules to allow, in addition to AC to the system objects, the IFC between these objects. This function controls information at access time and after its dissemination.

Figure 1. The HM-WSS

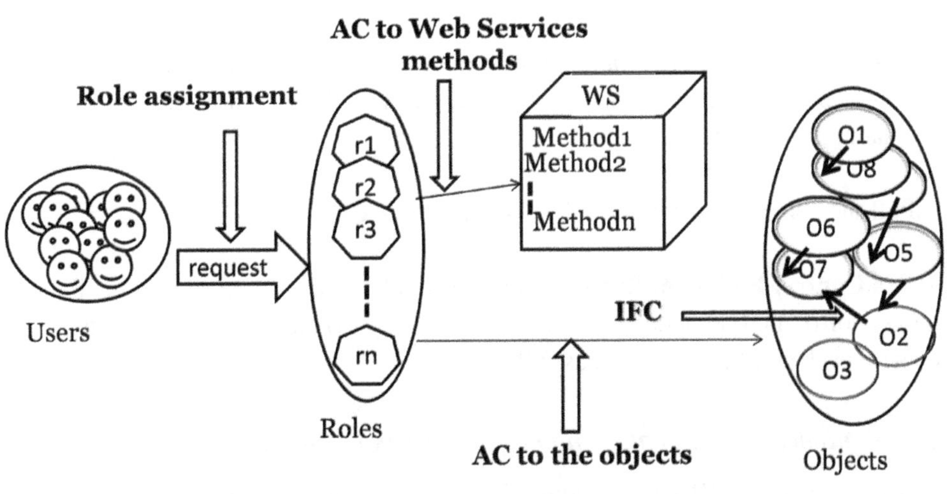

The solution consists of a set of definitions, rules, safety demonstration for the confidentiality and the integrity and the algorithms allowing their implementation.

The total sight of the model is illustrated by (Figure 1) which is explained in following section.

The Model Development

In this section, the AC and the IFC models are developed.

Access Control Components

In this section, the necessary concepts and definitions for AC model are presented:

1. **User:** A user can be a human being, an autonomous agent or a web service. Each user is defined by a set of attributes of the form: (attr_name, type) where:

attr_name is the attribute name (e.g. ID for identifier)

and type is the type of the attribute (e.g. String for the ID).

It is given by:

$$User_i = \{(ID, ID\_value^i), (key, key\_value^i), (attr\_name_1, value_1^i), \ldots, (attr\_name_m, value_m^i)\}$$

2. **Methods:** The web services methods (e.g. create(), consult(), update(), pre-book…etc.) are characterized by a set of parameters and their types of the form: (par_name, type).

Each method is given by:

$$method_i = \{(par\_name_1, value_1^i), (par\_name_2, value_2^i) \ldots, (par\_name, value_1^i)\}$$

3. **The Context Parameters:** They are parameters of the environment or situation where the access to a resource appears (e.g. dates, hour…). A parameter is given by its name, its type and its value: CP = (c_name, c_type, getvalue ()).

The set of all the context parameters is $C = \{CP_1, CP_2, \ldots, CP_t\}$

4. **An Access Control Policy (ACP):** A policy is a set of conditions on subject attributes (e.g. login name, password), method parameters (e.g. a system object) and context parameters (e.g. date and time) where each condition is given as follows:

$$cond_i = \begin{cases} (attr\_name_1, VA_1), \ldots, (attr\_name_m, VA_m), (par\_name_1, VP_1) \\ \ldots, (par\_name_n, VP_n), (c\_name_1, VC_1) \ldots, (c\_name_t, VC_t) \end{cases}$$

such as:

VA_i ($1 \leq i \leq m$) values of subject attributes

Vp_j ($1 \leq j \leq n$) values of method parameters

VC_h ($1 \leq h \leq t$) values of context parameters

5. **Role:** Corresponds to different job descriptions within an organization.

The set of roles in the system is:

Role = $\{R_1, R_2 \ldots, R_n\}$

There is a relation of partially ordered hierarchy between roles.
Formally:

$$R_i \leq R_j \Leftrightarrow R_i\ permissions \subseteq R_j\ permissions$$

6. **Permission:** Is an authorization to perform certain tasks on an object (e.g. reading).

The set of permissions is:

Permission $=\{P_1, P_2,\ldots,P_p\}$

where:

P_i = ($action_i$, $resource_i$)

and $action_i$; to read, write, add, create or remove $resource_i$; a system object.

7. **The Role-Condition Assignment Function:** The function of assignment between roles set (Role) and conditions set (Condition) gives conditions set defining a role of the system. In other words, this function defines the conditions which a request must check to activate a role in the system:

MapRC: $\begin{array}{l} Role \rightarrow Condition \\ MapRC(r_i) = Cond \end{array}$

Cond: subset of conditions

8. **Method Access Request:** An access request to a web service method by a requester must be in the form:

access_request = (subject_attr, method_par, context_par)

where subject_attr is the user's attributes who calls the method, method_par are the called method's parameters and context_par are the context parameters of the request execution.

9. **The User-Role Assignment Function:** When the AC system of service provider receives a request; it determines the role corresponding to the subject at the origin of the request.

This function is given by:

MapRR:

$$\mathrm{Re}\,quet \rightarrow Role$$

$$MapRR(access\_request) = \left\{ \begin{array}{l} R_i / \exists h\left(cond_h \in MapRC(r_i)\right) \\ \wedge \left[\begin{array}{l} \forall K\left(\left(parameter_k, value_k\right) \in cond_h\right) \\ \exists m \left(\begin{array}{l} \left(parameter_m, value_m\right) \in access\_request \\ \wedge parameter_m = parameter_k \\ \wedge value_m \in Vparameter_k \end{array} \right) \end{array} \right] \end{array} \right\}$$

where $parameter_i$ can be a subject attribute, a method parameter or a context parameter, and $V\ parameter_k$ is either VA_k, VP_k or VC_k.

10. **The Permission-Role Assignment Function:** This function allows determining the set of all roles, which have the privilege to use a given permission using the IFC rules. It ensures AC to objects and IFC between them. This function is given by:

MapPR: $$\begin{array}{l} Permission \rightarrow Role \\ MapPR(P_i) = Role' \end{array}$$

such as:

$$Role' \subseteq Role$$

11. **Separation of Duties (SOD):** The separation of duties aims at reducing the risk of frauds. It is generally represented by a set of mutually exclusive roles. The SOD prevents a user playing (or activating) two contradictory roles. The whole of the mutually exclusive roles is defined as follows:

$ER = \{R_1, R_2, \ldots, R_k\}$

such as:

$R_i \in Role$ and $0 \leq K < |Role|$

The security administrator specifies mutual exclusion operations for every resource, so when producing the permission set, the system also produces the mutual permission set MP. By using the permission-role assignment function, we obtain the set of mutually exclusive roles ER such as:

$$|Session.Srole \cap ER| = 1$$

where Session.Srole is the set of roles activated in one session (Session).

12. **Access Control Algorithm:** The algorithm 1 (Figure 2) summarizes steps of the access control.

Information Flow Control Components

As mentioned earlier, permission-role assignment function uses the rules defined by IFC model to allow not only AC to objects, as in the case of traditional RBAC and other models derived from the latter, but also the information flow control between these objects.

In what follows, the IFC elements are presented. Data items are objects, and subjects can be owners, readers and writers of those objects. Each object has a label where its owners specify their access policies. Each owner of an object may trust some of the other owners of the same object. Trust is described

Figure 2. Access control algorithm

```
                Algorithm 1: The access control algorithm

                Inputs : Requet_acces, action, resource  // the access request and the
                //action we want to perform //on the resource
Outputs : {authorize, not authorize}
Begin
        1. Role ← MapRR (Requet_acces)   // request to role assignment

        2. PerRoles ← MapPR (action, resource) // permission to role assignment

        3. If Role PerRoles then

            If Session (access_request. subject_attr) then   // if there is no session for the subject
            Session ← Create_Session (access_request. subject_attr)  // create a new session
            Else
            Session ←Recovery_session (access_request. subject_attr)    // recovery of the activated session
            End If
            End If
        4If |Session. Srole RE| >1     // separation of duties control

            then return (non authorize)       // the request is denied
            Else                               // add the activated role to the user session
                Session.AddRole (Role)
            Return (authorise)          // the request is granted
        End If
End.
```

by a binary variable, i.e. a subject can be trusted or untrusted. Each owner can nominate readers and writers of the object, as well as potential declassification recipient i.e. temporary readers and writers needed to accomplish transactions:

1. **Subjects:** The roles, which are defined in the system:

$R = \{R_1, R_2 \ldots, R_N\}$

The relation of hierarchy between these roles is defined by:

$HR = \{(R_1,R_2)/R_1,R_2 \in R(R_1 \geq R_2)\}$

2. **Objects:** The set of the objects manipulated by the web services methods is: $Q = \{Q_1, Q_2 \ldots, Q_m\}$. This set is also provided with a relation of hierarchy:

$HO = \{(Q_1,Q_2)/Q_1,Q_2 \in Q \wedge Q_2$ is a sub element of $Q_1\}$

3. **A Label:** to each object Q of the system is associated a label noted by $L(q) = \{K_1, K_2 \ldots, K_i \ldots, K_c\}$.

A label contains all the policies of the owners concerning the AC and the IFC for the corresponding object. It is a set of components where each component represents the policy of an owner on his object. A component in its turn is a 7-uplet: $K = \{K_o, TO_{q,Ko}, Re_{q,Ko}, W_{q,Ko}, P_{q,Ko}, DR_{q,Ko}, DW_{q,Ko}\}$ where:

- $\mathbf{K_o} \in \mathbf{O_q}$ is an owner of object q;
- $\mathbf{TO_{q,Ko}}$ is the trusted owners set defined by K_o;
- $\mathbf{Re_{q,Ko}}$ is the reader set defined by K_o;
- $\mathbf{W_{q,Ko}}$ is the writer set defined by K_o;
- $\mathbf{P_{q,Ko}}$ is the rule of propagation such as:

$P_{q,o} = (p_{accept}, p_{propagate})$

where the rule of acceptance p_{accept} defines when accept the policies propagation of the parent objects' labels and the rule of propagation $p_{propagate}$ defines when propagate policies of the parent objects towards the children ones:

- $\mathbf{DR_{q,Ko}}$ is declassification policy set for reading, such as $DR_{q,o}=\{\delta_1,\delta_2,\ldots,\delta_p\}$. Each component δ contains two parts:
  - $\delta_{init} \in Re_{q,o}$: The subject to which, declassification will appear:
  - $\delta_{inter} \subseteq R - Re_{q,o}$: The subset of intermediate subjects (roles) that perform declassification, such that: $\{\delta_{init}\} \cap \delta_{inter} = \varnothing$
- $\mathbf{DW_{q,Ko}}$ is declassification policies set for writing, such as: $DW_{q,o}=\{\delta_1,\delta_2,\ldots,\delta_p\}$ where each component δ contains two parts:
  - $\delta_{init} \in W_{q,o}$: The role to which, declassification will appear;

- $\delta_{inter} \subseteq R - W_{q,o}$: The subset of intermediate roles that perform declassification, such that $\{\delta_{init}\} \cap \delta_{inter} = \varnothing$

Note: A label allows applying the AC policies of all the object's owners and to control how information of an object can be disseminated (IFC).

4. **Permissions of Access:** Access permissions to the objects of the system and their labels are granted to the following subsets according to rules, which are described in the following section (Data access permissions):
   a. Owners set: Oq
   b. Effective owners set: $EOq = \bigcap_{o_i \in O_q} TO_{q,o_i}$
   c. Effective readers set: $ERq = \bigcap_{o_i \in O_q} \mathrm{Re}_{q,o_i}$
   d. Joint readers set: $JRq = Oq \cup ERq$
   e. Effective writers set: $EWq = \bigcap_{o_i \in O_q} W_{q,o_i}$
   f. Joint writers set: $JWq = Oq \cup EWq$
   g. Effective declassification set for reading: $EDRq = \bigcap_{o_i \in EO_q} DR_{q,o_i}$
   h. Effective declassification set for writing: $EDWq = \bigcap_{o_i \in EO_q} DW_{q,o_i}$
5. **Rules:** In this section, a set of rules are given. They manage access to objects in the system and to their labels, and maintain data confidentiality and integrity. Permission-to-roles assignments are represented by the function MapPR, its arguments being the permissions and the object.

Let us take again the permission-role assignment function defined previously:

MapPR (P_i) = *Role'* such as $Role' \subseteq Role$

where:

Role = R

We obtain *MapPR* (P_i) = *R'* such as $R' \subseteq R$:

- **Data Access Permissions:** Data can be accessed only by subjects who are authorized to perform the requested operation:
  Rule 1: $MapPR(read,q)=\{r/r \in JRq\}$ i.e. A role can read the object q if and only if the role belongs to the joint reader set of q;
  Rule 2: $MapPR(write,q)=\{r/r \in JWq\}$;
  Rule 3: $MapPR(create,q_2)=\{r/r \in Oq_1 \wedge q_1 \rightarrow ho\ q_2\}$;
  Rule 4: $MapPR(delete,q)=\{r/r \in O_q \wedge |O_q|=1\}$;

- **Label Access Permissions:** Labels can be manipulated only by authorized subjects, who maintain the integrity of labels and thereby the integrity of whole system:
  Rule 5: $MapPR(\{read, write, add, delete\}, K.Re_{q,Ko}) = \{K_o\}$ i.e. Only the owner of a component in a label can read, write, add and delete an element of the reader set of that component;
  Rule 6: $MapPR(\{read, write, add, delete\}, K.W_{q,Ko}) = \{K_o\}$;
  Rule 7: $MapPR(\{read, write, add, delete\}, K.TO_{q,Ko}) = \{K_o\}$;
  Rule 8: $MapPR(\{read, write, add, delete\}, K.DR_{q,Ko}) = \{K_o\}$;
  Rule 9: $MapPR(\{read, write, add, delete\}, K.DW_{q,Ko}) = \{K_o\}$;
  Rule 10: $MapPR(add, K.O_q)=\{r/r \in EO_q\}$:

$MapPR(delete, K.O_q.o) = \{r/r \in EO_q \wedge o \notin EO_q\}$

i.e. Only the effective owners of an object can extend the set of the owners of the object and can delete an owner. The owner to be deleted must not be an effective owner:

- **Propagation Rule:** this rule respect the hierarchy relationship:
  Rule 11: $q_1 \rightarrow_{oh} q_2 \wedge r \in O_{q_1} \Rightarrow add(r)\ to\ O_{q_2}$.

i.e. The owner of the object q_1 is the owner of the child object q_2:

- **Declassification Rule:** These rules allow the normal execution of transactions even if an intermediate subject is not authorized to read or write an object; they can be used if and only if the initiator of this transaction is an effective reader or writer respectively:
  Rule 12: $(r_1,\varepsilon) \in EDR_q \wedge r_1 \in ER_q \Rightarrow add(\varepsilon)$ to ER_q;
  Rule 13: $(r_1,\varepsilon) \in EDW_q \wedge r_1 \in EW_q \Rightarrow add(\varepsilon)$ to EW_q;
- **Safety of the information flow:**
  Rule 14: $q_s \rightarrow q_d \ is\ safe \Leftrightarrow \begin{cases} JR_{qd} \subseteq JR_{qs} \\ EDR_{qd} \subseteq EDR_{qs} \end{cases}$ and:

$$\begin{cases} JW_{qs} \subseteq JW_{qd} \\ EDW_{qs} \subseteq EDW_{qd} \end{cases} \text{ and } \begin{cases} JW'_{qd} \subseteq JW_{qd} \\ EDW'_{qd} \subseteq EDW_{qd} \end{cases}$$

where JW'_{qd} and EDW'_{qd} are the new sets calculated for q_d after the information flow, i.e. an information flow is safe, if it does not lead to:

1. Information disclosure i.e. the confidentiality of information contained in the source object is guaranteed. In other words, the number of authorized readers will not increase as a result of the information flow;
2. Non-authorized writing and the integrity of the recipient object will be maintained. This means that the number of authorized writers will not increase as a result of the information flow.

Figure 3. The label join

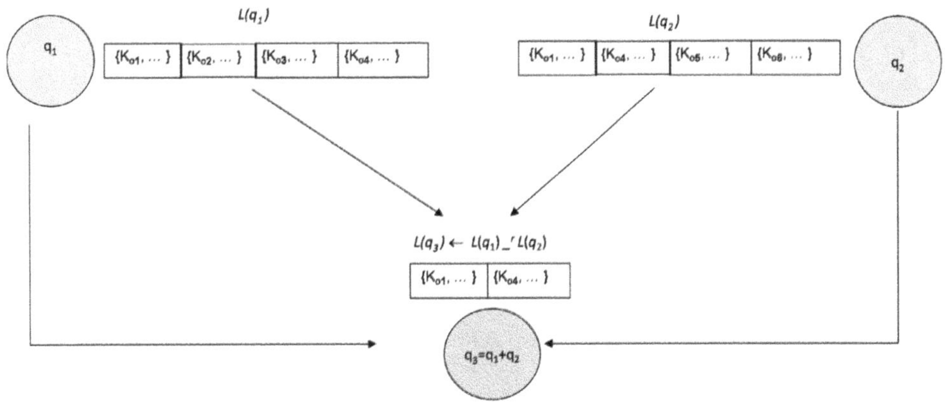

6. **Operations on Labels:** When performing operations on one or more objects, a result object with a new, derived label is produced. The operations on the labels can be associated with any operation on the objects themselves. In this section, operations for deriving a new label are described. J*oin* operations are defined, and the operator "_" to join labels is introduced.

For all label joins, let q1, q2, q3 ∈ Q, L(q1), L(q2) and L(q3) be the labels of q1, q2 and q3 respectively and L(x) a new label. Let us suppose that there is an operation on q1 and q2 that produces q3, i.e. L(q3) =L(q1) _Op L(q2) (see Figure 3).

There are three types of joins:

1. **Calculation Joins:** Assigning join, restrictive join and fusing join. They are used to update the label of object obtained after a calculation operation;
2. **Declassification Join:** Defines how to update the label of an object receiving declassified information in case of reading and the object written in case of writing;
3. **Propagation Join:** Defines how to update the labels of objects when applying propagation rule;
4. **Assigning Join (_[a]):** This operation is tailored to object assignment. Instead of inheriting all characteristics of source object, the result is a combination of both objects characteristics.

Assigning join giving a new label for the destination object is defined as follows:

$$O_x = O_{q1} \cup \left(O_{q2} \cap JR_{q1}\right)$$
$$\forall o_i \in O_x / O_{q1} \left(o_i \in O_x \ and \ o_i \notin O_{q1}\right) \ and \ \forall o_j \in O_{q1}$$
$$\mathrm{Re}_{x,oi} = ER_{q1} \cup \mathrm{Re}_{q2,oi}; \mathrm{Re}_{x,oj} = \mathrm{Re}_{q1,oj}$$
$$W_{x,oi} = W_{q2,oi}; W_{x,oj} = W_{q1,oj} \cap JW_{q2}$$
$$TO_{x,oi} = EO_{q1} \cup TO_{q2,oi}; TO_{x,oj} = TO_{q1,oj}$$
$$DR_{x,oi} = EDR_{q1} \cup DR_{q2,oi}; DR_{x,oj} = DR_{q1,oj}$$
$$DW_{x,oi} = DW_{q2,oi}; DW_{x,oj} = DW_{q1,oj} \cap EDW_{q2}$$
$$P_{x,oi} = P_{q2,oi}; P_{x,oj} = P_{q1,oj}$$
$$L(q_2) \leftarrow L(x)$$

5. **Restrictive Join (_^{r}):** This operation is appropriate when dealing with sensitive data.

It gives the resulting object properties from the properties of objects involved in the calculation operation but with more restrictions.

Restrictive join, which computes the label of object containing the result of operation using the labels of sources objects, is defined as follows:

$$O_x = O_{q1} \cap O_{q2}$$
$$If \ O_x \neq \emptyset \ then \ \forall o_i \in O_x$$

$$\mathrm{Re}_{x,oi} = \left(\mathrm{Re}_{q1,oi} \cup \mathrm{Re}_{q2,oi}\right) \cap \left(JR_{q1} \cap JR_{q2}\right)$$
$$W_{x,oi} = \left(W_{q1,oi} \cup W_{q2,oi}\right) \cap JW_{q3}$$
$$TO_{x,oi} = \left(TO_{q1,oi} \cup TO_{q2,oi}\right) \cap \left(EDR_{q1} \cap EDR_{q2}\right)$$
$$DR_{x,oi} = \left(DR_{q1,oi} \cup DR_{q2,oi}\right) \cap \left(EDR_{q1} \cap EDR_{q2}\right)$$
$$DW_{x,oi} = \left(DW_{q1,oi} \cup DW_{q2,oi}\right) \cap EDR_{q3}$$
$$P_{x,oi} = more \ \ restrictive \left(P_{q1,oi}, P_{q2,oi}\right)$$

$$Else\ \ O_x = O_{q3} \cap \left(JR_{q1} \cap JR_{q2} \right)$$
$$\forall o_i \in O_x$$
$$\mathrm{Re}_{x,oi} = \mathrm{Re}_{q3,oi} \cap \left(JR_{q1} \cap JR_{q2} \right)$$
$$W_{x,oi} = W_{q3,oi} \cap JW_{q3}$$
$$TO_{x,oi} = TO_{q3,oi}$$
$$DR_{x,oi} = DR_{q3,oi} \cap \left(EDR_{q1} \cap EDR_{q2} \right)$$
$$DW_{x,oi} = DW_{q3,oi} \cap EDW_{q3}$$
$$P_{x,oi} = P_{q3,oi}$$
$$L(q_3) \leftarrow L(x)$$

The table in (Figure 4) defines less/more restrictive operations for the propagation rules:

Figure 4. Less and more restrictive operations for the propagation rules

	acceptance rules	propagation rules
less restrictive operations	weak and weak = weak weak and strong = strong strong and weak = strong strong and strong = strong	weak and weak = weak weak and strong = weak strong and weak = weak strong and strong = strong
more restrictive operation	weak and weak = weak weak and strong = weak strong and weak = weak strong and strong = strong	weak and weak = weak weak and strong = strong strong and weak = strong strong and strong = strong

6. **Fusing join (_f):** This join is similar to restrictive join but is slightly less restrictive, because it keeps more owners in the new label. It calculates the label of object containing the result of operation as follows:

$$O_x = \left(O_{q1} \cup O_{q2}\right) \cap \left(JR_{q1} \cap JR_{q2}\right)$$
$$\forall o_i \in O_x \ and \ o_i \in \left(O_{q1} \cap O_{q2}\right)$$
$$\mathrm{Re}_{x,oi} = \left(\mathrm{Re}_{q1,oi} \cup \mathrm{Re}_{q2,oi}\right) \cap \left(JR_{q1} \cap JR_{q2}\right)$$
$$W_{x,oi} = \left(W_{q1,oi} \cup W_{q2,oi}\right) \cap JW_{q3}$$
$$TO_{x,oi} = \left(TO_{q1,oi} \cup TO_{q2,oi}\right) \cap \left(EO_{q1} \cap EO_{q2}\right)$$
$$DR_{x,oi} = \left(DR_{q1,oi} \cup DR_{q2,oi}\right) \cap \left(EDR_{q1} \cap EDR_{q2}\right)$$
$$DW_{x,oi} = \left(DW_{q1,oi} \cup DW_{q2,oi}\right) \cap EDW_{q3}$$
$$\forall K_i \ such \ that \ K_{io} \in \left(O_x / \left(O_{q1} \cap O_{q2}\right)\right)$$
$$L(x) \leftarrow L(x) \cup \{K_i\}$$
$$L(q_3) \leftarrow L(x)$$

7. **Declassification join (_d):** During the execution of a transaction, if a step cannot be carried out because a participant does not have access to an object, the whole transaction will be aborted. Allowing the operation to proceed by temporarily declassifying the object can solve this problem, but strict rules have to be introduced to avoid total loss of security.

The proposed solution is adding an intermediate subject to effective reader set of the requested object, if initiator of this transaction is already an effective reader of the object. For writing, intermediate subject to the effective writers is added, if the originator is already an effective writer. Declassification can proceed only, if all effective owners agree to it by nominating subjects in their declassification sets.

When reading is performed, the declassified information must not be saved or used later. This can be ensured by setting the label of the object receiving declassified information to empty $(\varnothing)$. In case of writing, label of the written object should not become less restrictive as a result. When declassification read or write is finished, the intermediate principal will be removed from effective reader or writer set respectively.

8. **Propagation join (_p):** Parent object owners are also owners of their child objects. Parent objects' labels can be propagated to children's labels. The propagation is not a default operation from parent to their children. Each owner of the parent object decides whether he propagates or not, and each owner of the child object decides also whether he accepts or no.

The policies propagation consists to apply the parent object policy if he is also an owner of the child object or simply insert its policy in the child label.

Let us suppose that $q_1, q_2 \in Q$, such that $q_1 \rightarrow_{oh} q_2$ (q_1 is the parent object and q_2 is the child object). The new label of q_2 after propagation is obtained as follows:

$$O_x = O_{q1} \cup O_{q2} \text{ and } L(x) = L(q_1) \cup L(q_2)$$

$$\forall o_i \in (O_{q1} \cap O_{q2})$$

1. If $P_{q2,oi} \cdot p_{accept} = weak \wedge P_{q1,oi} \cdot p_{propagate} = strong$ then

$$\mathrm{Re}_{x,oi} = (\mathrm{Re}_{q1,oi} \cup \mathrm{Re}_{q2,oi}) \cap (ER_{q1} \cup ER_{q2})$$

$$W_{x,oi} = (W_{q1,oi} \cup W_{q2,oi}) \cap (EW_{q1} \cup EW_{q2})$$

$$TO_{x,oi} = (TO_{q1,oi} \cup TO_{q2,oi}) \cap (EO_{q1} \cup EO_{q2})$$

$$DR_{x,oi} = (DR_{q1,oi} \cup DW_{q2,oi}) \cap (EDR_{q1} \cup EDR_{q2})$$

$$DW_{x,oi} = (DW_{q1,oi} \cup DW_{q2,oi}) \cap (EDW_{q1} \cup EDW_{q2})$$

$$P_{x,oi} = P_{q2,oi}$$

2. else

$$Re_{x,oi} = Re_{q2,oi}$$

$$W_{x,oi} = W_{q2,oi}$$

$$TO_{x,oi} = TO_{q2,oi}$$

$$DR_{x,oi} = DR_{q2,oi}$$

$$DW_{x,oi} = DW_{q2,oi}$$

$$P_{x,oi} = P_{q2,oi}$$

$$L(q_2) \leftarrow L(x)$$

9. **Verification of the Joins' Safety:** After having defined the join operations on labels, their safety must be demonstrated to show that information flows $q_s \rightarrow q_d$ caused by the arithmetic operations, declassification and propagation are safe.

By observing the rule of valid information flow and using set theory, we obtain assertion, which is necessary to demonstrate for each join:

$$q_s \rightarrow q_d \text{ is safe} \Leftrightarrow \begin{cases} JR_{qd} \subseteq JR_{qs} \\ EDR_{qd} \subseteq EDR_{qs} \end{cases}$$

and:

$$\begin{cases} JW_{qs} \subseteq JW_{qd} \\ EDW_{qs} \subseteq EDW_{qd} \end{cases} \text{ and } \begin{cases} JW'_{qd} \subseteq JW_{qd} \\ EDW'_{qd} \subseteq EDW_{qd} \end{cases}$$

where JW'_{qd} and EDW'_{qd} are the new sets calculated for q_d after information flow.

The projection of this assertion on different joins gives the following assertions that have been showed. In this paper, we present only the demonstration of the assigning join.

Assigning join:

$$L(q_2) \leftarrow L(q_1)\_^{a} L(q_2) \Rightarrow q_1 \rightarrow q_2 \text{ is safe} \Leftrightarrow \begin{cases} JR_x \subseteq JR_{q1} \text{ and } EDR_x \subseteq EDR_{q1} \\ JW_x \subseteq JW_{q2} \text{ and } EDW_x \subseteq EDW_{q2} \end{cases}$$

1. $JR_x \subseteq JR_{q1}$ and $EDR_x \subseteq EDR_{q1}$

According to the definition of the assigning join, we have:

$$O_x = O_{q1} \cup \left(O_{q2} \cap JR_{q1}\right)$$

We have:

$$\left(O_{q2} \cap JR_{q1}\right) \subseteq JR_{q1} \text{ and } O_{q1} \subseteq JR_{q1}$$

Therefore:

$$O_{q1} \cup \left(O_{q2} \cap JR_{q1}\right) \subseteq JR_{q1}$$

Then:

$$O_x \subseteq JR_{q1} \text{ (A.a)}$$

More:

$$\forall o_i \in \left(O_x / O_{q1}\right), \mathrm{Re}_{x,oi} = ER_{q1} \cup \mathrm{Re}_{q2,oi}$$

We can note that:

$$\left(O_x / O_{q1}\right) \subseteq O_{q2}$$

We have:

$$ER_x = \bigcap_{o_i \in O_x} \mathrm{Re}_{x,oi} = \left[\bigcap_{o_i \in O_{q1}} \mathrm{Re}_{q1,oi}\right] \cap \left[\bigcap_{o_i \in (O_x/O_{q1})} \left(ER_{q1} \cup \mathrm{Re}_{q2,oi}\right)\right]$$

$$ER_x = ER_{q1} \cap \left[\bigcap_{o_i \in (O_x/O_{q1})} \left(ER_{q1} \cup \mathrm{Re}_{q2,oi}\right)\right]$$

$$ER_{q1} \cap \left[\bigcap_{o_i \in (O_x/O_{q1})} \left(ER_{q1} \cup \mathrm{Re}_{q2,oi}\right)\right] \subseteq ER_{q1}$$

Therefore:

$$ER_x \subseteq ER_{q1}$$

Well, $ER_{q1} \subseteq JR_{q1}$. Then, $ER_x \subseteq JR_{q1}$ (A.b)
According to (A.a) and (A.b), we deduce that:

$$JR_x \subseteq JR_{q1} \text{ (A.c)}$$

On the other hand, we have:

$$\forall o_i \in \left(O_x/O_{q1}\right), DR_{x,oi} = EDR_{q1} \cup DR_{q2,oi}$$

and:

$$EDR_x = \bigcap_{o_i \in O_x} DR_{x,oi} = \left[\bigcap_{o_i \in O_{q1}} DR_{q1,oi}\right] \cap \left[\bigcap_{o_i \in (O_x/O_{q1})} \left(EDR_{q1} \cup DR_{q2,oi}\right)\right]$$

$$EDR_x = EDR_{ql} \cap \left[\bigcap_{o_1 \in (O_x/O_{q1})} \left(EDR_{q1} \cup DR_{q2,oi}\right)\right]$$

Well:

$$EDR_{q1} \cap \left[\bigcap_{o_i \in (O_x / O_{q1})} \left(EDR_{q1} \cup DR_{q2,oi} \right) \right] \subseteq EDR_{q1}$$

Therefore, we have:

$EDR_x \subseteq EDR_{q1}$ (A.d)

2. $JW_x \subseteq JW_{q2}$ and $EDW_x \subseteq EDW_{q2}$

We have before the information flow:

$JW_{q1} \subseteq JW_{q2}$

Therefore:

$\left(O_{q1} \cup EW_{q1} \right) \subseteq JW_{q2}$

Then:

$O_{q1} \subseteq JW_{q2}$ (A.a')

We have also:

$\left(O_{q2} \cap JR_{q1} \right) \subseteq O_{q2}$ and $O_{q2} \subseteq JW_{q2}$

Therefore:

$\left(O_{q2} \cap JR_{q1} \right) \subseteq JW_{q2}$ (A.b')

From (A.a') and (A.b'), we obtain:

$O_{q1} \cup \left(O_{q2} \cap JR_{q1} \right) \subseteq JW_{q2}$

We deduce that:

$$O_x \subseteq JW_{q2} \text{ (A.c')}$$

We have:

$$EW_x = \bigcap_{o_i \in O_x} W_{x,oi} = EW_x = \left[\bigcap_{o_i \in O_{q1}} \left(W_{q1,oi} \cap JW_{q2} \right) \right] \cap \left[\bigcap_{o_i \in (O_x/O_{q1})} W_{q2,oi} \right]$$

We have also:

$$\left(W_{q1,oi} \cap JW_{q2} \right) \subseteq JW_{q2}$$

Therefore:

$$\bigcap_{o_i \in O_{q1}} \left(W_{q1,oi} \cap JW_{q2} \right) \subseteq JW_{q2}$$

Thus:

$$\left[\bigcap_{o_i \in O_{q1}} \left(W_{q1,oi} \cap JW_{q2} \right) \right] \cap \left[\bigcap_{o_i \in (O_x/O_{q1})} W_{q2,oi} \right] \subseteq JW_{q2}$$

Consequently:

$$EW_x \subseteq JW_{q2} \text{ (A.d')}$$

From (A.c') and (A.d'), we obtain $JW_x \subseteq JW_{q2}$ (A.e')
On the other hand, we have:

$$EDW_x = \bigcap_{o_i \in O_x} DW_{x,oi} = \left[\bigcap_{o_i \in O_{q1}} \left(DW_{q1,oi} \cap EDW_{q2} \right) \right] \cap \left[\bigcap_{o_i \in (O_x/O_{q1})} DW_{q2,oi} \right]$$

We have:

$$\left(DW_{q1,oi} \cap EDW_{q2} \right) \subseteq EDW_{q2}$$

So:

$$\bigcap_{o_i \in O_{q1}} \left(DW_{q1,oi} \cap EDW_{q2}\right) \subseteq EDW_{q2}$$

Thus:

$$\left[\bigcap_{o_i \in O_{q1}} \left(DW_{q1,oi} \cap EDW_{q2}\right)\right] \cap \left[\bigcap_{o_i \in \left(O_x / O_{q1}\right)} DW_{q2,oi}\right] \subseteq EDW_{q2}$$

As a result, $EDW_x \subseteq EDW_{q2}$ (A.f')

Thus, according to (A.c), (A.d), (A.e'), (A.f') and ($L(q_2) \leftarrow L(x)$), we conclude that: $q_1 \rightarrow q_2$ is safe.

Restrictive Join:

$$\left(L(q_3) \leftarrow L(q_1) \_^{\,r} L(q_2) \Rightarrow \begin{pmatrix} q_1 \rightarrow q_3 \text{ is safe and} \\ q_2 \rightarrow q_3 \text{ is safe} \end{pmatrix}\right) \Leftrightarrow \begin{cases} JR_x \subseteq \left(JR_{q1} \cap JR_{q2}\right) \text{ and} \\ EDR_x \subseteq \left(EDR_{q1} \cap EDR_{q2}\right) \text{ and} \\ JW_x \subseteq JW_{q3} \text{ and } EDW_x \subseteq EDW_{q3} \end{cases}$$

Fusing Join:

$$\left(L(q_3) \leftarrow L(q_1) \_^{\,f} L(q_2) \Rightarrow \begin{pmatrix} q_1 \rightarrow q_3 \text{ is safe and} \\ q_2 \rightarrow q_3 \text{ is safe} \end{pmatrix}\right) \Leftrightarrow \begin{cases} JR_x \subseteq \left(JR_{q1} \cap JR_{q2}\right) \text{ and} \\ EDR_x \subseteq \left(EDR_{q1} \cap EDR_{q2}\right) \text{ and} \\ JW_x \subseteq JW_{q3} \text{ and } EDW_x \subseteq EDW_{q3} \end{cases}$$

Propagation Join:

$$q_1 \_^{\,p} q_2 \text{ is safe} \Leftrightarrow \begin{cases} ER_x \subseteq \left(ER_{q1} \cup ER_{q2}\right) \text{ and} \\ EDR_x \subseteq \left(EDR_{q1} \cup EDR_{q2}\right) \\ EW_x \subseteq \left(EW_{q1} \subseteq EW_{q2}\right) \text{ and} \\ EDW_x \subseteq \left(EDW_{q1} \subseteq EDW_{q2}\right) \end{cases}$$

Declassification join is safe because:

1. **Declassification is a Consensus of Effective Owners:** According to the definition of EDR_q and EDW_q, only effective owners of object q have the ability to declassify this item to roles that do not belong to the joint readers and joint writers. Then declassification is well controlled;
2. **Declassified Information in Case of Reading will not be Declassified Later:** Since label of the object carrying the declassified information is empty, set of effective declassification is empty. Thus, the object will not be declassified again;
3. **The Properties of the Object Declassified in Case of Writing will not be Altered:** Since the label of declassified object remains the same, its properties remain unchanged;
4. **Declassified Information is Used Only to Respond to Request of Transaction Initiator and will not be Saved:** This is achieved by assuming that HM-WSS modules in different service providers share a trust relationship between them.

MODELING

In this section, the main UML (Unified Modeling Language) diagrams are presented, which model the system, namely use case diagrams, class diagram and sequence diagrams.

Use Case Diagrams

The important actors of HM-WSS system are:

- **Administrator:** HM-WSS allows the administrator to define the different required roles, access control policies, mutually exclusive roles and possibly their updates (add, delete, modify);
- **Customer:** A customer may, in addition to the invocation of web services methods, manipulate information contained in the label of an object if system allows it after evaluation of its request and enforcement of the IFC rules.

The tow corresponding use case diagrams are given in (Figure 5) and (Figure 6).

Class Diagram

Static representation of the system is given by class diagram (Figure 7).

Sequence Diagram

Sequence diagram in (Figure 8) reflects the processing of a client request in HM-WSS system.

Security system is inserted between the main manager and system objects.

To control access to objects, the main manager first asks permission from access control module and forwards the required parameters. If the requested access is permitted, methods of the information flow control module have to be invoked for any access to or manipulation of objects in the sytem. After any modification of an object, its label is updated according to the corresponding join, in order to maintain the confidentiality and integrity of information.

Figure 5. Use case diagram of the administrator

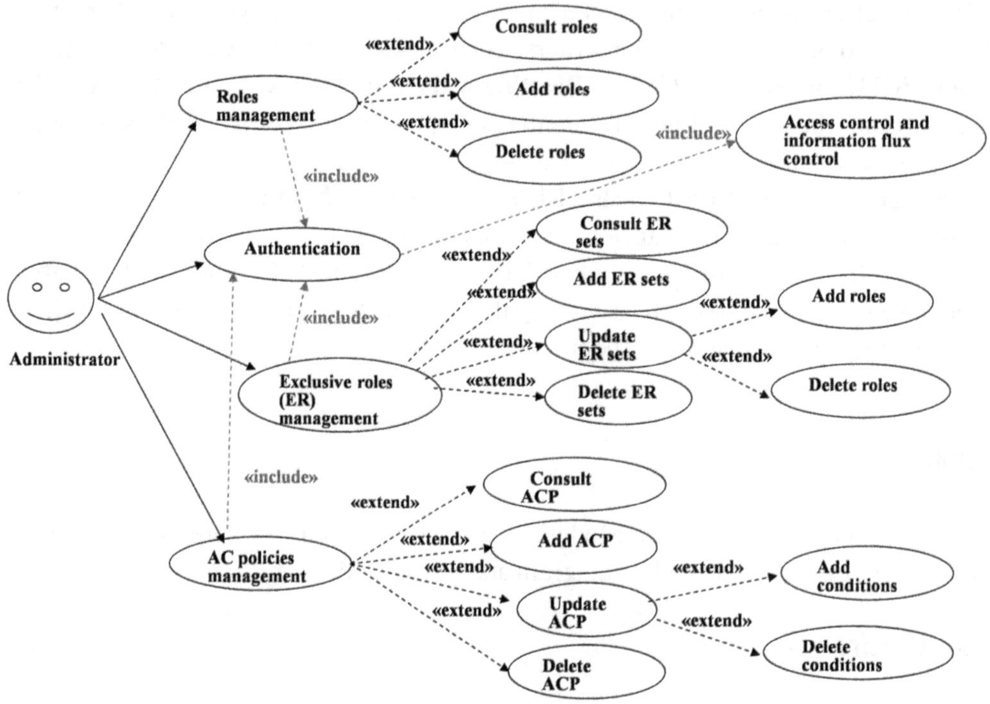

Figure 6. Use case diagram of the client

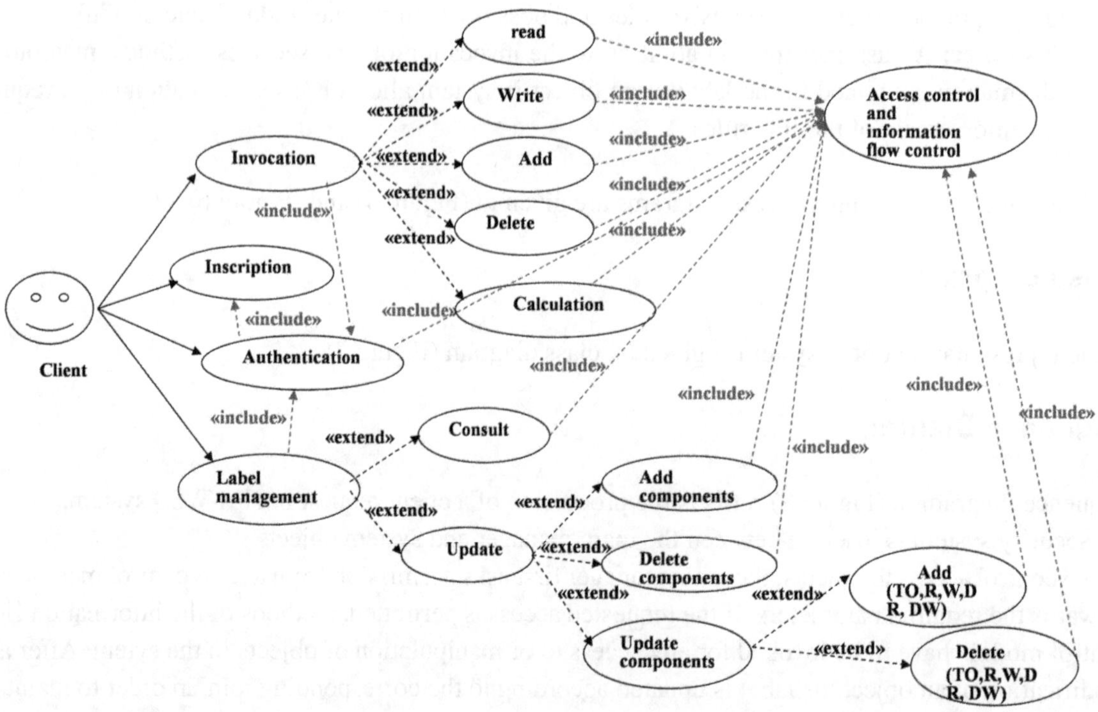

Figure 7. Class diagram

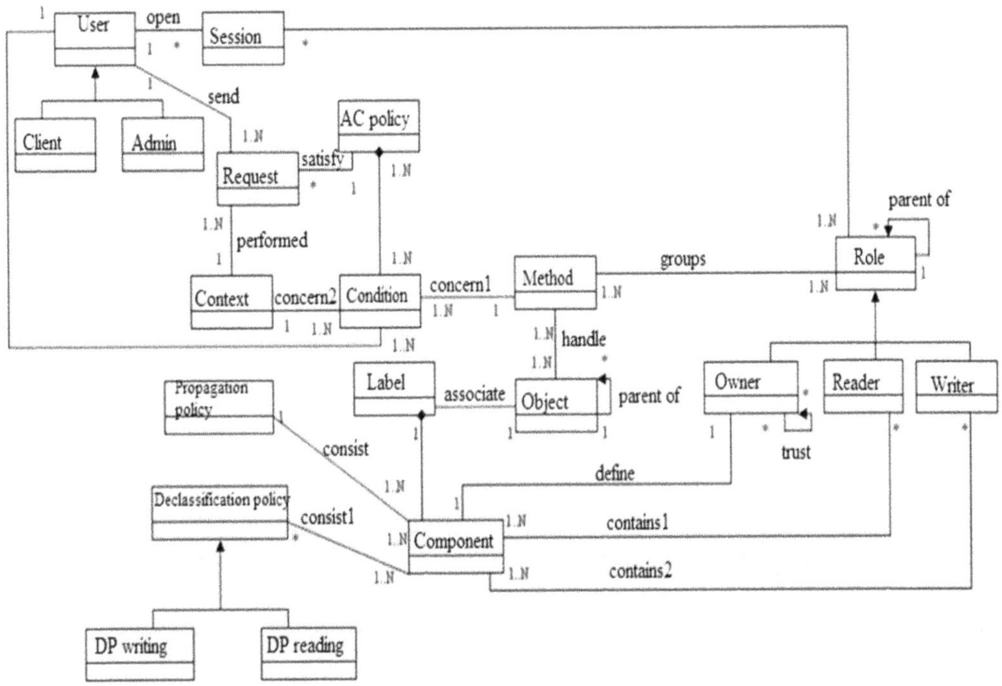

Figure 8. Sequence diagram

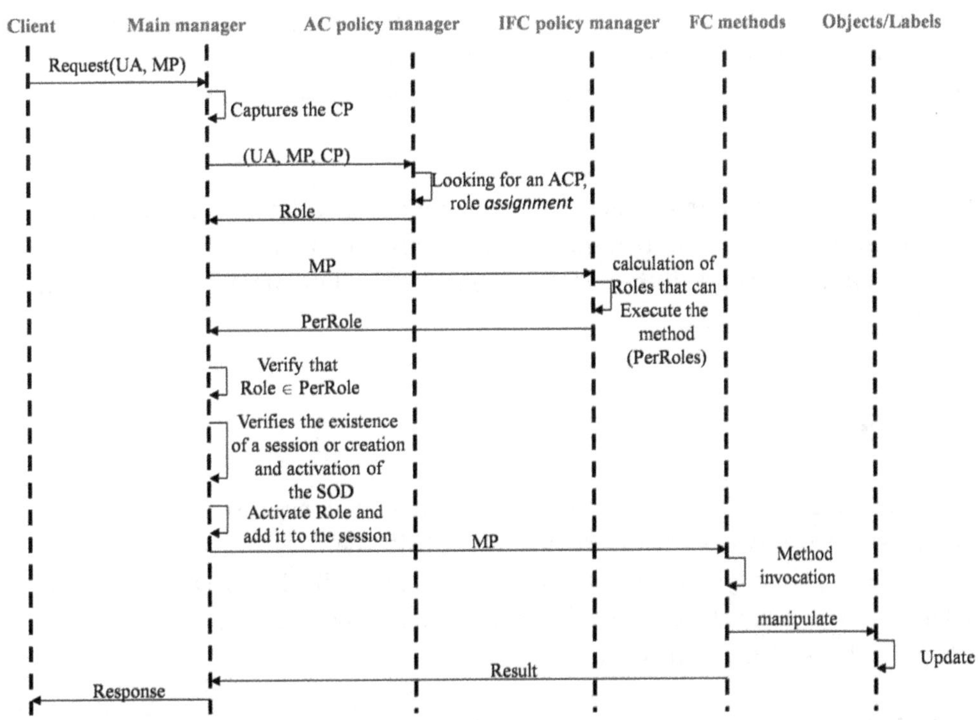

IMPLEMENTATION

The system consists of five main modules.

The Roles and AC Policies Manager

This module is responsible for the management of system roles and policies. A role is represented by an XML file and is characterized by a name "role-name", a parent role "parent_role" and a set of policies that allow its assignment to an access request. To assign a role to a request, this module should parse all policies of all roles until he finds the policy that satisfies this request and assigns this role. An access policy contains several conditions on the attributes of the access request.

This module contains two classes Role and Condition.

Example of methods of this module are:

- **create_role (role_name, ...):** This method adds a new role to the tree of existing roles with an activation policy;
- **add_attribute_condition (role_name, cond_num, ...):** It adds a condition on an attribute to a policy;
- **Map_RR (request):** This method activates the role corresponding to a request;
- ... etc.

Sessions Manager

When receiving a request from a client, this module performs a search of an open session for it.

If found, it applies the function of separation of duties to verify the role may or may not be activated. Otherwise, a new session is created for the client and the role enabled by the query is added.

Example of methods of this module are:

- **add_session (user, role_name):** Create a session for a user with the role activated by his request;
- **SOD ():** It creates a set of roles that should not be activated in the same session;
- **fc (user, role):** It returns true if the role can be enabled and false if the role is contradictory to one of the roles already activated;
- ...etc.

Labels Manager

The labels manager is a very important module in the system, it allows assigning a label to each object in a web services provider. A label is represented by an XML file.

To avoid overloading the system when a client accesses, EO, ER, EW, EDR, ERW, JR, JW are calculated and added to the label at the time of its creation and is updated with each change of label.

Example of methods of this module are:

- **create_label (object_name, ...):** Create a label for an object;
- **Add_component (object_name,...):** Add one component to the given object;

- **get_eff_owner (object_name):** It retrieves the set of effective owners of the given object;
- **EOq (object_name):** It calculates the set of effective owners of the given object;
- ...etc.

Joins Manager

This module is responsible for the implementation of the various joins, previously defined.

The main methods of this module are:

- **propagation_join (parent_object, child_object):** It implements the propagation join algorithm;
- **assigning_join (object_q1, object_q2):** It implements the assigning join algorithm;
- **restrictive_join (object_q1, object_q2, object_q3):** It implements the restrictive join algorithm;
- **fusing_join (object_q1, object_q2, object_q3):** It implements the fusing join algorithm;
- **DR_join (object_q, initiator, intermediate):** It implements the declassification join algorithm in case of reading;
- **DW_join (object_q, initiator, intermediate):** It implements the declassification join algorithm in case of writing.

Methods Manager

This module implements the IFC rules. Here are some examples:

- **MapPR_read_q(object):** This method returns the list of roles that can read an object;
- **MapPR_write_q(object):** This method returns the list of roles that can write an object;
- **MapPR_create_q(parent_object):** This method returns the list of roles that can create an object whose parent is parent_object;
- ...etc.

It implements also methods that perform the usual operations of web services by incorporating the IFC rules. The examples of methods that are redefined are: assignment, addition, subtraction and multiplication.

We explain here how we redefined the assignment and addition:

- **MapPR_copy (object1, object2):** It calculates the list of roles that can copy the contents of object1 in object2. This set is the intersection of roles that can read object1 and write in object2;
- **Copy (Role, object1, object2):** It implements the new definition of the copy method (object2 ← object1). It includes the flowing steps:
    - read (object1);
    - write (object2);
    - applying the assigning_join (object1, object2);
- **MapPR_addition (object1, object2, object3):** It calculates the list of roles that can perform addition on the contents of the object1 and object2. This set is the intersection of roles that can read object1 and object2 and can write in object3;

- **Addition (Role, object1, object2):** It implements the new definition of the addition operation (object2 + object1). It includes the flowing steps:
  - read (object1);
  - read (object2);
  - addition: object1 + object2;
  - write (object3);
  - applying the restrictive_join (object1, object2, object3) or fusing_join (object1, object2, object3).

CASE STUDY

The HM-WSS system is tested on a reservation system for a travel agency. This web services system is deployed at a company that offers services to its employees, a travel agency, a hotel, airline and car rental agency.

In this section, the web services system and its functioning by applying the security model are described with UML diagrams.

Company's Module

Use Case Diagram

There is four actors for the company's system:

- **Administrator:** He can define the main roles and their conditions to access the web services methods (consult, update, create, …) and system objects. He can also perform trips book for company employees;
- **Employee:** He has the ability to view various objects for which he has the access right as his payslip or his medical record;
- **Accountant:** His task is creating the payslip;
- **Doctor:** He can create the medical file of a company's employee and change it if necessary.

Every action performed, asking some confidentiality, will possibly invoke the HM-WSS modules, to perform the access control to methods and objects and the information flow control between them.

Their use case diagrams are given in (Figure 9) and (Figure 10).

Class Diagram

The (Figure 11) shows the class diagram of the company's module.

Travel Agency Module

The travel agency offers access to its Web service for its customers (company) for their help to make reservations.

Figure 9. Use case diagram of the company administrator

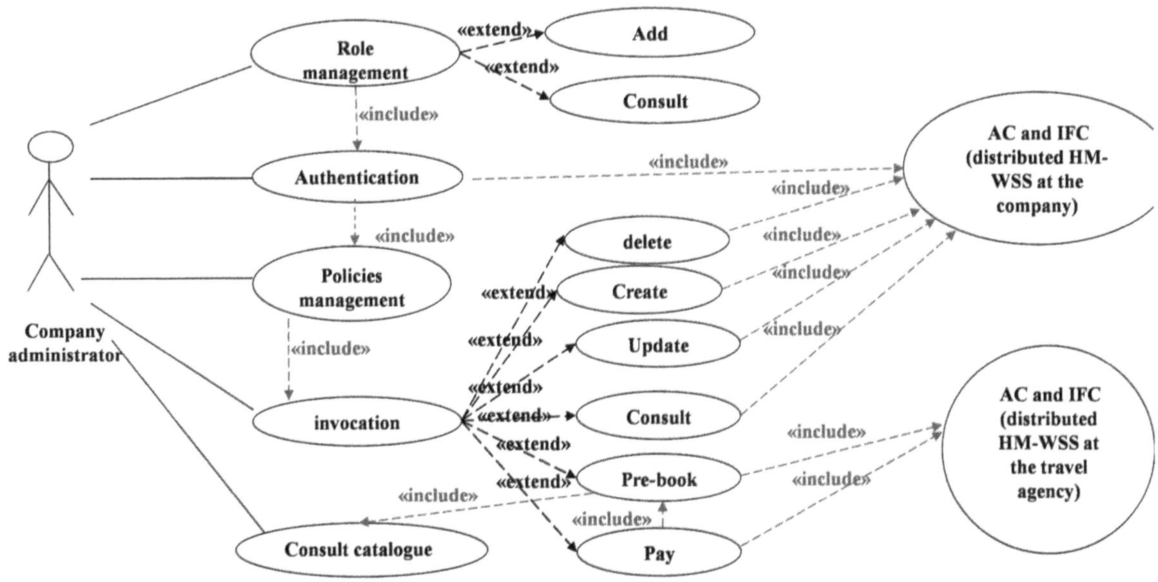

Figure 10. Use case diagram of the employee, the accountant and the doctor

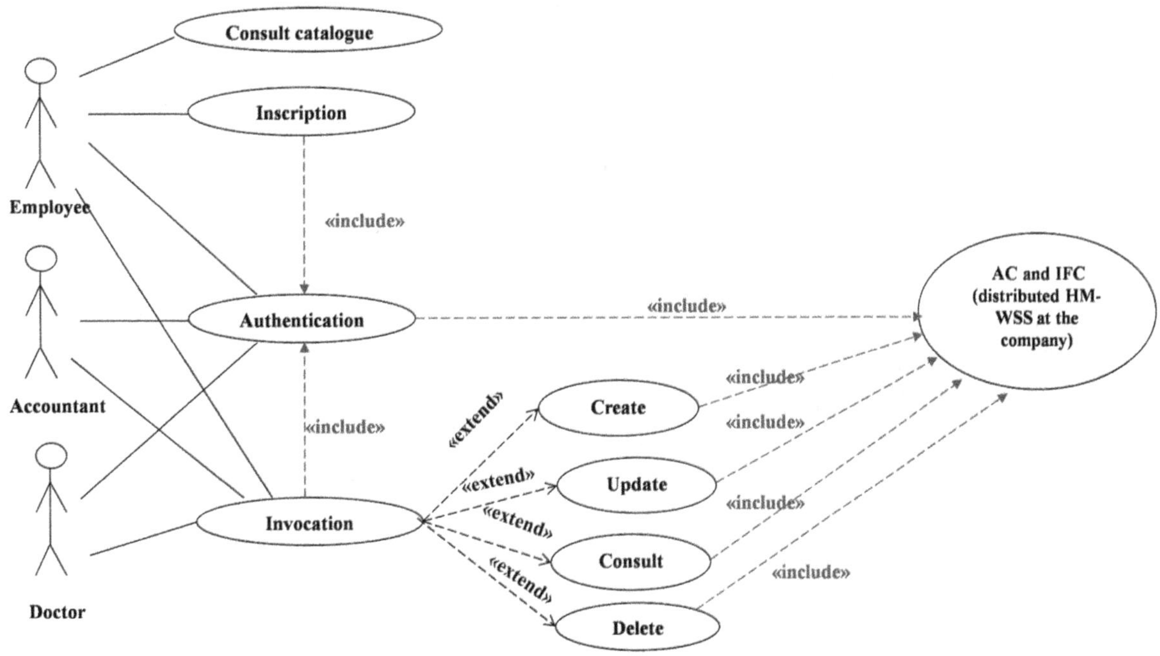

Figure 11. Class diagram of the company

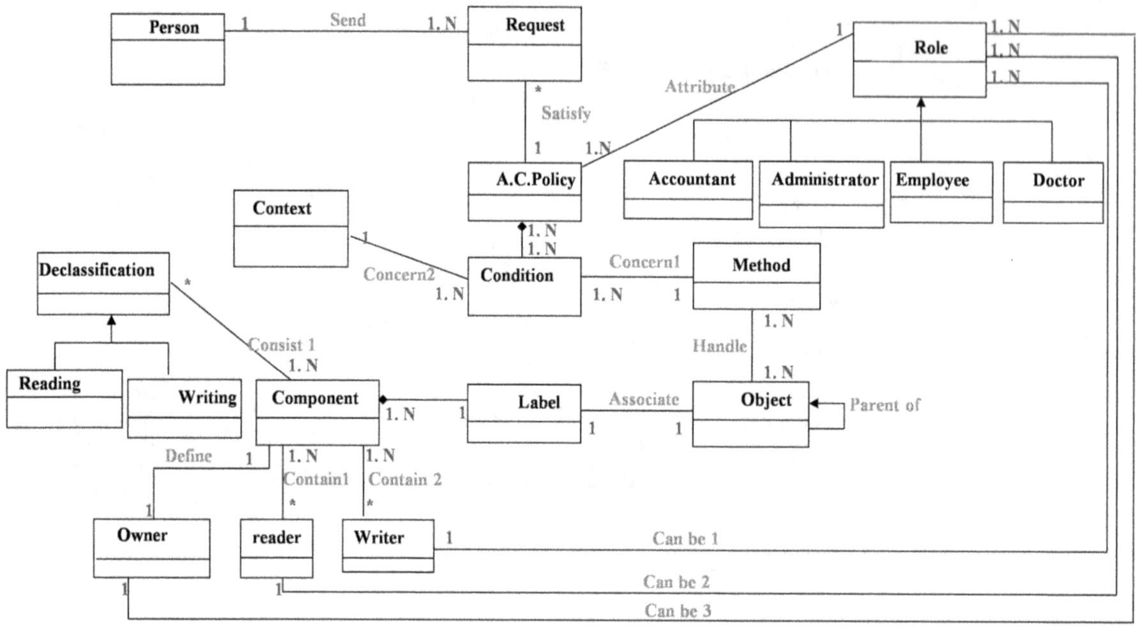

Figure 12. Use case diagram of the travel agency administrator

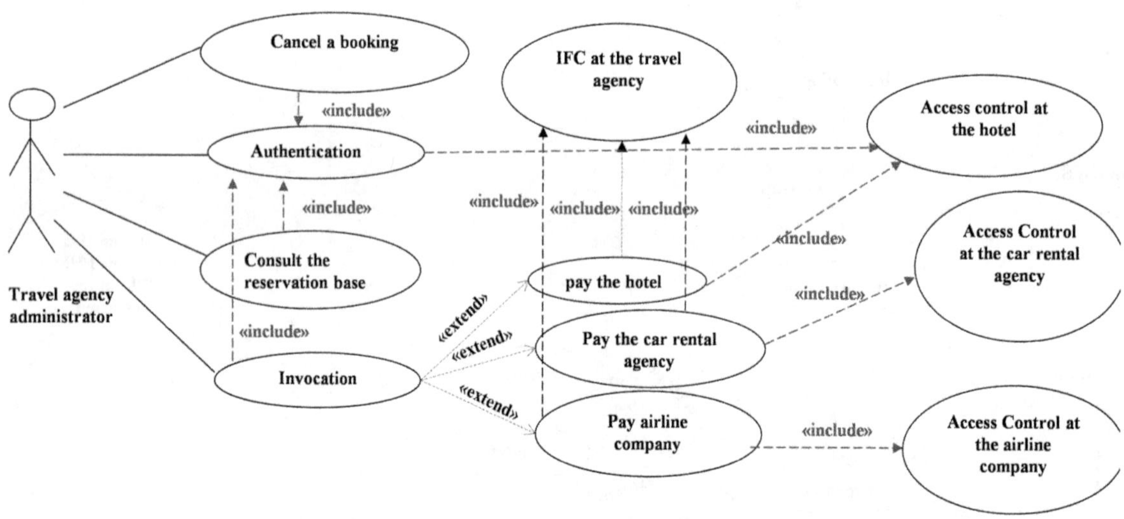

Figure 13. Use case diagram of the travel agency client

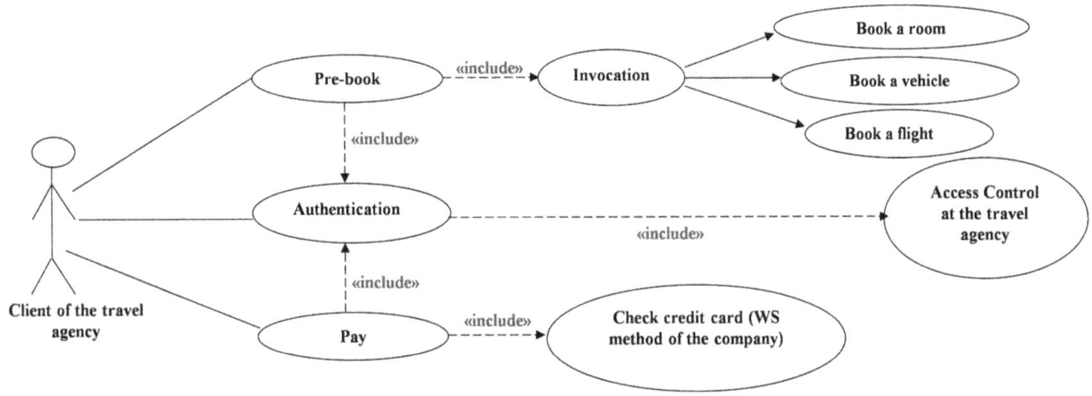

There is two actors for this module: the administrator and the client whose use case diagrams are illustrated in (Figure 12) and (Figure 13).

Hotel Module

The hotel offers a web service to book rooms and pay the reservation, according to the criteria specified by the customer and thereby update its database.

The (Figure 14) gives the use case diagram of its module.

Figure 14. Use case diagram of the hotel

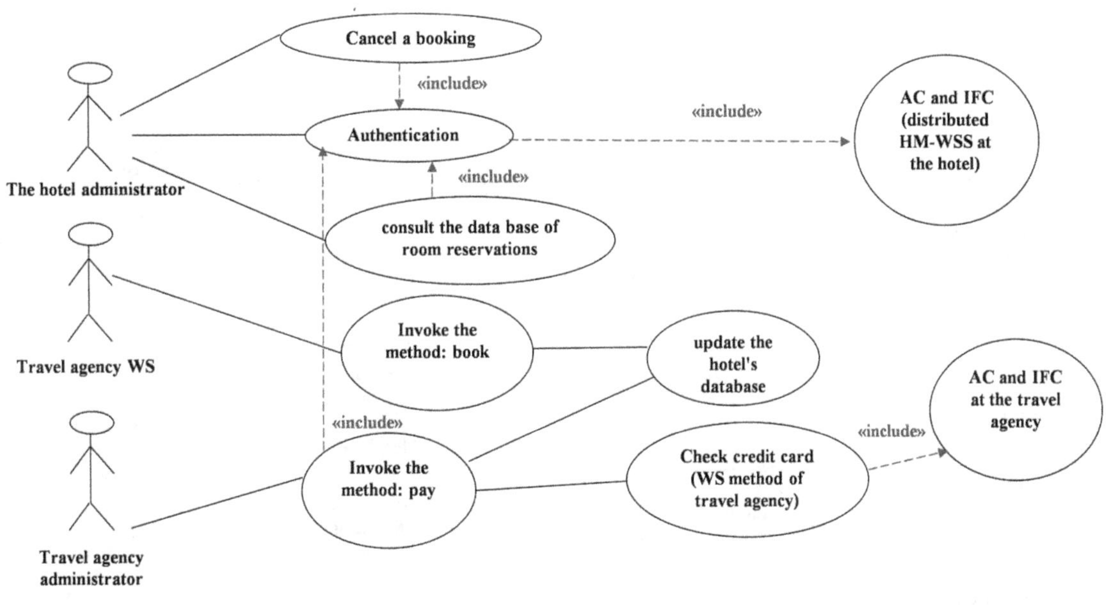

Car Rental Agency Module

This is the same principle as in the hotel, car rental agency gives also the possibility to rent vehicles and pay via its Web Service. The use case of its module is given in (Figure 15).

Airline Company Module

Through its Web Service, the client reserves flights, providing the information they need. The use case of its module is given in (Figure 16).

Interaction between Different Web Services

To illustrate the functioning of the web services by applying the security module (HM-WSS), sequence diagram of interactions between them is presented in (Figure 17).

SOFTWARE VALIDATION

The tools used to implement the HM-WSS and the reservation system for a travel agency are: NetBeans, JDK, JDOM API, Tomcat 6.0, Axis2 and JUDDI 0.9rc4.

Although this section will not be enough to show all the tests on the software, some examples of XML files (role, object, label, access control policy) and system responses to method access request, and information flow operation are presented.

Figure 15. Use case diagram of the car rental agency

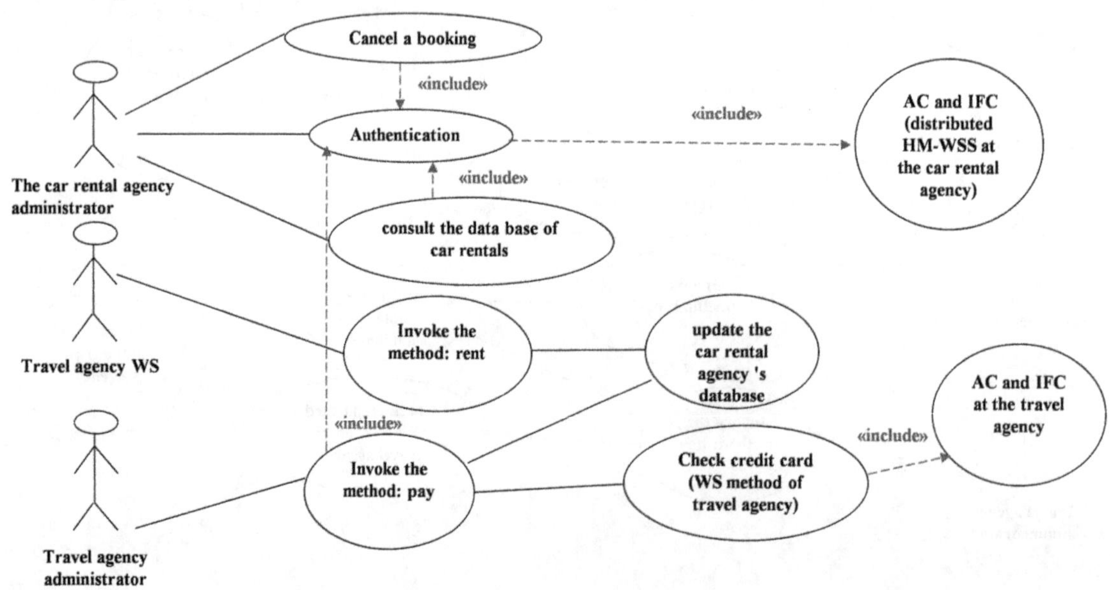

Figure 16. Use case diagram of the airline company

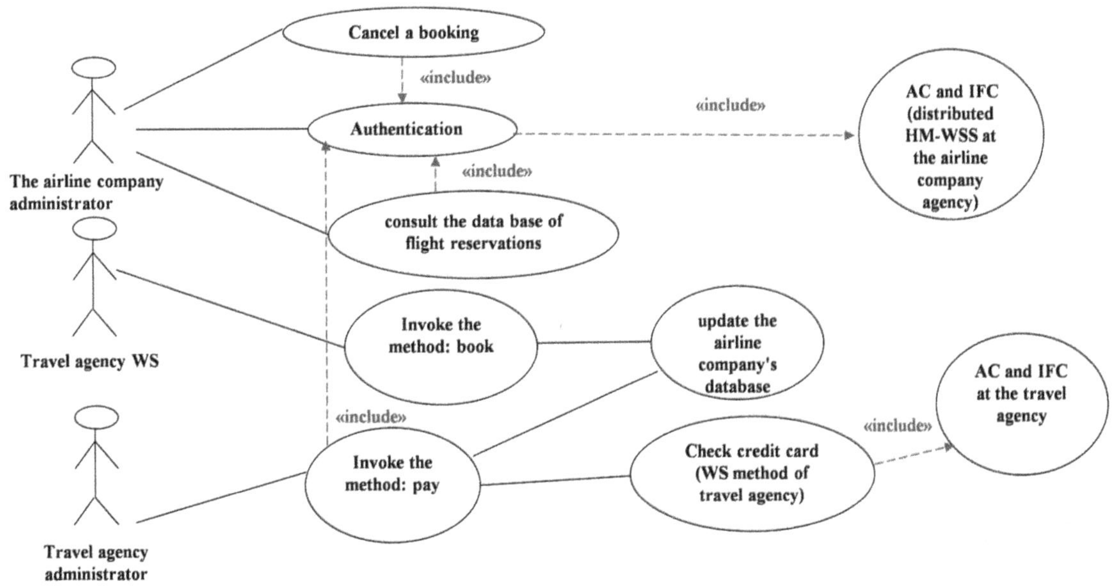

Figure 17. Sequence diagram of the interaction between different WS

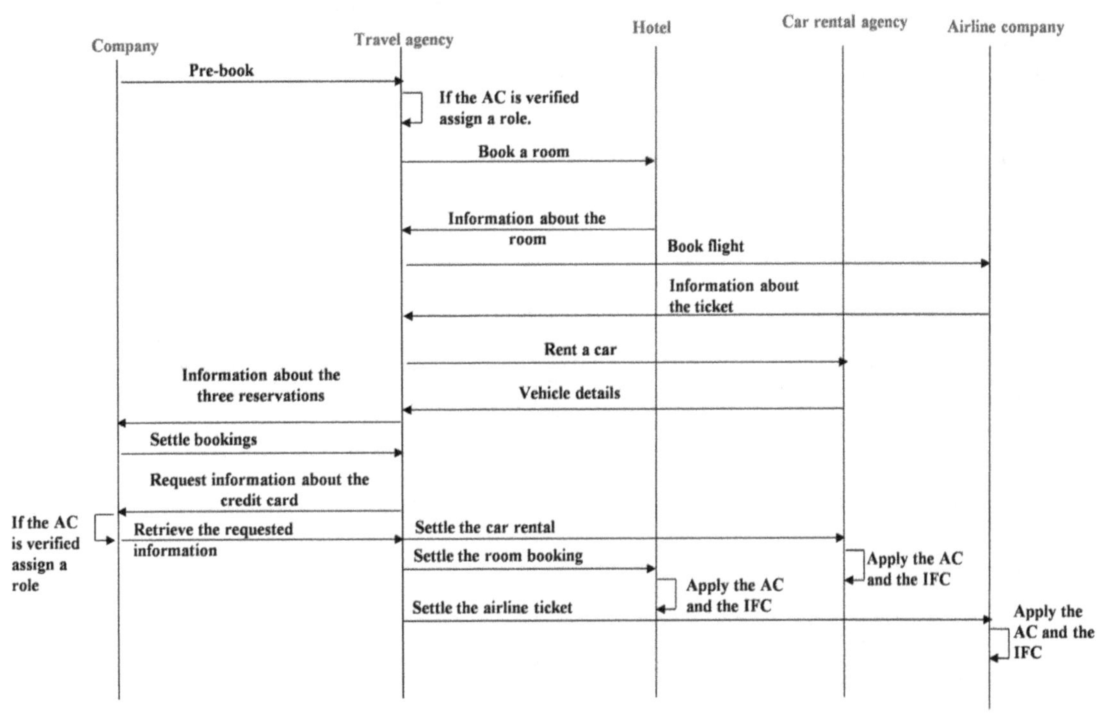

Data Structure Used

Objects, labels, subjects (roles) with their acces control policies are represented in XML files. Some examples are showed in (Figure 18):

Administrative Interfaces

Each service provider can configure the objects with their labels, the roles with their permissions on web services methods and objects. In (Figure 19), some interfaces of administration are presented.

Access Control and Information Flow Control Tests

In (Figure 20), an example of an access denied and an information flow not allowed is showed.

CONCLUSION

This paper present a hybrid model for Web services security (HM-WSS), which allows both the access control to web services methods, access control to objects and the information flow control between these objects. The proposed model is independent of the business logic of web services. It monitors web services and information at different levels of granularity. The mechanism of integrated access control allows the trust management between service requesters and service providers using the users'

Figure 18. Representation of data with XML files

```xml
<?xml version="1.0" encoding="UTF-8" ?>
<roles>
<role>
<role_name>employe</role_name>
<parent>administrateur</parent>
</role>
<policy>
<condition number="n1">
<attribute_name="pass_word">
<value>lmd</value>
<value>ilti</value>
<value>Saadia</value>
</attribute>
</condition>
<condition number="n2">
<attribute_name="method">
<value>modify</value>
<value>consult</value>
</attribute>
</condition>
</policy>
</roles>
```

a. The role « emplyee »

```xml
<?xml version="1.0" encoding="UTF-8" ?>
<infos_medicales>
<employee matricule="x060060" name= " KEDJAR" First_name= " Saadia"
social_security_number="88-5671-0065-25">
<diagnostic>
<desease>angina</desease>
<medicament>Ibuprofène</medicament>
<aptitude>not-apt</aptitude>
</diagnostic>
</employee>
</infos_medicales>
```

b. The object « medical_Saadia_KEDJAR »

```xml
<object>
<object_name>medical_Saadia_KEDJAR</object_name>
<object_parent>root</object_parent>
<label>
<components>
<component>
<owner>medecin</owner>
<trusted_owners>
<trusted_owner name="KEDJAR" First_name= " Saadia"> employee
</ trusted_owner >
</ trusted_owners>
<readers>
<reader>
<reader_name>administrator</reader_name>
</reader>
<reader>
<reader_name name="KEDJAR" First_name= " Saadia">employee</reader_name>
</reader>
</readers>
</component>
</components>
</label>
<Joint_Readers>
<effective_readers>
<reader_name name="KEDJAR" First_name="Saadia">employee</reader_name>
</effective_reader>
<owners>
< owners>medecin</ owners>
</ owners >
</ Joint_Readers >
< Joint_Writers>
<owners>
<owner>medecin</owner>
</owners>
</ Joint_Writers >
</object>
```

c. Label of the object « medical_Saadia_KEDJAR »

Figure 19. Some interfaces of administration

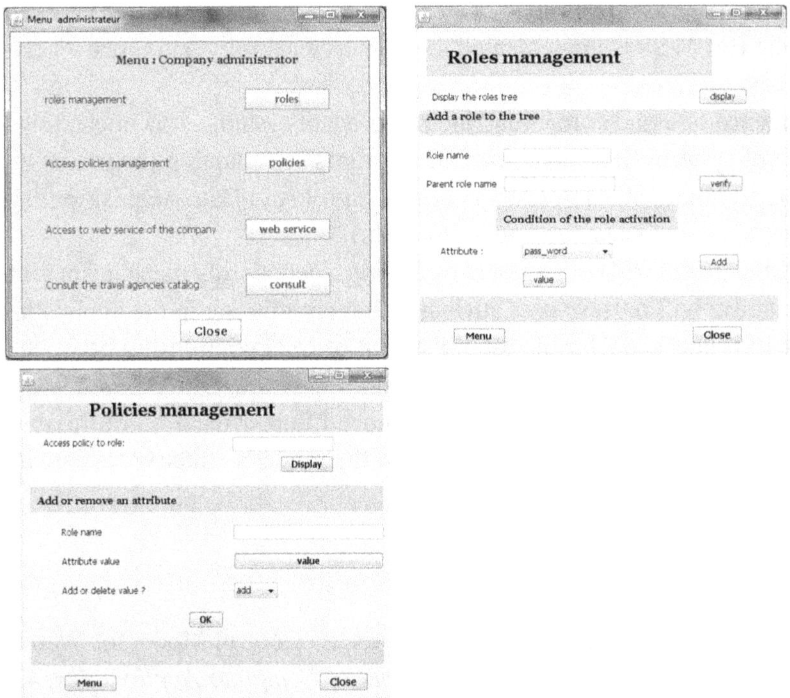

Figure 20. AC and IFC tests

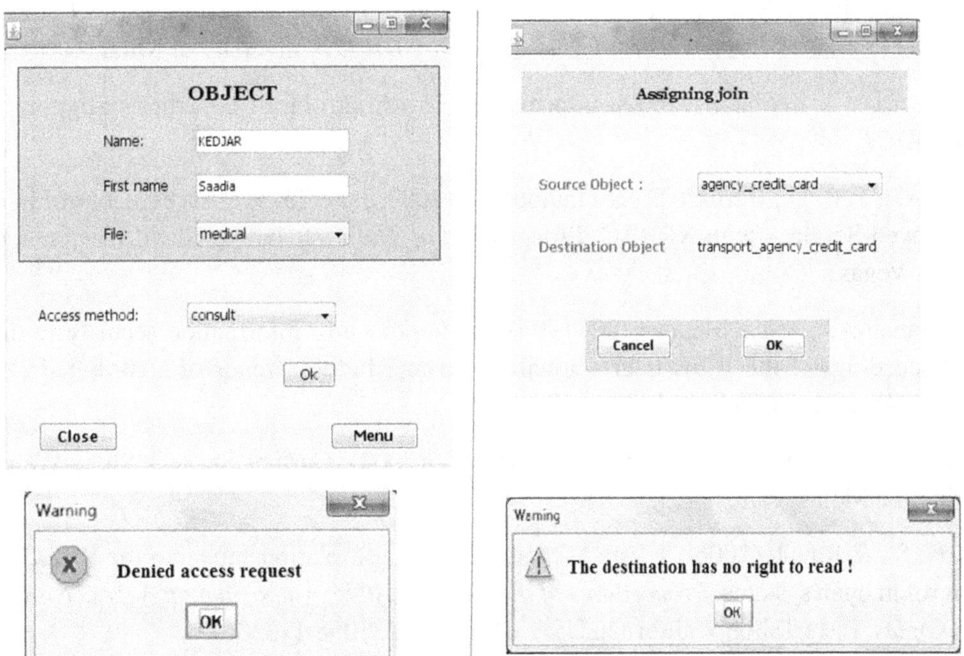

a. Access denied **b. Information flow not allowed**

attributes and it is flexible and extensible through the concept of role. The mechanism of information flow control allows the declassification if necessary and possible in order to continue normal execution of transactions. The HM-WSS is implemented to show its feasibility and prove its efficiency by testing it on a system of web services.

With the emergence of cloud computing and multi-agent systems, it is interesting to adapt the HM-WSS for this type of systems. For this reason, the authors are adapting the model to a particular type of distributed system namely SCADA (Supervisory Control And Data Acquisition) systems taking into account their constraints (response time, real time, etc.).

In future work, the model will be improved by adding a negotiating mechanism for the access control model. This mechanism will retrieve user attributes that are missing in the application of access rules. Another mechanism is necessary for the establishment of trust relationship between service providers and requesters when they are strangers to each other.

The information flow control's rules can be improved to provide a more flexible approach. Then, check the completeness of the model. Further tests of the model's effectiveness are also interesting.

REFERENCES

Alipour, H., Sabbari, M., & Nazemi, E. (2012). An Access Control Model for Web Services with Dynamic Separation of Duty Rules. *International Journal of Computer Applications*, 42(6).

Bertino, E., Martino, L., Paci, F., & Squicciarini, A. C. (2010). Security for Web Services and Service-Oriented Architectures. Springer. doi:10.1007/978-3-540-87742-4

Bertino, E., Squicciarini, A. C., Martino, L., & Paci, F. (2004). *A flexible access control model for web services. CERIAS and CS Department, Purdue University DICO*. University of Milano.

Bertok, P., Tari, A., & Kedjar, S. (2009). Information Flow Control for Cooperation Support in Virtual Enterprises. *AICT*, *307*, 581–590.

Bhatti, R., Joshi, J. B. D., Bertino, E., & Ghafoor, A. (2003, June 23-26). Access Control in Dynamic XML-based web-Services with XRBAC. *Proceedings of The First International Conference on web Services*, Las Vegas.

Bryce, C., Banatre, J., & Le Metayer, D. (1995). An approach to information security in distributed systems. Proceedings of the IEEE International Workshop, Future Trends of Distributed Computing Systems (p. 384). 10.1109/FTDCS.1995.525008

Cantara, M., Andrews, W., & Latimer-Livingston N.S. (2003). Gartner Surveys Show Web Services Are Entering the Mainstream.

Chakraborty, S., & Ray, I. (2006). TrustBAC: integrating trust relationships into the RBAC model for access control in open systems. *Proceedings of the eleventh ACM symposium on Access control models and technologies*. Lake Tahoe, California, USA. 10.1145/1133058.1133067

Chen, M. (2003). Factors affecting the adoption and diffusion of XML and Web services standards for E-business systems. *Int. J. Human-Computer Studies*, *58*(3), 259–279. doi:10.1016/S1071-5819(02)00140-4

Esfandi, A., & Sabbari, M. (2012). Study of Access Control Issue in Web Services. *International Journal of Computer Applications*, 49(1).

Ferrari, E., Samarati, P., Bertino, E., & Jajodia, S. (1997). Providing flexibility in information flow control for object-oriented systems. *Proceedings of the IEEE Symposium on Security and Privacy*. 10.1109/SECPRI.1997.601328

Gondara, M. (2011). Access Control Mechanisms for Semantic Web services-A Discussion on Requirements & Future Directions. *International journal of emerging technologies and applications in engineering, technology and sciences*, 4(1), 338-342.

Hai-bo, S., & Fan, H. (2006). An Attribute-Based Access Control Model for web Services. *Proceedings of the Seventh International Conference on Parallel and Distributed Computing, Applications and Technologies (PDCAT'06).*

Kedjar, S., & Tari, A. (2013). The hybrid model for web services security: access control and information flow control. *Proceedings of the 8th International Conference for Internet Technology and Secured Transactions (ICITST)* (pp. 194-202). 10.1109/ICITST.2013.6750190

Liu, M., & Guo, H., & SU, J. (2005). An attribute and role based access control model for web services. *Proceedings of the Fourth International Conference on Machine Learning and Cybernetics*, Guangzhou (pp. 18-21).

Myers, A. C., & Liskov, B. (1997). A decentralized model for information flow control. *Proc. of the 16th ACM Symposium on Operating Systems Principles*, Saint-Malo France. 10.1145/268998.266669

Tari, Z., Bertok, P., & Simic, D. (2006). A dynamic label checking approach for information flow control in web services. *International Journal of Web Services Research*, *3*(1), 1–28. doi:10.4018/jwsr.2006010101

Tari, Z., & Wonohoesodo, R. (2004). A role based access control for web services. *Proceedings of the IEEE International Conference on Services Computing (SCC'04).*

This research was previously published in the International Journal of Information Technology and Web Engineering (IJITWE), 11(1); edited by Ghazi I. Alkhatib; pages 44-76, copyright year 2016 by IGI Publishing (an imprint of IGI Global).

Chapter 12
The Politics of Access to Information:
Exploring the Development of Software Platforms and Communications Hardware in the Digital Age

Shefali Virkar
University of Oxford, UK

ABSTRACT

Over the last few decades, unprecedented advances in communications technology have collapsed vast spatial and temporal differences, and made it possible for people to form connections in a manner not thought possible before. Centred chiefly on information, this revolution has transformed the way in which people around the world think, work, share, and communicate. Information and Communication Technologies (ICTs) promise a future of a highly interconnected world, wherein action is not limited by physical boundaries, and constrained physical space is replaced by a virtual 'cyberspace' not subject to traditional hierarchies and power relations. But is the promise of ICTs chimerical? To tackle these issues, central to the global policy debate over the potential development contributions of Information and Communication Technologies, and to examine whether and the extent to which disparities in access to ICTs exist, this book chapter provides a demonstration of the ways in which ICTs may be used as tools to further global economic, social, and political advancement, to shape actor behaviour, and to enhance institutional functioning; particularly in the Third World.

INTRODUCTION

The age of Information Technology – IT as we call it – has arrived. I know of no other technological advantage which has brought together so many areas of rapid and exciting development. Computers and telecommunications are converging very rapidly, huge investments are being made, and the impact of information technology will be felt at every level in our society; in industry, in commerce, in our offices and in our homes. -Kenneth Baker (1982)

DOI: 10.4018/978-1-7998-0417-8.ch012

The closing years of the 20th century were a period of turbulent change for world politics, and stood witness to two major developments that critics agree played a key role in the sculpting of the political, economic and social landscape of the 21st century. The first was the dramatic unfolding of a series of events, beginning with the symbolic dismantling of the Berlin Wall in 1989, which signalled the beginning of the end for many of the central tenets of post-World War II international relations. A plethora of forces at work in the Soviet Union and Eastern Europe over previous decades unleashed dramatic upheavals in essentially all countries of the former Eastern Bloc, culminating in the unexpected collapse of Soviet statism in 1990-91 and the subsequent demise of international communism. At the forefront of these forces were the pressures of technological change on the internal structures of the Eastern Bloc nations and on their relationships with the outside world. These led to drastic economic restructuring to compete in the high technology global environment with huge shifts in the composition of the domestic economies, a rationalisation of military forces, and a seemingly unstoppable flood of information pouring unhindered through the erstwhile Iron Curtain.

The second development was less dramatic and, beyond a handful of scientific and academic circles, was less well recognised: the invention of Hyper Text Mark-up Language (HTML) and the creation of the World Wide Web. Although network computing had been around since the 1960s, the networks themselves were rudimentary – comprising of dispersed computers linked by packet-switching technology – and remained, till the end of the 1980s, the domain of scientists, academics and a handful of graduate students (Toulouse, 1998). The invention of HTML broke this user-monopoly by simplifying network programming and, together with the launch of the graphical browser Mosaic (and its descendants Netscape Navigator and Internet Explorer), made it possible for lay computer users to access Websites and communicate with people across the globe (Norris, 2001). Whilst seemingly unrelated, the developments of the late 1980s share a remarkable thread of commonality: they are both small historical footnotes in a much larger tale. A tale in which advances in science and technology, particularly developments in information and communications technology, have moulded the evolution of international affairs, and altered the relationships within and amongst nations and the fortunes of their peoples.

The starting point of this book chapter is the recognition of an apparently new way of conceiving contemporary society, and the acknowledgement of the pivotal roles that *information*, *communication*, and *technology* play within it. Social scientists have long seen 'information' as *the* distinctive feature of the modern world, however, what makes today's age distinct from before is the growing convergence of digital computing, telecommunications, and human infrastructure; reflected in the shift in terminology from *Information Technology* or *I.T.* to *Information and Communications Technology* or *I.C.T.* (Virkar, 2014). Popular and academic literature tells us that we stand on the edge of the Information Age, where both information and technology have become 'symbol(s) of political potency and economic prosperity' (Martin, 1998: 1). We live and work in 'weightless knowledge economies' and will soon be part of a 'global information society'.

These clichés are not used without reason. The world is continuing to witness the burgeoning growth of new electronic Information and Communications Technologies (ICTs) and their associated platforms and applications: the Internet and the World Wide Web have spawned multimedia and interactive technologies, video-conferencing, virtual realities, computer-aided design, the information superhighway, and technologies for consumer profiling and surveillance; all of which enable the electronic production, transmission, processing, communication, and consumption of increasingly vast quantities of information and know-how. Like their predecessors – the printing press, the telegraph, the radio, and black-and-white television – advanced ICTs have become an intrinsic part of our everyday social, political, and economic lives. They are embedded in an array of networks and services across the spectrum of human activity: from education to politics, from the arts to sport, from medicine to music, these technologies are set to transform the way in which people work, think, act, and interact.

HYPER CONNECTIVITY: GLOBALISATION, THE INTERNET, AND THE THREAT TO NATIONAL SOVEREIGNTY

All that is solid melts into air -Marshall Berman

Information has been feared by those in authority from time immemorial. The growth of the media and the spread of information have been regarded as sources of power and change ever since the time of James I of England, when the growth in the popularity of the printing press was watched with great suspicion by both the Crown and the Church. The nascent print media gave rise to the first stirrings of parliamentary democracy in Britain and allowed, for the first time, the old political order to be challenged by new ideas (Perritt, 1998). The subsequent development of new and improved forms of communication over the next few centuries, beginning with the invention of the radio and the telegraph, and moving thence to the telephone and to television, posed new and greater threats to central power and authority (Thussu, 2000). Writing in 1894, John Stuart Mill noted that "it is hardly possible to overrate the value, in this present low state of human improvement, of placing human beings in contact with persons dissimilar to themselves, and with modes of thought and action unlike those with which they are familiar… Such communication has always been, and is peculiarly in the present age, one of the main sources of progress" (Quoted in Grace et. al., 2001:1).

Today, it may be claimed concretely that the global spread of technology and the subsequent growth of the global media have definitely impacted nation-states in ways that would be seen as 'interference' by many in positions of authority. Globalisation has collapsed spatial and temporal barriers to economic and social exchange, and its convergence with two other trends, world-wide electronic connectivity and emergent knowledge networking practices, has reinforced the importance of the role played by knowledge and information in the global political, social, and economic arenas (Virkar, 2014). An oft-quoted example of such media power is the *CNN Effect*: the impact that live, round-the-clock, global news coverage by all-news cable television channels has on public opinion and on foreign policymaking (Virkar, 2004)[1]. Many International Relations theorists and self-styled *cyberenthusiasts* alike believe that the Internet, with its seemingly limitless possibilities for information transmission and access to knowledge, poses the strongest-ever technological challenge to state sovereignty than any other communications medium in living memory. Today, we live in knowledge-driven societies poised on the threshold of an Information Age.

Theoretical Frameworks of the Information Society

It is not surprising therefore, that advances in ICTs have been, and still are, regarded by many as the impetus behind radical, if not revolutionary, socio-economic changes, and are at the centre of many fierce debates raging across the world. The concept of an 'information society' and the uses of ICTs within such a community have themselves been sources of controversy (Mansell & Silverstone, 1996). To some commentators, the extensive use of ICTs constitutes the emergence of a truly efficient, open society, whilst to others it heralds the beginning of an Orwellian police-state and the gradual demise of key civil liberties; some see the flood of information as a precursor of a highly educated public, whilst others see in it a deluge of trivia, sensationalism and propaganda (Dutton, 1999).

Amidst the divergent opinions regarding the Information Society and ICTs one thing remains undisputed: the role and importance of information, and Information Technologies, have grown in the contemporary world. Given their potential to revolutionise social, economic, political and cultural life, recent advances in ICTs have generated many theoretical perspectives on the 'Information Revolution' and its implications for society. Early discussions of computers and telecommunications reflected the concern that modern technology would become an unstoppable force, supporting increasingly centralised control in organisations and society (Skolnikoff, 1993). Theories of technological determinism were particularly popular during the 1960s, and are still subscribed to by a number of commentators today.

Concurrent to the emergence of technological determinism was the emergence of modernisation theory, and the idea that technology could be used as a tool for development. Modernisation was concerned with the development gap between the North and South, and how best to close the gap so as enable quicker and more effective growth in the Third World. The most popular variant of the theory was an adaptation of Walt Whitman Rostow's views, popularised in his 1960 volume, *The Stages of Economic Growth: A Non-communist Manifesto* (Rodda, 2004). Rostow outlined five main stages of growth: the traditional society, the preconditions for take-off, the take-off, the drive to maturity, and the age of high mass consumption. This helped define where the constituent parts of the world stood in this scheme, and how best the South could climb the ladder of development. Essentially, information technology was considered an important precondition towards achieving a reformation of politics, society, and economy, and the ultimate emergence of a modern (typically capitalist) civilization.

With the turn of the decade, however, most social scientists discarded the linear models of cause-and-effect used by technological determinism and modernisation in favour of approaches that popularised the notion that a new sort of society was emerging, and which sought to explore the underlying processes of social and technical change (Silverstone & Haddon, 1996). Possibly the best known characterisation of the Information Society is, therefore, Daniel Bell's Theory of Post-Industrialism. In his seminal work *The Coming of the Post-Industrial Society* (1973), Bell asserted that information – not raw materials or financial capital – would become the key economic resource in the coming age.

Using the United States as his benchmark, Bell identified 3 major trends in the development of an Information Society: an Increased Employment in Information- and Knowledge-Driven Job Sectors, referring to the movement of a majority of the labour-force from the *primary* (agriculture-led) and *secondary* (manufacturing-led) sectors of an economy to jobs within the *tertiary* or the service sector that involve the creation, transmission, and consumption of information; an Increased Importance of 'Knowledge' and 'Information' in Society, including its integration into the everyday working of social, political, and economic institutions; and an Increased Centrality of Decision-making by Technologists to Technologists, implying a power shift in favour of those managers and professionals skilled in the use of information and technology for planning and analysis.

Bell's information-society thesis and its subsequent applicative relevance in the modern work world has been both criticised and has tested doubtful on many counts (Virkar, 2011). Firstly, there is a constant shifting of employment subject to demand-supply patterns for agricultural goods, manufactures and services, an economic given which may be completely unconnected with an Information Revolution. In addition, ICTs can bring about job losses in every sector of the economy, including the service sector, as manual labour is replaced by advanced technology. Finally, and most importantly, the value of information as a commodity itself is highly variable; certain kinds of information are not useful, and some parts can lose value whilst others retain it depending on the circumstances.

The Politics of Access to Information: Plugging in to the Information Age

In recent times, the focus of ICT scholarship has moved away from the centrality of information *per se* to the issues and processes that shape access to information and technology, and to the notion that the ability to control this access to information and the need to acquire an understanding of the institutions and hierarchies that do so are key to functioning in a knowledge-driven economy (Robins, 1992). In this context, questions concerned with *who* is 'connected' to information technology have grown in prominence over the last few decades. They now form an important element in the burgeoning canon of 'information age' literature, and are beginning to influence the policy agenda of industrialised, technologically-advanced countries such as the USA, the UK, and those of the European Union (Selwyn, 2002). The so-called 'techno-enthusiasm' of a whole host of analysts, politicians, and other policymakers has been tempered with concerns over the potentially divisive aspects of the Information Age, in particular the development of software platforms, communications hardware, and the related global inequalities of access to ICTs. Developing countries and pressure groups within some developed nations have become increasingly alarmed at the apparent emergence of a 'digital divide', wherein those without access to the latest and, ironically, the most expensive tools and technologies will find themselves at a great disadvantage, unable to compete in an increasingly hi-tech global socio-political marketplace. Decelerating economic progress has serious implications for the social and political development of these individuals, groups, and countries, circumstances which in turn threaten overall global peace and security.

In seeking to address the overarching question of whether the developing world is being left behind in the Information Revolution with regards to Information and Communication Technology Research and Development, the discussion covered in the subsequent sections of this chapter endeavours to succinctly answer three questions: 1) is there a gap in the access to ICTs between developed and developing countries; 2) is this gap growing or closing; and finally, 3) what are the implications of this *digital divide* for the overall development and global proliferation of communications hardware and software? The central hypothesis of this book chapter being, therefore, that a digital divide exists between developed and developing nations, and that it might be bridged through the increased development and greater use of ICTs worldwide. To tackle these issues, central to the global policy debate over the potential development contributions of Information and Communication Technologies, the chapter also provides a demonstration of the ways in which ICTs may be used as tools to further global economic, social, and political development, to shape actor behaviour, and to enhance institutional functioning particularly in the Third World. The work commences with a brief conceptualisation of the Digital Divide, examining its causes and critically reviewing current debates, moving forward to an assessment of the implied consequences that such a divide has for electronic government and for policy creation. The research therein seeks to analyse, in particular, the possible positive and negative consequences of bridging the Digital Divide for the betterment of public administrative practices and for the development of a more in-depth understanding of the applicative value that such a exploration holds for the future of the communications and software industry.

THE NETWORKING REVOLUTION: ICTs AND THE DIGITAL DIVIDE

The world at large is exactly what is at stake. Geographical borders seem to be of no importance whatsoever to the new media - they simply haven't been invited to the global ICT party.- Sarai Report to The Waag [2]

One of the most urgent issues today, and one of the questions central to global policy, is how ICTs affect global development, and whether they can be used to accelerate development in the Third World. Already, the spread of ICTs, in particular the Internet and telecommunications, is becoming visible: between 1995-1998, the global telecommunications markets added 200 million telephone lines, 263 million mobile subscribers and 10 million leased lines; and Internet connections increased to 88 million from 15 million in the early nineties. It took the telephone close to 50 years to reach 50 million users, a landmark which took the Internet only 4 years to surpass (World Bank, 2002).

The main reasons behind the recent explosion in ICTs are falling operating and hardware costs. These are, in turn, largely a result of technological innovations such as the use of *fibre optic cables,* able to transmit greater quantities of information across longer distances, *new mobile wireless technologies*, allowing users to stay connected regardless of location, and the adoption of *digital packet-switching* technology, making possible real-time networking and affordable computing power (Martin, 1998). Coupled with these developments, *regulatory reform* (increased privatisation and WTO-encouraged liberalisation of the global telecom market) has had a profound impact in both developed and developing countries.

Why ICTs?

There is no doubt that Information and Communication Technologies possess many basic characteristics that would enable them to play a significant role in the development process (Virkar, 2004).

1. **Increased and Faster Access to Knowledge:** Where reduced costs of producing and transmitting information lead, atleast in theory, to the greater availability of and access to information and help reduce uncertainty and risk to the benefit of all, particularly the poor, thereby *"[m]aking inefficient markets efficient"* as the management of online auctioneers eBay put it.
2. **Increased Efficiency and Precision:** Of working and of work processes, where the adoption of new ideas and inventions results in the streamlining of business activity, from production-lines to entire organisations, which in turn leads to greater productivity, increased profits, and more innovation.
3. **Overcoming Geography:** Through the harnessing of the innate ability of ICTs to function across national boundaries, and to collapse dislocations of space and time; thereby enabling people and organisations from diverse geographical regions to pool their resources, knowledge, and expertise. The bridging of temporal and spatial barriers to trade, commerce, travel and political action is particularly favourable for developing countries that, in addition to gaining access to larger markets and global supply networks, are also able to significantly benefit from new ideas and high-quality shared information.
4. **Openness:** A singular characteristic of the digital media that results in the key organisational process of *networking*, leading to greater and more effective information-sharing, and increased accountability and transparency. In this respect ICTs are potentially extremely powerful tools of

global empowerment for, as societies across the world become more and more interconnected and as information becomes more easily and readily available in digital form, they bring days of closed-door negotiations and secret repression closer and closer to an end.

Whilst many policymakers consider ICTs to be potent tools that empower poorer communities, societies, and countries, that are able to support long term economic and social development, and that are capable of bringing about 'a closer and more productive integration of affluent and developing nations, others consider them to be detrimental overall for global political, social, and economic development (Virkar, 2011). Under such circumstances, the need to answer questions regarding the utility and functionality of ICTs in development and the kind of goals that may be best achieved through their application becomes even more pressing. The impact of ICTs may be considered under three broad headings: their impact on economic growth, their created opportunities for the poor, and the role they play in improved governance and the delivery of government services.

Impact on Economic Growth

Economic data and anecdotal evidence suggest that growth and development of the Third World are increasingly being influenced by the availability of telecommunications hardware and informatics infrastructure, and that the benefits that ICTs can bring to the developing world are manifold (Katz, 2009). Improved information exchange benefits supply chains across industry sectors globally; giving producers, suppliers, and consumers access to market data, information on regulations and standards, prices, and potential customers. ICTs and their associated digital platforms can also help to promote the transnational marketing and distribution of goods and services: *e-commerce*, for example, is expected to benefit both local producers and international businesses by opening up the global marketplace and by enabling access to virtual digital markets, whilst simultaneously streamlining the structure and functioning of local businesses and institutions. In short, ICTs level the economic playing-field, as developed country producers become less insular in losing one of their key innate privileges – an unrestricted, verging on monopolistic, access to raw materials, human resources, and rich markets worldwide.

An advanced telecommunications infrastructure is, further, central to attracting foreign direct investment, particularly when applied to enhance a country's monetary system. In this respect, the adoption of Information and Communication Technologies facilitates both the modernisation of banking and financial systems, critical to developing countries access to the highly digitised world of international finance, and the expansion of local and transnational banking services and supply chains to previously underserved groups, countries, and regions (Virkar, 2004). Finally, ICT-based virtual applications and platforms, especially electronic messaging services and the Internet, enable countries to expand their service sectors, create jobs, and comply with international business practice standards through the outsourcing of professional services from different parts of the world. This presents enhanced employment opportunities for otherwise disadvantaged professionals, and provides for better pay and higher standards of living internationally (Andrianaivo & Kpodar, 2011). An oft-quoted example is that of the Indian services sector, where software professionals write code for American companies, medical transcribers decipher prescriptions and create dental and hospital records, and call-centres cater to customers all over the so-called Western world.

Opportunities for the Poor

ICTs have the potential to create diverse opportunities for the poor, and encourage the spread of equitable development within developing countries (Virkar, 2011). A majority of the poor of the Third World live in rural areas, and for them vital information and a wide range of services are either difficult to procure or are only available at prohibitive prices. ICTs provide an affordable, versatile mechanism by which the poor might access the global storehouse of knowledge, and use the information gained therein to improve their overall standard of living (Grace, 2003). Farmers and other rural entrepreneurs, for example, may use advanced software and hardware to source information about where they can obtain the highest possible prices for their goods, by-passing exploitative intermediaries and middle-men, rather than simply selling at the nearest market for convenience.

ICTs may be further used to boost agricultural productivity and food security. Schemes piloted in villages in Southern India enable farmers and fishermen to track weather patterns, to predict wave height, and to tackle crop disease (Le Page, 2002). ICTs can also provide increased business opportunities in rural areas and create jobs for more disadvantaged sections of a population. For example in North India, a group called Technology in Action for Rural Advancement (TARA) has pioneered a scheme that involves local people (mainly women) setting up computer centres in their villages, and earning money selling computer services to villagers (Prakash, 2012). Put this way, the pay-off from Information and Communication Technologies in terms of poverty reduction, say experts, could be dramatic. Indeed, as demonstrated above, in countries such as India and Thailand results have been self-evident for the last decade (Spence & Smith, 2010).

Improved Governance and the Delivery of Government Services

Many commentators believe that networking can potentially make a great impact on the public sector, as public services are still reliant on information flows and participation in governance may be facilitated by adequate communication infrastructure (Virkar, 2013). Broadly speaking, ICTs improve governance in three ways. Firstly, they help *enhance decision-making and public administration* by reducing administrative costs, by speeding up the day-to-day processing of information, and by increasing transparency and accountability. Secondly, ICTs *improve the provision of public utilities* such as water, electricity, and sanitation, and help speed up the allocation of permits and the dispensation of complaints. The proliferation and use of ICTs in political processes can also *bring a government closer to its people*, allowing for popular access to decision-making and facilitating communication on three levels – citizen to citizen, citizen to government, and government to citizen.

Information and Communication Technologies have also long been an integral part of the education system in developed countries, and today, new forms of hardware, applications, and platforms offer powerful tools for expanding educational access and improving knowledge and skill-transfer in the Third World (Kozma, 2008). The Internet, in particular, has helped in equalising access to knowledge, has improved teacher training, and has enhanced skills in some of the poorest parts of the world. ICTs may also increase the provision and efficiency of medical services through, amongst other things, the improved storage and transmission of data, the publication and dissemination of medical findings, and the amelioration of the surveillance and monitoring of epidemics (World Bank, 2002). Similarly, such technologies may contribute to the augmentation of efforts to boost environmental protection by enabling access to accurate data relating to global climate change and pollution levels.

MIND THE GAP: EXPLORING THE CONSEQUENCES OF THE DIGITAL DIVIDE FOR DEVELOPMENT

At first glance the digital divide appears to be a simple premise.-Neil Selwyn

It would be difficult to find a more apt real-life symbol for the inequitable distribution of digital technologies than the chasm that yawns between Silicon Valley's verdant Palo Alto, home to dot.com millionaires where the average price of a house is almost $700,000, and East Palo Alto, the squalid little town on the other side of Highway 101 that not long ago gained notoriety for having America's highest murder rate (Virkar, 2004). However, whilst it is largely agreed that there are disparities in access to ICTs, a fierce debate is raging within academic and policy circles as to whether this gap is actually growing or closing.

For developing countries, the potential benefits gained from advances in ICTs are immense, and their successful adoption would imply both an acceleration of economic and social development, and greater social, economic, and political integration of isolated (usually rural) populations into mainstream community, national, and global life. The ultimate vision for many *techno-enthusiasts* is thus that of the creation of an immense Global Information Infrastructure enabling the rapid acceleration of technology assimilation into political institutions and for economic development, one that will narrow gaps in poverty and eliminate obstacles to full social integration, to equality of opportunity, and to overall worldwide prosperity (Main, 2001).

The question stands clear: with the continued prevalence of existing inequalities in current institutions and infrastructure, will Information and Communication Technologies ever become truly global? With what consequences for political, social, and economic institutional reform and policy building? Many commentators fear that countries (and the individuals, groups, and communities within them) lacking access to fundamental resources essential for them to fully benefit from advances in technological hardware and software would only be further marginalised by the ICT Revolution (World Bank, 2002). This apprehension has been encapsulated succinctly in the phrase "**digital divide**", an amorphous term that may be defined as *the gap between those individuals and communities that have, and those that do not have, access to information, ICTs, and technological know-how.*

Understanding the Concept of the Digital Divide

It is plain to see that the conditions under which ICTs are diffusing in most countries are creating deep, more complex disparities in the way in which technology is developed and propagated across the world. Equally, it is not surprising that to many, bridging this so-called *digital divide* has become the single-most pervasive development issue of the new century. Concern has been expressed in various forums – from the UN and the Group of 8 at the very top of the development ladder to university departments and local community groups at the other end of the scale – that the developing world is being, and will continue to be, left behind in the digital stakes (UNDP, 2010). Commentators consider such disparities as evidence of an ever-widening gap between the information-rich and information-poor, see this divide as continuing to manifest itself along other, multiple axes: *between countries*, hindering the economic growth of some nations whilst aiding others; and *within countries*, differentially impacting the opportunities of various individuals and groups in society *vis-à-vis* each other.

A key issue central to arriving at a more nuanced understanding of the concept is, thus, how ICTs, and the associated digital divide, relate to global development. It is a welldocumented fact that during the 1990s, the world witnessed a substantial increase in social exclusion, poverty, and income inequality; statistics showed that 50% of the world's population (more so than in previous decades) subsisted on less than $2 a day, 20% of the global population generated 80% of the world's wealth, 80% of global youth lived in the developing world and lacked access to opportunity, and more women bore a larger part of the burden of poverty, illiteracy, and malnutrition than their male counterparts (Virkar, 2004). During the latter half of the decade, coinciding with the explosive growth in Information Technology and the rise of the network economy, and despite the spectacular strides made by certain developing countries as a result of the rapid proliferation of ICTs, the gap between the developed and developing world widened in terms of technology, productivity, income, social opportunity, and living standards.

The Digital Divide Debate

A growing number of scholars and specialists feel that the digital divide is no longer a crisis; indeed, some contend that it has never been as critical an issue as it was made out to be. These commentators believe that such a paradigm of 'frenetic urgency' is the product of the 'digital delirium' of the 1990s technological and dot-com booms, and argue that, whilst in *absolute* terms the degree of access to ICTs between nations might have widened, in *relative* terms developing countries continue to show faster rates of penetration of technology than developed societies. For example, between January 1997 and August 2000, North America's share of Internet users plummeted from 62.1% of the world total to 42.6%, whilst most other regions displayed impressive gains in their relative share. Overall, the number of Internet users worldwide increased by a factor of four (Castells, 2001).

Some scholars, in consequence, hold that *the gap between rich and poor countries is closing*, with the developing world quickly catching up in terms of numbers of the users able to access, comprehend, and use effectively new technologies and their associated platforms and applications (Virkar, 2004). Many feel that the digital divide today remains a popular cause amongst politicians and interested corporates only as a means of diverting attention from more pressing issues, such as national inequalities of income, education, access to services and benefits, and labour standards, and as means of benefiting from its emotional appeal in terms of either more votes or increased sales. As one critic observed of the American government: "The current political interest in the digital divide is an attempt to reverse the damage to race-relations caused by welfare reforms and by the retreat from affirmative action" (Strover, 2003: 276).

On the surface, it must be admitted that scholars on this side of the digital divide debate appear to have a point. Measured in terms of access, it is highly likely that we will, in the coming decades, witness the fast diffusion of the Internet and other ICTs around the world, and that the bulk of the users will indeed come from developing countries despite the deeper, more lopsided power relationships prevalent. However, that is only to be expected, simply because these countries account for 80%, and growing, of the world's population, soon to be highly educated and better professionally qualified.

Illustrated in more concrete terms, the digital divide runs as follows: whilst more telephone lines have been installed in the developing world over the past 5 years relative to the developed world, in the developed world technology has moved on from fixed analogue land-lines to digital broadband, to mobile networked access, and to 3G technology that allows people to process and access more information within shorter periods of time, and to harness quantum gains in productivity and efficiency (Fink & Kenny, 2003). The ability of a user-group population to access information is yet another facet to this

Table 1. An Integrative Framework for the Digital Divide

ACCESS	USE
Technological Access	**Technological Literacy**
ICT Infrastructure	Technological Skills
Hardware, Software, Bandwidth	Social and Cognitive Skills
Social Access	**Social Use**
Affordability	Information Seeking
Awareness	Resource Mobilisation
Language	Social Movements
Content/Usability	Civic Engagement
Location	Social Inclusion

(Source: Moorhead, 2004)

example, wherein the fact that the majority of the information accessible is available in English only (as documented earlier) is a substantial barrier for most people across the world.

Similarly, access to the Internet and other associated applications and platforms does not translate directly into a more *informed* use of those technologies, and people without sufficient education or skills will be unable to effectively harness informatics systems to uses that would benefit them (Virkar, 2011). Research conducted in the field by this researcher has highlighted a number of other equally pertinent social reasons behind the emergence of the digital divide. These include:

- **Socio-Economic Inequalities:** Such as not being able to afford to pay for access to computers or for associated network or connection charges.
- **Lack of Social Networks in Certain Key Areas:** Resulting in a lack of critical mass of people sharing information about the benefits of ICTs.
- **Inadequate Official Support:** Of low cost public access to technology, applications, networks, and associated infrastructure, particularly in developing countries, for want public institutions.
- **Other Social Issues:** Including gender differences involving unfavourable societal views of women accessing employment, the Internet, acquiring technical know-how, and of working outside the home.

One could therefore conclude that, whilst the digital divide measured simply in terms of the rate of penetration of ICTs is narrowing, the gap prevalent in terms of the *effectiveness* and the *ability* of ICTs to deliver on promises of increased efficiency, productivity, information processing and wealth creation continues to widen, reinforced by both technological and sociological factors, and needs to be addressed. Moreover, as Table 1 further illustrates, access to *hardware* is only one part of the digital divide; whilst the degree of density of penetration of ICTs in the Third World might remain low, there are many other factors that must be taken into consideration when judging the extent of technological differential, in particular differences in terms of networking capacity, hardware capability, and the ability of a population to access information round the clock.

THE POLITICS OF ACCESS TO INFORMATION: OF DIGITAL INEQUALITIES AND DIGITAL DIVIDES

While most observers extol the virtues of the information revolution, and cite its ability to "level the playing field" for all participants, it is not entirely clear that these are either realistic or likely results.- Geoffrey Kirkman

Most studies concerned with quantifying and analysing the digital divide examine inequality of access using a number of key set indicators, which can be broadly classified into two types: inter-country and intra-country.

Inter-Country Inequalities

The growth in proliferation of ICTs in the developing world over the past two decades has been impressive. From 1995-1998 alone, developing countries connected over 155 million phone lines, 4 million leased lines, and witnessed a cumulative increase of 105 million in the number mobile network subscribers. Most regions have also seen a spectacular expansion in the spread and area-coverage of the Internet and other associated technologies within the same period (Virkar, 2004). Information and Communications Technologies are reshaping the flow of investment, goods, and services in the global economy, doubling business investments and service revenues in the Third World.

However, such striking results have often masked the wide disparities prevalent between countries in terms of the degree of penetration, of investment in public and private infrastructure, of change in technological sophistication, and of differentials in content provision (see Figure 1). Consider the following: in 2004, ten years into the commercialisation of the World Wide Web, roughly two-thirds of the world's internet population resided in North America and Europe, with only 15% of the world's population constituting 88% of the world's Internet users. In contrast, South and East Asia was home to 23% of the

Figure 1. Who's Online Where?

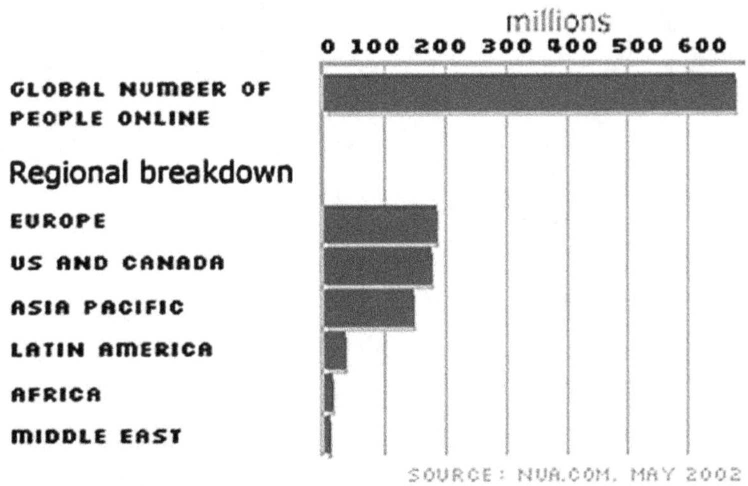

world's population but to only 1% of the world's internet users. 280 million people lived in the Middle East but only 1.1 million people were online, with half of those living in Israel alone. There were more telephone lines in Manhattan than in the entire geographical area of Sub-Saharan Africa (Virkar, 2004).

Internet User and Host Penetration and Density

For any technology or application to become a significant international development tool they must, first and foremost, be easily and readily accessible globally. In contrast, the diffusion of Information and Communication Technologies, particularly the Internet and its associated platforms, however rapid, has proceeded unevenly across the planet. For instance, in September 2000, of a total of 378 million Internet users or 6.2% of the world's population, North America's share of skilled technologist stood at 42.6%, Western Europe's at 23.8%, Asia's (including Japan) at 20.6%, Latin America's at 4%, the Middle East at 1.3% and Africa a meagre 0.4%. Recent data from NUA suggests that things haven't changed much since (NUA Online Surveys and Analysis, 2014).

Similarly, the level of penetration and market share of Internet broadcasters (hosts, nodes, and networks) within individual countries was much lower in the developing world – only 0.61% of India's population had access to the Internet in 2012 despite its growing software industry and increasing number of Internet users, as against over 41.5% of American households, and 30.8% of the population in the UK (Virkar, 2014). The geographical distribution of Internet hosts in 2012, illustrated by Figure 2, further demonstrates the gulf in connectivity between industrialised and developing countries.

Figure 2. Internet Hosts per 10,000 People (2012)

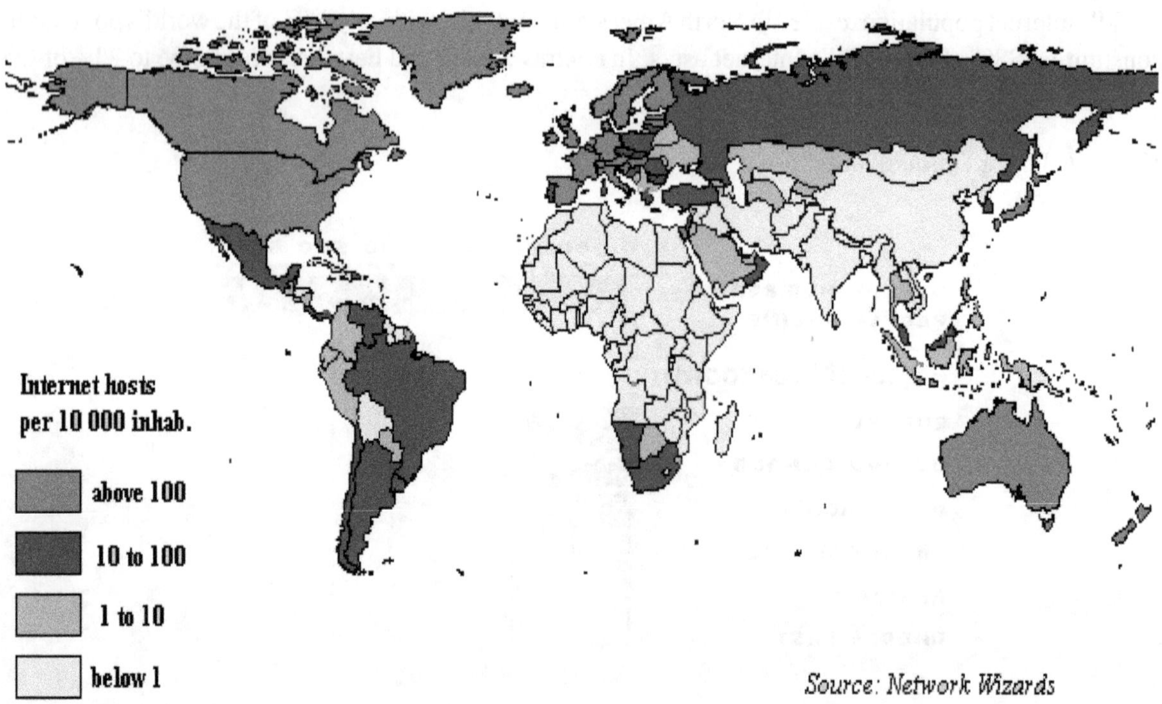

Infrastructure Investment and Technological Inputs

Recent studies suggest that the rate of investment in information technology infrastructure is greater for the wealthy as compared to low-income countries. Countries belonging to OECD are, for instance, on average estimated to be investing over $200 *per capita* on information infrastructure, technology, and software, whilst the rest of the world is investing only an average of $20 per capita on the same (OECD, 2012). Infrastructure investments need not, however, be related directly to Information and Communication Technologies, as a want of basic infrastructure such as reliable electricity and office environments, particularly in rural areas, also hampers network connectivity and human resource efficiency (Virkar, 2011).

In addition, as indicated by Table 2, many older basal studies stress the disparity of investment in 'soft infrastructures' – human capital (i.e. scientists and technicians) and research and development – which are as essential as the 'hard' components of ICTs (World Bank, 2002).

Internet Website and Content Languages

Another indicator of the developed world's technological superiority and dominance is the apparent lack of local language content on Internet websites. As seen in Figure 3, whilst English is the native tongue of just over one-third of the global Internet community, over half the websites online are in English solely to the exclusion of other languages.

Table 2. Spending on Infrastructure, Investment, and Technological Inputs by Region

Region	Spending on II (US$ per Capita)	R&D as Percent of GDP	Technicians	Scientists
OECD	129.11	1.8	1326.1	2649.1
Middle East	19.93	0.4	177.8	521
East Asia	13.49	0.8	235.8	1026
Latin America and the Caribbean	28.28	0.5	205.4	656.6
Eastern Europe and Transition Economies	22.89	0.9	577.2	1841.3
Sub-Saharan Africa	11.56	0.2	76.1	324.3
South Asia	13.49	0.8	59.5	161

Source: Pyramid Research (2000) and Wilson and Rodriguez (2000). Compiled by the World Bank and infoDev.
The figure for Investment II is the average of Asia Pacific; including East Asia and South Asia.
Note: Technicians and Scientists are per 1 million persons.

Figure 3. Language and the Internet

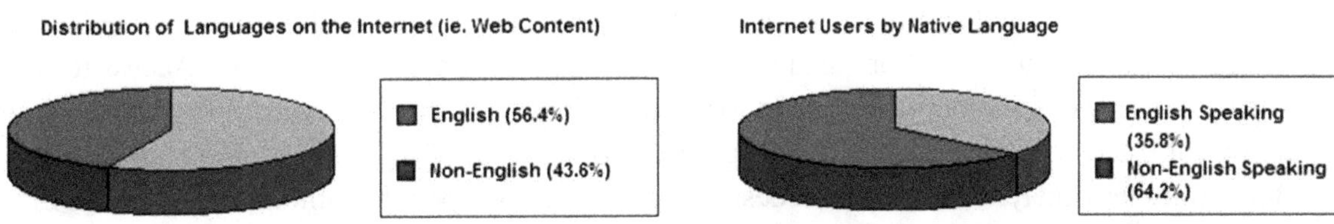

Compiled and Graphically Presented by the Author
Source: Internet World Stats, http://www.internetworldstats.com/stats7.htm

Internet content providers are still, according to numerous studies, concentrated in a few metropolitan areas of the developed world. A telling example is, for instance, the city of London that has for the last decade hosted more Internet domains than the whole of Africa (Castells, 2013).

Intra-Country Inequalities

Imbalanced access to ICTs and their associated platforms and applications is also visible within countries. Studies done in both developed and developing countries have identified several key within-country inequalities, including those of income, education, age, and disability, gender, and by geographic region (Virkar, 2011).

- **Income:** A recent OECD study concluded that individual or household income is an important determinant of the *presence* and of the *penetration* of Information and Communication Technologies; where higher income groups with greater purchasing power are the first to acquire and use new technology, and consequently have a head-start over persons from lower income groups who are concerned more with basic survival than with the acquisition of modern luxuries. This has been confirmed by the World Bank in stark results obtained from similar studies: in South Africa, for example, households in the wealthiest quintile are 125 times more likely to own a phone than those in the poorest quintile.
- **Gender:** In many developing countries, men have greater access to ICTs and the Internet than women do. In Latin America, for instance, *Wall Street Journal* polls targeting Internet users and technology use indicated that only 38% of the respondents polled were female. Likewise in Africa, surveys find that 86%, 83% and 64% of the Internet users in Ethiopia, Senegal, and Zambia respectively, were male. An analysis done by this author indicates that the degree to which women have access to technology seems to depend largely on societal and cultural values, particularly traditional expectations of a woman's role in the family and in society and the degree of opportunity such as the access to education to which they are exposed (Virkar, 2004). In societies where culture and/or religion places the most emphasis on a woman's reproductive and housekeeping functions, access to technology is likely to be low. By contrast, in the Western world, where there is greater emphasis on female literacy and equal of opportunity, the gender divide in access to technology is small but often highly acute. As women increasingly enter the labour force, differentials in physical and mental capabilities as a consequence of differences in race, background, and training have also led to a further polarisation in the degree of access within the female workforce.
- **Education, Age, and Disability:** Studies further indicate that the access and use of Information and Communication Technologies is related to a person's educational status and skill set. In Australia, data on average has shown that over 34% of people with a university degree were more likely to own a computer and to access the Internet than those without, whilst only 12% of those with a secondary school certificate as their highest qualification were likely to do so; a trend borne out by studies conducted in Europe and America over the last decade and a half. Access to ICTs is generally lower for older people than for persons from younger generations, the highest technological usage being prevalent in the age group 30-45 years of age. Disabled people are nearly three times less likely to have home access to the Internet than people without disabilities (Virkar, 2004).

- **Geographic Region:** Access to ICTs, again the Internet and its associated technologies, is greater in urban than in rural areas, in both developed and developing countries (Virkar, 2011). In the USA, for example, 42.3% of all urban households in 2010 had access to the Internet as compared with 38.9% of all rural establishments. Disparities such as these are even greater and more critical in developing countries, where up to 80% of the population lives in rural habitation.

FROM HUMAN FACTORS TO HUMAN ACTORS: THE DIGITAL DIVIDE AND PATTERNS OF HUMAN INTERACTION IN DEVELOPMENT

A concept of the user is fundamental to much of the research and practice of information systems design, development, and evaluation.- Roberta Lamb and Rob Kling

The design and implementation of complex computer systems requires a better understanding in practitioner circles of the users of such networks and the settings in which they work. Part of the problem resides in the implicit treatment of ordinary people as unskilled, non-specialist users of technology and their networks as comprising of elementary processes or *factors* that can be studied in isolation in a field laboratory setting (Bannon, 1991). Although psychology has a long tradition of contributing to computer systems design and implementation, it has been a neglected discipline in scholarly circles and key issues such as those relating to the underlying values of the people involved in large-scale system design and their motivation in the work setting have been missed out in recent computer science-based scholarly analysis (Salvendy, 2012).

Conceptualising and understanding people as *actors* in situations, on the other hand, with a set of skills and shared practices based on work experiences with others, requires a reorientation in the way in which the relationship between key elements of computer system design, namely people, technology, work requirements, and organisational constraints in work settings, is negotiated (Kuutti, 1996). The terms 'human factors' and 'human actors ' give a clue as to how people in system design clusters are and ought to be approached (Virkar, 2011). More particularly, the terms highlight differences in how people and their contributions are perceived, the former connotating a passive, fragmented, depersonalised, and somewhat automatic human contribution; the latter an active, controlling, involved one (Carayon et. al, 2012).

More precisely, within the *human factor* approach, the human element is more often than not reduced to being another system component with certain characteristics that need to be factored into the design equation for the overall human-machine system (Czaja & Nair, 2012). In doing so, however, the approach de-emphasises certain important elements of work design: the goals, the values, and the beliefs that technologists and system-users hold about life and about work (Jacko et. al., 2012). On the contrary,

Box 1. Winners and Losers of the Digital Age

Results of research on digital inequalities indicate that better-educated, young urban men living in developed countries are most likely to benefit from the ICT revolution; whilst less-educated, older rural women living in developing countries are most likely to be on the wrong side of the digital chasm.

(Source: Moorehead, 2004)

by using the term *human actors*, emphasis is placed on users and developers as autonomous agents possessing the capacity to control, to regulate, and to coordinate their behaviour; rather than them being on par and analysed as mere information processing automatons (Proctor & Vu, 2012).

Understanding Actor Behaviour: Winners and Losers in the Development Age

The central issue that needs to be understood whilst studying the Digital Divide, the development of ICT platforms, and the proliferation and implementation of such technologies in public sector organisations, through the additional lens of an analysis of actor interactions, is thus: *Why do people do what they do?* One approach to understanding behaviour is to look at the rationality of individual actors, rather than the system as a whole. This is largely because political actors especially are driven by a combination of organisational and institutional roles and duties and calculated self-interest, with political interaction being organised around the construction and interpretation of meaning as well as the making of choices.

Political actors, in general, have a complex set of goals including power, income, prestige, security, convenience, loyalty (to an idea, an institution or the nation), pride in work well done, and a desire to serve the public interest (as the individual actor conceives it). According to Downs (1964) actors range from being purely self-interested ('climbers' or 'conservers' motivated entirely by goals which benefit themselves and their status quo rather than their organizations or the society at large) to having mixed motives ('zealots', 'advocates' and 'statesmen' motivated by goals which combine self-interest and altruistic loyalty with larger values). An in-depth analysis of the ICT for development literature by this researcher identified five actor groups involved in games relating to the implementation of e-government projects:

1. **Politicians:** The first group identified comprises of elected representatives of various hues, guided and influenced chiefly by electoral imperatives and a need to maintain their public image, and are therefore concerned with directing both key economic policy issues as well as issues of public service delivery.
2. **Administrators / Civil Servants:** This group of actors is guided by their perceptions of existing institutional 'culture' and practices and their positive (or negative) attitudes towards internal bureaucratic reforms such as concerns about the down-sizing of administrative services to promote 'efficiency' and a sense of being policed by elected government through the introduction of ICTs.
3. **Organisations Dealing with Technical Designing of IT Systems for Tax Collection:** The approach private IT suppliers take to e-government might be considerably different to what the adopting government agency actually needs or wants from a system.
4. **Citizens:** This is another particularly interesting group of actors as one is never quite sure what their reaction to the implementation of e-government will be. Whilst in theory citizens should welcome the introduction of a system that simplifies administrative processes, in practice it is equally possible that some citizens might not be very happy if a more efficient system was put into place.
5. **International Donors:** This final actor group controls the purse-strings and oftentimes comes to the table with 'higher' ideals coloured by ideas prevalent in international politics (such as the desire to see a particular brand of 'good governance' in the developing world).

Introducing new technology and grassroots social media initiatives into political, social, and economic arenas is a tricky game to play, as computerisation alters the work-load, the work profile, and the overall level of literacy of the average public sector employee and citizen; impacting accountability, reducing the opportunities available for the exercising of discretion, making performance more visible, flattening the hierarchy, and often forcing the need for retraining and retooling and sometimes creating redundancy (Bhatnagar, 2004).

Many technology-based projects aimed at bridging digital divides often tend to face both external resistance from a general user population and internal resistance from staff recruited to run them, in particular from the middle to lower levels of a civil service, and especially when efforts are made to reengineer work-flow processes through the seamless integration of technology and to create a form of back-end computerisation that has a profound impact on the way civil servants and citizenry perform their duties and perceive their jobs. Very often in developing countries, it is the fear of the unknown that drives this resistance, especially if the introduction of new technology results in a change of procedures and the need for the acquisition of new skills and knowhow. Further, in corrupt service delivery departments, there may be pressure to slow down or delay the introduction of technology-led reforms due to the impending loss of additional incomes (Virkar, 2011).

Far from following new patterns, interactions behind efforts to bridge the current digital divide appear to reflect existing, oft-formulaic patterns of social, political, and economic inequality, and show little sign of altering drastically in the foreseeable future. Critics believe that the unequal spread of ICTs along old socio-political fault lines prompts the re-emergence of traditional set patterns of detrimental actor behaviour, engendering potentially cataclysmic consequences in terms of development prospects and policy processes in the Third World (Virkar, 2011). More particularly, such negative interactions would result in: **inhibited economic growth**, forcing poor countries into what the World Bank (2002) terms *ICT-related poverty traps*, as countries with little access get excluded from the highly digitised international trading and financial system; **increased internal tension and instability**, as poverty and increased feelings of helplessness and dependence on the West create resentment and drive people onto the streets in protest and other forms of civil unrest; **the emergence of a technologically disadvantaged workforce** that is, relative to their Western counterparts, inflexible and ill-equipped to deal with rapid external changes and, therefore, at a permanent relative disadvantage; and a **gradual erosion of global peace and security**, as countries that are unable to integrate equitably into the world trading system become increasingly poor and isolated, providing ideal breeding-grounds and hosts for extremism and terrorist networks.

BRIDGING THE DIGITAL DIVIDE: TOWARDS DEVELOPMENT OR DEPENDENCY?

ICTs represent a major opportunity for world development. However, this is an opportunity that must be promoted in full awareness of the risk that the benefits will be unevenly shared.-Robin Mansell

Today, it is widely recognised that the digital revolution holds many promises for developing countries, and that 'bridging the digital divide' has become the central developmental issue for an array of national, regional, and international organisations. Over the years, a number of governments, businesses, individuals, communities, and organisations have studied the issues at stake in the digital divide and have drafted reports ranging from statistical analyses to in-depth case studies, putting forward recommendations to address inherent problems. In general, these include specific ground-level initiatives and policy reforms, but also cover the wider issues that have had an impact on the array of digital advances and divides and that manifest themselves under the broad umbrella of the global ICT revolution, within *e-commerce*, *e-government*, *e-procurement*, and *international trade*.

Organisations and institutions, particularly those that form the political, societal, and economic core of a country, cannot afford to be left behind, as the people within those institutions are generally looked to as trendsetters and role models in addition to being responsible for societal welfare (Virkar, 2011b). Software platform and application development, therefore, needs to be able to respond swiftly and appropriately to these changes to meet need for equitable access to information and technology. The growing demand for cost-effective, high-quality programming, and the response from both the private and public sectors, has resulted in the emergence of several collaborative, cross-sectoral partnerships between software developers and government organisations globally (Virkar, 2011a). However, as illustrated in previous sections of this chapter, the underlying motivations for the individual partners and actors within these collaborations can be widely divergent, and may result in highly divisive and negative outcomes the world over.

A Summary of Current Efforts to Bridge the Digital Divide

A number of major international initiatives have been launched specifically to deal with the digital divide, such as the G-8 Summit's *Digital Opportunity Task* (DOT) *Force* and the *World Summit on the Information Society* (WSIS), which aim to bring together key leaders and policymakers from around the world for consultation, debate, and policy formulation. A variety of organisations have conducted 'e-readiness' assessments in developing countries to determine their preparedness to integrate technology and electronic work-flow best practice into the mainstream economy and into the public sector.

Elsewhere on the ground, efforts aimed at introducing new ICTs into less-developed parts of the world are concerned chiefly with putting technology to use in underserved populations through the provision of infrastructure and equipment (Main, 2001). Existing efforts range from projects that create public access centres and kiosks, where poor people can use telephones and computers, to those that incorporate ICT in healthcare and other essential public service sectors using innovative technology and small business applications to promote local entrepreneurship. Initiatives are driven by agencies that range from tiny Non-Governmental Organisations (NGOs) working in remote areas such as SchoolNet, Namibia's effort to put computers into rural schools, to multibillion-dollar multinational corporations, such as Hewlett Packard's $1 billion "e-Inclusion" scheme aimed at promoting hardware innovations especially suitable for developing country environments (Dunn & Yamashita, 2003). In order to meet connectivity needs, programmes are structured to tackle two basic issues: the need to increase developing country connectivity to international communications backbones and the need to improve internal connectivity infrastructure.

Promising technological solutions include the use of underwater cables, satellites, and Very Small Aperture Terminals or *VSATs*. Satellites, in particular, offer the cheapest form of high-speed, web-enabled connectivity to date, but their potential is still under-exploited (Graham, 2011). Another potential solution is the use of Wireless Application Protocol or WAP technologies and wireless devices, today seen as a way of digitally leapfrogging the lack of conventional telephones in developing countries. Recent years have seen an explosive growth in the number of mobile communications operators in poorer countries – Tanzania, for example, has more mobile telephone operators than the United Kingdom – and in conflict-zones such as Somalia and Rwanda, where prolonged fighting has destroyed most land-based fixed infrastructure and the number of mobile phones in circulation has exceeded the number of traditional phone lines owned by the local population (Poblet, 2011). Efforts are also being made come up with innovative schemes to expand traditional phone availability in impoverished areas, particularly by routing government funding through to successful private initiatives such as *Grameen Telecom* in Bangladesh.

A favourite solution with many international development projects involves the establishment of Internet cafés, public computer centres, kiosks, and telecentres (Virkar, 2011). Multipurpose community telecentres[3], in particular, have been set up by development agencies and national governments to counter low Internet and mobile technology penetration in a number of otherwise deprived localities such as rural Mexico and Senegal, whilst privately owned Internet cafés and gaming centres have sprung up all over the developing world. In addition, international organisations like the World Bank advocate the implementation of policy reforms in parallel to such developments and to complement improvements in infrastructure (World Bank, 2002). These reforms are generally market- and growth-oriented, and seek to create a satisfactory regulatory environment for the adoption of ICTs in developing countries. In particular, they focus on monitoring and altering the actors, the behaviours, and the interactions that encourage privatisation and competition in the telecom markets, and on providing fiscal incentives for the growth of e-commerce and its eventual mainstreaming into a country national economy (Virkar, 2011). Suggested measures deal with issues such as the management of intellectual property rights, the adoption of consumer protection policies, the development of guidelines for taxation in cyberspace, and the establishment of standards and regulatory systems for the development of technological hardware and software (Dutton, 1992).

The panoply of programmes initiated in recent years has yielded a range of benefits in the developing world (Virkar, 2014). These might be broadly summarised to include an improved standard of living for the poor through the adoption and propagation of better, automated work practices and regular access to information and connectivity with the outside world; a reduction in the vulnerabilities of the poor and a concurrent increase in their capacities and opportunities through schemes and pilot projects which promote ICT solutions for self-employment and micro-enterprises; enhanced government capacity, defined in terms of efficiency and accountability as well as enhanced political participation, leading eventually to enhanced democratisation, and the increased participation in civil society, together with the strengthening of the *body politic*, of previously disempowered groups and individuals; all resulting in the emergence of a large pool of technologically literate producers and consumers in the developing world who drive growth-led exports to the benefit of local, national, and global economies.

THE NETWORK SOCIETY: DIGITALLY EMPOWERED DEVELOPMENT

Small changes in ICTs trigger unexpectedly explosive changes in use.-John Gage

There are, however, potential downsides to being ICT-focused. Greater reliance on information technology increases the vulnerability of individuals, groups and communities within developing countries to the dangers of cyber-crime and other equally serious fraud and security risks through the reduction of manual functionality and the creation of machine-behaviour patterns of living and interaction. The transmission of viruses, worms, and spyware can seriously hamper the use of existing technological hardware and software, subvert morale, disrupt hierarchies, office-based interactions, and work-flow processes, compromise a country's e-commerce and digital government base, and potentially undermine national security in times of conflict or of diplomatic hostilities (Zin & Yunos, 2004).

There is also the danger that technology, given to self-serving governments for development purposes, may be clandestinely put to military uses or be sold by them to terrorists to further their own political agenda (Virkar, 2004). Dual-use technology particularly could, in the wrong hands, pose a serious threat to peace and security, a classic example being the supercomputer; networks of exceptionally powerful, advanced computing systems that are at once employed to predict large-scale weather patterns, to monitor seismic activity, and used in functionalities ranging from national security surveillance to genomic sequencing, but are equally capable of being behind the mass production of advanced nuclear, chemical, and biological weapons. The United States, the biggest producer of supercomputers, has imposed restrictions on its export for exactly these reasons.

Another grim reality is that the world's poorest face a variety of problems, all of them possessing broader global implications, and most of which cannot be solved through the mere provision of access to computers and technology-related infrastructure (Sklair, 2002). Key global developmental issues include people without access to clean drinking water or proper sanitation facilities, chronic food shortages, and illiterate populations. Furthermore, the HIV/AIDS pandemic is set to explode within the developing world, with the Asia-Pacific region alone predicted to account for 40% of new global infections by 2020. Prolonged armed conflicts, particularly in Africa, are devastating developing economies and resulting in massive humanitarian crises (UNDP, 2014). In the face of numerous efforts being made to combat the digital divide, therefore, the fundamental question must be asked: will simply investing in the development and dissemination of technological infrastructure in developing countries, both hard and soft, automatically lead to better lives for the people who live there?

Consequently, scholars emphasise that Information and Communication Technologies are increasingly becoming pre-requisites for rapid economic development, and are crucial in helping the South to digitally leapfrog conventional industrialisation and to catch up with the knowledge-based, knowledge-driven economies of the North (Virkar, 2004). Similarly, the competitiveness of developing countries in the international trading system will increasingly depend on their ability to exchange digital information globally. Scholarly literature contends that there is a strong positive correlation between poverty and a lack of access to ICTs, and argues that the more developed a country's infrastructure is, the greater its attractiveness to foreign investors becomes and the more probable rapid economic growth (Trujillo, 2003).

However, despite the number of reported success stories, evidence from the field indicates a high rate of information system failure in the developing world (Heeks, 2002). Whilst failures are in themselves a cause for concern, a lack of success in developing countries is even more alarming because of the large opportunity costs associated with failed projects and the inability of these countries to recover quickly from them independently. Developing countries, with their multitude of development problems, can ill afford to keep pouring scarce resources into projects that are likely fail. Some critics feel that allowing technological innovations to hog the development limelight would only further compound the problems of the Third World, diverting attention and funds away from other high-priority areas. Others maintain further that current efforts to bridge the digital divide are generally more talk than action, and are only likely to increase the dependency of poorer countries on the developed world its peoples (Virkar, 2011).

One line of critique focuses on currently popular 'trade-not-aid' policies, which many scholars feel could make the South more dependent on imports from the North, simply because Southern nations are not capable of selling enough national products and services in the global market to compete with their Northern counterparts (Stiglitz & Charlton, 2006). In the rapidly changing, winner-takes-all environment of the global economy, many feel that if left to free market forces, telecommunications and the Internet are likely to increase inequalities between advanced nations and the developing world

(McChesney, 1998). Some scholars suggest that technology could become instrumental in the creation of a transnational *virtual élite*, as the benefits of market-driven development in developing countries stay limited to a small minority of highly skilled professionals, further polarising the educated élite and the less-educated poor (Uimonen, 1997). Building on this, other commentators believe that developing countries are disadvantaged both by the set-up of, and power structures found within, current global ICT régimes and the ever-increasing complexity of international knowledge networks (Wade, 2002).

Another line of argument points out that the cornerstone of the global ICT-for-development campaign rests on the assumption that ICTs possess 'some inherent quality that enables them to leapfrog institutional obstacles and skill and resource deficiencies on the ground', an idea founded on the premise that technology is an objective, rational entity, and not something that incorporates, and is affected by, politics and culture (Virkar, 2004). The neutrality of technology is reinforced by repeated emphasis on innovation in today's world, stemming from theories of modernisation or the forcible (often incongruous) application of science and Western (or Northern) rationalism to human development in the Third World (Bessant, 1987). Adherents of this school of thought believe that as technology developed in the West spreads to the Third World, poor country users are increasingly caught in a hardware-software bind from which escape is limited, and user costs grow as user dependency increases. These scholars see this phenomenon as the beginning of a new form of international digital dependency, a modern-day equivalent of the 1970s Dependency Theory which contended that the problem of underdevelopment lay in the exploitative relationship between rich and poor nations, illustrated by the now-famous *centre-periphery* analogy (Lairson & Skidmore, 2003). The more recent, technological manifestations of this dependency are summarised and discussed below:

The North/Corporate Privilege in Software

Developing countries are caught in the middle of a growing 'software-hardware arms race' in the global technology market, the chief upshot of which is increased ICT complexity– extremely attractive to the younger, better-educated, wealthier user minority but intimidating for older, less well-educated, and poorer users who are not yet comfortable with even simpler models (Virkar, 2004). This can only prove detrimental to the North-South divide in ICT-based power relations, as technological improvements will continue to be pushed by the mega-corporations that profit from them, to the benefit of those Northern producers, users, and élite Southern groups that constitute the global demand for upgrades. Poorer countries, on the other hand, will either be unable to afford to keep upgrading their computer network systems, and so fall behind in terms of overall electronic competitiveness, or to sustain a reallocation of funds to such projects from priority areas such as healthcare and education.

The Northern Privilege in Internet Access and Telephone Services

Compared to the developed world, in particular the United States of America, developing countries operate at a cost disadvantage in Internet access and penetration (Roseman, 2003). Developing country *Internet Service Providers* (ISPs), being smaller and unable to invest in large capacity networks, experience more crashes and congestion than their First World counterparts, and are at the mercy of developed country ISPs which are not only larger and able to corner most of the digital traffic, but are also able to set prohibitively monopolistic access prices and global standards. Similarly, the international payments system for *Voice Over Internet Protocol* (VoIP) traffic is again dominated by America and a handful of major global firms, players who keep down the cost of telephonic services to the advantage of First World consumers in whose countries the primary digital exchanges are located. This is, however, detrimental to those Third World organisations and companies that, unable to charge prices that reflect the real costs of providing telephone services in those countries, are unable to invest in technology upgrades to remain competitive (Li et. al., 2011).

The North's Control over Development Ideology

Information and Communication Technologies, especially those platforms and applications that are Internet-enabled, have long been touted as *the* democratising force of the current age, contributing to the emergence of a new kind of 'networked politics' or 'networked governance' wherein the mobilisation of people into interest groups across physical boundaries and borders enhances participation in democratic processes and subverts traditional hierarchies of power and privilege (Virkar, 2011). However, it is widely argued that the infrastructure of the Internet and other networked communications systems is by-and-large dominated by a number of big commercial and governmental players who can potentially enforce their intellectual and political dominance over development discourse by capturing and monitoring a majority of technology users, and presenting them with selective information that suits their own singular purpose. For example, the World Bank has long been accused of popularising, through its new multistakeholder supersite *The Development Gateway*, issues and views that fit in well with the Bank's official diplomatic line, whilst using its global monetary influence to ensure that all opinions critical of the Bank's proclamations and policies are quietly ignored and remain unpublished (Wade, 2001). Seen as the most politically troubling form of technological dependency, critics worry that developing countries could remain passive recipients dependent on received Northern knowledge, rather than taking on an active role in the sharing and in creation of know-how and expertise themselves. The fallout of such a dependency may been seen today, in the constant, often-contentious North-South bickering over requirements and standards for technology transfer, intellectual-property rights, protectionism, the 'brain-drain', and the division of technological resources (Virkar, 2004). Those commentators who are highly critical of current discourse have even associated the manner in which developmental knowledge has proliferated with ideology accompanying the global re-expansion of capitalism and the re-emergence of Western neo-colonialism in the late 1990s-early 2000s.

The Threat of Cultural Neo-Colonialism

A final critique centres around current ICT-for-development discourse and the way in which the digital divide is demonstrated and is being addressed through the lens of actor interactions and social network behaviour (Virkar, 2004). Several development commentators, particularly adherents to Amartya Sen's Capabilities Approach and other theories of the New Institutionalism, contend that technology-driven development programmes in their current embodiment are oversold as agents of higher efficiency and better governance in favour of quantifiable access to ICTs, given their tendency to overlook the importance of actor interactions, actor motivations, and actor opinions, together with other individual actor differences, capabilities, and the role that choice also plays in the use, application, and ultimate valuation of new technologies (Virkar, 2011).

The result on the ground is a gap between 'hard' rational design and 'soft' socio-political actualities (see Table 3), and numerous situations where ICTs have done more harm than good (Heeks, 2002). The remoteness of project designs and the designers from the core context of the final user in physical, economic, cultural and other ways, further implies imminent ICT project failure given that project designs and actor realities are simply not built to withstand nor suit the prevailing local environment. When framed in socio-anthropological or culturally relativist terms, this gradual deterioration in the quality of interpersonal relationships, pre-empts the eventual decline of social and political capital in the developing world should ICTs not be introduced into their proposed diverse environments in a culturally sensitive manner (Virkar, 2004).

Many social anthropologists have warned that the erosion of the family and the degradation of the cultural ties that form the basis of many developing country societies will, in turn, have extremely negative effects on the behaviour and on the interactions of actors and actor groups co-existing at different levels of the various developmental and national arenas prevalent (Alampy, 2003).

Interestingly, to conclude, some of the more extreme technological optimists maintain that the rapidly falling price of both computing power and bandwidth will eventually result in a *digital deluge*, rendering any policy aimed at giving access to the so-called *information-poor* quite unnecessary and possibly even highly counter-productive. Emerging evidence is, however, likely to prove this view wrong (Virkar, 2014).

EXPLORING THE DEVELOPMENT DIVIDE IN THE DIGITAL AGE

You can put computers in community centres, but only the literate people are likely to go use them.- Esther Dyson

Table 3. The Difference Between 'Hard' Design and 'Soft' Actuality

Dimension	'Hard' Rational Design	'Soft' Political Actuality
Information	Emphasis on standardised, formal, quantitative information	Emphasis on contingent, informal, qualitative information
Technology	A simple, enabling mechanism	A complex value-laden entity; status symbol for some, tool of empowerment for some, tool of oppression for others
Processes	Stable, straight-forward, and formal; decision outcomes as optimal solutions based on logical criteria	Flexible, complex, constrained, and often informal; decision outcomes as compromises based on power games and influenced by existing power structures
Objectives and Values	Formal, organisational objectives	Multiple, informal, personal objectives
Staffing and Skills	Staff viewed as rational beings	Staff viewed as political beings in a definite hierarchy
Management Systems and Structures	Emphasis on formal, objective processes and structures	Emphasis on informal, subjective processes and structures
Other Resources: Time and Money	Used to achieve organisational objectives	Used to achieve personal objectives

(*Source: Heeks, 2002*)

Advances in Information and Communication Technologies have been the driving force behind the economic boom and global integration of financial markets and industry ever since their first commercial appearance in the late-1990s. Computer technology has transformed commerce and industry, society and politics; making possible such things as automated inventory control and just-in-time manufacturing, facilitating the emergence of new data networks, and enabling greater efficiency and productivity in virtually every aspect of human endeavour. E-mail and instant messaging have become ubiquitous in industrialised countries, and are also becoming increasingly popular in the developing world. Voice Over Internet Protocol and other communications technologies are also advancing in leaps and bounds, with new sound-enabled infrastructure and software spreading rapidly round the globe. Mobile connectivity is expanding particularly fast, with mobile phones expected to reach over 8.5 billion subscribers worldwide by end of 2016 (ITU, 2014). In addition, the provision of multiple digital services and computing platforms is fast becoming an important, rapidly growing sector of both developed and emerging economies.

Has Opportunity Come Calling...or Do We Have Our Wires Crossed?

The speed at which these transformations have occurred, the wealth that ICTs have generated, and the economic power wielded by major players in the technology industry are truly staggering and as yet unprecedented. Yet alongside such spectacular advancements are more sobering signs, particularly amongst the 3 billion people who constitute nearly half the world and who live on less than $2 a day (Shah, 2004). Poverty still persists in many regions of the world, including large pockets of industrialised nations, and a large number of people in Asia and Africa die from malnutrition and related diseases every year. The poorest areas of the world see regular surges in urban migration and populations still grow rapidly, putting greater pressure on already scarce natural resources, and illiteracy remains another major stumbling-block to prosperity in the Third World. The impact of these problems is now globally palpable. Armed conflicts erupt frequently over scarce resources, whilst law and order in many developing countries remains decidedly fragile. An upsurge in new forms of terrorism and the unchecked spread of deadly diseases such as HIV/AIDS both threaten to upset global peace and stability. On the whole, greater economic and technological progress seems only to increase disparities between the world's *haves* and *have-nots*.

An important illustration of this global 'development divide' is the growing gap that is opening up between those who are able to participate in the Information Revolution, sharing in the wealth and benefiting from the efficiency the use of technology creates, and those who are increasingly being left out of it. ICTs may be transforming the lives of the people who use them, but they do little for the large part of humanity that lacks access to them. The digital divide is therefore a multifaceted phenomenon that is both dynamic and complex, and exists at many levels: between groups and communities, between companies, between geographical regions, and between countries. As the world moves towards increasingly digitised societies, it is generally agreed by a large number of development experts, commentators, and policymakers that closing the digital divide is becoming imperative for the economic and social progress of the Third World. Whilst there is no denying that the developing world faces a multitude of other problems, it remains equally true that, given the growing importance of ICTs today, developing countries face the dilemma of either resetting some of their priorities or facing complete global exclusion.

Recent initiatives to bridge the divide within the extended context of global development have focussed on the provision of infrastructure together with the adoption of a number of macro-economic policies and improved work practices, all aimed at promoting effective free-market liberalism. However, after a number of high-profile failures, there is growing recognition amongst members of the development community that offering the world the latest in mobile technology and Internet-enabled computers will not in itself help bridge socio-economic or political disparities, and that encouraging economic growth is only a part of the larger policy response. Current discourse has failed to recognise that the digital divide is symptomatic of a much broader, much more complex set of interrelated inequalities, and that the lack of access to technology and software is connected to a wide array of unresolved problems, both within the developing world and current international systems. In consequence, current initiatives all too often neglect the crucial interrelation of factors that altogether stymy and limit success. For example, many community access projects that introduce computers into rural areas do not become self-sustaining simply because they fail to appreciate the central authority's role in the local economy, the need for locally relevant content, and the specific requirements of the local population.

Against the backdrop of a slew of project failures, it has become apparent that ICTs are not silver bullets that can magically make development problems vanish. With attention focused on the achievement of quantitative proliferation and penetration targets, as against a more holistic set of developmental goals, many feel that the ICT-for-development campaign in its present shape and form stands to lose credibility (Virkar, 2004). Technology alone is clearly not the automatic solution to the digital divide, to poverty and to other developmental problems, but a critical factor in their ultimate resolution may lie in ensuring that underserved groups and countries can harness and use built-in latent potential. If not consciously used to improve equity, therefore, new technologies may only serve to worsen prevailing socio-political divides, benefiting only those who possess sufficient skills and adequate know-how. In this vein, scholars argue that the introduction of ICTs into an arena of interaction is of particularly limited value unless people are equipped with the necessary skills and are provided with enough opportunity to exploit them to the full.

There is a need, therefore, to alter current development paradigms and, rather than seeking to find miraculous quick-fixes in technological hardware and software to deep-rooted problems, the focus ought be on understanding the reasons behind the polarisation of behaviour, both in society and in the workplace. The sheer intricacy and variety of interactions prevalent in human societies, and their relationship with Information and Communication Technologies, requires the constant local adaptation and improvisation of technological hardware and software if programmes involving Information Technology are to achieve and sustain high rates of success. The Internet, for instance, may prove extremely useful for villagers in the Indian state of Kerala where literacy levels and levels of village electrification are high, but the form the technology takes would not probably be of much use in Rwanda, where years of political instability and civil war have destroyed much of the basic infrastructure and have resulted in massive population displacements.

In summary, international ICT policy would do well to follow guidelines based on lessons learned in the field, and chief amongst these precepts is the idea that digital and developmental problems are interrelated and complex, primarily because of the variety of social and cultural contexts within which they occur. The interplay of national policies and different regulatory environments, circumscribed by a range of international forces, the power games prevalent within the international development machinery, and the fast evolving nature of ICTs themselves all add to this complexity. Again, installing volt-gobbling machines in areas that get only an erratic supply of electricity is problematic. In this context, investment in ICT-based initiatives needs be made keeping in mind prevailing socio-economic conditions, along with the necessary institutional structures and policy priorities that create, as discussed earlier, an enabling environment within which both technical artefacts and human actors succeed and flourish; an objective generally more difficult to attain than the mere sourcing of hardware and of software.

CONCLUSION

It is not ICT or food. It is ICT for food, for health, for teaching and for social and human development.- Vincezo Schioppa

In modern times, people and their governments have struggled to find easy, cheap, and effective ways to run and improve countries. ICT-based applications have the potential to revolutionise patterns of communication between authority and citizenry, radically restructuring politics, the economy and society at all levels by making systems more integrated, transparent, and efficient. However critics of hyperdigitisation, and more particularly of the introduction of new technologies into developing country contexts, contend that formulation of one-sided reform processes is not an important enough issue to justify exposing cash-strapped governments to the risks and opportunity costs associated with large-scale ICT projects. Today, technology can provide the world with new opportunities and potentialities. However, the way in which those opportunities are grasped is circumscribed by contextual factors: political, economic, socio-cultural, behavioural, and institutional. The current concept of a 'digital divide' has been unhelpful to understand and tackle global inequities insofar as it has diverted attention away from other high-priority divides that constitute development bottlenecks. For developing countries to benefit fully from the digital revolution, current attitudes must experience a paradigm shift away from current thinking and the appropriate policies be implemented, particularly those that promote the indigenisation of ICT-based systems and the interconnection of all ICT-related divides with other development priorities.

Although the development and application of new communications hardware and software does have some potentially harmful effects on nascent business, government and society – not all firms will survive increased competition, some traditional jobs may be lost to digital machines and work-process automation, self-serving governments could use technology to spread propaganda, and the effects of technological dependence on the industrialised world are unlikely to be mitigated for some time to come – the extreme *cyberpessimism* of many critics today is unwarranted. ICT-led reforms are often complex as they involve the amelioration of both organisations and of human behaviour, and cannot be made through legislation alone. Such reforms require a change in the way users think, act, how they view their work, and how they share information; together with a simultaneous reengineering of the working of government; its business processes within individual agencies, departments, and across different levels or strata. They work best when part of a broader reform agenda in which the *status quo* is broken down through delegation, decentralisation, and citizen empowerment. The development and adoption of the new digital technologies has thus become a large game within the greater 'meta-game' of a country's development, bringing with it not only an array of benefits but also numerous challenges and obstacles that shape and are shaped by the perceptions and motivations of a multitude of actors, groups, and organisations. When considered this way, Information and Communication Technologies, in drastically improving standards of living, can save lives; and also create new jobs, connect unemployed people to previously inaccessible work opportunities, facilitate meaningful participation in mainstream political processes, and enable the inhabitants of relatively isolated villages to leverage the outside world at the click of a button.

However, the discussion put forward in this chapter reveals that at the heart of the digital divide and in attempts to create equality of access to information lies a global power struggle, brought about through a deep-seated mistrust between different actor groups and lopsided inter-country politics. This holds particularly true for the process of software conception and design where, gaps in the quality and overall technical applicability of a technology arise because those with the power and authority to take design or implementation decisions are usually unwilling to allow any initiative to go ahead that would give other actor group(s) in the game more precedence or autonomy over the process or system. Further, certain key games with local impacts get played out in different arenas between actors influenced not only by local but also national and international factors. Problems arise if designers and top-level managers assume that localised outcomes result only from direct local, quantifiable influences, discounting the impact of other 'soft' factors external to the project at hand. Added to this, there is a tendency for power élites to lose touch with ground realities when devising projects for their organisations as well as for their citizens, especially when planners comprise the higher échelons of government and operate exclusively within a top-down command-and-control system of management. There is also a danger that high-level project planners will, in looking at macro-outcomes, ignore outliers and how these may precipitate unexpected turns of events. This holds particularly true when existing patterns of communication and information exchange are inequitable and fail to be flexible or unable to adapt to rapidly changing situations.

Whilst it is widely recognised that ICTs are strategically important to a country, it must be concluded that if the developing world is to benefit, experts must cease debating over whether countries should spend their budgets on the development and propagation of ICTs or other other basic infrastructural requirements altogether; instead they should explore as to how technology may be used effectively to solve developmental problems and to meet other policy objectives. Likewise, the applicative and practitioner focus whilst considering the ways and means to employ new hardware and software in bridging digital and developmental divides should not just be on forking out cheap computers or on connecting every home to the Internet. A single well-located and well-maintained computer with Internet connectivity in an isolated village in Southern India has proved adequate in providing its inhabitants with essential information and services – storm-warnings, crop prices, medical information, legal records and learning opportunities – and raising the standard of living for the entire the local area for a radius of 10 miles. In conclusion, if developing countries are to reap the full potential of the digital revolution, what is needed is a more holistic, multi-pronged approach when tackling the range of development issues they face, supported by the simultaneous creation of an enabling environment for the effective and sustainable integration of technology into local society. Information technology might have made '*all that is solid melt into air*', but digital bridges still require concrete foundations.

REFERENCES

Bessant, J. (1987). Information Technology and the North-South Divide. In R. Finnegan, G. Salaman, & K. Thompson (Eds.), *Information Technology: Social Issues – A Reader* (pp. 163–180). London: Hodder and Stoughton.

Castells, M. (2001). *The Internet Galaxy*. Oxford: Oxford University Press. doi:10.1007/978-3-322-89613-1

Castells, M. (2013). *Communication Power*. Oxford: Oxford University Press.

Dunn, D., & Yamashita, K. (2003). 'Microcapitalism and the Megacorporation'. *Harvard Business Review*, *81*(8), 46–54. PMID:12884667

Dutton, W. H. (1992). 'The Ecology of Games Shaping Telecommunications Policy'. *Communication Theory*, *2*(4), 303–328. doi:10.1111/j.1468-2885.1992.tb00046.x

Dutton, W. H. (1999). *Society on the Line: Information Politics in the Digital Age*. Oxford: Oxford University Press.

Fink, C., & Kenny, C. J. (2003). 'W(h)ither the Digital Divide?'. *Info: The Journal of Policy. Regulation and Strategy for Telecommunications*, *5*(6), 15–24. doi:10.1108/14636690310507180

Gage, J. (2002). Some Thoughts on How ICTs Could Really Change the World. In *Global Information Technology Report 2001-2002* (pp. 4–9). Readiness for the Networked World. Retrieved from www.cid.harvard.edu/cr/pdf/gitrr2002_ch01.pdf

Grace, J., Kenny, C., Qiang, C., Liu, J., & Reynolds, T. (2001). 'Information and Communication Technologies and Broad-Based Development: A Partial Review of the Evidence. *World Bank Resource Paper (2001)*. Retrieved from: http://poverty.worldbank.org/library/view/10214/

Graham, M. (2011). 'Time Machines and Virtual Portals: The Spatialities of the Digital Divide'. *Progress in Development Studies*, *11*(3), 211–227. doi:10.1177/146499341001100303

Heeks, R. (2002). 'Information Systems and Developing Countries: Failure, Success and Local Improvisations'. *The Information Society*, *18*(2), 101–112. doi:10.1080/01972240290075039

NUA Internet Surveys. (2014). *How Many Online?* Retrieved from: http://www.nua.ie/surveys/how_many_online/

Katz, R. L. (2009). 'The Economic and Social Impact of Telecommunications Output'. *Inter Economics*, *44*(1), 41–48. doi:10.100710272-009-0276-0

Kirkman, G. (1999). *Its More Than Just Being Connected: A Discussion of Some Issues of Information Technology and International Development*. Paper presented at the Development E-Commerce Workshop. Retrieved from: http://cyber.law.harvard.edu/itg/libpubs/beingconnected.pdf

Lairson, T. D., & Skidmore, D. (2003). *International Political Economy: The Struggle for Power and Wealth*. Belmont: Thompson and Wadsworth.

Lamb, R., & Kling, R. (2003). 'Reconceptualising Users as Social Actors in Information Systems Research'. *Management Information Systems Quarterly*, *27*(2), 197–235.

Le Page, M. (2002, May 4th). 'Village-Life.com'. New Scientist, 44–45.

Levis, K. (2009). Winners and Losers: Creators and Casualties of the Age of the Internet. London: Atlantic Books Ltd.

Li, B., Ma, M., & Jin, Z. (2011). 'A VoIP Traffic Identification Scheme Based On Host and Flow Behavior Analysis'. Journal of Network and Systems Management, 19(1), 111–129. doi:10.1007/s10922-010-9184-7 doi:10.100710922-010-9184-7

Main, L. (2001). 'The Global Information Infrastructure: Empowerment or Imperialism?'. Third World Quarterly, 22(1), 83–97. doi:10.1080/713701143 doi:10.1080/713701143

Martin, W. J. (1988). The Information Society. London: Aslib Press.

McChesney, R. W., Wood, E. M., & Foster, J. B. (1998). Capitalism and the Information Age: The Political Economy of the Global Communication Revolution. New York: Monthly Review Press.

Norris, P. (2001). Digital Divide: Civic Engagement, Information Poverty and the Internet Worldwide. Cambridge: Cambridge University Press. doi:10.1017/CBO9781139164887 doi:10.1017/CBO9781139164887

Odendaal, N. (2002). 'ICTs in Development – Who Benefits? Use of Geographic Information Systems on the Cato Manor Development Project, South Africa'. Journal of International Development, 4(1), 89–100. doi:10.1002/jid.867 doi:10.1002/jid.867

Organisation for Economic Co-operation and Development. (2000). *Learning to Bridge the Digital Divide*. Paris: OECD Publications.

Perrit, H. H. (1998). 'The Internet as a Threat to Sovereignty? Thoughts on the Internet's Role in Strengthening National and Global Governance'. *Indiana Journal of Global Legal Studies*, *5*(2), 431–444.

Poblet, M. (2011). *Mobile Technologies for Conflict Management: Online Dispute Resolution, Governance, Participation*. London: Springer Verlag. doi:10.1007/978-94-007-1384-0

Prakash, N. (2012). 'Empowering Women Using Environmentally Friendly Technology in Paper Recycling'. *Research in Political Sociology*, *20*(1), 125–136. doi:10.1108/S0895-9935(2012)0000020009

Robins, K. (1992). *Understanding Information: Business, Technology and Geography*. London: Belhaven Press.

Rodda, C. (2004). *'The Five Stages of Economic Growth'*. Retrieved from: http://www.cr1.dircon.co.uk/TB/5/fivestages.htm

Roseman, D. (2003). 'The Digital Divide and the Competitive Nature of ISPs: Part 1 – Issues and Arguments'. *Info: The Journal of Policy Regulation and Strategy for Telecommunications*, *5*(5), 25–37. doi:10.1108/14636690310500439

Selwyn, N. (2002). *'Defining the 'Digital Divide': Developing a Theoretical Understanding of Inequalities in the Information Age'*. Occasional Paper No. 49. Cardiff University.

Shah, A. (2004). *'Poverty Facts and Stats'*. Retrieved from: http://www.globalissues.org/TradeRelated/Facts.asp

Silverstone, R., & Haddon, L. (1996). Design and Domestication of Information and Communication Technologies: Technical Change and Everyday Life. In R. Mansell & R. Silverstone (Eds.), *Communication by Design: The Politics of Information and Communication Technologies* (pp. 16–44). Oxford: Oxford University Press.

Sklair, L. (2002). *Globalisation: Capitalism and its Alternatives*. Oxford: Oxford University Press.

Skolnikoff, E. B. (1993). *The Elusive Transformation: Science, Technology and the Evolution of International Politics*. Princeton: Princeton University Press.

Stiglitz, J. (1999). '*Scan Globally, Reinvent Locally: Knowledge Infrastructure and the Localisation of Knowledge*'. Keynote Address – First Global Development Network Conference, Bonn, Germany.

Strover, S. (2003). 'Remapping the Digital Divide'. *The Information Society*, *19*(4), 275–277. doi:10.1080/01972240309481

Toulouse, C., & Luke, T. W. (1998). *The Politics of Cyberspace*. New York, NY: Routledge.

Trujillo, M. F. (2003). *'Does the Global Digital Divide Have Anything to do with Progress in Development?'*. Research Paper on Development Gateway: ICTs for Development (April 2003). Retrieved from: http://topics.developmentgateway.org/ict/rc/filedownload.do~itemId=307577

Uimonen, P. (1997). *'The Internet as a Tool for Social Development'*. Paper presented at the Annual Conference of the Internet Society. Retrieved from: http://www.i-connect.ch/uimonen/INET97.htm

United Nations Development Programme. (2001). *Human Development Report (1996-2001)*. Retrieved from: http://hdr.undp.org/reports/view_reports.cfm?type=1

Wade, R. H. (2002). 'Bridging the Digital Divide: New Route to Development or New Form of Dependency?'. *Global Governance*, *8*(4), 443–466.

Webster, F. (2002). *Theories of the Information Society* (2nd ed.). London: Routledge Press. doi:10.4324/9780203426265

Woolgar, S. (2002). *Virtual Society? Technology, Cyberbole and Reality*. Oxford: Oxford University Press.

World Bank. (2002). *'The Networking Revolution: Opportunities and Challenges for Developing Countries'*. InfoDev Working Paper.

Zin, A. N. M., & Yunos, Z. (2004). *'Computer Viruses: Future Cyber Weapons'*. National ICT Security and Emergency Response Center (NISER) Resource Paper. Retrieved from: http://www.niser.org.my/resources/computer_virus.pdf

KEY TERMS AND DEFINITIONS

Design-Actuality Gap Model or Design-Actuality Gap Framework: Is a framework for project evaluation which contends that the major factor determining project outcome is the degree of mismatch between the current ground realities of a situation ('where are we now'), and the models, conceptions, and assumptions built into a project's design (the 'where the project wants to get us').

Development Divide (The): Refers to the divide, gap, division, or differential in overall levels of human development, measured against economic, socio-anthropological, cultural, and political variables, between the world's richest and poorest individuals, groups, regions, and countries. The broad constituent elements of the Development Divide can also be described against The Human Development Divide, The Digital Divide, and The Democratic Deficit or Divide.

Digital Divide (The): Refers to the divide, gap, division, or differential in the meaningful availability of and access to technology, in particular the new digital information and communication technologies, between individuals, groups, regions, and countries; encompassing not merely quantified variables technological and technical hardware, but also levels of physical, digital, human and socio-cultural resources.

Hard Factor(s) or Hard Element(s): Refers to the actual, true-to-life, rational design elements or constituent variables of a technology or of a similarly created, automated, and independently functioning system.

Hard-Soft Analytical Framework or Hard-Soft Gap: Refers to the difference between the *actual, rational design* of a technology or man-made system (hard) adopted within a location-based project or a national policy and the *actuality of the social context*, namely people, culture, politics, etc., within which the system operates (soft).

Human Actor Approach: Refers to the approach taken whilst describing and analysing how people operating and interacting within symbiotic technology-rich ecologies and environments and their contributions are perceived; connoting active, controlling, involved, and independent human action.

Human Factor Approach: Refers to the approach taken whilst describing and analysing how people operating and interacting within symbiotic technology-rich ecologies and environments and their contributions are perceived; connoting passive, fragmented, depersonalised, and somewhat automatic human action.

Information Economy (The): Refers to the global socio-economic paradigm prevalent from the late 1990s onward, characterised by centrality and the importance of *information*, and in particular *knowledge*, as a primary raw material or a base economic resource in the creation of economic value and of commercial productivity.

Information Poor: Refers to the descriptive term indicative of the degree of quality and quantity of content, of information, and of technological hardware and software readily accessible and directly present in circulation within a given population, geographical region, system ecology, symbiotic environment, or collaborative circumstance; in the general case, delineative of between adequate and detrimentally under par availability of and access to online resources and the latest digital Information and Communication Technologies.

Information Revolution (The): Refers to the global economic paradigm prevalent from the late 1990s onward, characterised collectively by unprecedented advancements in technological innovation and the rapid global proliferation, appropriation, application, and use of new digital Information and Communication Technologies in everyday life. The Information Revolution is further described against three constituent strands - the Computer Revolution, the Internet Revolution, and the Digital Revolution.

Information Rich: Refers to the descriptive term indicative of the degree of quality and quantity of content, of information, and of technological hardware and software readily accessible and directly present in circulation within a given population, geographical region, system ecology, symbiotic environment, or collaborative circumstance; in the general case, delineative of between adequate and excellent availability of and access to online resources and the latest digital Information and Communication Technologies.

Information Society (The Global): Refers to the global socio-economic paradigm prevalent from the late 1990s onward, characterised by the centrality and the importance of *information* and *Information and Communication Technologies* (*ICTs*) to human interaction and endeavour; conceptualised and evaluated along several distinct axes including *the technological*, *the economic*, *the occupational*, *the spatial*, and *the cultural*.

Open Access Movement (The): Refers to a political movement dedicated to the development and promotion of free operating systems, free software applications, and to the provision of free digital content; popularised to lessen the dominance of proprietary software, and to eventually replace them.

Open Knowledge or Open-Source Knowledge, or Open Content: Refers to freely and openly distributed digitised knowledge and/or rich content; disseminated online over the Internet or through other digital information and communications media or platforms, or via new digital technological hardware.

Soft Factor(s) or Soft Element(s): Refers to the human issues or socio-political, socio-economic, socio-cultural, socio-anthropological, and psycho-sociological variables or contexts – involving people, culture, politics, economics, and society - within which a rational technological or hard system operates.

ENDNOTES

1. The CNN Effect was first noted when the news channel CNN showed heartbreaking footage of starving children in Somalia that pressured U.S. officials to send troops there. Subsequent horrifying footage of Somalis dragging the body of a dead American soldier through the streets followed, turning US public opinion against the intervention and prompting U.S. officials to withdraw their troops.
2. Quoted in Mark Surman and Katherine Reilly, Appropriating the Internet for Social Change: Towards the Strategic Use of Networked Technologies by Transnational Civil Society Organisations, Social Science Research Council Report, November 2003, p. 62
3. Multipurpose Community Telecentres (MCTs) are facilities that provide public access to a variety of information and communication services including Web-enabled computing, phone and fax services.

This research was previously published in the Handbook of Research on Trends and Future Directions in Big Data and Web Intelligence edited by Fausto Pedro Garcia Marquez, Noor Zaman, Mohamed Elhassan Seliaman, and Mohd Fadzil Hassan; pages 233-265, copyright year 2015 by Information Science Reference (an imprint of IGI Global).

Chapter 13
Role-Based Access Control for Mobile Computing and Applications

Yaira K. Rivera Sánchez
University of Connecticut, USA

Steven A. Demurjian
University of Connecticut, USA

Joanne Conover
University of Connecticut, USA

Thomas P. Agresta
University of Connecticut Healthcare Center, USA

Xian Shao
University of Connecticut, USA

Michael Diamond
Pomona College, USA

ABSTRACT

The proliferation of mobile devices has changed the way that individuals access digital information with desktop applications now performed seamlessly in mobile applications. Mobile applications related to healthcare, finance/banking, etc., have highly sensitive data where unsecure access could have serious consequences. This chapter demonstrates an approach to Role-Based Access Control (RBAC) for mobile applications that allows an information owner to define who can do what by role, which is then enforced within a mobile application's infrastructure (UI, API, server/database). Towards this objective, the chapter: motivates the usage of RBAC for mobile applications; generalizes the structure and components of a mobile application so that it can be customized by role; defines a configurable framework of locations where RBAC can be realized in a mobile application's infrastructure; and, proposes an approach that realizes RBAC for mobile security. To demonstrate, the proposed RBAC approach is incorporated into the Connecticut Concussion Tracker mobile application.

DOI: 10.4018/978-1-7998-0417-8.ch013

INTRODUCTION

The proliferation of mobile devices in all aspects of daily living has fundamentally altered the way that individuals interact with mobile applications. Evidence includes: the worldwide shipments of 1.9 billion phones and 230 million tablets outpacing PC/laptop sales (300 million estimate) (Gartner, 2015; Cisco, 2014); a report of smartphone usage in the U.S. where 64% of adults own a Smartphone, 42% own a Tablet, and 32% own an e-reader (Pew Research Center, 2012; Smith, 2015); and, predictive statistics that tablet users will surpass 1 billion worldwide in 2015 (eMarketer, 2015) and total devices will exceed 12.1 billion by 2018 (Radicati, 2014). Mobile applications now span a broad spectrum of complexity, including games, social networking, email, web browsing, financial management, health and fitness, pharmaceutical, etc. For both personal and business usage, there is a need to protect secure information ranging from protected health information (PHI) and personally identifiable information (PII) to confidential work product that is displayed, accessed, modified, and stored. Mobile health (mHealth) applications in healthcare and fitness are numerous and diverse: tracking medications (myCVS (CVS Pharmacy, 2015), MedWatcher (2012), etc.); personal health records (PHR) (CAPZULE PHR (Capzule, 2012), MTBC PHR (2011), etc.); fitness applications that work with phones and wearables (Cohen, 2015); Apple's HealthKit app (iOS 9, 2014) and the Google Fit fitness tracker (Google Play, 2013), to track activity, heart rate, blood pressure, etc. (Kelly, 2014); and, Apple's ResearchKit (Apple, 2015), an open source framework for mobile applications to support medical research. Patients also seek to have access via their mobile devices to the electronic medical records (EMRs) utilized by medical providers and health information technology (HIT) systems that contain medical testing results (Care360, 2014) or results from imaging testing (My Imaging Records App, 2013). All of these systems must adhere to the Health Insurance Portability and Accountability Act (HIPAA) (HHS.gov, 2013) for the security, availability, transmission, and release of a patient's medical information.

To augment the usability of these mHealth applications, there is also a desire by patients to attain privacy control to different individuals at varying levels of granularity over their electronic health and fitness information in various locations (Caine & Hanania, 2013). For a given patient, this effort highlights the potential recipients of the information (e.g., primary physicians, spouse, family, emergency medical providers, etc.) and the type of information to be controlled (e.g., contact info, current conditions, medications, recent test results, genetic information, etc.). In such a setting, patients are also interested in actually defining specific fine-grained access control by role (Sujansky, Faus, Stone, & Brennan, 2010), for example: a family member may view my medication list (but not all of them), a medical provider may view my medication list and history of hospital visits (but not modify), my personal physician may both view and modify my health care and fitness data, etc. These efforts highlight a strong need to achieve fine grained role-based level of security to allow patients to define who can see and/or modify what portions of their health/fitness data, where the mobile application itself can be customized based on role to meet the permission definition provided by the patient (Peleg, Beimel, Dori, & Denekamp, 2008). Securing information of mHealth applications for a diverse set of stakeholders may benefit from the usage of role-based access control (RBAC) (Ferraiolo & Kuhn, 1992). Such an inclusion allows permissions established by the information owner to be defined for other authorized users by role and use this as a basis to have the mobile application deliver only authorized information, and permitted view and/or modify capabilities. Note also that RBAC has been heavily adopted in healthcare, where a recent published literature review (Fernández-Alemán, Señor, Lozoya, & Toval, 2013) had 35 efforts utilizing access control methods and 27 of these specifically utilized RBAC.

One challenge in such an approach is to identify locations where RBAC can be incorporated within the mobile application's infrastructure (UI, API, Server/Database), which can be conceptualized as a configurable framework for RBAC permission definition and enforcement for mobile applications, as shown in Figure 1. In the figure, there are three options for including RBAC. The first option, *direct UI modifications,* shown in the left side of Figure 1, would be to modify the existing mobile application itself with RBAC permissions on screens, UI widgets, etc., which would involve code-level changes so that the look-and-feel of the UI would change based on the user and his/her role. The second option, *intercepting API calls,* shown in the middle of Figure 1, would be to define RBAC permissions on the API (REST, web, cloud) and/or database calls of the mobile application and intercept them in order to include RBAC permission checks that determine the filtered information returned to the mobile application or control information that can be stored in the mobile application's server. This may require minimal changes on the way that the mobile application calls the backend or the way that the backend calls are intercepted by the access control code. Finally, the third option, *direct server modifications,* shown in the right side of Figure 1, involves making changes to the backend of the existing mobile application (e.g., server for database, cloud, web, etc.) that would retain the view of the mobile application's API to the mobile application and embed RBAC on the server side. There are different ways to realize the three options with the mobile application infrastructure. One approach is via *application containers*, which separates a group of mobile applications that share/contain highly-sensitive data by placing them in an encrypted virtual container at the device level. Another approach is *application wrappers*, which wrap security policies on individual mobile applications at the application level (Symantec, 2014). We believe that the usage of application wrappers is the preferred approach for the options for three reasons: wrappers can be used to realize finer-granularity security policies than could be attained using application containers; wrappers can be utilized on third-party mobile applications; and, wrappers have a lower potential of damaging the functionality of a mobile application. This paper primarily focuses on option 1, *direct UI modifications*; the other two options are discussed in part as they represent ongoing work.

The remainder of the chapter has five sections. In the *Background and Motivation* section we review the NIST RBAC standard, RBAC in the healthcare domain, and RBAC in mobile computing, including work by both researchers and practitioners in applying RBAC to healthcare. In the *RBAC Approach for Mobile Applications* section, we present a generalizable approach to achieve RBAC security for mobile applications in support of the direct UI modifications option of Figure 1 that is realized with a corresponding RBAC model in SQL, which can be utilized to both define and enforce security on a mobile

Figure 1. A configurable framework for RBAC and its interactions with the mobile application infrastructure

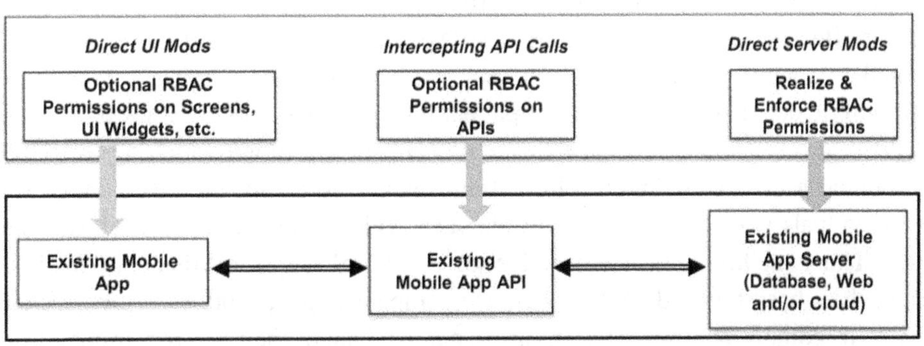

application. In the *RBAC in Connecticut Concussion Tracker Mobile Application* section, we demonstrate the attainment of the RBAC model of the prior section in the Connecticut Concussion Tracker (CT^2) application, providing detailed screen shots and a scenario of usage that fully demonstrates the ability to have the mobile application appear different to users based on their role. This includes the detailing of the direct UI modifications option as achieved by an application wrapper as well as a brief discussion of the intercepting API calls and direct server modifications options. Next, the *Future Trends* section presents emerging efforts that may impact RBAC for mobile applications, including: other types of access control such as Attribute-Based Access Control (NIST Computer Security Division, 2013), and BiLayer Access Control (Alshehri & Raj, 2013); as well as emerging approaches for mobile application security (MobileIron (2015)). Finally, the *Conclusion* section summarizes the contributions of the chapter.

BACKGROUND AND MOTIVATION

This section provides background information on: role-based access control (RBAC); security issues in healthcare; the usage of RBAC in healthcare; and, general security issues in mobile computing. To begin, *access control* is a security process and mechanism that allows user permissions to be granted or denied against the resources (objects) of a system or application. *Authorization,* a part of access control, is the process that is specifically associated with allowing or denying access to a resource (object). One of the dominant approaches, role-based access control (RBAC), was proposed by David Ferraiolo and Richard Kuhn (Ferraiolo & Kuhn, 1992) and transitioned to the National Institute for Standards and Technology (NIST) (Ferraiolo, Sandhu, Gavrila, Kuhn, & Chandramouli, 2001) that was adopted in 2004. The main concepts of the NIST RBAC standard (Sandhu, Ferraiolo, & Kuhn, 2000) are conceptualized in Figure 2 (SlideShare, 2012) with four reference models. $RBAC_0$ in the middle portion of Figure 2 is comprised of: *users* that perform a specific function within an organization, *roles* that are assigned to users based on their responsibilities, and *permissions* that define which operations/objects within a system/application a role can have access to. Users can have one or more roles, and roles can contain one or more permissions to objects. $RBAC_1$, shown in the upper middle portion of Figure 2, supports the ability of roles to be organized in a hierarchy. $RBAC_2$, shown in the upper left of Figure 2, provides the definition of constraints, such as separation of duty (SoD), mutual exclusion (ME), and cardinality. Lastly, $RBAC_3$, shown at the bottom part of Figure 2, captures the concept of sessions that represent the lifetime of a particular user, role, and permissions in a dynamic runtime application.

Next, we highlight two key issues involving security for healthcare. The first issue of incorporating health technologies such as Electronic Medical Records (EMRs) in healthcare organizations concerns privacy and security (Boonstra & Broekhuis, 2010). Improper disclosure of data in healthcare systems can have serious effects on patients, which can include personal embarrassment, prejudice, ostracization from family and community groups, as well as issues with insurability (Rindfleisch, 1997). In addition, unauthorized individuals that obtain access to patient information could use it for their own profit. For instance, in 2013, a billing technician at a hospital spent several months looking for people that had recently been in car accidents and then sold that information to an attorney. The attorney would then contact the individuals who were involved in the car accident and offered them legal representation (Wiech, 2013). This issue highlights the need for access control in systems that contain highly sensitive information, such as hospitals and health insurance companies. A second issue involves ensuring that healthcare systems comply with several security standards. One of the main requirements can be found

Figure 2. General structure of the RBAC model
SlideShare, 2012.

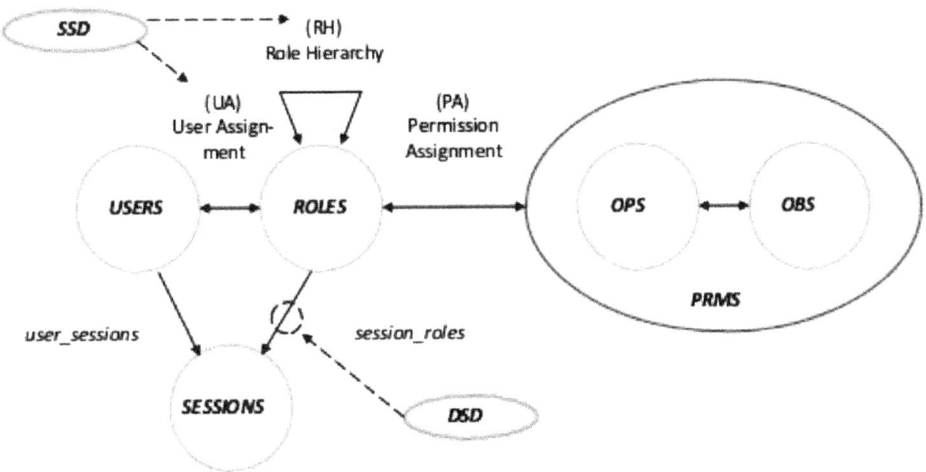

in §164.312(a)(1) of the standard (Scholl et al., 2008) that indicates that an approach for access control should be identified in order to allow access to authorized users and no one else. The HIPAA Privacy Rule also states that health care organizations should only disclose the minimum required information in order for the individual to realize an action (Health Information Privacy, 2002). In fact, as part of the Health Level Seven (HL7) International Standard (Health Level Seven International, 2010), a scenario-based role engineering process has been proposed and adopted (HL7 Security Technical Committee, 2007).

The third background area, RBAC in healthcare, has numerous efforts to extend RBAC to address limitations in regards to supporting healthcare. One effort extended RBAC in order to create an authorization model for Healthcare Information Systems (Hsu & Pan, 2013). The proposed model has the ability to assign different access permissions and to define new ones, with the consideration of roles having the ability to access certain permissions in emergent situations, and using RBAC to create an authorization mechanism for this case. Another approach proposes the creation of an access control model that contains elements from the mandatory, discretionary, and role-based access control models (Gajanayake, Iannella, & Samaha, 2014) for providing security and privacy to EMRs. On the practitioner side, one effort (Science Application International Corporation, 2004) in the United States involves the implementation of a large RBAC system for health care for Armed Service veterans and Native Americans: Kaiser Permanente, Department of Veterans Affairs, Department of Defense, and the Indian Health Service. Another example has added RBAC functionality to an existing medical database (Slevin & Macfie, 2007). This was done in order to observe the feasibility of the implementation, and to include RBAC as a security mechanism within the National Program for Information Technology (NPfIT) of the UK National Health Service (NHS). A third effort example implemented an Electronic Patient Record (EPR) in the Hospital S. João in Porto, Portugal using an RBAC model in order to provide a secure authorization mechanism (Ferreira, Chadwick, & Antunes, 2007).

The final background area involves security issues for mobile computing and applications. Mobile devices and computing are being improved on a seemingly daily basis in terms of hardware and software, increasing capabilities, features, and capacity. This in turn has resulted in the rise of new security risks. In the worst-case, a mobile device may be lost or stolen, necessitating the availability of techniques to control and securely access highly sensitive data. For example, healthcare data stored in a mobile device is being created, retrieved, and manipulated from multiple sources and by varied applications and this sensitive information must be protected from disclosure. This security requirement is juxtaposed against a recent survey (West & Miller, 2009) where the majority of people wanted email access with providers (74%), diagnostic test results electronically (67%), and access to their EMR (64%). These tasks will require a great amount of security as the information to be shared is highly sensitive and pertains to specific people from multiple sources and ultimately residing on a patient's mobile device.

From a security perspective, many high-end mobile devices contain biometric controls (e.g., fingerprint, voice recognition, facial recognition) and input controls (e.g., pattern, PIN, password) for authentication and authorization. All work under the assumption that one person is the owner of the device. To protect sensitive information many corporations are relying on the bring-your-own-device (BYOD) concept (e.g., corporate email, corporate applications) through their personal mobile devices or through a mobile device issued by the corporation itself. While this enhances productivity and increases employee satisfaction and engagement after hours (Wainwright, 2012), a study of mobile devices utilized in a corporate setting (Paganini, 2015) showed that approximately 14,000 applications installed on these devices were unsafe and compromised sensitive device data such as phone location, phone contacts, and SMS message logs. One of the methods that companies who have utilized BYOD policies have relied on to secure employees' mobile devices is to have defined roles for employees that limit access to mobile applications. This insures that employees only have access to what they need, and lowers the risk of downloading malicious applications. Finally, as part of BYOD, corporations utilize the concept of Mobile Device Management (MDM) (Gartner, 2012), which consists of software that manages software distribution, policies, inventory, security, and services.

RBAC APPROACH FOR MOBILE APPLICATIONS

In the literature, there are numerous access control models and approaches that utilize and extend RBAC (Motta & Furuie, 2003; Peleg, Beimel, Dori, & Denekamp, 2008; Russello, Dong, & Dulay, 2008). In addition, several approaches (Schefer-Wenzl & Strembeck, 2013; Santos-Pereira, Augusto, Correia, Ferreira, & Cruz-Correia, 2012; Abdunabi, Sun, & Ray, 2014) have emerged that propose RBAC for a mobile setting. However, while these approaches add capabilities such as spatio-temporal or context-aware techniques, they do not specifically address the way that the mobile application itself (UI, API, Server/Database) is impacted depending on the role that a user assumes for a particular mobile application session. To address this issue, this section provides an approach and detailed examination for achieving RBAC for mobile computing and applications by leveraging the NIST RBAC model, as presented in Figure 2, to the user interface (UI) of a mobile application; this is supporting the direct UI modifications option as shown in Figure 1. *User interface (UI)* can be defined as the means users utilize to interact with computer systems. The specific objective is to allow a mobile application to dynamically customize the capabilities of the mobile application's UI that are available based on a user's role, to both permit a user to perform needed tasks using the mobile application while simultaneously limiting and/or disabling and/or removing capabilities and features that are not allowed at certain times or in certain situations. In our approach, the "objects" of the NIST $RBAC_0$ will correspond to the various components of a mobile application's UI.

The remainder of this section is organized into a five-part discussion. In part one, we motivate the proposed RBAC approach by providing a sample mobile application in healthcare that illustrates the intended capabilities of our RBAC approach in terms of customizing the look-and-feel of the UI of a mobile application on a role-by-role basis. Part two generalizes the features and characteristics of the UI of a mobile application in order to be able to control what is viewable and/or modifiable on a role-by-role basis. Part three defines the different types of permissions that are available against the screens and components of a mobile application in order to allow a role to be defined with a set of permissions that limits the look-and-feel of the UI by role. Part four defines a relational database structure to store the content of a generalized mobile application that is comprised of a UI with screens and their components, to allow permissions to be defined that customize the mobile application look-and-feel based on role. Part five explains the programmatic changes that must be made to the mobile application itself to allow for the screens and their components to be customized.

In the first part of this section, we present a mobile application utilized by personnel at a pharmacy to fill and process prescriptions for customers with a UI that has five screens to: look up the status of a prescription (Screen 1), enter a new prescription to be filled (Screen 2), fill and dispense the prescription with the appropriate medication (Screen 3), look up to see if a medication is in inventory (Screen 4), and order medications for inventory (Screen 5). The five screens could be linked by next and back buttons or could be five different tabs on one screen. There are two types of users: *pharmacy technicians* that interact with the customer to receive and enter the prescription; and, *pharmacists* that have the legal authority to fill and dispense the prescription. A pharmacy technician would be limited to Screens 1, 2, and 4, while a pharmacist would have access to all five screens. To achieve this in practice, the mobile application's UI would have to be adaptable based on role in order to determine which components of the application the user with a role is allowed to see in order to avoid improper disclosure of information. Our solution in the proposed RBAC approach is to place these access control policies in a database where they will be easier to manage and change as permissions are created, modified, deleted, etc. To support such an approach, there is a need to control not only which screens are available to which users but to also control the actual capabilities on each screen which may limit some users to be able to view data on a screen while others could view/modify it.

This leads to the second part of this section that enumerates the general structure of a mobile application in terms of its features and characteristics so that the way that the mobile application looks and feels can be dynamically customized on a role-by-role basis. Specifically, a mobile application's UI will be comprised of a series of inter-connected *screens* where each screen contains a portion of the functionality. Each screen of the UI will have a set of different *components* consisting of information that is displayed (cannot be changed) and information that can be entered by a user including: text field (TF), button (BN), drop down (DD), checkboxes (CB), radio buttons (RB), spinner (SP), date picker (DP), etc. A mobile application can have one or more screens and screens can have one or more of the aforementioned components. Definitions 1 to 4 formalize these concepts:

Defn. 1: A mobile application, *MA*, consists of a user interface (UI) that contains a set of *n* screens, *S*, that are organized as either tabs (users can click among tabs) or a sequence of inter-connected screens which are linked with next and previous buttons.

Defn. 2: Each screen, S^i, has a set of *k* screen components, *SC*, denoted, SC_k^i, that allow a user to select, enter, and manipulate data in a MA.

Defn. 3: A component, *C,* is a portion of a screen that can be displayed and/or entered by users and includes but is not limited to: a text field (TF) to enter information; a button (BN) to effect the state of the application (save, cancel, next, previous, etc.); a drop down (DD) where one value is chosen; a set of checkboxes (CB) where multiple values can be chosen; a set of radio buttons (RB) to select only one of a number of options; a spinner (SP) to select values; a date picker (DP) to enter calendar dates; etc.

Defn. 4: Each MA has a screen set, *SS*, that is classified as either:

- A collection of tabs where each tab is a screen, where there is an order among the tabs in the way that they are displayed left to right within the MA.
- A collection of screens where each screen has an appropriate list of buttons to navigate among screens that is augmented with the *screen interactions, SI,* necessary to switch among the various screens.

Utilizing these definitions as a basis, users will be authorized to access a subset of the screens with defined permissions for each screen in order to limit and control the access to each screen's components, where our RBAC approach can enable/disable the components based on a user's role. As result, a user as owner by his/her role could have full access to the application (e.g., pharmacist in the prior can utilize all five screens) while another user would be restricted to a dynamically customized version of the mobile application (e.g., pharmacy technician limited to Screens 1, 2, and 4). The end result is the ability to control which components of the application's UI users can have access (view/edit) to depending on their role. The advantage of this is that user permissions can be configured based on his/her role; therefore, the application does not need to be configured for each individual user, but will operate by role against the user instance that has been authorized.

This third part of the proposed RBAC approach provides the ability to define permissions against a generalized structure of a mobile application's UI screens and their components that is capable of customizing which screens and their respective components are available in the mobile application, depending on the role a user assumes. Towards this end, the left side of Figure 3 contains a sample screen from the UI where a set of components (text fields, spinners, date pickers, drop down boxes, and buttons) is shown. The screens and the components are the objects in $RBAC_0$ that will be authorized as screen, component, and screen interaction permissions to a particular role. This essentially defines what a role can and cannot do in terms of screen, component, and screen interaction permissions and determines whether the user with such role can access and/or view a certain component. As an example, the screen with all capabilities on the left side of Figure 3 is customized as shown on the right side of Figure 3 where a text field (the search bar), the drop down, the checkboxes, and button number 2 have been disabled. In this case, the user with the role would be able to view information but would not be able to make any changes to the aforementioned disabled components. The permissions that are defined on the components of a screen are placed in two main categories: *on/off permissions* that are for components that can be 'on' (enabled) or 'off' (disabled); and, *data permissions* that are for components that can be 'view', 'edit', or 'edit once'. On/Off permissions are defined for the different components: button (BN), radio button (RB), drop down (DD), checkbox (CB), date picker (DP), spinner (SP), and text fields (TF), while data permissions are defined for text fields (TF). A text field has to be On in order for view/edit/edit once to be defined. A mobile application can have one or more screens and screens can have one or more of the aforementioned components and permissions on a user/role basis. Definitions 5 to 9 formalize these concepts:

Defn. 5: A screen permission, $sp=<s,p>$, where $s \in SS$ is a screen and p is permission, is utilized to define whether a screen s in SS as given in Defns. 2 and 4, that is part of a mobile application MA is allowable ($p=true$) or not ($p=false$).

Defn. 6: A component permission, $cp=<sc,p>$, where $sc \in SC_k^i$ is a screen component (Defn. 2), is utilized to define permissions on various components of each screen S (Defn. 3). There are two types of component permissions:

- On/off permissions for button (BN), radio button (RB), drop down (DD), checkbox (CB), date picker (DP), spinner (SP), or text field (TF). The permission values for each component are: $p=$*enabled* or *disabled.*
- Data permissions for text fields (TF). The permission values for a text field are: $p=$*view*, *edit*, or *edit once*.

Defn. 7: A screen interaction permission set, $SIP=<si_1,\ldots,si_e>$, defines all permitted screen interactions, where each $si=[s_z,s_y]$ is a pair of screens that means that screen s_x interacts with screen s_y.

Defn. 8: A role, R, is assigned a set of role permissions, R_p, for a subset $m \leq n$ screens of SS in MA as: $R_p=<\sigma,\chi,\delta>$ where: $\sigma=<sp_1,\ldots,sp_m>$ are the m screens (Defn. 5) assigned to the role R; $\chi=<cp_1,\ldots,cp_j>$ are j component permissions (Defn. 6) for all m screens; and $\delta=SIP$ are the screen interactions (Defn. 7) for non-tabbed UIs.

Defn. 9: A user, U, can be assigned a role R that customizes the UI of the MA based on the role permissions (Defn. 8).

The fourth part of the proposed RBAC approach is the design of an entity-relationship diagram representation of the database model in Figure 4 that is utilized to capture screen, component, and screen interaction permissions (see Defns. 5, 6, and 7), for each role (see Defn. 8), by representing the generalized structure of the mobile application (via the entities screens, screen_sequence, and screen_components) and the permissions (via the entities roles, screen_access, and component_access). In Figure 4, the *roles* entity contains the name of the roles that are available as well as a unique role_id assigned to each one of these. This role_id is utilized to determine if a role has access to a specific screen of a UI,

Figure 3. A screen with components (left) that are customized (right)

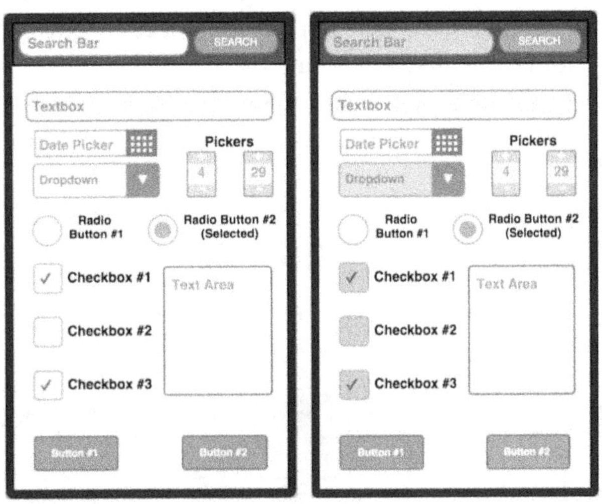

Figure 4. Proposed entity-relationship diagram for capturing permissions on screens and components

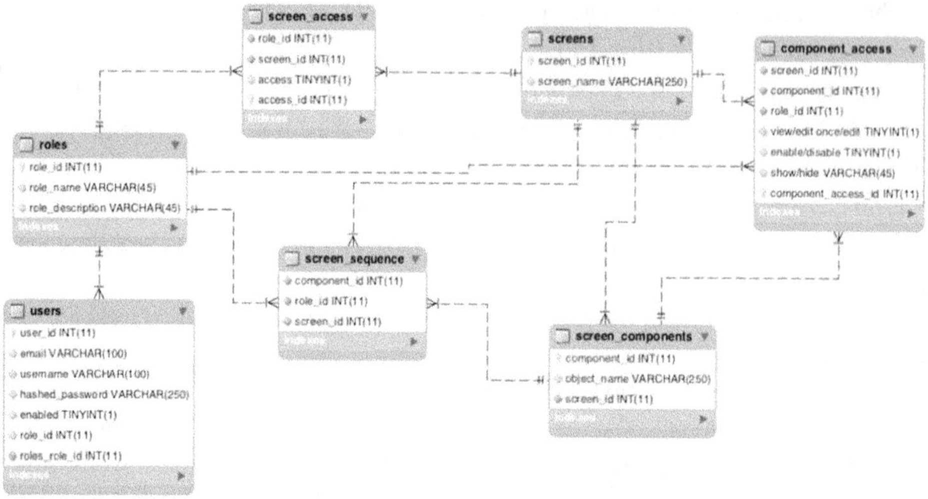

to a component in that UI screen, and the sequence of screens it is allowed to view. This role_id would leverage the prior pharmacy example, where the pharmacy technician role would only be allowed to access UI screens 1, 2, and 4. If a role by role_id has access to a specific screen, then the second step of the permission process would be to define components of the screen that such role can access; otherwise, if role_id is not assigned to a screen, the screen and its components are hidden. In this model, users can only have one role, and roles can have one or more permissions. In order to capture permissions, the entities screen_access and component_access are utilized, where: the *screen_access* entity supports the definition of the permission for a role with respect to the entire screen and the *component_access* entity supports the definition of the permissions of the role with respect to the components of a screen. To bring the concepts together, Figure 5 illustrates the authorization process that assigns a user one or more roles (while limiting a user to one identified role per session) and then defines screens, their components, and their interactions on a role-by-role basis against all mobile application screens/components. Note that both the on/off and data permissions are for the components that are captured in the component_access entity.

The authorization policies for a generalized mobile application as defined via the process in Figure 5 are then enforced as shown in Figure 6. The enforcement process begins with the mobile application authenticating the user, verifying the credentials, and then retrieving the role of the user to customize the mobile application (Defn. 9). The right hand side of Figure 6 (Proposed Approach box) utilizes the data in the screen access and component access entities (see Figure 4 again) to determine a custom

Figure 5. Authorization process for roles with respect to screens and components

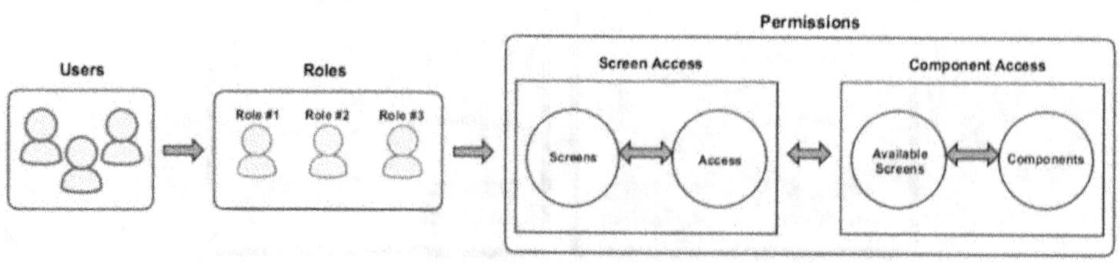

Figure 6. Enforcement process for a mobile application

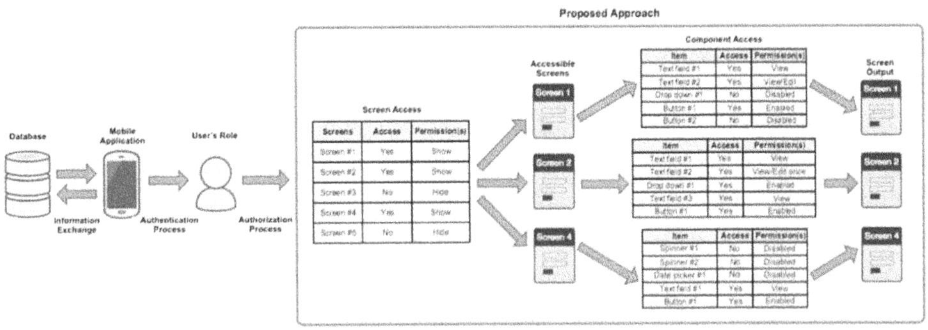

version of the UI of the mobile application by role (Defn. 8). Notice that the screen access instances are shown for a role (like the pharmacy technician role of the prior example), with screens 1, 2, and 4 authorized. The *Accessible Screens* part of Figure 6 illustrates a basic idea of the screen permissions (Defn. 5). Also, the *Component Access* table on the right side of Figure 6 illustrates the components of the aforementioned screens that have been authorized to a specific role, thereby realizing the component permissions (Defn. 6). There are no screen interaction permissions in Figure 6, since we assume the mobile application consists of a set of tabs.

The fifth part of our approach involves programmatic changes that are made just one time; since the permissions are taken from the database of Figure 4, these can be changed and the mobile application's UI will adjust the look-and-feel based on roles/permissions without any additional code-level changes. The entity-relationship diagram in Figure 4 was realized as a relational database using MySQL. To support interactions from the mobile application to the MySQL database of permissions, an RBAC Application Programming Interface (API) was created that can be utilized to support the application wrapper for the direct UI modifications option as illustrated in Figure 1. The RBAC API calls are invoked within the mobile application's source code and return data from the queries in JSON format. There are three main API calls that will constitute the wrapper that have been defined against the entities in Figure 4 and realized in the MySQL database, which are briefly described along with the incorporation of their usage within the code of the mobile application. The API calls are as follows:

- **Is_Screen_Allowable(role_id, screen_id):** returns a Boolean value true (JSON format: [{"access":"1"}]) if the role represented by role_id has the permission to display a particular UI screen screen_id, and false otherwise (JSON format: [{"access":"0"}]). This first API call queries the screen_access entity of Figure 4 which was illustrated in Figure 6, and would return true for screens 1, 2, and 4, and false for screens 3 and 5. This requires a change to the mobile application code to include a conditional statement that only displays a particular screen of the UI based on the screen_id and role_id if there is permission defined in the screen_access entity.
- **Return_Allowable_Components(role_id, screen_id):** Returns a table of component permissions for the role_id/screen_id combination that identifies the on/off and data permissions on buttons, spinners, date spinners, radio buttons, checkboxes, drop downs, and text fields. The API call begins by querying the component_access entity of Figure 4, which was illustrated in Figure 6 by the three permission tables for screens 1, 2, and 4 (*Component Access* table in the figure). Then, the API call retrieves the component permissions for a single screen of the UI that is autho-

rized to that role. Finally, the API call is invoked for the allowable screens following the API call Is_Screen_Allowable(role_id, screen_id). As part of the process to display an allowable screen **s**, the mobile application's code is modified with conditional statements for the various components of each screen. Specifically, for the on/off permissions, the button (BN), radio button (RB), drop down (DD), checkbox (CB), date picker (DP), and/or spinner (SP) components are disabled for all non-allowed actions which are the 'no' entries as shown in the component_access table of screen 1 for Figure 6. For the data permissions, each text box is set accordingly based on View, Edit, or Edit once. Note that the APIs are not called in sequence rather are utilized in multiple locations throughout the mobile application's source code.

- **Return_Allowable_Screen_Interactions(role_id):** Utilizes a role_id to look up all of the allowable screens (via a database query to the screen_access entity for role_id) and using this information, returns the sequences of permissible movement/interactions among all allowable screens of the UI. First, the API call utilizes the screen_sequence entity in Figure 4 in order to find all of the allowed interactions among screens of the UI for role_id and only enable those interactions that occur among the allowable screens. The API call is then utilized to set behavior related information to buttons (BN) on a particular screen. For a button that is enabled, the information in screen_sequence for the given role and its allowable screens will allow the button to cause the screen to be reached; a button not enabled will not link to another screen.

To this point, we have shown the different components that our approach contains and the way that these are incorporated in a mobile application in support of the direct UI modifications option via an application wrapper. Next, we review the way that a mobile application maintains its functionality after adding these direct changes. First, we identify the screens and the objects of a screen of the mobile application to which RBAC is to be applied. Then, we assign a unique id to each of these components and store them as tables in a database as shown in Figure 4. The role of the user is retrieved and stored in a secured session variable (passed over https) through the means of an API call (part of the application wrapper). Using this as a basis, to enforce the policies established in the database with the mobile application, we create a set of API calls. These calls will return if a component can be shown/edited or if it needs to be disabled/hidden. Each call will check if the component that we are trying to apply the policy to exists in the database; if it doesn't, then the API call will return that the component is enabled for the role that is in session as no RBAC permissions were found in the created policy. By making these changes, the functionality of the mobile application will not be affected since the API calls that are being added to the source code of the mobile application always return a value regardless if the component does not have a policy stored in the database anymore. In addition, storing the role of users in a secure session variable will prevent a user from tampering its role and it does not require any changes in the source code.

Lastly, note that the approach presented in this section supports the direct UI modifications option that was part of the Figure 1 configurable framework for RBAC. The direct UI modifications option focuses on RBAC of the UI of a mobile application's screens and their components, and then customizes the look-and-feel by role that is defined with varied screen, component, and screen interaction permissions stored in a database. When permissions change, only the database needs to be changed, and the mobile application will adjust appropriately. However, one disadvantage of the direct UI modifications option is that programmatic changes are required in the mobile application itself through the addition of condition statements and calls to APIs that return allowable screens and permissions on components in order to adjust the look-and-feel of the mobile application (via the application wrapper). The other two options in Figure 1, intercepting API calls and direct server modifications, are both under investigation in our work. Consider that the intercepting API calls option would require minimal or no changes to the UI of the mobile application other than for the need to identify a given role for a session being initiated by a user. In this case, we incorporate the functionality of our API calls into REST or API services that are utilized to intercept the API calls. Here, we are not changing the look-and-feel of the mobile application, but essentially disabling the delivery of content to the user. Recalling the pharmacy example, the pharmacy technician could see all five screens, but information on screens 3 and 5 would be blocked in the display of data. For the case where the pharmacy technician attempts to utilize screens 3 and 5, if they do attempt to take a positive action to search or insert information, this would be intercepted at the server side to disallow the attempt. Basically, the RBAC checks on defined permissions that have been discussed for the approach in this chapter would be before the REST/API calls in the case of the intercepting API calls option and after the REST/API calls for the direct server modifications options. For both of these options, insert/update actions need to be before in order to prevent changes to be made and inserts to be stopped. For retrieval actions that are not allowed, we perform the RBAC checks after the information is retrieved from the database to filter out some or all of the information; this would be done by intercepting the calls in the intercepting API calls option and by including these checks in the server code in the third option. By embedding these checks into the REST/API calls themselves at the server side for the direct server modifications option, the mobile application remains primarily unchanged other than requiring the mobile application to identify itself by role.

RBAC IN CONNECTICUT CONCUSSION TRACKER MOBILE APPLICATION

In order to evaluate the proposed RBAC approach for mobile computing and applications, we apply the model and algorithm as presented in the prior section to the Connecticut Concussion Tracker (CT^2) mobile application. CT^2 is a collaboration between the Departments of Physiology and Neurobiology, and Computer Science & Engineering at the University of Connecticut and Schools of Nursing and Medicine in support of a new law passed in the state of Connecticut to track concussions of kids between ages 7 to age 19 in public schools (CT Law HB6722) (Connecticut General Assembly, 2015). As shown in Figure 7, the Android mobile application CT^2 (first screenshot) consists of a UI with 7 additional tabbed screens: 'Home', 'List', and, 'Student', respectively, in the top row of the figure; and 'Cause', 'Symptoms', 'Follow-up', and 'Return', respectively, in the bottom row. Briefly, we explain each screen. The 'Home' tab allows the user to enter a concussion, to retrieve an open case, or to find a student by typing the student's last name and first name. If a user has access to 'Retrieve Open Cases', this returns the 'List' tab in the top row, which contains the list of students the user has permission to view and, for each student gives him/her the option to add a concussion or edit an existing one (if he/she has permission to access these components). The 'Student' tab, the last screenshot in the top row, allows the user to input the student's general information (e.g., name, birthdate, school) and the date that the incident occurred. The 'Cause' tab, the first screenshot of the bottom row, allows the user via drop down options to specify where the injury was caused, with what it was caused, etc. After the user saves the data he/she entered in the 'Cause' tab, he/she can proceed to the 'Symptoms' tab (second screenshot, bottom row), where the symptoms the student had within 48 hours and other pertinent data are entered. To finish, the 'Follow-up' and 'Return' (third and fourth screenshot, respectively, bottom row) tabs allow users to record the status of the student over time (Follow-up) and when the student can return to various activities at school (Return).

To illustrate the proposed approach of the chapter, four different roles for CT² are defined: the *Nurse* role represents the actions that a school nurse would take in order to manage a student's concussion incident from its occurrence to its resolution; the *Athletic Trainer* (*AT*) role represents the actions that a trainer would take at an athletic event including a limited preliminary assessment if a concussion incident occurs at the event; the *Coach* role represents the actions a coach of a sport would take to report a concussion incident at an athletic event with very limited information on the student; and, the *Parent* role which represents the actions to both report a concussion incident on his/her child while attending the athletic event or to track the current status of his/her children that have ongoing concussions. While all of these roles are allowed to enter basic information to report the concussion (fourth screenshot, top row in Figure 7), there are limitations in terms of the screens and the components on the screens that each role is allowed to utilize. For instance, a user with the role *AT* can add students (fourth screenshot, top row in Figure 7), input the cause of the concussion incident (first screenshot, bottom row) that are related to a sport, and add symptoms (second screenshot, bottom row). However, the *AT* role cannot edit information after it is saved (edit once permission), has access to view the *Follow Up* screen but can't edit it (third screenshot, bottom row), and does not have access to the *Return* screen (fourth screenshot, bottom row). On the other hand, a user with role *Nurse* has permission to utilize all of the tabs shown in Figure 7. *Coach* and *Parent* roles will have also limited access to view and/or edit information.

The four roles can be defined in terms of their ability to access the UI of the CT² application screens and the components (text fields, spinners, date pickers, drop down boxes, and buttons) on a screen-by-screen basis to establish both the on/off permissions and the data permissions as discussed in the prior section. This information represents the privileges or permissions that are authorized to each role, which when assigned to a given user, results in the CT² application being customized in terms of the screens

Figure 7. CT² mobile application

that are displayed and the components that are enabled. Figure 8 contains a table that summarizes all of the screen, on/off, and data permissions for all screens (tabs) and components for the CT^2 application for the four roles: Nurse, Athletic Trainer, Coach, and Parent with respect to their permissions. In terms of permissions, the entire screen can either be shown or hidden as a first level of control. For screens that are shown, the different components can be enabled/disabled (button (BN), radio button (RB), drop down (DD), checkbox (CB), date picker (DP), and/or spinner (SP)) or can be view, edit, or edit once (text field (TF)) via the on/off (values of enable and disable) and data (values of view, edit, and edit once) permissions. The edit once data permission means that the user can input data in the text field one time and, after he/she saves such data, he/she cannot modify it. The edit once option also applies to buttons, drop downs, and spinners, since there are cases where the user selects an option from one of these and it can't be modified later on by him/her. If a screen is hidden from the role, then all of the components of the screen are hidden by default. One of the benefits of our approach is that we can adjust the level of granularity we want to provide to the mobile application since we can add the RBAC proposed approach to specific screens, to specific components, or to all of these (as we do in this case).

The component permissions (Defn. 6) as defined in Figure 8 are inserted as tuples into the CT^2 database that manages all of the concussion incidents, students, and users. To accomplish this, the entity-relationship model as presented in Figure 4 was integrated into the CT^2 database that tracks all of the information on the tabs shown in Figure 7. This includes database tables for: a student, a student's concussion incident, the school and its location, symptoms, information for following up on the concussion, and tracking when the student can return to various activities; note that we have omitted these tables from this discussion since the issue is to authorize and define permissions with respect to information on the various screens and their components. For completeness, we review the entities in Figure 4 in greater detail from a database table perspective in order to support the discussion on the permission process. The roles table assigns a unique id to each of the roles and, stores the name of the role as well as an optional description. The users table in the CT^2 database models information on each user and it was modified to include the role_id foreign key in order to determine the role of the user once he/she logs in to the application. After a user logs in successfully, the role_id is obtained to determine which students and which screens of the UI the user has access to. The screens table assigns a unique screen_id to each of the screens of the UI as well as a name so that it would be easier to identify and manage them while the screen_components table stores the information that is used to view which components belong to which screen. The screen_access table contains the screen_id, the role_id, and a Boolean value named access, and determines if the specified role has access to the specified screen (access = 1) or not (access = 0). The screen_sequence table is utilized to determine the screen(s) that a role has access to once it modifies a component. Finally, the component_access table stores the information that specifies the screen in which a component is located, which role id can access the component, and the permissions the role has over this component in terms of on/off and data permissions that are utilized to enable/disable, view, edit, or edit once. The permissions as captured in the upgraded CT^2 database in Figure 4 support the three API calls of the prior section and are executed in the CT^2 mobile application's code to enforce the permissions of each role to determine the screens and their components for each user by role. CT^2 utilizes a MySQL database to store its data and relies on API commands to retrieve data for

Figure 8. Tabular summary of role permissions in CT²

Screens/Components	Roles and their Permissions			
	Nurse	Athletic Trainer	Coach	Parent
Home Tab	Show	Show	Show	Show
'Enter New Student' BN	Enabled	Enabled	Enabled	Enabled
'Retrieve Open Cases' BN	Enabled	Enabled	Enabled	Enabled
'Last Name' TF	View/Edit	View/Edit once	View/Edit once	View/Edit once
'First Name' TF	View/Edit	View/Edit once	View/Edit once	View/Edit once
'Search' BN	Enabled	Enabled	Enabled	Enabled
List Tab	Show	Show	Show	Show
'Enter New Student' BN	Enabled	Enabled	Enabled	Enabled
'View Student Info' BN	Enabled	Enabled	Enabled	Enabled
'Edit' BN	Enabled	Disabled	Disabled	Disabled
'Add' BN	Enabled	Enabled	Enabled	Enabled
Student Tab	Show	Show	Show	Show
'First Name' TF	View/Edit	View/Edit once	View/Edit once	View/Edit once
'Middle Initial' TF	View/Edit	View/Edit once	View/Edit once	View/Edit once
'Last Name' TF	View/Edit	View/Edit once	View/Edit once	View/Edit once
'Gender' DD	View/Edit	View/Edit once	View/Edit once	View/Edit once
'Date of Birth' DP	View/Edit	View/Edit once	View/Edit once	View/Edit once
'Date of Past Concussions' DP	View/Edit	View/Edit once	View/Edit once	View/Edit once
'State' DD	View/Edit	View/Edit once	View/Edit once	View/Edit once
'City/Town/Region' DD	View/Edit	View/Edit once	View/Edit once	View/Edit once
'District' DD	View/Edit	View/Edit once	View/Edit once	View/Edit once
'School' DD	View/Edit	View/Edit once	View/Edit once	View/Edit once
'Save' BN	Enabled	Enabled	Enabled	Enabled
'Cancel' BN	Enabled	Enabled	Enabled	Enabled
Cause Tab	Show	Show	Show	Show
'Location of Incident' DD	Enabled	View/Edit once	View/Edit once	View/Edit once
'If Sport' DD	Enabled	View/Edit once	View/Edit once	View/Edit once
'Others/Details' TF	View/Edit	View/Edit once	View/Edit once	View/Edit once
'Contact Mechanism' DD	Enabled	View/Edit once	View/Edit once	View/Edit once
'Impact Location of Head' DD	Enabled	View/Edit once	View/Edit once	View/Edit once
'Head Gear Usage' DD	Enabled	View/Edit once	View/Edit once	View/Edit once
'Save' BN	Enabled	Enabled	Enabled	Enabled
'Cancel' BN	Enabled	Enabled	Enabled	Enabled
Symptom Tab	Show	Show	Hide	Show
'Mild and Severe Symptoms' BN	Enabled	View/Edit once	-	View
'Hour' TF	View/Edit	View/Edit once	-	View
'Minute' TF	View/Edit	View/Edit once	-	View
'Second' TF	View/Edit	View/Edit once	-	View
'Were Parents Notified?' DD	Enabled	View/Edit once	-	View
'Removed From Activity' DD	Enabled	View/Edit once	-	View
'Removed by' DD	Enabled	View/Edit once	-	View
'Concussion Assessment Tool' DD	Enabled	View/Edit once	-	View
'Additional Comments' TF	View/Edit	View/Edit once	-	View
'Save' BN	Enabled	Enabled	-	Disabled
'Cancel' BN	Enabled	Enabled	-	Disabled
Follow Up Tab	Show	Show	Hide	Show
'Lingering Symptoms' BN	Enabled	View	-	View
'If Other, Please Specify' TF	View/Edit	View	-	View
'All Symptoms Resolved in' DD	Enabled	View	-	View
'Concussion Diagnosed by' DD	Enabled	View	-	View
'Post Concussive Syndrome Diagnosis' DD	Enabled	View	-	View
'Medical Imaging' DD	Enabled	View	-	View
'Additional Comments' TF	View/Edit	View	-	View
'Save' BN	Enabled	Disabled	-	Disabled
'Cancel' BN	Enabled	Disabled	-	Disabled
Return Tab	Show	Hide	Hide	Hide
'Days Absent From School' TF	View/Edit	-	-	-
'Schedule/Activity Modification' DD	Enabled	-	-	-
'504 Plan Required' DD	Enabled	-	-	-
'Date of Return to Learn' DP	Enabled	-	-	-
'Date of Return to Full Participation' DP	Enabled	-	-	-
'Save' BN	Enabled	-	-	-
'Cancel' BN	Enabled	-	-	-

display on the UI and to store new concussion incidents (or changes) into the database. Figure 9 illustrates the result of the screen and component permissions for the *Nurse*, *Parent*, and *Coach* roles. The *Nurse* role has all of the tabs active (first screen of figure 9). The *Parent* role has limited access to the tabs and also, although users with the *Parent* role can view the 'Symptom' and 'Follow Up' tabs, they are not allowed to update that information (second screen of Figure 9). Finally, the *Coach* role has the first four tabs active and has limited access to the information it can view/modify (third screen of Figure 9).

Figure 9. Result of RBAC in CT² (nurse, parents, and coach view)

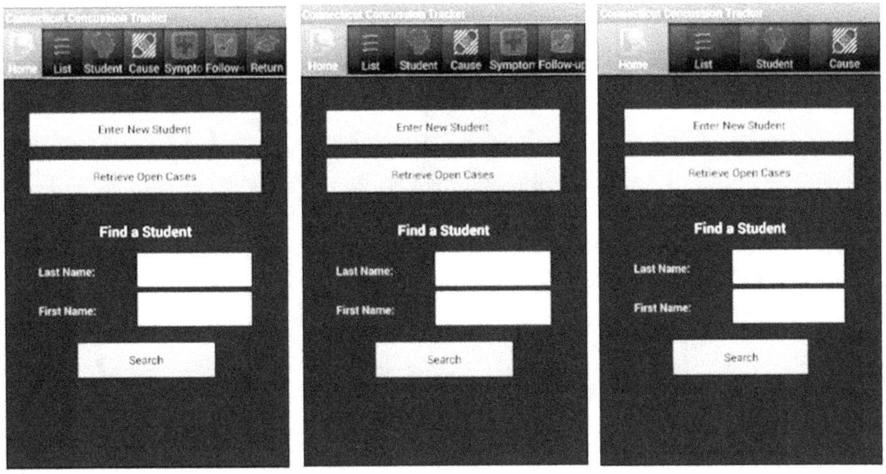

FUTURE TRENDS

This section explores future trends with a two-fold focus: novel access control methods that have the potential for future usage in a mobile setting; and, device level security methods related to authorization and authentication.

The Attribute-Based Access Control (ABAC) method (Coyne & Weil, 2013) is a context-aware approach that considers the user's responsibilities and can place users in groups/roles based on their attributes. For example, a physician has a different context when he/she is seeing patients in the medical practice, attending patients at a hospital or clinic, or answering phone calls after hours and on weekends; this context differs based on what he/she does. One of the main advantages of ABAC over RBAC is the ability of granting dynamic permissions by checking the user's attributes to determine if the user has access to that component at that particular moment. Figure 10 illustrates the overall architecture of the ABAC model where: a user tries to access a component and the Access Control Mechanism processes the user's attributes by analyzing these against an access control policy, subject attributes, component attributes, and environmental conditions (The Johns Hopkins University Applied Physics Laboratory, 2014).

The BiLayer Access Control (BLAC) method (Alshehri & Raj, 2013) provides secure authorization as a fusion between RBAC and ABAC that combines attributes with roles. BLAC has additional advantages to RBAC of supporting attributes and policies where is verified utilizing two layers. The first layer checks the individual against pseudo roles (i.e., the list of individual's attributes) while the second layer checks the requested component against rules within the policies that are related. Figure 11 illustrates the high-level components of the BLAC model that: assigns a pseudo role to the subject; evaluates this against the subject's attributes, the environmental attributes, and the component's attributes; verifies all attributes against the policy; and determines whether the subject has access to the requested component or not. The use of pseudo roles could be leveraged in the physician example of ABAC to define pseudo roles based on where the physician treats patients.

Figure 10. Overall architecture of the ABAC model

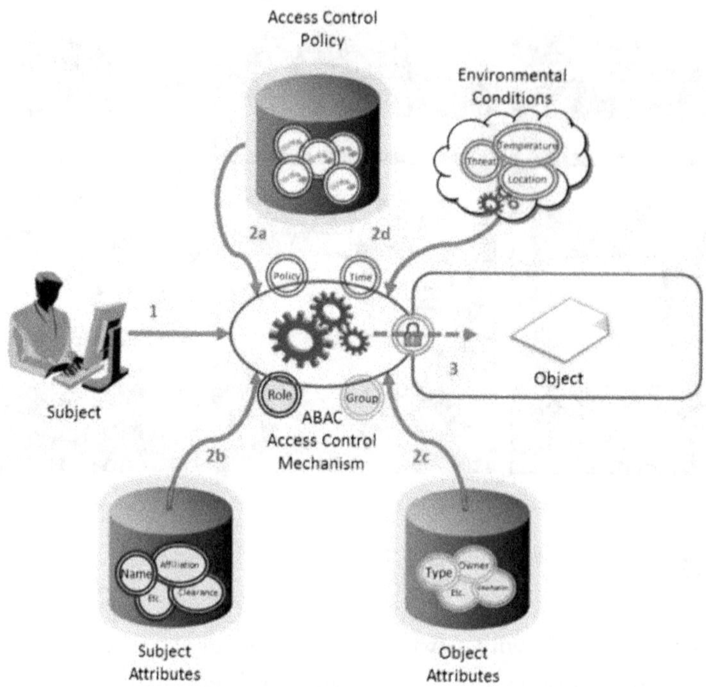

Figure 11. High-level components in BLAC model
Alshehri & Raj, 2013.

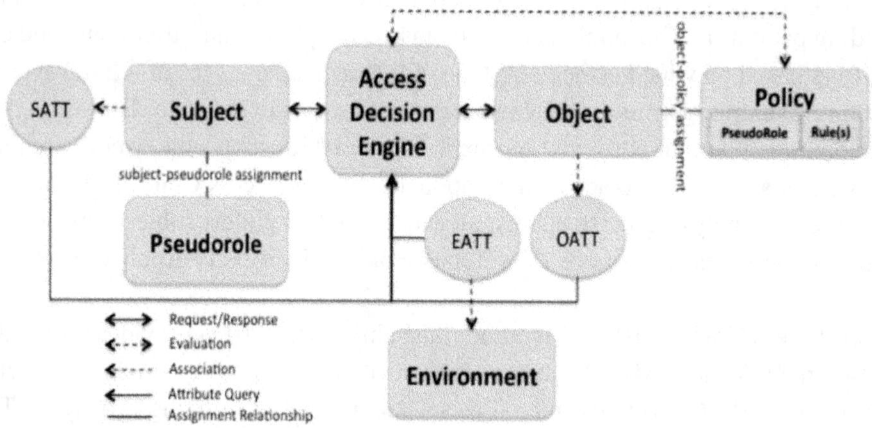

To complete this discussion, there are emerging device level security approaches for mobile computing related to authorization and authentication. The Oauth2 authorization framework (Hardt, 2012) has the purpose of granting access to a third-party application to obtain limited access to an HTTP service. One of the advantages of Oauth2 is that there is no need to store the user's credentials (e.g., username and password) to *reauthorize* in the future since an access token is employed. Such a process is performed through four different roles: *resource owner* manages the access to a protected source; *resource server* utilizes access tokens to determine which requested resources a user can view; *client* is the application that makes resource requests on behalf of the resource owner; and, *authorization server* issues access tokens to the client once it has properly authenticated the resource owner as well as obtained authorization. A good amount of websites that require users to authenticate (i.e., Facebook, Gmail, Twitter, etc.) utilize the Oauth2 protocol's API to authorize them after the authentication process takes place.

Another security solution for mobile devices is Stormpath (2011) (API and open source SDKs) that utilizes the OAuth2 password grant type scheme to authenticate users to manage part of the authentication process and to be able to issue an access token for the user that is requesting access to the mobile application. One of Stormpath's features is a user authorization management mechanism for mobile applications and support for single sign-on and multi-factor authentication (Stormpath, 2015). Another approach, MobileIron (2015), is a solution that seeks to secure a group of mobile applications that have highly secure information for a particular enterprise. MobileIron focuses on providing security on mobile devices, mobile applications, and mobile content of enterprises through the means of a solution called Enterprise Mobility Management (EMM) (MobileIron Solutions EMM, 2015). EMM is composed of three approaches: Mobile Device Management (MobileIron Solutions MDM, 2015), Mobile Application Management (MobileIron Solutions MAM, 2015), and Mobile Content Management (MobileIron Solutions MCM, 2015). These three approaches manage enterprise settings, which users can utilize to secure mobile apps and, to obtain enterprise access to corporate data via VPNs.

CONCLUSION

This chapter has presented a generalizable approach to RBAC for mobile applications that proposed a configurable framework of three options in Figure 1, which can be utilized to both define and enforce security on a mobile application in differing locations of the infrastructure. The direct UI modifications option was the focus of this chapter to the UI to be dynamically customized by role via the usage of an application wrapper. To organize the presentation, the *Background and Motivation* section reviewed NIST RBAC and the usage of RBAC in mobile computing and healthcare. With this as a basis, the *RBAC Approach for Mobile Applications* section presented an RBAC approach capable of defining roles with screen and component permissions of the mobile application's UI, realized with a corresponding RBAC model in SQL, to dynamically customize the UI of a mobile application in support of the direct UI modifications option. This included an API as an application wrapper which was employed to make programmatic changes to the mobile application with conditional statements that would enable/disable by role the screens and components of a UI. This also briefly discussed the intercepting API calls and direct server modifications options of the configurable framework of Figure 1, illustrating the other ways to include RBAC that has less of an impact on the mobile application itself. To demonstrate the feasibility and utility of our work, the *RBAC in Connecticut Concussion Tracker Mobile Application* section, implements our proposed approach in the CT^2 mobile application, making it appear different (in terms of UI) to users based on their role, with permissions illustrated for four different roles (Nurse, Parent, Coach, Athletic Trainer). To complete the chapter, the *Future Trends* section reviewed emerging RBAC approaches and security infrastructures for authorization and authentication.

REFERENCES

Abdunabi, R., Sun, W., & Ray, I. (2014). Enforcing spatio-temporal access control in mobile applications. *Computing*, *96*(4), 313–353. doi:10.100700607-013-0340-2

Alshehri, S., & Raj, R. (2013). Secure Access Control for Health Information Sharing Systems. *2013 IEEE International Conference on Healthcare Informatics, ICHI 2013*. 10.1109/ICHI.2013.40

Apple. (2015). *ResearchKit and CareKit*. Retrieved from http://www.apple.com/researchkit/

Boonstra, A., & Broekhuis, M. (2010). Barriers to the acceptance of electronic medical records by physicians from systematic review to taxonomy and interventions. *BMC Health Services Research BMC Health Serv Res*, *10*(1), 231. doi:10.1186/1472-6963-10-231 PMID:20691097

Caine, K., & Hanania, R. (2013). Patients want granular privacy control over health information in electronic medical records. *Journal of the American Medical Informatics Association*, *20*(1), 7–15. doi:10.1136/amiajnl-2012-001023 PMID:23184192

Capzule. (2012). *Capzule PHR*. Retrieved from http://www.capzule.com/

Care360. (2014). *MyQuest*. Retrieved from https://myquest.questdiagnostics.com/web/home

Cisco. (2014). *Cisco Visual Networking Index: Global Mobile Data Traffic Forecast Update, 2014-2019*. Retrieved from http://www.cisco.com/c/en/us/solutions/collateral/service-provider/visual-networking-index-vni/mobile-white-paper-c11-520862.html

Cohen, J. (2015, January 7). *11 Health And Fitness Apps That Achieve Top Results*. Retrieved from http://www.forbes.com/sites/jennifercohen/2015/01/07/the-11-top-health-fitness-apps-that-achieve-the-best-results/#11f5c21a1aca

Connecticut General Assembly. (2015). *Substitute for Raised H.B. No. 6722*. Retrieved from https://www.cga.ct.gov/asp/CGABillStatus/CGAbillstatus.asp?which_year=2015&selBillType=Bill&bill_num=HB6722

Coyne, E., & Weil, T. (2013). ABAC and RBAC: Scalable, Flexible, and Auditable Access Management. *IT Professional*, *15*(3), 14–16. doi:10.1109/MITP.2013.37

eMarketer. (2015, January 9). *Tablet Users to Surpass 1 Billion Worldwide in 2015*. Retrieved from http://www.emarketer.com/Article/Tablet-Users-Surpass-1-Billion-Worldwide-2015/1011806

Fernández-Alemán, J., Señor, I., Lozoya, P., & Toval, A. (2013). Security and privacy in electronic health records: A systematic literature review. *Journal of Biomedical Informatics*, *46*(3), 541–562. doi:10.1016/j.jbi.2012.12.003 PMID:23305810

Ferraiolo, D., & Kuhn, R. (1992). Role-Based Access Control. In *Proceedings of the NIST-NSA National (USA) Computer Security Conference*.

Ferraiolo, D., Sandhu, R., Gavrila, S., Kuhn, D., & Chandramouli, R. (2001). Proposed NIST standard for role-based access control. *ACM Transactions on Information and System Security*, *4*(3), 224–274. doi:10.1145/501978.501980

Ferreira, A., Chadwick, D., & Antunes, L. (2007). Modelling access control for healthcare information systems. In *Proceedings of the Doctoral Consortium at the 9th International Conference on Enterprise Information Systems (ICEIS)*.

Gajanayake, R., Iannella, R., & Sahama, T. (2014). Privacy oriented access control for electronic health records. *Electronic Journal of Health Informatics*, *8*(2), e15.

Gartner. (2012). *Mobile Device Management (MDM)*. Retrieved from http://www.gartner.com/it-glossary/mobile-device-management-mdm

Gartner. (2015, March 19). *Gartner Says Global Devices Shipments to Grow 2.8 Percent in 2015*. Retrieved from http://www.gartner.com/newsroom/id/3010017

Google Play. (2013). *Fitness Tracker*. Retrieved from https://play.google.com/store/apps/details?id=com.realitinc.fitnesstracker

HL7 Security Technical Committee. (2007, September). *HL7 Role-Based Access Control (RBAC) Role Engineering Process*. Retrieved from http://csrc.nist.gov/groups/SNS/rbac/documents/hl7_role-based_access_control_(rbac).pdf

Hardt, D. (Ed.). (2012). *The OAuth 2.0 Authorization Framework*. Internet Engineering Task Force (IETF). Retrieved from https://tools.ietf.org/html/rfc6749

Health Information Privacy. (2002). *Minimum Necessary Requirement*. Retrieved from http://www.hhs.gov/hipaa/for-professionals/privacy/guidance/minimum-necessary-requirement/index.html

Health Level Seven International. (2010). *Introduction to HL7 Standards*. Retrieved from http://www.hl7.org/implement/standards/

HHS.gov. (2013). *Health Information Privacy*. Retrieved from http://www.hhs.gov/hipaa/index.html

Hsu, W., & Pan, J. (2013). The Secure Authorization Model for Healthcare Information System. *Journal of Medical Systems*, *37*(5), 1–5. doi:10.100710916-013-9974-z PMID:24061706

iOS 9. (2014). *Health: An innovative new way to use your health and fitness information*. Retrieved from https://www.apple.com/ios/health/

Kelly, S. M. (2014, June 27). *In Google Fit vs. Apple HealthKit, Fitness Apps Stay Neutral*. Retrieved from http://mashable.com/2014/06/27/healthkit-google-fit-apps/#nf_r0U7flmqC

MedWatcher. (2012). *MedWatcher*. Retrieved from https://medwatcher.org/

MobileIron. (2015). *MobileIron*. Retrieved from https://www.mobileiron.com/en

MobileIron Solutions EMM. (2015). *Enable business transformation MobileIron's Enterprise Mobility Management (EMM) Platform*. Retrieved from https://www.mobileiron.com/en/solutions/enterprise-mobile-management-emm

MobileIron Solutions MAM. (2015). *Do more with secure mobile application management (MAM)*. Retrieved from https://www.mobileiron.com/en/solutions/mobile-application-management-mam

MobileIron Solutions MCM. (2015). *Secure mobile content management (MCM) keeps data safe and business moving*. Retrieved from https://www.mobileiron.com/en/solutions/mobile-content-management-mcm

MobileIron Solutions MDM. (2015). *Mobile Device Management (MDM): The foundation for a secure mobile enterprise*. Retrieved from https://www.mobileiron.com/en/solutions/mobile-device-management-mdm

Motta, G., & Furuie, S. (2003). A contextual role-based access control authorization model for electronic patient record. *Proceedings of the IEEE Transactions on Information Technology in Biomedicine*, *7*(3), 202–207. doi:10.1109/TITB.2003.816562 PMID:14518734

MTBC PHR. (2011). *MTBC PHR*. Retrieved from https://phr.mtbc.com/

My Imaging Records App. (2013). *My Imaging Records App*. Retrieved from http://myimagingrecords.com/index.html

NIST Computer Security Division. (2013). *Attribute-Based Access Control*. Retrieved from http://csrc.nist.gov/projects/abac/

Paganini, P. (2015, June 17). *Mobile App Security: Threats and Best Practices*. Retrieved from https://www.veracode.com/blog/2015/05/mobile-app-security-threats-and-best-practices-sw

Peleg, M., Beimel, D., Dori, D., & Denekamp, Y. (2008). Situation-Based Access Control: Privacy management via modeling of patient data access scenarios. *Journal of Biomedical Informatics*, *41*(6), 1028–1040. doi:10.1016/j.jbi.2008.03.014 PMID:18511349

Pew Research Center. (2012, February 23). *Mobile Technology Fact Sheet*. Retrieved from http://www.pewinternet.org/fact-sheets/mobile-technology-fact-sheet/

Pharmacy, C. V. S. (2015). *myCVS On the Go*. Retrieved from http://www.cvs.com/mobile-cvs

Radicati, S. (2014). *Mobile Statistics Report, 2014-2018*. Retrieved from http://www.radicati.com/wp/wp-content/uploads/2014/01/Mobile-Statistics-Report-2014-2018-Executive-Summary.pdf

Rindfleisch, T. C. (1997). Privacy, information technology, and health care. *Communications of the ACM*, *40*(8), 92–100. doi:10.1145/257874.257896

Russello, G., Dong, C., & Dulay, N. (2008). A Workflow-Based Access Control Framework for e-Health Applications. *22nd International Conference on Advanced Information Networking and Applications - Workshops (AINAW 2008)*. 10.1109/WAINA.2008.131

Sandhu, R., Ferraiolo, D. F., & Kuhn, R. (2000). The NIST Model for Role Based Access Control: Toward a Unified Standard. In *Proceedings of the Fifth ACM Workshop on Role-based Access Control (RBAC '00)*. 10.1145/344287.344301

Santos-Pereira, C., Augusto, A. B., Correia, M. E., Ferreira, A., & Cruz-Correia, R. (2012). A Mobile Based Authorization Mechanism for Patient Managed Role Based Access Control. LNCS, 7451, 54-68.

Schefer-Wenzl, S., & Strembeck, M. (2013). Modelling Context-Aware RBAC Models for Mobile Business Processes. *International Journal of Wireless and Mobile Computing*, *6*(5), 448. doi:10.1504/IJWMC.2013.057387

Scholl, M. A., Stine, K. M., Hash, J., Bowen, P., Johnson, L. A., Smith, C. D., & Steinberg, D. I. (2008). *An Introductory Resource Guide for Implementing the Health Insurance Portability and Accountability Act (HIPAA) Security Rule*. Gaithersburg, MD: National Institute of Standards & Technology. doi:10.6028/NIST.SP.800-66r1

Science Application International Corporation (SAIC). (2004, May 11). *Role-Based Access Control (RBAC) Role Engineering Process*. Retrieved from http://csrc.nist.gov/groups/SNS/rbac/documents/HealthcareRBACTFRoleEngineeringProcessv3.0.pdf

Slevin, L. A., & Macfie, A. (2007). Role Based Access Control for a Medical Database. In *Proceedings of Software Engineering and Applications* (pp. 195–199). SEA.

SlideShare. (2012). *Constrained RBAC diagram*. Retrieved from http://image.slidesharecdn.com/rbac6576-121205031439-phpapp01/95/rbac-18-638.jpg?cb=1354677352

Smith, A. (2015, April 1). *U.S. Smartphone Use in 2015*. Retrieved from http://www.pewinternet.org/2015/04/01/us-smartphone-use-in-2015/

Stormpath. (2011). *Stormpath*. Retrieved from https://stormpath.com/

Stormpath. (2015). *User Authorization Management*. Retrieved from https://stormpath.com/product/authorization

Sujansky, W. V., Faus, S. A., Stone, E., & Brennan, P. F. (2010). A method to implement fine-grained access control for personal health records through standard relational database queries. *Journal of Biomedical Informatics*, *43*(5), 46–50. doi:10.1016/j.jbi.2010.08.001 PMID:20696276

Symantec. (2014, October 7). *Securing Mobile App Data - Comparing Containers and App Wrappers*. Retrieved from https://www.symantec.com/content/en/us/enterprise/white_papers/b-securing-mobile-app-data-comparing-containers-wp-21333969.pdf

The Johns Hopkins University Applied Physics Laboratory. (2014, December 19). *Digital Policy Management Framework for Attribute-Based Access Control*. Retrieved from https://www.ise.gov/sites/default/files/DigitalPolicyFramework-ABAC.pdf

Wainwright, A. (2012, June 21). *7 Benefits of BYOD on Enterprise Wireless Networks*. Retrieved from http://www.securedgenetworks.com/blog/7-Benefits-of-BYOD-on-Enterprise-Wireless-Networks

West, D., & Miller, E. A. (2009). Digital Medicine: Health Care in the Internet Era. Brooking Institution Press.

Wiech, D. (2013, April 17). *Role-Based Access Control for Healthcare Data Security*. Retrieved from http://healthcare-executive-insight.advanceweb.com/Features/Articles/Role-based-Access-Control-for-Healthcare-Data-Security.aspx

KEY TERMS AND DEFINITIONS

Access Control: Method that determines who or what has access to resources in an environment.

Application Wrapper: Management layer applied to a mobile application in order to incorporate additional functionality that can be called by the application with a limited overhead and impact.

Authorization: Procedure that allows an individual to access/obtain something.

Electronic Medical Record (EMR): Digital version of a patient's paper health record.

Health Information Technology (HIT) systems: Electronic systems that are utilized with the expectation that they will lower costs, improve efficiency, and reduce errors, in addition to providing better care and services for consumers in the healthcare domain.

Health Insurance Portability and Accountability Act (HIPAA): Law which main purpose is to protect the confidentiality and security of healthcare information, as well as assist the healthcare industry to control administrative costs.

Health Level Seven International (HL7): Organization that delivers a framework and several standards in order to manage electronic health information.

Highly Sensitive Data: Information that if exposed or modified without proper authorization could lead in a critical effect on the performance, assets, or reputation of its owner (e.g., medical data, credit card data, social security number, etc.).

Mobile Computing: Devices that allow people to access software/data regardless of their location.

Role-Based Access Control (RBAC): Approach utilized to control access to a computer system through the means of roles assigned to the users of such system.

This research was previously published in Mobile Application Development, Usability, and Security edited by Sougata Mukherjea; pages 117-141, copyright year 2017 by Information Science Reference (an imprint of IGI Global).

Chapter 14
Analysis of Healthcare Workflows in Accordance with Access Control Policies

Sandeep Lakaraju
Dakota State University, USA

Dianxiang Xu
Boise State University, USA

Yong Wang
Dakota State University, USA

ABSTRACT

Healthcare information systems deal with sensitive data across complex workflows. They often allow various stakeholders from different environments to access data across organizational boundaries. This elevates the risk of exposing sensitive healthcare information to unauthorized personnel, leading 'controlling access to resources' a major concern. To prevent unwanted access to sensitive information, healthcare organizations need to adopt effective workflows and access control mechanisms. Many healthcare organizations are not yet considering or do not know how to accommodate the 'context' element as a crucial element in their workflows and access control policies. The authors envision the future of healthcare where 'context' will be considered as a crucial element. They can accommodate context through a new element 'environment' in workflows, and can accommodate context in policies through well-known attribute based access control mechanism (ABAC). This research mainly addresses these problems by proposing a model to integrate workflows and access control policies and thereby identifying workflow activities that are not being protected by access control policies and improving the workflow activities and/or existing access control policies using SARE (Subject, Action, Resource, and environment) elements.

DOI: 10.4018/978-1-7998-0417-8.ch014

INTRODUCTION

The wide adoption of information technology across healthcare organizations has increased the need for developing efficient workflows. Literature has shown that healthcare organizations with efficient workflows have more success rate in adopting healthcare information technology (HIT) into their organizations (Sittig, Krall, Kaalaas-Sittig, & Ash, 2005). Effective care delivery is possible through workflows with competent activities (Campbell, Sittig, Ash, Guappone, & Dykstra, 2006). Nevertheless, security and privacy of healthcare information have become major challenges for healthcare organizations (Akinyele et al., 2011; Alhaqbani & Fidge, 2007). In particular, effective access control mechanisms are needed to protect sensitive information from being exposed to unauthorized personnel.

Workflows

Workflows are used to describe the pattern of tasks to be executed by users to achieve business objectives. According to Welch (2014), "Efficient clinical workflow saves time, saves money, and saves lives. And in today's industry, workflow can have a significant effect on reimbursement". Workflows can be very complicated, especially in a complex environment like healthcare which may involve various subjects trying to perform actions on certain resources in multiple environments, thus requires controlling the access of resources by subjects. For a subject to perform an action on a resource in an environment, that subject should be authorized to perform the intended action. In this research, Business Process Modeling Notation (BPMN) has been used to develop workflows. BPMN (Business Process Modeling Notation) is visualization for business process workflows (Giaglis, 2001). The various elements of BPMN are given in Figure 1. We use four types of elements, defined as follows: Events that can be start or finish, distinguishable by size of circles; Activities (Tasks) have an "id" (A1; A2 etc.) and possibly user icons on the upper right corner of the rectangle, and groups indicate a group of activities; Gateways are diamond shaped, with multiple input channels; Conditional gateways are plain diamonds with only one output channel that is based on the evaluation of a condition; Parallel gateways have diamonds with a '+' sign inside. They have multiple input/output channels indicating that control flows on those channels in parallel; Sequences (flows) link tasks together, and associations are used to associate activities with flow objects; some of the extra events used are also shown in the Figure 1 representing Binding of Duties (BOD) policy and Separation of Duty (SOD) policy, and a release event.

Figure 1. Workflow elements

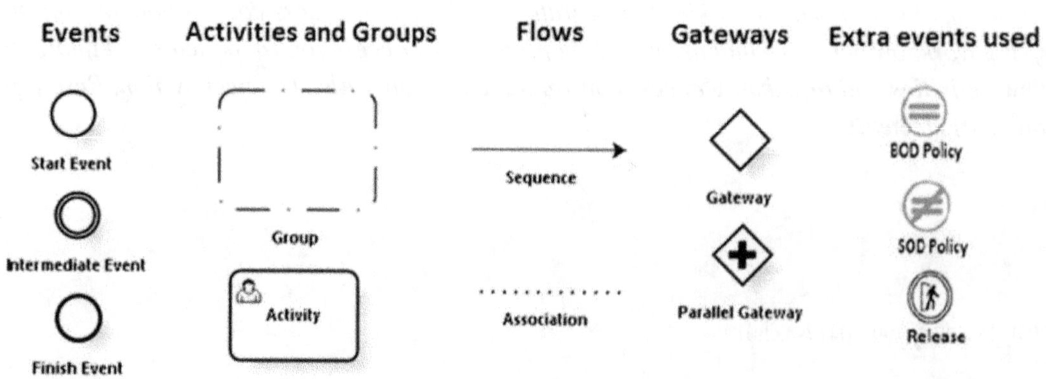

A workflow involves execution of a series of certain activities which help in achieving a goal (Chaari, Biennier, Amar, & Favrel, 2004). These workflows have to be executed in a secure way, which is made possible through access control.

Access Control

Inter-organizational systems allow users to access and share data beyond organizational boundaries and therefore needs proper authorization mechanisms to protect sensitive information from being exposed to unauthorized personnel. An access control policy defines the conditions to which access to resources can be granted and to whom (Ferreira, Cruz-Correia, Antunes, & Chadwick, 2007). With the increasing complexity of information systems, access control methods have evolved from Mandatory Access Control (MAC), Discretionary Access Control (DAC), Task Based Access Control (TBAC), Context Based Access Control (CBAC), Role-Based Access Control (RBAC), to Attribute-Based Access Control (ABAC) (Xu & Zhang, 2014).

Attribute Based Access Control (ABAC)

ABAC provides dynamic access control capability. ABAC does not depend on subject-resource relation, but on various attributes (of subject, resource, environment, etc.). National Institute of Standards and Technology (NIST) indicates ABAC as a recommended access control language which can improve 'information sharing within organizations and between diverse and disparate organizations while maintaining control of that information' (Hu, Scarfone, & Kuhn, 2013).

Coming to attribute base access control (ABAC), it is "an access control method where subject requests to perform operations on objects are granted or denied based on assigned attributes of the subject, assigned attributes of the object, environmental conditions, and a set of policies that are specified in terms of those attributes and conditions" (Hu et al., 2013). The preferability of ABAC over other access control mechanisms is demonstrated in detail in (Yuan & Tong, 2005). In ABAC, the authorization elements are defined in terms of attributes, rather than identities, of subjects, actions, resources, and environments (SARE). Attributes are characteristics of these entities that are predefined and pre-assigned by an authority. Subject attributes help in identifying a user (or an operation or a process) with its characteristics rather than its role; for example: job title, user name, age, etc. A resource attribute is a characteristic of a resource (record, data, etc.); for example: medical elements of patient record, non-medical elements of patient record, etc. Action attributes help in identifying the type of action the subject will perform on a resource; for example: read, write, etc. Environment attributes are operational or situational characteristics, such as current time and IP address. Consider the following access control rule: Any doctor can read and write into patient health record (PHR) only for his/her designated patients from internal network. The subject attributes include 'doctor', the action attribute is 'read' and 'write', and the resource attribute is 'patient health record', and the environment variable is 'internal network' and the condition is that the doctor can only access the health records of the patients designated to him/her.

HIPAA Compliance of Workflows and Access Control

Implementing HIPAA compliance involves the steps below: (i) establishing a process to develop/improve policies (ii) administering security functions (iii) actively tracking personnel changes, and (iv) examining and recording the policy application (K. Cole, 2002).

The privacy rule involves: (i) Minimum necessary use: where an organization should delineate people who may request to have their hands on PHI. Organizations should also delineate the health information into various categories and should define the level of access an employee should have to access that particular information, and any other specific regulations that may apply; (ii) notice of privacy practice: Organizations should make understand the employees and any other stakeholders about their privacy practices, (iii) it also provides the patients with advanced rights of access about their health information. Upon patient's request, a healthcare entity should provide information sharing policies, and patients can request with whom their information may be shared or not shared.

The security rule involves confidentiality, integrity, and availability of information. Confidentiality involves restriction of access to information. Integrity imposes strict restrictions on type of modifications that can be performed on the protected health information. Availability ensures that recognized users have access to PHI whenever they require. This can be implemented in three ways as shown in this research: developing policies in plain English, implementing through computer models (such as workflows and ABAC), and using technical mechanisms. In this research, the access control policies and workflow activities are HIPAA compliant because:

1. This methodology requires to develop and use uniform SARE standards
2. Workflow activities and access control policies use same SARE attributes
3. Access control policies consider environment variables to allow or deny access
4. Policies can be modified based on patient's interests
5. The privacy will be enhanced by considering the environment attributes, which would further allow the administrator to know what information has been accessed from which location and by whom.

Integrating Access Control and Workflow

Many organizations treat access control and workflow as two separate issues. As both workflow specifications and access control polices can be complex, it is likely that there exists discrepancy between workflow activities and access control policies. For example, some workflow activities may not be adequately regulated by the access control policies. To address this issue, we propose a methodology for integrated modeling and analysis of workflows and ABAC policies.

The proposed methodology views workflow activities in terms of subject, resource, action, and environment. Specifying environment attributes in a workflow will provide more contextual information for analysis. It is also consistent with the ABAC concepts. Through cross-examination of inter-organizational workflow activities and access control policies, the proposed methodology can identify: (a) Whether there are workflow activities that are not covered by the access control policies, (b) whether there are unused access control policies, (c) how many policies are covering an activity, and (d) whether the workflow activities and the access control policies need to be modified or refined.

Organizational Implementation of ABAC

An access control policy defines the conditions to which access to resources can be granted and to whom (Ferreira et al., 2007). With the increasing complexity of information systems, access control methods have evolved from Mandatory Access Control (MAC), Discretionary Access Control MAC (DAC), Access Control List (ACL), Role-Based Access Control (RBAC), to Attribute-Based Access Control (ABAC) (Xu & Zhang, 2014). The preferability of ABAC over other access control mechanisms is demonstrated in detail in (Yuan & Tong, 2005). In ABAC, the authorization elements are defined in terms of attributes, rather than identities, of subjects, actions, resources, and environments (SARE). Attributes are characteristics of these entities that are predefined and pre-assigned by an authority. A sample organizational ABAC implementation has been shown in Figure 2. It mainly involves certain functional 'points': Policy Enforcement Point (PEP), Policy Decision Point (PDP), Policy Administration Point (PDP), and Policy Information Point (PIP). Considering a particular scenario where a subject requests access to a resource under certain environment, this is sent as a request into a policy enforcement point (PEP) where a decision is taken whether to 'allow' that access or 'deny' the access based on certain attributes (user, action, resource, and environment). PEP sends that request to PDP where the request is broken into subject attributes, resource attributes, action attributes and environmental attributes.

Initially, each of those attributes is stored in their respective attribute stores managed at the policy information point (PIP). And the Policy Administration Point (PAP) is the point where policies are managed by the administrators. PDP will validate the request based on the available policies from PAP and the attributes available from PIP. Once the PDP is able to validate the request, it will send a notification

Figure 2. Access control mechanism distribution in a sample organizational ABAC implementation (Hu et al., 2013)

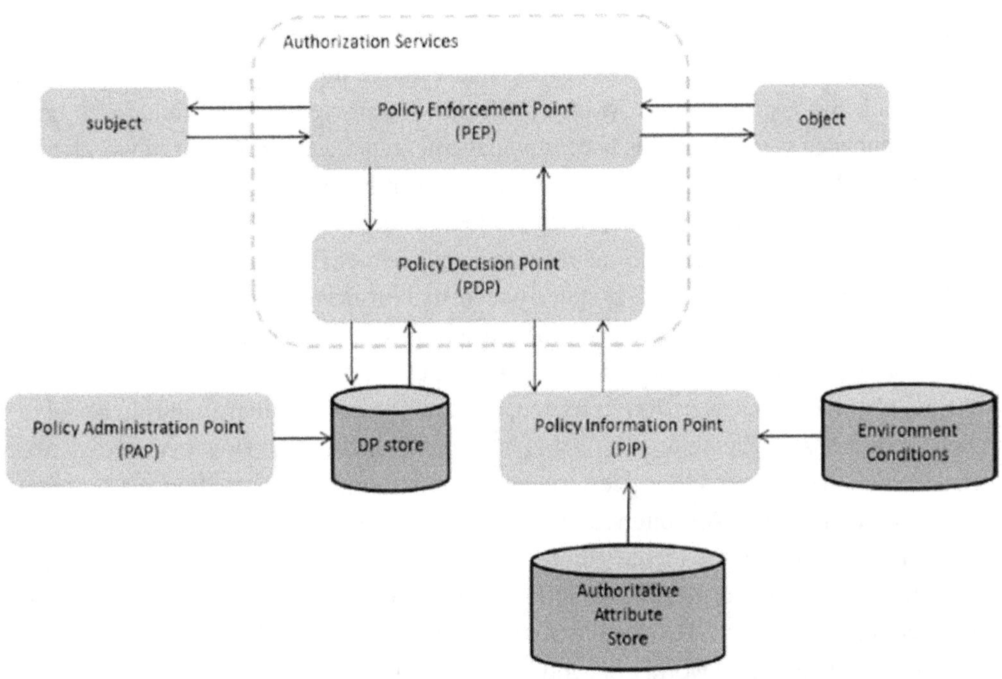

to PEP suggesting to 'allow' the access, otherwise 'denies' the request. To support ABAC, OASIS has developed the eXtensible Access Control Markup Language (XACML) standard (Identifier, 2005). Consider the following access control rule: *Any doctor can read and write into patient health record (PHR) only for his/her designated patients from internal network.* The subject attributes include 'doctor', the action attribute is 'read' and 'write', and the resource attribute is 'patient health record', and the environment variable is 'internal network' and the condition is that the doctor can only access the health records of the patients designated to him/her.

Literature Review

A workflow involves execution of a series of certain activities which help in achieving a goal (Chaari et al., 2004). These workflows must be executed in a secure way, which is possible through access control. To achieve these secured workflows, various access control techniques have been studied in accordance with the workflows, but none of the works have shown an integrated analysis and have only dealt with workflows and access controls separately. In (Chaari et al., 2004), authors have extended role based access control and proposed an authorization and access control model for workflows. Research by Chaari et al. (2004) mainly focuses on the user's role and the task the user has to execute; but it does not consider any other contextual information or user attributes except the role. Russello et al. (2008) have proposed a workflow based access control framework for e-health applications, where permission is granted to a user based on the necessity of the task that the users have to execute. Russello et al. (2008)'s research mainly focuses on the 'need' of the user to execute the task, but does not consider any of the environment or resource or subject attributes except the role. Russello et al. (2008) indicates that 'access rights must be granted only to entities that require access to a given resource and just for the amount of time that access is necessary', but healthcare is rather dynamic environment where access is required in varying contexts which requires precise contextual information to allow a user to access certain resource. This research will address this issue by focusing on importance of 'environment' attributes and our methodology will demonstrate the integrated analysis of workflow and access control which can grant access rights only to the entities that require access to a given resource under certain context where access is necessary. Le, Doll, Barbosu, Luque, & Wang (2012) have improved the traditional role based access control model to enhance the information access management in the environment of workflow and team collaboration in healthcare programs. Le et al. (2012)'s research has mainly concentrated on traditional RBAC and is an extension of RBAC. This research deals with ABAC, which not only deals with user attributes such as 'role' but also with various resource, environment and action attributes. Lu, Zhang, & Sun (2009) have developed a framework to specify security constraints in workflow by improving business process management notation model. Authors have improved the workflow model to aid role based access, separation of duty, history based task assignment, etc. Compared to this work, our model deals with the attributes of the subjects, action, resource, and environments rather than role based or SOD or history based or task based. Zhang & Liu (2011) have developed a workflow oriented attribute based access control model that provides 'Service-Oriented Computing', where any device's functionality can be offered as a standard service. Although Zhang & Liu (2011) talk about attribute based access control, they have not considered the need to identify unused policies or the need to identify unprotected workflow activities. XiangPeng, Cerone, & Krishnan (2006) have developed a framework integrating workflows (BPEL) and access control (RBAC) to execute security constraints through 'temporal logic'. Though the framework deals with integrating workflows and RBAC through temporal logic; regular people may not exercise the logic to execute security restraints. Compared to their work, our model deals with enforcing ABAC policies on the workflow activities which is not covered in (XiangPeng et al., 2006).

None of the above mentioned literature talks about integrated analysis of workflow and ABAC policies. One of the main takeaways from our research is that it is possible to identify any unused policies and also it is possible to identify any workflow activities that are not being protected by access control policies.

Assumptions

Some of the assumptions in developing the current model are discussed below. We are not developing a new modeling language. We are adding a new element 'environment' to the activity of the workflow. We are suggesting breaking down an activity in the workflow in terms of 'Subject, Action, Resource, and Environment' (SARE) elements as shown in Figure 3. Not every activity may have all of the four (SARE) elements, i.e. each activity may have any of the SARE elements. We identify common themes between the workflow and ABAC policies in terms of SARE elements. In any given situation to integrate a workflow and policies, we assume that workflow and policies will have any or all of the SARE elements. We assume workflow is a valid one without any deadlocks. Organization will define the SARE elements to be used commonly by both workflow and the ABAC policies.

Figure 3. Workflow activity breakdown

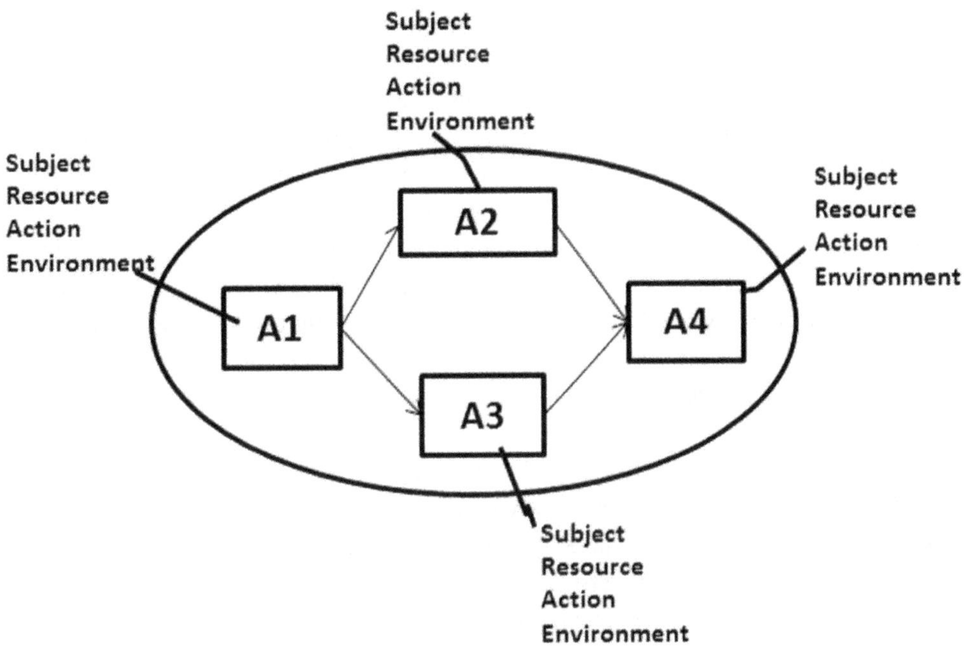

Methodology

The general idea of integrated modeling and analysis is as follows: (a) specify workflow activities in terms of SARE elements, (b) specify ABAC policies, (c) cross-examine the workflow activities and ABAC policies to identify discrepancy, (d) if there is no discrepancy, then terminate, otherwise go back to (a) if the discrepancy is about the workflow activities, or go back to (b) if the discrepancy is about the ABAC policies. In the following, we focus on the cross-examination of workflow activities and ABAC policies, as illustrated in Figure 4.

Step 1: The given workflow may include many activities (A1, A2, A3…). Each activity has to be individually identified from the given workflow as (A1), (A2), and (A3) ….

Step 2: From the individual activity that has been identified from the workflow (say A1), subject resource action and environment (SARE) attributes have to be identified, i.e. each activity (A1) has to be broken down into SARE (subject action resource and environment) elements (Figure 4's break the activity in terms of SARE).

Step 3: ABAC policies will be written targeting the Subject and/or Resource elements of the SARE attributes. An ABAC policy is represented by the target which the policy is intended to cover. It is seen in Figure 4 where P1 is represented by R1, where R1 is the resource1 targeting any workflow activity which involves the resource1. All the workflow activities that involves resource1 (R1) will be covered by this policy. Therefore, in this step, the target element from the policy is extracted and used to represent the policy to match with the respective attribute in the workflow activity.

Step 4: Once the workflow activities are broken into SARE elements, and the targets are extracted from the Policies, each of the 'subject and resource' attributes of the workflow activity are cross examined across the available ABAC policies that are targeting the respective subject and/or resource attributes.

Step 5: It is important to identify all the policies that can be applied on an activity. Once the policies are applied on the activity of the workflow, record each of those policies per workflow activity into a table (Table 1). Identify all of the policies that are being applied on each of the activity of the workflow and develop a table (Policies applicable on each activity of the workflow: Table 1).

Step 6: Once the policies are applied on the activity of the workflow, identify all of the policies that are not being used on the workflow (Policies that are not being used on the workflow: Table 2).

Implementing the Approach

Figure 4 represents the integrated model of the workflow and ABAC policies. It is evident from the Figure 4 that the 'workflow' denotes a workflow with four activities: A1, A2, A3, and A4. Each of these activities has 'subject, resource, action, and environment attributes'. Once there is the workflow, each of the activities of the workflow is extracted from the workflow as shown under the 'Identify each activity from workflow' task in Figure 4 ({A1}, {A2}, {A3}, and {A4}). Following this, break each of these activities into the subject, action, resource, and environment elements (SARE).

{A1} => {S1, A, R1, E}; {A2} => {S1, A, R1, E}; {A3} => {S2, A, R2, E}; and {A4} => {S3, A, R3, E}

Figure 4. Model to integrate workflow and ABAC policies

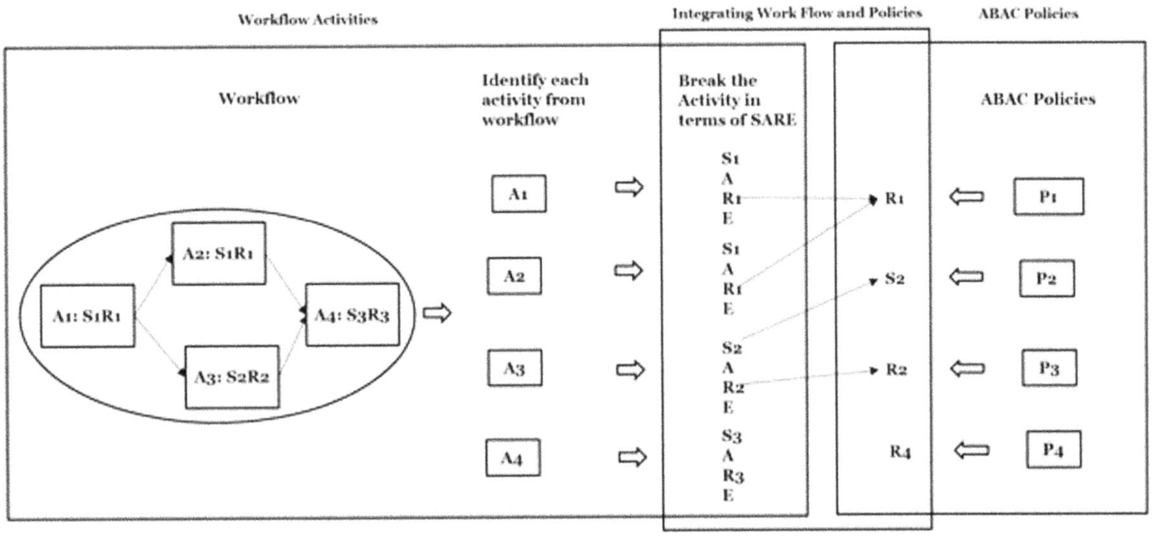

Similarly, from the given ABAC policies {P1, P2, P3, and P4}, identify individual policies. Each of these policies will further include multiple rules which are written targeting either a subject or a Resource. Based on the target, each of these policies may be targeted to either subject or resource. Therefore, each of these policies can be shown as under 'ABAC Policies' in Figure 4, P1=>R1, P2=>S2, P3=>R2, P4=>R4. Once the subject and resource elements are found from the workflow activities, the policies with respective subject or resource targets must be imposed on that particular activity as shown below.

As {A1} has subject S1 and Resource R1, any of the policies that target Subject S1 or Resource R1 can be imposed. From the given policies, only P1 is applicable. This case is a special example where there is no policy specified on subject S1, and therefore this activity of the workflow is **incompletely covered (partial)** by the access control policy. It is the same case with A2.

Whereas {A3} has a subject S2 and Resource R2, and therefore, policies P2 and P3 can be applied on the activity A2 showing that A2 is completely covered.

Coming to the activity {A4}, it has subject S3 and Resource R3, but there is no policy targeting either subject S3 or Resource R3. Therefore, this activity is not at all covered. Similarly, Policy P4 is targeting resource R4, which has no occurrence in the workflow, resulting in no use of this policy. The outputs from the current model are shown in the below Tables 1 and 2. Based on these outputs, the workflow developers and access control policy administrators can make the necessary changes to the respective workflows and policies.

Expected Results of the Integration Model

Based on these outputs from Tables 1 and 2, it is evident that (i) Activities A1 and A2 are each covered by one Policy P1, whereas Activity A3 is covered by two policies P2 and P3, (ii) The workflow administrators that the 'IOS workflow activity A4 is not being covered by any ABAC policy and therefore it is recommended to re-evaluate the activity A4, (iii) the Policy P4 is not covering any workflow activity and therefore it needs re-evaluation, (iv) in re-evaluation, policy administrators may re-evaluate the un-

Table 1. Policies applicable on each activity of the workflow

Activity Name	Policy applicable (Yes/ N0/ Partial)?	If applicable, Policy Name
A1	Partial	P1
A2	Partial	P1
A3	Yes	P2, P3
A4	No	-

Table 2. Policies in use (Y/N)

Policy	Policy in use (Y/N)?
P1	Y
P2	Y
P3	Y
P4	N

covered workflow activity and the policies that are not in use, and based on the need, they may suggest the organizations to add new SARE elements using which the administrators may develop new policies or workflow activities.

Demonstrating the Methodology in a Healthcare Scenario

Manipal hospital is located in Bangalore, India with 54 bed count and can accommodate up to 91 beds when fully equipped. It is located in the center of the city. The hospital has six departments: administration department, inpatient/outpatient department, pharmacy department, laboratory department, emergency department, and surgical ward. The hospital accommodates both inpatients and outpatients. The pharmacy department provides medications for both the inpatients and outpatients. The scientific staff of the hospital include: front desk specialists, doctors, nurse specialists, lab specialists, pharmacists, and surgical specialists. This hospital has recently implemented and mandated to use electronic health records across the hospital. The main parts of the electronic health records may include: administrative record, clinical record, pharmacist record, patient record, and surgical record. Administrative record of the EHR mainly includes patient demographic information (such as age, sex, first and last names, email addresses, physical addresses, etc.), date of admission and discharge, patient registration information, etc. This administrative record is restricted to be accessed only by the front desk personnel, nurse specialists and doctors. The clinical record stores the health related information of the patient. The clinical record may include detailed information of pathology reports, blood reports, ENT reports, doctor notes, nurse notes, prescriptions, etc. The pharmacist record includes prescription ids, patient ids, physician ids, and pharmacist notes. The surgical record of the EHR includes the surgical information, images (like Xrays, etc.), surgery specialist, and patient information. The subject, action, resource, and environment (SARE) attributes are provided by the hospital and are discussed below.

Subject attributes may include: department id (which includes an administration department, pharmacy department, emergency department, etc.); specialty id (which includes doctors, nurses, pharmacists, etc.); user id (which includes patient ids, doctor ids, nurse ids, etc.). Action attributes may include: read, write, update, delete, fill, validate, approve, reject, etc.; resource attributes include: electronic health record, patient health record, pharmacist record, clinical record, administrative record, surgical record, etc.; environment attributes include: ip addresses (92.92.1.1, 93.93.1.1, etc.), inpatient ward, outpatient ward, laboratory, surgery ward, doctor office, etc. Each of the departments of the hospital is assigned with different IP address as mentioned below: for hospital administration department: 92.92.1.1; for inpatient and outpatient wards, doctors' offices, and nurse quarters, the IP range is from 91.91.1.1 to 91.91.1.5; the internet protocol address for pharmacy department is 93.93.1.1, and for laboratory department is 94.94.1.1, for emergency department is 95.95.1.1, and for surgical ward is 91.91.1.6.

This case study contains multiple workflows which are developed for various causes. A basic scenario in a hospital starts when a patient walks in for an appointment with the doctor (Figure 5). This workflow mainly involves five workflow activities. Subjects involved in this workflow are patient and front desk person (FDP). FDP uses a system which has been configured for the IP address 92.92.1.1 and the FDP is allowed only to use this system from this IP address. The FDP cannot access any other systems configured with other IP addresses. Also the FDP can only access administrative record but not any other clinical information of the patient's electronic health record. When a patient walks in, the front desk person (FDP) asks the patient for his/her demographic information and tries to retrieve the patient information, if the patient is coming in for the first time, the FDP will request the patient to fill in the registration form and FDP validates the form, and thereby registers the patient into the hospital system followed by scheduling an appointment with a doctor.

This particular scenario can be considered as an example for separation of duties (SOD) and also binding of duties (BOD). There are mainly two roles: patient and FDP. A patient will check for an appointment with the FDP. FDP will check if the patient is valid, and then checks for doctor's schedule, and schedules an appointment. For this example, separation of duties applies between patient and receptionist. Main assumptions for a given scenario of patient's appointment with doctor to be static SOD are: (i) receptionist cannot be the patient; (ii) patient himself/herself cannot act as receptionist. If a receptionist is a patient, the receptionist cannot perform tasks checking the validity of the patient, checking for doctor's schedule and scheduling an appointment. Only another receptionist can perform those tasks.

As shown in the Figure 6, subject attributes to activity allocation can be seen, where multiple users with usernames (such as Tresa, Mary, etc) are allocated to subject attributes (role) and are thereby connected to their respective workflow activities.

As shown in the Figure 6, it is evident that activities 'FDP requests for patient demographic information...' and 'Patient fills the patient registration form...' cannot be completed by the same subject, accommodating separation of duty constraint. Similarly, activity 'FDP validates patient info in the admin record…' and activity 'FDP schedules appointment time with doctor…' should be done by the same subject, accommodating binding of duties constraint.

Once the patient has an appointment with the doctor, the workflow in Figure 5will begin. Activities of the workflow given in Figure 5 are discussed in detail. This particular scenario begins when a patient has an appointment with a practitioner and the practitioner recommends a diagnostic procedure.

This workflow starts with (activity A1) identifying the requirements for the diagnostic procedures to be performed (e.g. tests to evaluate a patient's health). Here the doctor will identify the tests and treatments for the patient from ip address 91.91.1.1-91.91.1.5;

Once the diagnostic procedures are identified, the recommended diagnostic procedures will be validated and performed in accordance with the Medicaid/Medicare regulations. This activity (A2) involves conducting the procedure validation to check for appropriate diagnosis in comparison with the Medicaid/Medicare regulations by another practitioner2 from 91.91.1.1-91.91.1.5. After that, if the procedure validation is correct and performed, the workflow will be carried on to Activity 4, otherwise diagnostic procedures will be reviewed and will be recommended to re-assess by the practitioner1 based on the Medicaid/Medicare regulations;

Figure 5. Patient walks in for an appointment

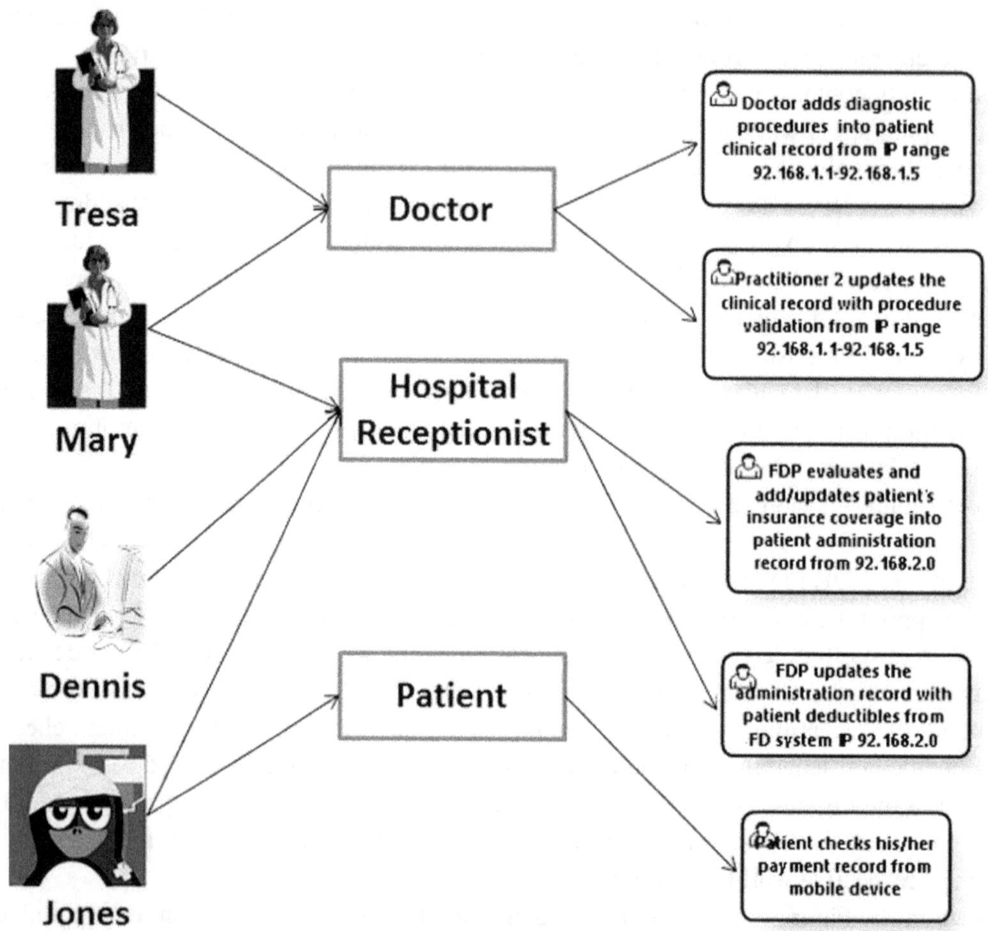

Then the patient's insurance will be evaluated by the front desk person of the hospital staff (e.g. by a receptionist) (A3) from ip address 92.92.1.1. Based on the patient's information, his/her insurance will be evaluated to verify whether his/her current insurance policy would cover that particular test (for example, an eye or a dental exam). If the insurance covers that particular test, workflow will move on to the next activity (A4). If the insurance will not cover the test, the patient may go back and check for a secondary insurance policy which will cover that test;

Activity 4 (A4) is where the financial administrator will calculate the patient's deductibles, once the patient's insurance is validated. This includes the percentage of the total bill that the insurance company would bear (e.g. 85%-15% deductible) vs the amount the patient is liable to pay.

Activity 5 (A5) is where the patient will access his/her payment record. The computed quote is available in the payment record and the patient will access it through a mobile device.

Figure 6. Subject attributes to resource allocation

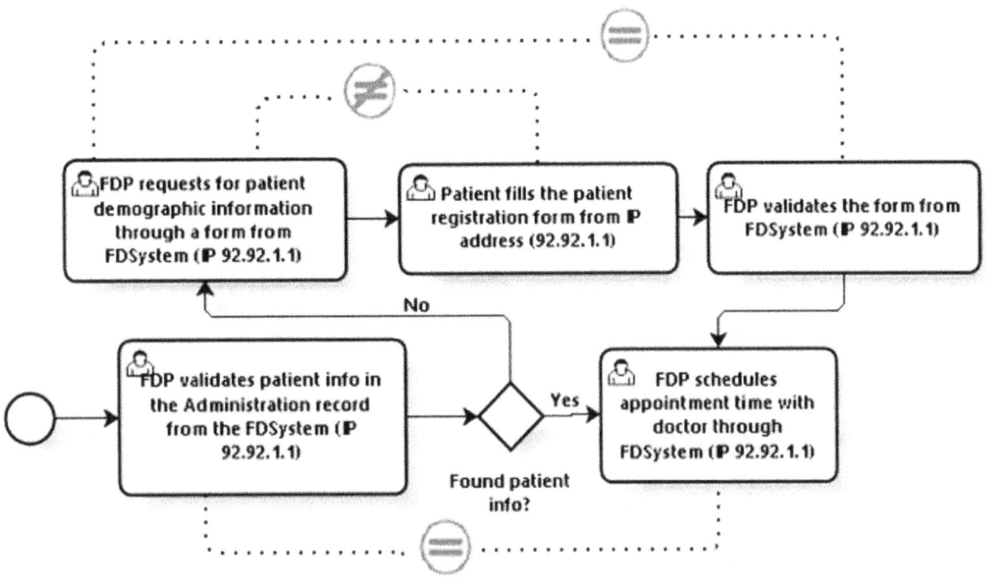

Attribute based Access Control Policies

The following is a subset of the access control rules in the case study: Some of the ABAC policies for the proposed case study may include:

PPrac: Any user with the position Practitioner/SupervisorPractitioner and an employee of the Organization, and are assigned to the patient, can read/write a Patient record from 91.91.1.1-91.91.1.5

SARE: Target is Subject: Practitioner, Resource: Patient Record, Action: read/write, Environment: 91.91.1.1-91.91.1.5

PN: A Nurse who is working under a practitioner can access patient record from internet network (e.g., IP range: 91.91.1.1-91.91.1.5)

SARE: Target is Subject: Nurse, Resource: patient record, Action: access, Environment: 91.91.1.1-91.91.1.5.

PFDP: Any user with Position: FrontDeskPerson from Department Front Desk with UserID Receptionist can 'access' the 'insurance information' of a patient and thereby 'validate' the Insurance of a patient and add/update it to the payment record, from 92.92.1.1.

SARE: Target is Subject: FrontDeskPerson, Resource: Payment Record, Action: Add/Update, Environment: 92.92.1.1

PPR: Patient Record cannot be accessed by any user with Position: FrontDeskPerson from the IP 92.92.1.1.

If tried to access, email to the Supervisor 'FrontdeskPerson with name X has tried to access Clinical Record X from ip address 92.92.1.1.

SARE: Target is Resource: 'Patient Record', Subject: FrontdeskPerson, action: access, Environment: 92.92.1.1.

PPayR1: Any user with Designation: Patient whose age is greater than 16 can read his/her own Payment Record from internal network or from his/her mobile device at any time.

SARE: Target is Resource: Payment Record, Subject: Patient, Action: read, Environment: Hospital's internal network or from his/her mobile device

PPayR2: Any user with Designation: guardian or parent can read Payment Record of a Patient whose age is less than 16 from hospital's internal network or from his/her mobile device.

SARE: Target is Resource: Payment Record, Subject: Gaurdian/Parent, Action: read, Environment: hospital's internal network or from his/her mobile device.

PIN1: Practitioner/Nurse/SupervisorPractitioner can only read/write patient record from 91.91.1.1-91.91.1.5.

SARE: Target is Subject: Practitioner or Nurse or SupervisorPractitioner, Resource: Patient Record, Action: read/write, Environment: 91.91.1.1-91.91.1.5

PFDD1: Only FDPerson can be logged into 'FDDesktop', and read PatientInsuranceInformation.

SARE: Target is Subject: FDPerson; Resource: Patient Insurance Information, Action: login, Environment: 92.92.1.1;

WSO2

WSO2 identity server is an open source application, which hosts a web service and a web application. It offers a user interface with multiple features where a user can log into the system and create, edit, read, or delete an access control policy. A user can login as an administrator to create and manage access control policies which can be tested in another user interface in which the user can send a request in terms of SARE attributes. For example, if a practitioner tries to access a patient health record, the practitioner's credentials are validated against the access control policy file which is located on a XACML engine in the identity server, and after validation the engine will permit/deny the user's request. A detailed demonstration of the WSO2 identity server with an example is discussed below.

Demonstrating the Case Study using WSO2

The process of validation of policies on workflow activities is shown in the above Figure 7. To validate the model, we have used case study analysis in which we've used Business Process Management Notation (BPMN) to develop the workflow and WSO2 Identity Server to administer the ABAC policies. The steps involved in applying these two for our integrated model are discussed below: ABAC policies written in plain English are entered into the WSO2 Identity server's Policy Administration Point (PAP) through their admin interface, and workflow is developed using BPMN. Once we have policies in WSO2 Identity Server and the workflow, each of the workflow activities is individually identified. Each of the identified workflow activities are extracted from the workflow and the SARE elements are derived from each activity. A request is formulated from the workflow activity's SARE elements, and that request is sent to the WSO2 Identity server's Policy Decision Point. Once the request is sent, WSO2 Identity server will evaluate the request. Based on the policies specification, the server will generate a response containing either 'permit' or 'denied' or 'indeterminate'.

Figure 7. Demonstrating the approach using WSO2

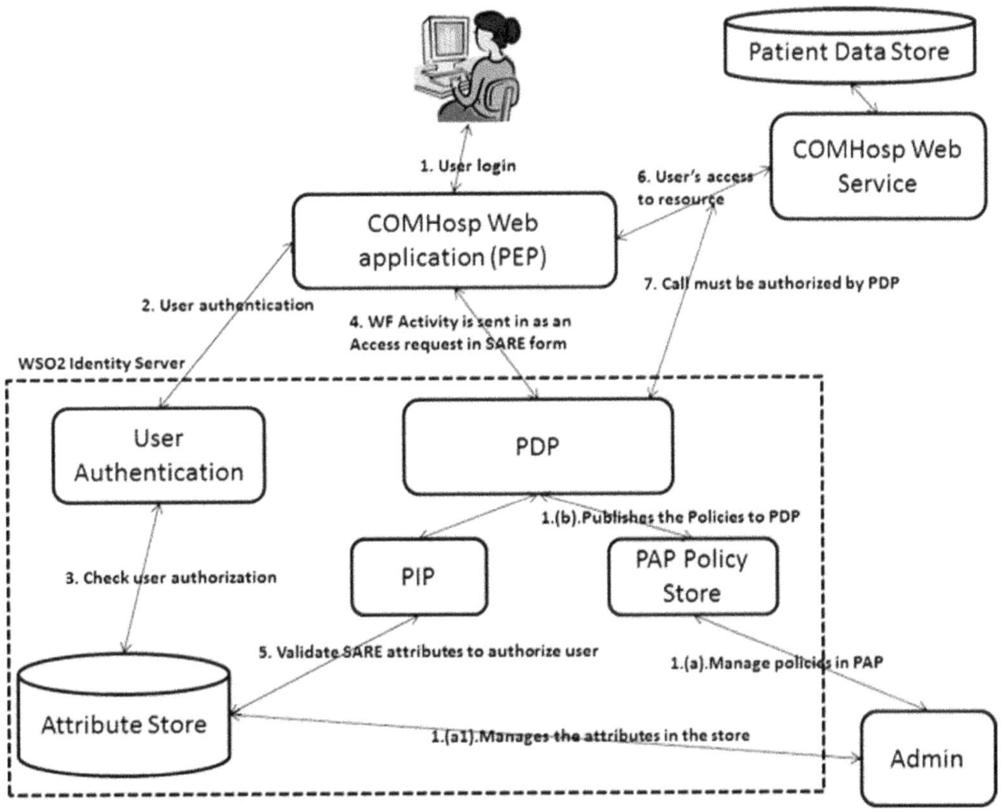

- A 'permit' response will denote that the intended actions by the subject under certain environmental conditions are allowed.
- A 'deny' response will denote that the intended actions by the subject under certain environmental conditions are not allowed.
- An 'indeterminate' response will denote that the activity is not fully covered by the policies defined.

To accommodate complex ABAC policies, more coding is required to modify and accommodate more complex WSO2 features. With some coding into WSO2, it is possible to identify which policies are being enforced on the request (workflow activity).

WSO2 in Action

Here, we'll demonstrate the proposed research methodology using WSO2 Identity server. If we consider activity A1: A Practitioner adds diagnostic procedure into EHR from hospital's internal network, we send this as a request through WSO2 Identity server (in Figure 8). Once the request is evaluated, we can see the result 'permit' in the below Figure 9.

Figure 8. PPrac Policy in WSO2

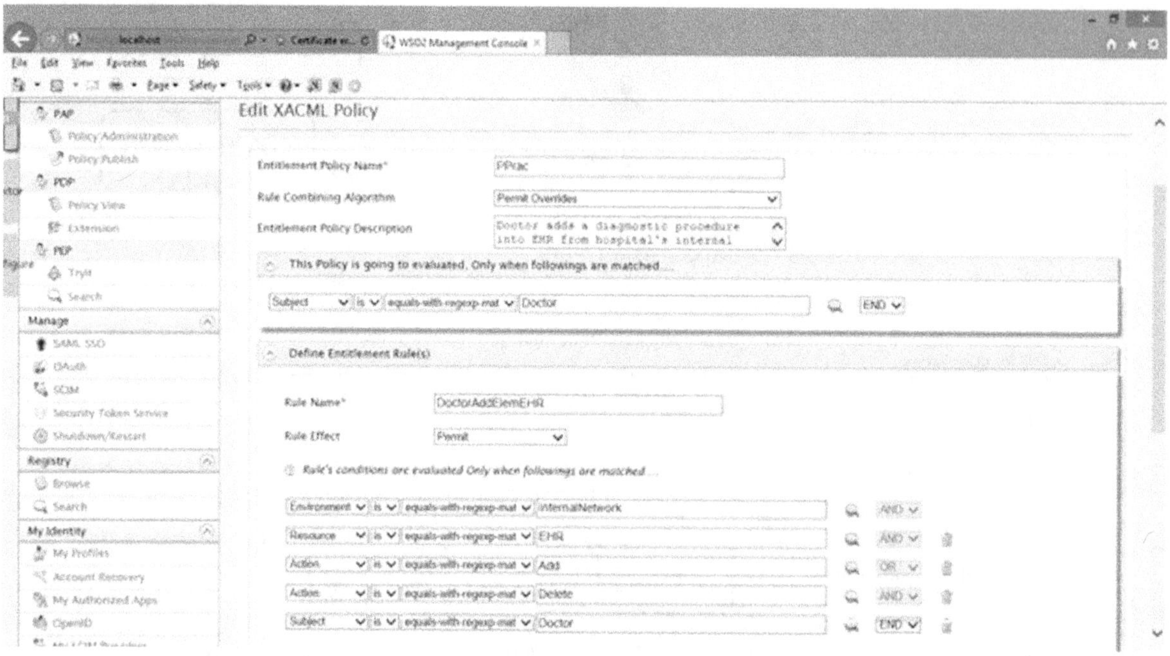

Figure 9. Policy PPrac in action

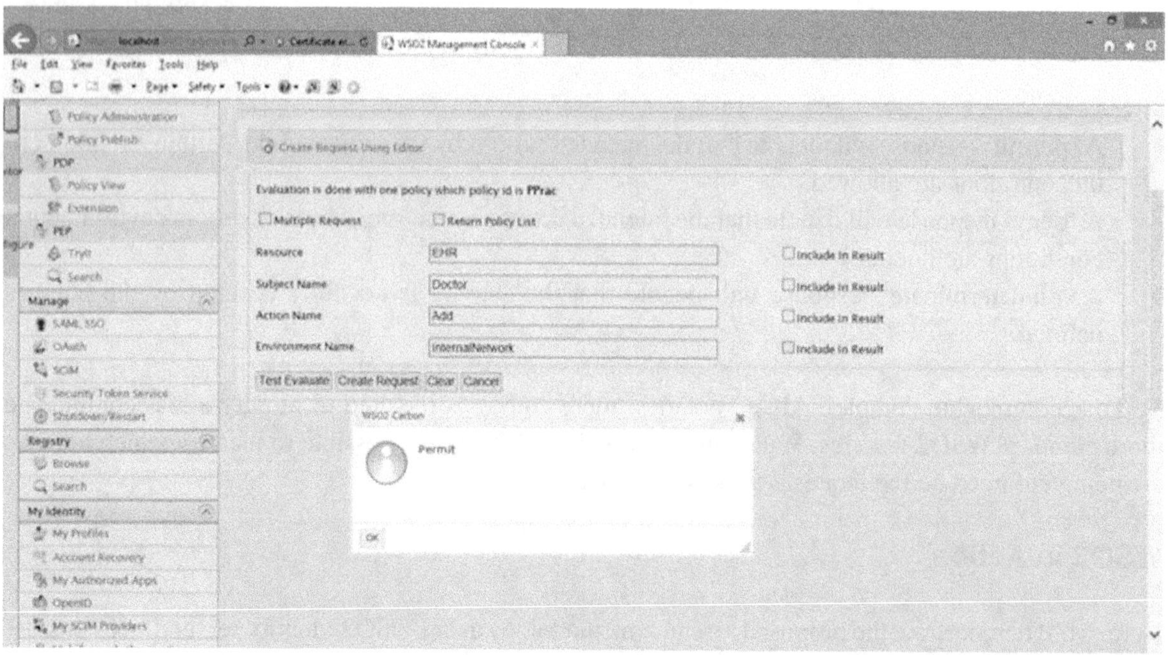

Testing Results

All of the available ABAC policies are: PPrac, PPR, PFDP, PPayR1, PPayR2, and PN. The activity analysis helps in understanding that not all of the policies are being used across the activities of the workflow, and can be seen in Table 4. The policies (y) that are not being used at least once include: PN. The policies that are applicable on each activity of the workflow can be found in Table 3 and the policies that are being used (not used) on the workflow activities can be found in Table 4.

GUIDELINES FOR HOSPITALS TO IMPLEMENT THE APPROACH

Purpose

This guide contains the necessary specifications for the integration of workflows and access control policies in a healthcare setting. An integrated methodology will allow efficient and accurate specification and modification of access control policies and workflow activities while reducing the burden on dealing with access control and workflow activities separately. This guide defines how healthcare organizations can define attribute based access control policies; define the implementation of XACML through WSO2; defining and creating a policy administration point; defining the method to extract workflow activities from workflows.

Audience

The intended audiences for this guide are hospital personnel who intend to improve their current access control mechanisms by making environment element their organizational priority. This guide helps in integrating workflow activities and ABAC policies through WSO2 Identity server.

Table 3. Policies applicable on each activity of the workflow

Activity Name	Policy applicable (Yes/ NO/ Partial)?	If applicable, Policy Name
A1	Yes	PPrac, PPR, PIN1
A2	Yes	PPrac, PPR, PIN1
A3	Yes	PFDP, PPayR1, PPayR2, PFDD1
A4	Partial	PPayR1, PPayR2, PFDD1
A5	Partial	PPayR1, PPayR2

Table 4. Policies that are being used (or not used) on the workflow activities

Policy	Policy in use (Y/N)?
PPrac	Y
PPR	Y
PFDP	Y
PN	N
PPayR1	Y
PPayR2	Y
PIN1	Y
PFDD1	Y

Steps to Implement the Proposed Approach

Assess Current Practice

Some of the elements to assess current practice at a healthcare facility may include: (a) performing an analysis on both workflows and access control policies in the organization; (b) performing an analysis on current type of access control mechanism (c) validating the clinical workflows to check if they are developed based on SARE elements; (d) are access control policies and workflow activities using same SARE elements; (e) does the organization considers environment element as a crucial element.

Setting the Goals

After assessing the current practice, healthcare organization should set clear goals. To implement the proposed methodology, organization is recommended to set and pursue 'specific' 'measurable' 'attainable' 'relevant' and 'time bound' (SMART) goals (Robert, 2005). The healthcare organization is recommended to make the 'environment' element an organizational priority. Some of the goals to be set by the healthcare organization include: (a) identifying and developing SARE elements across the organization, (b) developing workflow activities in terms of SARE elements, (c) developing ABAC policies in terms of SARE elements, (d) developing policy to use same SARE elements across the development teams, (e) making the environment element an organizational priority, (f) providing training and support to the workflow and policy developer team.

Planning the Process

Once the goals are identified, the organizational executive team should develop a plan to implement the methodology and should identify the necessary steps to analyze the process of implementation.

Forming an Expert Team to Identify SARE Elements Which Can Be Used Across the Workflow Development Team and Access Control Developing Team

Healthcare organization should identify an expert team to analyze current working process and identify the required SARE attributes so that the same SARE attributes can be used across the teams that develop workflows and access control policies. The purpose of this team is to define the SARE elements to be used commonly by both workflow and the ABAC policies. This team is recommended to have regular meetings to review and add/modify/delete the existing SARE attributes.

Creating a Policy Statement for SARE Elements Usage Across the Organization

To follow uniform standards of data usage across various electronic platforms, healthcare organization should make a policy statement about SARE elements across the organizational development teams. The organization should also make the policy statement available to the development teams and should work on making the teams to understand the statement.

Training on Developing Workflow Activities in Terms of SARE Elements

Proper training to the workflow developers on how to develop workflow activities in terms of SARE elements should be given. It is an important task to develop workflow activities in terms of SARE elements as these are the elements which would help in integrating the workflow activities with the ABAC policies.

Plan to Implement ABAC through WSO2 Identity Server

As WSO2 identity server is an open source application and accommodates healthcare requirements, WSO2 identity server has been used to implement the approach in this research. As the WSO2 identity server is an open source application and with proper coding knowledge, it can be easily modified based on the organization's requirement. It is recommended by the author to the organization to plan to implement ABAC policies through WSO2 identity server.

Employing an ABAC Policy and WSO2 Identity Server Expert

To implement and develop ABAC policies through WSO2, the developer team should have sufficient knowledge about the concept, which requires having an ABAC policy and WSO2 Identity server expert on team. ABAC policies should be developed from the SARE elements recognized by the expert team. The policy expert can provide required support and guidance to the policy developing team.

Training on ABAC and WSO2 Identity Server

In order to implement ABAC through WSO2 Identity server, the team should have proper training about ABAC concepts, how to implement WSO2, how WSO2 works, how to write ABAC policies in WSO2, how to validate requests through WSO2, and also how to edit the WSO2 identity server.

Summary

This research addresses crucial problem for future healthcare organizations which accommodate environment into workflow activities and access control policies; we have addressed a crucial objective: integrating the workflows and access control policies; and our integrated methodology can identify workflow activities that are not being protected by access control policies. They can further be improved by modifying the workflow activities and access control policies through integrating workflow activities and attribute based access control policies using SARE (Subject, Action, Resource, and environment) elements.

Our main contributions include: (i) proposing 'environment' as a crucial element in a workflow activity along with Subject, Action, and Resource, (ii) a methodology to integrate workflow activities and access control policies, using this methodology to address below questions: (a) Whether there are any workflow activities that are not covered by the access control policies, (b) Whether there are any unused access control policies, (c) How many policies are covering each activity, and (d) Whether the workflow activities and the access control policies need to be modified or refined, (e) Demonstrating the methodology with WSO2 Identity Server; (iv) guidelines for healthcare organizations to implement the approach.

As a part of our future work we have plans to work on: (i) extend the case study to perform in-depth testing and analysis with multiple healthcare scenarios, (ii) modifications to WSO2 identity server are needed to accommodate extended policy sets, (iii) modifications to WSO2 are needed to view the policies that are effecting a workflow activity, (iv) identify any policy related conflict issues, (v) perform in-depth analysis of the integrated methodology.

REFERENCES

Akinyele, J. A., Pagano, M. W., Green, M. D., Lehmann, C. U., Peterson, Z. N. J., & Rubin, A. D. (2011). Securing electronic medical records using attribute-based encryption on mobile devices. *Proceedings of the 1st ACM Workshop on Security and Privacy in Smartphones and Mobile Devices SPSM '11* (pp. 75–86). 10.1145/2046614.2046628

Alhaqbani, B., & Fidge, C. (2007). Access control requirements for processing electronic health records. *Proceedings of the 2007 International Conference on Business Process Management BPM'07* (pp. 371–382). doi:10.1007/978-3-540-78238-4_38

Basin, D., Burri, S. J., & Karjoth, G. (2011). Obstruction-free authorization enforcement: Aligning security with business objectives. *Proceedings of the IEEE Computer Security Foundations Symposium* (pp. 99–113).

Bertino, E., Ferrari, E., & Atluri, V. (1999). The specification and enforcement of authorization constraints in workflow management systems. *ACM Transactions on Information and System Security*, *2*(1), 65–104. doi:10.1145/300830.300837

Campbell, E. M., Sittig, D. F., Ash, J. S., Guappone, K. P., & Dykstra, R. H. (2006). Types of unintended consequences related to computerized provider order entry. *Journal of the American Medical Informatics Association*, *13*(5), 547–556. doi:10.1197/jamia.M2042 PMID:16799128

Chaari, S., Biennier, F., Ben Amar, C., & Favrel, J. (2004). An authorization and access control model for workflow. *Proceedings of the First International Symposium on Control, Communications and Signal Processing*. 10.1109/ISCCSP.2004.1296239

Cole, K. (2002). HIPAA Compliance: Role Based Access Control. *Global Information Assurance Certification Paper - SANS Institute*.

Cole, R., Purao, S., Rossi, M., & Sein, M. K. (2005). Being proactive: where action research meets design research. *Proceedings of the TwentySixth International Conference on Information Systems* (pp. 1–21). Association for Information Systems.

Eekels, J., & Roozenburg, N. F. M. (1991). A methodological comparison of the structures of scientific research and engineering design: Their similarities and differences. *Design Studies*, *12*(4), 197–203. doi:10.1016/0142-694X(91)90031-Q

Ferraiolo, D. F., Sandhu, R., Gavrila, S., Kuhn, D. R., & Chandramouli, R. (2001). Proposed NIST Standard for RBAC. *ACM Transactions on Information and System Security*, *4*(3). doi:10.1145/501978.501980

Ferreira, A., Cruz-Correia, R., Antunes, L., & Chadwick, D. (2007). Access control: How can it improve patients' healthcare? *Studies in Health Technology and Informatics*, *127*, 65–76. PMID:17901600

Giaglis, G. M. (2001). A taxonomy of business process modeling and information systems modeling techniques. *International Journal of Flexible Manufacturing Systems*, *13*(2), 209–228. doi:10.1023/A:1011139719773

Hevner, A. R., March, S. T., Park, J., & Ram, S. (2004). Design Science in Information Systems Research. *Management Information Systems Quarterly*, *28*(1), 75–105. doi:10.2307/249422

HHS.Gov. (n. d.). Health Information Privacy - HIPAA Privacy Rule., U.S. Department of Health & Human Services, HHS.gov (2003).

Hu, V. C., Scarfone, K., & Kuhn, R. (2013). *NIST Special Publication 800-162 DRAFT - FINAL Guide to Attribute Based Access Control (ABAC) Definition and Considerations NIST Special Publication 800-162 DRAFT - FINAL Guide to Attribute Based Access Control (ABAC)*. Definition and Considerations.

Identifier, D. (2005). eXtensible Access Control Markup Language. *Oasis Standard,* February, 23.

Janssen, C. (2014). *Security Breach*. TechoPedia.

Lakkaraju, S. (2013). *Context Aware Mobile Knowledge Management System in Healthcare* (pp. 1–10). MWAIS.

Lakkaraju, S., & Lakkaraju, S. K. (2011). Mobile Device Application in Healthcare. In Cases on Healthcare Information Technology for Patient Care Management (p. 22).

Lakkaraju, S., & Moran, M. (2011). *A Framework to Investigate the Role of Mobile Technology in the Healthcare Organizations*. MWAIS.

Lakkaraju, S., & Xu, D. (2014). Integrated Modeling and Analysis of Attribute based Access Control Policies and Workflows in Healthcare. *Proc. of the 1st International Conference on Trustworthy Systems and Their Applications TSA '14*, Taiwan (p. 8). 10.1109/TSA.2014.15

Le, X. H., Doll, T., Barbosu, M., Luque, A., & Wang, D. (2012). An enhancement of the Role-Based Access Control model to facilitate information access management in context of team collaboration and workflow. *Journal of Biomedical Informatics*, *45*(6), 1084–1107. doi:10.1016/j.jbi.2012.06.001 PMID:22732236

Leyva, C. (2014). Hitech Act Summary. *HIPAA Survival Guide*. Retrieved from http://www.hipaasurvivalguide.com/hitech-act-summary.php

Ligatti, J., Bauer, L., & Walker, D. (2005). Edit automata: Enforcement mechanisms for run-time security policies. *International Journal of Information Security*, *4*(1-2), 2–16. doi:10.100710207-004-0046-8

Lowe, G. (1996). Some new attacks upon security protocols. *Proceedings of the 9th IEEE Computer Security Foundations Workshop* (pp. 162–169). 10.1109/CSFW.1996.503701

Lu, Y., Zhang, L., & Sun, J. (2009). Task-activity based access control for process collaboration environments. *Computers in Industry*, *60*(6), 403–415. doi:10.1016/j.compind.2009.02.009

March, S. T., & Smith, G. F. (1995). Design and natural science research on information technology. *Decision Support Systems*, *15*(4), 251–266. doi:10.1016/0167-9236(94)00041-2

Peffers, K., Tuunanen, T., Rothenberger, M. A., & Chatterjee, S. (2007). A Design Science Research Methodology for Information Systems Research. *Journal of Management Information Systems*, *24*(3), 45–77. doi:10.2753/MIS0742-1222240302

Robert, B. (2005). Use S.M.A.R.T Goals to Launch Management by Objectives Plan. *TechRepublic*. Retrieved from http://www.techrepublic.com/article/use-smart-goals-to-launch-management-by-objectives-plan/

Roscoe, A. W. (2005). The Theory and Practice of Concurrency. *Theory into Practice*, *216*.

Russello, G., Dong, C. D. C., & Dulay, N. (2008). A Workflow-Based Access Control Framework for e-Health Applications. *Proceedings of the 22nd International Conference on Advanced Information Networking and Applications - Workshops (AINA Workshops '08)*. 10.1109/WAINA.2008.131

Sandhu, R. (1988). *Transaction control expressions for separation of duties*. Fourth Aerospace Computer Security Applications. doi:10.1109/ACSAC.1988.113349

Schneider, F. B. (2003). Enforceable security policies. *Proceedings of the Foundations of Intrusion Tolerant Systems '03*.

Siriwardena, P. (2013). Understanding HIPAA. *Facilelogin*. Retrieved from http://blog.facilelogin.com/2013/02/understanding-hipaa.html

Sittig, D. F., Krall, M., Kaalaas-Sittig, J., & Ash, J. S. (2005). Emotional Aspects of Computer-based Provider Order Entry: A Qualitative Study. *Journal of the American Medical Informatics Association*, *12*(5), 561–567. doi:10.1197/jamia.M1711 PMID:15905478

Spear, N., Malladi, S., & Lakkaraju, S. (2012). Analyzing Workflows in Business Processes for Obstructions Due to Authorization Policies. *Proceedings of the 45th Hawaii International Conference on System Sciences* (pp. 5340–5349). 10.1109/HICSS.2012.112

Tan, K., Crampton, J., & Gunter, C. A. (2004). The consistency of task-based authorization constraints in workflow. *Proceedings of the 17th IEEE Computer Security Foundations Workshop* '04.

United States Department of Defense DoD. (1985). Trusted Computer System Evaluation Criteria

Van Der Aalst, W.M.P. (1998). The application of petri nets to workflow management. *Journal of Circuits, Systems, and Computers*.

van der Aalst, W. M. P. (2004). Business process management: A personal view. *Business Process Management Journal*, *10*(2), 135–139. doi:10.1108/bpmj.2004.15710baa.001

Welch, J. (2014). Improving Clinical Workflow: An Example from the Emergency Department. *Health Catalyst*. Retrieved from https://www.healthcatalyst.com/improve-clinical-workflow-emergency-department

Wolter, C., Schaad, A., & Meinel, C. (2008). Task-based entailment constraints for basic workflow patterns. *Proceedings of the 13th ACM symposium on Access control models and technologies - SACMAT '08* (pp. 51–60). ACM Press. 10.1145/1377836.1377844

XiangPeng. Z., Cerone, A., & Krishnan, P. (2006). Verifying BPEL Workflows Under Authorization Constraints. *Proceedings of the 4th International Conference Business Process Management BPM* (pp. 439–444).

Xu, D., & Zhang, Y. (2014). Specification and Analysis of Attribute-Based Access Control Policies: An Overview. *Proceedings of the International Workshop on Information Assurance, in Conjunction with the 8th International Conference on Software Security and Reliability (SERE'14).* 10.1109/SERE-C.2014.21

Yuan, E., & Tong, J. (2005). Attributed based access control (ABAC) for Web services. *Proceedings of the IEEE International Conference on Web Services ICWS '05.* 10.1109/ICWS.2005.25

Zhang, G., & Liu, J. (2011). A Model of Workflow-oriented Attributed Based Access Control. *International Journal of Computer Network and Information Security, 1*(February), 47–53. doi:10.5815/ijcnis.2011.01.07

This research was previously published in the International Journal of Healthcare Information Systems and Informatics (IJHISI), 11(1); edited by Qiang (Shawn) Cheng and Joseph Tan; pages 1-20, copyright year 2016 by IGI Publishing (an imprint of IGI Global).

Chapter 15
Information Control, Transparency, and Social Media:
Implications for Corruption

Chandan Kumar Jha
Madden School of Business, Le Moyne College, USA

ABSTRACT

Although the research linking social media and corruption is still in infancy, it provides important insights. It has been shown that social media can prove to be an important tool in fighting corruption. At the same time, freedom on the net is under threat in many parts of the world with governments using a variety of methods, including designing vague and flexible security laws as well as employing technological means, to censor the content that can be shared and accessed by net users. This chapter discusses the implications that government control over information can have for the effects of social media on corruption. It suggests that freedom on the net and the anonymity of net users must be protected if the effects of social media on corruption are to be fully realized.

INTRODUCTION

One of the greatest advantages of the Internet is to disseminate information, and social media has played an instrumental role in facilitating the spread of information. The reason is simple: social media platforms cannot only be used to disseminate new, user-generated information but can also be used to spread the information that originally appeared elsewhere. A significant amount of the content shared on social media platforms originates elsewhere on the Internet and even off-Internet. People routinely share links to online news articles, blog posts, pictures, and audio and video clips from radios, televisions, and several Internet source as well as photos and audio and video clips recorded by themselves using mobile phones or other electronic devices, and even pages from printed books, leaflets, and newspapers. Social media, thus, enables individuals to share information in a quick and cheap manner that was never possible before, to an audience that was never so big and diverse, and in a way that no one could have imagined a decade or so ago!

DOI: 10.4018/978-1-7998-0417-8.ch015

Since the primary objective of social media is to facilitate the communication and interaction between users and allowing them to edit and share content, social media platforms are designed to facilitate the exchange of information, even when users are geographically separated (Tepper, 2003; Porter, 2008). Social media platforms are, thus, intended to be dialogue platforms as opposed to traditional media such as newspapers, radio, and television, which serves as a broadcast platform (Porter, 2008). The new information and communication technologies (ICTs), such as computer, Internet, mobile phones, social media platforms such as Facebook, Google Plus, and Twitter, and numerous applications that are used for communication have an important advantage over radio and television: While radio and television can be used for only one-way communication, the new ICTs allow for a two-way and even multi-way communication (Diamond, 2010). Many Internet users rely on social media platforms to communicate–sharing photos and videos, links to news and other stories, sharing their status updates–with their friends, family members, and a growing network of contacts (Madden, 2010). The popularity of and the reliance of Internet users on social media for communication have been increasing rapidly over time as reflected by the impressive growth in the number of social media users in recent years among both teens and adults in the United States (Madden, 2010; Lenhart, 2015). Worldwide, the number of Facebook users has increased massively in the last decade – from 1 million in 2004 to 1230 million by the end of 2013 (The Guardian, 2014). According to Statista, one of the world's leading statistics database, the total number of social media users increased by more than 230 percent in past 5 years – from under 1 billion in 2010 to 2.34 billion in 2015 (Statista, 2016). It is then not surprising that the exponential growth of social media users, not only in developed but also in developing and underdeveloped world, has drawn the attention of the academics. As a result, a significant body of research that evaluates whether social media (a form of the new ICT) can have causal effects on democratic, economic, and political outcomes[1] has emerged.

There are obvious advantages of such technologies that can facilitate and quicken the exchange of information. By allowing people to anonymously share their ideas and beliefs on multiple online platforms such as webpages, chat rooms, bulletin boards, blogs (Salbu, 2001), and, more recently social media websites, the ICTs augment the freedom of speech and the freedom of expression. The new ICTs enable the "citizens to report news, expose wrongdoing, express opinions, mobilize protest, monitor elections, scrutinize government, deepen participation, and expand the horizons of freedom" (Diamond, 2010). Therefore, in many cases, the governments, especially (but not only) autocratic regimes, may feel the need for controlling certain types of information such as those related to political and bureaucratic corruption, police brutality, and judicial failures. Countries such as China, Malaysia, and Iran have been censoring information related to corruption, human rights violations, and policy brutality by controlling or even owning the print and broadcast media (Freedom House, 2009a). For example, in Malaysia, the government had a clear dominance over print and broadcast media through direct ownership and monopoly practices (Freedom House, 2009b). The 2009 Freedom of the Press Report documents that all of the 11 dominant national daily newspapers were owned by either the ruling coalition or individuals closely associated with the government. The report further points out that the state-owned Radio Television Malaysia operated a large number of radio stations along with two television channels (providing the government substantial control over the diffusion of information).

Indeed, the new ICTs have been recognized to be playing an instrumental role in promoting transparency and accountability and acting as deterrents for human rights violations and the abuses of democratic rights of the citizens (Diamond, 2010). The advent of the Internet and, more recently, social media has expanded the audience to which information can be shared and therefore has made controlling the diffusion of information much more difficult (Jha & Sarangi, 2014). The Internet and social media not only make it possible for the information to flow very quickly to a large number of people but also enable grassroots organizing (Diamond, 2010). Consequently, the cases of human rights violations and corruption in many of these countries have started to come out to the public through blogs and social media sites, which often find places in international media (Freedom House, 2009a). The online media thus challenges the monopoly of the government over information. In several countries, *e.g.,* Malaysia, with a greater share of the population gaining access to the Internet and the use of online media has provided the public with the alternative sources of information and has resulted in the loss of government control over information (Freedom House, 2009b). Furthermore, social media, by allowing the transmission of messages through social networks increases the "shared awareness" where each member of a group understands the situation at hand and knows that everyone else is aware of the situation too (Shirky, 2011). Thus, social media plays a key role in facilitating the coordination among public with common agendas such as movements against corruption, human rights violations, and police brutality. Therefore, it has become even more important for autocratic (and democratic) regimes to censor the content that can threaten the power held by the rulers. Expectedly, then, not only autocratic but even democratic countries have placed restrictions on the exchange of information over the Internet directly or indirectly (Freedom House, 2015).

This chapter briefly reviews the literature on the effects of information technologies, with a focus on social media, on democratic and political outcomes, with an emphasis on corruption. The chapter goes on to discuss the recent attempts made by the governments around the world targeted to curtail the freedom on the net and discusses the implications that the government control over information can have on the effects of social media on corruption. Finally, based on the existing evidence, some policy conclusions are drawn and the avenues for further research are identified and discussed.

INFORMATION ACCESS, TRANSPARENCY, AND CORRUPTION

The availability and transparency of information can play an important role in reducing corruption for a variety of reasons. The first and foremost reason is the obvious fact that free and easy availability of information increases transparency making it more likely that any financial irregularities will be caught and, hence, increases the likelihood that both the bribe-taker and the bribe-giver will be caught (Salbu, 2001). As a result, the cost of committing corrupt practices rises discouraging the corrupt activities. The end result is a decline in corruption. The transparency of laws has long been recognized as one of the most important tools in the fight against corruption (Tanzi, 1998). It has also been argued that the lack of transparency acts as a deterrent for the honest and efficient people to be selected as public employees and undermines social norms and reduces trust (Kolstad & Wiig, 2009). While it is easy to imagine that with dishonest people entering government jobs, corruption is likely to rise; it has been found that corruption thrives in the presence of mistrust (Uslaner, 2005).

Furthermore, it has been suggested by the previous studies that a greater competition adversely affects corruption. Ades and Di Tella (1999), for instance, contend that a greater competition implies that firms enjoy little rents and hence smaller is the bribe that can be extracted from them by bureaucrats and politicians. Consistent with their argument, the authors find that corruption levels are higher in countries where firms extract larger rents. An easy access to information will reduce the scope of bribing by the firms in the same way: An easy access to and the transparency of information is likely to boost competition by increasing the applications for tenders for public contracts, which, in turn, will increase the bidding for these projects, leaving little room for bribing.

An enhanced access to information and a greater transparency through the use of online portals can also be utilized by the governments to raise awareness regarding different public projects and welfare schemes, which will reduce the scope of misappropriation by government officials. An online system that facilitates public's access to government programs and services reduces the discretion of public officials, increases the likelihood of exposure of wrongdoing and, therefore, makes the demand of bribes less likely (Bhatnagar, 2003; Lio, 2011). In addition to that, political corruption is likely to be adversely affected if the public has an easy and unhindered access to information regarding the corrupt activities of politicians. In democratic countries, the politicians are under pressure not to get involved in corrupt practices in order to ensure their re-election. There are instances when corruption has been an important issue in elections. In the 2014 Indian General Election, for example, corruption was the main election issue raised by the Bharatiya Janta Party-led National Democratic Alliance (NDA) that culminated in the historic defeat of the Indian National Congress-led United Progressive Alliance (UPA). It has widely been argued that the Indian population, fed up with the stories of all the financial scams involving the ministers of the incumbent UPA government, decided to vote against the incumbent government, which ultimately led to the grand defeat of the UPA and resulted in the lowest ever parliamentary seats secured by the INC since independence (Chakrabarty & Hazra, 2016). Corruption has also been an issue in the ongoing U.S. presidential elections 2016 (Zurcher, 2016). On the other hand, in autocratic regimes, the dictators would want to keep the frustrations of the public under the threshold such that the demand for democracy does not take the form of a revolution that succeeds in overthrowing the government as it happened in several middle-east countries such as Tunisia and Egypt. A greater access to information thus forces the ruling party to keep corruption in check not only by the bureaucrats but also by their own members. In China, for example, the famous crackdown on corruption by the president Xi Jinping convicted several leaders from his own communist party (The Atlantic, 2015)

Figure 1 shows the relationship between access to information (proxied by the Internet penetration, defined as the proportion of the population with Internet access) and the Control of Corruption Index (henceforth, CCI) across countries. The CCI is an index published by the World Bank that measures the extent of corruption across countries and is designed to capture the "perceptions of the extent to which public power is exercised for private gain, including both petty and grand forms of corruption, as well as "capture" of the state by elites and private interests" (Kaufmann et al., 2010)[2]. Note that the CCI takes values in the range of -2.5 to 2.5, with greater values indicating lower corruption. I have adjusted the scale of the CCI such that higher values of the index imply greater corruption. A strong, negative correlation is clearly visible in Figure 1, suggesting that corruption levels are lower in countries with greater access to information.

Quite possibly, however, the access to and the transparency of information alone may not be sufficient to have desirable effects on corruption. Consider, for example, that the government in a country provides information on the net and/or through newspapers or television regarding a welfare scheme that the poor are entitled to. In many developing countries, literacy rates are very low among the poor and they may not have the ability to access and process that information to understand and claim their rights. In several developing countries, such a situation may give rise to a group of individuals that demands a share of the benefits provided by the government. Usually, government officials encourage such groups and form a nexus in order to share part of the benefits. In countries like India, such nexuses are widespread in rural areas. The beneficiaries of several government schemes receive a mere fraction of the benefits that they are entitled to, yet these recipients are forced to sign acknowledging that they received the full amount. For example, the Public Distribution System (PDS) in India that is targeted to provide subsidized food

Figure 1. Internet penetration and corruption in 2012

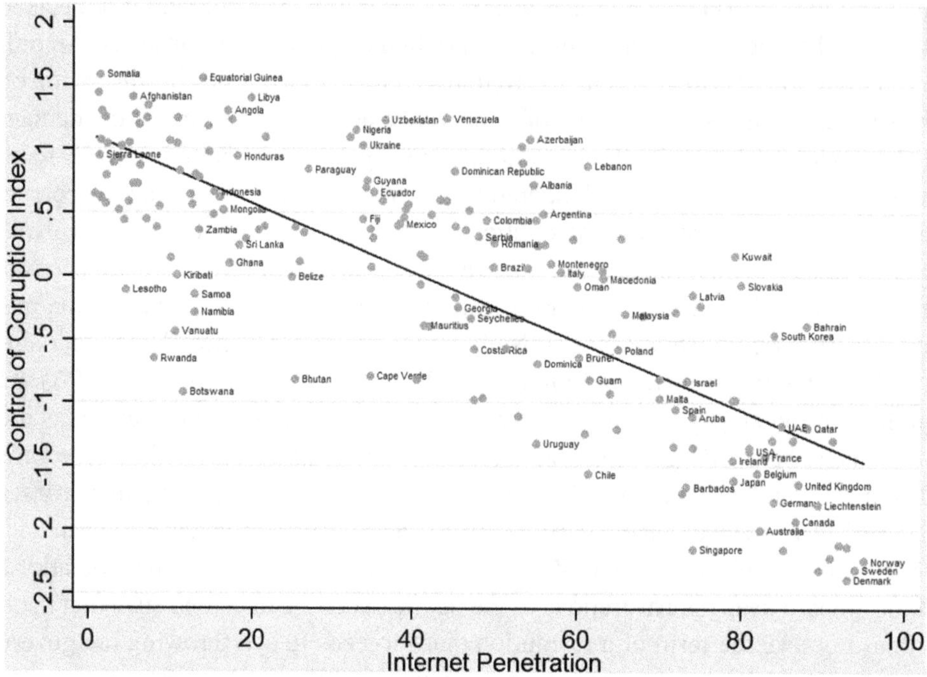

products to the poor is deeply mired in corruption. The complex procedures, even for simple tasks, are conducive to the flourishing of the middlemen and touts. The beneficiaries of the PDS, besides having to pay bribes for even getting a ration card, often do not get the quantity that they are entitled to (Kumari & Kumari, 2016). An increased access to information in such situations may even lead to an increase in corruption by increasing the number of beneficiaries.

Recently, some authors have raised this important issue contending that the transparency of information is not a sufficient condition for tackling government and bureaucratic corruption and have noted that the new ICTs have failed to show desirable effects on corruption in some countries for various reasons. These studies, *e.g.*, Bertot et al. (2010), have argued that the success of the ICTs depends on factors such as effective implementation, education, and the culture concerning the acceptance of the ICTs among the public. Furthermore, Kolstad and Wiig (2009) argue that transparency will have desirable effects on corruption only if the agents, whose access to information has been enhanced, have both the ability to process the information and the incentives to act on that information such that they can benefit from the newly available information. It is obvious from the above discussion that, along with providing the infrastructure that eases the access to information, implementing policies that raise awareness by increasing literacy rates (and other measures) is essential to realize the full potential of an increased access to and enhanced transparency of information on corruption.

TRADITIONAL MEDIA VS. ICT AND CORRUPTION

Although the traditional – print and broadcast – media has been serving the purpose of information dissemination, the advent of the modern ICTs has revolutionized the information industry. The modern ICTs are much more inclusive than the traditional media and have provided access to information to the marginalized sections of the society that previously faced many obstacles in the access to information and was deprived of consuming and acting on many relevant information and projects that were targeted towards their betterment. Thus, besides promoting transparency and accountability of governments and businesses, social media has played a crucial role in the inclusive social and economic development (United Nations, 2014).

One of the earliest studies investigating the link between access to information and corruption, DiRienzo et al. (2007), found that a greater access to information is associated with lower levels of corruption across countries. Authors use the digital access index (DAI) as a proxy for information access. The DAI is constructed on the basis of the number of users of fixed telephone, mobile phones, and the Internet, affordability of Internet access, knowledge to use these technologies as measured by literacy and school enrolment levels, and the quality of information and communication technology services. Since then there have been a number of studies that have investigated the impact of the ICTs, especially Internet penetration, on corruption. The impact of Internet penetration (defined as the proportion of the population with access to the Internet) on corruption has been explored more extensively than any other form of the ICT (Lio et al., 2011; Andersen et al., 2011; Elbahnasawy, 2014; Jha & Sarangi, 2014). It has been argued that the Internet can impact corruption by facilitating the exchange of information and promoting transparency. Note that these studies use various empirical techniques, including instrumental variables analysis (Jha & Sarangi, 2014; Andersen et al., 2011) and dynamic panel estimation (Lio et al., 2011; Elbahnasawy, 2014), to ascertain whether the relationship between Internet penetration and corruption is causal. Furthermore, these studies have controlled for a number of economic, political, institutional, and cultural factors that may potentially be correlated with Internet penetration and/or corruption to address the concerns that their results may be confounded due to the omission of factors that are potentially correlated with Internet penetration and/or corruption. Most of these studies, for example, control for the political rights enjoyed by the citizens of the country to ensure that the results are not driven by the omission of the institutional quality (see, for example, Jha & Sarangi, 2014, Elbahnasawy, 2014). In order to ensure that the results are not driven by the omission of cultural factors, studies often include the proportions of the population belonging to different religions in the empirical specification (Jha & Sarangi, 2014). Furthermore, almost all the studies control for per capita income in order to rule out the possibility that the results may be driven by economic disparities across countries. Finally, studies have also controlled for several other variables (such as education, press freedom, inflation, telecom infrastructure, urbanization) to account for heterogeneity across countries (Elbahnasawy, 2014; Jha & Sarangi, 2014; Lio et al., 2011).

One of the primary ways in which the Internet can be used to combat corruption is through the use of electronic-government (in short, e-government) services. E-government services can be used to provide public services online that eliminate or diminish the need for a direct interaction between public officials and the applicants and, hence, make the exchange of bribes more difficult or even impossible in certain cases. Furthermore, since online system is based on standardized rules and procedures, it reduces the discretion of civil servants and increases transparency (Lio et al., 2011; Bhatnagar, 2003). Bhatnagar (2003) discusses several case studies that underscore the importance of e-government for transparency and corruption. For instance, the Online Procedures Enhancement for Civil Applications (known as OPEN), adopted by Seoul Municipality in South Korea, allows for online checking of individual applications for municipal licenses. In a survey, it was found that OPEN has resulted in greater transparency and lower corruption. In India, the computerization of land records, under the *Bhoomi* (meaning land) project, was very effective in combating corruption because it reduced the discretion of public officials significantly. Elbahnasawy (2014) studies the effect of e-government on corruption using a dynamic panel data model. His results suggest that e-government has a causal, negative effect on corruption. Moreover, Banerjee et al. (2014) find evidence from a field experiment that e-governance reduces leakages of public funds.

Furthermore, the ICTs have been used by the governments and non-government organizations to design websites that allow people to share their bribery experiences anonymously. Sometimes, the statistics collected from such websites are used to gauge the extent of corruption in a region, which are then used to pressurize policymakers to take actions to constrain corruption. For instance, in India, "I Paid a Bribe" encourages people to report the details (nature, location, frequency, values) of any bribes they were forced to pay and uses the information "to argue for improving governance systems and procedures, tightening law enforcement and regulation and thereby reduce the scope for corruption in obtaining services from the government" ("I Paid a Bribe" 2016). As of September 23, 2016, 100,412 cases of bribes amounting 2873.19 crores Indian rupees (about USD 430.67 million) were reported in 1,071 cities across India. Following the success of this portal, similar websites now exist for many countries around the world and are underway for several others. Even the governments have used online portals to allow anonymous reporting of bribes. One such initiative has been taken by the Anti-Corruption Commission of the Kingdom of Bhutan in the form of a web-page that can be used to report corruption anonymously.[3]

SOCIAL MEDIA, DEMOCRACY, AND CORRUPTION: SOME RECENT CASES

On December 17, 2010, a young vegetable merchant set himself ablaze in front of a municipal building in Tunisia to protest against the corrupt system and the government. The fire that he set upon himself would not only burn him but in months and years to come it would result in the entire Tunisia and most part of the Arab world burning. Since then an extensive body of research has emerged trying to explain the factors that made large-scale protests seeking democracy in Tunisia possible, which would spread over other Arab countries. And, the most important factor that undoubtedly emerges is the presence and an extensive use of social media.

So how did the self-immolation of a street vendor turn into the large-scale protests across Tunisia that paved the way for democracy in the country? There were restrictions on the Internet in Tunisia, including on YouTube, at the time of the incident. However, Facebook was not under close watch by the authorities at the time allowing a blogger to share a video recorded using a mobile phone that captured the protest held by the public in front of Sidi Bouzid's city hall against the way vendors were treated.[4] Within days the video was posted on Facebook, protesters across the country took to the street demanding the prosecution of the corrupt officials. Howard et al. (2011) have analyzed the data collected from Facebook, Twitter, and YouTube. Their analysis underscores the importance of social media in overthrowing the dictator in Tunisia. The tech-savvy young population (median age in Tunisia is 30 years) was able to effectively use social media. Social media also facilitated the participation of women in political debates–41 percent of Facebook and 30 percent of Twitter users in Tunisia were women. The protesters used social media extensively for political conversation and to share ideas in favor of democracy. Social media thus played an important role in shaping the political debate regarding democracy and helped the protestors pressurize the government. Furthermore, social media was also used to connect with the outside world not only the foreign news channels were provided with the information regarding what was happening in the country but the protesters also attracted followers and got support from people around the world. The role of the Internet and social media in the Tunisian revolution is further confirmed in a study by (Bruer et al., 2015). The authors find that the digital elites used the Internet and social media to bypass the barriers that prevented the transmission of information and aggregated and shared the stories of government abuses and oppressions to the masses.

In the same year on June 8, another revolution began on Facebook, a popular social media website, when a Google marketing executive named Wael Ghonim came across the photo of a bloodied and disfigured face while browsing Facebook. The disfigured face belonged to a 28-year-old Khaled Said, who was killed by the Egyptian police. Ghonim created a Facebook page titled "Kullena Khaled Said" (translated as "We are all Khaled Said") that was joined by more than 250,000 people in the next three months (The New York Times, 2012). Ghonim also used Twitter to spread the information to English-speaking audience abroad. On January 25, 2011, thousands of protesters gathered on Tahrir Square demanding the President Hosni Mubarak to step down. Social media was again recognized to be playing a key role in the success of the revolution that culminated in the overthrow of the Egyptian president (Howard et al., 2011). Like Tunisia, Egypt also has a young, tech-savvy population and women actively participated in the democracy debate – the median age is 24, and 36 percent of the Facebook users and 33 percent of actively tweeting Egyptian were females (Howard et al., 2011). An Egyptian protester's statement further sheds light on the importance of social media in the revolution: "We use Facebook to schedule the protests, Twitter to coordinate, and YouTube to tell the world." (The Guardian, 2016).

Next year, in 2011, the anti-corruption movement in India was placed among the top 10 news stories of the year by Time (2011) magazine. The movement gained huge support from the masses that was frustrated by reading the cases of corruption in newspapers every day. The protesters took advantage of the extensive use of social media, especially by the youth of the country, to mobilize support for the anti-corruption movement. A Facebook page titled "India Against Corruption" was created that provided a platform to the protesters to share their activities. The page was liked by more than 1.37 million people as of September 24, 2016. Social media has been recognized to be the most important factor that facilitated the largest anti-corruption movement possible and led to the huge crowds appearing to demand the passage of anti-corruption bill famously known as "Jan Lokpal Bill" (Bong et al., 2012; Jha, 2014).

Social media was said to have played a role in overthrowing the Communist Party in Moldova in 2009. Social media sites such as Facebook and Twitter provided means that facilitated coordination among the people against the fraudulent elections and resulted in the massive protests in the country (Shirky, 2011). Some scholars (*e.g.*, Hale, 2013) have, however, argued that the role of social media was much-hyped and overestimated in the 2009 Moldovan political upheaval and the social media played a secondary role at best. There have been other instances when the dissents were not successful, even though social media was employed to disseminate information and organize demonstrations. For instance, the Green Movement in Iran, where activists used technological means to coordinate against the miscount of votes for Mir Hossein Mousavi, failed in June 2009 due to the violent crackdown (Shirky, 2011). Another notable failure was the "Red Shirt" protest that erupted in Thailand in March 2010, where tech-savvy protesters used social media platforms such as Facebook and Twitter to share the information regarding protests and demonstrations throughout the country (Newley, 2011). A military crackdown on the protesters resulted in at least 90 deaths and more than 2,000 injuries. Yet, the charges against the Prime Minister Abhisit Vejjajiva, along with his deputy Suthep Thaugsuban and former army chief General Anupong Paojinda were dropped by the National Anti-Corruption Commission (NACC) on December 29, 2015, which was recognized as "a serious setback for accountability in the country" by Humans Rights Watch (hrw.org, 2016). These instances emphasize that while social media has the potential to affect political and democratic outcomes, political accountability and the strength of civil society is important for this potential to be realized. In Shirky (2011)'s words "the potential of social media lies mainly in their support of civil society and the public sphere."

INFORMATION CONTROL, SOCIAL MEDIA, AND CORRUPTION

Traditional media such as newspapers and television can easily be controlled and, hence, curbed or manipulated or both by corrupt and authoritarian governments. Authoritarian regimes in many countries have filtered public's access to information by controlling and even owning the media channels (Freedom House, 2009a). On the other hand, it is often very difficult, though not impossible, to control the information that is available on the Internet and can be shared through social media websites, blogs, and other ways. Furthermore, studies have argued that the ICTs can have significant impacts on democratic outcomes even under strict government controls and even when the activities on the net are under close watch (Sunstein, 2009).

Moreover, the ICTs allow for multi-way communication as opposed to only one-way communication facilitated by the traditional media. It has the potential to strengthen democracy by empowering individuals, facilitating the exchange of information and mobilization for a given cause (Diamond, 2010). Individuals can not only share corruption stories that were published in major newspapers but they can also share their own personal experience related to corruption (Jha & Sarangi, 2014). Social media thus enables individuals to share their experiences regarding petty corruption, which was not possible through traditional media. Besides the spread of information, social media also enables people to organize and protest against corrupt activities. For instance, Facebook can be used to create pages for a cause such as corruption, which can be shared by the creators to their friends and others. Those who are interested in anti-corruption movement can become members of the page and invite others to join. The platform, then, can be used to share corruption related stories to create awareness and organize protests against corruption. The page allows people to communicate about the location where anti-corruption activists can gather to protest against corruption in large numbers, which the policymakers may find difficult to ignore. Other social media sites such as Twitter and Google+ can be used to circulate the information about the upcoming events to the public. And, finally, YouTube and other video sharing sites can be used to share the videos of the events that may include any police brutality on activists. In recent years, multiple cases of police violence against citizens have been evidenced by activists using videos even in democratic countries such as the United States[5]. As discussed earlier, the Facebook page "India Against Corruption" was heavily used for communicating and organizing protests by the activists of the anti-corruption movement in India. Social media has another important advantage over traditional media. It enables individuals to share their personal experiences with friends and family and even strangers who have been in similar situations and therefore can empathize with the victims of corruption (Jha & Sarangi, 2014).

Qin et al. (2016) find social media to be an effective surveillance tool and provide further evidence on the role of social media in spreading the information regarding corrupt stories and organizing protests. They find that millions of posts published on Sina Weibo – the most widely used microblogging platform in China – explicitly discussed the cases of corruption. They further find that a greater use of Sina Weibo is positively associated with the likelihood of the occurrence of protest and large-scale conflicts.

Based on these characteristics of social media, some studies have recently linked social media with corruption. Figure 2 shows that there is a strong, negative correlation between Facebook penetration (data obtained from Jha & Sarangi, 2014) defined as the percentage of the population using Facebook and corruption. Though research on social media and corruption is still in infancy, the available evidence indicates that social media can be used as a powerful weapon against corruption.

The obvious reason behind the lack of studies exploring the relationship between social media and corruption is the presence of endogeneity – it is possible that not only social media affects corruption, but corrupt countries are also more likely to curb information dissemination, and hence, social media usage. In fact, even the democratic governments have recently placed restrictions on the information and the content that can be published and shared online. While some countries such as China, Belarus, and Iran have developed technologies that are used to filter and control the content that can be shared on the Internet, others have enacted vague laws that can be used to stifle the freedom of speech on the Internet (Freedom House, 2009a; Diamond, 2010).

Recently, some of the democratic countries that are considered to be the pioneers of the freedom of speech such as the United States and the United Kingdom have been subject to criticism for attacking freedom on the net by spying on users' activities online. One of the biggest stories of 2013 was the information leaked by Edward Snowden (the former National Security Agency contractor) who revealed that the National

Figure 2. Facebook penetration and corruption in 2012

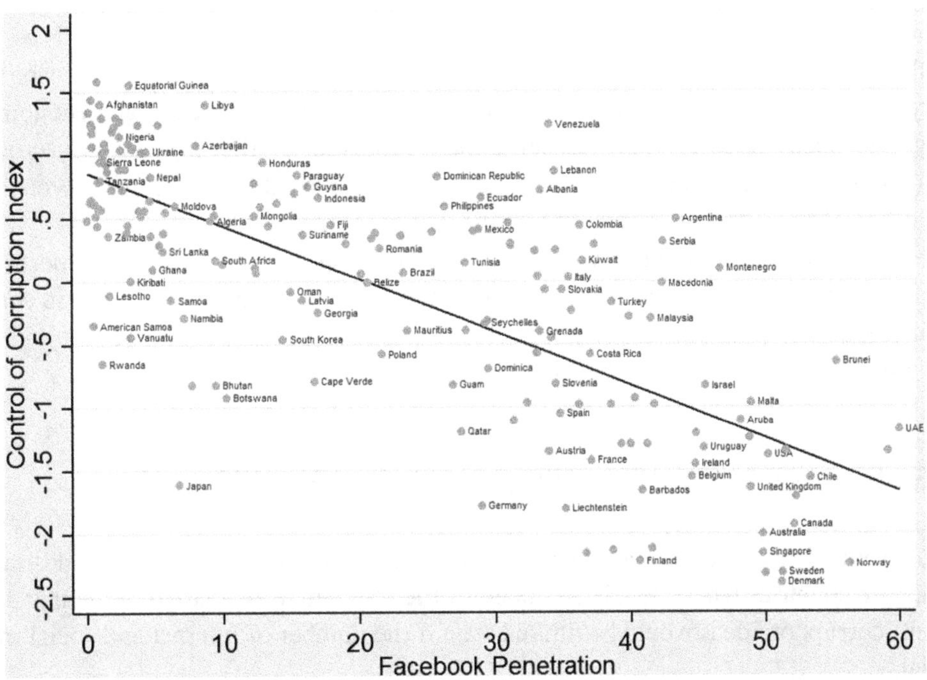

Security Agency (NSA) of the United States was running several surveillance programs that violated the privacy of Internet users. Government Communications Headquarters (GCHQ) of the United Kingdom has also been engaged in activities that compromise the privacy of the users and violates the promise that their private data would be inaccessible to criminals or the government. Both the NSA and the GCHQ have been accused of working on developing technologies that undermine the efficacy of Internet anonymizing tools and can be used to access encrypted traffic (Freedom House, 2015)[6]. Many Internet users may resort to self-censorship if they are afraid of being watched. For example, Freedom House (2015) documents that in the United States, one of the freest countries in the world, Internet users have resorted to stricter self-censorship after the information regarding government surveillance of online communications was leaked.

In many countries, there is a constant ongoing battle between the government and the public to control access to information that can potentially be harmful to the government. In such countries, while the government tries to conceal/censor specific information through technological means, social activists are quick to find a way to share relevant information. Bloggers and social activists have been able to share information regarding government corruption and human rights violations stealthily, sometimes anonymously and using virtual private networks (VPN). In many cases, by the time the government is able to take the information out of the net, it is already accessed by millions of the people and the harm is already done. For instance, millions of people already viewed "Under the Dome", an environmental documentary, before it was censored in China (Washington Post, 2015)·

Additionally, studies also encounter important identification issues such as the data availability and the reliability of available data. Initial studies exploring the relationship between social media and corruption have attempted to overcome some of these issues to the extent possible and, despite their limitations, have provided important insights into the link between social media and corruption. For instance, Jha and Sarangi (2014) use Facebook penetration across countries as a proxy for social media since the data on the latter was not available. In order to address endogeneity concerns, the study employs the adoption of communication technology in 1500 AD as an instrument for today's Internet penetration. Their identification assumption is that Internet penetration is responsible for the endogeneity in exploring the relationship between social media and corruption. The authors' argument behind this assumption is that while the exclusion of Internet penetration leads to omitted variables bias, its inclusion introduces endogeneity in the model. The authors show that social media has statistically and economically significant negative impact on corruption. The authors show that this relationship is robust across different samples of countries, including and excluding those which have placed severe restrictions on information dissemination, in general, and on Facebook or social media usage, in particular.

In another notable study, Enikolopov et al. (2016) show that anti-corruption blog posts negatively impacted the market returns of state-controlled companies in Russia. The authors go on to conclude that social media has the potential to negatively impact corruption even in countries where political competition is very limited and mass media is heavily controlled.

INTERNET FREEDOM, SOCIAL MEDIA, AND CORRUPTION

It is obvious from the above discussion that freedom on the net is critical for having desirable effects on corruption. In countries where people do not enjoy the freedom to share their opinion and views, the spread of anti-corruption ideas would be limited even if the number of Internet and social media users is substantial.

Freedom House collects information on the freedom that net users enjoy in different countries and assigns numerical scores on the basis of three broad categories. The first category, obstacles to access, evaluates the barriers to access to information created by infrastructural and economic limitations, legal and ownership controls as well as the freedom enjoyed by regulatory institutions. The second category, limits on content, measures the freedom to share contents on the net and analyzes the legal restrictions and technological means that are used to control the contents that can be published or shared, whether certain websites are blocked, as well as takes into account the diversity of online news media and the extent to which the use of digital technology is used to mobilize citizens. The final category, violations of user rights, deals with the "surveillance, privacy, and repercussions for online speech and activities, such as imprisonment, extralegal harassment, or cyberattacks" ("Freedom House Report" 2016). The score ranges from 0 (most free) to 100 (not free). Note that the index, besides freedom on the net, also includes the access to and the freedom that users enjoy in using technologies such as mobile phones and text messaging services that can be used to exchange information.

Figure 3 plots the relationship between Internet freedom using the index from Freedom House and corruption. In the figure, I have adjusted the scale of the index such that a higher value implies greater freedom on the net. Expectedly, we can see that there is a strong and negative correlation between freedom on the net and corruption across countries. The observed correlation in the figure indicates the need for further research to ascertain whether the observed correlation between Internet freedom and corruption is causal.

As argued earlier, although social media has undermined the government's ability to control the dissemination of information, governments around the world still censor the content that can be shared on the net using technological means and vague security laws (Freedom House, 2009a; Freedom House, 2015). Some countries, such as China (where the Chinese Communist Party exercises tight control over the traditional media), have actively launched crackdown on social media activism to eliminate the threat imposed by social media (Fortune, 2013). Hence, one should expect that in countries with greater Internet freedom, social media should have a stronger effect on corruption because in such countries bloggers and journalists can share news exposing corrupt practices without fear. On the other hand, countries where the government has near monopoly over information or where there is a threat to those who share articles and news exposing the corrupt practices of the government officials, cases involving political and bureaucratic corruption are unlikely to come out to the public and hence the effects of social media on corruption might be very limited. Future research should investigate the implications that the government's control over information can have for the effects of social media on corruption.

It is also noteworthy here that studies have found the evidence that a free press can have significant negative impacts on corruption (Brunetti & Weder, 2003). Arguably, free press reduces the cost of fighting corruption and acts as an external control of corruption. In many countries, journalists and bloggers are under threat of legal actions and being imprisoned (Freedom House, 2015). Although sharing information on the net provides more anonymity than newspaper and TV journalism, it is not entirely anonymous given recent developments in technology that are used by governments to attack the anonymity of net users. Under these circumstances, it is plausible that an increased anonymity and greater freedom on the net will result in a much greater effect of social media on corruption than the effect that we observe now.

Figure 3. Freedom on the net and corruption in 2014

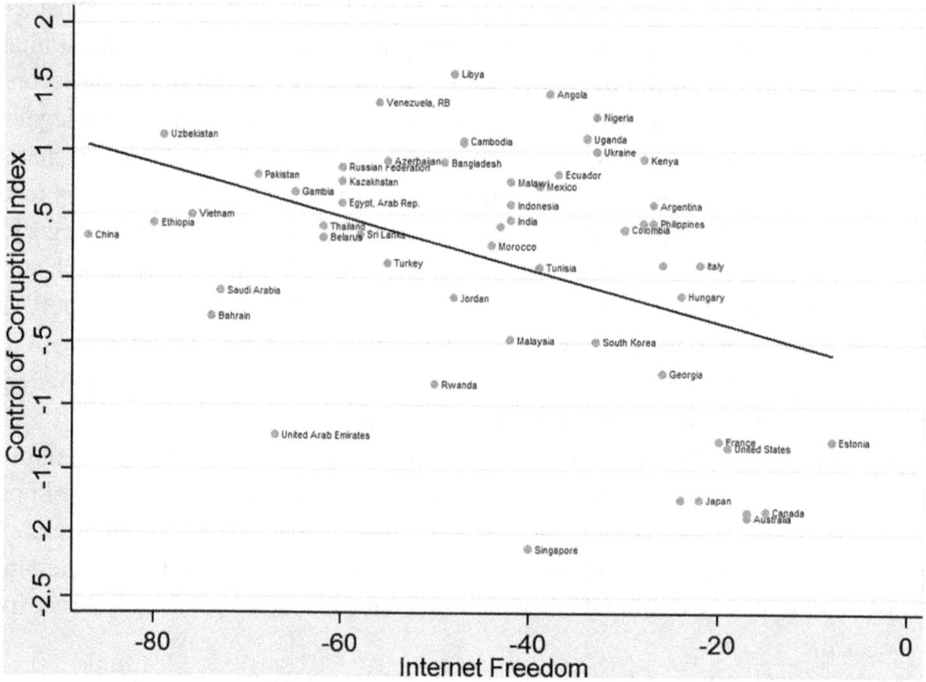

DISCUSSION AND CONCLUSION

The Internet freedom is in danger across the world. According to Freedom House's "Freedom on the Net 2015" report, freedom on the net has been declining over time around the world for last 5 consecutive years. Out of 65 countries, more than 40 have some restrictions in place relating to political, religious, and social issues that can be shared on the web. Many countries have imprisoned people for sharing information related to such issues. Not only the authoritarian regimes but also democracies have been criticized for spying on the activities of net users and violating their privacy.

The role of the new ICTs in augmenting the individual freedom has been so significant that Diamond (2010) goes as far as terming them the "liberation technology" – defined as "any form of information and communication technology (ICT) that can expand political, social, and economic freedom." In recent years, social media has played a profound role in promoting democracy around the world and therefore has been subject to restrictions. The activities of net users have been scrutinized and spied upon. A greater control over what can be shared will discourage people to use the Internet and join social media platforms. In many countries, the governments have attempted to stifle the freedom of speech on social media sites and blogs using legal means and by designing vague laws. Such laws are likely to prevent people from becoming members of social media sites and hence limit the exchange of information. The privacy settings of social media can play an important role in alleviating these concerns. Recently, many social media sites and short messaging services have developed and adopted technology to preserve the anonymity of individuals, which may partially address some of these concerns. For instance, Whatsapp, a leading short messaging services provider, has enabled end-to-end encryption that ensures that the conversation between two people cannot be ready by anyone else, not even Whatsapp ("Whats

App FAQ" 2016). End-to-end encryption is now also offered by other communication platforms such as Facebook messenger and Viber (Wired, 2016). The civil society must fight to preserve the freedom of speech and the freedom to share ideas, and the degree of anonymity enjoyed by net users is significant in this regard. As Diamond (2010) states, technological progress alone will not decide the winner in the race of democrats versus autocrats. Rather, the role of political organizations and economic forces will be significant in determining the outcome and it is people, organization, and governments that will decide who wins. The democratic governments around the world must support the freedom on the net not only in their own countries but also in other countries. Towards this end, Hillary Clinton, secretary of state of the United States, declared in her famous speech delivered on January 21, 2010: "We stand for a single Internet where all of humanity has equal access to knowledge and ideas" (Foreign Policy, 2010).

Corruption is an important concern for both the policymakers and the citizens around the globe because of its undesirable effects on outcomes such as economic growth, poverty, and inequality (Mauro, 1985; Gupta et al., 2002). A number of factors such as the quality of institutions, economic development, democratic and cultural factors, and openness among others (see Treisman (2000) for a review) and, more recently, the ICTs have been identified to be the determinants of corruption. Social media is amongst the newest factors that have been shown by researchers to negatively impact corruption.

At the same time, freedom on the net is under threat in many parts of the world. Freedom on the net is critical for the effects of social media on corruption to be fully realized. With countries around the world trying to control the way information is being shared, the effects of social media on corruption is likely to be undermined. It is also important to note that some authoritarian regimes may allow some independent reporting simply because it may actually help them by unearthing any upcoming threat, information regarding which can be used to pacify discontented citizens by improving local level governance. For example, the Chinese Communist Party leaders in China use media as a watchdog to monitor the activities of subordinate officials so the problems can be identified and solved before they turn into popular public unrest. The media is, however, prevented from reporting the wrongdoings of higher levels of government (Shirk, 2011). Recent studies have developed models to help explain such censorship practices. For instance, Lorentzen (2014), using a formal model, shows that an authoritarian regime may benefit from allowing the media to report the misconducts of low-level officials, while, at the same time, controlling the amount of information such that citizens do not have enough information to determine whether a revolt will be successful. Regarding social media, Qin et al. (2016) find evidence that the Chinese government regulates social media to ensure that there is no threat to the stability of the regime. It is important for the civil society to recognize and act against such censorship practices.

There is a need for further research that explores the complementarity between Internet freedom and social media usage in the context of their effects on corruption. It will also be an important exercise to investigate the implications of the interaction between institutional quality and social media on corruption. Furthermore, while there is ample evidence that the Internet is being used by the governments around the world to promote transparency, the use of social media by governments in promoting e-participation is still in infancy (Bonsón et al., 2012). The use of the ICTs and social media is not ubiquitous and there is a room for many countries to improve infrastructural quality that enhances public's access to the ICTs (Dutta et al., 2015). Since many of these countries are mired in corruption, it would be advisable for the governments in these countries to implement policies that enhance the access to the ICTs and use them to promote transparency and accountability.

REFERENCES

Ades, A., & Di Tella, R. (1999). Rents, Competition, and Corruption. *The American Economic Review, 89*(4), 982–993. doi:10.1257/aer.89.4.982

Andersen, T. B., Bentzen, J., Dalgaard, C. J., & Selaya, P. (2011). Does the Internet Reduce Corruption? Evidence from US States and across Countries. *The World Bank Economic Review, 25*(3), 387–417. doi:10.1093/wber/lhr025

Banerjee, A., Duflo, E., Imbert, C., Mathew, S., & Pande, R. (2014). Can E-Governance Reduce Capture of Public Programs? *Poverty Action Lab*. Retrieved from https://www.povertyactionlab.org/evaluation/enhancing-local-public-service-delivery-through-financial-reform-india%E2%80%99s-employment

Bertot, J. C., Jaeger, P. T., & Grimes, J. M. (2010). Using ICTs to Create a Culture of Transparency: E-government and Social Media as Openness and Anti-corruption Tools for Societies. *Government Information Quarterly, 27*(3), 264–271. doi:10.1016/j.giq.2010.03.001

Bhatnagar, S. (2003). E-government and Access to Information. *Global Corruption Report, 2003*, 24–32.

Bong, S., Chung, K., Parkinson, K., Peppard, A., Rabbach, J., & Thiher, N. (2012). *Analyzing Social Media Momentum*. Workshop in International Public Affairs.

Bonsón, E., Torres, L., Royo, S., & Flores, F. (2012). Local E-government 2.0: Social Media and Corporate Transparency in Municipalities. *Government Information Quarterly, 29*(2), 123–132. doi:10.1016/j.giq.2011.10.001

Bruer, A., Landman, T., & Farquhar, D. (2015). Social Media and Protest Mobilization: Evidence from the Tunisian Revolution. *Democratization, 22*(4), 764–792. doi:10.1080/13510347.2014.885505

Brunetti, A., & Weder, B. (2003). A Free Press is Bad News for Corruption. *Journal of Public Economics, 87*(7), 1801–1824. doi:10.1016/S0047-2727(01)00186-4

Caselli, F., & Coleman, W. J. II. (2001). Cross-Country Technology Diffusion: The Case of Computers. *The American Economic Review, 91*(2), 328–335. doi:10.1257/aer.91.2.328

Chakrabarty, B., & Hazra, S. (2016). *Winning the Mandate: The Indian Experience*. India: SAGE Publications.

Diamond, L. (2010). Liberation Technology. *Journal of Democracy, 21*(3), 69–83. doi:10.1353/jod.0.0190

DiRienzo, C. E., Das, J., Cort, K. T., & Burbridge, J. Jr. (2007). Corruption and the Role of Information. *Journal of International Business Studies, 38*(2), 320–332. doi:10.1057/palgrave.jibs.8400262

Dutta, S., López-Claros, A., & Mia, I. (Eds.). (2015). *The Global Information Technology Report: ICTs for Inclusive Growth.* World Economic Forum.

Elbahnasawy, N. G. (2014). E-government, Internet Adoption, and Corruption: An Empirical Investigation. *World Development, 57*, 114–126. doi:10.1016/j.worlddev.2013.12.005

Enikolopov, R., Petrova, M., & Sonin, K. (2016). Social Media and Corruption. *CEPR Discussion Paper No. DP11263*. Retrieved from http://ssrn.com/abstract=2777570

Foreignpolicy.com. (2010). Internet freedom. Retrieved from http://foreignpolicy.com/2010/01/21/internet-freedom/

Fortune (2013). Social media activism. Retrieved from http://fortune.com/2013/09/12/chinas-tragic-crackdown-on-social-media-activism/

Freedom House (2009a). Freedom on the Net: A Global Assessment of Internet and Digital Media.

Freedom House (2009b). Freedom of the Press 2009.

Freedom House (2015). Freedom on the Net 2015.

Greenberg, A. (2016). 'Secret conversations:' end-to-end encryption comes to Facebook messenger. *Wired*. Retrieved from https://www.wired.com/2016/07/secret-conversations-end-end-encryption-facebook-messenger-arrived/

Gupta, S., Davoodi, H., & Alonso-Terme, R. (2002). Does Corruption Affect Income Inequality and Poverty? *Economics of Governance*, *3*(1), 23–45. doi:10.1007101010100039

Hale, H. E. (2013). Did the Internet Break the Political Machine? Moldova's 2009 "Twitter Revolution that Wasn't". *Demokratizatsiya (Washington, D.C.)*, *21*(4), 481–505.

Howard, P. N., Duffy, A., Freelon, D., Hussain, M. M., Mari, W., & Maziad, M. (2011). Opening Closed Regimes: What was the Role of Social Media during the Arab Spring? Retrieved from http://ssrn.com/abstract=2595096

Hrw.org. (2016). *Thailand: New whitewash of 2010 political violence.* Retrieved from https://www.hrw.org/news/2016/01/07/thailand-new-whitewash-2010-political-violence

I Paid a Bribe (2016). *I Paid a Bribe.* Retrieved from http://www.ipaidabribe.com/#gsc.tab=0F

Jha, C. K. (2014). Can Social Media and Internet Help Reduce Corruption? *Ideas for India.* Retrieved from http://ideasforindia.in/article.aspx?article_id=353

Jha, C. K., & Sarangi, S. (2014). Social Media, Internet and Corruption. Retrieved from http://ssrn.com/abstract=2391904

Jorgenson, D. W. (2001). Information Technology and the US Economy. *The American Economic Review*, *91*(1), 1–32. doi:10.1257/aer.91.1.1

Kaufmann, D., Kraay, A., & Mastruzzi, M. (2010). *The Worldwide Governance Indicators: A Summary of Methodology, Data and Analytical Issues.* World Bank Policy Research Working Paper.

Keliher, M., & Wu, H. (2015). How to discipline 90 million people. *The Atlantic*. Retrieved from http://www.theatlantic.com/international/archive/2015/04/xi-jinping-china-corruption-political-culture/389787/

Kolstad, I., & Wiig, A. (2009). Is transparency the key to reducing corruption in resource-rich countries? *World Development*, *37*(3), 521–532. doi:10.1016/j.worlddev.2008.07.002

Kumari, D. L., & Kumari, K. S. (2016). Public Distribution System in India: An Overview. *Indian Journal of Applied Research*, *5*(5).

Lenhart, A. (2015). *Teens, Social Media & Technology Overview 2015*. Washington, DC: Pew Research Center.

Lio, M.-C., Liu, M.-C., & Ou, Y.-P. (2011). Can the Internet Reduce Corruption? A Cross-country Study based on Dynamic Panel Data Models. *Government Information Quarterly*, *28*(1), 47–53. doi:10.1016/j.giq.2010.01.005

Lorentzen, P. (2014). China's Strategic Censorship. *American Journal of Political Science*, *58*(2), 402–414. doi:10.1111/ajps.12065

Madden, M. (2010). *Older Adults and Social Media*. Washington, DC: Pew Research Center.

Mauro, P. (1995). Corruption and Growth. *The Quarterly Journal of Economics*, *110*(3), 681–712. doi:10.2307/2946696

Mufson, S. (2015). This documentary went viral in China. Then it was censored. It won't be forgotten. *Washington Post*. Retrieved from https://www.washingtonpost.com/news/energy-environment/wp/2015/03/16/this-documentary-went-viral-in-china-then-it-was-censored-it-wont-be-forgotten/?utm_term=.fdbb8ae67fb4

Newley. (2011). *Social media and Thailand's red shirt protests*. Retrieved from http://newley.com/2011/01/25/social-media-and-thailand%E2%80%99s-red-shirt-protests/

Oliner, S. D., & Sichel, D. E. (2000). The Resurgence of Growth in the Late 1990s: Is Information Technology the Story? *The Journal of Economic Perspectives*, *14*(4), 3–22. doi:10.1257/jep.14.4.3

Porter, J. (2008). *Designing for the Social Web*. New Riders Press.

Qin, B., Strömberg, D., & Wu, Y. (2016). The Political Economy of Social Media in China.

Salbu, S. R. (2001). Information Technology in the War against International Bribery and Corruption: The Next Frontier of Institutional Reform. *Harvard Journal on Legislation*, *38*(1), 67–102.

Shirk, S. (2011). Changing Media, Changing China. In S. Shirk (Ed.), Changing Media, Changing China, 1–37. New York: Oxford University Press.

Shirky, C. (2011). The Political Power of Social Media: Technology, the Public Sphere, and Political Change. In *Foreign Affairs* (pp. 28–41).

Statista (2016). Number of worldwide social network users. Retrieved from https://www.statista.com/statistics/278414/number-of-worldwide-social-network-users/

Sunstein, C. R. (2009). *Republic.com 2.0*. Princeton University Press.

Tanzi, V. (1998). Corruption Around the World: Causes, Consequences, Scope, and Cures. *IMF Staff Papers*, *45*(4), 559–594. doi:10.2307/3867585

Tepper, M. (2003). The Rise of Social Software. *netWorker*, *7*(3), 18–23. doi:10.1145/940830.940831

Sedghi, A. (2014). Facebook: 10 years of social networking, in numbers. *The Guardian*. Retrieved from https://www.theguardian.com/news/datablog/2014/feb/04/facebook-in-numbers-statistics

Shearlaw, M. (2016). Egypt five years on: was it ever a 'social media revolution'? *The Guardian*. Retrieved from https://www.theguardian.com/world/2016/jan/25/egypt-5-years-on-was-it-ever-a-social-media-revolution

Vargas, J.A. (2012). Spring Awakening: How an Egyptian revolution began on Facebook. The New York Times. Retrieved from http://www.nytimes.com/2012/02/19/books/review/how-an-egyptian-revolution-began-on-facebook.html

Time (2011). The Top 10 Everything of 2011. Retrieved from http://content.time.com/time/specials/packages/article/0,28804,2101344_2101368_2101650,00.html

Treisman, D. (2000). The Causes of Corruption: A Cross-National Study. *Journal of Public Economics*, *76*(3), 399–457. doi:10.1016/S0047-2727(99)00092-4

United Nations. (2014). Information and Communications Technologies for Inclusive Social and Economic Development. Geneva: UN.

Uslaner, E. M. (2005). Trust and Corruption. In J. G. Lambsdorff, M. Taube & M. Schramm (Eds.) The New Institutional Economics of Corruption (pp. 76-92). USA: Routledge.

WhatsApp. (2016). End-to-end Encryption. Retrieved from: https://www.whatsapp.com/faq/en/general/28030015

Zurcher, A. (2016). US election: Why is Clinton's foundation so controversial? *BBC*. Retrieved from http://www.bbc.com/news/election-us-2016-37168505

KEY TERMS AND DEFINITIONS

Corruption: The misuse of entrusted power by government officials or elected political leaders for illegitimate personal gains.

Facebook: A popular social media website.

Information and Communication Technology: The forms of technology that allow people to transmit information and communicate with one another and/or a broad general audience.

Information Control: Restrictions placed by the government authorities on the content, the audience, or the way the information can be shared on the Internet, social media, traditional media, and elsewhere.

Internet Freedom: The ability of Internet users to express their opinions and share ideas and content freely and without restrictions using social media websites, news portals, blogs, and other means using the Internet.

Multi-Way Communication: A form of communication in which more than one (often several) involved parties can exchange information with one another.

Social Media: A form of the information and communication technologies that enables users to access, create, and share information with the members from both within and outside their network.

Traditional Media: The form of media such as the print and broadcast media that has traditionally (before recent developments in information and communication technologies) been used to transmit information and can be used for only one-way communication.

ENDNOTES

1 This chapter focuses on the effects of the ICTs, in general, and social media—in particular—on democratic and political outcomes, with an emphasis on corruption. The effects of the ICTs on economic outcomes, such as economic growth, productivity, human capital and manufacturing trade openness, are well documented in the literature (Oliner & Sichel, 2000; Jorgenson, 2001; Caselli & Coleman, 2001). Readers interested in the effects of the ICTs on economic outcomes may refer to these studies.

2 Visit http://info.worldbank.org/governance/wgi/index.aspx#home for details regarding the construction of the CCI.

3 http://www.anti-corruption.org.bt/?q=node/295

4 See the link for details about the protest: https://www.washingtonpost.com/world/in-tunisia-act-of-one-fruit-vendor-sparks-wave-of-revolution-through-arab-world/2011/03/16/AFjfsueB_story.html (Retrieved August 8, 2016)

5 One such example can be found at: http://www.npr.org/2016/07/07/485138688/activists-use-video-to-document-police-violence

6 Also see https://www.theguardian.com/world/2013/sep/05/nsa-gchq-encryption-codes-security?CMP=share_btn_tw

This research was previously published in Political Scandal, Corruption, and Legitimacy in the Age of Social Media edited by Derya Çakır-Demirhan and Kamil Demirhan; pages 51-75, copyright year 2017 by Information Science Reference (an imprint of IGI Global).

Chapter 16
A Survey on Access Control Techniques for Social Networks

Yousra Asim
COMSATS Institute of Information Technology, Pakistan

Ahmad Kamran Malik
COMSATS Institute of Information Technology, Pakistan

ABSTRACT

Online Social Networks (OSN) are getting popular day by day. Users share their information in OSN with others users. Access control is required to prevent unauthorized access to this information. Several studies have been conducted for access control in social networks. This chapter is a survey of available access control models/techniques based on social networks. Available access control models can be categorized as relationship-based, attributes-based, community structure-based and user activity centric model. A number of techniques have been proposed by several authors for access control in social networks. Most of the approaches use Social Network Analysis (SNA) techniques, others use user related information, for example, attributes or activities, the rest use a combination of approaches.

INTRODUCTION

"Man is a social animal" is a well-known quote by a renowned Greek philosopher, Aristotle (n.d.). Historically, human beings invented many ways to communicate with each other. The communication journey started from letter writing and kept on moving through telegraph, radio, TV, Computer, Internet, messenger up to the social network. Users of every age keep themselves connected with their friends and relatives via social networks e.g. Facebook, Twitter etc. Online Social Network (OSN) provides value and immediacy to its users. Users of this platform like to share their interests, activities, personal information and enjoy to increase their friendship circles but they also don't like to let their private information distorted. Proper and efficient access control strategies can fulfill their dreams in this regard.

DOI: 10.4018/978-1-7998-0417-8.ch016

Access control process basically involves authentication and authorization. It may also include identification and access approval. Authentication addresses the question: Who are you? It can uniquely identify a user. Authorization addresses the question: What can you do? It is the process which manages the resources that authenticated client is permitted to do. Normally access control is used to perform the following functions: granting access right, limiting access rights, preventing access rights and revoking access rights. Access control administration can be centralized or decentralized. In centralized approach of administration, central authority is responsible for granting or denying access to user. It is more restricted approach in which all decisions are depending upon a central authority. If central authority fails due to some technical problem, no access to resources will be granted by anybody. Moreover, if a single authority fails to satisfy all the requests then it will disappoint users. In decentralized approach of administration, users are responsible for their resource policies, this approach has no single point of failure but user's privacy is at risk. It is very difficult to maintain security of resources at each node of the social network.

Access control models and techniques prior to social network are described in this paragraph. These models and techniques are not the subject of this chapter yet they are the basis of most access control implementations and also used in combination with social network techniques. Access policies are defined to map different access rights. Historically, researchers used different access control structures like access control matrix (Graham & Denning, 1972), access control lists (Sandhu & Samarati, 1994) and many other access control models to implement access policies. The use of these techniques depends upon the scenario and feasibility of proposed approach. Access control can be categorized into different types from the administration point of view. For example, MAC and DAC (US Department of Defense standard, 1985). Mandatory Access Control (MAC) is the strategy in which rules are strictly controlled and enforced by system administrator. Access to resource is granted according to that rules. Discretionary Access Control (DAC) is the strategy in which access is granted to resources depending upon the policy specified by its owner. The NIST standard Role-based Access Control (RBAC) model (Ferraiolo, Sandhu, Gavrila, Kuhn & Chandramouli, 2001) is the strategy in which access is granted to resources depending upon the roles of users. Rule-based access control, for example (Carminati, Ferrari & Perego, 2006) is the strategy in which access is granted to resources depending upon rules specified for access. Attribute-based Access Control (ABAC) model, for example (Hu, Kuhn & Ferraiolo, 2015) is the strategy in which access is granted depending upon different properties of subject, object and other related data.

Recent access control techniques, mainly for social networks, are based on community structure and relationship patterns. They apply different techniques, for example, Social Network Analysis (SNA) techniques to find out social network structure like clique, k-core etc. In this case, access can be granted by applying rules to a cluster found after the application of above described techniques. Social network requires proper access control techniques to manage the resources of it users. Researchers have proposed different access control techniques/models for online social networks, different architectures for these models, access rules and policy specification languages. This study is all about them. Social network based access control techniques available in literature can be classified into the following categories according to their characteristics; Relationship-based access control model, Attribute-based access control models, Community centric and User activity centric techniques.

The remainder of this chapter is organized as follows. Relationship-based access control models/ techniques for OSN is further organized into sub sections according to access control models for OSN. Attribute-based, Community centric and User activity centric access control models/techniques are described in the following sections. Discussion of the access control techniques for OSN is described before the conclusion section.

Relationship-Based Access Control for OSN

Relationship based access control is based on user to user relations in a social network. Social network of users can have many different types of relations among connecting users. It creates a social network graph between actors having ties/relationships among them. These graphs can be analyzed using graph algorithms and SNA based techniques to find hidden patterns of relations, significance of actors and much more. These findings can help to implement access control in social network effectively. Relationship based access control models are further classified into the following categories; Relationship Type, Trust and Depth of a relationship.

Relationship-Type Based Access Control

Researchers proposed access control models based on relationship-type. As in OSN, users make relationships with other users, for example, close friend, friend-of-friend etc., close friends of owner have more access to resources of owner than friend-of-friend relationship. It means relationship type of owner with requester can provide base for access control. Here, in this section we discuss some proposed studies in this context.

The study (Gollu, Saroiu & Wolman, 2007) presents social relationship-based strategy of access control as well as describes importance of access control policies for online personal data sharing for three applications; Google Calendar, Social BitTorrent and Social Firewalls. For social networking-based access control, authors introduced the concept of social attestations and social access control lists. Social attestation will verify social relationship of a user with another user and social ACL concept consists of three things: owner's public key, public key of all people who can access an information and a social relationship. Author says that when a person wants to access any object, he will use his public key that is listed already in social ACL or he will have to show the attestation that is given by owner which will be verified by the social relationship specified in ACL. Authors suggest a concept that a user can use social attestation to enforce different views of his calendar. View of calendar will totally depend upon his social relationship which means he can create different view of his activities and his schedule for different people. Authors suggest this access control scheme for BitTorrent for sharing multimedia content among people. Moreover, they propose social attestation to bypass firewall which will be verified the relevant social relationship mentioned in social ACL.

In both studies (Tootoonchian, Saroiu, Ganjali, & Wolman, 2009) and (Tootoonchian, Gollu, Saroiu, et al., 2008), social ACL concept is also used. ACLs are associated with resources and having two fields; set of authorized user identifiers and required relationship to access that resource. Further, authors propose relationship certificate approach named social attestation to apply authorizations. In mentioned approach, relationship information between two users is recorded by extracting identifiers of two users and their relationship type. The study (Cheng, Park & Sandhu, 2012a) represents user to user relationship based access control model for online social networks. Writers use different notations to develop the proposed model, $\sum$ for the set of relationship types having bi-directional relationship identifiers, "action" for active action and "action^{-1}" for passive action. This model has five components including: Accessing user (It has access control polices and user to user relationships with other users), Target (can be target user which has its own policies and U2U relationship information or target resource has ownership information with controlling user), Access request (action of user against target), Action (initiated by accessing user) and Policy (rules for authorization). According to authors, policies can be user specified or system specified. User specified polices are related to users and resources whereas System specified polices are implemented and owned by online social system and are not separate for incoming and outgoing actions. Incoming actions are evaluated by Target resource policies. User specified policies can be accessing user policy (for out-going action) or target user policy (for incoming action). They model social graph which was directed (arc representing relationship from user to user), labeled (with relationship type) and simple (having no multiple arcs or loops). This model supposes that every user has set of resources and mentions set of policies for users and their resources as well. A requester is granted access to target if he has user to user relationship mentioned in the policy of target.

This study (Cheng, Park & Sandhu, 2012a) also presents a policy language based on regular expression. It is the first model having such capabilities. It provides access evaluation procedure algorithm as well. According to algorithm, when a user request for target, policies of accessing user, policies of target user and system policies against that particular action are extracted by system. Access control policy consists of requested action and required graph rule, where graph rule consists of a pair (start, path rule); start shows the start of path evaluation and path rule can have many path specs. Proposed algorithm uses depth first search algorithm to traverse the graph.

From each policy in the policy set, graph rule is extracted by algorithm then by the help of graph rule path checking algorithm extracts every path spec where path spec consists of pair (path, hop count); path shows pattern of relationship path between two users and hop count limits the maximum number of edges found in the path. In order to get result of particular policy, algorithm combines all path spec. Finally for granting access, results of all path spec for all policies in the policy set is combined. Authors do not discuss conflict resolution policies here and assume that system specified policies will handle multi user policy conflicts. Moreover, this model doesn't consider repeating nodes for prevention of unnecessary iterations.

The study (Cheng, Park & Sandhu, 2012b) proposes access control model for not only user to user based relationship but also includes user to resource relationship and resource to resource relationships. It is the extension of their previous work .This access control model covers administrative activities which are rare in previous literature. Regular expression based policy is extended to U2R and R2R relationships in it. This model consists of six components; Users (accessing user and target user with their policies), Sessions (Active instance of user; can be target session or accessing session), Resources (can be any object or target user session), Policies (rules to access targets), social graph (network of users, sessions, objects and their access control policies) and decision module (decides about granting access by keeping an eye to all specified policies and if conflicts then resolved by system policies). Policies in the proposed model are system defined and user defined. System defined policies can be authorization polices and conflict resolution policies. User defined policies are classified into: access user policy, target user policy, accessing session policy, object policy and policy for policy.

Authors propose policy language for model in (Cheng, Park & Sandhu, 2012b) where accessing user and accessing session policies consists of pair (act, graph rule) and target user policy, target session policy, object policy, policy for policy, system policy for user all consist of pair (act^{-1}, graph rule).System policy for resource consists of pair (act^{-1},o.type, graph rule) in proposed language. Authors specify grammar for proposed model just like before. Here, two hop counts are calculated; local hopcount and global hopcount whereas in previous model there was only hopcount. Global hopcount shows the distance between accessing user and target on the graph whereas within each path segment there is local hopcount which shows maximum distance requirement for specific relationship type expression. Local hopcount is not counted in global hopcount to omit distances created by resources.

For conflict resolution, three different approaches are suggested in (Cheng, Park & Sandhu, 2012b); Firstly disjunctive approach which says if any policy is satisfied then access is granted. Secondly conjunctive approach in which access is granted by satisfying the requirement of every policy and finally prioritized approach in which parent's policies are having higher precedence than their child's.

Access evaluation procedure of this model (Cheng, Park & Sandhu, 2012b) works as follows: When a user requests an action against target in his session then decision module collects all the relevant policies including accessing user session policy for that action, target policy, system wide policies about that action and object type (if target is object), then it extracts each path spec from graph rule and runs path checking algorithm as in previous study and evaluates result. By resolving conflicts according conflict resolution policies, decision module finalize about access (grant/deny).

The Facebook is very popular social platform in these days. The study (Pang & Zhang, 2014) provide mechanism for the Facebook access control. It focuses on not only the user relationships but also on public information of users in online social networks. The proposed model consists of three kinds of information; users and their relationships, public information and their connections (extracted from external databases) and link between user and public information. With the help of this model user can focus on their social relations and public information for access control requirements. Authors give concept of user graph, public information graph and links between both of them for their model. Moreover, they used hybrid logic to define access control policies.

The study (Du, Liu, & Wang, 2013) provides relation based access control. This model is for campus social network system. Relation based access control is done by the collaboration of system designer, system administrator and users of the system in this study. In this model access control can be user centered or group centered. In user centered approach, When a user visits a web page for getting any service, then system will get the information of friends, followers and followed users of the requester with the resources released by these contacts and then page is generated based on this information. In group centered approach, when a user visits web page for group services then system gets the information about the groups who created or managed this web page and resources released by these group members and page is displayed based on collected information.

The studies (Hu, Ahn & Jorgensen, 2013), (Carminati, Ferrari & Perego, 2006), (Carminati, Ferrari, Heatherly, et al., 2009), (Carminati, Ferrari, Heatherly, et al., 2011), (Carminati & Ferrari, 2009), and (Carminati & Ferrari, 2008) described in this survey are also on relationship type based access control.

Trust-Based Access Control for OSN

Access control models based on trust for online social networks depend upon the calculation of trust value of requester that is calculated by some trust algorithms. These algorithms are based on the values of trust calculated by other users for that requester. Many researchers have proposed their access control models based on trust relationship. For example, the study (Ali, Villegas & Maheswaran, 2007) proposes multi-level access control solution. In this approach, users and resources are arranged in different security levels and access grant is based on the relationship between security levels of both. To organize user in the security levels, Every user is attached with a reputation value that is calculated by the average of trust ratings for that user by others in the network and for resource's security level, system automatically assigns security level 'SL' to resource. Users are only allowed to access the resources with a security level less than or equal to SL. For every resource, owner generates a key K, Encrypt it, split it into 'k' portions and divide it in 'n' nodes of the social network by hashing algorithm. If a requester wants to access that resource, resource owner sends that encrypted key to requester. If the requester retrieves k portions of key K from n nodes by fulfilling the trust requirement enforced by resource owner and reconstruct key K by k portions, then he is granted access to resource otherwise denied.

Some studies involve some other factors with combination of trust. For example, the studies (Shehab, Squicciarini & Ahn, 2008) and (Carminati, Ferrari & Perego, 2009) say that access control policies for shared information in online social networks should not only be based on relationships but also on depth of relationship and trust level between users. This study suggests rule based access control model of social networks which allows access to resources based on relationship type, depth of relation and trust level existing between users of OSN. Authors say that relationship may be direct or indirect; can be of two types. If a person has straight arc to another person then it is direct relationship. If a person is not directly connected to another then there may be more than one intermediate nodes between them. Depth of relationship between users is the length of path between them. Trust levels of each user will define the extent to which a user is trust worthy to another user. Trust is divided into two categories; Topical trust which refers to the extent to which a user trust the opinion of another user about a particular topic. Absolute trust refers to the extent to which a user consider other user's opinion trust worthy independently from a topic. Here, relationship is considered as entity as it has three attributes: type, depth and trust. In proposed model, three actors are mentioned: owner of the resource, person requested resource and social network management system. In rule based model, when a requester requests against a resource of an owner then requester receives set of access rules. By these rules, the requester has to show that he has which type of relationship with owner, with which depth and with which trust level. Decision to grant access of resource is taken on these access rules provided by requester. The information given by requester is verified by certificates which were created when two new owner and requester communicate. So, to assure owner about correct relationship of requester, he has to provide all chains of relationship between requester and owner to verify relationship path. To make it sure that requester has not omitted any chain of low trust level intentionally and has provided all possible chains of trust level, central node is proposed which is responsible for managing all certificates and verify all possible chains from certificate repository to social network management system.

Proposed architecture for model consists of two main services (Carminati, Ferrari & Perego, 2006). Firstly, central node service that is run by social network management system. It consists of two modules: Certificate manager which receives all certificates from network and Certificate retrieval module which is in charge of replying chain requests between two nodes of the social network and also calculates the trusted level of relationship based on the information of chain of certificates. Second service of architecture is peripheral nodes run by server or end user machine. It consists of four modules: Certificate manager (in charge of all certificates created by user), Rule manager (manages and store all access rules specified by user), Access control module (in charge of replying to access requests submitted by user) and Access request module (in charge of communication with central node and access control modules of other peripheral nodes).This study has a limitation that it does not talk about topical trust and certificate protection access rules.

The study (Carminati, Ferrari, Raymond, et. al, 2009) is the extension of (Carminati, Ferrari & Perego, 2006) is based on semantic web rules. Authors propose to model user profiles, their relationships, resources, actions and relationship between user and resources in social network by semantic web technologies. By exploiting the knowledge from OSN author enforce access control mechanism. Authors use FOAF ontology for modelling personal data which is OWL based format where OWL is semantic web language to represent complex knowledge about things. Personal relationships were modelled by n-array relation pattern. Resources, actions (modelled in hierarchies) and user/resource relationship were modelled by OWL. Access control policies here, are also based on type, depth and trust level of relationship between owner and requester just described in (Carminati, Ferrari & Perego, 2006). Moreover, they suggest filtering policies in this studies which can enable a user to filter out unwanted data during social website browsing. Filtering policies are proposed in two different ways; Firstly user can apply filtering on the content which she can access. Secondly, user can apply filtering to social network pages fetched by target users. They say access control policies and filtering policies differ each other because access control policy is specified by the resource owner but filtering policy is specified by target user or supervisor himself. Writers of this study also propose admin policies for social administrator to authorize users for access control and filtering policies. The framework supports three types of security policies so need three types of authorizations named: access control authorizations (for access control policies), admin authorizations (for admin policies), and prohibitions (for filtering policies).All of these authorization were also modelled and implemented on SAKB (Security authorization Knowledge Base) which acts as reference monitor in this framework. When a request is submitted to SAKB then authorization and prohibitions are retrieved from SAKB and if authorization returns with some value and prohibition with empty value then access is granted otherwise denied. Authors use SWRL to encode security rules.

Some authors have used semantic Web technologies for their proposed trust-based access control models. For example, the study (Carminati, Ferrari, Heatherly, et al., 2011) is basically the extension of (Carminati, Ferrari, Raymond, et. al, 2009) by same authors. In this study, authors implemented their semantic web based access control model. They generated large size of dataset having 350 million nodes by data generator and created social network. They performed experiments after implementing the proposed model. Their results show that for semantic inference of their access control model, social networks require sound data partitioning. The study (Hu, Ahn & Jorgensen, 2013) is a methodology to provide security to shared data of multiple users (collaborative environment) in online social networks. Authors propose an access control model for multiparty authorization requirements, its policies and policy enforcement mechanism. In this study, writers identify different sharing patterns available in sharing content where different users may have different authorization requirement to a single resource. They analyzed three scenarios; profile sharing, relationship sharing and content sharing. They studied accessor (application accessing content), owner of content and disseminator (person using owner content and sharing it to others), contributor (person sharing something to other's space) and stakeholder (tagged user) roles of user on OSN.As disseminator's content after sharing can also be re-disseminated by his friends so authors suggest that access control policies should be implemented without keeping an eye on the number of steps the content being re-disseminated. To evaluate access request over multi party access policies, two steps are involved.

First step is to check whether policy is applicable to request or not, if yes then second step is performed to find out the decision (permit or deny) of each controller (owner, contributor, disseminator and stakeholder) about access request and their decision is aggregated to allow or deny access. If policy is not applicable to request then without checking controllers decisions, access is denied. But there may be policy conflict because different controllers may have different policies on shared data item. Authors use voting scheme to resolve policy conflicts in decision making process. There are two types of voting schemes used for this purpose: Firstly, Decision voting scheme in which weight DV (aggregation of trust level of data owner and reputation value for collaborative control) is assigned to each controller according to his importance and secondly Sensitive voting in which each controller is assigned a sensitive level "Sc" for shared data item to show his privacy concern. Decision is taken according to resulted weighted voting value and sensitive level value respectively. Finally, threshold based conflict resolution scheme (combination of above voting schemes) is used to resolve policy conflict. In this approach, sensitive level value is taken as threshold for decision. If sensitive level value is higher than weighted voting value then access will be denied otherwise granted. Any controller can change his policy or sensitive level anytime and again both values of "Sc" and DV will be calculated and decision will be made according. Author also suggests strategy based conflict resolution having three policies: In first policy owner's decision has highest policy. If owner permits then access is granted whether other controllers agree for permission or not. In second approach, if any controller denies access then access is denied. In last approach, access is denied if the number of controllers who permit is less than the number of controllers who deny. This study also proposes solution for conflict about disseminated content. In this approach, access is granted if both owner and disseminator permit access otherwise denied. Authors also implemented a prototype named MController in the Facebook to verify proposed approach which helps different authors to specify their own policies regarding shared data item. This prototype was only restricted to photo sharing and is also a third party application. All the policy conflict resolution techniques were implemented in MController and on its basis module deny or grant access to shared data item. Module has capability to recognize malicious users in social network as well which can be eliminated after detection. To check the usability of that module a survey was also conducted by authors. For survey purpose, participants used Facebook with and without MController for a few days and they answered questions of the survey about likeability, simplicity and control of MController. Results of this study show that average user declares 80% positivity about likeability and control and 67% simplicity of MController which means positive opinion of users about MController use in Facebook.

The study (Carminati & Ferrari, 2011) is focusing on collaborative access control for resources as many users can be related to a single resource in online social network. This study proposes collaborative access control policy that rely on the collaborative set of users which can be identified by their relationship for resource and semantic web based technologies (RDF Documents) are used to identify collaborative users. Model of online social network has actors, arcs with relationship 'rt' and a further label for trust level. Every resources in model is associated with set of access conditions and each access condition is associated with maximum depth and minimum trust level. Depth depends upon the length of shortest distance between two nodes and trust level was calculated by TidalTrust algorithm. In this approach, every user is assumed to manage his resources and relationships. In this model, when a requester requests for a resource, owner will take help from social manager to check whether requester satisfies access rule for that resource or not. Social manager will collect all the opinions about resource release from collaborative set of users related to that resource. Collaborative security policies are implemented on both social manager and user side. Collaborative set of users can perform resource access evaluation as well as collaborative access rules administration. Social manager has RDF repository of RDF files which have information about all resources and relationships of users with resources. Model classified access control policies into admin side access control policies (implemented on social manager) and user defined access control policies (defined on user side).Policy language for this model consists of three components; subject specification (which specify the collaborative users to whom policy applies), object specification (which specify the resources to which policy applies) and Mode (which specifies how many user's positive opinion required at minimum to release resource).

Algorithm implemented for the proposed model (Carminati & Ferrari, 2011) works as follows: When a user creates a new resource, then he send its RDF description and access control policy for that resource to social manager. RDF description is added up to RDF repository by social manager. To approve resource access control policy, social manager computes collaborative users by collaborative administrator policies for that resource. When collaborative set of users is retrieved then algorithm requests for feedback from each user of collaborative set by sending them RDF description of new resource and policy to be approved. Algorithm waits until response from each collaborative user is gathered then it checks mode value. If mode=1 (when a single feedback required only) or if all responses are positive and mode="all" or if more than half responses are positive and mode="majority" then it returns approval message and it returns denial message when policy exist and there are no sufficient feedbacks. As a result of approval, requester inserts the new access control policy in his local policy base. This model focus on resource confidentiality but not user privacy.

Encryption is a technique that is used to produce cipher text that is not understandable by attackers. Some authors also used this technique for providing access control. For example, the study (Beato, Kohlweiss, & Wouters, 2009) by authors provides access control rule enforcement by Firefox extension. This extension enforce access control by encryption according to user choice. They used OPENPGP standard to provide access control. They secure user contents from social network provider especially as well as from other possible invaders. Contents of user are only visible to only selective group of users which are also called local trusted circle of user. There is public key transfer between users when they connect to each other and these keys are stored locally on their sites. The study (Zhang, He, Zhao, et al., 2015) proposed pro-active access control model for social networks named PAC. This study presents a framework based on trust for preventing malicious attacks in the social network. This model provide mechanism for detecting malicious attempts and denial to such repeated attempts in future as well. Authors used constraint mechanism provided by feedback component and evaluation component. Moreover, they used Game Theory for pro- active approach to give response to malicious attacks. The studies (Smari, Clemente, & Lalande, 2014), (Carminati & Ferrari, 2009), (Carminati & Ferrari, 2008) and (Bruns, Fong, Siahaan, et al., 2012) described later are also based on trust value.

Depth-Based Access Control for OSN

These models provide access control based on the distance between owner and requester. Researchers used encryption, digital signatures, cryptography and hybrid logic techniques for these type of access control models. For example, the authors of study (Shehab, Squicciarini & Ahn, 2008) also presents (Villegas, Ali & Maheswaran, 2008) in which distance between owner and requester is the base of access control rights. In this approach requesters are classified into three zones: Acceptance zone: The requesters whose requests will be accepted instantly. Attesting zone: This zone has those requesters whose requests will be considered after further evaluation. Rejection zone: The requesters whose request will be instantly rejected. These three zones are based on trusted distance. This model PDAC was also implemented and its usability was checked on some graphs from myspace.com. The study (Carminati & Ferrari, 2009) provides collaborative access control to resources. In this approach anonymous path is calculated by EIGamal cryptosystem (an encryption algorithm) when a user requests for resource. By anonymous path, resource owner is able to match the path according to resource access rules without the disclosure of path participants. Moreover, relationship trust value is also calculated for the resource owner without disclosure of trust of each relationship in the path. It can be called as anonymous trust value. Proposed algorithm checks depth of path found between requester and owner, decrypted trust value and anonymous path's both ends(must be owner and requester).If access rules are satisfied by depth and trust value then access is granted. This process is repeated for all nodes of collaboration, and access is denied if algorithm does not find any suitable path after checking each path associated with collaboration nodes.

Different groups can provide access control to their shared resources. For example, the study (Carminati & Ferrari, 2008) focuses on collaborative access control by using cryptography and digital signatures. By the collaboration of different selected nodes, relationship type, trust level and depth of relationship stated by owner in his access rules are checked to grant access. If resource has more than one access rules then all the rules are checked to grant access. Encrypted trust level is signed by each node to avoid fake trust level problem and owner public key is used to encrypt the trust level to avoid disclosure of trust level to intermediate nodes. If a node satisfies distributed rules related to all the relationships of the current path between owner and requester, then it will take part in collaboration. So, a node is required to check this condition before requesting its neighbor for collaboration.

Authors propose hybrid logic for access control in study (Bruns, Fong, Siahaan, et al., 2012). They say that hybrid logic is better than modal logic in expressing relationships. They provided different policies regarding relationship based access control in this study. They have provided many policy examples based on trust and depth of relationship. The studies (Carminati, Ferrari & Perego, 2006), (Carminati, Ferrari, Heatherly, et al., 2009), (Carminati & Ferrari, 2011), (Carminati, Ferrari, Heatherly, et al., 2011), (Cheng, Park & Sandhu, 2012a), and (Cheng, Park & Sandhu, 2012b) described above also represents depth relationship based access control models.

Attribute-Based Access Control in OSN

Attributes of profiles in online social networks have personal information of users. Different researchers proposed access control models based on these attributes. Here, in this section, we will briefly discuss about them.

Online social networks support API's which are the applications that can be added to platforms like Facebook, and by extracting data from user profiles, these application can perform specific tasks e.g. horoscope application can use birth date of user for reminding his friends on particular date. These applications are based on all or nothing rule. If a user grants full access of profile data to application then it is installed otherwise not. It indicates that due to these applications, user personal information has high risk of leakage which may cause disclosure about his particulars to strangers. The study (Shehab, Squicciarini & Ahn, 2008) proposes an access control model regarding such applications which may help users to enjoy such applications without disclosing their personal data. Access control framework developed by M. Shehab and his fellows consists of two components; Applications and user profiles. They say that user information's set of attributes should be generic rather than specific to provide abstraction to private information e.g. In address field only show zip code but not the complete address. The second component of social network is application that have set of defined functions (called API's) which application can call. Proposed API framework consists of three main phases:

- Firstly, Application registration; in this phase application developers provides application API calls and Application business state diagram to social network server to register the application with server. As a result, application sheet is formed having all list of attributes required by app and application is made available to users of social network for using in their profiles.

- Second phase is User application addition; when a user selects the application then application sheet is shown to user by giving him three options to use; opt-in, opt-out and generalize. If a user choose opt-in,it allows application to use all profile data, If user choose opt-out and does not select some data then application will have to work without some fields and finally generalize option will make app use just generalized attributes of user. According to user selection of option, user sheet is formed.
- User application adaptation is the last phase of framework. In this phase, application version is generated by using the input of profile data items mentioned in user sheet.

As user can enable generalized attributes or can ignore some options by not selecting them so due to missing data application can face problem in successfully providing the desired service. To address this problem author proposed reduced application transition system which includes only the state transitions permitted by user preferences and the possible reachable states after applying user preferences to application.

The study (Cheng, Park, & Sandhu, 2014) by authors propose a model $UURAC_A$ which integrate attribute-based policies in relationship based access control. It is basically the extension of UURAC model of (Cheng, Park & Sandhu, 2012b) study with attributes aware access control. It specifies three types of attributes: Node attributes (user or resource are taken as nodes), Edge attributes (show characteristic of edge like weight etc.) and Count attributes (specify the lower bound of occurrence of attribute-based path).Authors added attribute-based rules to existing model (Cheng, Park & Sandhu, 2012b). As far as algorithm for access evaluation is concerned, when a requester requests to access a resource then system fetches accessing user policy for that action, resource policy and system specified policy for that action. Decision module extracts path specification and attribute-based rules for these policies. Then result of each policy is found by running path checking algorithm and during this process decision module makes sure that all involved attributes satisfy attribute-based policies. The results of all policies are integrated to find final result. Authors say that attribute-based approach is an additional overhead to algorithm and it is directly proportional to number of attributes and type of attribute function.

The OSNs are very useful for cooperation in practical life. The study (Jung & Joshi, 2014) presents CPBAC (Community-centric Property Based Access Control) to support secure cooperation among users in social networks. OSN can help better than traditional methods in disaster conditions like finding lost child or disaster relief because information can spread more quickly with social network. Limited help (as emergency condition just known by friend circle of victim if he post it on OSN), naive cooperation and disclosure of highly sensitive and private information to others are the key limitations in OSN cooperation. Finding a trusted group which can help better the victim in a disaster is a big issue. Authors suggest three requirements for secure cooperation in OSN; Organization of a community of eligible users only, Anonymous cooperation and Time-based control (all the resources and permissions should remain valid during cooperation only).CPBAC model specifies four properties of user; User context which represent a user status (age, gender, job, reputation, and social relationships), User tasks which are the functions user can perform in OSN like posting messages, User resources which a user owns, and User policies which can be of two types; Access control policy which decides authorized users to his own properties and Filtering policy which filters unwanted contents from all authorized contents of his choice.

The CPBAC model specifies six properties of a community formed for cooperation; Community Context (goal of community), Community tasks (creation and termination of community), Community resources, Cooperation process for any situation and Community policies where Policies in community can be of three types. Firstly, access control policy which allow access to community properties, recruiting policy specify eligibility rule to perform role in community and last separation of duty policy which must be checked before assigning any role to a person because two roles can be assigned to a person by mistake. Sixth property of community is the community member who has permission to perform a role in community. The CPBAC model also specifies four properties of society that represents online social network supporting secure cooperation. These properties are Contexts, Tasks, Resources and Policies. The CPBAC model categorizes permission into context oriented, task oriented, resource oriented, policy oriented and user oriented permissions. To address subject's property there are four predicate functions in the CPBAC model named hascnt,, hastsk, hasrsc and haspol.

This paper (Jung & Joshi, 2014) also suggests administration model for the CPBAC named ACPBAC. In the ACPBAC, administrator responsibilities are divided into three types of admins: Society Manager which control access to OSN's properties such as virtual space, Community Manager which is responsible for community life cycle and user. In an OSN, SM and CM each role is assigned to only one person each. In this approach, first user registers himself to OSN, Community manager adds users to different communities according to their roles, register communities and provide access control to community properties in cooperation environment. Once society manager receives the registration of community or departure request of user or community manager, it deletes virtual space given to the requester. Society properties are also managed by society manager. Community manager can also take help from society manager to recommend users for community and society manager nominate them from registered users. To cope with conflict resolution based on property based access control, CPBAC enforces three types of constraints; Cardinality constraint which limits no. of users assigned to a community, SOD constraint that avoid problems in assigning different roles to the same person and eligibility constraint which qualify a user to take community role or permission. CPBAC architecture is also suggested by authors. It has three components; a) Community repository which contains information about necessary community roles, community policies and cooperation process among members. b) CPBAC engine which controls all types of access during interaction whether they are of OSN system, communities or members) SeCON application which is a Facebook app helping its users to perform secure cooperation by using CPBAC model.SeCON app was implemented and used to validate the concept of CPBAC model and results successful application of proposed model in real world scenarios. There are two limitation to this study: The application developed to validate the proposed work is only applicable to Facebook. It should be applicable to other applications as well. Security analysis of CPBAC is also not the part of this study. The study (Guesmia & Boustia, 2015) proposes contextual based access control model. Users can specify different rules with the help of contexts. They used T J classic as description language. This model helps user in two ways; Firstly, when user specify his privacy setting for shared resource, he can include temporal conditions and secondly it makes access control decision dynamically when request is made. Model is composed of four parts: Access control related entities (entity can be subject, object, action and environment), Attributes of entities, policy representation and Policy evaluation. Policy evaluation is the process for granting access to any resource for which the subject has requested. In this model, if the attribute values of entities in the request meet the attribute values declared in the policy rule, then access to resource is granted. Otherwise access is not granted. Authors also propose architecture for this model that has some components: Policy Administration Point (PAP) which is the database of all policies specified by user. Policy Information Point (PIP) which provide information for evaluating policies. Policy Decision Point (PDP) which decides about permission grant or denial and

Policy Enforcement Point (PEP).When a user requests for a resource, policy enforcement point sends all attributes of requested subject, requested object, action and environment to PDP. The PDP checks all attributes against owner specified rules and sends request to PIP for additional information if required. Policy is evaluated by the PDP and sends its response back to the PEP.

Some researchers has provided access control by combining attributes and other factors like trust etc. For example, the study (Smari, Clemente, & Lalande, 2014) proposes attribute-based access control model including trust and privacy. It is a general framework for access control models. Basic components of this model are as follows: Subjects, Objects, attributes, operation, permission, permission assignment functions, trust and privacy. Every subject and object have their attributes, trust and purpose of privacy. Extended ABAC decision module has context, trust algorithm, permission granted functions and privacy preserving algorithm. When requester requests for operation on an object then ABAC decision module evaluates request by attributes of subject and object and attribute-based access control rules and contexts are evaluated. Trust algorithm computes the value of trust for subject and module decides about operation execution based on these factors. Trust algorithm calculates the value of trust (trust level) for subject based on his previous behavior. This model (Smari, Clemente, & Lalande, 2014) include trust in two ways: Direct trust and indirect trust. In direct trust, trust level of subject directly affects the access control decision and in indirect approach, trust level of subject will affect the attributes but not directly the access control decision. Privacy policies are categorized in three classes in this model; subject privacy, object privacy and policy privacy. The model (Smari, Clemente, & Lalande, 2014) includes highly dynamic conditions in collaborative domain. Authors also implemented a prototype for this model which guarantees the privacy of object attributes with the help of trust level of subjects.

The study (Jin, Krishnan, & Sandhu, 2012) presents an access based access control model that has formal connections between discretionary access control, mandatory access control and role based access control. They say that there are three entities to be mentioned in this model; Subject, Object and user. All of them have attributes associated with them where each attribute can have two types of ranges; atomic valued or set valued. Different components of the proposed model are described here.

Users are associated with different attribute functions. Subjects are created by users only. Objects are resources with their attributes and their values can be based on subject and object values. User attributes, Subject attributes, Object attribute, permissions, authorization policies and constraint checking policies. Authors suggests four policy configuration points in this approach; authorization policies, constraints for subject attribute assignment, constraints for object attribute assignment and constraints for object attribute modification. This study (Jin, Krishnan, & Sandhu, 2012) suggests an ABAC model that can be easily used for discretionary access control, mandatory access control and role based access control.

Third party applications provide ease to users of a social network and these type of applications are embedded with social networks. Privacy regarding these applications is also mandatory when we talk about social network access control. The study (Shehab, Squicciarini, Ahn & Kokkinou, 2012) by authors is focusing on privacy concerns of third party applications which are open interfaces for public developers regarding social networks. Authors proposed framework in which user can specify the data attributes for sharing with the applications and degree of specificity for these attributes as well. They also implemented their solution and find out user feedback which shows that users need such type of solutions to enjoy applications securely. Participants under study also found this approach easy to use.

Encryption technique can also be used for attribute-based access control. For example, the study (Jahid, Mittal & Borisov, 2011) proposed architecture named "EASIER" which provides access control by attribute-based encryption. It suggests that if we want to remove access from a user then there are two ways that can be used for this purpose; Generate new keys for users whom you want to grant access or re-encrypt the existing already encrypted keys. They also implemented a prototype with proposed approach for the Facebook.

Community-Centric Access Control for OSN

Social networks have different groups of users that have similar interests. Such type of groups are having more interactions. Some models are based on these communities for providing access control. Amin and Muthucumaru, the authors of study (Ranjbar & Maheswaran, 2010) used the idea of community-centric control to estimate the users who will get information in the community. For estimating such users, they found sharing patterns in the community based on grouping of users depending upon their communication patterns. They refer this sharing set of users named "myCommunity". In this idea, OSN will compute group of users in myCommunity of user and that user can approve or ban any person in the available set. Moreover, when a user banns somebody then risk of leaking information to that person is also calculated. If calculated risk is above acceptable threshold then person can reduce sharing to that person or simply eliminate him from his myCommunity. The myCommunity is the subset of users who are dense part of the network. Here myCommunity is the friends of user who have frequent interactions and can be for each user independently. For estimating myCommunity authors used Clique and k-plex algorithms, where Clique is the maximal complete subnetwork of users in which no other user can be added and k-plex is a group in which each member have no less than n-k friendships (neighbors) in n size community. Two datasets from Facebook and Flicker were selected for analysis. From these datasets they made three different networks named friendship network (undirected network), interaction network (directed network) and weighted interaction network (based on interaction network by giving weights on arcs). Authors performed two studies in parallel. Firstly, they studied behavior of users whether inside or outside of their community. Results show that there are more interactions inside myCommunity than outside which means members of community are used to keep maximum information inside community. Flicker data has 12 times more interaction than the Facebook dataset. Number of interactions within and inside to outside of myCommunity in friendship network is larger than other two networks. Secondly, they focused on the interactions within communities. Results show that almost 50% of community members are active in participation with more than 90% of activities inside community in both the Facebook and the Flicker networks. Author suggest that only active persons should have access to private data only. In this study, how to control information leak is discussed by identifying communities but different possible information leaks is not discussed.

Confidentiality approach can also provide access control because it consists of constraints to limit access to anything. The study (Ranjbar & Maheswaran, 2014) propose community centric confidentiality control scheme for online social networks. This study also estimates the exact risk of information disclosure related to user's access control decision. Here, Algorithm 1 finds sub graph named α-myCommunity against a user which shows that information of user can reach that sub graph without leaking where α shows number of interactions between users. Algorithm 2 suggests method for calculating set of friends who can disclose information to opponents. Algorithm 3 limits this set of friends to avoid information flow to opponents. Results show that if α is high then α-myCommunity size will be small. Opponents can receive information from indirect links even if we block direct links from user to opponent. By historical information of interactions and computation of α-myCommunity again and again, stable α- myCommunities can be calculated. Authors also used Facebook and Flicker datasets to compute α-myCommunity. They say that blocking list is not effected by random changes in interaction intensity up to 60% of Facebook and 50% of Flicker. This study works fine only by including opponents in the network. It doesn't include physical contacts of a user with others for information sharing; only focus contact by social network. Moreover, it says that all the users are concerned for a single topic while in real life users are concerned to different topics.

The study (Toomim, Zhang, Fogarty, et al., 2008) is about simple social access control where community of users is not based on cliques or any other technique like structure of network etc. But only based on a test questions about shared knowledge. Here, in this study, the set of friends are only based on specific questions instead of any complex techniques like attestation, trust value calculation etc. They also implemented a prototype on its basis for Facebook. The study (Jung & Joshi, 2014) has also used community-centric approach with attribute defined approach.

User-Activity Centric Access Control for OSN

Users of OSN perform many activities on social networking websites. Authors have proposed different access control models for these activities. Here, in this section we will study some of them. The study by Jaehong Park, Ravi Sandhu, and Yuan Cheng (Park, Sandhu, & Cheng, 2011a) is related to both user control policies and system automated activities in social networks. This study provides ACON (Activity centric access control for social computing). Authors classify activities of social computing system (SCS) in three categories: User activities, SCS's activities and SCS's administrator activities (manual activities performed by administrators to manage overall system). User activities are further divided into User's usage activity (user can read, write modify resources or poke other users), User's control activities on resources, user's control activities on users and user's control activities on sessions. SCS's activities are further classified into SCS's Service Activities, SCS's Control Activities (to control users, resources and sessions) and SCS's Decision Activities. ACON framework proposed by (Park, Sandhu, & Cheng, 2011a) consists of nine components:

- Users are human being performing different activities in social computing system. User can have his attribute (his name, address etc.) and policies (his limit set).
- Sessions represents the user who is logged into SCS.
- Activities can be of user, SCS or SCS administrator. Action is the fourth component which can be any notion of the user (read, write, poke etc.).Action can be against any target user, target resource or both.
- Target User is the one who receives an action from the sender. Target resources are the resources which are used in action.
- SCS's Decision Activity helps SCS to take a decision against an activity permission or denial by considering individual policies of users and SCS's own policies and attributes.
- SCS's Activity Module are the functions that perform control activities of SCS.
- SCS Administrators is the last component of ACON which represent a person with management role in SCS.

The ACON Framework has some characteristics suggested by authors. Policy individualization is one of them which says that policies of user is combined with policies of SCS to perform any decision. It means user's specified policy is important just like SCS specified policy. Another characteristic in

ACON is a separation of user and resource policies. In this study (Park, Sandhu, & Cheng, 2011a), Authors present two models; ACON user activity control model and a model of session management with examples. Limitation to this work is that model only considers static session but not dynamic session. It means that during a session, policy and attributes of session remain unchanged.

The study (Park, Sandhu, & Cheng, 2011b) by Jaehong Park, Ravi Sandhu, and Yuan Cheng proposed "A User-Activity Centric Framework for Access Control". This study is specific version of ACON framework described above. It is not discussing social computer system activities as well as social computer system administrator activities. It is just focusing on user activities. This framework contains three components: users, sessions and activities. User maintain session for different activities while activities can be of two types: general user activities and user's control activities. In a session user can perform different activities whereas Activity can contain action, target resources, and target users. Action is any function performed by user in a session. Target resources can be any shared content like picture, videos, profile information etc. Target user receives action from other user. This framework has some extra ordinary features: it can distinguish session from a user, it provides conceptual model to understand OSN access control, it helps user to control activity notification by specifying either user policies or resource policies, and it also supports enhanced control in active user sessions which are not available in previous studies.

DISCUSSION

The OSN providers want to mine information from user population to extract useful business information which puts personal information of users on risk; against privacy. On the other hand, users want to provide privacy to their data and resources. To enforce access control to resources in the social network, researchers used many techniques. Every approach has its pros and cons, which are discussed in the following.

As we have seen that access control models depend on relationship-type, for example (Gollu, Saroiu & Wolman, 2007), trust between users, for example (Ali, Villegas & Maheswaran, 2007) and relationship-depth between users, for example (Barbara & Elena, 2008) or a combination of them, for example (Carminati, Ferrari, Heatherly, et al.,, 2009). Moreover, access control models are also based on community-centric approach for example (Ranjbar & Maheswaran, 2014), community-centric property based approach for example (Jung & Joshi, 2014), attribute-based approach for example (Jung & Joshi, 2014) and user-activity centric approach for example (Park, Sandhu, & Cheng, 2011b).

Social network is the collection of millions of actors. Every actor is used to communicate frequently with some specific persons but not all. So, in social network some actors have more interactions than others. Access control can be enforced on such groups by finding them. Community centric access control approach seems efficient method to estimate such groups in which communication can be carried out without leaking as in (Ranjbar & Maheswaran, 2010). It is useful in the way that by such technique more controlled environment for accessing resources can be granted to more dense part of the network. Limitation to this approach is that in this scheme access control methods are limited to specific actors (clusters or groups) of the network, it should be applied to all actors.

As we have seen, some approaches for access control are used in collaborations, for example, (Carminati & Ferrari, 2011). Resources of the network can have one or many owners. Collaborative approach focuses on such scenarios as present social networks are also providing more options to users than the previous ones like poking, tagging etc. The owner and all somehow related users of a resource have rights to specify their policies for a single resource and this approach seems good enough in this regard. Very few models are available in this dimension. One major issue in this approach is the calculation of collaborative set of users, rare algorithms in this context are found; efficient algorithms should be proposed in this context.

We have also seen that some of the available access control models have used semantic web technologies, for example (Carminati, Ferrari, Raymond, et. al, 2009). Semantic web technologies provide better way to extract information about complex relationships and also facilitate users to write rules for handling data. These technologies are not platform dependent and can be extended to multiple OSNs. This technique is more flexible than HTML. To fulfill the evolving needs of social network users, this approach based models seems notable but models based on semantic approach are difficult to implement. Those approaches that cannot be easily implemented remain theories with no practical justifications.

User-activity centric access control models provide the facility that users can affect control decisions on other users or system's activities. The studies, for example (Park, Sandhu, & Cheng, 2011b) are based on user activities. Generally speaking, RBAC models do not facilitate users to have effect in control decisions on other user activities or system activities, so user activity based access control models are better in this context. Relationship-based access control models are easy to use for users. They provide access control by depth of relationship, trust parameter or type of relationship. They do not focus on history based access control in which access can be granted to requester on his history basis (whether on his previous interaction with owner or with a trusted value which other users have calculated for him). Moreover, they use ACL technique to provide access control which is easier technique to check the authorized users but its maintenance is an additional overhead for the system on which it is implemented.

Relationship-based access control can be categorized as user to user, user to resource and resource to resource. User to user relationship based access control (Hu, Ahn & Jorgensen, 2013), (Shehab, Squicciarini & Ahn, 2008) and (Cheng, Park & Sandhu, 2012a) provides authorization if there is a U2U relationship between requester and granter depending upon their depth of relationship or type of relationship. But, current OSN needs to manage authorizations for U2R and R2R relationships as well. User to resource relationship based approaches not only facilitate user to specify policies for their own but also the activities of other related users whereas U2U relationship based models only allow users to specify policies for their own contents and activities. Very few studies (Carminati, Ferrari, Raymond, et. al, 2009), (Carminati & Ferrari, 2011), (Carminati, Ferrari, Heatherly, et al., 2011), (Cheng, Park & Sandhu, 2012b) and (Cheng, Park, & Sandhu, 2014) are available which provides mechanisms for both U2U and U2R relationships.

The attribute-based access control is an extension to relationship based access control model. A user may have different attributes like age, gender and location; these attributes must be considered in granting access to that user and this approach is used in these models. For example, "mutual friend" relationship is found in the Facebook but "Mutual friend named Ali" cannot be specified until and unless attributes of mutual friend (name) is not considered. A mixture of both schemes provides more adaptable and flexible access control to their data. But one thing to mention is, a user can have many attributes, which attributes are to consider for granting access is the big question. Moreover, when more number of attributes will be under consideration for granting access then there will be more overhead for algorithm used for this approach and processing will be slow and response time for user might be increased. The access control models that are based on user activities are described in (Park, Sandhu, & Cheng, 2011a) and (Park, Sandhu, & Cheng, 2011b) are based on user activities. It is the strength of these studies as social network is all about users and their activities.

Trust-based access control models are totally based on the calculation of the trust value between two users. Algorithms available for trust computation are described in (Xin, Leyi, Yao, et al., 2013), (Gambhir, Doja & Moinuddin, 2014), (Chakraborty & Karform, 2012) and (Faisal, Alsumait & Al-ameer, 2014). These algorithms are suggested almost in the last four years, it means that trust-based algorithms has become area of research but available algorithms are very few. More work is required in this field. Generalized and standard trust based algorithms are yet to be developed.

The Table 1 classifies all available access control models/techniques with their strategy. Some studies like (Beato, Kohlweiss, & Wouters, 2009) use encryption technique for access control enforcement but as encryption produce cipher text from simple text, cipher text size is very important in this regard. Higher the cypher size require more processing and protection of keys is also a big issue. The studies in which access control is based on shared knowledge seems interesting and easy to implement but bias exists here in term of security of questions. Attackers can guess answer to precise question and can be part of cluster.

Authors of study (Anwar, Fong, Yang, et al., 2010) proposed a tool for users of OSN to visualize their extended neighborhood. Owner of the profile is facilitated by providing some functions by this tool for policy assessment; user can specify its neighborhood size, user can examine his profile view by other user's point of view and user is provided help in different access scenarios to specify its neighborhood. These types of tools are needed to help user by visualizing their access policies for better understanding of their relationships with other users. Limited number of studies proposing such kind of visualizing tools is available. Researchers have to concentrate on this perspective.

A different type of study regarding general perspectives of access control is also available for researchers and users of OSN. Authors of the study (Prabhakar & Santhaiah, 2013) have discussed that there is the need of multi- party access control in the OSN. They briefly explained different types of social media like blogs, social networking sites etc. They proposed that community structure can be found on the basis of density of group, similarity of vertex between group, similarity of group actions and similarity of frequent action of users. Further, the categories of algorithms are discussed which are community detection algorithms, hierarchal clustering algorithms, partitioned clustering algorithms, modularity based algorithms and spectral clustering. They focused on the analysis of social network with respect to emerging research areas. Such kinds of study can help beginners to understand about overall aspects related to access control and to recognize the techniques that can be used to detect clusters in a social network.

A study (Oo, 2013) propose an approach in which system is able to construct access rules for resources itself based on user's already mentioned profile settings. In this model, options are provided to user for access rules for his friends and by considering his options access decision tree is formed by system. Community structure of a user's neighborhood is calculated by system itself. This approach seems to provide minimum effort for the user to specify rules for access control. Very little work is available in this concern. Distributed access control technique (Ahmad & Whitworth, 2011) define social requirements for access control as ownership, local roles, local object classes, usability and flexibility and delegating view rights. Further it also designs a technical solution to fulfill these social requirements. It requires no overall administration and is based on issuance of distributed certificates. It has less points of failure. As users of OSN cannot actually have understanding of policy specification related to access control of their resources. Beta version of ACPT tool is released by NIST (National Institute of Standard and Technology) in 2015 for access control policy specification. More tools should be developed in this area with proper user guides to help users.

Table 1. Categories of different access control models and their related studies

Access Control techniques for OSN	Trust	Relationship type	Depth	Attributes	Community centric	Activity centric
(Ali, Villegas & Maheswaran, 2007)	Yes	No	No	No	No	No
(Carminati, Ferrari & Perego, 2006)	Yes	Yes	Yes	No	No	No
(Carminati, Ferrari & Perego, 2009)	Yes	No	No	No	No	No
(Carminati, Ferrari, et al., 2009)	Yes	Yes	Yes	No	No	No
(Carminati, Ferrari, et al., 2011)	Yes	Yes	Yes	No	No	No
(Hu, Ahn & Jorgensen, 2013)	Yes	Yes	No	No	No	No
(Carminati & Ferrari,2011)	Yes	No	Yes	No	No	No
(Smari, Clemente, & Lalande, 2014)	Yes	No	No	Yes	No	No
(Beato, Kohlweiss, & Wouters, 2009)	Yes	No	No	No	No	No
(Zhang, He, Zhao, et al., 2015)	Yes	No	No	No	No	No
(Carminati & Ferrari, 2008)	Yes	Yes	Yes	No	No	No
(Carminati & Ferrari, 2009)	Yes	Yes	Yes	No	No	No
(Bruns, Fong, Siahaan, et al., 2012)	Yes	No	Yes	No	No	No
(Gollu, Saroiu & Wolman, 2007)	No	Yes	No	No	No	No
(Tootoonchian, Saroiu, et al., 2009)	No	Yes	No	No	No	No
(Tootoonchian, Gollu, et al., 2008)	No	Yes	No	No	No	No
(Cheng, Park & Sandhu, 2012a)	No	Yes	Yes	No	No	No
(Cheng, Park & Sandhu, 2012b)	No	Yes	Yes	No	No	No
(Pang & Zhang, 2014)	No	Yes	No	No	No	No
(Du, Liu, & Wang, 2013)	No	Yes	No	No	No	No
(Villegas, Ali & Maheswaran, 2008)	No	No	Yes	No	No	No
(Shehab, Squicciarini & Ahn, 2008)	No	No	No	Yes	No	No
(Cheng, Park, & Sandhu, 2014)	No	No	No	Yes	No	No
(Jung & Joshi, 2014)	No	No	No	Yes	Yes	No
(Guesmia & Boustia, 2015)	No	No	No	Yes	No	No
(Jin, Krishnan, & Sandhu, 2012)	No	No	No	Yes	No	No
(Shehab, Squicciarini et al., 2012)	No	No	No	Yes	No	No
(Jahid, Mittal & Borisov, 2011)	No	No	No	Yes	No	No
(Ranjbar & Maheswaran, 2010)	No	No	No	No	Yes	No
(Ranjbar & Maheswaran, 2014)	No	No	No	No	Yes	No
(Toomim, Zhang, Fogarty, et al., 2008)	No	No	No	No	Yes	No
(Park, Sandhu, & Cheng, 2011a)	No	No	No	No	No	Yes
(Park, Sandhu, & Cheng, 2011b)	No	No	No	No	No	Yes

The valuable work done by (Carminati & Ferrari, 2010) is related to privacy aware access control and available for future directions for researchers. Authors discussed about access control requirements and did literature review according. They say access control policy has requirements like trust, depth of relation, efficient and scalable implementation of strategies, subject and object specification. Then they discuss privacy issues in access control; disclosure of personal information during relationships, protection of trust level and calculation of trust value. Moreover, study (Carminati & Ferrari, 2010) suggests some future direction for researchers in access control regarding OSN.

Most of the available access control models and techniques for OSN based on various characteristics and aspects are discussed. We have to focus on evolving needs of access control related to social network because if we do not put efforts for this concern, attackers will have more power to disclose user's personal information. Different social platforms have different functionalities and access control should be focused for all the facilities provided by such platforms.

CONCLUSION

A number of techniques have been proposed by several authors of access control for OSN. Every approach has different idea but one thing is common among them; all of them are facilitating users of online social networks to provide security measure for their activities and contents. The journey of access control administration started from centralized approach and now it has reached to decentralized approaches. User wants more power and freedom for access control and they don't want to be restricted to system specified control. There is more need to focus on decentralized approaches for access control, models for automatically generated access control rules, access control models for professional networks, visualizing tools for user neighborhood structure and collaborative access control models. Moreover, a common user has rarely aware of policy specification advantages and disadvantages. Further, when a user specifies his policies then to check the effects of that policy, guideline is very rare. There must be supportive tools available for OSN users to enable them for efficient policy specification with real life examples. Access Control Models with their proper implementation must be focused for all kinds of available social network platforms.

REFERENCES

Ahmad, A. & Whitworth, B. (2011). Distributed Access Control for Social Networks. In *Proceedings of Information Assurance and Security*, (pp.68-73). Melaka: IEEE.

Ali, B., Villegas, W., & Maheswaran, M. (2007). A trust-based approach for protecting user data in Social networks. In *Proceedings of the 2007 Conference of the Center for Advanced Studies on Collaborative research*. New York, NY: ACM. 10.1145/1321211.1321251

Anwar, M., Fong, P. W. L., Yang, X. D., & Hamilton, H. (2010). Visualizing Privacy Implications of Access Control Policies in Social Network Systems. *Data Privacy Management and Autonomous Spontaneous Security, SETOP, 2009*, 106–120. doi:10.1007/978-3-642-11207-2_9

Aristotle. (n.d.) Retrieved from: http://www.goodreads.com/quotes/183896-man-is-by-nature-a-social-animal-an-individual-who

Beato, F., Kohlweiss, K., & Wouters, K. (2009). Enforcing Access Control in Social Network Sites. *GoogleScholar, Hot Topics in Privacy Enhancing Technologies*, (HotPETS).

Bruns, G., Fong, P., Siahaan, I., & Huth, M. (2012). Relationship-Based Access Control: Its Expression and Enforcement through Hybrid Logic. In *Proceedings of the second ACM conference on Data and Application Security and Privacy*, (pp. 117-124). ACM.

Carminati, B., & Ferrari, E. (2008). Privacy-Aware Collaborative Access Control In Web-Based Social Networks. Data and Applications Security XXII. *LNCS*, *5094*, 81–96.

Carminati, B. & Ferrari, E. (2009). Enforcing Relationships Privacy through Collaborative Access Control in Web-based Social Networks. In *Proceedings of CollaborateCom, Collaborative Computing: Networking, Applications and Worksharing*, (pp. 1-9). Washington, DC: IEEE.

Carminati, B. & Ferrari, E. (2010). Privacy-Aware Access Control in Social Networks: Issues and Solutions. *Privacy and Anonymity in Information Management Systems*, (pp. 181-195). Springer London.

Carminati, B. & Ferrari, E. (2011). Collaborative Access Control in On-line Social Networks. *IEEE Collaborative Computing: Networking, Applications and Worksharing,* (pp. 231 - 240). Orlando, FL: CollaborateCom.

Carminati, B., Ferrari, E., Heatherly, R., Kantarcioglu, M., & Thuraisingham, B. (2009). A semantic Web based framework for social network access control. In *Proceedings of the 14th ACM symposium on Access control models and technologies*, (pp. 177-186). ACM.

Carminati, B., Ferrari, E., Heatherly, R., Kantarcioglu, M., & Thuraisingham, B. (2011). Semantic web-based social network access control. Computers & Security, 30(2-3), 108-115.

Carminati, B., Ferrari, E. & Perego, A. (2006). Rule-Based Access Control for Social Networks. *OTM Workshops* (vol. 4278, pp. 1734–1744). Springer.

Carminati, B., Ferrari, E., & Perego, A. (2009). Enforcing access control in web-based social networks. *ACM Transactions on Information and System Security*, *13*(1), 6. doi:10.1145/1609956.1609962

Chakraborty, P. S., & Karform, S. (2012). Designing Trust Propagation Algorithms based on Simple Multiplicative Strategy for Social Networks. *Procedia Technology,* (6), 534–539.

Cheng, Y., Park, J., & Sandhu, R. (2012a). A User-to-User Relationship-based Access Control Model for Online Social Networks. *Data and Applications Security and Privacy*, *26*(7371), 8–24.

Cheng, Y., Park, J., & Sandhu, R. (2012b). Relationship-based Access Control for Online Social Networks: Beyond User-to-User Relationships. In *International Conference on Social Computing, Privacy, Security, Risk and Trust*, (pp. 646 – 655). Amsterdam: IEEE. 10.1109/SocialCom-PASSAT.2012.57

Cheng, Y., Park, J., & Sandhu, R. (2014). *Attribute-aware Relationship-based Access Control for Online Social Networks. Data and Applications Security and Privacy XXVIII, 28th Annual IFIP WG 11.3 Working Conference, DBSec 2014* (pp. 292–306). Vienna, Austria: Springer Berlin Heidelberg.

Du, Z., Liu, Y., & Wang, Y. (2013). Relation Based Access Control in Campus Social Network System. *First International Conference on Information Technology and Quantitative Management, Procedia Computer Science*. ScienceDirect. 10.1016/j.procs.2013.05.003

Faisal, M., Alsumait, A., & Al-ameer, Z. (2014, March). Trust inference algorithms for social networks. *Journal of Engineering Research, 2*(2), 3. doi:10.760340632-014-0003-2

Ferraiolo, D. F., Sandhu, R., Gavrila, S., Kuhn, R., & Chandramouli, R. (2001). Proposed NIST standard for role-based access control. *ACM Transactions on Information and System Security, 4*(3), 224–274. doi:10.1145/501978.501980

Gambhir, M., Doja, M.N., & Moinuddin. (2014). Action-Based Trust Computation Algorithm for Online Social Network. In *Advanced Computing & Communication Technologies*, (pp. 451 – 458). Rohtak: IEEE.

Gollu, K. K., Saroiu, S., & Wolman, A. (2007). A Social Networking-Based Access Control Scheme for Personal Content. In *Proceedings of the 21st ACM Symposium on Operating Systems Principles.* Skamania Lodge Stevenson, WA: ACM.

Graham, G. S., & Denning, P. J. (1972). Protection: principles and practice. In *Proceedings of the ACM Spring Joint Computer Conference*, (pp. 417–429). New York, NY: ACM.

Guesmia, K. & Boustia, N. (2015). A Contextual Attribute-based Access Control Model based on T – Jclassic. *ISPS, Programming and Systems*, (pp. 1-6). Algiers: IEEE.

Hu, H., Ahn, G.H. & Jorgensen, J. (2013). Multiparty Access Control for Online Social Networks: Model and Mechanisms. *Knowledge And Data Engineering, 25*(7), 1614 – 1627.

Hu, V. C., Kuhn, D. R., & Ferraiolo, D. F. (2015). Attribute-Based Access Control. *Computer, 48*(2), 85–88. doi:10.1109/MC.2015.33

Jung, Y., & Joshi, J. B. D. (2014, March). CPBAC: Property-based access control model for secure co-operation in online social networks. *Computers & Security, 41*, 19–39. doi:10.1016/j.cose.2013.08.004

Jin, X., Krishnan, R., & Sandhu, R. (2012). A Unified Attribute-Based Access Control Model Covering. In *D. A. C. MAC and RBAC. Data and Applications Security and Privacy XXVI, 26th Annual IFIP WG 11.3 Conference, DBSec 2012*. Springer Berlin Heidelberg.

Jahid, S., Mittal, P., & Borisov, N. (2011). EASiER: Encryption-based Access Control in Social Networks with Efficient Revocation. In *Proceedings of the 6th ACM Symposium on Information, Computer and Communications Security*, (pp. 411-415). ACM. 10.1145/1966913.1966970

Oo, S. H. P. (2013, June). Intelligent access control policies for social network site. *International Journal of Computer Science & Information Technology, 5*, 3.

Pang, J., & Zhang, Y. (2014). A new access control scheme for Facebook-style social networks. In *Proceedings of Availability, Reliability and Security*, (pp. 1 – 10). Fribourg: IEEE.

Park, J., Sandhu, R., & Cheng, Y. (2011a). ACON: Activity-Centric Access Control for Social Computing. In *Proceedings of Availability, Reliability and Security 2011 Sixth International Conference* (pp. 242 – 247). Vienna: IEEE.

Park, J., Sandhu, R., & Cheng, Y. (2011b). A User-Activity-Centric Framework for Access Control in Online Social Networks. *IEEE Internet Computing*, *15*(5), 62–65. doi:10.1109/MIC.2011.30

Prabhakar, R., & Santhaiah, C. H. (2013, August). Structural Model and Dynamics Mechanisms of Social Network Analysis. *International Journal of Engineering Trends and Technology*, *4*, 8.

Ranjbar, A. & Maheswaran, M., (2010). A Case for Community-Centric Controls for Information Sharing on Online Social Network. In *Proceedings of IEEE GLOBECOM Workshops* (pp. 373 – 377). Miami, FL: GCWkshps.

Ranjbar, A., & Maheswaran, M. (2014, March). Using community structure to control information sharing in online social networks. *Computer Communications*, *41*, 11–21. doi:10.1016/j.comcom.2014.01.002

Sandhu, R.S. & Samarati, P. (1994). Access control: principle and practice. *Communications Magazine*, *32*(9), 40–48.

Shehab, M., Squicciarini, A., Ahn, G.H., & Kokkinou, I. (2012). Access control for online social networks third party Applications. *Computers & Security*, *31*(8), 897–911.

Shehab, M., Squicciarini, A.C., & Ahn, G.J. (2008). Beyond User-to-User Access Control for Online Social Networks. *Information and Communications Security*, *5308*, 174–189.

Smari, W. W., Clemente, P., & Lalande, J. F. (2014, February). An extended attribute-based access control model with trust and privacy: Application to a collaborative crisis management system. *Future Generation Computer Systems*, *31*, 147–168. doi:10.1016/j.future.2013.05.010

Toomim, M., Zhang, X., Fogarty, J., Landay, J. A., & Morris, N. (2008). Access Control by Testing for Shared Knowledge. In *CHI '08 Proceedings of the SIGCHI Conference on Human*. ACM.

Tootoonchian, A., Ganjali, Y., Saroiu, S., & Wolman, A. (2009). Lockr: Better privacy for social networks. In *Proceedings of the 5th ACM International Conference on emerging Networking Experiments and Technologies*, (pp. 169-180). New York, NY: ACM.

Tootoonchian, A., Gollu, K.K., Saroiu, S., Ganjali, Y., & Wolman, A. (2008). Lockr: social access Control for web 2.0. In *Proceedings of WOSN'08* (pp. 43–48). Washington, DC: ACM.

U.S. Department of Defense. (1985). *Trusted Computer System Evaluation Criteria, 5200.28-STD*. Author.

Villegas, W., Ali, B., & Maheswaran, M. (2008). An access control scheme for protecting personal Data. In *Proceedings of the 2008 Sixth Annual Conference on Privacy, Security and Trust*, (pp. 24–35). IEEE. 10.1109/PST.2008.14

Xin, L., Leyi, S., Yao, W., Zhaojun, X., & Wenjing, F. (2013). A Dynamic Trust Conference Algorithm for Social Network. In *Proceedings of P2P, Parallel, Grid, Cloud and Internet Computing*, (pp. 340 – 346). Compiegne: IEEE.

Zhang, Y., He, J., Zhao, B., Huang, Z., & Liu, R. (2015, March). Towards more pro-active access control in computer systems and networks. *Computers & Security*, *49*, 132–146. doi:10.1016/j.cose.2014.12.001

KEY TERMS AND DEFINITIONS

Access Control: Authentication and authorization are collectively called access control.

Algorithm: Series of steps used for problem solving approach is called algorithm.

Attributes: Any property related to a person or user of social network is known as attribute. For example, name, age etc.

Community: Group of people (cluster) having same characteristics or interests is called community.

Relationship: Type of association between two or more users is called relationship.

Social Network: Collection of actors and their relationships is called a social network.

This research was previously published in Innovative Solutions for Access Control Management edited by Ahmad Kamran Malik, Adeel Anjum, and Basit Raza; pages 1-32, copyright year 2016 by Information Science Reference (an imprint of IGI Global).

Section 4
Knowledge Sharing in Business

Chapter 17
Knowledge Sharing:
At the Heart of Knowledge Management

John S. Edwards
Aston University, UK

ABSTRACT

Knowledge sharing is central to knowledge management in organizations. The more tacit the knowledge, the harder it is to share. However, successful knowledge sharing means looking not just at the content of the knowledge, and the people and technology concerned in the sharing, but the context in which that sharing takes place. This chapter discusses relevant theories from knowledge management and other fields. It goes on to present a model covering the time, place and context of the knowledge sharing activity, developed using theories about decision support systems. This forms the final part of a three-stage approach intended to help managers (and others) make decisions about how to support knowledge sharing activities in organizations. Each stage takes the form of a question to be answered, as follows: 1) What are the business processes concerned? 2) What is the knowledge to be shared related to - knowledge creation, knowledge acquisition, knowledge refinement, knowledge storage, or knowledge use? 3) What does this mean for the time, place and context of the knowledge sharing?

INTRODUCTION

Knowledge sharing is a fundamental part of almost any knowledge management (KM) initiative. Not surprisingly therefore, it has been the most researched topic in knowledge management. Ribière and Walter (2013) demonstrate this for papers published in one journal, *Knowledge Management Research & Practice*, and any literature search will confirm that this is true more generally. However, knowledge sharing is by no means fully understood at the moment. It is a complex activity whose characteristics need to depend on the specifics of each particular situation in which the sharing might take place. Only then will knowledge sharing help an organization to achieve its goals or improve its performance. This chapter begins by considering what the key characteristics of knowledge sharing are. This includes the contentious terminological issue of what the relationship is between knowledge sharing and knowledge

DOI: 10.4018/978-1-7998-0417-8.ch017

transfer. It goes on to explain the difference between tacit and explicit knowledge. Next comes a discussion of the barriers to knowledge sharing. To capture the complexity of knowledge sharing, far from it being the simple concept of a message passing from one party to another, the chapter then presents a detailed view of knowledge sharing as a process, based on wider theories of business processes.

The key characteristics of knowledge sharing are next identified as depending on time, place and context, as well as the content of the knowledge itself. These are brought together into a proposed model for thinking about knowledge sharing in organizations. Only in very special cases does this amount to something as simple as transmitting a message.

KNOWLEDGE SHARING (AND KNOWLEDGE TRANSFER)

Anyone writing about knowledge sharing has to face the problem of inconsistency of terminology. There are (at least) three different stances distinguishable in the literature, each of which is inconsistent with the other two. This confusion is well illustrated by articles such as that by Lee (2001) who refers to knowledge sharing as "activities of transferring or disseminating knowledge from one person, group or organization to another." The easiest of the three positions to explain is that many authors use the terms knowledge sharing and knowledge transfer interchangeably (Klein, 2008). However, by contrast, there is a widely-accepted school of thought that regards sharing as being a broader and more complex process than transfer. This school distinguishes between the two along the lines of the definition offered by King (2006): "transfer implies focus, a clear objective, and unidirectionality, while knowledge may be shared in unintended ways multiple-directionally without a specific objective" (p. 493).

Similarly, Berends (2005) observes that "knowledge sharing and knowledge transfer cannot be treated as equals. Knowledge sharing encompasses more than only the transfer of descriptions containing justified factual information" (p. 104). Unfortunately, there is another school of thought, also widely-accepted, which calls this wider activity knowledge transfer, and does not use the phrase knowledge sharing at all. For example, Szulanski (2000), one of our key sources for this chapter, was writing about what he calls knowledge transfer, but he clearly means the wider process we are calling knowledge sharing: "Knowledge transfer is seen as a process in which an organization recreates and maintains a complex, causally ambiguous set of routines in a new setting" (p.10). His latest paper on the topic still follows this view (Szulanski, Ringov, & Jensen, 2016).

Others also use knowledge transfer for the wider activity, such as Levine and Prietula (2012), who refer to the "transfer (or exchange) of knowledge" and from their discussion, and the references they cite, evidently are addressing what we call knowledge sharing. Neither Szulanski nor Levine and Prietula use the phrase knowledge sharing in their articles. The approach that we will take in this chapter regards knowledge transfer as one-way and top-down – usually controlled by the source, whereas knowledge sharing is a broader, more interactive process, including the narrower knowledge transfer as a special case. The quote from Szulanski above raises the prospect that it may be more helpful to think of knowledge sharing as a process than as the transmission of a message, but let us first consider where the latter, mechanistic view comes from.

Shannon and Weaver and the Mechanistic View

Many articles on knowledge sharing still cite the work on communication theory of Shannon and Weaver (1949). The original work by Shannon and Weaver was about the transmission of codes, but crucially it did not take into account the meaning of the symbols in the codes. They assumed, for example, that each symbol in the code was equally likely to be transmitted, which is not true for any code related to natural languages, and also assumed that there was no problem in interpreting what each code meant. It is all the more surprising that these citations are common within the human resource management and organizational studies literatures, given the entirely impersonal and mathematical nature of the original theory. Szulanski et al. (2016) ascribe the popularity of this view in those fields to the work of Boland and Tenkasi (1995) and call their contribution the "conduit model".

Further confusion seems to have arisen in the KM field, in that several often-cited KM authors have referred to the work of Shannon and Weaver, including Boisot (1995) and Davenport and Prusak (1998), but they were not using the theory of communication *per se*. For example, Boisot cited them while discussing entropy. Berends (2005) comments "Informed by the linear communication model (Shannon & Weaver, 1949), knowledge sharing is often interpreted as the transfer of knowledge from a source to a recipient" (p.97). Linearity is, of course, a tempting simplification to make, even when it is not appropriate.

Mingers pointed out as long ago as 1996 that this theory of communication was really about data, and was not even the most useful conception of information for information systems research (Mingers, 1996). In later work, he explains how moving from information to knowledge just compounds the weaknesses of this and similar theories: "they all suffer from inadequate and unclear conceptualizations of the nature of information and its possible relationships to knowledge" (Mingers, 2008, p.65). Szulanski (2000) perhaps has it right - he refers to communication theory as providing a useful metaphor, rather than a model. That therefore gives us the elements of source, recipient, and perhaps channel to think about when considering knowledge sharing, as well as the knowledge itself, the content – but remember as mentioned above that Shannon and Weaver assumed that all codes were equally likely to be transmitted.

TACIT AND EXPLICIT KNOWLEDGE

The principal distinction in terms of knowledge content is that between tacit knowledge and explicit knowledge, usually credited to Polanyi (1966). Knowledge sharing needs to cover both types. Explicit knowledge can be set out in the form of documents or rules and so can be easily stored and retrieved, and hence shared. Tacit knowledge remains in the mind of the knower and is difficult, often impossible to articulate. At best it may be demonstrated in action, but even this is not always possible. Polanyi makes the important point that this knowledge is not even readily accessible to the knower, let alone anyone else.

A misunderstanding often seen in the knowledge management literature is to treat tacit and explicit knowledge as a simple binary categorization. Far from it; most knowledge has both tacit and explicit elements. Knowledge of how to ride a bicycle is mainly tacit, but not entirely so: "sit on the saddle and hold the handlebars" is relevant explicit knowledge, but there is little more. By contrast, the majority of the knowledge of how to fill in most types of form is explicit, and normally to be seen as a set of instructions. But any tacit knowledge that is relevant can be vital. Many years ago, when the author was a student, he ticked a box on a government form to say that he had been "unemployed" during part of the summer vacation, when he should have ticked the box for "not employed", although this was not apparent from the instructions given. It took twelve months to sort out the problems which resulted! Records management, by definition, only deals with explicit knowledge. Preserving and sharing the associated tacit knowledge is therefore a major problem. A basic but essential element of this tacit knowledge is knowing that the explicit knowledge exists, how to find it and when to access it.

WHAT MAKES KNOWLEDGE SHARING DIFFICULT?

There has been a great deal of work on barriers to knowledge sharing, far more than on its enablers (Collier, Edwards, & Shaw, 2004; Dyer & Hatch, 2006; Inkpen, 1996; Schwartz, 2007; Szulanski, 1996; Teece, 1998). Despite more than a generation of published research into knowledge sharing, it remains difficult to explain why some attempts to share knowledge succeed whilst others fail (Szulanski et al., 2016). Space does not permit us to discuss all of the work in detail in this chapter. Instead, we will concentrate on the work of Szulanski and his co-authors (Szulanski, 1996; Szulanski, 2000; Szulanski et al., 2016). It is significant to note that the 1996 paper refers to the topic as research on the transfer of best practices. The label "knowledge transfer" appears in the extension of the original work (Szulanski, 2000) and is the one used in all the subsequent work, though it continues to be on the transfer of best practices.

A Sticky Situation

One of Szulanski's main contributions is the idea of sticky knowledge - knowledge that is hard to share even when there is the willingness to do so by both parties. One theme of his research has been understanding the factors that affect this stickiness. The starting point, which has remained the same throughout, is that the degree of stickiness depends on four sets of factors representing attributes of: the practices/knowledge itself, the source unit, the recipient unit and the context in which the sharing/transfer takes place. The specific attributes whose effects Szulanski tested for in his studies (Szulanski, 1996; Szulanski, 2000; Szulanski et al., 2016) are listed below. Most of them are self-explanatory.

Knowledge Attributes

- Causal Ambiguity: The extent to which the members of the organization understand the relationship between the inputs to a practice and its outcomes (King, 2007). This is related to the tacitness of the knowledge: the greater the tacit element of the knowledge, the less likely it is that there is a widely-shared common understanding.
- Unprovenness of knowledge.

Source Attributes

- Source lacks motivation.
- Source not perceived as reliable.

Recipient Attributes

- Recipient lacks motivation.
- Recipient lacks absorptive capacity - originally defined at the organizational level "a firm's ability to recognize the value of new, external information, assimilate it, and apply it to commercial ends" (Cohen & Levinthal, 1990, p.128) and later also adopted in the literature at the level of the individual.
- Recipient lacks retentive capacity.

Context Attributes

- **Barren Organizational Context:** A lack of support for the sharing process.
- **Arduous Relationship:** Especially prior to the sharing/transfer in question.
- **Spontaneity:** 2000 study only - a binary variable denoting whether the sharing was ordered from above, or decided at the level of the people involved.

Causal ambiguity and lack of absorptive capacity are consistently found to be the most significant predictors of stickiness problems. Not knowing what explicit knowledge might be available, as mentioned earlier, is one form of causal ambiguity.

PROCESS PERSPECTIVES ON KNOWLEDGE SHARING

As we have seen, in addition to the concept of sticky knowledge, Szulanski (1996) was also one of the first to propose that knowledge sharing should be treated as a process. He suggested a process comprising four stages which he termed initiation, implementation (essentially the decision to proceed), ramp-up (when the recipient starts to use the shared knowledge) and integration. His later paper (Szulanski, 2000) decomposes the effects of the "stickiness" factors at these various stages, and thus serves as a partial validation of this four-stage model. Burns, Acar, and Datta (2011) observe that this model matches the stages of a typical product development cycle well.

However, it is important to note that Szulanski's focus was entirely on knowledge sharing within an organization; within-firm knowledge transfer, as he called it. Chen, Duan, and Edwards (2006) have extended this model to inter-organizational knowledge sharing/transfer for SMEs, with a framework of five stages: identification, negotiation, selection, interaction and conversion. This is the description from the perspective of the "receiving" organization; the "source" organization is only involved in the middle three of these stages. In both cases this is concerned with the exploitation of existing knowledge, and thus incremental innovation, rather than new knowledge creation and radical change. Absorptive capacity itself has been developed from a process perspective, principally by Zahra and George (2002). They identify the four sub-processes as acquiring, assimilating, transforming and exploiting the knowledge.

These models/frameworks are undoubtedly useful, but they treat knowledge sharing as a self-contained process. For a full understanding, especially of the context, it is important to consider the wider question of why anyone wants this sharing to be taking place at all. This first necessitates a broader look at processes and knowledge management more generally.

PROCESSES AND KM

A common way of thinking about KM, and especially about KM systems, is in terms of the three elements people, processes and technology (Edwards, 2005; Rodriguez & Edwards, 2010). This applies both at the level of the business processes, and of the KM processes that support them (Edwards, 2016). Arguably, thinking about the linkages between the three elements is even more important than the elements themselves.

The linkages relevant to this chapter are comprised of two complementary pairs; those between processes and people, and those between processes and technology.

Two of the linkages are the same at both the business process and KM process levels:

- People help design and then operate processes.
- Processes determine the need for technology.

The other two linkages are subtly different at the two levels. At the level of the business processes they are:

- Processes define the roles of people, and the knowledge needed by them.
- Technology makes possible new kinds of processes.

While at the level of the KM processes supporting the business processes, they become:

- Processes define the roles of people, and the contributions expected from them.
- Technology makes possible new ways to implement processes.

A model such as "people, processes and technology" helps us to think about the question "What is the business process that the knowledge sharing activity is connected with?" This gives an overview of some contextual factors, but having answered this question, we then need to go into more detail and ask "What precisely is the role of the knowledge that is to be shared?" This leads us on to knowledge lifecycle models, also known as KM process models.

KM PROCESS MODELS

Two well-known descriptions of the KM process, although they are really only intended as lists of knowledge-related activities, especially Heisig's, are:

- Creation, storage/retrieval, transfer, application (Alavi & Leidner, 2001).
- Use, identify, create, acquire, share, store (Heisig, 2009).

New versions continue to appear. For example, Jimenez-Jimenez and Sanz-Valle (2013) present a model of the KM process comprising knowledge acquisition, distribution, interpretation and memory, which they attribute to Huber (1991). Now, Huber was working before the term KM had come into widespread use, so it is not surprising that at the time he described these activities as relating to orga-

Figure 1. KM process model
Source: Modified from Edwards, 2001

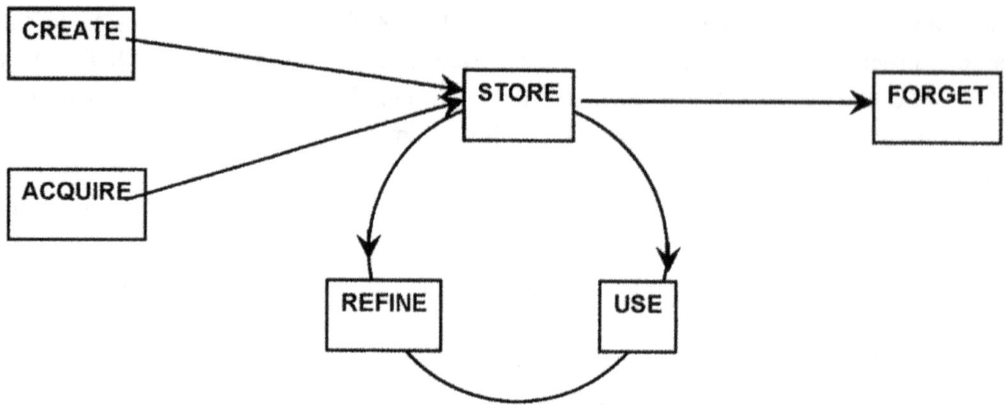

nizational learning. However, Jimenez-Jimenez and Sanz-Valle (2013) have made significant changes to the names of the constructs: originally they were knowledge acquisition, information distribution, information interpretation, and organizational memory. Changing "information" to "knowledge" is a non-trivial difference!

There are many other such lists/models. Naturally we prefer our own, as shown in Figure 1: note that the store-refine-use loop runs in both directions. This is not simply bias, but because the model in Figure 1 does not include either knowledge sharing or transfer as activities in themselves. We believe this difference in focus is important, since we do not regard knowledge sharing, at least in an organizational context, as an end in itself, but as a means to some wider purpose. That purpose can be addressed in two stages: first, the business process or processes to which the knowledge is relevant; and second, the knowledge-related activity, which is one or more of creation, acquisition, storage, refinement and use - forgetting is a specialized activity and so beyond the scope of this chapter.

Zahra and George's model of absorptive capacity (2002) can be mapped onto the model in Figure 1 straightforwardly. Acquisition is the same. Assimilation maps to storage, transformation to refinement and exploitation to use. Knowledge creation is the production of new knowledge. Many studies of knowledge sharing/transfer, including those of Szulanski, do not cover this activity. It may nevertheless still be partly inspired by knowledge sharing "…many knowledge sharing episodes contribute to the creation of knowledge, by formulating a problem, suggesting a potential solution, contributing to the justification of solutions or stimulating someone to reflect on something" (Berends, 2005, p.104). Once the knowledge-related activities have been identified, the final step is to look at the type of knowledge sharing more closely. To develop the typology, we first look back into work from the 1980s and 1990s.

WHY KNOWLEDGE SHARING?

The specific question that has not been addressed so far is: why share knowledge at all? Put another way, how does it help an organization? The simple answers are first, that knowledge sharing is crucial to the related concepts of organizational learning (Argyris & Schön, 1978) and the learning organization (Senge, 1990). Second, knowledge-related activities, such as those described in the previous section, almost always have a knowledge sharing dimension; the "lone wolf" is a rare character in modern business. This is not to say that lone wolves are completely absent, but while individual contributions are important, from the organizational perspective there is a huge risk in leaving knowledge with just one individual. Additionally, knowledge is not a resource like (say) capital, where sharing that resource inevitably means that some of the parties involved have less of it. Sharing knowledge with someone else does not devalue it, and theories of intellectual capital suggest that in fact knowledge sharing can have a multiplier effect on the value of that knowledge.

DESCRIBING TYPES OF KNOWLEDGE SHARING

Some of the most relevant concepts for describing knowledge sharing were developed in related fields before the term "knowledge management" was even in widespread use, especially those of Group Decision Support Systems (GDSS) and Computer-Supported Cooperative Work (CSCW). The first two elements came from work by DeSanctis and Gallupe (1985) as part of a typology of different types of GDSS. Originally these related to the duration of the decision-making session (limited or ongoing) and the proximity of the group members (close, i.e. face to face, or dispersed). The categorization has evolved somewhat from the original research, but the dimensions remain as time and place. For our purposes, we have categorized each of these factors as being either the same or different time when and place where the sharing occurs, producing a 2x2 matrix as shown in Table 1. These two factors capture some of the most salient points about the relationship between the parties to the knowledge sharing (source and recipient, in mechanistic knowledge transfer terms).

Grudin (1994), working in the CSCW field, added a third category to each of the two factors by introducing the issue of the predictability of the two dimensions of time and place. This splits the "different" category in each case. For place, different but predictable means the cooperative work is being carried out in several places, all known to the participants. Predictability of time also encompassed the element of constraint or expectation, for example expecting that something would be done by the end of the following day.

We propose to add a third dimension, that of context, with a similar division into three possible values: same; different but predictable; different and unpredictable. This will give three versions of a 3x3 matrix, as shown in Tables 2, 3 and 4. We have tried representing them as a three-dimensional cuboid, but it did not prove to be easy to read.

Context includes the elements from the earlier section on stickiness, and also those which Schwartz (2007) listed under organization. These include the role, experience and education level of the parties

Table 1. 2x2 matrix

		Time	
		same	different
Place	same	same time, same place	different time, same place
	different	same time, different place	different time, different place

Developed from the work of DeSanctis and Gallupe, 1985

involved, and also their motivation. Osterloh and Frey (2000), looking at motivation in the transfer of tacit knowledge, make the important point that intrinsic motivation and extrinsic motivation cannot simply be added to each other. There is actually a potential conflict when both are present, which they term "crowding out" of one by the other.

Another element of the context relates to codification and especially decodification. Hall (2006) studied decodification in a KM initiative at the UK Post Office. He stresses that "decodification is not simply one of understanding words at face value, but also requires a recipient to possess or acquire context-dependent knowledge necessary both to decodify the codes themselves, and the knowledge codified using them" (p.120). This then ties in with experience and prior knowledge, so that "even to some within the group, the codes had limited meaning because they lacked the underlying knowledge and experience of postal operations" (p.124). This is a crucial element of absorptive capacity, in the assimilation step (Zahra & George, 2002), and also indicates a context high in causal ambiguity.

Parallel issues occur with the sharing of more tacit knowledge. Klein (2008) points out that "The advantage offered by stories is much clearer in the way in which they allow implicit knowledge to be shared, by invoking the framework of assumptions possessed by their audience." (p.42) but also adds that it is vital that the story teller does understand the assumptions that the audience possesses. This makes sharing over time especially difficult: the author is surely not the only professor to find that a teaching example "story" used successfully for many years suddenly (it seemed) no longer conveyed the desired learning point to the students in the class. Even though none of the elements of the story had actually dated (it did not depend on a specific technology, for example), the students' shared assumptions had gradually changed until a tipping point was reached and it no longer worked for them.

There are also issues of differences in language, but they are beyond the scope of this chapter.

SUGGESTIONS FOR A MODEL AND AN APPROACH

Tables 2, 3, and 4 show the matrices of the three factors time, place and context, together with some examples of knowledge sharing situations, often embodying the support provided, to fill the cells.

These examples are still a work in progress: indeed, they will in any case need to change as technology advances and business practices change. For example, e-mail no longer implies a predictable place as it did for Grudin (1994), when it could only be accessed from one's desktop at work, though there are still expectations about reply habits that put it in the "different but predictable" time column. There

Table 2. Time and place varying; same context

	Context: **Same**	**Time**		
		Same	Different but predictable	Different and unpredictable
Place	Same	Face-to-face, similar expertise	Work shifts with good relationship between shifts	Machine operating sheets
	Different but predictable	Video conferencing, similar expertise	Pre-prepared set of slides	Pokayoke
	Different and unpredictable	Engineer in the field telephoning a colleague	Guidelines for fellow professionals	Low-level admin procedures

Table 3. Time and place varying; context different but predictable

Context: **Different but predictable**		**Time**		
		Same	Different but predictable	Different and unpredictable
Place	Same	Face-to-face, different expertise (e.g. different roles within one organization)	Work shifts with arduous relationship between shifts	Team rooms
	Different but predictable	Video conferencing, different expertise	Campus-wide learning labs	Collaborative writing
	Different and unpredictable	Video lecture	E-mail	FAQs, workflow

Table 4. Time and place varying; context different and unpredictable

Context: **Different and unpredictable**		**Time**		
		Same	Different but predictable	Different and unpredictable
Place	Same	Hospital emergency department	Advice centre	Public notice board (physical)
	Different but predictable	Information kiosk	Teaching material sold on DVD	Equipment manual
	Different and unpredictable	Webcasts, vodcasts (open)	Computer bulletin boards (open)	Blog post

are some very general "rules": when interaction is possible, then it is better to do that, especially if it can be immediate (same time). Much research on knowledge sharing therefore assumes same time: this is better still, because the greater interactivity improves the chances of sharing tacit knowledge. The "narrow" one-way knowledge transfer literature always assumes predictability, at least, if not sameness.

So, to summarise the approach, there are three stages, each in the form of a question to be answered. as follows.

1. What are the business processes concerned?
2. What is the knowledge to be shared related to - knowledge use, knowledge acquisition, knowledge refinement, knowledge storage, or knowledge creation?
3. What does this mean for the time, place and context of the knowledge sharing?

FUTURE RESEARCH DIRECTIONS

There are three directions in which more research would seem to be most fruitful. In no particular order, the first is the relationship between context and knowledge sharing. What are the effects of the continuing technology-enabled shift from predictable to unpredictable place, and to a lesser extent from predictable to unpredictable time? The second is the effect of the sequencing of different knowledge sharing activities and supporting technologies. Szulanski et al. (2016) raise the latter as a potential future direction for their research into stickiness. The third is to look more closely at the role of knowledge sharing in knowledge creation, perhaps by linking the operational support for knowledge sharing covered in Tables 2, 3 and 4 above to the strategic support for knowledge creation described by Nonaka and co-workers in the theories of *ba* (Nonaka & Konno, 1998).

CONCLUSION

Knowledge sharing is at the heart of knowledge management, but can only be purposeful as part of another knowledge-related activity. Just as the emphasis in KM generally needed to shift from the knowledge to the knower, representing a move from object to process, so the emphasis in knowledge sharing or transfer still needs to shift further from the message (the knowledge) to the process of sharing. However, this should not be limited by viewing knowledge sharing as a process in and of itself. In fact, consideration of knowledge sharing needs to be driven by its ultimate purpose, which is most probably knowledge use or knowledge acquisition, though it could be knowledge refinement or knowledge storage, or even knowledge creation. At the more detailed level, we have offered some suggestions for an approach, stressing the need to consider the three attributes of time, place and context, not just the knowledge content. Of course, when it can be done face to face and interactively, then it's much easier(!).

REFERENCES

Alavi, M., & Leidner, D. E. (2001). Review: Knowledge management and knowledge management systems: Conceptual foundations and research issues. *Management Information Systems Quarterly*, *25*(1), 107–136. doi:10.2307/3250961

Argyris, C., & Schön, D. A. (1978). *Organizational learning: A theory of action perspective*. Reading, MA: Addison-Wesley.

Berends, H. (2005). Exploring knowledge sharing: Moves, problem solving and justification. *Knowledge Management Research & Practice*, *3*(2), 97–105. doi:10.1057/palgrave.kmrp.8500056

Boisot, M. H. (1995). *Information space, framework for learning in organizations, institutions and culture*. London: Routledge.

Boland, R. J. Jr, & Tenkasi, R. V. (1995). Perspective making and perspective taking in communities of knowing. *Organization Science*, *6*(4), 350–372. doi:10.1287/orsc.6.4.350

Burns, A. T., Acar, W., & Datta, P. (2011). A qualitative exploration of entrepreneurial knowledge transfers. *Journal of Knowledge Management*, *15*(2), 270–298. doi:10.1108/13673271111119691

Chen, S., Duan, Y., & Edwards, J. S. (2006). Inter-organisational knowledge transfer process model. In E. Coakes & S. Clarke (Eds.), *Encyclopedia of communities of practice in information and knowledge management* (pp. 239–245). Hershey, PA: Idea Group. doi:10.4018/978-1-59140-556-6.ch043

Cohen, W. M., & Levinthal, D. A. (1990). Absorptive capacity: A new perspective on learning and innovation. *Administrative Science Quarterly*, *35*(1), 128–152. doi:10.2307/2393553

Collier, P. M., Edwards, J. S., & Shaw, D. (2004). Communicating knowledge about police performance. *International Journal of Productivity and Performance Management, 53*(5), 458–467. doi:10.1108/17410400410545923

Davenport, T. H., & Prusak, L. (1998). *Working knowledge: How organizations manage what they know*. Boston, Mass: Harvard Business School Press.

DeSanctis, G., & Gallupe, B. (1985). Group decision support systems: A new frontier. *ACM SIGMIS Database, 16*(2), 3–10. doi:10.1145/1040688.1040689

Dyer, J. H., & Hatch, N. W. (2006). Relation-specific capabilities and barriers to knowledge transfers: Creating advantage through network relationships. *Strategic Management Journal, 27*(8), 701–719. doi:10.1002mj.543

Edwards, J. S. (2001). *Knowledge life-cycles: What to keep and what to throw away?* Paper presented at Knowledge Management in O.R. Groups, Farnborough, UK.

Edwards, J. S. (2005). Business processes and knowledge management. In M. Khosrow-Pour (Ed.), *Encyclopedia of information science and technology* (Vol. I, pp. 350–355). Hershey, PA: Idea Group. doi:10.4018/978-1-59140-553-5.ch062

Edwards, J. S. (2016). Processes: Still the poor relation in the knowledge management family? In J. Liebowitz (Ed.), *Successes and failures of knowledge management* (pp. 59–69). San Francisco, CA: Morgan Kaufmann/Elsevier. doi:10.1016/B978-0-12-805187-0.00004-8

Grudin, J. (1994). Computer supported cooperative work: Its history and focus. *IEEE Computer, 27*(5), 19–26. doi:10.1109/2.291294

Hall, M. (2006). Knowledge management and the limits of knowledge codification. *Journal of Knowledge Management, 10*(3), 117–126. doi:10.1108/13673270610670894

Heisig, P. (2009). Harmonisation of knowledge management. *Journal of Knowledge Management, 13*(4), 4–31. doi:10.1108/13673270910971798

Huber, G. P. (1991). Organizational learning: The contributing processes and the literatures. *Organization Science, 2*(1), 88–115. doi:10.1287/orsc.2.1.88

Inkpen, A. (1996). Creating knowledge through collaboration. *California Management Review, 39*(1), 123–140. doi:10.2307/41165879

Jimenez-Jimenez, D., & Sanz-Valle, R. (2013). Studying the effect of HRM practices on the knowledge management process. *Personnel Review, 42*(1-2), 28–49. doi:10.1108/00483481311285219

King, A. W. (2007). Disentangling interfirm and intrafirm causal ambiguity: A conceptual model of causal ambiguity and sustainable competitive advantage. *Academy of Management Review, 32*(1), 156–178. doi:10.5465/AMR.2007.23464002

King, W. R. (2006). Knowledge sharing. In D. G. Schwartz (Ed.), *The encyclopedia of knowledge management* (pp. 493–498). Hershey, PA: Idea Group Publishing Ltd. doi:10.4018/978-1-59140-573-3.ch064

Klein, J. H. (2008). Some directions for research in knowledge sharing. *Knowledge Management Research & Practice*, *6*(1), 41–46. doi:10.1057/palgrave.kmrp.8500159

Lee, J. N. (2001). The impact of knowledge sharing, organisational capability and partnership quality on IS outsourcing success. *Information & Management*, *38*(5), 323–335. doi:10.1016/S0378-7206(00)00074-4

Levine, S. S., & Prietula, M. J. (2012). How knowledge transfer impacts performance: A multilevel model of benefits and liabilities. *Organization Science*, *23*(6), 1748–1766. doi:10.1287/orsc.1110.0697

Mingers, J. (1996). An evaluation of theories of information with regard to the semantic and pragmatic aspects of information systems. *Systems Practice*, *9*(3), 187–209. doi:10.1007/BF02169014

Mingers, J. (2008). Management knowledge and knowledge management: Realism and forms of truth. *Knowledge Management Research & Practice*, *6*(1), 62–76. doi:10.1057/palgrave.kmrp.8500161

Nonaka, I., & Konno, N. (1998). The concept of ba: Building a foundation for knowledge creation. *California Management Review*, *40*(3), 40–54. doi:10.2307/41165942

Osterloh, M., & Frey, B. S. (2000). Motivation, knowledge transfer, and organizational forms. *Organization Science*, *11*(5), 538–550. doi:10.1287/orsc.11.5.538.15204

Polanyi, M. (1966). *The tacit dimension*. Garden City, NY: Doubleday.

Ribière, V., & Walter, C. (2013). 10 years of KM theory and practices. *Knowledge Management Research & Practice*, *11*(1), 4–9. doi:10.1057/kmrp.2012.64

Rodriguez, E., & Edwards, J. S. (2010). People, technology, processes and risk knowledge sharing. *Electronic Journal of Knowledge Management*, *8*(1), 139–150.

Schwartz, D. G. (2007). Integrating knowledge transfer and computer-mediated communication: Categorizing barriers and possible responses. *Knowledge Management Research & Practice*, *5*(4), 249–259. doi:10.1057/palgrave.kmrp.8500153

Senge, P. M. (1990). *The fifth discipline, the art and practice of the learning organization*. New York: Doubleday.

Shannon, C. E., & Weaver, W. (1949). *The mathematical theory of communication*. Urbana, IL: University of Illinois Press.

Szulanski, G. (1996). Exploring internal stickiness: Impediments to the transfer of best practice within the firm. *Strategic Management Journal, 17*(Winter Special Issue), 27-43.

Szulanski, G. (2000). The process of knowledge transfer: A diachronic analysis of stickiness. *Organizational Behavior and Human Decision Processes*, *82*(1), 9–27. doi:10.1006/obhd.2000.2884

Szulanski, G., Ringov, D., & Jensen, R. J. (2016). *Overcoming stickiness: How the timing of knowledge transfer methods affects transfer difficulty*. Organization Science, Articles in Advance.

Teece, D. (1998). Research directions for knowledge management. *California Management Review*, *40*(3), 289–292. doi:10.2307/41165957

Zahra, S. A., & George, G. (2002). Absorptive capacity: A review, reconceptualization, and extension. *Academy of Management Review*, *27*(2), 185–203.

KEY TERMS AND DEFINITIONS

Absorptive Capacity: An organization's ability to acquire, store, refine and use knowledge from elsewhere.

Business Processes: The activities that an organization performs, for its customers and internally, that literally determine what kind of organization it is.

Explicit Knowledge: Knowledge set out in a form such as documents or rules, also known as codified knowledge.

Knowledge Management Process Model: The activities involved in carrying out knowledge management within an organization.

Knowledge Sharing: A process, usually interactive, by which one person, unit or organization acquires knowledge from another person, unit or organization.

Sticky Knowledge: Knowledge that is difficult to share, even when both parties are willing.

Tacit Knowledge: Knowledge that is difficult or impossible to express.

This research was previously published in Managing Knowledge Resources and Records in Modern Organizations edited by Priti Jain and Nathan Mnjama; pages 1-14, copyright year 2017 by Business Science Reference (an imprint of IGI Global).

Chapter 18
Understanding Knowledge Sharing in an Organization:
A Perspective of Actor-Network Theory

Michael Twum-Darko
Cape Peninsula University of Technology, South Africa

Lee-Anne Lesley Harker
Cape Peninsula University of Technology, South Africa

ABSTRACT

This paper set out to propose the actor-network theory (ANT) as a lens through which to understand and interpret the sociotechnical knowledge sharing challenges in organisations. The methodology for this study was developed within the context of ANT by adopting its ideals and principles. The findings demonstrate that using the concept of the Moments of Translation as a lens to study this phenomenon is indeed a novel way of investigating the reason why there is still difficulty with sharing and managing knowledge. This perspective is proposed to transform the way that knowledge sharing factors are perceived. By utilising a normative approach, this research looked at how knowledge sharing as an ideal can be achieved when taking into account the existing constraints within an organisation. A general framework is proposed to guide the formation of a network of aligned interest for knowledge sharing.

INTRODUCTION

This qualitative-based knowledge management study is an approach to research that facilitates the understanding of a social construct within the context of knowledge management using Actor Network Theory (ANT). As a social theory, ANT can be used as a lens through which to interpret the phenomenon of knowledge sharing challenges in organisations. Although knowledge management can be studied by a variety of lenses, this paper argues that it can well be understood through the single lens of the concept of Moments of Translation of ANT. Knowledge management was conceptualised in the 1980s, but still draws significant attention in research and industry today (Baskerville & Dulipovici, 2006). The effective

DOI: 10.4018/978-1-7998-0417-8.ch018

management of knowledge seems to be a primary concern for organisations in various industries and in academia due to the value that an organisation can derive from knowledge (Malik, 2005; Lubega, Omona & Van der Weide, 2010; Sulisworo, 2012; Tan & Wong, 2015). Knowledge is considered to be a valuable asset as it can improve performance in terms of productivity, efficiency and effectiveness, thus enabling an organisation to be more competitive (Holsapple, 2001; Liao, 2003; Bush & Tiwana, 2005; Durcikova & Gray, 2005; Hewett & Watson, 2006; Lubega et al., 2010). However, such benefits are not derived from knowledge management unless organisations manage their knowledge efficiently (Meso & Smith, 2000). Knowledge is context-specific because it is derived from the accumulated individual experiences of employees within an organisation (Chen & Mohamed, 2010). Various methods, techniques and tools are employed to harness the knowledge of individuals through capturing, storing, sharing and using of knowledge (Lee, 2001; Liao, 2003). However, these techniques do not guarantee the flow of knowledge and social structures make it difficult to manage these processes (Lauring & Selmer, 2012). This is why knowledge management strategies are so widespread (Davenport & Prusak, 2000; Hislop, 2013).

The question, then, is why after all these years are organisations, including academia, still struggling to share and manage knowledge? Given the works of Chen & Mohamed (2010), Lee (2001); Liao (2003), Polanyi (1967), Hong, Kim & Suh, (2012) and Lauring & Selmer (2012), it is agreeable to consider individuals creating the accumulated knowledge as actors in a network of aligned interest. This paper argues that knowledge sharing is influenced by facilitating factors of technology, processes, and a knowledge sharing strategy (Twum-Darko & Harker, 2015) which form part of a network of aligned interests to share the accumulated knowledge. Given the contextual and sociotechnical nature of knowledge sharing, this paper employs the actor-network theory (ANT) as a methodology to understand and interpret the sociotechnical processes of knowledge sharing challenges in organisations. The paper draws on the findings of an interpretive case study conducted at a selected University of Technology in South Africa.

OVERVIEW OF LITERATURE REVIEWED

Barriers and facilitators constitute the core themes within knowledge sharing literature (Schauer, Vasconcelos & Sen, 2015). This is due to the need to understand the factors that influence knowledge sharing for its stimulation and to manage knowledge sharing processes more effectively (Ma, Huang, Wu, Dong & Qi, 2014). Even though the literature highlights individual, organisational and technological factors as the most important enablers for knowledge sharing, the relationship between these factors need to be explored (Cavaliere, Lombardi & Giustiniano, 2015). Consequently, studies on knowledge sharing have spanned several decades (Alavi, Kayworth & Leidner, 2006; Bontis & Serenko, 2009; Ma & Yu, 2010). The review of current literature suggests that findings are divergent, but there is consensus that individual and organisational factors determine the success of knowledge sharing (Israilidis, Siachou, Cooke & Lock, 2015). This speaks to the very contextual nature of knowledge and the individuals that are central to knowledge sharing. While individual (or personal) factors are found to significantly affect knowledge sharing, organisational factors, such as management, structure and cultural influences, are found to be influential too (Israilidis et al., 2015). Whether barriers are considered in terms of individual factors, or environmental (organisational) factors, their applicability spans different countries, industries and organisation types and sizes (Martin, 2000; Chuang & Hung, 2009; Ma et al., 2014).

While there are several perspectives to knowledge management literature, people, processes and technology constitute the core components of these perspectives (Carayannis & Alexander, 2002). In addition, more recent studies have alluded to the lack of institutionalisation and the failure to develop proper knowledge management strategies, to influence knowledge sharing too (Fong & Lee, 2009; Khalil, 2012).

Studies on knowledge sharing have either been undertaken at the organisational level, individual level or a combination of the two (Schauer et al., 2015). Studies focusing on one or the other present limitations on how to provide guidelines for knowledge-sharing practices, as individuals' perceptions about knowledge sharing are not nearly enough to address willingness to share knowledge and the organisational perceptions about knowledge sharing are inherently abstracted. While organisations must pay attention to individual enablers to foster effective knowledge sharing, knowledge is found not only to be embedded in individuals, but also in the organisational and technological domains (Cavaliere et al., 2015). Furthermore, focusing on the interplay between the individual and organisational level may reveal problems of integration between hierarchical structures within the organisation. This will ensure that the organisation designs their knowledge sharing processes to align to the environment and the necessary levels of interaction (Cavaliere et al., 2015).

Individual level, or social factors, relates mainly to individuals' motivations to share knowledge and it's agreeable to consider individuals' motivations to share as a precursor for developing a successful knowledge management strategy (Iskoujina & Roberts, 2015). Factors influencing individuals' motivations to share are culture, opportunities to share, motivations to share, trust, beliefs, self-efficacy, enjoyment in helping others and experience (Bock & Kim, 2002; Ipe, 2003; Cabrera, Collins, & Salgado, 2006; Lin, 2007; Aulawi, Sudirman, Suryadi, & Govindaraju, 2009). The uptake, promotion and sustaining of knowledge sharing is hugely influenced by these factors, particularly the organisational culture (Twum-Darko & Harker, 2015). Culture and other social factors are conditions for sharing which is brought about by management influences and practices (Iskoujina & Roberts, 2015). This means that management should be amenable to individuals' suggestions so that their practices are aligned to individuals' motivations to share. The role of management in ensuring knowledge sharing success is twofold: management must be a role model and facilitator for knowledge sharing (Huysman & de Wit, 2003). This is because of the importance of management influence on the knowledge sharing culture and the appropriate management of processes and technology to facilitate sharing and how interests are given authority (Iskoujina & Roberts, 2015, Heizmann and Olsson, 2015:757-758).

A knowledge sharing strategy has been emphasised as a way of improving the effectiveness of knowledge sharing initiatives, ensuring alignment to individuals' motivations to share, and for having a positive influence on the uptake of knowledge sharing (Tan & Wong, 2015; Iskoujina & Roberts, 2015; Twum-Darko & Harker, 2015). Furthermore, it "provides insights into the problems that should become the focus of the strategy before implementation" (Tan & Wong, 2015:819). The strategy addresses knowledge sharing factors before it's able to deal with operational issues pertaining to processes, technology, infrastructure and other knowledge resources (ibid.). The strategy also describes how best to leverage the knowledge of employees in order to manage knowledge sharing better, thereby deriving its maximum potential.

Arguably, while low-level knowledge management activities are taking place, there is a lack of institutionalisation of knowledge sharing (Fong & Lee, 2009; Khalil, 2012). Twum-Darko and Harker (2015) found institutionalisation to be an enabler for knowledge sharing and contributing positively to knowledge sharing sustainability. Institutionalisation not only enables a culture for sharing, but provides a systematic means for sharing knowledge, thereby enabling more effective and efficient sharing of knowledge (ibid.). While the influence of insitutionalisation on knowledge sharing has not received much explicit focus in the literature, there are some factors reported to impact on knowledge sharing, such as the lack of policies, procedures and guidelines (Lu, Lueng & Koch, 2006), which are matters of institutionalisation.

From the review of literature, it is evident that these aforementioned factors influence knowledge sharing. However, it is pointless knowing what the factors are unless there is a network of aligned interest within the organisation for knowledge sharing. It is therefore proposed that without a network of aligned interest, any strategies for knowledge sharing would not be successful. Essentially, it is important to understand why there is no network of aligned interest and how this network can be created. Power to influence knowledge sharing is non-existent without a network of aligned interest. Therefore, the actor-network theory (ANT) was used to unpack this phenomenon, thereby allowing for an increased understanding of the dynamics influencing the formation and growth of a network of aligned interest for knowledge sharing. Of the literature reviewed, few studies have used social theories to unpack this issue. Anthropologists contend that social theories should be used to study social phenomena, as it will strengthen the relevance of the study and provide meaning to social behaviour. Therefore, using ANT, the objectives of this study is twofold: To determine why there is no network of aligned interest and to determine how to create a network of aligned interest.

OVERVIEW OF ACTOR NETWORK THEORY

The actor network theory (ANT) is a social theory which examines the interplay between human and non-human entities in an actor network, thereby allowing technical, organisational and social aspects of an actor-network to be considered and studied together (Diedrich & Guzman, 2015). To date, most of the knowledge management literature has focused on one perspective at the expense of the other, and at the expense of the relationship between these variables (ibid.). Knowledge sharing is therefore a phenomenon that ideally should be explained using a framework that can encompass categories of influences from both the organisational and individual level.

The actor-network theory (ANT) examines the shifting relationships between the actors (or members) of a network. These shifting relationships are examined in respect of the four moments of translation. Translation is the alignment of interests of the actors in a network with that of a focal actor. The four moments of translation include: Problematisation, interessement, enrolment and mobilisation (Sarker, Sarker, & Sidorova, 2006). They address the formation, growth and stability of a network of aligned interest. Successful network formation is dependent on the successful implementation of the four moments of translation, which is driven by a focal actor. The four moments of translation involve the rallying of support from all the actors in a network and maintaining alignment with the obligatory passage point (OPP) (ibid.). The OPP is "[a] situation that has to occur for all of the actors to be able to achieve their interests, as defined by the focal actor" (Sarker et al., 2006:56). In this context, the OPP would be knowledge sharing. Organisational efforts to introduce and develop knowledge sharing is conceptualised as the continuous application of the processes of translation to produce stable networks, while generating the actors' identities and interests within the network (Diedrich & Guzman, 2015).

Problematisation is when a focal actor frames a problem, considers possible ways to address this problem, and in doing so will establish an OPP as a solution. During the problematision phase the focal actor identifies the actors that are affected by this problem, and uses the problem as a catalyst for the alignment of the actors' interest to that of the focal actor, that is, for the actors to pass through the OPP. Interessement involves a process of negotiation between the focal actor and the identified actors in order to maintain their alignment with the interests of the focal actor. The process of enrolment is a means to record (formerly define) the commitments made by each actor that has been enrolled and to make this part of the shared memory of the social system. It is possible that actors can betray the actor-network after enrolment, therefore it enrolment can involve inscription, which is a way to inscribe the interests of the actor-network in the form of artefacts which serve to protect the interests of the actor-network and thus serves to stabilise the network. Mobilisation is to assume a state of readiness, so to speak. The focal actor assumes the role of representative for the network actors and seeks to mobilise them into action. Inscription can therefore be considered as a precursor, and thus an enabler, for mobilisation.

Using ANT as a theoretical lens can unpack this social phenomenon by revealing how humans resist, allow, deny or assist courses of events (Diedrich & Guzman, 2015). Thus, it is only through following human actors, and their associations with nonhuman entities, that this phenomenon can be better understood (Latour, 1987, 1996, 2005). Context has always played an important role in knowledge sharing. ANT does well to reveal the differences in such contexts because the moments of translation, through inscription of the purpose of an actor-network by delegating the actor roles, responsibilities and identities, as well as assigning the attachment of resources to the actor-network to enable its purpose (Latour, 1991), reveal such differences for a given context. Moments of Translation underpin the formation of the actor-network, but as the aligned interest of the actor's progress through these processes, the stability of the network improves and increased network growth is achieved (Twum-Darko, Noruwana & Sewchurran, 2015).

PROBLEM CONCEPTUALISATION

Drawing on the findings of the review of literature and the concepts of Moments of Transformation of ANT as the underpinning theory to study the given phenomenon, a conceptual framework was developed to guide the design and collection of the data. A knowledge sharing strategy is developed from the knowledge-related problems unique to an organisation and industry. ANT as a methodology not only frames a problem, but also enables an organisation to seek out the best way to rally the support of actors in their knowledge sharing network to align to their knowledge sharing interests, and to institutionalise knowledge sharing as an organisational culture. ANT can reveal ways that the organisation can influence individuals' motivations to share knowledge through understanding what motivates them to share knowledge. It is proposed that the problematisation and interessement stages enable researchers to understand what motivates individuals to share their knowledge or what will 'get' them to share their knowledge, while the enrolment and mobilization stages reveal the antecedents for mobilising the actors into action.

Figure 1 conceptualises the proposed problem. The formation of the network of aligned interest is initiated by management as a focal actor, given that management hold a unique position not only to act as a role model to influence organisational culture, but also to act as a facilitator to influence the appropriate use of processes and technology. The formation of the network is preceded with the development of a knowledge sharing strategy as this constitutes the obligatory passage point. During problematisation the focal actor identifies the relevant actors and establishes how they are affected. The focal actor will look at possible ways to address the problem and in doing so will establish an OPP. Therefore, the knowledge sharing strategy is developed during the problematisation phase of translation. The strategy

Figure 1. Problem conceptualisation

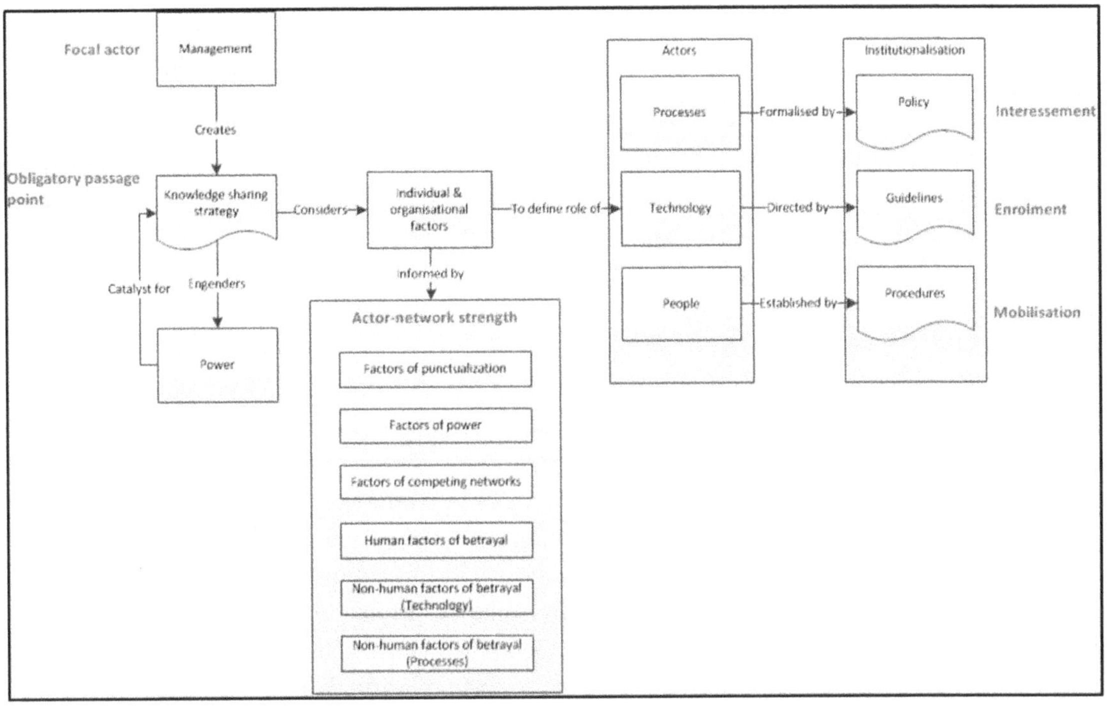

serves to define the role of the actors in the network of aligned interest. Alliances are strengthened by artifacts which are inscriptions of the interests of the network and its actors. The knowledge sharing strategy therefore serves as the first phase towards strengthening the alliance.

Translation involves not only the rallying of support from identified actors, but also the maintenance of the alignment with the obligatory passage point. Policy helps to maintain this alignment by formalising the roles of the actors. Therefore, interessement should be achieved through policy. Given that stabilisation of the actor-network must be ensured during translation, particularly because actors can betray the network despite successful interessement, the commitments made by each actor is inscribed in the form of guidelines to direct the role of the actors. This inscription, as a precursor and enabler for mobilisation helps to mobilise actors into action through documented procedures, based on the guidelines. The procedures help to establish the roles of the actors.

The factors to determine actor-network strength constitute both individual and organisational factors. Therefore, a knowledge sharing strategy is informed by both levels of influence. Each actor has been enrolled based on an aligned interest. Essentially, in considering the factors of actor-network strength, the knowledge sharing strategy is a way to inform actors on what to share, how to share and provides for facilitation and support.

METHODOLOGY

Research Approach

Knowledge sharing is considered to be influenced by the unique dynamic of each organisation. The contextual nature of knowledge, and thus the knowledge-sharing phenomenon, calls for a qualitative approach to obtain an in-depth understanding of the phenomenon based on the subjective accounts of the units of analysis. According to Perry and Coote (1994:3):

In many areas of the social sciences existing deductive, theory testing research methods do not adequately capture the complexity and dynamism of the context of organisational settings.

While deductive theory-testing and positivist research methodologies aim to formulate theories using large data samples to ensure their validity, these approaches limit the richness of data that is generated through qualitative case studies (Leonard & McAdam, 2001). Moreover, positivist methodologies, due to their focus on generalisability, do not use data collection methods such as interviews, observations, documentation, and the like, which provide the richness of data that qualitative research seeks to obtain. On the other hand, the most developed inductive inquiry, grounded theory, involves minimalist a prior constructs, seeking to gradually test and form theoretical constructs, grounded in the data (Glaser and Strauss, 1967). This research was conducted in the form of inductive inquiry, underpinned by the theoretical framework of ANT. The methodology was underpinned by a theoretical framework, as its purpose was to direct the work and provide a basis for the methodology (Rubenstein-Montano, Liebowitz, Buchwalter, McCaw, Newman & Rebeck, 2001). This research draws on the perceptions of Borgström (2012), who contends that a rigorous and thorough study is underpinned by strong theoretical foundations, where a body of strong theory is matched to the empirical matter which is used to guide the research. The intention of the researcher was to use the inductive approach to link the themes to the data, and not to any preexisting coding frame (Patton, 1990; Braun & Clarke, 2006). Therefore the theoretical framework did not guide the data collection, but the research was guided by the data. The underpinning theory helped to put the data into context. Therefore, the factors were explored inductively, using ANT as a deductive analysis to conceptualise the factors and explain them in relation to each other. Thus, a combination of deductive and inductive reasoning was used (William, 2006). This approach therefore drew on the benefits of inductive inquiry to adequately capture the dynamics of the given context, while exploring the interplay between variables which positivist research fails to achieve, and deductive inquiry through exploring the concepts of ANT to reveal the interplay between the elements of a knowledge sharing actor network.

Due to the theoretical orientation of this research, it is classified as an interpretive case study (Laws & McLeod, 2004). This case study research provided an intensive description and analysis (Smith, 1978), enabling the acquisition of tacit knowledge about the phenomenon under study (Stake, 1995). The breadth and depth of knowledge about a phenomenon that can be achieved through case study research is demonstrated in this statement made by Chelly (1996:77): "Good story telling about a single case would provide better theoretical insights than multiple case research based on creating good constructs". Not only is the case itself the main product of the research, but the case can be instrumental in broader investigations into this phenomenon (ibid.). ANT has underpinned this research to provide a guiding framework, or set of guiding principles. The methodology for this study was developed within the context of ANT by adopting its ideals and principles. However, a methodology must be specific by providing detail on how to carry out the ideas and objectives set forth (Rubenstein-Montano et al., 2001). Therefore, the research methods, discussed next, will detail the collection and analysis of the data.

Overview of Case Study

The case is a selected University of Technology (UoT) in South Africa with diverse cultural and race groups of academic and non-academic staff and students. The case has been in existence for at least 10 years as a University of Technology. A UoT is mandated to offer programmes that are aimed at producing practitioner graduates, focusing on career-oriented training and applied research. The UoT faces competition from the traditional, well-established universities and is in the process of recurriculating their programmes across the institution. Teaching and learning constitutes the largest part of what the UoT does, given that the bulk of students are at undergraduate level. However, research features very prominently, particularly because research informs teaching and learning and contributes to the academic community at large. This creates a connection between the activities that take place at the institution.

The knowledge which is pertinent to the job of an academic in higher education is related to teaching and learning, curriculum development, assessment and examination, academic administration and research. The challenge is to create organisational memory in a formal and systematic manner, which can store policies, procedures, best practice and know-how to make this knowledge accessible to more than one individual across the institution. As it currently stands, informal methods of creating and managing knowledge are utilised by academics, and this is mostly on an individual, fragmented basis. When an academic staff member leaves, they often leave with the knowledge that they have accumulated over the term of their tenure. This knowledge base has to be re-built by a new staff member. This is why knowledge sharing should be nurtured, as the first step to achieving an organisational memory.

Figure 2 shows a concept map which outlines the relationships between the main entities within the environment of a UoT. Given the fact that the UoT is one of the largest in South Africa, with several campuses to manage as well as an ongoing recurriculation process, a fair amount of harmonisation is required for the UoT to compete. This, however, cannot occur unless a culture of knowledge sharing is nurtured. Sharing, however, should not only occur at the subject level, but across departments and faculties.

The population included all academic staff members from the selected UoT who are actively participating in teaching and learning activities and are appointed at a level of junior lecturer, lecturer and senior lecturer. The participants were predetermined based on their involvement in teaching and learning activities that would utilise the 'operational' knowledge that is the focus of this research. Hence, the population is determined based on a common element, being their degree of participation in teaching and learning activities, which is relevant to the research objectives. Respondents at varying levels of tenure were selected to ensure that the units of analysis spanned several different disciplines or varying areas of expertise, that is, from different faculties, in order to obtain a well-rounded view of the academic domain. This would also reveal the potential differences in perceptions that each staff member would offer.

Research Methods

A purposive sampling method was applied as this is usually the preferred method of sampling for case study research (Kruger & Welman, 2001:189) as the units of analysis will be data rich. Face-to-face interviews, with semi-structured interview questions, were used for data collection. Semi-structured

Figure 2. Concept map of UoT context

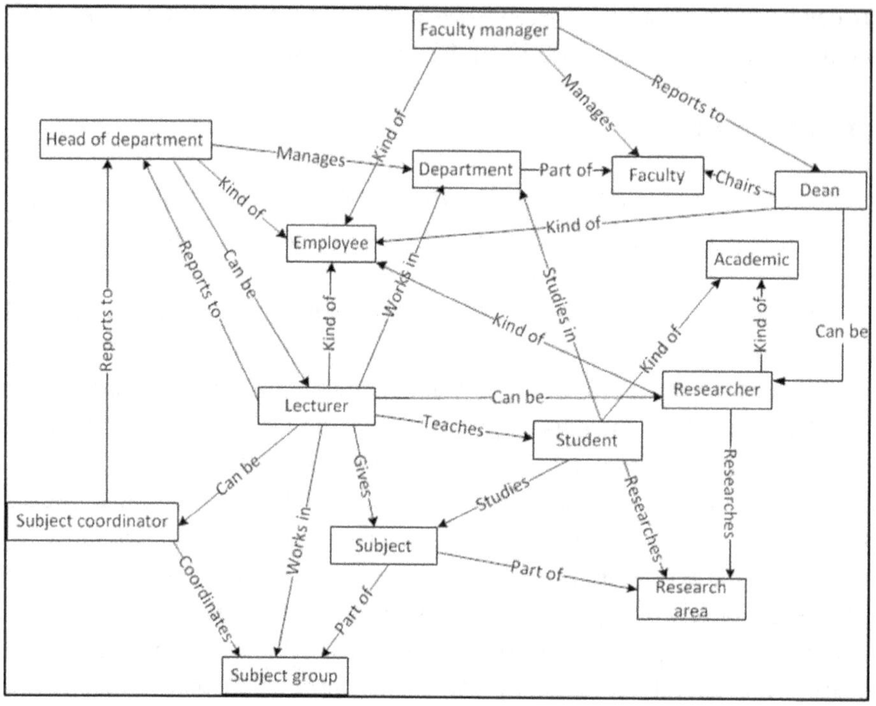

questions served to explore the views of the academics, while providing guidance to the kind of answers expected in relation to the concepts of ANT and to validate and/ or extend the proposed conceptual framework. The sample size was contingent on the theoretical saturation point (Glaser & Strauss, 1967). This was the point at which "no additional data are being found whereby the (researcher) can develop properties of the category" (Glaser & Strauss, 1967:65). This means that when similar codes are seen repeatedly within a category, the researcher was satisfied that a level of saturation was reached for that category. The researcher was therefore satisfied with the sample size of eighteen academic staff members, representing a variation of the population in terms of level of tenure and work context based on the selection from each faculty.

The main themes identified in the literature were social, process and technology factors. These themes were therefore classified in relation to the individual and organisational levels of influence, and in relation to the concepts of ANT. Thus, the problem conceptualisation in Figure 1 was a basis for constructing the interview questions and these questions are aligned to the main objectives of the research. This allowed for the researcher to begin the investigation with a clear focus, rather than just a general notion of what to research, therefore addressing more specific issues (Malbon, 1999) of knowledge sharing as a network of aligned interests. Not only do the questions reflect the research objectives by suggesting the themes of discussion, but also values the point of view of the respondent (Malbon, 1999; Kruger & Welman, 2001). Maxwell (2013) contends that a 'genuinely' qualitative study should also account for the perspectives of the respondents, or the 'theories' of the phenomenon of focus, as developed by the respondents, rather than relying entirely on the theoretical orientation of the researcher (see Table 1).

Table 1. Interview questions

Research Objective: Determine why there is no Network of Aligned Interest
Which personal factors would impede on your ability to share knowledge or lead to your abandonment of knowledge sharing? Which technology factors would impede on your ability to share knowledge or lead to your abandonment of knowledge sharing? Which process factors would impede on your ability to share knowledge or lead to your abandonment of knowledge sharing? Would your willingness to share knowledge be influenced by whether or not you were compelled to do so? Which work environment-related factors would impact negatively on your ability/opportunity to share knowledge? What is your perception of the impact of centralisation on the support and preservation of knowledge sharing? What is your perception about the influence of power on the support and preservation of knowledge sharing?
Research Objective: Determine how to Create a Network of Aligned Interest
What would you consider as influencing/ motivating factors on your decision to share knowledge? What enablers should be in place to ensure successful implementation of knowledge sharing processes? What do you consider as effective strategies for gaining academic staff commitment to knowledge sharing? What do you think could sustain knowledge sharing within your subject, department or faculty? How can knowledge sharing as a process be formalised/ institutionalised?

Data Analysis

The results of this paper emanated from a primary study which intended to determine the factors that influence knowledge sharing within an academic institution. The original study applied data analysis involving organising the data, summarising the data, and interpreting the data (Ary, Jacobs & Razavieh, 2002). Data organisation was performed using Microsoft Excel. The responses were condensed into a list, organised by question. Each interview question was typed into a separate worksheet and each response was labelled according to the interview number. The analytic relevance of traditional variables such as gender was not assumed, but only considered if and when the data showed it to be relevant.

Summarising was done by grouping similar coded categories in relation to the concepts of ANT. This provided a meaningful summary and reconstruction of the collected data for interpretation (Ary et al., 2002:465). Coding for a concept involved looking for words grouped into a conceptual cluster (or idea). These words would have a strong link to the proposed concept. Therefore, coding was dependent on: Something that was repeated in several places, anything that the respondent explicitly stated as important, or themes identified in the literature. The rules for coding were formulated beforehand and applied consistently to ensure reliability and validity of the analysis (Berg, 2007). These rules were for identifying the characteristics of categories. The conceptualisation and operationalization was based on the interaction between the theoretical and empirical observations (Berg, 2007:248). Theoretical observations were instrumental in being able to identify obvious characteristics for categories in the data. However, some form of inductive categorisation was required for those characteristics which were implied. This is where both inductive and deductive reasoning come into play. As Schatzman and Strauss (1973:12) point out, although some categorisation is worked out in advance and some is developed later, consistency is key in both.

The number for concepts coded was determined based on the interaction with the data (Busch, De Maret, Flynn, Kellum, Le, Meyers, Saunders, White, Palmquist, 1994 – 2012). Thus, there was a degree of flexibility applied in the coding to inductively discover important material to be incorporated into the research which could have a significant impact on the results. A set of subcategories were created based on the codes, which mapped to the main categories identified in the literature or that emerged from the qualitative interviews. These subcategories were saturated until no other new categories, or variables, emerged. Once this was completed, similar categories were grouped together to form abstracted categories. After identifying the categories, it was important to establish the links between the categories. These relationships were grounded in ANT. The interpretation of the text was guided by the theoretical orientation of the researcher. Therefore, in contradiction to a phenomenological orientation, which seeks to understand the meaning behind the patterns, the intention of this research was to uncover these patterns.

Thus, while the initial intention of the research was to determine the manifest content through directed content analysis, latent content emerged due to the interpretive orientation of the research, guided by the underpinning theory. Additional attributes emerged which provided an alternative means of evaluating the relationships between variables and the dynamics at play within the organisation which could address the research questions posed in this paper. The following section discusses the results that emerged to determine why there is no network of aligned interest.

RESULTS AND DISCUSSION

Problematisation

Which personal factors would impede on your ability to share knowledge or lead to your abandonment of knowledge sharing?

The personal inhibitors to sharing amongst the respondents were generally external triggers. For the most part the respondents are willing to partake in knowledge sharing activities, but are discouraged from sharing mainly because of the lack of management. The misalignment between management and staff is in fact one of the more significant inhibitors for staff personally. One respondent asserted that "The way that they operate does not resonate with staff", while another suggested that "If there is enough encouragement and support from management, it will assist one to rise above the issues". In general, management support is lacking. There is not only a lack of trust amongst staff, but also toward management. The culture of the organisation has engendered this lack of trust. Similarly, a positive culture can engender trust within the organisation. Management support could be a catalyst for change when staff are not motivated to do so, whether due to a lack of trust or a resistance to change. In addition, management support should be extended to the proper management of the process of knowledge sharing, as the respondents are apprehensive to share when it is not a shared interest of the organisation. In other words, there must be a fair distribution of responsibility to share knowledge.

Which technology factors would impede on your ability to share knowledge or lead to your abandonment of knowledge sharing?

Technology is well-established as a facilitator of knowledge sharing due to its capability to provide a systematic way of sharing knowledge and immediate access to knowledge. Often it is an obvious choice to incorporate the use of technology in knowledge-sharing processes. Many of the respondents, however, indicated that a potential hindrance to sharing knowledge through technology would be the lack of skills amongst staff to use technology. Without the necessary skills staff would not be able to use technology optimally. As one respondent mentioned, "Success lies in the way people use it". This could create a negative attitude toward sharing, especially if the organisation does not apply a two-pronged approach to knowledge sharing by enabling sharing through online and offline methods. It is arguable that technology makes it easier to share knowledge, but, as one respondent pointed out, "Technology must be balanced, as too much reliance is bad".

There is a sense that staff are overwhelmed by the plethora of tools that must be balanced to enable tasks. On the one hand, some respondents felt that there is not enough time for training, while on the other, some felt that features are often not linked to the intended use, making it difficult for them to use the technology. In addition, it was proposed that the organisation should keep technology simple, thereby enabling staff to master the use of the technology. Organisations should choose an appropriate platform for their staff that aligns not only to the facilitation of the necessary task, but which also complies with the way people work.

While training and skills present a major stumbling block to the use of technology for sharing knowledge, unreliable systems and accessibility issues present a significant bone of contention amongst the respondents as far as technology is concerned. A respondent asserted that "If technology does not work, or is unreliable, it creates a barrier to sharing". Essentially, it is about getting the basics right. On the matter of technology, management should put some conscious thought into the use of technology to enable sharing, as these systems will contribute to either the encouragement or discouragement of sharing knowledge.

Which process factors would impede on your ability to share knowledge or lead to your abandonment of knowledge sharing?

The respondents felt that there is simply a lack of processes around sharing knowledge, and these processes should exist first. Management, or those in a position to effect change, are not taking note of where improvements can be implemented. As pointed out by a respondent, "Management take too long to implement decisions, with no proper concept of what one wants to achieve". Staff interest tends to waiver when there are long lead times to implementation. Knowledge sharing strategies should therefore precede the implementation of processes, and should cater to these processes.

Processes should provide guidelines on how to share knowledge, and staff should be trained on how to share, what to share, and how to use mechanisms in place for knowledge sharing. Processes should be consciously and intentionally formulated. As a respondent said, "Everyone must play a role and understand its importance", while another respondent pointed out that "Not everyone contributing [will impede on sharing] because they have got people working in the same department and they may decide they won't do it because someone else will".

A lack of planning, arrangement and coordination will impede on knowledge sharing processes. There must be adequate management of the processes for it to be successful. One respondent mentioned "If people aren't into it, it won't matter what processes there are and if [management] don't do their thing, it won't work".

While a knowledge sharing strategy is proposed as a catalyst for sharing, it should carefully consider the processes that will engender sharing, as a respondent contended that "People will prioritise other work over knowledge sharing when time is a factor". Processes should therefore be planned around people's work. It should not be a departure from how people have previously worked.

Would your willingness to share knowledge be influenced by whether or not you were compelled to do so?

The findings on mandating knowledge sharing, despite being divergent, reveal that power and influence alone will not foster knowledge sharing. The respondents views included "Convincing or encouraging highly educated people to share their knowledge by making it compulsory won't work as [we] hate being pushed into a corner", and "I hate anything that is compulsory". The perceptions amongst the respondents centre on the fact that people will share if they want to and if it is in their nature to do so, or if it is perceived to be important to them or to benefit them. Additionally, making knowledge sharing compulsory brings with it the notion that staff will not have input in the process. This approach is deemed to be prescriptive, and thus met with resentment. The respondents' views, however, allude to the structure and format of knowledge sharing to be more likely to stimulate sharing.

Which work environment-related factors would impact negatively on your ability/opportunity to share knowledge?

The overwhelming perception amongst the respondents is that knowledge sharing, despite being an imperative, will not be prioritised over their primary work. Essentially, it comes down to management's approach toward balancing workloads to accommodate the inclusion of knowledge sharing as a recognised form of work. Inadequate support has led to the notion that work is simply "added on". The perception is that knowledge sharing initiatives would follow this precedent. It would be imprudent to implement knowledge sharing strategies without a pragmatic plan for its implementation where management have consulted with staff and put conscious thought into the implications for how they work. One view was that sharing is less likely to occur when there is a "lack of any real guidance on what to share, how to share and what is appropriate to share. There needs to be clear guidelines". It would also be counterproductive to have these guidelines while the systems (which also impact on the overall work environment), do not adequately respond to the needs of staff.

Staff are often those called upon to recognise the value of knowledge sharing, while this responsibility equally rests with management. Management's appreciation of its value should manifest in the guidelines for its implementation. The entrenched a culture of non-participation and indifference has been nurtured through increased workloads with no corresponding growth in recognition or support, or inconsistencies in workloads amongst staff. As one respondent stated, "You just do everything, including all the admin. You are the secretary and the academic", while another respondent mentioned that "Some people work hard and others are lazy, so I'm not going to give someone my [work] that I spent hours preparing". Inconsistent workloads, coupled with management's lack of involvement and management of work, magnifies this culture, and the respondents feel that this would negatively impact on their willingness to share. A respondent contended "If other people are not sharing, it will impact on my willingness to share knowledge". It was asserted that if management were more supportive on the whole, this culture is more likely to dissipate, but it will not happen without intervention.

What is your perception of the impact of centralisation on the support and preservation of knowledge sharing?

The perception amongst the respondents is when a person or management in general have centralised control over processes there is an opportunity for incompetence to erode the intended goals or to make unilateral changes which may not speak to the needs of the staff. For example, a respondent said "People start acting like power maniacs. They usually just start instituting systems". In addition, when initiatives are instituted, there should be tangible benefits that emanate from the contributions of staff. As one respondent pointed out "It must not be an exercise in admin (or window dressing) … we were required to compile files that documented what we do in our subjects. However, no one else ever looks at these files". The role of management should be to support and direct, rather than control processes. Centralisation is perceived to be positive when it is to ensure that knowledge is indeed filtered down and to oversee the implementation of knowledge sharing. The views are that centralisation should be applied to the structures and systems, that is, location of and access to knowledge. When processes and control are centralised, the perception is that staff are out of touch with their direct line managers on a departmental level. There is a perceived loss of control linked to centralisation from a process perspective in particular.

What is your perception about the influence of power on the support and preservation of knowledge sharing?

The perception is that power is a catalyst for the acceptance of the obligatory passage point. However, the findings suggest that perceptions are that power can be abused to make management indispensable. When power is exerted to bring about change and progress, the outcome is usually counterproductive. In fact, centralisation is seen to be a catalyst for power. As one respondent pointed out "Centralising would lead to power issues" while another respondent said "People want to run everything themselves out of fear of being challenged or their value is tied to how much control they have". Perceptions also reveal that power does not exist in parallel with collaborative efforts. If a focal actor were to exert power to form a network of aligned interest, it is perceived to be to institute practices without the input of the actors. Responses like "If someone is heading something they want to run it their way, even if other people offer their guidance, goods ideas get ignored", or "They do not teach, so they do not know what we need" demonstrate that the respondents believe that knowledge sharing should be autonomous.

An approach to rallying support that would make staff more amenable to sharing would be to create an environment for knowledge sharing where the matter of control is eliminated, and this should be consciously directed by management. As a respondent mentioned, "Establish a situation where these issues won't come up, such as letting sharing happen lower down where sharing issues is not a problem, as opposed to where it could be a problem, such as at management level". In doing so, management are demonstrating their involvement in a collaborative, rather than forceful, manner.

Interessement

What would you consider as influencing/ motivating factors on your decision to share knowledge?

The respondents are aware of the benefits of sharing knowledge. In fact, they believe it is their responsibility to share knowledge. They recognise the potential for growth and development when sharing occurs, as well as the improvement of operational efficiency and effectiveness. One respondent indicated "We simply cannot compartmentalise knowledge" and another said "The only way that I could get the job done was to get staff to share their knowledge". The respondents therefore feel there is no need to force this decision on them, or make unilateral decisions for them, but the credibility lies in the way that it is approached. This might start with making provision for sharing in the form of workload capacity and systems. In addition, everyone should be participating in sharing for its stimulation amongst colleagues, as one respondent pointed out "We need to have the buy-in from everybody, making things easier for everybody. There is very little admin assistance, you have to do everything. You basically have to be lecturer, admin person, photocopier, everything. If we work together a little bit more, it will make everyone's lives easier". Influence should extend to all staff to ensure that the formation of the network of aligned interest is successful. Thus, proper leadership is imperative for influence.

Enrolment

What enablers should be in place to ensure successful implementation of knowledge sharing processes?

The findings here support the assertion that technology and processes are enablers for knowledge sharing. In general, the infrastructure to support knowledge sharing must exist before knowledge sharing can occur. It does not, however, suggest that both processes and technology must be in place simultaneously. What should exist are standardised processes, and anything that will facilitate these processes. As one respondent suggested "It must be organised, not happen in an ad hoc manner" and another added "The people in charge should create a space, time and opportunity to share". Technology does, however, feature prominently amongst the respondents as a platform to facilitate the ease of access to relevant knowledge and thus reducing workload. As a respondent stated "The learner management system – it fits my philosophy to reduce my carbon footprint and it saves me time and reduces my administrative work, so should any knowledge-sharing platforms that are in place. If it can satisfy these requirements, then it will fit my needs", while another respondent asserted "There must be technology that works and it must be in place before gaining staff commitment".

In addition to these enablers, the respondents reveal that knowledge sharing as an initiative must have a driver (focal actor), so that there is ownership over its implementation and responsiveness throughout the (translation) process, which is demonstrated in this respondents view "It must not just be an idea. For knowledge sharing to be taken seriously after gaining staff commitment, there must be a combination of a person and a platform in place. Without a face to the initiative, the ball won't get rolling" and another mentioned "There should be a person with a 'listening ear'. If knowledge is to improve the way that we work, people should be 'listening', particularly those that have the influence to effect change". Furthermore, the driver must not only represent the institution, but the staff who will partake in the initiative to ensure that the respective goals align, as one respondents pointed out "There is disconnect between the institution and the goals of the academic staff".

What is pivotal for successful translation, however, is that the enablers must be planned and provided for as a precursor for sharing to take place. This is the only perceived way for knowledge sharing to become a standardised practice which could advance progress toward a culture for sharing. What might potentially break down a culture of participation is if new initiatives are mandated without consultation of staff, and more importantly without a responsible party to ensure that staff are serviced adequately in terms of support. In other words, there is no process of (engaging) translation.

What do you consider as effective strategies for gaining academic staff commitment to knowledge sharing?

Despite the fact that new initiatives are often introduced by management, staff are expected to be instrumental in its implementation. Management is perceived to have an equal responsibility in the implementation of such initiatives. Strategies which are perceived to be effective for gaining staff commitment have a strong link to the enablers for successful implementation. This alludes to the fact that a good strategy would ensure that the enablers are in place and would consider input from staff in defining the appropriate processes and infrastructure for its implementation. As one respondent pointed out "Management say 'this is our vision' but we are just there to make it work, without knowing how to do it. There is no follow through on the plans by management" and another respondent said "There needs to be persons put in place to drive knowledge sharing that are accessible (do not sit on the top floor and never interact with staff). They need to get a feel for what people are doing and what they need". Findings further reveal that management's participation should be on-going to gain staff buy in.

Mobilisation

What do you think could sustain knowledge sharing within your subject, department or faculty?

The respondents reveal that sustainability cannot be achieved if knowledge sharing as an initiative is viewed by staff as a "fad". Their views affirm that the structure and facilities for knowledge sharing must be implemented and there must be a way forward that will ensure that it happens. This alludes to not only the existence of a strategy, but implementation in the form of institutionalisation. In this context, institutionalisation will manifest in the work environment if knowledge sharing is integrated into daily operations and facilities to enable knowledge sharing exist. As one respondent pointed out, "Make knowledge sharing processes part of the main operational processes by integrating it. That way it won't just be a new thing for now" and another respondent said "If it becomes part of your work environment, it will naturally sustain itself and if it is a generally accepted thing". In addition, there should be continuous reflection and evaluation of the knowledge sharing strategy which is responsive to the needs of the staff. As one respondent said "You are only really going to buy into something if you have an interest or you get something out of it". If staff find that the strategies are not responsive to their needs, then interest will diminish. Furthermore, unless staff are getting the specific knowledge that they need, this would impact on their sustained knowledge sharing, as a respondent pointed out "It must be split up in terms of areas of interest – so you share based on what you are interested in".

In terms of management, good leadership will also sustain knowledge sharing. A good leader will not just be a person, but the right person to drive such an initiative. Good leadership manifests itself in the form of creating consistent awareness around knowledge sharing initiatives, meaning there is constant buy-in from the staff. A leader that ensures that knowledge sharing is reinforced as an imperative through reflection and evaluation will reinvigorate interest. It is also proposed that the driver of knowledge sharing must be rotated, as anyone that holds a position for a prolonged period is perceived to stagnate and this will not bode well for the constant buy-in of staff participation. As a respondent asserted, "Being in the same position for long gives you the idea that you don't need to learn anything else" while another respondent said "The network of knowledge sharing cannot grow by itself unless management continuously nurtures it." In addition, a respondent said "We need encouragement to deal with issues to prevent knowledge sharing from stagnating". Essentially, sustainability is highly contingent on management's leadership abilities. Aspects of leadership that were brought to the fore include having the appropriate vision, providing the guidelines and methods for implementation, coordination of the initiative, and balancing the interests of staff.

How can knowledge sharing as a process be formalised/ institutionalised?

For knowledge sharing to become an entrenched culture, the respondents consider strategy as important to guide the implementation of facilities to enable sharing. Policies are also proposed to further affirm these strategies. One respondent, however, mentioned "There must be a culture of sharing. If not, nothing will be done. The culture must be institutionalised for knowledge to be shared at all levels". The entrenchment of this culture is preceded by the aforementioned initiatives for implementation and the constant efforts to obtain buy-in, revision and coordination would likely lead to this entrenched culture. In particular, there are observations that the integration of knowledge sharing into operations may lead to such entrenchment, and thus institutionalisation, as one respondent said "Here our timetables are filled to the brim. There are no slots for staff development. It should be there, they should make provision for sharing" and another contended "A regular formalised meeting…must be scheduled on the timetable". Furthermore, the respondents feel that policies should be written in consultation with staff, and there should be continuous revision until these policies align to the way that staff work, for example, respondents said "We need to discuss new policies and how it affects us" and "There must be consultation and there must be a process until you finalise your policy."

Structure seems to feature very strongly as an enabler for institutionalisation. This corresponds with the above view that continuously applying knowledge sharing methods as part of how staff work and in a systematic manner will lead to the institutionalisation, and thus culture, of knowledge sharing. Structure is considered to be created through defined processes, structure of knowledge in terms of its relevancy, systems to facilitate the access to knowledge, and training. In particular, a respondent said "Very often people need to be re-orientated and trained to undergo a paradigm shift. There should be deliberate training, especially for new people coming in". In this context, training seems to be the catalyst for obtaining the buy-in from an institutionalisation perspective, i.e. that the institutionalisation at its inception is achieved through training as the first step toward formalising knowledge sharing processes. This view is further supported by this statement made by a respondent: "Institutionalisation is paramount, as it displays that there is a buy-in from management which is important for convincing staff that they should participate".

CONCLUSION AND RECOMMENDATIONS

Introduction

This paper set out to employ the actor-network theory (ANT) as a methodology to understand and interpret the sociotechnical knowledge sharing challenges in organisations. Although knowledge management can be studied by a variety of lenses, this paper argued that it can well be understood through the single lens of the concept of Moments of Translation of ANT. Thus, using ANT, the objective of this study was twofold: To determine why there is no network of aligned interest and to determine how to create a network of aligned interest. The methodology for this study was developed within the context of ANT by adopting its ideals and principles to understand how to introduce and develop knowledge sharing within an organisation, using the moments of translation.

The findings demonstrate that using the concept of the Moments of Translation as a lens to study this phenomenon is indeed a novel way of investigating the reason why there is still difficulty with sharing and managing knowledge. New perspectives were explored, thereby transforming the way that knowledge sharing dynamics are perceived. By utilising a normative approach, this research looked at how knowledge sharing as an ideal can be achieved when taking into account the existing constraints. The culture of the institution, as revealed by the views of the respondents, has determined the suitable knowledge sharing approaches that should be employed, impacting on processes and technology factors.

The discussion of the findings served to determine why there is no network of aligned interest, while the refinement of the problem conceptualisation, as informed by the findings, was used to develop a general framework which served to determine how to create a network of aligned interest. This framework is discussed in the next section.

Research Implications and Recommendations

Figure 3 is a general framework, which is a refinement of the problem conceptualisation in Figure 1. The problem conceptualisation was derived from the theory and findings from the literature review. The research questions which were aligned to the research objectives served to verify whether the proposed conceptual framework indeed represented the views of the respondents. The general framework has not only been validated, but extended to represent the view of the respondents on how to create and sustain a network of aligned interest for knowledge sharing.

Management is not only identified to be the focal actor, but a leader, facilitator and coordinator too. Therefore, management must drive knowledge sharing as an initiative, and must demonstrate continuous leadership from the initial phase of problematisation, through to mobilisation. Management's role should be that of a coordinator to oversee knowledge sharing processes, making knowledge sharing a shared interest of the entire organisation. In order for management to be a facilitator, rather than an enforcer, the role of power must be replaced with collaboration. This will bring about the "capacity" for management to influence the actors. In other words, this will give management the credibility for gaining buy-in from staff. Continuous support from management manifests in the continuous oversight and coordination of knowledge sharing processes, measurement of knowledge sharing success, and the continuous revision of the role of people, technology and processes through the revision of policies, standards and procedures to be responsive to the needs of staff to ensure alignment to how they work.

Given that a particular concern is the misalignment between management and staff, a knowledge sharing strategy is a necessary precursor for knowledge sharing initiatives. Pivotal for successful translation are the enablers for sharing, which must be planned and provided for. This is why a knowledge sharing strategy should consider the variables related to actor-network strength. The strength of the network is not only influenced by human factors and organisational factors that are technology, process, or power driven, but factors of punctualisation and competing networks too. All of these variables should be given due consideration during the problematisation phase and should be negotiated in the interessement phase. A good strategy would also consider input from staff in defining the appropriate processes and infrastructure for its implementation, but not be too prescriptive. A new initiative cannot be mandated without consultation of staff, and more importantly without a responsible party to ensure that staffs are serviced adequately in terms of support. This would make the process of translation an engaging one. A process of negotiation will ensure that staff needs are balanced, and that the role of non-human actors is carefully thought out too. For example, organisations should choose an appropriate platform for their staff that aligns not only to the facilitation of the necessary task, but which also complies with the way people work, while processes should not be a departure from how people have previously worked. In addition, balancing workloads to accommodate the inclusion of knowledge sharing as a recognised form of work should be addressed in this process.

Figure 3. General framework

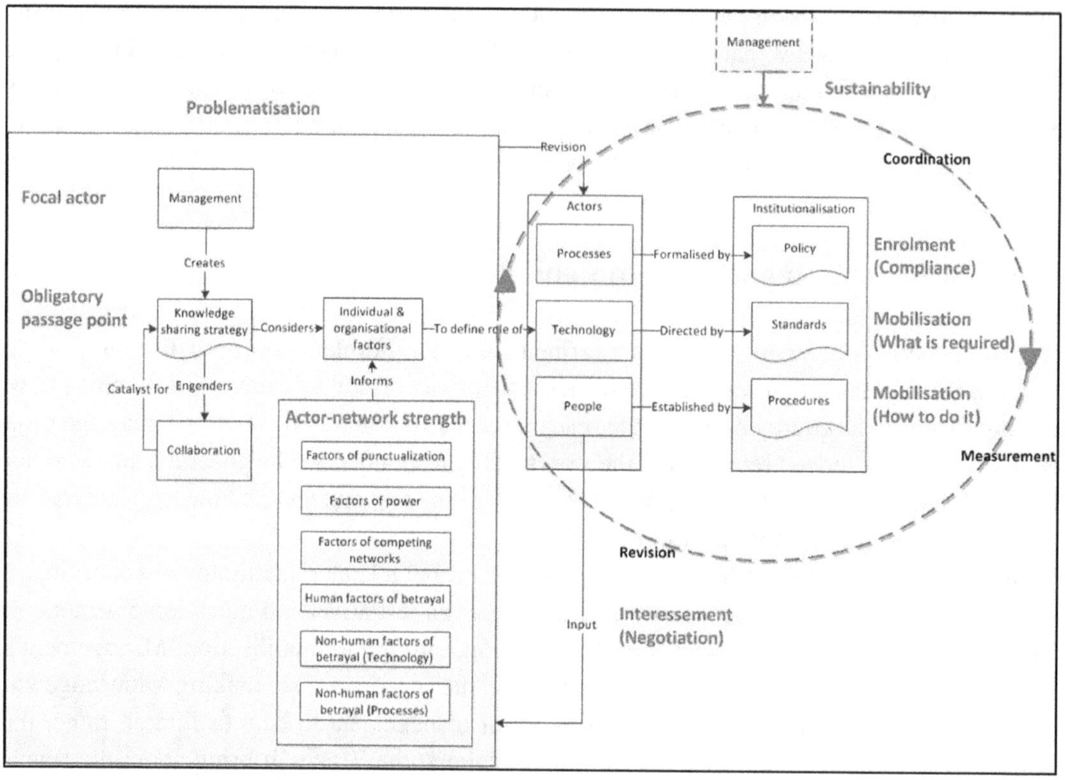

The structure and facilities for knowledge sharing must be implemented and there must be a way forward that will ensure that it happens. This alludes to not only the existence of a strategy, but implementation in the form of institutionalisation. Once the knowledge sharing strategy is ratified by staff and management, it is further formerly defined by a policy which serves as the inscription of the commitments made by each party. However, a policy merely serves as a reminder of the scope and issues identified. Knowledge sharing strategies cannot succeed without a pragmatic plan for its implementation. Thus, standards and procedures serve as important means to ensure what must be done and how it will be done, respectively. Without standards, it would be difficult to determine what to measure and whether the processes are effective. Thus, standards add a quantifiable aspect to the framework. Procedures (or processes) serve to ensure that there are step-by-step instructions that will eventually become an established way of doing things. These processes will include the use of mechanisms put in place for knowledge sharing. Standards and procedures constitute the process of mobilisation. By having the proper standards and procedures, staff can mobilise into action as they will have assumed a state of readiness. An entrenched culture for sharing will not only manifest out of the policies, standards and procedures, which are the catalysts for institutionalisation, but the constant efforts to obtain buy-in, revision and coordination would likely lead to this entrenched culture. In addition, the aforementioned are perceived to contribute to the sustainability of the knowledge sharing initiative.

Research Limitations and Future Research

This was a qualitative study that was conducted at one higher education institution. Despite the fact that this study could shed a new light on the matter of knowledge sharing, the findings cannot be generalised beyond the context of this study. However, it is context that has enabled a deeper understanding of this social phenomenon to demonstrate the actor-network theory (ANT) as a suitable methodology to understand and interpret the socio-technical knowledge sharing challenges in organisations. The rigorous processes employed to collect, analysis and interpret the data furthermore strengthen the validity of the findings. Thus, it is proposed that this study be replicated in different contexts to either prove or refute the relevancy of the general framework for different contexts.

REFERENCES

Alavi, M., Kayworth, T. R., & Leidner, D. E. (2006). An empirical examination of the Influence of organizational culture on knowledge management practices. *Journal of Management Information Systems*, *22*(3), 191–224. doi:10.2753/MIS0742-1222220307

Ary, D., Jacobs, L. C., & Razavieh, A. (2002). *Introduction to research in education*. Belmont: Wadsworth/ Thompson.

Aulawi, H., Sudirman, I., Suryadi, K., & Govindaraju, R. (2009). Knowledge sharing behavior, antecedents and their impact on the individual innovation capability. *Journal of Applied Sciences Research*, *5*(12), 2238–2246.

Baskerville, R., & Dulipovici, A. (2006). The theoretical foundations of knowledge management. *Knowledge Management Research & Practice*, *4*(2), 83–105. doi:10.1057/palgrave.kmrp.8500090

Berg, B. L. (2007). *Qualitative research methods for the social sciences*. Boston, MA: Allyn & Bacon.

Bock, G. W., & Kim, Y.-G. (2002). Breaking the myths of rewards: An exploratory research of attitudes about knowledge sharing. *Information Resources Management Journal*, *15*(2), 14–21. doi:10.4018/irmj.2002040102

Bontis, N., & Serenko, A. (2009). A follow-up ranking of academic journals. *Journal of Knowledge Management*, *13*(1), 16–26. doi:10.1108/13673270910931134

Borgström, B. (2012). Towards a methodology for studying supply chain practice. *International Journal of Physical Distribution & Logistics Management*, *42*(8/9), 843–862. doi:10.1108/09600031211269785

Braun, V., & Clarke, V. (2006). Using thematic analysis in psychology. *Qualitative Research in Psychology*, *3*(2), 77–101. doi:10.1191/1478088706qp063oa

Busch, C., De Maret, P. S., Flynn, T., Kellum, R., Le, S., Meyers, B., . . . Palmquist, M. (2012). *Content analysis*. Retrieved from http://writing.colostate.edu/guides/guide.cfm?guideid=61

Bush, A. A., & Tiwana, A. (2005). Continuance in expertise-sharing networks: A social perspective. *Transactions on Engineering Management*, *52*(1), 85–101. doi:10.1109/TEM.2004.839956

Cabrera, A., Collins, W. C., & Salgado, J. F. (2006). Determinants of individual engagement in knowledge sharing. *International Journal of Human Resource Management, 17*(2), 245–264. doi:10.1080/09585190500404614

Carayannis, E., & Alexander, J. (2002). Is technological learning a firm core competence, when, how and why? A longitudinal, multi-industry study of firm technological learning and market performance. *Technovation, 22*(1), 625–643. doi:10.1016/S0166-4972(01)00047-5

Cavaliere, V., Lombardi, S., & Giustiniano, L. (2015). Knowledge sharing in knowledge-intensive manufacturing firms. An empirical study of its enablers. *Journal of Knowledge Management, 19*(6), 1124–1145. doi:10.1108/JKM-12-2014-0538

Chelly, S. (1996). The case study method for research in small and medium sized firms. *International Small Business Journal, 15*(1), 73–85. doi:10.1177/0266242696151005

Chen, L., & Mohamed, S. (2010). The strategic importance of tacit knowledge management activities in construction. *Construction Innovation, 10*(2), 138–163. doi:10.1108/14714171011037165

Chuang, Y.-H., & Hung, Y.-C. (2009, July 30 – August 1). Factors affecting knowledge sharing behavior: A content analysis of empirical findings. *Proceedings of the International Conference of Pacific Rim Management*, San Francisco, USA.

Davenport, T. H., & Prusak, L. (2000). *Working knowledge. How organisations manage what they know.* Boston, MA: Harvard Business School.

Diedrich, A., & Guzman, G. (2015). From implementation to appropriation: Understanding knowledge management system development and introduction as a process of translation. *Journal of Knowledge Management, 19*(6), 1273–1294. doi:10.1108/JKM-02-2015-0055

Durcikova, A., & Gray, P. H. (2005). The role of knowledge repositories in technical support environments: Speed versus learning in user performance. *Journal of Management Information Systems, 22*(3), 159–190.

Fong, P. S. W., & Lee, H. F. (2009). Acquisition, reuse and sharing of knowledge in property management firms. *Facilities, 27*(7/8), 291–314. doi:10.1108/02632770910956148

Glaser, B., & Strauss, A. (1967). *The discovery of grounded theory: Strategies for qualitative research.* New York: Aldine.

Heizmann, H., & Olsson, M. R. (2015). Power matters: The importance of Foucaults power/knowledge as a conceptual lens in KM research and practice. *Journal of Knowledge Management, 19*(4), 756–769. doi:10.1108/JKM-12-2014-0511

Hewett, K., & Watson, S. (2006). A multi-theoretical model of knowledge transfer in organizations: Determinants of knowledge contribution and knowledge reuse. *Journal of Management Studies, 43*(2), 141–173. doi:10.1111/j.1467-6486.2006.00586.x

Hislop, D. (2013). *Knowledge Management in Organizations. A Critical Introduction.* Oxford: Oxford University Press.

Holsapple, C. W. (2001). Knowledge management support of decision making. *Decision Support Systems, 31*(1), 1–3. doi:10.1016/S0167-9236(00)00115-9

Hong, J., Kim, S., & Suh, E. (2012). A diagnosis framework for identifying the current knowledge sharing activity status in a community of practice. *Expert Systems with Applications, 39*(18), 13093–13107. doi:10.1016/j.eswa.2012.05.092

Huysman, M., & de Wit, D. (2003). A critical evaluation of knowledge management practices. In M. S. Ackerman, V. Pipek, & V. Wulf (Eds.), *Sharing Expertise: Beyond Knowledge Management* (pp. 27–55). Cambridge, MA: The MIT Press.

Ipe, M. (2003). Knowledge sharing in organizations: A conceptual framework. *Human Resource Development Review, 2*(4), 337–359. doi:10.1177/1534484303257985

Iskoujina, Z., & Roberts, J. (2015). Knowledge sharing in open source software communities: Motivations and management. *Journal of Knowledge Management, 19*(4), 791–813. doi:10.1108/JKM-10-2014-0446

Israilidis, J., Siachou, E., Cooke, L., & Lock, R. (2015). Individual variables with an impact on knowledge sharing: The critical role of employees ignorance. *Journal of Knowledge Management, 19*(6), 1–32. doi:10.1108/JKM-04-2015-0153

Khalil, O. E. M., & Shea, T. (2012). Knowledge sharing barriers and effectiveness at a higher education institution. [April-June.]. *International Journal of Knowledge Management, 8*(2), 43–64. doi:10.4018/jkm.2012040103

Kruger, S. J., & Welman, J. C. (2001). *Research methodology*. South Africa: Oxford university press.

Latour, B. (1987). *Science in action: How to follow scientists and engineers through society*. Cambridge, MA: Harvard university press.

Latour, B. (1991). Technology is society made durable. *The Sociological Review, 38*(1), 103–131.

Latour, B. (1996). *Aramis, or, the love of technology*. Cambridge, MA: Harvard University Press.

Latour, B. (2005). *Reassembling the social-an introduction to actor-network-theory*. Oxford: Oxford University Press.

Lauring, J., & Selmer, J. (2012). Knowledge sharing in diverse organisations. *Human Resource Management Journal, 22*(1), 89–105. doi:10.1111/j.1748-8583.2010.00158.x

Laws, K., & McLeod, R. (2004, July 25 – 29). Case research and grounded theory: Sharing some alternative qualitative research methodologies with systems professionals. *Paper presented at the 22nd International Conference of the Systems Dynamics Society.*

Lee, J. (2001). The impact of knowledge sharing, organizational capability and partnership quality on IS outsourcing success. *Information & Management, 38*(5), 323–335. doi:10.1016/S0378-7206(00)00074-4

Leonard, D., & McAdam, R. (2001). Grounded theory methodology and practitioner reflexivity in TQM research. *International Journal of Quality & Reliability Management, 18*(2), 180–194. doi:10.1108/02656710110377301

Liao, S. (2003). Knowledge management technologies and applications-literature review from 1995 to 2002. *Expert Systems with Applications*, *25*(2), 155–164. doi:10.1016/S0957-4174(03)00043-5

Lin, H. (2007). Knowledge sharing and firm innovation capability: An empirical study. *International Journal of Manpower*, *28*(3/4), 315–332. doi:10.1108/01437720710755272

Lu, L., Lueng, K., & Koch, P. T. (2006). Managerial knowledge sharing: The role of individual, interpersonal and organizational factors. *Management and Organization Review*, *2*(1), 15–41. doi:10.1111/j.1740-8784.2006.00029.x

Lubega, J., Omona, W. & Van der Weide, T. (2010). Using ICT to enhance knowledge management in higher education: A conceptual framework and research agenda. *International Journal of Education and Development using Information and Communication Technology*, 6(4), 83-101.

Ma, Z., Huang, Y., Wu, J., Dong, W., & Qi, L. (2014). What matters for knowledge sharing in collectivistic cultures? Empirical evidence from China. *Journal of Knowledge Management*, *18*(5), 1004–1019. doi:10.1108/JKM-06-2014-0252

Ma, Z., & Yu, K. (2010). Research paradigms of contemporary knowledge management studies: 19982007. *Journal of Knowledge Management*, *14*(2), 175–189. doi:10.1108/13673271011032337

Malbon, B. (1999). *Interviewing in qualitative research*. Retrieved from http://www.comp.dit.ie/dgordon/Podcasts/Interviews/chap15.pdf

Malik, M. (2005, November 10-11). Improvement in higher education through KM. *Paper presented at the 3rd Convention PLANNER'05*, Assam University, Silchar, 2005.

Martin, B. (2000). Knowledge management within the context of management: An evolving relationship. *Singapore Management Review*, *22*(2), 17–36.

Maxwell, J. A. (2013). *Qualitative research design: An interactive approach*. Thousand Oaks, CA: Sage.

Meso, P., & Smith, R. (2000). A resource-based view of organizational knowledge management systems. *Journal of Knowledge Management*, *4*(3), 224–234. doi:10.1108/13673270010350020

Patton, M. Q. (1990). *Qualitative evaluation and research methods*. Newbury Park, CA: Sage.

Perry, C., & Coote, L. (1994). Processes of a new case study research methodology: tool for management development? *Paper presented at the National Conference of Australian and New Zealand Association for Management*. Victoria University of Wellington, Wellington.

Polanyi, M. (1967). *The Tacit Dimension*. London: Routledge and Kegan Paul.

Rubenstein-Montano, B., Liebowitz, J., Buchwalter, J., McCaw, D., Newman, B., & Rebeck, K. (2001). SMARTVision: A knowledge-management methodology. *Journal of Knowledge Management*, *5*(4), 300–310. doi:10.1108/13673270110411724

Sarker, S., Sarker, S., & Sidorova, A. (2006). Understanding business process change failure: An Actor-Network perspective. *Journal of Management Information Systems*, *23*(1), 51–86. doi:10.2753/MIS0742-1222230102

Schauer, A., Vasconcelos, A. C., & Sen, B. (2015). The ShaRInK framework: A holistic perspective on key categories of influences shaping individual perceptions of knowledge sharing. *Journal of Knowledge Management, 19*(4), 770–790. doi:10.1108/JKM-12-2014-0519

Stake, R. E. (1995). *The art of case study research.* Thousand Oaks, CA: Sage.

Sulisworo, D. (2012). Enabling ICT and knowledge management to enhance competitiveness of higher education institutions. *International Journal of Education, 4*(1), 112–121. doi:10.5296/ije.v4i1.1207

Tan, L. P., & Wong, K. Y. (2015). Linkage between knowledge management and manufacturing performance: A structural equation modeling approach. *Journal of Knowledge Management, 19*(4), 814–835. doi:10.1108/JKM-11-2014-0487

Twum-Darko, M., & Harker, L. L. (2015). Factors influencing knowledge sharing amongst higher education academics at a university in South Africa. *Journal of Corporate Ownership & Control, 12*(2), 280–292.

Twum-Darko, M., Noruwana, N., & Sewchurran, K. (2015). Theoretical interpretation of e-government implementation challenges in South Africa: A case study of a selected provincial government. *Journal of Governance and Regulation, 4*(1), 175–185. doi:10.22495/jgr_v4_i1_c2_p2

William, M. K. (2006). *Research methods knowledge base: Deduction and induction.* Retrieved from http://www.socialresearchmethods.net/kb/dedind.php

This research was previously published in the International Journal of Knowledge Management (IJKM), 13(1); edited by Murray E. Jennex; pages 53-74, copyright year 2017 by IGI Publishing (an imprint of IGI Global).

Chapter 19
Business Intelligence System Design and its Consequences for Knowledge Sharing, Collaboration, and Decision-Making:
An Exploratory Study

Lapo Mola
SKEMA Business School, LSMRC, France

Cecilia Rossignoli
Università degli Studi di Verona, Italy

Andrea Carugati
Aarhus University, Denmark & IESEG School of Management (LEM - CNRS UMR 9221), France

Antonio Giangreco
IESEG School of Management (LEM-CNRS UMR 9221), Catholic University of Lille, France

ABSTRACT

This exploratory study analyses the effects of the technical and organisational characteristics of business intelligence systems (BIS) on knowledge sharing, collaboration, and decision-making processes. The authors conducted a two-phase multi-method investigation. First, we surveyed 30 enterprises using BIS on a regular basis; then, we engaged in an in-depth case study with one of the respondent companies. Our results show that, on average, the technical and organisational characteristics of the BIS are positively associated with an increase in knowledge sharing, leading to an improvement in internal collaboration that subsequently brings improvement in the quality of decision-making. This case study adds that the way the BIS is designed and appropriated in organisations is important in obtaining such results is. A BIS being designed so that it can be appropriated by the general employee base is key in obtaining the desired organizational impacts. This suggests some requirements for BIS design that we will discuss in terms of theoretical and managerial implications.

DOI: 10.4018/978-1-7998-0417-8.ch019

INTRODUCTION

Business intelligence was first defined as "the ability to apprehend the interrelationships of presented facts in such a way as to guide action towards a desired goal" (Luhn, 1958, p. 315). Even in this new era of big data,[1] this definition still holds true today, for the way business intelligence systems (BIS) are perceived, interpreted and used, in the large majority of organisations (that are not ready nor need big data analysis). Business intelligence covers several processes and technologies (data mining, data warehouses and online analytical processing [OLAP]), and involves the tools and systems that play a vital role in information dissemination, knowledge sharing and action guiding in organisations (Barakat, et al., 2013). These systems allow a company to gather, store, access and analyse corporate data to aid decision-making. As highlighted by Parry and Graves, "knowledge is a fluid mix of experiences, value, contextual information and expert insight offering a framework to evaluate and integrate new experiences and information" (2008, p. 429). BIS help organisations generate meaningful knowledge shared across the whole organisation, in order to perform short and long-term strategic planning (Williams & Williams, 2006).

However, the fact that BIS—as the systems that support and provide business intelligence—focus so heavily on the interrelationship of facts has clearly influenced the way the applications and databases have been built—namely, to provide cross-functional, cross divisional, interrelated data analysis. Over time, BIS have become more complex, and have started to include knowledge management systems and executive information systems (Clark, et al., 2007). In turn, the interrelated nature of the data analysis has increased the expectation for interrelated results. Indeed, BIS have often been assumed, in theory and practice, to take the role of the collaboration processes facilitators (Clark et al., 2007). This is achieved through the ability of BIS to promote a knowledge-sharing process, defined as the actual process of sharing information, skills and expertise across the members of different groups or organisations (Barakat et al. 2013). Computer-based systems help facilitate such activities (Tsui, 2003), and BIS, in particular, tend to emphasise these aspects. In other words, knowledge sharing can be considered the ability to transform the information into an asset, shared across different levels and departments of the organisation independently, by the person or organisation unit where the information was created.

Over time, the study of the effect of technology on organisational and decision processes has become very varied, including multiple types of technologies (Leidner & Kayworth 2006; Bailey, Leonardi & Chong, 2010). The result of this evolution has been that the role of BIS—as systems that allow increased knowledge sharing, enable an increased level of collaboration and favour quality decision processes—has been often equalised to that of all other information technologies. Whether by design, research or simple wishful thinking, the relationship between BIS and collaboration and knowledge sharing has been black-boxed, in favour of the rather deterministic view that BIS, if simply implemented correctly, will lead to improved decision-making processes.

The phenomenon of black boxing information technology is well known, and surprisingly common in information systems research (Orlikowski & Iacono, 2001; Leonardi & Barley, 2008). Only recently have researchers attempted to unpack the relationship between technology and collaboration, knowledge sharing and decision-making processes in organisations (Bailey et al., 2010; Chen, et al., 2012). However, relatively few studies directly address the relationship between BIS technical features and organisational demands, and their effect on decision-making processes. This problem appears to be increasingly serious in this period in which big data, as the latest incarnation of BI, is slowly rising as the new analysis paradigm. Organisations are experiencing a transitional period between traditional data analysis and big data (Magoulas & Lorica, 2009), and need tools and knowledge to decide whether the investment in BI technologies is justifiable, in terms of organisational returns. This paper aims to investigate this transitional period, particularly the relationship between the characteristics of BIS and its different organisational impacts. This is done by analysing the effects produced by BIS on the quality of the decision-making process, through the ability of BIS to support knowledge sharing. Our research question can be formalised as follows:

How do BIS technical and organisational characteristics affect the level of collaboration in organisations, and subsequently the quality of decision-making?

To answer this research question, we designed an exploratory multi-method research project. First, we built and tested a number of hypotheses, to verify whether a relationship exists between the characteristics of BIS and the quality of decision-making in organisations. We used data from 30 companies, in which at least 15 employees had been using BIS across various departments for at least a year after implementation. We then conducted an in-depth case study, to validate the model emerging from the survey, and to explore the nature of the relationships that emerged, in depth. We used a combination of quantitative and qualitative research methods to provide information about *what* happened and *why*.

Our findings suggest that BIS technical and organisational characteristics affect increased knowledge sharing, which in turn affect better internal collaboration, that subsequently affect better quality decision-making. While these results may confirm a functionalist/deterministic view of the expected results of BIS, our case study demonstrates that a main component in obtaining such results is the way that a BIS is designed and appropriated in organisations. We show that a conscious design of the different aspects of BIS is instrumental for how the BIS is appropriated by the general employee base, rather than by a restricted number of information technology (IT) employees. If BIS are designed for widespread availability and ease of manipulation, they can become the basic building block allowing connection between BIS, knowledge exchange, collaboration and decision-making.

The rest of the article is organised as follows. The next section analyses the literature on BIS, knowledge sharing and collaboration. Then, we introduce the relationships tested in the study. In the second part of the paper, we first outline the research context, methods and results of the quantitative study. Then, we present the case study. We conclude by discussing the theoretical contributions, future directions of research and managerial implications.

BACKGROUND LITERATURE

The literature deals with BIS from two perspectives that rarely communicate between each other: (i) a technological view, focused on the characteristics of the IT artefact, embodied in the systems built and used in organisations to obtain intelligence; and (ii) a functional or organisational view that is focused on the process of creating intelligence.

From a technological perspective, business intelligence is considered a collection of data storage, manipulation algorithms and interfaces, which bring intelligence to users (Negash, 2004). These systems start from an extract, transform, and load processes that transfer data from a variety of applications to the data-warehouse (DWH) and data-marts. On the usage side, we find OLAP, querying and reporting systems and data mining systems that are designed to enable the flexible and goal-driven transformation and integration of data (Chamoni & Gluchowski, 2004, Prado, et al. 2010). Within this view, the important result is the technological design, which allows certain actions, rather than the business result itself.

From a functional/organisational perspective, business intelligence can be considered an analytic process, designed to transform data into information that supports the decision-making of corporate management, both the middle and top management. Typically, these complex and expensive BIS are aimed at supporting corporate, strategically relevant goals (Negash, 2004). In this view, the important topic is the business result achieved, rather than the technology and design that enabled the result.

Despite the numerous contributions identified in the literature that address BIS as an area of study (for example, Jourdan, et al., 2008), during the last 15 years, the information systems (IS) literature has focused primarily on the technological characteristics (Chen et al., 2000) and dynamics relevant to knowledge sharing and management decision-making processes (Yeoh & Koronios, 2010, Boh, 2014). Only recently have some scholars begun to investigate the relationships between decision processes and the technical features of BIS (such as Elbashir, et al., 2008,). In attempting to do so, the literature has sought to position BIS in relation to other classic systems geared towards helping decision-making, such as decision support systems, executive support systems, group decision support systems and knowledge management systems (Dalkir, 2013; Arnott, 2004). Following these works, BIS represent the natural evolution of a series of earlier technologies developed to support decision-making (Clark et al., 2007).

The reason for this interest in better understanding the relationship between BIS and organisational processes is that today, more than ever, the availability of DWH technology, improved hardware and software performance and increased adoption of web-based technology in business transactions have contributed to creating BIS environments rarely available in the past (Negash, 2004; Chen et al., 2012). Contemporary BIS can process information with a quality and speed that has the potential to improve dramatically decision-making processes at all levels of organisations.

The literature offers numerous examples demonstrating how the adoption of BIS enables the creation of flexible organisational structures and mechanisms. BIS is studied, not only as an instrument able to support decision-making processes, but also in relation to its organisational effects—measured in terms of the reduction of complexity and uncertainty within the user organisation (Arnott & Pervan, 2005; Elbashir, Collier & Sutton, 2011). Following this trend, the study of BIS cannot be limited exclusively to its technological characteristics without an adequate evaluation of its organisational effects on the user organisation. Even if the main objective in adopting BIS is to improve decision-making processes, this could be accompanied by better communication among co-workers, and better coordination of interdependencies within the organisation. BIS can help streamline and optimise the process of creation, management and diffusion of information relative to decision-making (Elbashir et al., 2008).

With greater support for decision-making and greater communication and knowledge sharing, the collaboration among different organisational units and departments should be more efficient, thereby allowing the actors in the organisation to better perform their tasks and complete their processes. Previous research has found that this relationship between IT support for processes and coordination conceives technology as a fundamental enabler of flexible business cooperation (Venkatraman, 1994). This is supported by similar results regarding the adoption of software applications for computer support cooperative work, and its influence on various forms of coordination (Gattiker & Goodhue, 2005).

Although promising, this stream of research suffers from two problems. First, IT is black-boxed, and therefore limited conclusions can be reached regarding practices with and around the artefact (Orlikowski & Iacono, 2001). Second, systems implemented in organisations go through an initial period, in which they are adapted in bursts to suit the organisation's needs (Tyre & Orlikowski, 1994). Accordingly, it is important to both highlight the specific characteristics of technology, hence avoiding black boxing, but also to account for technological change in the organisation over time, hence avoiding a stable view of the technological artefact.

Thus, to avoid the black boxing approach of organisational research in IS, and the stable approach of technical studies of IS, in this study we adopted a multi-method approach. First, we undertook a survey, to investigate the relationship that the organisational and technical characteristics of BIS have with the ability of organisations to enhance and reinforce knowledge-sharing processes among organisational members, thereby improving the internal collaboration, and subsequently the quality of decisions. To discount the effects of technology changes in the initial phases of BIS use, we only considered cases in which BIS had been in use for more than one year. Second, to validate the model emerging from the analysis of the survey, we conducted an in-depth case study, aimed at understanding how and why organisations take advantage of the potential changes enabled by the introduction and use of BIS.

AN EXPLORATORY MODEL

Figure 1 presents this study's research model. The technical and organisational characteristics of BIS should facilitate the knowledge sharing within the organisation. Then, partaking in a common patrimony of information enhances the level of internal collaboration between units and people. Finally, the establishment of a more positive collaborative environment enhances the quality of decision-making.

Before introducing the model, we provide the definition of the macro-variables. Table 2 in the Appendix provides a detailed explanation of variable construct description and references used.

- Technical Organisational Characteristics (TOC) are related to the ability of BIS to structure data coming from different sources, such as ERP, CRM, Excel files and so on, providing homogeneity, consistency and correctness. The data structuration allows the integration across different types of users and departments.
- Increased Knowledge Sharing (IKS) is the ability to transform information about organisations' assets, shared across levels and departments of the organisation, and used independently by the person or organisation unit where the information originated.
- Improved Internal Collaboration (IIC) describes the level of inter- and intra-departmental collaboration enabled by the use and diffusion within the organisation of BIS.
- Improved Decision-Making Quality (IDMQ) refers to the reliability and speed of decision process, derived by the availability of shared data, which concurrently reduces the need for the mutual adjustment as coordination mechanism.

Figure 1. Research model

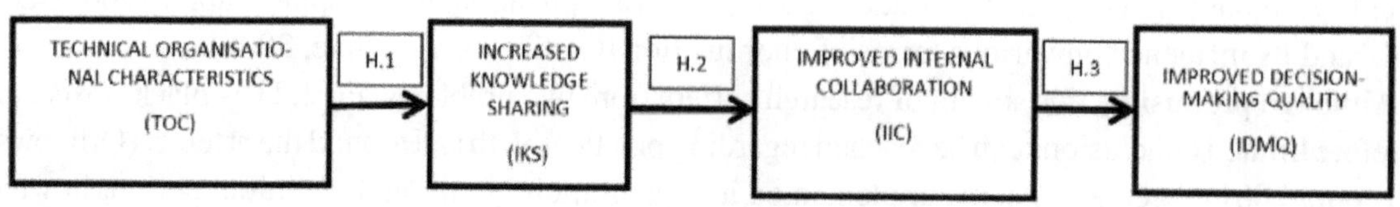

Technical Organisational Characteristics of BIS and Increased Knowledge Sharing

At the outset, we wanted to test whether the technical characteristics of BIS affect the facilitation of knowledge sharing for multiple units in the same organisation. BIS allow the design of collaborative, cross-functional decision processes, to provide a solution for several possible decision alternatives. Such decision processes might be structured or unstructured. However, if the process is difficult to structure, BIS might provide a helpful means of supporting formal decision processes, because they can integrate and make available information gathered across different units and/or departments (Bowers & Benford, 1991; Goldberg, et al., 1992; Raghu, et al., 2001).

Depending on the type of TOC, BIS provide significant access to data, information and knowledge, specific to the needs of individuals and groups facilitating the knowledge-sharing process (Alavi & Leidner, 2001; Kankanhalli, et al., 2005; Barakat, et al. 2013). Here, we aim to explore the relationship between BIS and knowledge sharing in organisations. BIS enables organisations to generate knowledge about their environments (Gold, et al., 2001), mostly by gathering knowledge possessed by individual members of the organisation (Grover & Davenport, 2001). Knowledgeable people "have information within the context of their experience, expertise and judgment" (Grover & Davenport, 2001, p. 6). Users can enhance their knowledge by using and framing the support provided by the BIS to address their problems, and then incorporate this usage back into the BIS (Clark et al. 2007; Leclercq, 2007). Therefore, we measured whether BIS improve knowledge and knowledge sharing. We capture these arguments in the first of our study hypotheses:

Hypothesis H.1: Technical organisational characteristics (TOC) of BIS are positively related to increased knowledge sharing (IKS).

Increased Knowledge Sharing and Improved Internal Collaboration

One assumption that has been taken for granted until now is that the more knowledge shared across an organisation, the better the collaboration within the organisation. To verify this assumption, we tested whether a BIS is able to increase coordination and communication among different business units/departments. BIS standardise the way knowledge is collected, processed and shared. In other words, it represents a move from a mutual adjustment logic to one based on standard input/output, because it is able to provide a common language across the organisation (Eckerson, 1999; Dias, 2001). On this basis, we proposed the following hypothesis:

Hypothesis H.2: Increased knowledge sharing (IKS) is positively related to improved internal collaboration (IIC).

Improved Internal Collaboration and Improved Decision-Making Quality

A well-established collaboration among individual actors and across business units, especially in the initial phases of an innovation process, may enable people to offer knowledge contributions. These contributions not only pertain to operational information, but also planning and control, which should increase an organisation's ability to engage in innovation processes, reduce related costs and stay within budget.

Further, Aoki (1986) suggests that decentralisation of decision-making is necessary when organisations need to be responsive to changing technologies or an uncertain environment, even if centralisation may have beneficial coordination effects (Zabojnik, 2002). Thus, we wanted to test whether improving collaboration affects the quality of decision-making. This was the basis for our third and last study hypothesis:

Hypothesis H.3: Improved internal collaboration (IIC) is positively related to improved decision-making quality (IDMQ).

CONTEXT AND QUANTITATIVE RESEARCH METHODS

Research Context and Sample

We conducted an explorative/pilot study in Veneto, a region in the northern part of Italy. We asked the local *Confindustria*—the Italian association representing manufacturing and service companies—to provide a random sample of 1,000 companies. From those 1,000 companies, we randomly selected 380 companies that covered the different industrial sectors, according to the Italian Institute of Statistics. Each had a turnover of more than 10 million Euros, and more than 15 employees. We contacted these 380 companies by email, asking whether they used BIS. From those 380, 180 confirmed the use of BIS. Of the latter, 83 confirmed their participation in the survey via an initial round of telephone interviews, between March 2007 and July 2008. We guaranteed that no names of the companies would be disclosed.

We used telephone interviews, rather than other survey methods (such as email), for two reasons. First, given the relatively small size of the sample of companies wishing to participate in the survey (83), we thought that direct contact would maximise the response rate. Our rate of 36 per cent is consistent with, or even slightly higher than, that usually obtained in the information system literature (for example, 12 per cent response rate in Bhattacherjee [2001] and Baruch [1999]). Second, we thought that given the high technicality of some questions, direct telephone contact would ensure that the interviewee was the appropriate respondent.

We first asked the respondents to identify the type of BIS that their organisation had been using for at least one year. Only 30 companies could identify their system as using BIS that complied with our definition, based on the technical and organisational elements defined in the theory section. The technologies used in these organisations are presented in Table 1. The remaining 53 organisations employed applications such as Microsoft Excel and Access as their BIS, which did not align with the definition. Subsequently, these organisations were excluded from the study.

Table 1. Technical components adopted by the companies

Technical Component	% of Companies
Query and reporting	100
Tableau de board, dashboard, scorecard	57
OLAP	47
Data mining	27
Analytic applications	20

Although our sample was relatively small, the companies were heterogeneous in their industry and size. Specifically, the sample consisted of eight manufacturing, five service, four trade and distribution, three chemical/pharmaceutical, three food, two textile/clothing, two healthcare, and two automotive firms, and one public administration firm. In terms of their 2006 turnover, we differentiated the companies by size, as follows: 37 per cent earned more than 500 million Euros, 10 per cent earned between 251 to 500 million Euros, 23 per cent earned 101 to 250 million Euros, 13 per cent earned 51 to 100 million Euros, and seven per cent earned 11 to 50 million Euros.

Data Collection

For each of the 30 companies, we identified and selected the person responsible for the BIS of their companies, from both the technical and organisational points of view. It was important to interact with a person with this double competence, as the survey included both technical and organisational questions. With the help of the holders of this key role, we submitted a questionnaire using telephone interviews, to different BIS key role players in these 30 organisations. According to the different cases, we interviewed the Chief Performance Officer, Business Intelligence Officer, Chief Financial Officer or Chief Information Officer (CIO).

Given that the survey was conducted via telephone, we developed and put into place a protocol to minimise eventual biases coming from the direct interaction between the interviewer and the interviewee. The protocol is summarised in the following points:

- We explained to the first contact in each company (the person in charge of the BIS) that participation was on the voluntary basis, and anonymous.
- When requested, we sent the list of questions to the person in charge of the BIS, so that the most appropriate interviewee could be selected.
- We asked to the person in charge of the BIS to have the email contact of the interviewee so that we could fix a telephone appointment in the following days; in the message to the interviewee, we presented ourselves, and clarified the objective of the survey and the methods used. We also explained that the participation was on the voluntary basis and anonymous.
- Each question was asked to each interviewee in the same way, using the same words and at the same pace. At the end of each question, we asked whether it was clear to the interviewee, or whether there was any need to repeat them question.
- In reading the different response options, we left time between one option and the following, and at the end, we asked the question: "To this question you answered with option X, do you confirm your choice?"
- Once we completed the interview, we asked if the interviewee confirmed her/his participation to the survey. We also clarified that at any moment the person could withdraw from the study. So far, none have taken this option.

Measures

The telephone interview questionnaire pertained to the four main variables used in this project, following Mackenzie, et al. (2011): TOC, IKS, IIC and IDMQ. We used existing scales that were translated from English into Italian, and adapted to the respondents. To ensure the correctness of the translation, we asked a native English speaker with knowledge of Italian to translate the Italian version of the questionnaire back into English. The items used, and relative sources, are presented in Table 2 in the Appendix. All variables were measured with Likert scales, from one (very low) to five (very high).

Control Variables

We inserted several control variables into the questionnaire, related to the types of industry, function, turnover, type of organisational chart, personnel size and time of adoption of the BIS. However, for the data analysis, we chose to use only the time of adoption of the BIS, due to the size of the sample and the data analysis technique employed. The combination of the small sample size and the partial least square modelling technique employed indicated that we should minimise the number of variables affecting the dependent variable to three, as suggested by Ringle, et al. (2005). This is also the reason that, although the length of adoption of BIS was operationalised through four different intervals (1=less than one year; 2=between one and three years; 3=between three and five years; 4=more than five years), they were grouped into two intervals (1=between zero and three years; 2=between three and five years; 3=more than five years) and then encoded, using thermometer encoding in TA1 and TA2 (Dejaeger, et al., 2012).

Data Analysis

For the data analysis, we used partial least square (PLS) modelling, with the support of SmartPLS 2.0. We identified the level of significance in 200 bootstrapped iterations. The main reason for selecting the PLS technique was that it provides less severe constraints for small samples (Ringle, 2005), such as ours. Moreover, PLS provides the possibility of verifying both the measurement and structural models at the same time (Addas & Pinsonneault, 2013), without enforcing normality requirements or multivariate homogeneity (Hair, et al., 2011). In presenting their overview of 33 research papers published in top journals in the 2000s, across the disciplines of marketing, consumer behaviour, human resources management, organisational behaviour and IS, Henseler, et al. state that "PLS path modelling avoids small sample size problems and can therefore be applied in some situations when other methods cannot" (2009, p. 283). Moreover, "depending on the effect sizes for paths and loadings, the case can be made that sample size can be extremely small relative to the complexity of the model" (Chin, 2009, p. 662).

The use of relatively old data (2006-2007) for the quantitative analysis has the distinct disadvantage of not taking into account the evolution that BIS experienced from the time of our empirical investigation. However, some distinct advantages can be identified in leaving time between the survey and the time of the analysis and discussion of the results. Analogous to what has been explained by Lee and Barua (1999) in their study about management productivity information technology, the study of BIS today is much more complex than in 2006, given the role played by big data and predictive analytics (Chen et al., 2012). Moreover, as for any information technology system at the beginning of its evolution, BIS were first conceived as a tool for higher efficiency, rather than a strategic choice. By examining earlier data, we have the possibility of detecting more tangible paths and outcomes. Indeed, our qualitative empirical investigation took place between 2010 and 2011, therefore around five years after the quantitative data collection. The elapsed time provides the possibility of a clearer interpretation, as it is certain that the observed phenomenon had finished.

THE MODEL TESTED

This section first presents the results of the PLS measurement model, and then those of the structural model. The latter are also schematised in Figure 2.

PLS Measurement Model

The reliabilities, means, standard deviations, average variance explained (AVE) and correlations among the constructs are displayed in Table 3 in the Appendix. The composite reliability showed values higher than the required value of 0.7 (Fornell & Larcker, 1981). Similarly, the indicator reliability showed expected values, with two exceptions: the first item of IDMQ ("decreases the time required to process information"), and the fourth item of the TOC ("integration across different types of users, including the ability of the system to spread and share analyses and results"). These respectively showed values of 0.59 and 0.66. However, we decided to keep these in the model, in order to attain a more rounded picture of the correspondent construct.

The results of the convergence validity, tested through the AVE, were correct, as values were greater than 0.5 for all variables. The results of the discriminant validity measured through the squared AVE values were correct overall, as they were higher than the correlations of each construct with the others. The only exception was in the correlation between IIC and IDMQ, which showed a value slightly higher than the squared AVE of IDMQ (0.7718 and 0.7664, respectively). A reason for this could be connected to our earlier choice of retaining the two items for which the reliability test was slightly unsatisfactory. However, as explained in the next section, retaining these items added significance to the results of the PLS structural model. Additionally, the eventual problem of multicollinearity linked to this issue should be minimised, as we used PLS as an estimation technique, which is very robust for multicollinearity among predictors (Cassel, et al., 1999). Finally, the cross-matrix discriminant validity showed proper results, as all the items loaded higher on their focal variable. At the end of this process, four items resulted from the model.

PLS Structural Model

The results of the PLS structural model essentially confirmed the three hypotheses of our research model (see figure 2). The TOC of the BIS showed a positive influence on the level of knowledge sharing (IKS, Hypothesis 1), which subsequently positively influenced the level of internal collaboration (IIC, Hypothesis 2). Moreover, the latter was found to affect the quality of decision-making (IDMQ, Hypothesis 3). Finally, both control variables were found to have no effect on the IDMQ. The R^2 of the model was 0.64.

Figure 2. Research model results

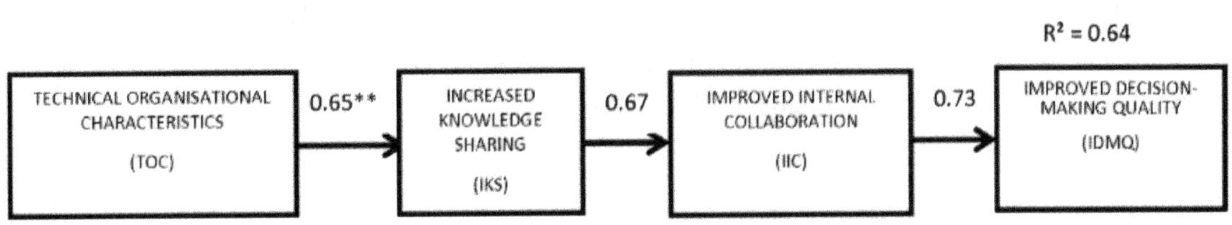

THE CASE STUDY

While the overall results of the survey showed a general positive association between the different stages of effects of BIS, they also showed high variability between those companies that achieved the best results from their BIS, and those that were worse off. To understand better these variations in the quantitative investigation, we undertook an in-depth analysis of one of the organisations that took part in the survey—company Alpha. Qualitative data was collected, to understand why certain usage patterns emerged in this study.

In particular, we wanted to understand why and how the BIS positively affected the knowledge-sharing processes, the internal collaboration and quality of the decision-making processes in a company such as Alpha, but not in other companies. We chose the case study method because of its usefulness in examining a phenomenon in its natural setting (Benbasat, 1984). We chose Alpha because of its history of mergers and acquisitions, which place an additional strain on harvesting organisational results from BIS.

The Company

Company Alpha was founded in 2005, because of a series of mergers and acquisitions in the textile industry, a vocational sector of the region. Alpha's headquarters is located in Vicenza, with six subsidiaries in Germany, France, Spain, the United Kingdom and Poland. Alpha has 150 employees, 50 representatives and consultants and, in 2012, had a turnover of 110 million euros. Its core business is the design and distribution of several brands of clothing (Italian and otherwise). The production processes are outsourced abroad, and its products distributed to department stores and shops. Past seasons' inventories are sold in outlets in the northern part of Italy, owned by Alpha. Alpha has a flat organisation structure on three macro levels: the Chief Executive Officer (CEO) and General Manager; the Operating Managers (Chief Financial Officer [CFO], Chief Operating Officer [COO], Chief Marketing Officer [CMO], CIO and so forth); and the operating teams.

Data Collection and Analysis

The data was collected between November 2010 and March 2011. We conducted two rounds of interviews with the CEO, CIO, CMO and Sales Manager. Additionally, we organised a focus group with some of the system's users. The interviews and focus group focused on questions on the connection between BIS and IKS, IIC and IDMQ. Data collected during the interviews was tape recorded and transcribed. The case was analysed with simple thematic coding, given the already established relationship between the variables. The focus of this second analysis was to understand the reasons behind the observed correlations.

Case Analysis

Our results indicated that organisations that used BIS declared a general high level of satisfaction with the system. The following sections discuss the results emerging from the qualitative investigation, in connection with the outcomes of the quantitative study.

Techno-Organisational Characteristics of BIS and Increased Knowledge Sharing

The technical components of the BIS provide an improved availability and correctness of data, which would subsequently provide a better capacity for data analysis, and in turn lead to improved information sharing (Beta 0.65; p<0.01). These results align with previous studies of BIS as systems supporting decision-making (Clark et al., 2007; Chen et al., 2012). The availability of DWH technology, improved hardware and software performances and increased adoption of web-based technology can be associated with the creation of business intelligence environments (Negash, 2004), whose principal aim is to improve the quality and speed of useful information processing. However, when interviewing participants at Alpha about the quality and speed of information, they largely underlined the widespread availability for all employees of reporting and querying, as the main advantage point of the BIS:

There is no reason anymore to go to the IT guys and ask for a report or a query. All managers are able to use the systems and browse the data. This means that everyone has the information when needed, as needed (Alpha Sales Manager 2011).

Moreover, when asked about knowledge sharing, they reiterated this point, stating the importance of a user interface allowing easy access to other departments' data:

The system implemented uses the multidimensional futures of a data-warehouse. The graphic user interface allows each user to generate their own report, even if the data required belongs to other departments. The DWH has created a shared environment that can be seen as the repository of the organisational knowledge (Alpha CIO 2010).

These statements raise a design issue for BIS beyond the functional result that BIS highlighted in the quantitative analysis. BIS are still considered quite advanced technologies, and even large organisations are taking their first steps towards implementation of these. As such, the manipulation of the BIS often remains in the hands of IT departments. However, the Alpha experience tells us that, despite their complexity, BIS must be given to all employees so that a greater number of people are able to capitalise on its use. The easier the BIS system, and the more cross-departmental data is available, the more knowledge-sharing organisations will develop.

Increased Knowledge Sharing and Improved Internal Collaboration

Our results suggest that IKS derived by the use of BIS can be associated with IIC (Beta 0.67; p < 0.01). When we enquired about this issue at Alpha, the CEO explained the importance for Alpha of sharing data that is simple to handle, easy to access and understandable across functions:

In a contest where the competition requires a real-time reaction to the market or consumer changes, organisations need to react with actions that have to consider marketing aspects, as well as financial or operating ones. Different departments have to cooperate and operate starting from the same data that must be simple, shared, and understandable. Our BI infrastructure can be considered as a common language, known and spoken across all departments. We have designed a system where the access and the, let me say, the distribution of the organisational knowledge, has become easier, faster, and, last but not least, cheaper (Alpha CEO 2011).

Alpha used its organisational structure as a blueprint, upon which the BIS data was based. While this is a reasonably normal process in enterprise resource planning (ERP) implementations or enterprise architecture efforts, Alpha went a step further by also focusing on 'simple' and 'easy' access, rather than only the single set of data. Therefore, collaboration stems not only from an innate feature of BIS, but also from a design choice that facilitates and enables collaboration. Some companies may accidentally end up with good design choice, while others, such as Alpha, may be required to engage purposefully in such design because of their complexity. The outcome of these findings is that the effect of BIS on collaboration is partially the result of the TOC of BIS, and partially the result of a design choice. As such, the design of BIS must be carefully managed.

Improved Internal Collaboration and Improved Decision-Making Quality

Finally, our findings also suggest that IIC arising from the use of BIS is associated with improved quality in the decision-making process (Beta 0.73; $p<0.01$). The decision process is based upon data generated by processes designed to respond to the needs of efficacy and efficiency at the operating level. When we enquired at Alpha about the origin of operational and strategic decisions because of BIS, they answered:

The marketing department operates under the supervision of the CEO. The introduction of the BI system didn't change this structure. What has changed is the quality of the relationship between CMO—me—and the CEO. We don't need to gather and waste time in creating 'ad hoc' documentation in order to justify our proposal. We show and discuss the data that everyone can extract from the system and now we discuss on the action, rather than on the correctness or reliability of the data (Alpha CMO 2010).

Here, we evince the same principle used for the data structure: at Alpha, the BIS did not alter the organisational assets, but was adapted to it. The idea of design adaptation to the organisational context's needs seems to be pervasive in the Alpha case. Additionally, in the decision-making case, respondents reiterated the idea of everybody being able to extract data. This again underlies the importance of providing common access to decision-making tools, rather than only focusing on the sophistication of the system. Therefore, the decision-making question highlights another dimension in the design of BIS. BIS can be very sophisticated, but sophistication is subordinate to appropriation. The BIS must first be appropriated by employees and managers alike, and only once this has occurred can the sophistication of the system increase.

DISCUSSION

Several implications arise from the results of this exploratory study. From a theoretical perspective, we contribute to the existing literature that offers numerous examples demonstrating how the adoption of BIS enables the creation of flexible organisational structures (Arnott & Pervan, 2005; Barakat et al., 2013). In our study, this is furthered, by stating how this knowledge-sharing process affects the internal collaboration, and thus the quality of the decision process.

As users retain the power to accept, alter, or reject any potential advantage offered by BIS (Leidner & Kayworth, 2006), they appear to be collaborative when the TOC of the system facilitates the process of sharing knowledge, without altering the equilibrium of the decision process. In other words, as shown in the Alpha case study, the process of knowledge sharing enabled by the BIS does not change who is in charge of the decisions—unless BIS is designed to do so—but only how the decisions are taken. From our findings, the role of the BIS seems that of a tool facilitating the process of gathering and structuring information, providing a common decision environment that aids collaboration among different departments and increasing the quality of the decision process.

The internal equilibrium among decision makers is not influenced by such systems. This could explain why there are no signs of resistance to the adoption of these systems, both in the companies surveyed and in Alpha. In contrast to previous studies, where users showed resistance to systems requiring them to share knowledge (Orlikowski, 1993; Kankanhalli et al., 2005), our results suggest that BIS are not necessarily associated with a reshaping and redistribution of power deriving from knowledge sharing. This is because the specific design of the technology allows top managers to govern the effects of sharing information without sharing power, or at least to respect extant organisational power structures.

On the issue of the division between the technical and the organisational characteristics of BIS, our results allow us to conclude that this division is mainly the result of the academic approach to BIS, and that this division does not appear relevant in practice. Our results are aligned with the theoretical considerations of Leonardi (2009) on the socially construed nature of the implementation line. Previous studies show that the dividing line between implementing and using a technology is artificial. Our study confirms these results, but also shows, through the specific case of BIS, that technologies that are seemingly created to exist outside traditional organisational process need to be integrated in the organisation, if organisations wish to obtain organisational impacts such as knowledge sharing or enhanced collaboration from the use of BIS.

Finally, our results confirm for BIS that to obtain the most of any specific technology, IT cannot be black-boxed (Orlikowski & Iacono, 2001). We show that technology needs to be unpacked for both the technological and the organisational characteristics, and that these two sets need to be integrated in a conscious design process. While this has implications for the way research examines technology in organisations in the future, it also has important practical consequences.

In many organisations, IT implementation in general and BIS implementation in particular are conducted with the help of external partners, either vendors or IT consultants. This division of labour may also be responsible for the division between technical features and organisational needs. In virtue of this division, many implementations risk focusing more on implementation issues as a technical exercise, rather than on issues of designing the integration between BIS and the organisation.

However, we show that the unpacking of the components of BIS and their careful integration in the existing organisational structures is a responsibility that management cannot outsource, and that needs to be carefully designed. This is for two reasons. First, because organisations gain much more from knowledge sharing, increased collaboration and improved decision-making respect enhanced decision-making. Second, because BIS touch upon issues of power, professionalism and organisational welfare that are extremely sensitive in organisations, and can ultimately lead to implementation failures (Orlikowski, 1993).

Managers need to evaluate carefully their choices and options to obtain the advantages of the first, while avoiding the problems of the second. We believe that our research contributes to such practical knowledge for managers.

CONCLUSION

This research contributes to the present literature on BIS by confirming, in practice, the hypothesised relationship between the technical and organisational characteristics of BIS, and knowledge sharing, collaboration and decision process quality. However, we also move beyond these results to an in-depth analysis of a successful case study. We used this case study to indicate the general design principles of successful BIS implementations. We showed that, despite their technical complexity, BIS must be designed to fit the organisational context, along with two design principles regarding the accessibility of the data, and two design principles regarding the use of data.

Regarding accessibility BIS must be designed so that data is (i) easily accessible through easy to use interfaces and structured queries, and (ii) globally accessible from all functions and levels in the organisation. Regarding the use of data for collaboration and decision-making, BIS must be designed so that (i) the data fits the existing organisational structure, and (ii) the decisions emerging from the data are closely related to the organisational hierarchy.

This study has opened up the black-box of BIS to demonstrate not only practical evidence of the relationships between knowledge sharing, collaboration and decision process quality, but also the effect of design choices on how and why these relationships work within a specific organisation. Our results can be useful to managers and practitioners who need to implement or reshape such complex systems within an organisation, providing meaningful design guidelines for alignment between the technology chosen and its effect on knowledge sharing, internal collaboration and decision process reconfiguration.

We are aware of the limitations of this study, deriving from its reliance on the limited sample size of the survey. However, starting from the results of the present exploratory study, we aim to extend our research on this topic to make the model more comprehensive. This will include employing a set of variables able to measure emerging issues, such as the neutral effect of BIS on power reconfiguration, and the dynamism of the interpretation of BIS by users, including the variable of time of use as dependent variable instead of control ones.

REFERENCES

Addas, S., & Pinsonneault, A. (2013). "IT interruptions and coordination effectiveness in software development groups: a conceptual, multilevel model." *SIGHCI 2013 Proceedings*, Paper 26, http://aisel.aisnet.org/sighci2013/26

Alavi, M., & Leidner, D. (2001). Review: knowledge management and knowledge management systems: conceptual foundations and research issues. *Management Information Systems Quarterly*, *25*(1), 107–136. doi:10.2307/3250961

Aoki, M. (1986). Horizontal vs. vertical information structure of the firm. *The American Economic Review*, *76*, 971–983.

Arnott, D. (2004). Decision support systems evolutions: Framework, case study, and research agenda. *European Journal of Information Systems*, *13*(4), 247–259. doi:10.1057/palgrave.ejis.3000509

Arnott, D., & Pervan, G. (2005). A critical analysis of decision support systems research. *Journal of Information Technology*, *20*(2), 67–87. doi:10.1057/palgrave.jit.2000035

Bailey, D. E., Leonardi, P. M., & Chong, J. (2010). Minding the gaps: Understanding technology interdependence and coordination in knowledge work. *Organization Science*, *21*(3), 713–730. doi:10.1287/orsc.1090.0473

Barakat, S., Al-Zu'bit, H. A., & Al-Zegaier, H. (2013). The role of business intelligence in knowledge sharing: A case study at Al-Hikma Pharmaceutical Manufacturing Company. *European Journal of Business and Management*, *5*(2), 237–242.

Baruch, Y. (1999). Response rate in academic studies—a comparative analysis. *Human Relations*, *52*(4), 421–438. doi:10.1177/001872679905200401

Benbasat, I. (1984). An analysis of research methodologies. In F. W. McFarlan (Ed.), *The Information Systems Research Challenge* (pp. 47–85). Boston, MA: Harvard Business School Press.

Bhattacherjee, A. (2001). Understanding information systems continuance: An expectation-confirmation model. *Management Information Systems Quarterly*, *25*(3), 351–370. doi:10.2307/3250921

Boh, W. F. (2014). Knowledge sharing in communities of practice: Examining usefulness of knowledge from discussion forums versus repositories. *ACM SIGMIS Database, Vo*, *45*(2), 8–31. doi:10.1145/2621906.2621908

Bowers, J. M., & Benford, S. D. (1991). *Studies in computer supported cooperative work: theory, practice and design*. Amsterdam: North-Holland.

Cassel, C., Hackl, P., & Westlund, A. H. (1999). PLS for estimating latent variable quality structures: Finite sample robustness properties. *Journal of Applied Statistics*, *26*(4), 435–446. doi:10.1080/02664769922322

Chamoni, P., & Gluchowski, P. (2004). Integrationstrends bei business-intelligence-systemen. empiriche untersuchung auf basis des business intelligence maturity model. *Wirtschaftsinformatik*, *46*(2), 119–128. doi:10.1007/BF03250931

Chaudhuri, S., Dayal, U., & Ganti, V. (2001). Database technology for decision support systems. *Computer*, *34*(12), 48–55. doi:10.1109/2.970575

Chen, H., Chiang, R. H., & Storey, V. C. (2012). Business intelligence and analytics: From big data to big impact. *Management Information Systems Quarterly*, *36*(4), 1165–1188.

Chen, L., Soliman, K. S., Mao, E., & Frolick, M. N. (2000). Measuring user satisfaction with data warehouses: An exploratory study. *Information & Management*, *37*(3), 103–110. doi:10.1016/S0378-7206(99)00042-7

Chin, W. W. (2009). How to write up and report PLS analyses. In V. E. Vinzi, W. W. Chin, J. Henseler, & H. Wang (Eds.), *Handbook of partial least squares: concepts, methods and applications* (pp. 655–691). Berlin: Springer.

Clark, T. D., Jones, M. C., & Armstrong, C. P. (2007). The dynamic structure of management support systems: Theory development, research focus, and direction. *Management Information Systems Quarterly*, *31*(3), 579–615.

Dalkir, K. (2013). *Knowledge management in theory and practice*. Burlington, MA: Routledge.

Dejaeger, K., Goethals, F., Giangreco, A., Mola, L., & Baesens, B. (2012). "Gaining insight into student satisfaction using comprehensible data mining techniques." *European Journal of Operational Research*, Vo. 218, No. 2: pp. 548–562.Dias, C. (2001). "Corporate portals: a literature review of a new concept. *International Journal of Information Management, 21*(4), 269–287.

Eckerson, W. (1999). *Business portals: drivers, definitions, and rules*. Boston, MA: Patricia Seyhold Group.

Elbashir, M. Z., Collier, P. A., & Davern, M. J. (2008). Measuring the effects of business intelligence systems: The relationship between business process and organizational performance. *International Journal of Accounting Information Systems, 9*(3), 135–153. doi:10.1016/j.accinf.2008.03.001

Elbashir, M. Z., Collier, P. A., & Sutton, S. C. (2011). The role of organizational absorptive capacity in strategic use of business intelligence to support integrated management control systems. *Accounting Review, 86*(1), 155–184. doi:10.2308/accr.00000010

Fornell, C., & Larcker, D. F. (1981). Evaluating structural equation models with unobservable variables and measurement error. *JMR, Journal of Marketing Research, 18*(1), 39–50. doi:10.2307/3151312

Gattiker, T. F., & Goodhue, D. L. (2005). What happens after ERP implementation: Understanding the impact of interdependence and differentiation on plant-level outcomes. *Management Information Systems Quarterly, 29*(3), 559–585.

Gold, A. H., Malhotra, A., & Segars, A. H. (2001). Knowledge management: An organizational capabilities perspective. *Journal of Management Information Systems, 18*(1), 185–214.

Goldberg, D., Oki, B., Nichols, D., & Terry, D. B. (1992). Using collaborative filtering to weave an information tapestry. *Communications of the ACM, 35*(12), 61–70. doi:10.1145/138859.138867

Grover, V., & Davenport, T. D. (2001). General perspectives on knowledge management: Fostering a research agenda. *Journal of Management Information Systems, 18*(1), 5–21.

Hair, J. F., Ringle, C. M., & Sarstedt, M. (2011). PLS-SEM: Indeed a silver bullet. *Journal of Marketing Theory and Practice, 19*(2), 139–151. doi:10.2753/MTP1069-6679190202

Henseler, C., Ringle, M., & Sinkovics, R. R. (2009). The use of partial least squares path modeling in international marketing. *Advances in International Marketing, 20*, 277–320.

Jourdan, Z., Rainer, R. K., & Marshall, T. E. (2008). Business intelligence: An analysis of the literature. *Information Systems Management, 25*(2), 21–13. doi:10.1080/10580530801941512

Kankanhalli, A., Tan, B. C. Y., & Wei, K. K. (2005). Contributing knowledge to electronic knowledge repositories: An empirical investigation. *Management Information Systems Quarterly, 29*(1), 113–143.

Leclercq, A. (2007). The perceptual evaluation of information systems using the construct of user satisfaction: Case study of a large French group. *ACM SIGMIS Database, 38*(2), 27–60. doi:10.1145/1240616.1240621

Lee, B., & Barua, A. (1999). An integrated assessment of productivity and efficiency impacts of information technology investments: Old data, new analysis and evidence. *Journal of Productivity Analysis, 12*(1), 21–43. doi:10.1023/A:1007898906629

Leidner, D. E., & Kayworth, T. (2006). A review of culture in information systems research: Toward a theory of information technology cultural conflict. *Management Information Systems Quarterly*, *30*(2), 357–399.

Leonardi, P. M. (2009). Crossing the implementation line: The mutual constitution of technology and organizing across development and use activities. *Communication Theory*, *19*(3), 277–310. doi:10.1111/j.1468-2885.2009.01344.x

Leonardi, P. M., & Barley, S. R. (2008). Materiality and change: Challenges to building better theory about technology and organizing. *Information and Organization*, *18*(3), 159–176. doi:10.1016/j.infoandorg.2008.03.001

Luhn, H. P. (1958). A business intelligence system. *IBM Journal of Research and Development, Vo.*, *2*(4), 314–319. doi:10.1147/rd.24.0314

MacKenzie, S. B., Podsakoff, P. M., & Podsakoff, N. P. (2011). Construct measurement and validation procedures in mis and behavioral research: Integrating new and existing techniques. *Management Information Systems Quarterly*, *35*(2), 293–334.

Magoulas, R., & Lorica, B. (2009). Introduction to big data, *Release 2.0.* Sebastopol, CA: O'Reilly Media. Negash, S. (2004) Business intelligence. *Communications of the Association for Information Systems*, *13*(1), 177–195.

Orlikowski, W. J. (1993). Learning from notes: Organizational issues in Groupware implementation. *The Information Society*, *9*(3), 237–250. doi:10.1080/01972243.1993.9960143

Orlikowski, W. J., & Iacono, C. S. (2001). Research commentary: Desperately seeking the 'IT' in IT research—a call to theorizing the IT artefact. *Information Systems Research*, *12*(2), 121–134. doi:10.1287/isre.12.2.121.9700

Parry, G., & Graves, A. (2008). The importance of knowledge management for ERP systems. *International Journal of Logistics: Research and Applications*, *11*(6), 427–441. doi:10.1080/13675560802340992

Prado, A. B., Freitas, C., & Sbrici, T. R. (2010). Using OLAP Tools for e-HRM: A Case Study. [IJTHI]. *International Journal of Technology and Human Interaction*, *6*(4), 49–62. doi:10.4018/jthi.2010100104

Raghu, T. S., Ramesh, R., Chang, A. M., & Whinston, A. B. (2001). Collaborative decision making: A connectionist paradigm for dialectical support. *Information Systems Research*, *12*(4), 363–383. doi:10.1287/isre.12.4.363.9705

Ringle, C. M., Wende, S., & Will, A. (2005). *SmartPLS 2.0*, Hamburg. www.smartpls.de

Tsui, E. (2003). Tracking the role and evolution of commercial knowledge management software. *Handbook on Knowledge Management*, *2*, 5–27.

Tyre, M. J., & Orlikowski, W. J. (1994). Windows of opportunity: Temporal patterns of technological adaptation in organizations. *Organization Science*, *5*(1), 98–118. doi:10.1287/orsc.5.1.98

Venkatraman, N. (1994). IT-enabled business transformation: From automation to business scope redefinition. *Sloan Management Review*, *35*(2), 72–87.

Williams, S., & Williams, N. (2006). *The Profit Impact of Business Intelligence*. San Francisco, CA: Morgan Kaufmann.

Yeoh, W., & Koronios, A. (2010). Critical success factors for business intelligence systems. *Journal of Computer Information Systems*, (Spring): 23–32.

Zabojnik, J. (2002). Centralized and decentralized decision making in organizations. *Journal of Labor Economics*, *20*(1), 1–22. doi:10.1086/323929

ENDNOTES

1 See, for example: 'IBM What is big data?-Bringing big data to the enterprise'. www.ibm.com. (Retrieved 25 May, 2014).

This research was previously published in the International Journal of Technology and Human Interaction (IJTHI), 11(4); edited by Anabela Mesquita and Chia-Wen Tsai; pages 1-25, copyright year 2015 by IGI Publishing (an imprint of IGI Global).

APPENDIX

Table 2. Variables used and relative items

Name of Variable	Construct Description	Item as asked (Adapted from Sources of References)	REFERENCES
TOC of BI			
TOC1	Level of structure and organisation of data.	How do you evaluate the current level of structuration and organisation of the data, taking into account the issues of insufficient data homogeneity, dismantling, delocalisation, incorrectness, inconsistency, unclearness and ambiguity of data?	Chaudhuri et al. (2001) and Bendoly (2003).
TOC2	Interoperability level of the BIS.	How do you consider the interoperability of the BIS in terms of ability to access data from other applications and systems (e.g. ERP and CRM)?	Vernadat, (2007)
TOC3	Level of excellence of the system technology.	How do you assess the level of technology quality of the BIS in terms of data security, continuity of service, time of access, capability of adequacy to future needs and continuing updating?	Davis (1989) and Shackel (1991).
TOC4	Integration across different types of users.	How do you assess the ability of the BIS to integrate different type of users by spreading and sharing analyses and results?	Raghu et al. (2001), Bowers and Benford (1991), Goldberg et al. (1992).
IIC			
IIC1	Level of inter-departmental communication.	To what extent has the BIS enhanced inter-departmental communication?	Thompson (1967) and Mintzberg (1979).
IIC2	Level of coordination and collaboration in inter-departmental processes.	Because of the BIS, to what extent has the level of coordination and collaboration in inter-departmental processes increased?	Eckerson (1999) and Dias (2001).
IIC3	Number of meetings and time needed for each meeting (positive if declining).	To what extent, thanks to the BIS, has there been a decrease in the number of meetings of the different teams and in the length of each meeting?	Eckerson (1999) and Dias (2001).
IIC4	Results obtained from meetings.	To what extent, thanks to the BIS, have meetings been more effective and efficient, and experienced lower conflict levels?	Yeh and Tsai (2001).
IDMQ			
IDMQ1	Time required to process information.	To what extent, thanks to the BIS, the time to process information are shorter?	Arnott (2004) and Arnott and Pervan (2005).
IDMQ2	Level of identification and formalisation of strategic, tactical, and operational decisions.	To what extent, thanks to the BIS, are the identification and formalisation of strategic, tactical, and operational decisions smoother?	Clark et al. (2007).
IDMQ3	Time required for decision processes.	To what extent, thanks to the BIS, are the decision processes shorter?	Scott-Morton (1984).
IDMQ4	Level of support to operation processes.	To what extent does the BIS provide superior decisional support to the operational processes?	Clark et al. (2007).

Table 2. Continued

Name of Variable	Construct Description	Item as asked (Adapted from Sources of References)	REFERENCES
IKS			
IKS1	Value of corporate information assets, supporting the organisation's competitiveness.	To what extent, thanks to the BIS, have the corporate information assets enhanced the competitiveness of the organisation?	Gold et al. (2001).
IKS2	Level of information sharing at all organisational levels.	To what extent, thanks to the BIS, has culture sharing information at all levels of the organisation been promoted?	Grover and Davenport (2001).
IKS3	Decisional autonomy due to the availability of information.	To what practical extent are users who are decisions makers better supported by the BIS?	Zabojnik (2002).

Table 3. Correlations matrix and composite reliability scores

Variable	Reliability	AVE	Mean	STD	1	2	3	4	5	6
7. Time of adoption 1	1	1	0.23	0.43	1					
8. Time of adoption 2	1	1	0.30	0.47	-0.19	1				
9. TOC	0.81	0.52	3.62	0.64	-0.19	-0.14	**0.72**			
10. IKS	0.89	0.73	3.20	0.83	-0.10	-0.12	0.65**	**0.85**		
11. IIC	0.88	0.64	2.74	0.89	-0.12	-0.23	0.45*	0.67**	**0.80**	
12. IDMQ	0.85	0.59	3.47	0.64	-0.30	-0.19	0.60*	0.62**	0.77**	**0.77**
*p 0.01; **p 0.001										
AVE^2 in bold along the diagonal										

Chapter 20
Knowledge Sharing between Enterprises of the Same Group

Nuno Carvalho
Universidade de Coimbra, Portugal

Isabel Gomes
ISCTE, Portugal

ABSTRACT

This exploratory study seeks to promote investigation about knowledge sharing between enterprises of the same enterprise group and is motivated by the growing importance of knowledge management (KM) to businesses. The data was collected from Community Innovation Survey (CIS) 2012 and three linear regressions were performed (one to all enterprises, one to SME and one to large enterprises). The results show that cooperation for product or process innovation and service innovation influence knowledge sharing between enterprises of the same enterprise group, contributing to learning organizations. The present paper clarifies the importance of innovation and cooperation for innovation in KM practices between enterprises of the same enterprise group. The results are only valid to SME, since large enterprises have different practices of KM.

INTRODUCTION

Knowledge management is the science of managing the intellectual capital that is controlled by a given company (Petty & Guthrie, 2000). It is a systematic process used by organizations and individuals to locate, store, retrieve, share, adapt and use knowledge in order to promote the objectives of the organization, having always been regarded as a powerful tool for organizations (Karamitri, Talias, & Bellali, 2015).

The objectives of KM are making organizations act in a way as smart as possible, in order to ensure its viability and success, and allowing organizations to get the best value added from their knowledge resources. To achieve these goals, organizations build, transform, organize, deploy and use knowledge

DOI: 10.4018/978-1-7998-0417-8.ch020

resources effectively (Wiig, 1997). Another objective of KM is to improve the effectiveness and sustain the viability of any organization, whether it is a commercial one or a part of a society, a country or a single individual (Wiig, 2002).

This work is motivated by the growing importance of KM for enterprises, particularly, knowledge sharing, and intents to answer the following question: does innovation and cooperation for innovation influences cooperation between enterprises of the same enterprise group and, consequently, knowledge sharing between enterprises of the same enterprise group? The work is focused on SMEs, aiming to shed new insights about this type of enterprises, since KM research is, traditionally, centered in large enterprises.

This work is divided in a first part with a literature review about KM, innovation and about the importance of KM and innovation to organizational performance, and then in a second part the methodology will be presented followed by the results, the discussion and the conclusion.

KNOWLEDGE MANAGEMENT

The growing relevance of intangible assets can be found in the evaluation of enterprises over the past decades, in which the ratio between the market value and the accounting value of a company has been steadily increasing, especially since the 90´s. This demonstrates that the financial accounting systems are not appropriate indicators of economic or resources value (John, 2009). Progressively, KM is seen as an intangible asset that maximizes profits and provides a comparative advantage to those who hold it, so the interest for this area of research has been growing (Karamitri et al., 2015; Sensuse, Sucahyo, Rohajawati, & Anggia, 2014).

The sharing and transfer of knowledge have gained an increasingly central role, believing that they play a pioneering role in organizations (Asrar-ul-haq & Anwar, 2016). The demand for success in an ever-increasing competitive market leads organizations to implement strategies that help in the acquisition, maintenance, storage and dissemination of knowledge, in order to be reused when needed (Barros, Ramos, & Perez, 2015). To achieve this, many organizations feel the need to acquire technologies that allow sharing and efficient access to knowledge (Diamantini et al., 2013).

The constant process of acquisition and exploitation of knowledge in organizations contributes to the development of knowledge sharing practices within the company and increases the ability to solve problems, to create new knowledge and to innovate (D'Arrigo et al., 2015). Knowledge management is considered essential for the increase of productivity and flexibility in both the public and private sectors (Martensson, 2000).

The majority of research in the field of KM tends to emphasize large companies but, assuming that small and medium size enterprises (SMEs) are the "Engines" of most nations, this situation is not satisfactory. The existing empirical literature provides only fragmented information about KM in SMEs (Durst & Edvardsson, 2012), emphasizing that KM in SMEs is a facilitator of the longevity of the business, where learning emerges through an evolutionary process that begins in the family and continues inside and outside the business (Chirico, 2008).

In SMEs, the majority of the identification of knowledge is made through informal networks and, as organizations grow, these networks can be aware of all the knowledge that is necessary to manage. Many SMEs seem to have efficient communication networks with rapid response capacities in relation to the resolution of internal problems. However, often they do not have the time or resources to identify and use important sources of scientific and technological knowledge (Egbu, Hari, & Renukappa, 2005).

Almost all SMEs feel the need to be involved in the transfer of knowledge, in particular, by attending regular meetings with the major customers (or suppliers), by receiving advice from friends or colleagues from other organizations, or by dealing with complaints and even by sharing knowledge with competitors (Chen, Duan, Edwards, & Lehaney, 2006). Structurally, when compared to large enterprises, SMEs are typically more informal, with more flat organizational structures. Are often more weak in terms of financing, planning, training and use and exploitation of advanced information technologies, due to lack of resources (Egbu et al., 2005; Perez-Araos, Barber, Munive-Hernandez, & Eldridge, 2007).

Small and medium size enterprises are creators of knowledge, but are weak on taking advantage of it. Due to lack of resources, SMEs feel the need to share costs in KM activities, sometimes by cooperating and competing at the same time, since they can share knowledge that can be an important source of competitive advantage, but the knowledge obtained by cooperation can also be used for competition (Levy, Loebbecke, & Powell, 2003). That is why it is necessary to control the critical knowledge that is shared in order to avoid counterproductive effects for the organization (Ritala, Olander, Michailova, & Husted, 2015).

Organizational learning involves the process of assimilation of new knowledge in the knowledge base of the organization, thus the sharing of knowledge is central to the rapid internationalization of SMEs (Fletcher & Prashantham, 2011) and, consequently, knowledge is recognized as being the most important feature to cause competitive advantages and to maximize innovation (Al-Husseini, 2015; Meihami & Meihami, 2014).

INNOVATION

With the phenomenon of globalization, knowledge has become the main factor of competitive advantage, which requires acquisition and use of knowledge for innovation and technical change in a systematic way. This is only possible in a "learning" organization (Kharbanda, 2002) so, KM is fundamental to increase the systematic innovative capacity of organizations (Gloet & Samson, 2013).

Innovation is crucial to the economic performance of countries, and empirical evidences confirm the positive relationship between innovation and growth. Innovation involves the production of new knowledge from research and development (R&D), software, human capital and organizational structures. This way, these intangible assets have become strategic factors in creating value for enterprises (OECD, 2010b; Sivak, Caplanova, & Hudson, 2011).

Increasing productivity is the key to economic success in the global knowledge-based economy. Productivity can be increased through a reduction in the cost of production and/or increasing the value of what is produced. This requires innovation, i.e. the introduction of new products, services or processes that increase the value of what is produced in relation to their cost (Sadek, 2015). Circulation of knowledge is essential for innovation. New ideas emerge from the combination of existing knowledge from multiple sources. Circulation of knowledge makes it possible to confront, mix, test and improve ideas, share and explore data sources and transfer knowledge to contexts where might be developed and applied (OECD, 2010a). Both the capacity of creation of internal knowledge and the absorption capacity of knowledge have a positive effect on innovative performance (Forés & Camisón, 2016; Yeşil, Koska, & Büyükbeşe, 2013).

Experience shows that sacrificing innovation investments due to financial restrictions, in the long term, is counterproductive. The solution for single companies to continue their innovation agenda without overloading their scarce internal resources is adopting a system of strategic networking innovation to bolster external resources. It is an approach with a focus on the outside and that is based on the exploitation of resources and capacities of external networks to enlarge or improve the quality of the results of innovation by fostering, in this way, the creation and dissemination of knowledge (Nambisan & Sawhney, 2010). However, the technological and innovative features of a company depend on the education and experience level of their employees (Hitt, Biermant, Shimizu, & Kochhar, 2001), and on the ability of the managers to effectively use these resources (Herrera, Muñoz-Doyague, & Nieto, 2010). Empowered and experienced human resources are an essential requirement for a high level of innovative activities so as to generate new knowledge and absorb the existing one. Employees with higher education, training and experience are especially important in science-based industries (Luo, Koput, & Powell, 2009).

Given the close connection between the knowledge possessed by the human capital of the company and its products and services, it is clear that the ability of a company to produce new products is inextricably linked to its human capital (Cabello-Medina, López-Cabrales, & Valle-Cabrera, 2011) and to its internal R&D that functions as a base to create assets and complementary capabilities that allow opportunities for future acquisitions or combinations of technology (Denicolai, Ramirez, & Tidd, 2016). On the other hand, access to external knowledge is also essential to improve the innovation of businesses in emerging markets. R&D and marketing efforts, by affecting the ability of firms in the process of absorption of external knowledge, increase the positive effects of external knowledge, contributing to innovation in enterprises (Li, Chen, & Shapiro, 2009).

New technologies can play an important role in the dissemination of this knowledge and, consequently, in the promotion of new innovations. Technology is, increasingly, becoming strategically important for companies seeking competitive advantages thought innovation (Durmuşoğlu & Barczak, 2011; Huang, Lai, & Lin, 2011; Lee, Jeon, & Park, 2011). Modern economies base its competitiveness in science, technological development and knowledge, which are the driving forces of the innovation capacity of a nation (Gust-Bardon, 2015; Sultan, 2013). These aspects and KM will contribute to product innovations. Suppliers will contribute to the improvement of the design (process innovation), and customers increase performance of design and of the market, so, cooperation with third parties is beneficial for the emergence of innovations (Lai, Chen, Chiu, & Pai, 2011). On the other hand, process innovators, usually, depend on the access to external sources of knowledge, reflecting their weak internal capacities, demonstrating a completely different pattern than product innovators - which normally innovate on the basis of internal R&D activities (Hervas-Oliver, Sempere-Ripoll, & Boronat-Moll, 2014).

Organizational innovation is leveraged by practices of KM and cooperation, and is a fundamental element for the successful completion of innovation projects (Cobo-Benita, Rodríguez-Segura, Ortiz-Marcos, & Ballesteros-Sánchez, 2016). So, it´s important to highlight that organizational cooperation to exploit the value of knowledge through innovation of new products is at the heart of the knowledge-based economy. The integration of new knowledge, resulting from these acts of cooperation, has a strong positive impact on the development of new innovative products (Lin & Chen, 2006), thus cooperation enables to share costs and risks, potentiating innovation activities of organizations (Nunes, Carvalho, & Costa, 2013).

THE IMPORTANCE OF KM, COOPERATION AND INNOVATION TO ORGANIZATIONAL PERFORMANCE

The creation of innovative products positively affects the performance of companies, i.e. the fact of being the first to reach the market creates a competitive advantage, with positive effects on market share and financial return (Molina-Castillo, Jimenez-Jimenez, & Munuera-Aleman, 2011; Otero-Neira, Varela, & Garcia, 2010). The development of new products, therefore, is the key to achieve competitive advantages and sustained growth of enterprises. The high innovative capacity of a company will cause a "snowball effect" contributing to new innovations, due to the organizational memory effect (know-how accumulated by the organization). The organizational memory contributes to the success of new products, but the mere stock of memory is not enough if not shared, since the memory must be dispersed throughout the organization in the form of individual knowledge, routines of behavior and organizational structures (Chang & Cho, 2008). Innovative products positively affect the results of the companies, and a culture of organizational innovation stimulates and encourages creativity and risk taking on the part of employees, thereby, contributing to the emergence of innovations (Augusto & Coelho, 2009).

Organizational innovations may aim to increase the performance of the company, reducing administrative costs or transaction costs, improving the satisfaction at work (and therefore the productivity of work), gaining access to non-marketable assets (as, for example, external knowledge), or reducing the costs of supplies (OECD, 2005). However, it is necessary to take into account that innovation can have negative impacts on organizational performance, in particular, when the newly inserted knowledge is not compatible with the previous knowledge of the organization. In this case, the organization may experience loss of knowledge that can be avoided if organizations recognize, in good time, the incompatibility between the new and the prior knowledge and then, reformulate the newly inserted knowledge (Mariano & Casey, 2015). In this aspect, organizational culture plays a fundamental role in relation to innovation, enhancing it if certain characteristics are present (creativity, autonomy, positive attitude toward the risk), or constituting a barrier to innovation, if the above characteristics are not present in the culture of the organization (Naranjo-Valencia, Jiménez-Jiménez, & Sanz-Valle, 2015).

Organizational learning encourages innovation, because an organization committed to learning tries to deeply understand its environment, which includes customers, competitors and emerging technologies. Innovation also involves the desire to embrace new ideas. This means that a climate of learning is valuable for companies looking to overcome their competitors through various processes of innovation. Managers should, therefore, create and promote the desire to learn among their employees, to develop new skills and to share existing knowledge (Salim & Sulaiman, 2011). These practices of open innovation positively affect organizational performance (Wang, Chang, & Shen, 2015).

Practices of knowledge sharing positively contribute to the operational and financial performance of organizations, whether directly or by increasing the speed and quality of innovation (Wang & Wang, 2012). Therefore, external acquisition strategies of expertise have impact on the performance of innovation and their need is mainly caused by the observation that the acquisition of new knowledge is a prerequisite for successful innovative activities. That's why, many organizations, in addition to its own internal R&D, are normally involved in the acquisition of knowledge and in cooperation activities, whose result is expected to positively influence organizational performance (Arvanitis, Lokshin, Mohnen, & Woerter, 2015). Knowledge sharing in organizations improves organizational performance and allows to achieve competitive advantages. It also positively influences organizational human capital (empowers employees), which in its turn, positively affects organizational performance (Hsu, 2008).

Collaboration with other enterprises (of the same group or others) fosters continuous learning, adapting and upgrading, being a key success factor (Dyer & Nobeoka, 2000). This collaboration or cooperation in an organization is necessary to achieve the desired objectives of such an organization (Jiacheng, Lu, & Francesco, 2010) and many times is essential for their existence (Michailova & Minbaeva, 2012) because innovation is built on collective knowledge sharing activities (Bica, Constantinescu, & Bica, 2015), depending on workplace innovation (Pot, Totterdill, & Dhondt, 2016) and on the environmental conditions that allow employees competences to flourish in the process of improvement, innovation and change (Junquera & Del Brio, 2009).

Cooperating between colleagues of the same enterprise group fosters knowledge sharing as part of the ongoing innovation and development efforts of the enterprise and enables knowledge transfer between enterprises of the same enterprise group (Gooderham, Minbaeva, & Pedersen, 2011), to enable this knowledge sharing practices, managers should create trustworthy relationships within the organization based on social interaction and on a shared knowledge sharing vision (Hsu & Chang, 2014; Wang & Wang, 2012) because internal knowledge sharing needs this informal lateral relations to flourish (Tsai, 2002).

In an enterprise group, the different units can learn from each other and benefit from new knowledge developed by other units. This intra organizational transfer of knowledge provides opportunities for mutual learning and intra cooperation, that in turn stimulates the creation of new knowledge and, at the same time, contributes to the ability of organizations to innovate (Tsai, 2001) because an organization with a broad knowledge base is more likely to achieve innovations through their own internal knowledge (Zhou & Li, 2012).

Innovation contributes to the increase of the capacity of firms in applying knowledge and to the development of new products and new services that create value for organizations (Lai & Lin, 2012; Vaccaro, Parente, & Veloso, 2010). Currently, the ability to intelligently use knowledge determines the future. So, KM is delineated for presenting the strategy, processes and technologies that allow to increase organizational learning and performance, also contributing to develop the capacity of organizational innovation (Mehrabani & Shajari, 2012).

Managers should be aware of the total impact of innovation in the value of the company, instead of focusing its impact only on sales, profits or returns of actions. The direct impact of innovation in the value of the company is stronger than its impact through financial and market positions, because the markets are able to recognize the innovative efforts of a given company, rewarding them, even before the new innovative products are ready to be marketed (Rubera & Kirca, 2012).

METHODOLOGY

This paper aims to perform a cross-sectional study to several European countries. A linear regression will be performed in order to find out what are the variables that influence cooperation between enterprises of the same enterprise group.

To increase the predictive power of the results, after performing a linear regression to all enterprises, a linear regression will be executed just to SMEs and another one just to large enterprises. This will also allow to uncover possible differences related to enterprise dimension.

Table 1. Variables and acronyms

Variable	Acronym
Enterprises cooperating with other enterprises within the enterprise group	COOP
Enterprises that introduced new business practices organizing procedures	ORGANIZATIONAL_INOV
Enterprises that developed goods innovation	GOODS_INOV
Enterprises that developed service innovation	SERVICES_INOV
Enterprises that developed product and or process innovation with other enterprises - non R&D performers	COOP_PROD_PROC_INOV_ NON_R_D
Enterprises that developed product and or process innovation with other enterprises - R&D performers	COOP_PROD_PROC_INOV_R_D

The independent variable is "Enterprises cooperating with other enterprises within the enterprise group" than, there are three more variables relating to single innovation activities and the last two variables relating to cooperation for innovation with other enterprises. The variables of the model and their acronyms are displayed in Table 1.

Data was collected from Community Innovation Survey (CIS) 2012 from Eurostat website. The CIS based innovation statistics are part of the EU science and technology statistics. Surveys are carried out with two years' frequency. The CIS is a survey of innovation activity in enterprises. The harmonized survey is designed to provide information on the innovativeness of sectors by type of enterprises, on the different types of innovation and on various aspects of the development of an innovation, such as the objectives, the sources of information, the public funding, the innovation expenditures etc. The CIS provides statistics broken down by countries, type of innovators, economic activities and size classes.

The countries for which there was available data are: Belgium, Czech Republic, Estonia, Greece, Spain, France, Croatia, Italy, Cyprus, Lithuania, Luxembourg, Hungary, Malta, Austria and Portugal. The total number of enterprises and the total number of large enterprises is presented in Table 2.

SPSS 23 was utilized to perform all the statistics calculations of the present paper.

After testing several methods, the best results were obtained through a Backward regression. This method consists in starting with fitting a model with all the variables of interest then, the least significant variable is dropped, so long as it is not significant at our chosen critical level (in our case 5%).

The obtained results to all enterprises are in Tables 3-7, and the best possible model occur in the third iteration (model number 3).

The control variable firm size was utilized and the obtained results for SMEs are in Appendix A (see Tables 8-14). Regarding Large enterprises, the obtained results are not statistical significant (Appendix B, Tables 15-20).

RESULTS

Pearson correlation between GOODS_INOV and SERVICES_INOV is -0,645 and significant at 1% level (Table 4). This could indicate possible multicollinearity problems between these two variables but, fortunately, only one of these variables is statistically significant (SERVICES_INOV), both in the linear regression to all enterprises and in the one to SMEs.

Table 2. Sample

Country	Total Number of Enterprises in the Population in 2012	Total Number of Large Enterprises in the Population in 2012
Belgium	14.286	593
Czech Republic	22.253	1.141
Estonia	3.485	88
Greece	14.987	270
Spain	71.801	1.720
France	70.962	3.050
Croatia	6.953	268
Italy	116.621	2.294
Cyprus	1.588	37
Lithuania	7.296	217
Luxembourg	1.618	83
Hungary	15.160	592
Malta	779	30
Austria	16.451	776
Portugal	17.660	432

Table 3. Descriptive statistics

	N	Minimum	Maximum	Mean	Std. Deviation
COOP	15	3,0	23,2	13,727	6,1004
ORGANIZATIONAL_INOV	15	24,5	54,2	37,453	10,3141
GOODS_INOV	15	56,4	85,2	73,467	8,2921
SERVICES_INOV	15	36,2	72,8	54,373	10,0995
COOP_PROD_PROC_INOV_NON_R_D	15	5,5	52,0	17,993	11,4621
COOP_PROD_PROC_INOV_R_D	15	8,2	49,3	26,140	10,4098
Valid N (listwise)	15				

According to the results from all enterprises, the R^2 from model 3 is 62,5% (Table 5), with three significant variables - SERVICES_INOV, COOP_PROD_proc_INOV_non_R_D and COOP_PROD_proc_INOV_R_D with, respectably, 0.013, 0.018 and 0.008 significance levels (Table 7).

The model is significant with a p-value of 0.011 (Table 6). The variables ORGANIZATIONAL_INOV and GOODS_INOV were excluded from the model due to lack of significance. The obtained equation from the model (Table 7) is: COOP = 18,588 – 0,378 SERVICES_INOV + 0,333 COOP_PROD_proc_INOV_non_R_D + 0,372 COOP_PROD_proc_INOV_R_D.

The results from SMEs confirm this effects having the same three variables being considered significant, although the R^2 is slightly lower (59.1%) and the statistical significance of the variables isn´t as powerful, respectably, 0.039, 0.06 and 0.006 (Appendix A). In this case, the best possible model was also obtained by a backward regression in the third iteration.

Table 4. Pearson correlations

	COOP	ORGANIZATIONAL_INOV	GOODS_INOV	SERVICES_INOV	COOP_PROD_PROC_INOV_NON_R_D	COOP_PROD_PROC_INOV_R_D
COOP	1	,119	-,052	-,408	,094	,490
		,671	,855	,131	,740	,063
ORGANIZATIONAL_INOV	,119	1	-,123	-,161	,294	-,197
	,671		,662	,567	,288	,483
GOODS_INOV	-,052	-,123	1	-,645**	-,378	-,137
	,855	,662		,009	,165	,627
SERVICES_INOV	-,408	-,161	-,645**	1	,482	-,131
	,131	,567	,009		,069	,642
COOP_PROD_PROC_INOV_NON_R_D	,094	,294	-,378	,482	1	-,362
	,740	,288	,165	,069		,185
COOP_PROD_PROC_INOV_R_D	,490	-,197	-,137	-,131	-,362	1
	,063	,483	,627	,642	,185	

**. Correlation is significant at the 0.01 level (2-tailed).

Table 5. Model summary

Model	R	R Square	Dalys R Square	Std. Error of the Estimate
3	,791 c	,625	,523	4,2120

Table 6. ANOVA

Model		Sum of Squares	Df	Mean Square	F	Sig.
3	Regression	325,862	3	108,621	6,123	,011d
	Residual	195,148	11	17,741		
	Total	521,009	14			

Table 7. Coefficients

Model		Unstandardized Coefficients		Smr Coefficients	T	Sig.
		B	Std. Error	Beta		
3	(Constant)	18,588	7,159		2.597	.025
	SERVICES_INOV	-,378	,127	-,626	-2,970	,013
	COOP_PROD_proc_INOV_non_R_D	,333	,119	,626	2,789	,018
	COOP_PROD_proc_INOV_R_D	,372	,116	,635	3.202	Clearance .008

With regard to large enterprises, the results are not statistically significant (Appendix B).

DISCUSSION

The results demonstrate that SMEs that are sharing knowledge with other enterprises of the same enterprise group are very negatively influenced by services innovation and positively by cooperation for product or process innovation. The fact that these enterprises are in a constant internal process of exploitation of knowledge for innovation seems to contribute to the development of knowledge sharing practices within the company (D'Arrigo et al., 2015).

Cooperation is leveraged by the necessity of enterprises to seek knowledge (Chen et al., 2006), which in turn, will foster organizational learning thought the assimilation of new knowledge in the knowledge base of the organization (Fletcher & Prashantham, 2011). This external knowledge is essential to improve the innovation of businesses (Li et al., 2009). Results show that cooperation for product or process innovation is essential to practices of knowledge sharing because enterprises believe that this practices positively contribute to the operational and financial performance (Wang & Wang, 2012) and that with cooperation more new knowledge will be created (Lin & Chen, 2006).

Enterprises privilege cooperation in order to decrease costs and risks, potentiating innovation activities (Nunes et al., 2013). Enterprises that share knowledge within the same enterprise group can be considered learning organizations, since they are constantly involved in other innovation activities (Kharbanda, 2002), like, for example, cooperation for innovation with external enterprises, according to the obtained results. Services innovation has a negative impact on intern knowledge sharing practices, suggesting that product innovators are the ones that most pursue internal knowledge sharing practices.

As to large companies, this study confirms that they have different KM practices, if compared with SMEs, this is in agreement with the literature (Egbu et al., 2005; Perez-Araos et al., 2007).

CONCLUSION

This study intents to promote the debate about knowledge sharing between enterprises of the same enterprise group and it permitted to discover some variables that influence this knowledge sharing practices. This study confirms that SMEs and large companies have different forms of sharing knowledge, probably because large companies have the necessary funds to hire the best human capital and to buy or create knowledge without the "dangers" of cooperation.

It seems that enterprises that pursue services innovation have a smaller tendency to follow this knowledge sharing practices. Cooperation for product or process innovation is, probably, more "goods innovation type" and has a huge impact in internal knowledge sharing practices. So, product innovators seem to privilege more this practices than services innovators. Further sectorial investigation will be necessary to confirm these assumptions.

As to R&D and non R&D performers, their cooperation activities influence knowledge sharing so, despite not having a R&D department, enterprises can adopt KM practices and cooperate for innovation.

The weaknesses of this study are: using data from a single period and from a limited number of countries, lack of sectorial analysis and of information about the relationships that originate the necessity to share knowledge between enterprises of the same enterprise group.

This exploratory study has many gaps and raises many questions so; future research should focus on discovering the differences between SMEs and large enterprises, and between goods innovation and service innovation enterprises. A comparative analysis between R&D and non R&D performers should also be pursued. Other potential areas of research are:

- Inter-country differences with respect to enterprise cooperation/knowledge sharing;
- Specific industry differences;
- Examining other (non-European) markets, such as the U.S. and China;
- Examining cooperation/knowledge sharing between enterprises of different groups.

REFERENCES

Al-Husseini, S. (2015). Knowledge Sharing Practices as a Basis of Product Innovation: A Case of Higher Education in Iraq. *International Journal of Social Science and Humanity, 5*(January 2014), 182–185. doi:10.7763/ijssh.2015.v5.449

Arvanitis, S., Lokshin, B., Mohnen, P., & Woerter, M. (2015). Impact of External Knowledge Acquisition Strategies on Innovation: A Comparative Study Based on Dutch and Swiss Panel Data. *Review of Industrial Organization, 46*(4), 359–382. doi:10.100711151-015-9450-7

Asrar-ul-haq, M., & Anwar, S. (2016). A systematic review of knowledge management and knowledge sharing : Trends, issues, and challenges. *Cogent Business & Management*. doi:10.1080/23311975.2015.1127744

Augusto, M., & Coelho, F. (2009). Market orientation and new-to-the-world products: Exploring the moderating effects of innovativeness, competitive strength, and environmental forces. *Industrial Marketing Management, 38*(1), 94–108. doi:10.1016/j.indmarman.2007.09.007

Barros, V. F. de A., Ramos, I., & Perez, G. (2015). Information Systems and Organizational Memory: A Literature Review. *Journal of Information Systems and Technology Management, 12*(1), 45–63. doi:10.4301/S1807-17752015000100003

Bica, G., Constantinescu, M., & Bica, E. (2015). Innovation and knowledge management in a knowledge--based economy. *World Review of Entrepreneurship, Management and Sustainable Development, 11*(2–3), 156–171.

Cabello-Medina, C., López-Cabrales, Á., & Valle-Cabrera, R. (2011). Leveraging the innovative performance of human capital through HRM and social capital in Spanish firms. *International Journal of Human Resource Management, 22*(4), 807–828. doi:10.1080/09585192.2011.555125

Chang, D. R., & Cho, H. (2008). Organizational memory influences new product success. *Journal of Business Research, 61*(1), 13–23. doi:10.1016/j.jbusres.2006.05.005

Chen, S., Duan, Y., Edwards, J. S., & Lehaney, B. (2006). Toward understanding inter-organizational knowledge transfer needs in SMEs: Insight from a UK investigation. *Journal of Knowledge Management, 10*(3), 6–23. doi:10.1108/13673270610670821

Chirico, F. (2008). Knowledge accumulation in family firms evidence from four case studies. *International Small Business Journal, 26*(4), 433–462. doi:10.1177/0266242608091173

Cobo-Benita, J. R., Rodríguez-Segura, E., Ortiz-Marcos, I., & Ballesteros-Sánchez, L. (2016). Innovation projects performance: Analyzing the impact of organizational characteristics☆. *Journal of Business Research, 69*(4), 1357–1360. doi:10.1016/j.jbusres.2015.10.107

D'Arrigo, F., Virginia, A., Bertolini, G., Prantz, C., Fachinelli, A. C., & Camargo, M. E. (2015). The Influence Of Knowledge Sharing Intention In The Process Of Knowledge Acquisition And Exploitation: A Study with Young Entrepreneurs. *Business and Management Review*, 2015, 642–651.

Denicolai, S., Ramirez, M., & Tidd, J. (2016). Overcoming the false dichotomy between internal R&D and external knowledge acquisition: Absorptive capacity dynamics over time. *Technological Forecasting and Social Change, 104*, 57–65. doi:10.1016/j.techfore.2015.11.025

Diamantini, C., Potena, D., Proietti, M., Smith, F., Storti, E., & Taglino, F. (2013). A Semantic Framework for Knowledge Management in Virtual Innovation Factories. *International Journal of Information System Modeling and Design, 4*(December), 70–92. doi:10.4018/ijismd.2013100104

Durmuşoğlu, S. S., & Barczak, G. (2011). The use of information technology tools in new product development phases: Analysis of effects on new product innovativeness, quality, and market performance. *Industrial Marketing Management, 40*(2), 321–330. doi:10.1016/j.indmarman.2010.08.009

Durst, S., & Edvardsson, I. R. (2012). Knowledge management in SMEs: A literature review. *Journal of Knowledge Management, 16*(6), 879–903. doi:10.1108/13673271211276173

Dyer, J. H., & Nobeoka, K. (2000). Creating and Managing a High-Performance Knowledge-Sharing Network: The Toyota Case. *Source: Strategic Management Journal, 21*(21), 345–367. doi:10.1002/(SICI)1097-0266(200003)21

Ebrahimi Mehrabani, S., & Shajari, M. (2012). Knowledge Management and Innovation Capacity. *Journal of Management Research, 4*(2), 164–177. doi:10.5296/jmr.v4i2.1390

Egbu, C. O., Hari, S., & Renukappa, S. H. (2005). Knowledge management for sustainable competitiveness in small and medium surveying practices. *Structural Survey, 23*(1), 7–21. doi:10.1108/02630800510586871

Fletcher, M., & Prashantham, S. (2011). Knowledge assimilation processes of rapidly internationalising firms: Longitudinal case studies of Scottish SMEs. *Journal of Small Business and Enterprise Development, 18*(3), 475–501. doi:10.1108/14626001111155673

Forés, B., & Camisón, C. (2016). Does incremental and radical innovation performance depend on different types of knowledge accumulation capabilities and organizational size? *Journal of Business Research, 69*(2), 831–848. doi:10.1016/j.jbusres.2015.07.006

Gloet, M., & Samson, D. (2013). Knowledge Management to Support Systematic Innovation Capability. *Proceedings of the 2013 46th Hawaii International Conference on System Sciences (HICSS)* (pp. 3685–3694). doi:10.1109/HICSS.2013.374

Gooderham, P., Minbaeva, D. B., & Pedersen, T. (2011). Governance Mechanisms for the Promotion of Social Capital for Knowledge Transfer in Multinational Corporations. *Journal of Management Studies, 48*(1), 123–150. doi:10.1111/j.1467-6486.2009.00910.x

Gust-Bardon, N. I. (2015). The structural and functional analysis of innovation systems: Outline of the Polish case. *International Journal of Innovation and Regional Development, 6*(1), 31–60. doi:10.1504/IJIRD.2015.067646

Herrera, L., Muñoz-Doyague, M. F., & Nieto, M. (2010). Mobility of public researchers, scientific knowledge transfer, and the firms innovation process. *Journal of Business Research, 63*(5), 510–518. doi:10.1016/j.jbusres.2009.04.010

Hervas-Oliver, J. L., Sempere-Ripoll, F., & Boronat-Moll, C. (2014). Process innovation strategy in SMEs, organizational innovation and performance: A misleading debate? *Small Business Economics*. doi:10.100711187-014-9567-3

Hitt, M. A., Biermant, L., Shimizu, K., & Kochhar, R. (2001). Direct and moderating effects of human capital on strategy and performance in professional service firms: A resource-based perspective. *Academy of Management Journal, 44*(1), 13–28. doi:10.2307/3069334

Hsu, I. C. (2008). Knowledge sharing practices as a facilitating factor for improving organizational performance through human capital: A preliminary test. *Expert Systems with Applications, 35*(3), 1316–1326. doi:10.1016/j.eswa.2007.08.012

Hsu, M. H., & Chang, C. M. (2014). Examining interpersonal trust as a facilitator and uncertainty as an inhibitor of intra-organisational knowledge sharing. *Information Systems Journal, 24*(2), 119–142. doi:10.1111/isj.12000

Huang, H.-C., Lai, M.-C., & Lin, T.-H. (2011). Aligning intangible assets to innovation in biopharmaceutical industry. *Expert Systems with Applications, 38*(4), 3827–3834. doi:10.1016/j.eswa.2010.09.043

Jiacheng, W., Lu, L., & Francesco, C. A. (2010). A cognitive model of intra-organizational knowledge-sharing motivations in the view of cross-culture. *International Journal of Information Management, 30*(3), 220–230. doi:10.1016/j.ijinfomgt.2009.08.007

John, C. D. (2009). Intellectual capital measurement: A critical approach. *Journal of Intellectual Capital, 10*(2), 190–210. doi:10.1108/14691930910952614

Junquera, B., & Del Brio, J. A. (2009). Environmental concurrent engineering: A way to competitive advantage? *World Review of Entrepreneurship. Management and Sustainable Development, 5*(3), 256–270.

Karamitri, I., Talias, M. A., & Bellali, T. (2015). Knowledge management practices in healthcare settings: A systematic review. *The International Journal of Health Planning and Management*. doi:10.1002/hpm.2303 PMID:26153388

Kharbanda, V. P. (2002). Learning Organisations: The Process of Innovation and Technological Change. *AI & Society*, 2002, 89–99.

Lai, C.-S., Chen, C.-S., Chiu, C.-J., & Pai, D.-C. (2011). The impact of trust on the relationship between inter-organisational collaboration and product innovation performance. *Technology Analysis and Strategic Management, 23*(1), 65–74. doi:10.1080/09537325.2011.537107

Lai, Y.-L., & Lin, F.-J. (2012). The Effects of Knowledge Management and Technology Innovation on New Product Development Performance An Empirical Study of Taiwanese Machine Tools Industry. *Procedia: Social and Behavioral Sciences, 40*, 157–164. doi:10.1016/j.sbspro.2012.03.176

Lee, C., Jeon, J., & Park, Y. (2011). Monitoring trends of technological changes based on the dynamic patent lattice: A modified formal concept analysis approach. *Technological Forecasting and Social Change, 78*(4), 690–702. doi:10.1016/j.techfore.2010.11.010

Levy, M., Loebbecke, C., & Powell, P. (2003). SMEs, co-opetition and knowledge sharing: The role of information systems1. *European Journal of Information Systems, 12*(1), 3–17. doi:10.1057/palgrave.ejis.3000439

Li, J., Chen, D., & Shapiro, D. M. (2009). Product Innovations in Emerging Economies: The Role of Foreign Knowledge Access Channels and Internal Efforts in Chinese Firms. *Management and Organization Review, 6*(2), 243–266. doi:10.1111/j.1740-8784.2009.00155.x

Lin, B. W., & Chen, C. J. (2006). Fostering product innovation in industry networks: The mediating role of knowledge integration. *International Journal of Human Resource Management, 17*(1), 155–173. doi:10.1080/09585190500367472

Luo, X. R., Koput, K. W., & Powell, W. W. (2009). Intellectual capital or signal? The effects of scientists on alliance formation in knowledge-intensive industries. *Research Policy, 38*(8), 1313–1325. doi:10.1016/j.respol.2009.06.001

Mariano, S., & Casey, A. (2015). Is organizational innovation always a good thing? *Management Learning, 46*(5), 530–545. doi:10.1177/1350507615569429

Martensson, M. (2000). A critical review of knowledge management as a management tool. *Journal of Knowledge Management, 4*(3), 204–216. doi:10.1108/13673270010350002

Meihami, B., & Meihami, H. (2014). Knowledge Management a way to gain a competitive advantage in firms (evidence of manufacturing companies). *International Letters of Social and Humanistic, 3*, 80–91. doi:10.18052/www.scipress.com/ILSHS.14.80

Michailova, S., & Minbaeva, D. B. (2012). Organizational values and knowledge sharing in multinational corporations: The Danisco case. *International Business Review, 21*(1), 59–70. doi:10.1016/j.ibusrev.2010.11.006

Molina-Castillo, F.-J., Jimenez-Jimenez, D., & Munuera-Aleman, J.-L. (2011). Product competence exploitation and exploration strategies: The impact on new product performance through quality and innovativeness. *Industrial Marketing Management, 40*(7), 1172–1182. doi:10.1016/j.indmarman.2010.12.017

Nambisan, S., & Sawhney, M. (2010). Making the Most of the Global Brain for Innovation. *International Commerce Review, 8*(2–4), 128–135. doi:10.100712146-010-0042-z

Naranjo-Valencia, J. C., Jiménez-Jiménez, D., & Sanz-Valle, R. (2015). Studying the links between organizational culture, innovation, and performance in Spanish companies. *Revista Latinoamericana de Psicología, 48*(1), 30–41. doi:10.1016/j.rlp.2015.09.009

Nunes, S., Carvalho, L., & Costa, T. (2013). Cooperation for innovation: evidence from southern European countries. *International Journal of Innovation and Regional Development 7, 5*(2), 226–241.

OECD. (2005). Oslo Manual: Guidelines for Collecting and Interpreting Innovation Data. OECD Publishing. Retrieved from http://www.oecd.org/document/23/0,3746,en_2825_30453906_35595607_1_1_1_1,00.html

OECD. (2010a). *OECD Science, Technology and Industry Outlook*. OECD Publishing; doi:10.1787ti_outlook-2004-en

OECD. (2010b). *The OECD Innovation Strategy*. OECD Publishing. doi:10.1787/9789264083479-en

Otero-Neira, C., Varela, J., & Garcia, T. (2010). Competitive reaction to the introduction of a new product: An exploratory market signalling study. *Journal of Strategic Marketing, 18*(5), 379–394. doi:10.1080/0965254X.2010.497847

Perez-Araos, A., Barber, K. D., Eduardo Munive-Hernandez, J., & Eldridge, S. (2007). Designing a knowledge management tool to support knowledge sharing networks. *Journal of Manufacturing Technology Management, 18*(2), 153–168. doi:10.1108/17410380710722872

Petty, R., & Guthrie, J. (2000). Intellectual capital literature review: Measurement, reporting and management. *Journal of Intellectual Capital, 1*(2), 155–176. doi:10.1108/14691930010348731

Pot, F., Totterdill, P., & Dhondt, S. (2016). Workplace innovation: European policy and theoretical foundation. *World Review of Entrepreneurship. Management and Sustainable Development, 12*(1), 13–32.

Ritala, P., Olander, H., Michailova, S., & Husted, K. (2015). Knowledge sharing, knowledge leaking and relative innovation performance: An empirical study. *Technovation, 35*, 22–31. doi:10.1016/j.technovation.2014.07.011

Rubera, G., & Kirca, A. H. (2012). Firm Innovativeness and Its Performance Outcomes: A Meta-Analytic Review and Theoretical Integration. *Journal of Marketing, 76*(3), 130–147. doi:10.1509/jm.10.0494

Sadek, T., Kleiman, R., & Loutfy, R. (2015). The role of technology transfer offices in growing new entrepreneurial ecosystems around mid-sized universities. *International Journal of Innovation and Regional Development, 6*(1), 61–79. doi:10.1504/IJIRD.2015.067648

Salim, I. M., & Sulaiman, M. (2011). Organizational Learning, Innovation and Performance: A Study of Malaysian Small and Medium Sized Enterprises. *International Journal of Business and Management, 6*(12), 118–125. doi:10.5539/ijbm.v6n12p118

Sensuse, D. I., Sucahyo, Y. G., Rohajawati, S., & Anggia, P. (2014). Models and frameworks of knowledge management: A literature review. *Proceedings of the 2014 International Conference on Information Science, Electronics and Electrical Engineering (ISEEE)* (Vol. 2, pp. 1166–1170). doi:10.1109/InfoSEEE.2014.6947854

Sivak, R., Caplanova, A., & Hudson, J. (2011). The impact of governance and infrastructure on innovation. *Post-Communist Economies*, *23*(2), 203–217. doi:10.1080/14631377.2011.570050

Sultan, N. (2013). Knowledge management in the age of cloud computing and Web 2.0: Experiencing the power of disruptive innovations. *International Journal of Information Management*, *33*(1), 160–165. doi:10.1016/j.ijinfomgt.2012.08.006

Tsai, W. (2001). Knowledge Transfer in Intraorganizational Networks: Effects of Network Position and Absorptive Gapagity on Business Unit Innovation and Performance. ®. *Academy of Management Journal*, *44*(5), 996–1004. doi:10.2307/3069443

Tsai, W. (2002). Social Structure of Coopetition Within a Multiunit Organization: Coordination, Competition, and Intraorganizational Knowledge Sharing. *Organization Science*, *13*(2), 179–190. doi:10.1287/orsc.13.2.179.536

Vaccaro, A., Parente, R., & Veloso, F. M. (2010). Knowledge Management Tools, Inter-Organizational Relationships, Innovation and Firm Performance. *Technological Forecasting and Social Change*, *77*(7), 1076–1089. doi:10.1016/j.techfore.2010.02.006

Wang, C.-H., Chang, C.-H., & Shen, G. C. (2015). The effect of inbound open innovation on firm performance: Evidence from high-tech industry. *Technological Forecasting and Social Change*, *99*, 222–230. doi:10.1016/j.techfore.2015.07.006

Wang, Z., & Wang, N. (2012). Knowledge sharing, innovation and firm performance. *Expert Systems with Applications*, *39*(10), 8899–8908. doi:10.1016/j.eswa.2012.02.017

Wiig, K. M. (1997). Knowledge management: Where did it come from and where will it go? *Expert Systems with Applications*, *13*(1), 1–14. doi:10.1016/S0957-4174(97)00018-3

Wiig, K. M. (2002). Knowledge management in public administration. *Journal of Knowledge Management*, *6*(3), 224–239. doi:10.1108/13673270210434331

Yeşil, S., Koska, A., & Büyükbeşe, T. (2013). Knowledge Sharing Process, Innovation Capability and Innovation Performance: An Empirical Study. *Procedia: Social and Behavioral Sciences*, *75*, 217–225. doi:10.1016/j.sbspro.2013.04.025

Zhou, K. Z., & Li, C. B. (2012). How knowledge affects radical innovation: Knowledge base, market knowledge acquisition, and internal knowledge sharing. *Strategic Management Journal*, *33*(9), 1090–1102. doi:10.1002mj.1959

This research was previously published in the International Journal of Knowledge Management (IJKM), 13(1); edited by Murray E. Jennex; pages 34-52, copyright year 2017 by IGI Publishing (an imprint of IGI Global).

APPENDIX A - SMES STATISTICAL ANALYSIS

Table 8. Descriptive statistics

	N	Minimum	Maximum	Mean	Std. Deviation
GOODS_INOV	15	59,6	84,9	72,587	7,2724
SERVICES_INOV	15	38,8	70,2	56,060	9,2770
COOP_PROD_PROC_INOV_NON_R_D	15	4,7	56,4	18,153	12,6506
COOP_PROD_PROC_INOV_R_D	15	6,4	42,1	21,380	8,9636
ORGANIZATIONAL_INOV	15	23,6	61,3	46,133	12,4914
COOP	15	5,3	32,4	19,607	8,1161
Valid N (listwise)	15				

Table 9. Correlations[c]

		GOODS_INOV	SERVICES_INOV	COOP_PROD_PROC_INOV_NON_R_D	COOP_PROD_PROC_INOV_R_D	ORGANIZATIONAL_INOV	COOP
GOODS_INOV	Pearson Correlation	1	-,531*	-,185	-,312	-,246	-,137
	Sig. (2-tailed)		,042	,509	,257	,377	,626
SERVICES_INOV	Pearson Correlation	-,531*	1	,370	,000	,749**	-,321
	Sig. (2-tailed)	,042		,175	,999	,001	,243
COOP_PROD_PROC_INOV_NON_R_D	Pearson Correlation	-,185	,370	1	-,214	,156	,125
	Sig. (2-tailed)	,509	,175		,443	,578	,657
COOP_PROD_PROC_INOV_R_D	Pearson Correlation	-,312	,000	-,214	1	-,178	,569*
	Sig. (2-tailed)	,257	,999	,443		,525	,027
ORGANIZATIONAL_INOV	Pearson Correlation	-,246	,749**	,156	-,178	1	-,355
	Sig. (2-tailed)	,377	,001	,578	,525		,195
COOP	Pearson Correlation	-,137	-,321	,125	,569*	-,355	1
	Sig. (2-tailed)	,626	,243	,657	,027	,195	

*. Correlation is significant at the 0.05 level (2-tailed).

**. Correlation is significant at the 0.01 level (2-tailed).

c. Listwise N=15

Table 10. Variables entered/removed[a]

Model	Variables Entered	Variables Removed	Method
1	ORGANIZATIONAL_INOV, COOP_PROD_PROC_INOV_NON_R_D, COOP_PROD_PROC_INOV_R_D, GOODS_INOV, SERVICES_INOV[b]		Enter
2		ORGANIZATIONAL_INOV	Backward (criterion: Probability of F-to-remove >=, 100).
3		GOODS_INOV	Backward (criterion: Probability of F-to-remove >=, 100).

a. Dependent Variable: COOP

b. All requested variables entered.

Table 11. Model summary

Model	R	R Square	Adjusted R Square	Std. Error of the Estimate
1	,790[a]	,624	,415	6,2055
2	,781[b]	,609	,453	6,0022
3	,769[c]	,591	,480	5,8528

a. Predictors: (Constant), ORGANIZATIONAL_INOV, COOP_PROD_PROC_INOV_NON_R_D, COOP_PROD_PROC_INOV_R_D, GOODS_INOV, SERVICES_INOV

b. Predictors: (Constant), COOP_PROD_PROC_INOV_NON_R_D, COOP_PROD_PROC_INOV_R_D, GOODS_INOV, SERVICES_INOV

c. Predictors: (Constant), COOP_PROD_PROC_INOV_NON_R_D, COOP_PROD_PROC_INOV_R_D, SERVICES_INOV

Table 12. ANOVA[a]

Model		Sum of Squares	df	Mean Square	F	Sig.
1	Regression	575,612	5	115,122	2,990	,073[b]
	Residual	346,578	9	38,509		
	Total	922,189	14			
2	Regression	561,929	4	140,482	3,899	,037[c]
	Residual	360,260	10	36,026		
	Total	922,189	14			
3	Regression	545,376	3	181,792	5,307	,017[d]
	Residual	376,813	11	34,256		
	Total	922,189	14			

a. Dependent Variable: COOP

b. Predictors: (Constant), ORGANIZATIONAL_INOV, COOP_PROD_PROC_INOV_NON_R_D, COOP_PROD_PROC_INOV_R_D, GOODS_INOV, SERVICES_INOV

c. Predictors: (Constant), COOP_PROD_PROC_INOV_NON_R_D, COOP_PROD_PROC_INOV_R_D, GOODS_INOV, SERVICES_INOV

d. Predictors: (Constant), COOP_PROD_PROC_INOV_NON_R_D, COOP_PROD_PROC_INOV_R_D, SERVICES_INOV

Table 13. Coefficients[a]

Model		Unstandardized Coefficients		Standardized Coefficients	t	Sig.
		B	Std. Error	Beta		
1	(Constant)	48,560	32,007		1,517	,164
	GOODS_INOV	-,221	,295	-,198	-,750	,472
	SERVICES_INOV	-,659	,347	-,753	-1,901	,090
	COOP_PROD_PROC_INOV_NON_R_D	,304	,151	,474	2,013	,075
	COOP_PROD_PROC_INOV_R_D	,584	,212	,645	2,755	,022
	ORGANIZATIONAL_INOV	,131	,220	,202	,596	,566
2	(Constant)	44,664	30,306		1,474	,171
	GOODS_INOV	-,190	,281	-,171	-,678	,513
	SERVICES_INOV	-,502	,217	-,573	-2,307	,044
	COOP_PROD_PROC_INOV_NON_R_D	,280	,141	,436	1,989	,075
	COOP_PROD_PROC_INOV_R_D	,552	,198	,610	2,783	,019
3	(Constant)	25,406	10,285		2,470	,031
	SERVICES_INOV	-,426	,182	-,487	-2,340	,039
	COOP_PROD_PROC_INOV_NON_R_D	,287	,137	,448	2,100	,060
	COOP_PROD_PROC_INOV_R_D	,603	,179	,665	3,360	,006

a. Dependent Variable: COOP

Table 14. Excluded variables[a]

Model		Beta In	t	Sig.	Partial Correlation	Collinearity Statistics
						Tolerance
2	ORGANIZATIONAL_INOV	,202[b]	,596	,566	,195	,364
3	ORGANIZATIONAL_INOV	,157[c]	,482	,640	,151	,376
	GOODS_INOV	-,171[c]	-,678	,513	-,210	,617

a. Dependent Variable: COOP

b. Predictors in the Model: (Constant), COOP_PROD_PROC_INOV_NON_R_D, COOP_PROD_PROC_INOV_R_D, GOODS_INOV, SERVICES_INOV

c. Predictors in the Model: (Constant), COOP_PROD_PROC_INOV_NON_R_D, COOP_PROD_PROC_INOV_R_D, SERVICES_INOV

APPENDIX B- LARGE ENTERPRISES STATISTICAL ANALYSIS

Table 15. Descriptive statistics

	N	Minimum	Maximum	Mean	Std. Deviation
GOODS_INOV	15	31,6	90,9	74,467	15,0068
SERVICES_INOV	15	36,2	100,0	56,320	14,7540
COOP_PROD_PROC_INOV_NON_R_D	15	5,3	37,1	12,833	7,4402
COOP_PROD_PROC_INOV_R_D	15	6,0	71,6	50,127	16,1447
ORGANIZATIONAL_INOV	15	39,5	69,8	59,273	9,0598
COOP	15	20,8	59,4	39,380	10,9838
Valid N (listwise)	15				

Table 16. Correlations

		GOODS_INOV	SERVICES_INOV	COOP_PROD_PROC_INOV_NON_R_D	COOP_PROD_PROC_INOV_R_D	ORGANIZATIONAL_INOV	COOP
GOODS_INOV	Pearson Correlation	1	-,752**	-,052	,010	-,126	,136
	Sig. (2-tailed)		,001	,853	,973	,656	,630
	N	15	15	15	15	15	15
SERVICES_INOV	Pearson Correlation	-,752**	1	-,033	-,044	,518*	-,503
	Sig. (2-tailed)	,001		,907	,876	,048	,056
	N	15	15	15	15	15	15
COOP_PROD_PROC_INOV_NON_R_D	Pearson Correlation	-,052	-,033	1	-,798**	-,351	-,105
	Sig. (2-tailed)	,853	,907		,000	,200	,710
	N	15	15	15	15	15	15
COOP_PROD_PROC_INOV_R_D	Pearson Correlation	,010	-,044	-,798**	1	,150	,336
	Sig. (2-tailed)	,973	,876	,000		,594	,221
	N	15	15	15	15	15	15
ORGANIZATIONAL_INOV	Pearson Correlation	-,126	,518*	-,351	,150	1	-,393
	Sig. (2-tailed)	,656	,048	,200	,594		,147
	N	15	15	15	15	15	15
COOP	Pearson Correlation	,136	-,503	-,105	,336	-,393	1
	Sig. (2-tailed)	,630	,056	,710	,221	,147	
	N	15	15	15	15	15	15

**. Correlation is significant at the 0.01 level (2-tailed).

*. Correlation is significant at the 0.05 level (2-tailed).

Table 17. Variables entered/removed[a]

Model	Variables Entered	Variables Removed	Method
1	ORGANIZATIONAL_INOV, GOODS_INOV, COOP_PROD_PROC_INOV_R_D, COOP_PROD_PROC_INOV_NON_R_D, SERVICES_INOV[b]	.	Enter

a. Dependent Variable: COOP
b. All requested variables entered.

Table 18. Model summary

Model	R	R Square	Adjusted R Square	Std. Error of the Estimate
1	,705[a]	,497	,217	9,7182

a. Predictors: (Constant), ORGANIZATIONAL_INOV, GOODS_INOV, COOP_PROD_PROC_INOV_R_D, COOP_PROD_PROC_INOV_NON_R_D, SERVICES_INOV

Table 19. ANOVA[a]

Model		Sum of Squares	df	Mean Square	F	Sig.
1	Regression	839,032	5	167,806	1,777	,214[b]
	Residual	849,992	9	94,444		
	Total	1689,024	14			

a. Dependent Variable: COOP
b. Predictors: (Constant), ORGANIZATIONAL_INOV, GOODS_INOV, COOP_PROD_PROC_INOV_R_D, COOP_PROD_PROC_INOV_NON_R_D, SERVICES_INOV

Table 20. Coefficients[a]

Model		Unstandardized Coefficients		Standardized Coefficients	t	Sig.
		B	Std. Error	Beta		
1	(Constant)	80,812	44,323		1,823	,102
	GOODS_INOV	-,351	,302	-,479	-1,164	,274
	SERVICES_INOV	-,613	,358	-,823	-1,710	,121
	COOP_PROD_PROC_INOV_NON_R_D	,329	,635	,223	,517	,617
	COOP_PROD_PROC_INOV_R_D	,330	,278	,485	1,189	,265
	ORGANIZATIONAL_INOV	-,026	,413	-,021	-,063	,951

a. Dependent Variable: COOP

Chapter 21
How Do Institution-Based Trust and Interpersonal Trust Affect Interdepartmental Knowledge Sharing?

Xinwei Yuan
Xi'an University of Technology, China

Lorne Olfman
Claremont Graduate University, USA

Jingbing Yi
Xi'an Jiaotong University, China

ABSTRACT

There are two typical forms of trust in organisational settings—institution-based trust and interpersonal trust. The role of interpersonal trust in promoting interdepartmental knowledge sharing has been investigated. The effect of institution-based trust, especially the joint effect of institution-based and interpersonal trust, on interdepartmental knowledge sharing has not been adequately described. This article builds a conceptual model to describe the independent and joint effects of these two forms of trust on the satisfaction and success of interdepartmental knowledge sharing. The moderating role of knowledge tacitness is also described in this model, which is tested on 294 collaborative task scenarios between departments within Chinese IT firms. The empirical results essentially support the proposed model and contribute to organisational trust and interdepartmental knowledge-sharing discussions by clarifying the substantial roles of these two forms of trust in the context of interdepartmental collaboration and knowledge sharing.

DOI: 10.4018/978-1-7998-0417-8.ch021

INTRODUCTION

Knowledge-sharing obstacles between departments are usually more prominent than those within a single department. The 'group consciousness' formed during the long-term collaboration between employees in a single department makes it easy to share knowledge within a department, but it also makes it difficult to transfer knowledge outside of a department. Communication gaps are more likely to appear between departments than within a department, thus forming barriers to interdepartmental knowledge sharing (Suckley et al., 2013). Therefore, social interaction is an indispensable channel for improving interdepartmental knowledge sharing (Noorderhaven & Harzing, 2009). Social interactions between employees from different departments promote knowledge inflows and outflows across departmental boundaries (Jasimuddin, 2014; Jasimuddin et al., 2006). In this process, trust is a core factor that influences the effectiveness of social interaction and knowledge sharing (Willem et al., 2006). As a social phenomenon, trust is almost ubiquitous in our social and economic activities (Lewis & Weigert, 1985). In dynamic and fluid work settings such as interdepartmental collaborative tasks, trust is particularly important to co-workers' collaboration and knowledge sharing (Rousseau et al., 1998).

The acknowledgement of the importance of trust has led to many studies that focus on the role of trust in promoting interdepartmental knowledge sharing (Willem et al., 2006; Willem & Buelens, 2007; Ford, 2004; Levin & Cross, 2004; Hsu & Chang, 2014). The primary form of trust that most of these studies mention, either explicitly or implicitly, is that of interpersonal trust. As a type of individual choice with social interactions, interpersonal trust primarily arises out of interpersonal relations and networks (Rousseau et al., 1998; Singh, 2012). Another important form of trust in the context of interdepartmental knowledge sharing is institution-based trust (Ford, 2004). Different from the 'individual choice' characteristic of interpersonal trust, institution-based trust is based on the belief that necessary impersonal structures—such as norms, regulations, contracts and guarantees—are in place to ensure individual members' trustworthy behaviour (McKnight et al., 1998). In an interdepartmental context, interpersonal trust and institution-based trust jointly influence interdepartmental knowledge sharing. Many studies have shown that the level of interpersonal trust often determines the success or failure of interdepartmental knowledge sharing (Willem et al., 2006; Willem & Buelens, 2007; Mäkelä & Brewster, 2009). However, little empirical work has been undertaken to investigate the effect of institution-based trust and, in particular, the joint effect of institution-based and interpersonal trust on interdepartmental knowledge sharing. Therefore, there is a gap in the current research on the relationship among institution-based trust, interpersonal trust and interdepartmental knowledge sharing. To address this gap, this study conducts an empirical examination of the effects of institution-based and interpersonal trust on interdepartmental knowledge sharing and aims to answer the following research question: *How do institution-based trust and interpersonal trust independently and jointly influence interdepartmental knowledge sharing?* We also explore the role of knowledge tacitness in this process. The following section presents a literature review of the key concepts about interpersonal trust, institution-based trust and knowledge sharing in an interdepartmental context.

LITERATURE REVIEW

Interpersonal Trust and Institution-Based Trust in an Interdepartmental Context

According to Rousseau, Sitkin, Burt, & Camerer (1998), trust is 'a psychological state comprising the intention to accept vulnerability based upon positive expectations of the intentions or behaviour of another' (p. 395). In organisational settings, interpersonal interactions are the main source of this type of 'psychological state', namely interpersonal trust. Impersonal systems or structures are another important source of this type of 'psychological state'—namely, institution-based trust—especially between unfamiliar individuals (Rousseau et al., 1998).

Table 1 compares interpersonal trust with institution-based trust in an interdepartmental context. As shown in Table 1, although these two forms of trust come from different sources, they jointly influence individuals' behaviour in interdepartmental collaboration.

Interpersonal Trust

Interpersonal trust, following Zand (1972), is defined as one person's willingness to increase his or her vulnerability to the actions of another person whose behaviour he or she cannot control. Mayer, Davis, & Schoorman (1995) similarly define interpersonal trust as 'the willingness of a party to be vulnerable to the actions of another party based on the expectation that the other will perform a particular action important to the trustor, irrespective of the ability to monitor or control that other party' (p. 712). Interpersonal trust arises out of interpersonal relations and tends to be developed through repeated, positive interpersonal interactions (Shapiro et al., 1992). In organisational settings, interpersonal trust varies

Table 1. Comparison of interpersonal trust and institution-based trust

	Interpersonal Trust	Institution-Based Trust
Definition	The willingness of one person to increase his or her vulnerability to the actions of another person whose behaviour he or she cannot control (Zand, 1972).	The belief that the necessary impersonal structures are in place to ensure the trustworthy behaviours of individual members (McKnight et al. 1998).
Sources (construct) of trust	Interpersonal interactions and individual choices based on the trustee's ability, benevolence, and integrity (Mayer et al., 1995). Other categories of interpersonal trust: calculus-based (also called calculative trust), knowledge-based (similar to cognition-based) and identification-based (the same as relational or affect-based trust) (Shapiro et al., 1992; McAllister, 1995; Rousseau et al., 1998; Maguire et al., 2001).	Structural assurance and situational normality from impersonal structures, including perceived monitoring, feedback and co-operative norms (McKnight et al., 1998; Pavlou, 2002).
At which level does it work	Micro-organisational (individual) level.	From the macro-organisational (collective) level to the micro-organisational (individual) level.
How to influence individual behaviour	Influence individuals' intentions and expectations, leading to individuals' rational/non-rational behaviour.	Impersonal structures and institutional factors are internalised in individuals, leading to collective rational behaviour.
How to facilitate interdepartmental collaboration	Facilitate spontaneous co-ordination and co-operation among participants.	Create a shared understanding among all participants that co-operation will most likely be reciprocated.

with the task, the situation, and the other person and is shown as individual choice behaviour, which has been described as either a rational choice (Kramer, 1999) or a non-rational choice (Hosmer, 1995).

The literature identifies interpersonal trust as a complex construct. Mayer, Davis, & Schoorman (1995) note that the trustee's perceived ability, benevolence, and integrity explain a major portion of trustworthiness. Ability is 'a group of skills, competencies, and characteristics that enable a party to have influence within some specific domain' (p. 717). Benevolence is 'the extent to which a trustee is believed to want to do good to the trustor, aside from an egocentric profit motive' (p. 718). Integrity is 'the trustor's perception that the trustee adheres to a set of principles that the trustor finds acceptable' (p. 719). McAllister (1995) identifies two principal sub-constructs of interpersonal trust—cognition-based trust and affect-based trust. Cognition-based trust is built based on individual beliefs about peer reliability and dependability. Affect-based trust comes from reciprocated interpersonal care and concern. Shapiro, Sheppard, & Cheraskin (1992) specify two sub-constructs of interpersonal trust—knowledge-based trust and identification-based trust.[1] Knowledge-based trust is derived from getting to know the other individual and being able to predict his or her behaviour. Identification-based trust is based on empathy and mutual understanding between individuals. Rousseau, Sitkin, Burt, & Camerer (1998) propose two sub-constructs of interpersonal trust—calculative trust and relational trust. Summarising the existing literature of interpersonal trust, Maguire, Phillips, & Hardy (2001) provide a slightly more complete set of categories of interpersonal trust—calculus-based (also called calculative trust), knowledge-based (similar to cognition-based trust), and identification-based (same as affect-based or relational trust). The development of interpersonal trust is a dynamic process. Trust between two parties tends to be calculus-based trust grounded in rational choice and economic exchange in the early stage of development, and with repeated interactions, it tends to become identification-based trust grounded in interpersonal attachment and identification (Rousseau et al., 1998; Maguire et al., 2001).

In an interdepartmental context, interpersonal trust is found to facilitate spontaneous co-ordination and co-operation among participants, and significantly increases a series of relationship outcomes, such as satisfaction, loyalty (Matzler & Renzl, 2006), and knowledge sharing (Mooradian et al., 2006).

Institution-Based Trust

Institution-based trust is defined by McKnight, Cummings, & Chervany (1998) as the belief that the necessary impersonal structures are in place to ensure the trustworthy behaviours of individual members. It is also termed 'impersonal trust' (Shapiro, 1987), 'institutional trust' (Rousseau et al., 1998), or 'system trust' (Bachmann, 2001). Institution-based trust emerges when one member believes that impersonal structures support his or her anticipation of the other's trustworthiness. Scholars argue that because of the existence of impersonal structures, institution-based trust increases one's sense of security in a given situation (Shapiro, 1987; Zucker, 1986). Thus, institution-based trust depends on individuals' acceptance and internalisation of impersonal structures and affects individuals' interactions in a relatively subconscious manner. It is the reflection of collective structures in individuals' trusting beliefs which allows it to be analysed at the individual level.

Zucker (1986) describes two types of mechanisms that contribute to institution-based trust in general economic activities—third-party certification and escrows. Third-party certification refers to impersonal structures, such as licenses, regulations, and laws, which define a party's trustworthiness and expected behaviour. Escrows refer to the mechanism in which money is held by a third party on behalf of transacting parties, thus guaranteeing the expected outcome of a transaction. McKnight, Cummings,

& Chervany (1998) specify two sources of institution-based trust in organisational settings—situational normality and structural assurance. Situational normality is the belief that the other party is trustworthy and that success is likely because the situation is normal. Structural assurance is the belief that the other party is trustworthy and that success is likely because contextual conditions such as promises, contracts, regulations, and guarantees are in place. Drawing upon Zucker (1986) and McKnight et al. (1998), Pavlou (2002) proposes five specific sub-constructs of institution-based trust in the background of online marketplaces: perceived monitoring, perceived accreditation, perceived legal bonds, perceived feedback, and perceived co-operative norms. Monitoring is described as the set of activities undertaken to assure that all activities are performed as specified by a predetermined set of widely accepted agreements and rules. Accreditation is described as the scope of efforts undertaken to verify the ability of an entity or organisation to perform as expected. Legal bonds are defined as lawful contracts that govern economic activity. Feedback is described as a mechanism to react quickly to signals that have been sent by others. Co-operative norms are the values, standards, and principles to which all parties adhere.

In an interdepartmental context, we argue that monitoring, feedback, and co-operative norms remain important impersonal structures that help to create a shared understanding among all participants and contribute to institution-based trust, though accreditation and legal bonds are usually unsuitable for interdepartmental situations.

Perceived Monitoring

Monitoring is a core managerial activity for procuring co-operative behaviour (Ferrin et al., 2007). Organisation-level monitoring for all of the parties involved in an interdepartmental task helps to assure that the collaborative task is conducted according to established standards for process, quality, and performance. Huemer, Boström, & Felzensztein (2009) argue that intended purpose and perceived legitimacy need to be considered in co-ordinating interdepartmental relationships. An effective monitoring system can play an important role in implementing such a 'purpose' or 'legitimacy'. Organisation-level monitoring is also frequently viewed as an effective third-party mechanism in resolving interdepartmental conflicts and cultivating trust (Nugent & Broedling, 2002). Although most organisations have their own monitoring mechanism for interdepartmental tasks, employees' perceptions of the effectiveness of the monitoring mechanism are likely to vary. An effective monitoring system can improve employees' positive expectations for others by clearly defined rules and the sanction of uncooperative behaviour, which then contribute to trust (Bijlsma-Frankema & Costa, 2005). Thus, in an interdepartmental context, organisation-level monitoring can be viewed as a form of structural assurance that promotes institution-based trust (McKnight et al., 1998).

Perceived Feedback

Effective feedback mechanisms are also emphasised by scholars as an important enabler to induce co-operation and trust between departments. Effective feedback promotes information exchange and learning, which are important antecedent factors of organisational trust (Hart et al., 1986; Buskens & Raub, 2002). Coletti, Sedatole, & Towry (2005) argue that feedback mechanisms in control-induced co-operation can reinforce trust. Song, Sommer, & Hartman (1998) also note that external supervisors' feedback regarding interdepartmental co-operative behaviour may lead to positive attitudes toward co-operation between departments. In interdepartmental collaboration, when control-induced co-operative behaviours are observed by participants through an effective feedback mechanism, co-operators' beliefs about partner trustworthiness can be strengthened. In addition, feedback regarding participants' non-cooperative behaviours, combined with effective monitoring and sanctioning systems, can help managers intervene and correct corresponding behaviours, which provides structural assurance in discouraging opportunistic behaviour and building trust (McKnight et al., 1998; Coletti et al., 2005).

Perceived Co-Operative Norms

Co-operative norms facilitate interdepartmental collaboration and trust. A norm represents a degree of consensus in the social system (Nahapiet & Ghoshal, 1998). Co-operative norms can establish a strong foundation for the building of institution-based trust, as a type of situational normality (McKnight et al., 1998). As mentioned by Posner, Randolph, & Schmidt (1987), employees in a department tend to easily develop a shared value because of frequent interaction, which is likely to be different from other departments' values because of less contact. Differences in values between departments lead to different acceptable behaviours and increase the risks of interdepartmental conflicts and distrust (Elangovan & Shapiro, 1998). Organisational co-operative norms facilitate trusting intentions across departments by creating comfort with each other's expected behaviour patterns and building shared values among all parties. Therefore, as a form of impersonal structure, organisational co-operative norms are effective adhesives that bind different departments and engender trust. Organisational co-operative norms also enhance the effectiveness of monitoring and feedback systems by making it easier to match monitoring and feedback information with employees' internal criteria (Herold & Greller, 1977).

Interdepartmental Knowledge Sharing

Due to the 'internal stickiness' of knowledge, knowledge sharing across departmental boundaries is often more difficult than it is within departments (Szulanski, 1996). Thus, corresponding interaction mechanisms between departments, such as formal systems and informal networks, are essential to urge interdepartmental knowledge sharing (Willem & Buelens, 2007; Hansen, 2002). By its nature, knowledge sharing is also a form of social interaction (Chen & Huang, 2007; Noorderhaven & Harsing, 2009). Thus, we argue that the quality of social interaction based on corresponding interaction mechanisms can lead to distinct effects of knowledge sharing. Because trust is a key determinant of the quality of social interaction, the importance of trust is therefore highlighted in interdepartmental knowledge sharing. Many studies have recognised the importance of trust in interdepartmental knowledge sharing (Willem & Buelens, 2007; Willem et al., 2006); however, the joint influencing mechanism of institution-based and interpersonal trust on interdepartmental knowledge sharing is seldom discussed. Thus, we create a conceptual model to depict the relationships of related factors, and then we examine the model empirically.

CONCEPTUAL MODEL AND HYPOTHESES

This paper focuses on the effect, especially the joint effect, of institution-based and interpersonal trust on interdepartmental knowledge sharing. A conceptual model (see Figure 1) is created to depict the relationships of related variables. Interdepartmental knowledge sharing is assessed in terms of two outcome dimensions—satisfaction and success. Satisfaction is selected as a dimension of interdepartmental knowledge sharing because trust may lead to a psychologically comfortable or safe status, which usually results

Figure 1. Conceptual research model

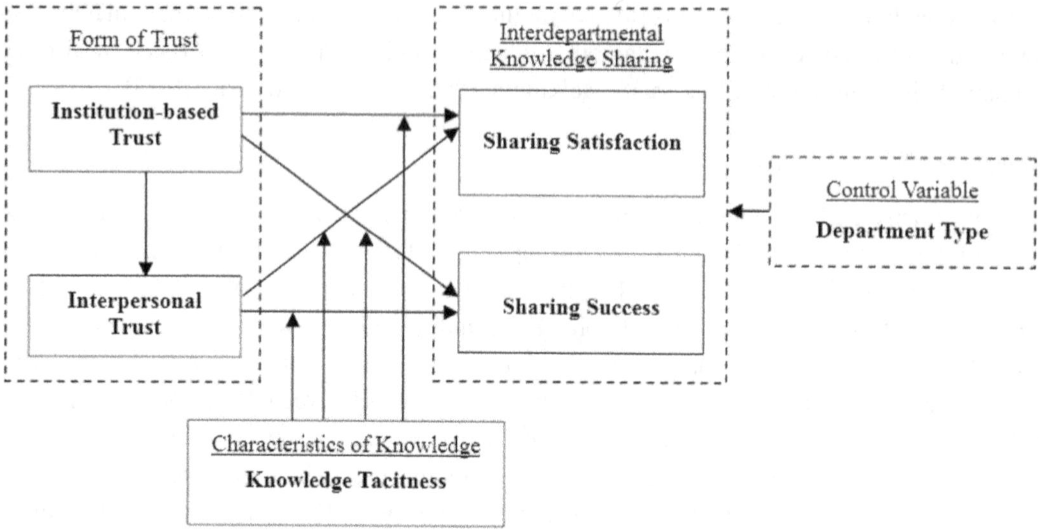

in more positive attitudes such as satisfaction (Matzler & Renzl, 2006). As a more objective dimension, success is selected to judge the real effect of interdepartmental knowledge sharing, that is, the extent to which interdepartmental knowledge sharing achieves success. Institution-based and interpersonal trust are viewed as the enablers of the two outcome dimensions (satisfaction and success). Their joint effects and mediation effects on satisfaction and success are described. Additionally, the moderating effects of knowledge tacitness are depicted. Department type is considered as the control variable. A set of testable hypotheses is developed. The first several hypotheses address the effect of institution-based and interpersonal trust, respectively, on interdepartmental knowledge sharing. Several hypotheses address the joint effects and mediation effects of these two forms of trust on interdepartmental knowledge sharing. Additional hypotheses address the moderating effects of knowledge tacitness.

The Effects of Institution-Based Trust on Sharing Satisfaction and Success

Institution-based trust comes from organisational impersonal structures or institutional factors. Adhering to the 'impersonal' characteristic, building of institution-based trust does not depend on specific individuals but instead relies more on employees' roles or positions in a well-functioning structure (Ford, 2004). Coleman (1988) argues that this type of structure constitutes a powerful, although sometimes fragile, social capital. Based on this type of social capital, institution-based trust makes individuals be willing to take risks and to implement trust behaviour, thus effectively decreasing employees' perceived risks in knowledge sharing. Therefore, when interdepartmental collaboration is encouraged and institutionalised in an organisation, institution-based trust can effectively overcome the public goods dilemma of knowledge sharing and promote employees' knowledge sharing between departments. Interdepartmental collaborative tasks impose higher requirements for group collaborations and corresponding group-level knowledge structures (Laframboise et al., 2007). Institution-based trust, along with a specific group knowledge structure, can become the solid foundation of interdepartmental knowledge sharing. Institution-based trust also provides employees with the sense of a safe co-operation environment. This will make it easier to expect co-operative behaviours from other employees in interdepartmental collaboration, and thus contributes to the satisfaction and success of interdepartmental knowledge sharing (Fukuyama, 1995; McKnight et al., 1998; Pavlou, 2002). Thus, we state the above arguments as the following hypotheses:

Hypothesis 1a: Institution-based trust positively influences sharing satisfaction in interdepartmental knowledge sharing.

Hypothesis 1b: Institution-based trust positively influences sharing success in interdepartmental knowledge sharing.

Effects of Interpersonal Trust on Sharing Satisfaction and Success

Interpersonal trust is engendered in employees' social interactions and is an important source of social capital (Nahapiet & Ghoshal, 1998). Numerous scholars agree that interpersonal trust is an important facilitator of interdepartmental knowledge sharing (Abrams et al., 2003; Bakker, 2006; Mäkelä & Brewster, 2009; Hsu & Chang, 2014). Mayer, Davis, & Schoorman (1995) argue that one's ability, benevolence, and integrity explain a major portion of his or her trustworthiness in interpersonal interaction. Drawing upon Mayer et al. (1995), Abrams, Cross, Lesser, & Levin (2003) argue that ability and benevolence strongly promote interdepartmental knowledge sharing. Bakker (2006) finds that integrity is also a positive facilitator of knowledge sharing. Empirical evidence also confirms the value of interpersonal trust in knowledge sharing (Mooradian et al., 2006). Based on this evidence, we argue that interpersonal trust can effectively promote the satisfaction and success of interdepartmental knowledge sharing. Thus, we state the above arguments as the following hypotheses:

Hypothesis 2a: Interpersonal trust positively influences sharing satisfaction in interdepartmental knowledge sharing.

Hypothesis 2b: Interpersonal trust positively influences sharing success in interdepartmental knowledge sharing.

The Joint Effects of Institution-Based and Interpersonal Trust on Sharing Satisfaction and Success

As two typical forms of trust, institution-based and interpersonal trust jointly influence interdepartmental knowledge sharing within an organisation. Based on different sources (see Table 1), the combination of institution-based and interpersonal trust enriches organisational trust at both the individual and collective levels, which will further improve the satisfaction and success of interdepartmental knowledge sharing. Thus, we argue that the combination of institution-based and interpersonal trust should be expected to be more influential on both satisfaction and success than either variable alone. We state the above arguments as the following hypotheses:

Hypothesis 3a: Institution-based trust and interpersonal trust will jointly influence sharing satisfaction more than either variable alone in interdepartmental knowledge sharing.

Hypothesis 3b: Institution-based trust and interpersonal trust will jointly influence sharing success more than either variable alone in interdepartmental knowledge sharing.

To further reveal the joint effect of institution-based and interpersonal trust on interdepartmental knowledge sharing, the relationship between institution-based and interpersonal trust needs to be clarified. A considerable amount of research emphasises the positive role of institution-based trust in promoting interpersonal trust (McKnight et al., 1998; Rousseau et al., 1998; Lewicki et al., 2006). About the formation and development of interpersonal trust, some scholars support the 'zero-baseline assumption', which postulates that interpersonal trust begins at zero (when two actors have no prior information about each other) and develops gradually (Jones & George, 1998). Therefore, interpersonal trust is often considered to start at a calculus-based stage based on calculating the costs and benefits of trust relationships. With repeated interactions, interpersonal trust gradually evolves from calculus-based to identification-based trust. In the formation and transformation process of interpersonal trust, institution-based trust can play a positive role by establishing a context conducive to interpersonal trusting relationships. Rousseau, Sitkin, Burt, & Camerer (1998) argue that 'Institution-based trust can ease the way to formulating both calculus-based and relational trust' (p. 400). Some scholars argue that interpersonal trust also may begin at a high initial trust level under the influence of some factors such as institution-based trust (Lewicki et al., 2006). McKnight, Cummings, & Chervany (1998) also argue that interpersonal trusting intention at the beginning of a relationship may be high because of high institution-based trust. Pearce, Branyiczki, & Bigley (2000) argue that institution-based trust promotes 'trust in strangers'. Without institution-based trust, interpersonal trust can easily fall into a 'limited clusters' trap and lead to distrust in employees from other departments, who may be viewed as 'outsiders' (Pearce et al., 2000).

Based on the relationship of institution-based and interpersonal trust, we expect that institution-based trust will reinforce interpersonal trust to improve the satisfaction and success of interdepartmental knowledge sharing. This implies that interpersonal trust is expected to be a mediating variable between institution-based trust and the two outcome dimensions of interdepartmental knowledge sharing. This leads to the following hypotheses:

Hypothesis 4a: Interpersonal trust mediates between institution-based trust and sharing satisfaction in interdepartmental knowledge sharing.

Hypothesis 4b: Interpersonal trust mediates between institution-based trust and sharing success in interdepartmental knowledge sharing.

The Moderating Effect of Knowledge Tacitness

According to our arguments in the previous sections, both institution-based and interpersonal trust are important for interdepartmental knowledge sharing. In this section, we suggest that these two forms of trust will have different relationships with sharing satisfaction and success when knowledge becomes more tacit.

In general, these two forms of trust facilitate the sharing of both explicit and tacit knowledge between departments. However, considering different sources, these two forms of trust might have different effects on explicit and tacit knowledge sharing. Levin, Cross, Abrams, & Lesser (2002) argue that different types of knowledge require different forms of trust. Compared with explicit or codified knowledge, tacit knowledge is 'the entire category of knowledge that is not easy to be conveyed by means of codified and symbolic representations' (p. 212), i.e., 'non-codifiable knowledge' (Cowan et al., 2000). Knowledge tacitness has been identified as a natural impediment to knowledge sharing between individuals and departments (Tsoukas, 1996; Szulanski, 1996; Levin & Cross, 2004). Close and frequent interaction between individuals has been considered an effective mechanism to overcome the obstacles of tacit knowledge sharing (Cavusgil et al., 2003). Compared to institution-based trust, interpersonal trust usually comes from intensive interpersonal interaction and is likely to be more helpful for tacit knowledge sharing. Many scholars also emphasise the value of interpersonal trust in the sharing of tacit knowledge. Holste & Fields (2010) find that interpersonal trust plays an important role in facilitating the willingness to share and use tacit knowledge. Interpersonal trust makes one believe the trustworthiness of the knowledge provider as a reliable knowledge source, which is critical to tacit knowledge sharing (Levin et al., 2002; Levin & Cross, 2004). Thus, we surmise that interpersonal trust should be more strongly associated with the satisfaction and success of interdepartmental knowledge sharing when such knowledge is tacit and difficult to articulate. Therefore, we propose the following hypotheses:

Hypothesis 5a: In interdepartmental knowledge sharing, as knowledge tacitness increases, the positive relationship between interpersonal trust and sharing satisfaction will strengthen.
Hypothesis 5b: In interdepartmental knowledge sharing, as knowledge tacitness increases, the positive relationship between interpersonal trust and sharing success will strengthen.

Institution-based trust stems from organisational impersonal structures. Compared with interpersonal trust at the individual level, the effect of institution-based trust primarily comes from the collective level. By nature, tacit knowledge is more suitable to be shared by individuals than collectives. Inkpen & Dinur (1998) argue that initiatives of tacit knowledge sharing from the collective often fail. Compared with tacit knowledge, explicit knowledge can be codified and understood apart from the knowledge source (Levin et al., 2002; Levin & Cross, 2004). Therefore, explicit knowledge sharing is less dependent on individuals' relationships and is relatively easy to initiate at the collective level. Thus, according to the 'collective' characteristic of institution-based trust, we speculate that institution-based trust might have less impact on the sharing of tacit knowledge than explicit knowledge. Ford (2004) also argues that institution-based trust is associated with explicit knowledge sharing. Therefore, we contend that institution-based trust is less important in tacit knowledge sharing. When knowledge is tacit, institution-based trust should be more weakly associated with the satisfaction and success of interdepartmental knowledge sharing. This leads to the following hypotheses:

Hypothesis 5c: In interdepartmental knowledge sharing, as knowledge tacitness increases, the positive relationship between institution-based trust and sharing satisfaction will weaken.
Hypothesis 5d: In interdepartmental knowledge sharing, as knowledge tacitness increases, the positive relationship between institution-based trust and sharing success will weaken.

Control Variables

The characteristics of knowledge from different departments are shown to be different (Choi & Lee, 2002). In interdepartmental collaboration, task knowledge characteristics are related to department types. Therefore, different types of departments involved in a collaborative task are likely to influence the outcomes of interdepartmental knowledge sharing. Thus, this study controls for the effects of department type on the satisfaction and success of interdepartmental knowledge sharing.

RESEARCH METHODOLOGY

Sample

Data were collected from employees of Chinese IT firms using a pre-tested, self-administered questionnaire. The IT sector was selected because IT firms are knowledge-intensive firms that frequently adopt interdepartmental collaborative tasks to manage competition (Mendelson, 2000). This study focuses on knowledge sharing between departments when interdepartmental collaborative tasks are implemented. Thus, following Willem & Buelens (2007), we asked each respondent to consider an interdepartmental collaborative task in which he or she is currently involved or that ended recently (in the past three months) in his or her firm. All items in the questionnaire were asked to be answered about that interdepartmental collaborative task. Questionnaires were collected from two sources. First, based on a non-random snowball selection method, 50 MBA part-time students from IT firms in Shaanxi, Beijing, and Shandong were asked to select respondents from either their own firm or their friends in other IT firms. Second, an online questionnaire via an embedded URL was sent to IT workers from Chinese IT professional online communities. Three hundred and twenty-eight respondents returned the questionnaires. After sorting out the invalid questionnaires, 294 valid questionnaires were used for the analysis.

The characteristics of the respondents are described in Table 2. The respondents were well educated, with 89.2% having earned at least a bachelor's degree. Respondents also had spent a considerable amount of time in their firms, with 84.7% working there for more than 3 years. Departments were grouped into five categories: Management/Planning, Research & Development, Marketing/Sales, Engineering/Technical Support, and Consulting/Services.

Measures

Research constructs were operationalised through scales drawn and modified from existing literature. A multiple-item self-report method was used with a seven-point Likert scale from 1 (completely disagree) to 7 (completely agree). Because a Chinese version of the questionnaire was necessary for our respondents in China, items from the previous studies were translated into Chinese. Next, the questionnaire was pretested using three professors familiar with organisational behaviour and knowledge sharing, who assessed its wording clarity and question item sequence. Those professors' comments were used to reword or remove inappropriate items. Following the pre-test, a pilot test involving 30 employees from an IT firm was conducted to test the feasibility of the questionnaire. According to those employees' comments, the questionnaire was then modified slightly. All of the operational definitions of instruments, together with the related literature, are summarised in Table 3.

The measurement of institution-based trust was based on the scales and work of Pavlou (2002), McKnight et al. (2002) and Zucker (1986), adapted to our research context. To measure interpersonal trust, the scales of Cook & Wall (1980), Mayer et al. (1995) and Bakker (2006) were adapted to our research purpose. To measure sharing satisfaction and success, the scales of Willem et al. (2006) were adopted with wording changes tailored to the context of interdepartmental knowledge sharing. To measure knowledge tacitness, the scales and work of Levin & Cross (2004), Willem et al. (2006), and Tsoukas (1996) were adapted. All the survey items used in this study are shown in the Appendix.

Table 2. Demographics of samples (N=294)

Category		Frequency	%
Gender	Male	165	56.1%
	Female	129	43.9%
Age	20 years or less	1	0.3%
	21-30 years	160	54.4%
	31-40 years	127	43.2%
	41 years or more	6	2.1%
Education	Less than bachelor's	32	10.8%
	Bachelor's	198	67.3%
	Master's	55	18.7%
	Doctorate	9	3.2%
Years at firm	3 years or less	45	15.3%
	4-6 years	140	47.6%
	7-9 years	81	27.6%
	10 years or more	28	9.5%
Departments	Management/Planning	53	18.1%
	Research & Development	92	31.3%
	Marketing/Sales	60	20.4%
	Engineering/Technical Support	66	22.4%
	Consulting/Services	23	7.8%

Table 3. Operational definition and related literatures

Variables	Operational Definition	Item Number	Related Literature
Institution-based trust	Perceived degree of monitoring, feedback, and co-operative norms in interdepartmental collaboration	4	Pavlou (2002), McKnight et al. (2002), Zucker (1986)
Interpersonal trust	Perceived degree of ability, benevolence, and integrity of co-workers from the other department	4	Cook & Wall (1980), Mayer et al. (1995), Bakker (2006)
Sharing satisfaction	Perceived degree of satisfaction with information exchange, experience sharing, co-operative status, and meeting task standards in collaboration with co-workers from the other department	4	Willem et al. (2006)
Sharing success	Perceived degree of failure in task progress, information communication, problem solving, and time frame during collaboration with co-workers from the other department (reverse scaled)	4	Willem et al. (2006)
Knowledge tacitness	Perceived degree of expressiveness in speech or writing about task knowledge (reverse scaled)	4	Levin & Cross (2004), Willem et al. (2006), Tsoukas (1996)

DATA ANALYSIS AND RESULTS

Reliability and Validity

Table 4 outlines the results of reliability and validity tests for survey items. The content validity of the instruments was established by adopting the constructs that had already been validated by other studies. Reliability was assessed using Cronbach's α (minimum 0.7). For convergent validity, item-to-total correlation scores of all items were greater than 0.4. Discriminant validity was checked by a factor analysis (minimum loading 0.40). The factor loadings show that as expected, the respondents discriminated among corresponding constructs. All items were acceptable and retained for further analysis.

Hypothesis Testing

Hypotheses were tested using hierarchical multiple regression. Table 5 shows means, standard deviations, and Pearson correlations of the variables used in the regression analysis.

Table 4. Reliability and convergent validity (N=294)

Construct		Items	Factor Loading	Eigenvalue	Variance Explained	Item-Total Correlation	α
Form of trust	Institution-based trust	INST1	0.744	2.732	34.152%	0.707	0.847
		INST2	0.783			0.722	
		INST3	0.760			0.676	
		INST4	0.868			0.638	
	Interpersonal trust	PERT1	0.736	2.700	67.906%	0.663	0.819
		PERT2	0.784			0.665	
		PERT3	0.763			0.707	
		PERT4	0.817			0.547	
Interdepartmental knowledge sharing	Sharing satisfaction	SAT1	0.839	2.998	37.481%	0.749	0.872
		SAT2	0.859			0.787	
		SAT3	0.846			0.700	
		SAT4	0.808			0.679	
	Sharing success	SUC1	0.847	2.912	73.875%	0.750	0.886
		SUC2	0.875			0.756	
		SUC3	0.858			0.765	
		SUC4	0.817			0.731	
Characteristics of knowledge	Knowledge Tacitness	TACI1	0.762	2.719	67.969%	0.597	0.842
		TACI2	0.856			0.721	
		TACI3	0.861			0.729	
		TACI4	0.816			0.663	

Table 5. Means, standard deviations, and correlations (N=294)

Variable	Mean	S.D.	1	2	3	4	5	6	7	8
Department type (Management/planning)										
1. Research/development	0.31	0.46								
2. Marketing/sales	0.20	0.40	-0.342**							
3. Engineering/technical support	0.22	0.42	-0.363**	-0.272**						
4. Consulting/services	0.08	0.27	-0.197**	-0.148**	-0.157**					
5. **Knowledge tacitness**	3.26	0.91	-0.059	0.026	-0.029	0.184**				
6. **Institution-based trust**	5.20	0.92	0.151**	-0.093	0.026	-0.167**	-0.674**			
7. **Interpersonal trust**	5.23	0.91	0.103	-0.068	-0.011	-0.138*	-0.675**	0.751**		
8. **Sharing satisfaction**	5.38	0.88	0.139*	-0.137*	0.006	-0.142*	-0.625**	0.759**	0.701**	
9. **Sharing success**	4.17	1.28	0.086	-0.043	-0.051	-0.047	-0.245**	0.325**	0.329**	0.348**

*P<0.05,**P<0.01 (2-tailed)

Pearson correlation coefficients show that both institution-based and interpersonal trust significantly correlate with both satisfaction and success. To account for the effects of different departments, we included four dummy variables to represent these five types of department: Management/Planning, Research & Development, Marketing/Sales, Engineering/Technical Support, and Consulting/Services. We also tested multicollinearity using the variance inflation factor (VIF). The VIF values for all independent variables were found to be less than 3 (maximum 2.680), which is well below the standard cut-off of 10 (Hair et al., 1995). When testing the moderating effects of knowledge tacitness, the variables were mean-centred (Aiken & West, 1991) to minimise the distortion due to high correlations between the interaction term and its component variables. Table 6 shows regression analysis results.

Table 6. Hierarchical regression analysis results

Variable	Sharing Satisfaction					
	M 1	M 2	M 3	M 4	M 5	M 6
Department type (Management/planning)						
Research/development	0.035 (0.567)	-0.030 (-0.591)	0.022 (0.409)	-0.022 (-0.446)	-0.017 (-0.342)	-0.020 (-0.393)
Marketing/sales	-0.127* (-2.161)	-0.107* (-2.214)	-0.100 (-1.914)	-0.098* (-2.079)	-0.101* (-2.163)	-0.100* (-2.122)
Engineering/technical support	-0.041 (-0.690)	-0.061 (-1.248)	-0.021 (-0.407)	-0.047 (-0.985)	-0.045 (-0.940)	-0.046 (-0.964)
Consulting/services	-0.047 (-0.896)	-0.033 (-0.753)	-0.035 (-0.758)	-0.030 (-0.710)	-0.021 (-0.490)	-0.023 (-0.544)
Knowledge tacitness (TACI)	-0.612*** (-13.281)	-0.210*** (-4.153)	-0.278*** (-5.106)	-0.134* (-2.555)	-0.135* (-2.578)	-0.128* (-2.443)
Institution-based trust (INST)		0.608*** (11.960)		0.475*** (8.094)	0.466*** (7.944)	0.472*** (8.052)
Interpersonal trust (PERT)			0.499*** (9.204)	0.246*** (4.223)	0.242*** (4.175)	0.245*** (4.220)
INST×TACI					0.059 (1.580)	
PERT×TACI						0.045 (1.224)
R^2	0.411	0.607	0.545	0.630	0.633	0.632
Adjust R^2	0.401	0.599	0.536	0.621	0.623	0.622
F	40.240***	73.913***	57.398***	69.617***	61.546***	61.209***

Variable	Sharing Success						Interpersonal Trust	
	M 7	M 8	M 9	M 10	M 11	M 12	M 13	M 14
Department type (Management/planning)								
Research/development	0.032 (0.411)	0.001 (0.016)	0.025 (0.322)	0.008 (0.099)	-0.007 (-0.088)	-0.001 (-0.010)	0.026 (0.434)	-0.033 (-0.647)
Marketing/sales	-0.044 (-0.595)	-0.034 (-0.475)	-0.028 (-0.384)	-0.027 (-0.376)	-0.017 (-0.235)	-0.021 (-0.292)	-0.056 (-0.990)	-0.038 (-0.788)

continues on following page

Table 6. Continued

Variable	Sharing Satisfaction							
	M 1	M 2		M 3	M 4		M 5	M 6
Engineering/technical support	-0.061 (-0.808)	-0.070 (-0.953)	-0.049 (-0.669)	-0.059 (-0.805)	-0.065 (-0.899)	-0.062 (-0.857)	-0.040 (-0.695)	-0.057 (-1.189)
Consulting/services	-0.012 (-0.176)	-0.005 (-0.072)	-0.005 (-0.071)	-0.003 (-0.039)	-0.028 (-0.429)	-0.024 (-0.374)	-0.024 (-0.480)	-0.011 (-0.259)
Knowledge tacitness (TACI)	-0.242*** (-4.172)	-0.052 (-0.682)	-0.047 (-0.616)	0.008 (0.105)	0.011 (0.137)	-0.009 (-0.112)	-0.669*** (-15.187)	-0.310*** (-6.222)
Institution-based trust (INST)		0.287*** (3.759)		0.182* (2.016)	0.204* (2.286)	0.190* (2.126)		0.543*** (10.829)
Interpersonal trust (PERT)			0.292*** (3.850)	0.195* (2.175)	0.204* (2.303)	0.196* (2.209)		
INST×TACI					-0.162** (-2.863)			
PERT×TACI						-0.144* (-2.546)		
R^2	0.068	0.111	0.113	0.126	0.150	0.145	0.462	0.618
Adjust R^2	0.051	0.093	0.095	0.104	0.126	0.121	0.453	0.610
F	4.181**	5.998***	6.121***	5.884***	6.302***	6.057***	49.456***	77.394***

* P<0.05, ** P<0.01, *** P<0.001; *t*-statistics in parentheses

1. The effects of institution-based trust on sharing satisfaction and success.

Hypothesis *1a* proposes that institution-based trust will positively influence sharing satisfaction. In the test of Hypothesis *1a*, the result of M 2 shows a significant and positive relationship ($\beta = 0.608$, $p < 0.001$) between institution-based trust and sharing satisfaction. Therefore, *Hypothesis 1a* is supported.

Hypothesis *1b* proposes that institution-based trust will positively influence sharing success. In the test of Hypothesis *1b*, the result of M 8 shows a significant and positive relationship ($\beta = 0.287$, $p < 0.001$) between institution-based trust and sharing success. Thus, *Hypothesis 1b* is supported.

2. The effects of interpersonal trust on sharing satisfaction and success.

Hypothesis *2a* proposes that interpersonal trust will positively influence sharing satisfaction. In the test of Hypothesis *2a*, the result of M 3 shows a significant and positive relationship ($\beta = 0.499$, $p < 0.001$) between interpersonal trust and sharing satisfaction. Thus, *Hypothesis 2a* is supported.

Hypothesis *2b* proposes that interpersonal trust will positively influence sharing success. In the test of Hypothesis *2b*, the result of M 9 shows a significant and positive relationship ($\beta = 0.292$, $p < 0.001$) between interpersonal trust and sharing success. Thus, *Hypothesis 2b* is supported.

3. The joint effects of institution-based and interpersonal trust on sharing satisfaction and success.

Hypothesis *3a* proposes that institution-based and interpersonal trust will explain more variance in sharing satisfaction than either variable alone. To test Hypothesis *3a*, R^2 changes of M 4 (both institution-based and interpersonal trust) relative to M 2 (only institution-based trust) and M 3 (only interpersonal trust) were analysed. In M 2, institution-based trust and other controlled variables were regressed on sharing satisfaction, resulting in an F-statistic of 73.913 ($p < 0.001$) and an adjusted R^2 of 0.599. In M 3, interpersonal trust and other controlled variables were regressed on sharing satisfaction resulting in an F-statistic of 57.398 ($p < 0.001$) and an adjusted R^2 of 0.536. Next, compared to M 2, M 4 added interpersonal trust to produce an F change of 17.833 ($p < 0.001$) for an R^2 change of 0.023. Compared to M 3, M 4 added institution-based trust to produce an F change of 65.518 ($p < 0.001$) for an R^2 change of 0.085. These results indicate that the combination of these two forms of trust explains significant additional variance in sharing satisfaction than does each alone. Therefore, ***Hypothesis 3a*** is supported.

Hypothesis *3b* proposes that institution-based and interpersonal trust will explain more variance in sharing success than either variable alone. To test Hypothesis *3b*, R^2 changes of M 10 (both institution-based and interpersonal trust) relative to M 8 (only institution-based trust) and M 9 (only interpersonal trust) were analysed. In M 8, institution-based trust and other controlled variables were regressed on sharing success, resulting in an F-statistic of 5.998 ($p < 0.001$) and an adjusted R^2 of 0.093. In M 9, interpersonal trust and other controlled variables were regressed on sharing success, resulting in an F-statistic of 6.121 ($p < 0.001$) and an adjusted R^2 of 0.095. Compared to M 8, M 10 added interpersonal trust to produce an F change of 4.730 ($p < 0.05$) for an R^2 change of 0.015. Compared to M 9, M 10 added institution-based trust to produce an F change of 4.066 ($p < 0.05$) for an R^2 change of 0.013. These results indicate that the combination of these two forms of trust explains significant additional variance in sharing success than does each alone. Thus, ***Hypothesis 3b*** is supported.

4. Interpersonal trust as a mediator.

Hypothesis *4a* tests the mediation effect of interpersonal trust between institution-based trust and sharing satisfaction. The mediator effect testing approach with a three-step process, as described by Baron & Kenny (1986), was utilised to test this relationship: first, the presumed mediator variable (interpersonal trust) was regressed on the independent variable (institution-based trust), as shown in M 14; second, the dependent variable (sharing satisfaction) was regressed on the independent variable (as shown in M 2); and third, the dependent variable was simultaneously regressed on both the independent and mediator variables (as shown in M 4). The results of M 14, M 2, and M 4 indicate that interpersonal trust is a partial mediator between institution-based trust and sharing satisfaction. Institution-based trust is significant in M 14 and M 2. Additionally, interpersonal trust is significant in M 4. Moreover, the β value of institution-based trust is lower in M 4 ($\beta = 0.475, p < 0.001$) than in M 2 ($\beta = 0.608, p < 0.001$), which meets the condition of partial mediation. The mediation effect explains 14.8% of the variance in sharing satisfaction. Thus, ***Hypothesis 4a*** is supported.

Hypothesis *4b* tests the mediation effect of interpersonal trust between institution-based trust and sharing success. The mediator effect testing approach of Baron & Kenny (1986) was also used to test Hypothesis *4b*. As shown in Table 6, the results of M 14, M 8 and M 10 indicate that interpersonal trust is a partial mediator between institution-based trust and sharing success. Institution-based trust is significant in M 14 and M 8. Additionally, interpersonal trust is significant in M 10. Moreover, the β value of institution-based trust is lower in M 10 ($\beta = 0.182, p < 0.05$) than in M 8 ($\beta = 0.287, p < 0.001$), which meets the condition of partial mediation. The mediation effect explains 10.5% of the variance in sharing success. Thus, ***Hypothesis 4b*** is supported.

5. Moderating effects of knowledge tacitness.

Hypothesis *5a* tests the moderating effect of knowledge tacitness on the relationship between interpersonal trust and sharing satisfaction. According to M 6 shown in Table 6, the interpersonal trust × knowledge tacitness interaction is not significant ($p = 0.222$), which indicates that knowledge tacitness does not moderate the relationship between interpersonal trust and sharing satisfaction. Thus, ***Hypothesis 5a*** is not supported.

Hypothesis *5b* tests the moderating effect of knowledge tacitness on the relationship between interpersonal trust and sharing success. M 12 indicates that knowledge tacitness does indeed moderate the relationship between interpersonal trust and sharing success ($\beta = -0.144, p < 0.05$). However, inconsistent with our hypothesis, this interaction effect has an unexpected impact. Following the recommendations of Aiken & West (1991), we used the slope test to examine the specific nature of this interaction. Controlling for everything else in equation M 12, a high (one standard deviation above the mean), average (the mean) and low (one standard deviation below the mean) value for knowledge tacitness were inserted, respectively, into this equation. The simple slope test showed that the slope (i.e., the unstandardised regression coefficient) of interpersonal trust was decreasingly steep from low knowledge tacitness (slope = 0.404, $p < 0.01$) to average tacitness (slope = 0.277, $p < 0.05$) to high tacitness (slope = 0.149, $p = 0.268$). This indicates that as knowledge tacitness increases, the positive relationship between interpersonal trust and sharing success becomes weaker, which is contrary to our hypothesis. Therefore, ***Hypothesis 5b*** is not supported.

Hypothesis *5c* tests the moderating effect of knowledge tacitness on the relationship between institution-based trust and sharing satisfaction. M 5 shows that the institution-based trust × knowledge tacitness interaction is not significant ($p = 0.115$), which indicates that knowledge tacitness does not moderate the relationship between institution-based trust and sharing satisfaction. Thus, ***Hypothesis 5c*** is not supported.

Hypothesis *5d* tests the moderating effect of knowledge tacitness on the relationship between institution-based trust and sharing success. M 11 indicates that knowledge tacitness moderates the relationship between institution-based trust and sharing success ($\beta = -0.162$, $p < 0.01$). Consistent with our hypothesis, the slope test using equation M 11 showed that the slope of institution-based trust was decreasingly steep from low knowledge tacitness (slope = 0.428, $p < 0.01$) to average tacitness (slope = 0.285, $p < 0.05$) to high tacitness (slope = 0.142, $p = 0.276$). This indicates that the positive relationship between institution-based trust and sharing success becomes weaker as knowledge tacitness increases. Therefore, ***Hypothesis 5d*** is supported.

DISCUSSION

This study was conducted to integrate organisational trust research in interdepartmental knowledge sharing. Thus, two typical forms of trust within an organisation—interpersonal trust grounded in interpersonal interaction and institution-based trust grounded in impersonal structures—are integrated into the context of interdepartmental knowledge sharing, and their joint effects on sharing satisfaction and success are analysed. Although the importance of trust has been shown in prior research on interdepartmental knowledge sharing (Willem & Buelens, 2007; Willem et al., 2006; Abrams et al., 2003; Mäkelä & Brewster, 2009; Hsu & Chang, 2014), most prior studies have focused on interpersonal trust and neglected institution-based trust. To our knowledge, nobody has integrated institution-based and interpersonal trust to investigate their joint effect on interdepartmental knowledge sharing, and explore the moderating role of knowledge tacitness in this process. By offering empirical support for the proposed conceptual model, this study provides three key findings on the role of institution-based and interpersonal trust in interdepartmental knowledge sharing. First, this study shows that both institution-based and interpersonal trust are significant predictor variables of interdepartmental knowledge sharing satisfaction and success. This finding is essentially consistent with McKnight et al.'s (1998) arguments about institution-based trust and is in accordance with Willem & Buelens's (2007) empirical test about the role of interpersonal trust in interdepartmental knowledge sharing. More importantly, this research highlights the joint effects of institution-based and interpersonal trust on sharing satisfaction and success. This finding indicates that these two forms of trust are (to some extent) indispensable in promoting interdepartmental knowledge sharing. Second, this study confirms that interpersonal trust partially mediates the relationship between institution-based trust and the outcomes of interdepartmental knowledge sharing—sharing satisfaction and success. This finding means that sharing satisfaction and success are not only indirectly affected by institution-based trust via interpersonal trust but are also directly affected by institution-based trust. Extending McKnight et al.'s (1998) arguments about institution-based trust to the context of interdepartmental knowledge sharing, this finding underlines the importance of institution-based trust and also confirms interpersonal trust as a critical mediator. Third, this study explores the moderating role of knowledge tacitness between institution-based trust and sharing success. As knowledge tacitness increases, the positive relationship between institution-based trust and sharing success weakens. This finding is consistent with Ford's (2004) arguments. Unexpectedly, and contrary to our expectations, knowledge tacitness has also been found to play a similar role in moderating the relationship between interpersonal trust and sharing success. As knowledge tacitness increases, the positive relationship between interpersonal trust and sharing success also weakens. This finding appears to show that the impact of high knowledge tacitness, as a potential obstacle to successful interdepartmental knowledge sharing, is not easily alleviated by either interpersonal or institution-based trust. Based on these findings, this study makes a theoretical and empirical contribution to the emerging literature on the role of institution-based and interpersonal trust in the context of interdepartmental knowledge sharing.

Theoretical Implications

This study makes a theoretical contribution to clarifying the role of institution-based and interpersonal trust in interdepartmental knowledge sharing by integrating the institution-based trust literature (Zucker, 1986; McKnight et al., 1998; Pavlou, 2002), interpersonal trust literature (Mayer et al., 1995; McAllister, 1995; Rousseau et al., 1998), and interdepartmental knowledge-sharing literature (Willem & Buelens, 2007; Willem et al., 2006; Laframboise et al., 2007). We also show how these two forms of trust interact with typical knowledge characteristics such as knowledge tacitness. Thus, this study contributes to both the organisational trust and the knowledge management literature. For the organisational trust literature, we reinterpret Pavlou's (2002) specific constructs of institution-based trust (perceived monitoring, feedback and co-operative norms) in an interdepartmental context. On the basis of this reinterpretation, we examine the relationship between institution-based and interpersonal trust. McKnight, Cummings, & Chervany (1998) argue that institution-based trust is a vital antecedent of interpersonal trust. This study empirically corroborates the proposition of McKnight et al. (1998). This study also extends McKnight et al.'s (1998) theoretical work by empirically demonstrating that institution-based and interpersonal trust jointly contribute to trust outcomes (interdepartmental sharing satisfaction and success). With respect to our contribution to the knowledge management literature, we propose and test a conceptual model (see Figure 1) to provide a more detailed understanding about how two specific forms of trust influence the outcomes of interdepartmental knowledge sharing with different degree of knowledge tacitness. We show the value of the combination of institution-based and interpersonal trust in facilitating interdepartmental knowledge sharing. We also call for a renewed focus on institution-based trust in the context of interdepartmental knowledge sharing. Although scholars have suggested that institutional (impersonal) factors are important for acquiring knowledge (Grant, 1996), few have focused on the role of institution-based trust in interdepartmental knowledge sharing. Our study provides a better understanding of how institution-based trust improves interdepartmental knowledge sharing both directly and indirectly. Our study also finds that knowledge tacitness will weaken the positive impacts of institution-based and interpersonal trust on the success of interdepartmental knowledge sharing. That indicates that these two forms of trust might not be sufficient to cope with the potentially disadvantageous impact of high knowledge tacitness on sharing success. In addition to trust, strong co-ordination and intensive interaction should be considered for successful tacit knowledge sharing (Willem et al., 2006; Seidler-de Alwis & Hartmann, 2008).

Managerial Implications

Our work provides three main insights that can be helpful to managers interested in improving interdepartmental knowledge sharing through trust building. First, this study reminds managers to pay attention to the sources of trust in organisational settings: Compared to interpersonal interaction (interpersonal trust), impersonal structures (institution-based trust) are shown in this study to be even more important within an organisation. More importantly, managers should realise the value of the combination of these two forms of trust. Such an understanding might help managers to vigorously promote these two forms of trust and obtain good outcomes in interdepartmental knowledge sharing. Second, extending the arguments of McKnight et al. (1998), we offer evidence for the role of institution-based trust in promoting interpersonal trust. Awareness of this can help managers focus their efforts on appropriate management activities through a trade-off between interpersonal interaction (interpersonal trust) and impersonal structures (institution-based trust) to facilitate interdepartmental knowledge sharing. Compared to interpersonal interaction with the characteristics of self-organisation and emergence, impersonal structures or institutional factors are more likely to be planned, designed, and applied by managers. We suggest that managers should pay more attention to organisational design than making a direct intervention to influence interpersonal interaction. Third, this study reminds managers that both institution-based and interpersonal trust are limited when sharing highly tacit knowledge. Our findings indicate that, in addition to trust, it is necessary to engage in more forceful actions, such as strong co-ordination and intensive interaction, to facilitate tacit knowledge sharing between departments.

Limitations and Suggestions for Future Research

Although our work is useful and potentially important for researchers and managers, this study has some limitations that should be acknowledged. One limitation of this study is its self-report bias based on the sample selection methodology. Some steps were taken to reduce this type of bias. For example, respondents were not asked to give their names or any other identifying data. We also instructed respondents to answer trust- and knowledge sharing-related questions based on careful recollection and perception about 'an interdepartmental collaborative task that you are currently involved with or that ended recently (in the past three months) in your firm'. Another limitation of this study comes from the sample selection. Our findings are likely to only represent IT firms in China. There is no evidence to support that trust has the same or similar characteristics in different industries. Indeed, some scholars argue that certain industries, such as investment banking, have their own typical patterns of trust (Rousseau et al., 1998). Meanwhile, there is evidence to indicate that the level of organisational trust might differ between China and some other countries (Huff & Kelley, 2003). Thus, further study is required to assess the applicability of our research framework to other industries and countries. This study is cross-sectional. Therefore, it is difficult to capture the dynamic interaction between institution-based and interpersonal trust and their corresponding effects on interdepartmental knowledge sharing. A longitudinal study can trace the long-term effects of trust and interdepartmental knowledge sharing and further enrich empirical findings. Finally, our study is limited in scope. Only a small subset of the many possible relationships among institution-based trust, interpersonal trust, and interdepartmental knowledge sharing was examined in this paper. For interdepartmental knowledge sharing, we only studied knowledge sharing between departments in the process of interdepartmental collaboration and the corresponding sharing satisfaction and success. For institution-based and interpersonal trust, only a few characteristics, such as perceived monitoring, feedback, and co-operative norms (for institution-based trust), along with co-workers' ability, benevolence, and integrity (for interpersonal trust), were considered. Future research may consider other interdepartmental knowledge-sharing activities and outcome dimensions, and other characteristics of institution-based and interpersonal trust.

ACKNOWLEDGMENT

The authors would like to acknowledge funding from the Humanities and Social Science Foundation of Ministry of Education of China (grant No. 13YJAZH123) and Scientific Research Program Funded by Shaanxi Provincial Education Department (grant No. 13JK0180).

REFERENCES

Abrams, L. C., Cross, R., Lesser, E., & Levin, D. Z. (2003). Nurturing interpersonal trust in knowledge-sharing networks. *The Academy of Management Executive*, *17*(4), 64–77. doi:10.5465/AME.2003.11851845

Aiken, L. S., & West, S. G. (1991). *Multiple regression: Testing and interpreting interactions*. Thousand Oaks, CA: Sage.

Bachmann, R. (2001). Trust, power and control in trans-organizational relations. *Organization Studies*, *22*(2), 337–365. doi:10.1177/0170840601222007

Bakker, M., Leenders, R. T. A., Gabbay, S. M., Kratzer, J., & Van Engelen, J. M. (2006). Is trust really social capital? Knowledge sharing in product development projects. *The Learning Organization*, *13*(6), 594–605. doi:10.1108/09696470610705479

Baron, R. M., & Kenny, D. A. (1986). The moderator–mediator variable distinction in social psychological research: Conceptual, strategic, and statistical considerations. *Journal of Personality and Social Psychology, 51*(6), 1173–1182. doi:10.1037/0022-3514.51.6.1173 PMID:3806354

Bijlsma-Frankema, K., & Costa, A. C. (2005). Understanding the trust-control nexus. *International Sociology, 20*(3), 259–282. doi:10.1177/0268580905055477

Buskens, V., & Raub, W. (2002). Embedded trust: Control and learning. In E. Lawler & S. Thye (Eds.), *Advances in Group Processes* (Vol. 19, pp. 167–202). Emerald Group Publishing Limited.

Cavusgil, S. T., Calantone, R. J., & Zhao, Y. (2003). Tacit knowledge transfer and firm innovation capability. *Journal of Business and Industrial Marketing, 18*(1), 6–21. doi:10.1108/08858620310458615

Chen, C. J., & Huang, J. W. (2007). How organizational climate and structure affect knowledge management—The social interaction perspective. *International Journal of Information Management, 27*(2), 104–118. doi:10.1016/j.ijinfomgt.2006.11.001

Choi, B., & Lee, H. (2002). Knowledge management strategy and its link to knowledge creation process. *Expert Systems with Applications, 23*(3), 173–187. doi:10.1016/S0957-4174(02)00038-6

Coleman, J. S. (1988). Social capital in the creation of human capital. *American Journal of Sociology, 94*(s1), S95–S120. doi:10.1086/228943

Coletti, A. L., Sedatole, K. L., & Towry, K. L. (2005). The effect of control systems on trust and cooperation in collaborative environments. *Accounting Review, 80*(2), 477–500. doi:10.2308/accr.2005.80.2.477

Cook, J., & Wall, T. (1980). New work attitude measures of trust, organizational commitment and personal need non-fulfilment. *Journal of Occupational Psychology, 53*(1), 39–52. doi:10.1111/j.2044-8325.1980.tb00005.x

Cowan, R., David, P. A., & Foray, D. (2000). The explicit economics of knowledge codification and tacitness. *Industrial and Corporate Change, 9*(2), 211–253. doi:10.1093/icc/9.2.211

Elangovan, A. R., & Shapiro, D. L. (1998). Betrayal of trust in organizations. *Academy of Management Review, 23*(3), 547–566.

Ferrin, D. L., Bligh, M. C., & Kohles, J. C. (2007). Can I trust you to trust me? A theory of trust, monitoring, and cooperation in interpersonal and intergroup relationships. *Group & Organization Management, 32*(4), 465–499. doi:10.1177/1059601106293960

Ford, D. P. (2004). Trust and knowledge management: the seeds of success. In C. Holsapple (Ed.), *Handbook on Knowledge Management 1* (pp. 553–575). Springer Berlin Heidelberg. doi:10.1007/978-3-540-24746-3_29

Fukuyama, F. (1995). *Trust: The social virtues and the creation of prosperity*. New York: Free Press.

Grant, R. M. (1996). Toward a knowledge-based theory of the firm. *Strategic Management Journal, 17*(S2), 109–122. doi:10.1002mj.4250171110

Hair, J. F., Anderson, R. E., Tatham, R. L., & Black, W. C. (1995). *Multivariate data analysis: with readings*. Englewood Cliffs, NJ: Prentice-Hall.

Hansen, M. T. (2002). Knowledge networks: Explaining effective knowledge sharing in multiunit companies. *Organization Science*, *13*(3), 232–248. doi:10.1287/orsc.13.3.232.2771

Hart, K. M., Capps, H. R., Cangemi, J. P., & Caillouet, L. M. (1986). Exploring organizational trust and its multiple dimensions: A case study of General Motors. *Organization Development Journal*, *4*(2), 31–39.

Herold, D. M., & Greller, M. M. (1977). Feedback: The definition of a construct. *Academy of Management Journal*, *20*(1), 142–147. doi:10.2307/255468

Holste, J. S., & Fields, D. (2010). Trust and tacit knowledge sharing and use. *Journal of Knowledge Management*, *14*(1), 128–140. doi:10.1108/13673271011015615

Hosmer, L. T. (1995). Trust: The connecting link between organizational theory and philosophical ethics. *Academy of Management Review*, *20*(2), 379–403.

Hsu, M. H., & Chang, C. M. (2014). Examining interpersonal trust as a facilitator and uncertainty as an inhibitor of intra-organisational knowledge sharing. *Information Systems Journal*, *24*(2), 119–142. doi:10.1111/isj.12000

Huemer, L., Boström, G., & Felzensztein, C. (2009). Control–trust interplays and the influence paradox: A comparative study of MNC-subsidiary relationships. *Industrial Marketing Management*, *38*(5), 520–528. doi:10.1016/j.indmarman.2008.12.019

Huff, L., & Kelley, L. (2003). Levels of organizational trust in individualist versus collectivist societies: A seven-nation study. *Organization Science*, *14*(1), 81–90. doi:10.1287/orsc.14.1.81.12807

Inkpen, A. C., & Dinur, A. (1998). Knowledge management processes and international joint ventures. *Organization Science*, *9*(4), 454–468. doi:10.1287/orsc.9.4.454

Jasimuddin, S. M. (2014). Face-to-face interface in software development: Empirical evidence from a geographically dispersed high-tech laboratory. *International Journal of Technology and Human Interaction*, *10*(1), 48–60. doi:10.4018/ijthi.2014010104

Jasimuddin, S. M., Connell, N. A. D., & Klein, J. H. (2006). What motivates organizational knowledge transfer? Some lessons from a UK-based multinational. *Journal of Information and Knowledge Management*, *5*(2), 165–171. doi:10.1142/S0219649206001414

Jones, G. R., & George, J. M. (1998). The experience and evolution of trust: Implications for cooperation and teamwork. *Academy of Management Review*, *23*(3), 531–546.

Kramer, R. M. (1999). Trust and distrust in organizations: Emerging perspectives, enduring questions. *Annual Review of Psychology*, *50*(1), 569–598. doi:10.1146/annurev.psych.50.1.569 PMID:15012464

Laframboise, K., Croteau, A. M., Beaudry, A., & Manovas, M. (2007). Interdepartmental knowledge transfer success during information technology projects. *International Journal of Knowledge Management*, *3*(2), 47–67. doi:10.4018/jkm.2007040103

Levin, D. Z., & Cross, R. (2004). The strength of weak ties you can trust: The mediating role of trust in effective knowledge transfer. *Management Science*, *50*(11), 1477–1490. doi:10.1287/mnsc.1030.0136

Levin, D. Z., Cross, R., Abrams, L. C., & Lesser, E. L. (2002). Trust and knowledge sharing: A critical combination. *IBM Institute for Knowledge-Based Organizations*, 1-9.

Lewicki, R. J., Tomlinson, E. C., & Gillespie, N. (2006). Models of interpersonal trust development: Theoretical approaches, empirical evidence, and future directions. *Journal of Management, 32*(6), 991–1022. doi:10.1177/0149206306294405

Lewis, J. D., & Weigert, A. (1985). Trust as a social reality. *Social Forces, 63*(4), 967–985. doi:10.1093f/63.4.967

Maguire, S., Phillips, N., & Hardy, C. (2001). When 'Silence = Death', keep talking: Trust, control and the discursive construction of identity in the Canadian HIV/AIDS treatment domain. *Organization Studies, 22*(2), 285–310. doi:10.1177/0170840601222005

Mäkelä, K., & Brewster, C. (2009). Interunit interaction contexts, interpersonal social capital, and the differing levels of knowledge sharing. *Human Resource Management, 48*(4), 591–613. doi:10.1002/hrm.20300

Matzler, K., & Renzl, B. (2006). The relationship between interpersonal trust, employee satisfaction, and employee loyalty. *Total quality management and business excellence, 17*(10), 1261-1271.

Mayer, R. C., Davis, J. H., & Schoorman, F. D. (1995). An integrative model of organizational trust. *Academy of Management Review, 20*(3), 709–734.

McAllister, D. J. (1995). Affect-and cognition-based trust as foundations for interpersonal cooperation in organizations. *Academy of Management Journal, 38*(1), 24–59. doi:10.2307/256727

McKnight, D. H., Cummings, L. L., & Chervany, N. L. (1998). Initial trust formation in new organizational relationships. *Academy of Management Review, 23*(3), 473–490.

Mendelson, H. (2000). Organizational architecture and success in the information technology industry. *Management Science, 46*(4), 513–529. doi:10.1287/mnsc.46.4.513.12060

Mooradian, T., Renzl, B., & Matzler, K. (2006). Who trusts? Personality, trust and knowledge sharing. *Management Learning, 37*(4), 523–540. doi:10.1177/1350507606073424

Nahapiet, J., & Ghoshal, S. (1998). Social capital, intellectual capital, and the organizational advantage. *Academy of Management Review, 23*(2), 242–266.

Noorderhaven, N., & Harzing, A. W. (2009). Knowledge-sharing and social interaction within MNEs. *Journal of International Business Studies, 40*(5), 719–741. doi:10.1057/jibs.2008.106

Nugent, P. S., & Broedling, L. A. (2002). Managing conflict: Third-party interventions for managers. *The Academy of Management Executive, 16*(1), 139–154. doi:10.5465/AME.2002.6640226

Pavlou, P. A. (2002). Institution-based trust in interorganizational exchange relationships: The role of online B2B marketplaces on trust formation. *The Journal of Strategic Information Systems, 11*(3), 215–243. doi:10.1016/S0963-8687(02)00017-3

Pearce, J. L., Branyiczki, I., & Bigley, G. A. (2000). Insufficient bureaucracy: Trust and commitment in particularistic organizations. *Organization Science, 11*(2), 148–162. doi:10.1287/orsc.11.2.148.12508

Posner, B. Z., Randolph, W. A., & Schmidt, W. H. (1987). Managerial values across functions: A source of organizational problems. *Group & Organization Management*, *12*(4), 373–385. doi:10.1177/105960118701200402

Rousseau, D. M., Sitkin, S. B., Burt, R. S., & Camerer, C. (1998). Not so different after all: A cross-discipline view of trust. *Academy of Management Review*, *23*(3), 393–404. doi:10.5465/AMR.1998.926617

Seidler-de Alwis, R., & Hartmann, E. (2008). The use of tacit knowledge within innovative companies: Knowledge management in innovative enterprises. *Journal of Knowledge Management*, *12*(1), 133–147. doi:10.1108/13673270810852449

Shapiro, D. L., Sheppard, B. H., & Cheraskin, L. (1992). Business on a handshake. *Negotiation Journal*, *8*(4), 365–377. doi:10.1111/j.1571-9979.1992.tb00679.x

Shapiro, S. P. (1987). The social control of impersonal trust. *American Journal of Sociology*, *93*(3), 623–658. doi:10.1086/228791

Singh, T. B. (2012). A social interactions perspective on trust and its determinants. *Journal of Trust Research*, *2*(2), 107–135. doi:10.1080/21515581.2012.708496

Song, C., Sommer, S. M., & Hartman, A. E. (1998). The impact of adding an external rater on interdepartmental cooperative behaviors of workers. *The International Journal of Conflict Management*, *9*(2), 117–138. doi:10.1108/eb022806

Suckley, L. J., Price, I., & Sharpe, J. (2013). Exploring inter-departmental barriers between production and quality. *Journal of Organizational Ethnography*, *2*(2), 173–190. doi:10.1108/JOE-09-2012-0038

Szulanski, G. (1996). Exploring internal stickiness: Impediments to the transfer of best practice within the firm. *Strategic Management Journal*, *17*(S2), 27–43. doi:10.1002mj.4250171105

Tsoukas, H. (1996). The firm as a distributed knowledge system: A constructionist approach. *Strategic Management Journal*, *17*(S2), 11–25. doi:10.1002mj.4250171104

Willem, A., & Buelens, M. (2007). Knowledge sharing in public sector organizations: The effect of organizational characteristics on interdepartmental knowledge sharing. *Journal of Public Administration: Research and Theory*, *17*(4), 581–606. doi:10.1093/jopart/mul021

Willem, A., Buelens, M., & Scarbrough, H. (2006). The role of inter-unit coordination mechanisms in knowledge sharing: A case study of a British MNC. *Journal of Information Science*, *32*(6), 539–561. doi:10.1177/0165551506067128

Zand, D. E. (1972). Trust and managerial problem solving. *Administrative Science Quarterly*, *17*(2), 229–239. doi:10.2307/2393957

Zucker, L. G. (1986). Production of trust: Institutional sources of economic structure, 1840–1920. In B. Straw & L. Cummings (Eds.), *Research in organization behavior* (pp. 53–112). Greenwich, CT: JAI Press.

ENDNOTES

1 Following Rousseau, Sitkin, Burt, & Camerer (1998), we also insist that deterrence is not trust and rule out the 'deterrence-based trust' discussed by Shapiro, Sheppard, & Cheraskin (1992).

2 Reverse scaled

This research was previously published in the Information Resources Management Journal (IRMJ), 29(1); edited by George Kelley; pages 15-38, copyright year 2016 by IGI Publishing (an imprint of IGI Global).

APPENDIX: QUESTIONNAIRE ITEMS

Institution-Based Trust (INST)

INST1: My firm can effectively monitor interdepartmental collaboration and help resolve conflicts.

INST2: In my firm, if any individual engages in misconduct in an interdepartmental collaborative task, a reliable feedback mechanism is provided to inform supervisors and co-workers.

INST3: In my firm, most departments are willing to make co-operative adjustments to implement interdepartmental collaborative tasks successfully.

INST4: My firm promotes co-operative norms to resolve any interdepartmental collaboration disputes.

Interpersonal Trust (PERT)

PERT1: In interdepartmental collaboration, we have confidence in the skills of our co-workers from the other department.

PERT2: In interdepartmental collaboration, we can rely on co-workers from the other department to make our job easier.

PERT3: In interdepartmental collaboration, if we face difficulties at work, we know that our co-workers from the other department will try to help us.

PERT4: In interdepartmental collaboration, co-workers from the other department do not try to deceive us for their own benefit.

Sharing Satisfaction (SAT)

SAT1: We are satisfied with the exchange of information and experience during collaboration with the other department.

SAT2: In general, we are satisfied with the collaboration with the other department.

SAT3: In interdepartmental collaboration, co-workers from the other department meet our expectations or task standards.

SAT4: Interdepartmental collaboration has been an opportunity to share more of our experiences and ideas with the other department.

Sharing Success (SUC) [2]

SUC1: In interdepartmental collaboration, we often encounter interruptions or delays in the flow of work, resources or services from or to the other department.

SUC2: In interdepartmental collaboration, exceptions or problems often arise in sending or receiving work, resources, or services to or from the other department.

SUC3: Some specific information that was not shared between departments leads to delays or lower performance of the collaborative task.

SUC4: In performing the collaborative task, we spend more time than actually planned.

Knowledge Tacitness (TACI) [2]

TACI1: We can clearly explain what knowledge and skills lead to task success.
TACI2: We are able to express what we know to explain that knowledge to co-workers from the other department.
TACI3: Explaining to co-workers from the other department how we do things is easy.
TACI4: Expressing our experiences in speech or writing to the other department is easy.

Index

A

absorptive capacity 348, 350, 352, 357
abstracting 155, 157-158, 163, 165, 170, 173
access control 98, 185-188, 191, 205, 210, 214, 216, 218, 253-259, 269, 275-283, 285, 289-290, 293-295, 319-336, 338, 342, 485
access control policies 259, 277, 280, 283, 289-290, 293-295, 321-326
accreditation 27, 31-32, 34, 37, 43, 428
ACEJMC 27-28, 31-32, 34, 37, 43
actor-network theory 358-359, 361, 374, 377
affordance 850, 853
altruism 514-515, 527, 763-764, 772-774, 787, 792
Antiquity 135-138, 142, 144
application wrapper 256, 263-264, 271, 276
applications 1-2, 8, 18, 36, 39, 71, 85, 87, 94-96, 98-101, 103-105, 112, 179, 186, 221, 226-227, 229-230, 234, 238, 242, 246, 251, 253-258, 265, 271, 282, 301-302, 306, 321, 328, 330-331, 383-385, 388, 453-454, 480-482, 485, 493-494, 498, 537, 573, 591, 604, 623-624, 627-630, 634, 643-644, 652, 685, 714, 749, 754, 759, 764, 767, 774, 787, 789, 797-798, 824, 827, 837, 858-859
attributes 3, 13, 20, 46, 50, 57, 113-114, 123, 158, 173, 185-186, 190, 208, 218, 269, 279-282, 284, 286-287, 289-290, 294, 319, 324, 328-331, 334-335, 342, 347, 354, 368, 540, 546, 605, 711, 717-721, 814-815, 828, 882
authorization 186, 256-258, 262, 269-271, 276, 279, 281-282, 320-322, 325, 331, 335, 342, 481

B

B2B 469
big data 76, 383-384, 390, 879-881
black box arguments 850-854
blogs 31, 70, 73, 81, 118, 301-302, 308, 312, 317, 336, 537, 624, 629, 665, 712, 714-715, 720, 726-728, 730-733, 737, 745, 747, 751, 753, 759, 764, 767, 771, 844, 900
business processes 1, 246, 344-345, 349, 357, 493, 658

C

call for papers 135-138, 141-146, 151-153, 651
cataloguing 155, 157-163, 167, 170, 173, 737
classification 17, 155, 157-158, 164, 167-170, 173, 479-480, 544, 561, 651, 737, 768, 794, 898, 900, 904
cloud-based applications 94-96, 99-100, 104, 112
cloudlets 96, 112
CODE 123, 162, 167, 169, 226, 255, 263-265, 267, 328, 346, 533-534, 543-544, 546, 548
cognitive niches 844, 846-848, 850, 852, 854
collaboration 66-71, 75, 82, 85-86, 93, 99, 103, 146, 151, 175, 265, 282, 323, 328, 375, 382-388, 391-396, 408, 424-426, 428-431, 433, 444, 452-454, 463, 473, 477-479, 481-485, 498, 502, 535-536, 538, 542-543, 569, 588, 592, 624, 629, 635, 643, 646-647, 665, 668, 715, 717, 728, 730, 732, 734, 744, 748, 750, 761-762, 764-765, 767-768, 771, 774, 778, 784, 787-788, 796-797, 799, 806, 912
collective action 114-115
communication studies 28, 35, 43
Communities of Practice (CoP) 66-68, 70-71, 87, 93, 496-499, 503-505, 536, 563, 676, 679, 712, 714, 716, 720
compartmental model 879, 886
compatibility 3, 6, 8-10, 12, 15, 20, 570-571, 662
competence 68, 389, 454, 565, 578, 587, 662, 747, 755, 770, 785, 789, 791, 794-795, 806
competition 48-49, 174-175, 239, 246, 302, 310, 365, 393, 405, 434, 452, 455, 458, 460, 462-463, 471, 534, 538, 547, 561, 577, 751, 809, 813, 889

complexity 3-4, 8-10, 12, 20, 49, 55, 241, 245, 254, 279, 281, 345, 364, 385, 390, 393-394, 396, 456, 490, 502, 534, 537, 540-541, 720, 862, 880, 885
conflict studies 642-643, 645, 647-652, 655
congenital heart disease 690, 692, 695
congresses 135-138, 140, 142-146, 150-151
cooperation for innovation 403-404, 409, 412
corruption 116, 120, 123, 300-313, 317, 889, 892
Cosmopolite 25
coupon information-sharing 823, 825, 827-830, 832, 834, 837
curriculum 27-28, 30, 32, 37-39, 43-44, 86, 365, 591, 625, 727, 733

D

Design-Actuality Gap Framework 250
Design-Actuality Gap Model 250
Development Divide 243-244, 250
Diffusion of Innovation/Information Theory 43
diffusion of innovations 2, 9, 12-14, 16, 23, 50
digital divide 224-225, 228-231, 235-238, 240, 242, 244-246, 250
Digital Literacy 43
dissemination 26, 50, 68, 75, 85, 117, 144-146, 155, 157, 186, 227, 240, 305, 309-311, 383, 404, 406, 452, 463, 470, 578, 659, 736, 762, 769, 796, 809, 827, 837
distance learners 590, 597, 600
Document Coding/Classification 157, 168, 173
Document description 155-158, 161, 170, 173
dynamic learning process 557-558, 587

E

Eastern Bloc countries 557-558, 587
E-Learning 2.0 community 605-607, 609-610, 616, 618-619
electronic commerce 45-46, 49
Electronic Medical Record (EMR) 276
E-Marketplace 469
emotional intelligence 764, 773, 785, 789-793, 795-798, 800, 806
employee voice 557, 559, 566-568, 574-576, 578
EPISTEMOLOGY OF IGNORANCE 844-845
Everett M. Rogers 14, 26
explicit knowledge 67, 93, 345-348, 357, 433, 492-496, 498-499, 503, 507-508, 511-512, 537-538, 547, 558, 561-562, 577-578, 608, 626, 664-665, 667, 711-713, 716, 718, 720, 744, 749-750, 762, 786
extranet 469

F

Facebook 85, 118, 143-145, 151, 153, 271, 301, 306-310, 313, 317, 319, 323, 326, 328, 330, 332-333, 335, 474, 480, 498, 624, 627-628, 633-634, 650, 703, 713-715, 726-728, 732-733, 735-737, 746-747, 751-755, 761, 767, 775, 777, 779, 797, 799, 808, 812-813, 825-826, 837, 843, 845, 847-850, 858, 861, 897-898, 910-911
Fasti Congressuum 135-136, 138-139, 142-150, 153
Femtocell 96, 112
filter bubble 844, 849-850, 853

G

Generation X 767, 769, 774-775, 777-779, 793, 796-799
Generation Y 767, 769, 774-775, 777, 779, 793, 796-799
generations 117, 646, 714, 761-762, 766-767, 769, 774, 779, 784-785, 792-793, 796, 798, 806
governance 114, 117, 119, 121, 123-124, 127-129, 226-227, 242, 306, 313, 503, 643, 668, 752
green characteristics 1-2, 6, 8-10, 12
groupware 483, 537, 764, 771

H

hard elelment(s) 251
Hard Factor(s) 251
Hard-Soft Analytical Framework 251
Hard-Soft Gap 251
HBCU 31-32, 37, 43
Health Information Technology (HIT) systems 254, 276
Health Insurance Portability and Accountability Act (HIPAA) 254, 276
Health Level Seven International (HL7) 276
health sector 658-660, 664-669
Healthcare Workflows 277
higher education 31, 43, 365, 377, 406, 588, 592, 624, 631, 735, 825, 871
highly sensitive data 253, 258, 276
HR practices 453, 455-456, 458-463, 471
Human Actor Approach 251
Human Factor Approach 235, 251
Human Resource Management 346, 495-496, 511
human resources 47, 226, 390, 406, 490-491, 512, 669
humanities 138, 144, 150, 444, 655, 733

I

ICT-for-development 241-242, 245

implementation 7-9, 14, 16, 19-20, 27, 31, 39, 49-50, 55, 87, 175, 185-186, 188, 208-209, 235-236, 239, 247, 257, 281, 293-294, 304, 338, 348, 360-361, 369-376, 384, 393, 395, 453-455, 483, 507, 539, 569-570, 611, 625, 629, 662, 669, 677-678, 685, 739, 747-748, 764, 768, 771, 777, 794, 799, 816, 849-850, 852
indexing 155, 157-159, 163, 170, 173
Influence Maximization 900, 908
Information and Communication Technologies (ICTs) 113, 116, 127, 179, 220, 224-228, 232-233, 240, 242, 244-246, 250-251, 301, 305, 312, 317, 490, 512, 534, 624, 643, 646, 711
Information Control 300, 308, 317
information diffusion 30, 807-808, 810-813, 816, 818-819, 824, 853, 859, 879-881, 903, 916
information diffusion theory 30
Information Economy 251
information flow control 185-187, 191, 205, 210, 216, 218
information friction 114, 118, 129
Information Management 155, 157, 168, 170, 174, 176-180, 537, 576, 664, 732
Information Poor 251
information retrieval 157, 159, 162, 643, 652, 882
Information Revolution 223-224, 231, 244, 251, 643
Information Rich 251
information society 145, 221-223, 238, 251, 625
information storage 155, 158, 167, 173
institution-based trust 424-430, 432-434, 439-444, 450
interdepartmental collaboration 424, 426, 428-431, 433, 444
interdepartmental knowledge sharing 424-425, 429-434, 441-444
international relations 221-222, 642-643, 645, 647-648, 650-652, 655
Internet freedom 310-313, 317
inter-organizational knowledge sharing system 658, 668
interpersonal trust 424-427, 429-434, 438-444, 450, 559, 569-570
Intranet 469, 498, 503, 507, 537, 763, 770, 774, 786, 797
IT firms 424, 434, 444

J

journalism 28, 31-33, 37, 43-44, 311, 482, 860

K

k-Neighbors 807, 816, 818-819
knowledge continuity 490-491, 493, 496, 498, 500, 503, 506, 512
Knowledge Continuity Management (KCM) 490-491, 512
knowledge exchange 384, 455, 462, 478, 588, 600, 611, 662
Knowledge loss 495
Knowledge Management (KM) 66-68, 70-71, 87, 93, 155-157, 178, 344, 346, 348, 351, 354, 357-361, 374, 383, 385, 403-404, 442-443, 470, 483, 485, 490-492, 512, 515, 524, 533-534, 558, 561, 563-564, 605-607, 625-626, 631, 643, 645-648, 652, 659, 662, 669, 676, 680, 684, 688, 726-727, 732, 744-752, 754-756, 759, 761-762, 766, 768-769, 774, 784, 786, 788, 793-794, 796, 806
Knowledge Management Process Model 357
knowledge production 642, 655, 791-792
knowledge quality 677, 688
Knowledge Sharing (KS) 69-70, 73-74, 87, 344-354, 357-377, 382-387, 391, 393, 395-396, 403-404, 407-408, 412, 424-425, 427, 429-434, 441-444, 452-458, 460-463, 471, 485, 490, 492-501, 503, 507-508, 512-515, 517-518, 525, 527, 533-536, 538-539, 543-548, 557-559, 561-571, 573-578, 588-591, 597, 599-600, 603-612, 616-619, 623-625, 627-628, 630-638, 642, 645-648, 652, 655, 658, 660-665, 668, 676-677, 679-680, 683-684, 688, 711-720, 726-730, 732, 735, 739, 744-746, 748, 750-752, 761-766, 768-776, 778-779, 784-788, 791-800, 806, 826
knowledge sharing behaviour 566, 568, 660-661, 663, 668, 676-677, 680, 683-684, 688, 762-763, 772-773, 784, 786-787, 791-792, 798, 800, 806
knowledge sharing platform 623, 625, 627, 630, 633-634, 638
knowledge transfer 26, 344-345, 347-348, 351, 353, 408, 484, 490, 492, 535-538, 544, 558, 588, 591, 648, 762
knowledge workers 477, 495, 534, 658-663, 665-669, 713-715, 727, 761-762, 772
KPMG 767-770, 772-773, 775, 778, 796, 799

L

learning organization 85, 350, 746
loss of knowledge power 764, 774

M

marketing strategy 85
Mass Communication Education 43-44
mass media 15-16, 23, 30, 33, 38, 310, 729, 746-747
Media Education 28, 44
media literacy 27-39, 44
media studies 27, 34-35
mindfulness 858-859, 861-862, 864-865, 867-871, 877
mobile computing 253, 255-258, 265, 270-271, 276
mobile devices 94-100, 102-105, 112, 114, 253-254, 257-258, 271, 627, 644, 767
Mobile Healthcare (M-Healthcare) 99, 112
Mobile Learning (M-Learning) 98, 112
mobile security 253
mobile-cloud technology 94-96, 98-105, 112
modeling 185-186, 205, 278, 280, 283-284, 603, 818, 865, 881, 888-889, 893, 897, 902, 904
motivating language 565, 573-574, 578
motivation 22, 68-70, 114, 235, 255-256, 271, 352, 453, 483, 495, 500, 536, 560, 563, 565, 576-577, 587, 589, 600, 604, 608, 610-611, 618, 629, 692, 717-718, 732, 739, 748, 761, 763, 766, 772, 778, 787, 792, 800, 806, 809, 826
multi-way communication 301, 308, 317

N

national culture 514-515, 517, 524-525, 539-540, 542-544
natural language processing 827, 879-880, 882, 888-889, 893
news propagation 879-881, 883, 889
newsletter 120, 145, 153

O

Obesegenic 26
observability 3, 6-10, 12
online social networks 319-321, 323-325, 328, 332, 338, 476, 479-480, 482, 624, 807-810, 813, 815, 819, 916
Open Access Movement 251
Open Content 252
Open Knowledge 252
Open-Source Knowledge 252
organisational characteristics 382, 384, 386-387, 395-396, 541, 545, 799
organisational commitment 563, 576, 587, 791
organisational culture 360, 362, 533-534, 539, 541-545, 548, 557, 559, 562-563, 565-569, 571, 578
organizational climate 603, 605-607, 610-612, 616-619
organizational learning 350, 405, 407-408, 412, 453, 495, 508, 591
organizational performance 404, 407, 786
organizational reward 764, 774

P

P/HIS 44
perception of psychological safety 557, 569-570
Petrides 773, 789-792
PLS model 683, 865, 867
Politics of Access to Information 220, 224, 231
processing 2, 43-44, 51-52, 94-95, 98-100, 102, 104-105, 179, 205, 221, 227, 230, 236, 335-336, 383, 393, 537, 678, 745, 824, 827, 861-862, 869, 871, 879-880, 882, 888-889, 893
public opinion 222, 827, 879, 893

Q

qualitative research methods 384
QUANTITATIVE RESEARCH METHODS 388

R

random forests 807
RBAC 186-187, 191, 253-261, 263-265, 267, 269, 271, 276, 279, 281-282, 320, 335
reciprocity 478, 515, 518-519, 526, 535, 603, 610, 616, 618, 715, 717, 763-764, 772, 774, 787
relative advantage 3, 6-10, 12, 15, 20, 49
reputation 69, 276, 323, 325, 329, 477-479, 483, 502, 515, 524, 544, 604, 728, 763-764, 774, 787, 798, 808-809, 825-826
retweet 700, 704, 809, 814, 816-817, 824, 826-827, 860, 904, 906, 913
RFID 1-2, 4, 6-10, 12
Rhizomatic 746, 759
Role-Based Access Control (RBAC) 253-254, 256, 276, 279, 281, 320
rumors 483, 845, 859-861, 870-871, 897-904, 906-908, 912-913, 916-917

S

scholars 27-29, 31, 39, 114, 116, 122, 136, 141, 143, 165, 229, 240-241, 245, 307, 385, 427-428, 431-433, 443-444, 515, 525, 534, 539, 642, 645-646, 648, 655, 736, 860, 870
school administrators 557, 559, 566-568, 574-575
seminar 36, 136, 151, 153
sentiment 807-808, 812-819, 823-832, 834, 836-837, 850, 879-880, 882, 888-889, 893, 901
sentiment analysis 823, 825, 827-829, 834, 837, 879-880, 882, 888-889, 893, 901
Sina Weibo microblogging 879-881, 888-889
skepticism 858, 862, 864-865, 867-871, 877
Skype 624, 634, 644, 713, 717, 746, 779
SMEs 45-54, 56-58, 348, 404-405, 408-410, 412-413, 419, 452-456, 460, 462-463, 785, 793-797, 799-800
social capital 430-431, 473-475, 478, 481, 485, 506, 561, 604, 714-716, 746, 751, 779, 811
Social Exchange Theory 456, 514-515, 567, 604
Social Media (SM) 28-29, 31, 33, 38, 79, 85, 119, 151, 236, 300-302, 305-313, 317, 336, 473-474, 481-484, 497-498, 507, 512, 536-537, 548, 588, 624, 630, 642-653, 655-656, 690-694, 704, 711, 713-718, 726-729, 731-739, 744-756, 759, 761-762, 764-768, 771, 774-779, 784-785, 787-788, 796-800, 806-809, 812-813, 818-819, 823-827, 834, 837, 843, 846-848, 850, 858-862, 864-865, 867-872, 877, 879-880, 893, 897-898, 900, 903-904, 907-908
social media technologies 715, 745-750, 754, 762, 764, 768, 771, 774-775, 778-779, 787, 796-797, 800
social media tools 588, 644, 650, 728, 732-733, 736, 745-748, 750-753, 756, 761-762, 765, 767-768, 776-779, 784-785, 797, 799-800, 806
social movements 114, 116-119, 123
social network analysis 319-320, 474, 483-484, 500, 506
social network services 824
Social Networking (SN) 744
social networks 70, 143-146, 148, 150, 153, 302, 319-321, 323-325, 327-329, 331-334, 338, 452, 456, 463, 470, 473-476, 479-483, 485, 498, 512, 536, 570, 607, 623-624, 627-629, 635, 642-646, 648, 712-713, 715, 726, 728, 730-733, 735, 750, 753, 766, 776, 788-789, 807-811, 813, 815, 819, 827, 844, 849-851, 854, 897-898, 915-917
social unrest 113-114, 116, 118-123, 125, 127-130
soft elements 252
soft factors 252
sticky knowledge 347-348, 357
strategic planning 178-180, 383, 511
subject cataloguing 158-159, 173
subject headings 159, 164, 167, 737
Supply Chain Management 174, 470, 485, 592
supply chains 1, 4, 226, 477, 588, 601
support vector regression 813, 817-819
Suscriptor 153
system success factors 603, 607-609, 616, 618-619

T

tacit knowledge 67, 93, 346-347, 352-353, 357, 364, 432-433, 443, 455-456, 490, 492-508, 512, 536-537, 547, 557-559, 561-568, 570-571, 573-578, 608, 711-720, 750-751, 762, 766, 786, 788, 792
tacit knowledge sharing 432-433, 443, 490, 493, 495, 497-499, 501, 507-508, 536, 557, 559, 561-568, 570-571, 573-578, 711, 714, 716-718, 750, 766, 788
Talent Management 495, 512
technological characteristics 57, 385
TEIQue 790-791, 795
tertiary education 623-625, 630-631, 638
Theory of Planned Behavior 604-605
traditional media 118-119, 301, 305, 308, 311, 317, 808, 858-860, 870
transaction costs 113-114, 117-118, 127, 129, 407
trialability 3, 8-10, 12
tweets 118, 144, 690-692, 694-698, 700-705, 754, 807-808, 812-816, 818, 823-832, 836-837, 898-899, 902-903, 907, 914
TWIS/PWIS 44
Twitter 85, 119, 143-144, 151, 271, 301, 306-308, 319, 480, 498, 627, 634, 650-651, 690-693, 695, 698, 701, 703-705, 713-715, 728, 732-733, 735, 737, 746-747, 749, 751-755, 767, 808-810, 812-816, 818, 823-830, 837, 848, 858, 860-861, 880, 897-902, 904, 906-907, 914, 917

U

usability 74, 254, 326-327, 336

V

VCoPs evaluation 677, 689
VCoPs Outcomes 689
virtual community 93, 684, 688, 717
Virtual Organizations 473, 477, 479, 485

Virtual Teams 473-474, 477, 479, 483-484
Virtual worlds 588-592, 601
vlogs 728, 733, 745, 759

W

Web 2.0 66-67, 70-71, 75, 85, 87, 452-456, 458, 460-463, 470-471, 481-482, 498, 604, 623-625, 627-638, 644, 665, 668, 727, 730, 744, 764-765, 897
Web 2.0 technologies 66-67, 70, 85, 87, 452-453, 456, 458, 463, 482, 624, 629, 634, 665, 668, 727, 730, 744
wikis 70, 74, 85, 452, 503, 537, 665, 712, 714-715, 727-728, 730, 733, 735-736, 747, 752
World Wide Web 70-71, 221, 231, 726

Y

YouTube 306-308, 497, 593-594, 598, 627-628, 633, 692, 726-728, 731, 733-734, 736, 748, 754-755, 767, 826, 898

www.ingramcontent.com/pod-product-compliance
Lightning Source LLC
LaVergne TN
LVHW062107300926
849161LV00010B/2393